KELANTAN
*Religion, Society and Politics
in a Malay State*

To' Kenali (*circa* 1920s)

kelantan
Religion, Society and Politics
in a Malay State

Edited by
WILLIAM R. ROFF
Columbia University, New York

KUALA LUMPUR
OXFORD UNIVERSITY PRESS
MELBOURNE LONDON NEW YORK
1974

Oxford University Press, Ely House, London W.1.
GLASGOW NEW YORK TORONTO MELBOURNE WELLINGTON
CAPE TOWN IBADAN NAIROBI DAR ES SALAAM LUSAKA ADDIS ABABA
DELHI BOMBAY CALCUTTA MADRAS KARACHI LAHORE DACCA
KUALA LUMPUR SINGAPORE JAKARTA HONG KONG TOKYO
Bangunan Loke Yew, Kuala Lumpur
● Oxford University Press 1974

All rights reserved. No part of this publication may be reproduced,
stored in a retrieval system, or transmitted, in any form or by any means,
electronic, mechanical, photocopying, recording or otherwise,
without the prior permission of Oxford University Press.

Printed in Malaysia by
ART PRINTING WORKS, KUALA LUMPUR

PREFACE

KELANTAN, the most populous of the peninsular Malay states in the early nineteenth century, is still the home of one of the largest concentrations of specifically Malay population in Malaysia—637,012 out of a total state population of 686,286, or nearly 93 per cent. The vast majority of the Malay inhabitants—more than half a million—live as peasant rice farmers on the 600 square mile alluvial plain created by the Kelantan River, constituting the most numerous settled Malay community in the peninsula. Most have been born and bred in the state (Malay immigrants are no more common than the Chinese and Indians who together form the remaining 7 per cent of the population), and this demographic concentration, which is in part the product of Kelantan's geographical isolation, cut off as it is from the western peninsula by heavily forested mountain terrain (though as will be seen it is an isolation often exaggerated or misunderstood), has undoubtedly given the state some of its more important cultural and social characteristics.

Situated in the north-east corner of peninsular Malaysia, bordering the ethnically Malay provinces of southern Thailand and with a fifty mile coastline on the South China Sea, Kelantan has come for many Malaysians and others to symbolize remoteness and beauty (of women, arts and crafts, and casuarina fringed beaches) in about equal proportion, allied with what is regarded as economic backwardness and religious puritanism. Only in Kelantan, today, do the Malay shadow play (*wayang kulit*), the traditional folk play (*Mak Yong*, with its Thai variant *menora*), the ritual psycho-drama (*main puteri*), and other dramaticforms still flourish. Kelantan silver-work and silk weaving, long the finest in the peninsula, continue to command wide admiration, and Kelantan artists and craftsmen are invited to design and execute artifacts as various as the new state throne in Pahang and the symbol for Malaysia's international airline, a stylized Kelantan *wau* or kite. In the realm of religion, Kelantan has since at least the mid-nineteenth century been well known for the number and size of its *pondok* (traditional religious schools), for a succession of notable Islamic scholars, and, though this is less recognized, for important innovations in the institutionalization of Islam that have been followed elsewhere in the peninsula. The state is also the heartland of the national Partai Islam Sa-Malaya, or Pan-Malayan Islamic Party (now sometimes Partai Islam), which since 1959 has controlled the state legislature and has been the largest party in opposition in the federal parliament. Economically, while it is true that Kelantan, the vast majority of whose population are wet-rice farmers or coastal fishermen with negligible surplus incomes, is one of the poorer states in Malaysia in per capita income, irrigation and other land and stock development schemes are already bringing about improvement, and its people have an unchallenged reputation for industry and application. In recent years, Kelantanese have been disproportionately numerous among young Malays entering institutions of higher learning, despite a local school system that, far from the centres of national power, acknowledgedly leaves much to be desired. General literacy (though current figures are not available) appears to be still rather low—if vastly above the 8 per cent for over-15 males achieved by 1931 under colonial rule—but for more than half a century Kelantan has been known as one of the principal centres of Malay publication in the peninsula for books and periodicals alike.

It is with these people, then, the Kelantan Malays, that the present collection of essays is concerned, and more especially with their history, their social organization and religious life, and their politics—all of which mark them out among the Malay peoples and make them, like the Minangkabau of Sumatra (or the Scots in Britain), of particular interest and influence well beyond their own borders.

Historically, the state, or *negeri*, of Kelantan—that is to say, the expanding and contracting area controlled from the port town at the mouth of the great Kelantan river—has existed as a locus of power on the east coast of the peninsula for at least a thousand years, and probably longer. Subject to, and at times subjecting, its northern and southern neighbours Patani and Trengganu, and latterly suffering a fluctuating relationship of tribute to the kingdom of Siam, Negeri Kelantan appears also to have enjoyed considerable periods of autonomy and independent prosperity, the latter based on the export of gold, tin, pepper, rice, and forest produce. In the course of the early part of the nineteenth century the state's political position began to change for the worse, as expansionist Siam assumed control over Patani, ultimately breaking it up into a number of directly ruled provinces, and, as Kelantan became involved in Malay resistance to encroachments of Siamese power in both Patani and Kedah, suffering punitive financial and other exactions as a result. Compounding these difficulties, the long reign of Sultan Muhammad I, which had lasted nearly half a century, was drawing to a close, with the old man in his nineties and indecisive. On his death early in 1838 there ensued a struggle for the succession, of a kind then characteristic of Malay politics, which caused much upheaval in the state and was brought to an end only with the assistance of Siam, thereby placing the state further under Siamese influence. The new ruler, Muhammad II, remained on the throne until his death in 1886, and after the settlement in the early 1840s of the 'civil war', was able to give the state another prolonged period of political calm, during which both economic and administrative development was able to take place. Though the mid-century saw increasing British involvement in the peninsula, culminating in the assumption of control over Perak in 1874, the first of the 'Protected Malay States', interest throughout the nineteenth century was confined almost entirely to the tin-rich west coast states, sparing for the time being the east coast, while helping to keep the Siamese at bay there. Sultan Muhammad II's death in 1886 was followed by another lengthy period of unrest, no fewer than four rulers coming to the throne before 1900, and at the time of his succession in that year Raja Long Senik (later Muhammad IV) was in no position to withstand the combined pressures of British and Thai rivalries and the enhanced power of major landed families within the state. Forced, in 1903, to accept a Siamese 'Adviser' (actually the Englishman Graham, in the service of the Siamese government), he was presented six years later, as a result of the Anglo-Siamese Treaty of 1909, with the *fait accompli* of a British Adviser on the model of the Residents earlier installed in the west coast states and Pahang, with wide-ranging powers over administration and finance.

Despite this concatenation of events, Kelantan, like the other 'unfederated' states in the peninsula, retained a measure of autonomy (if a decreasing one) in its internal affairs, and, subject to fewer British demands, proceeded upon a more leisurely road to modernization, eventually entering the post-war Federation of Malaya with much of its individual character and sense of identity still intact. During the colonial period, which lasted from 1909 to 1957, a branch of the main peninsular railway was built through Kelantan into southern Siam but, symbolically enough, skirting the capital, Kota Bharu, to the north of the river and connected to it only with some difficulty and by boat. Before the Second World War, road communications with the rest of Malaya were non-existent, and as recently as a decade ago the 400 mile journey from Kuala Lumpur to Kota Bharu required no fewer than thirteen ferry crossings. This, then, is what has conferred on Kelantan its 'isolation', but it is often forgotten that though links between the state and its south-western hinterland have in the past been poor, it has enjoyed many contacts to the north with the ethnically Malay and culturally influential Malay states of Thailand, with Thailand itself, and overseas to the Middle East and Islamic India, so that in many instances external forces have been somewhat different from those impinging on the rest of Malay Malaysia, but not necessarily less important—often acting, indeed, to reinforce and strengthen existing cultural patterns, and to confer a vitality independent from that derived from Kuala Lumpur.

Scholarly work on Kelantan has in the past been far from voluminous. The first ethnographic researches in the area, conducted by Skeat and Annandale in the late 1890s and early 1900s, were followed only in the 1930s by the studies undertaken by Jeanne Cuisinier and the Firths, with a further long gap until the recent past. Historiographically, Kelantan has been almost entirely neglected, notwithstanding its intrinsic interest and importance and its relevance for Malay historiography generally. The absence of any studies at all of Islam in the state does little more than emphasize the poverty of scholarly work on Islam in the peninsula as a whole. The linguistic, musical, and artistic culture of Kelantan, and its expression in the corpus of *wayang kulit*, *Mak Yong*, *main puteri*, and *selampit*—and even more the mythic structures and folk religion to which these aspects of cultural life relate so closely—though they have been the subject of brief and often colourful descriptive writing over the years, have seldom received the analytical study they deserve.

Seldom, that is to say, outside Kelantan itself, where the living nature of its history and traditional culture has not gone unobserved or undiscussed, and where intense interest has been and continues to be manifested in most aspects of social and religious life. Apart from a handful of pioneers from the University of Malaya (Muhammad Taib Osman, Kassim Ahmad, Ismail Hussein, Nik Safiah Haji Abdul Karim, and others), much of whose work has not been published, it is only recently that a more general recognition of Kelantan's unique attributes and interest has begun to find reflection in scholarly work by non-Kelantanese. In the past few years a striking number of scholars—Western as well as Malaysian—has undertaken substantial field research in Kelantan in the disciplines of history, social and cultural anthropology, linguistics, literature, musicology, and the dramatic arts. The present collection of essays, commissioned and prepared especially for this volume, and conceived as a whole, represents some of the first fruits of this research and brings together for the first time and in English a substantial body of original material on Kelantan society, its growth, its present features, and the direction in which it appears to be heading. That an enormous amount remains to be done is self-evident—the contributors to the present volume believe that the limitations of their own work do no more than testify to this. Concerning existing research, it is especially regretted that because of problems of production and length, papers on Kelantan musicology by William P. Malm and on the shadow play by Amin Sweeney, have had to be omitted. For other reasons, Ismail Hussein, on Kelantan mythology, and Nik Safiah Haji Abdul Karim, on linguistics, were unable to take part. What is offered here, accordingly, is a cross-section—it is hoped a useful and instructive one—of work that was approaching completion at the time when its collection was first discussed by the editor and others in 1970.

In an important sense, the present volume is a cooperative endeavour between Kelantan Malays and outsiders, and between scholars from two major disciplines, history and social anthropology. The work of three of the contributors—Nik Muhammad b. Haji Wan Musa, Abdullah Al-Qari b. Haji Salleh, and Abdul Rahman Al-Ahmadi—has not so far appeared in English, though all have written prolifically in Malay. The two other Malays taking part, Nik Mohamed b. Nik Mohd. Salleh and Nik Ibrahim Nik Mahmood, though writing in English, are both from Kelantan and look at their society from within. The outsiders all have close relationships with Kelantan, in varying degree, and share a common affection for its people and a common gratitude for being permitted access to their lives—from behind the *wayang kulit* screen as well as in front of it. While it is hoped that the privilege thus accorded has not been abused, it must be said that all the contributors alike, whatever their origin, believe that there is some value in looking at things from several different points of view. In this sense, perhaps, the present volume may be likened to a kind of prismatic lens, through which, according to the cultural background, scholarly discipline, or territorial standpoint of those taking part, the light emanating from the changeable and complex phenomenon of Kelantan Malay society may be focussed and analyzed.

Translations from the Malay have been made by the editor, who must in consequence be held responsible for any inaccuracies or infelicities that may have resulted. In this connection particular gratitude is due to Muhammad Kamal Hassan of the Department of Middle East Languages and Cultures of Columbia University, who, as the only Kelantanese in New York and as an Islamic scholar, bore the burden of frequent consultation and requests for advice, the latter not always taken. The contributors, collectively, wish to thank a large number of friends and colleagues in Kelantan and Kuala Lumpur (and elsewhere) for assistance of a variety of kinds. Though it is not possible to acknowledge them individually, we hope they will accept the remembrance for the deed, and not feel their kindness to have been misplaced.

Columbia University, New York, 1971 W.R.R.
Kota Bharu, Kelantan, 1972

NOTE

All currency is stated in Malaysian dollars.

CONTENTS

Preface		v
Maps		xii
Notes on Contributors		xiii
1.	NINETEENTH CENTURY KELANTAN: A THAI VIEW David K. Wyatt	1
2.	KELANTAN IN TRANSITION: 1891–1910 Mohamed b. Nik Mohd. Salleh	22
3.	THE TO' JANGGUT REBELLION OF 1915 Ibrahim Nik Mahmood	62
4.	TO' KENALI: HIS LIFE AND INFLUENCE Abdullah Al-Qari b. Haji Salleh	87
5.	THE ORIGINS AND EARLY YEARS OF THE *MAJLIS UGAMA* William R. Roff	101
6.	THEOLOGICAL DEBATES: WAN MUSA b. HAJI ABDUL SAMAD & HIS FAMILY Muhammad Salleh b. Wan Musa (with S. Othman Kelantan)	153
7.	NOTES TOWARDS A HISTORY OF MALAY PERIODICALS IN KELANTAN Abdul Rahman Al-Ahmadi	170

CONTENTS

8. FAITH AND SCEPTICISM IN KELANTAN VILLAGE MAGIC
   Raymond Firth ... 190

9. SOCIAL STRESS AND SOCIAL STRUCTURE IN KELANTAN VILLAGE LIFE
   Douglas A. Raybeck ... 225

10. ETHNICITY, CENTRALITY AND EDUCATION IN PASIR MAS
    Manning Nash ... 243

11. THE SOCIAL ORGANIZATION OF ISLAM IN KELANTAN
    Robert L. Winzeler ... 259

12. MUSLIM IDENTITY AND POLITICAL BEHAVIOUR IN KELANTAN
    Clive S. Kessler ... 272

    Glossary ... 315

    Bibliography of Kelantan ... 319

    Index ... 351

MAPS

1. The Malay Peninsula and Southern Thailand ... xviii
2. Kelantan ... xix

NOTES ON CONTRIBUTORS

ABDULLAH AL-QARI BIN HAJI SALLEH ('A.Q.HA.S), born 1937 at Kubang Kerian, Kelantan, and educated at Malay and Islamic schools there and in Kota Bharu. In 1953, aged fifteen, began teaching at Kubang Kerian Malay School, and started a publishing firm, Pustaka Angkatan Sayap Islam, which by the late 1960s had produced some 34 books on Islamic subjects. In addition to teaching Islam and Malay (certificated for the latter by the Language Institute in Kuala Lumpur) at various primary and middle schools in Kota Bharu, has also been part-time Lecturer in Malay Language and Literature at the Nilam Puri Centre of Higher Islamic Studies (1965–66). Has published more than fifty books in Malay (including translations from the Arabic), among them *Duta2 Allah di-Bumi* (Kota Bharu, Pustaka Dian, 1965); *Pengajian Sejarah Islam* (Kota Bharu, Pustaka Aman Press, 1968); *Peribahasa Modan* (Kota Bharu, Pustaka Aman Press, 1966); and two studies of his kinsman, *Sejarah Hidup To' Kenali* (Kota Bharu, Pustaka Aman Press, 1967), and *Cherpen To' Kenali* (Pustaka Dian, 1969). None of his work has previously appeared in English.

AL-AHMADI, ABDUL RAHMAN (Abdul Rahman b. Haji Muhammad Al-Ahmadi), born 1931 at Pasir Mas, Kelantan, and educated at Malay and Islamic schools in Kota Bharu. From 1947 attended high schools in Bukit Tinggi, Sumatra, and Jogjakarta, Java, later entering Gadjah Mada University in Jogjakarta, graduating with a Doctorandus (M.A.) degree in International Relations from the Faculty of Sociology and Politics in 1962. From 1966 to 1970 was as assistant editor at Pustaka Dian, Kota Bharu, and wrote frequently for *Majal-*

lah Dian, *Mingguan Kota Bharu*, and other Malay journals, also acting, from 1968, as part-time Lecturer in Sociology at the Nilam Puri Centre of Higher Islamic Studies. In 1970 became Principal of the Maktab Kadir Adabi (College) in Kota Bharu, and now lives in Pasir Mas. In addition to numerous articles on historical and sociological topics, he has published a study of literature and society in the Malay world, *Pengantar Sastera* (Kota Bharu, Pustaka Aman Press, 1966).

FIRTH, RAYMOND, *Sir*, born 1901 in New Zealand, educated there and at the London School of Economics and Political Science, from which he graduated Ph.D. in 1927. After teaching anthropology at the University of Sydney, he returned to lecture in the London School of Economics, becoming Professor of Anthropology in 1944, and from 1968 Emeritus Professor. Has since taught as visiting professor in the United States and Canada. Has done field work in West Africa, New Guinea and the Solomon Islands, and in particular has carried out extensive research in Tikopia and Kelantan. Has been awarded the Rivers Memorial Medal and the Huxley Memorial Medal by the Royal Anthropological Institute, the Viking Fund Medal by the Wenner-Gren Foundation for Anthropological Research, is a Fellow of the British Academy, and was knighted in 1973. His numerous publications include *Primitive Economics of the New Zealand Maori* (London, Routledge, 1929); *We, The Tikopia: A Sociological Study of Kinship in Primitive Polynesia* (London, Allen & Unwin, 1936); *Human Types* (London, Nelson, 1938); *Malay Fishermen: Their Peasant Economy* (London, Kegan Paul, 1946, revised ed. 1966); *Elements of Social Organization* (London, Watts, 1951); *Social Change in Tikopia: Restudy of a Polynesian Community after a Generation* (London, Allen & Unwin, 1959), and *Rank and Religion in Tikopia* (London, Allen & Unwin, 1970).

KESSLER, CLIVE S., born 1942 at Sydney, Australia, and educated at the University of Sydney (B.A. First Class Honours, and University Medal in Anthropology, 1965), and at the London School of Economics and Political Science (1966–67). Did field research in Kelantan from mid-1967 to mid-1969. Appointed Lecturer in Social Anthropology, London School of Economics, 1968–70, and in September 1970 became Assistant Professor of Anthropology at Barnard College, Columbia University, New York. Is at present completing for the University of London a doctoral dissertation on Islam and peasant radicalism in Kelantan, and has had articles published in the *British Journal of Sociology* and *Mankind*.

IBRAHIM NIK MAHMOOD, NIK, born 1940 at Kota Bharu, Kelantan, and educated there, at the Teachers' College in Penang, and at the University of Malaya in Kuala Lumpur (B.A., Honours in History, 1969), where he also obtained a Diploma in Public Administration in 1972. Was a schoolteacher in Kelantan for some years before attending the University of Malaya, and is now an official with the Malaysian Home and Foreign Service in Kuala Lumpur. This is his first publication.

MOHAMED BIN NIK MOHD. SALLEH, NIK, born 1935 at Kota Bharu, Kelantan, and educated at the University of Malaya in Singapore (B.A., Honours in History, 1960), later obtaining a Diploma in International Relations from the Institute of Social Studies at The Hague (1970). Has been a member of the Malaysian Home and Foreign Service since 1960, serving in Perak, Kelantan, and Kuala Lumpur, and is now a Principal Assistant Secretary with the Prime Minister's Department. Founder-member of the Persatuan Sejarah Kelantan (Kelantan Historical Society) in 1964, and joint editor of the society's journal for its first and only issue (1964/65). Has published articles on Kelantan history and society in this and other journals, and is at present engaged on a larger study of Kelantan history.

MUHAMMAD SALLEH BIN HAJI WAN MUSA, HAJI NIK, born 1920 at Kota Bharu, Kelantan, and educated there by his father, brother, and other Islamic teachers before going to Mecca in 1936, to the Darul-Ulum in Deoband (India) from 1937–39, and to the Jāmiʻa Miliyya in Delhi from 1939–43. Returning to Kelantan in 1946, he lived and taught in Kota Bharu until his death from illness in 1971. Among his publications are *Sinaran I'tiqad* (Kota Bharu, Majlis Ugama Press, 1938); *Risalah Masalah Fitrah dan Fitrah Kanak2 yang belum Baligh* (Kota Bharu, Al-Kamaliah Press, 1947); *Filsafat Berumahtangga* (Kota Bharu, Mustafa Press, 1947); and *Rahsia Kelahiran Nabi Muhammad* (Kota Bharu, Al-Ahliah Press, 2 vols., 1947).

NASH, MANNING, born 1924 in Pennsylvania, educated at Temple University, Philadelphia (B.S. 1949, Honours), and at the University of Chicago (M.A., 1952, Ph.D., 1955). Has taught anthropology at the University of Chicago, University of California at Los Angeles, and University of Washington, Seattle, and since 1964 has been Professor of Anthropology at the University of Chicago. He has done field research in Guatemala, Mexico, and Burma, as well as in Kelantan, which he visited three times between 1964 and 1968. He edited the journal *Economic Development and Culture Change* from 1958 to 1963, and is a Fellow of the American Anthropological Association, the Royal Anthropological Institute, and the American Association for the Advancement of Science. His numerous publications include *Machine Age Maya: The Industrialization of a Guatemalan Community* (Glencoe, Ill., Free Press, 1958); *The Golden Road to Modernity: Village Life in Contemporary Burma* (New York, John Wiley & Sons, 1965); *Primitive and Peasant Economic Systems* (Chicago, Chandler Publishing Co., 1966); and a forthcoming monograph on modernization in Kelantan.

OTHMAN KELANTAN, S. (Sayyid Othman b. Sayyid Omar), born 1938 at Kota Bharu, Kelantan, and educated at Malay and Islamic schools there. He has been a school teacher since 1952. Best known in Malaysia as a writer of fiction, he has published three novels: *Pengertian* (Machang, Pustaka Murni, 1966); *Pertentangan* (Kuala Lumpur, Pustaka Antara, 1967); and *Angin Timor Laut* (Kuala Lumpur, Utusan Melayu Press, 1969); and a collection of short stories, *13 Cherpen* (Kota Bharu, Pustaka Dian, 1970); as well as contributing numerous articles and other pieces to a wide variety of Malay periodicals.

RAYBECK, DOUGLAS A., born 1941 at Jamestown, New York, and educated at Dartmouth College (B.A. 1964, Honours in Anthropology). Did field work in Kelantan for eighteen months in 1968–69, on a National Institute of Mental Health Predoctoral Research Fellowship, and is at present completing a doctoral dissertation in anthropology for Cornell University, dealing with Kelantan cultural and social values. For the past year he has taught anthropology at Kirkland College, Clinton, New York. This is his first publication.

ROFF, WILLIAM R., born 1929 at Glasgow, Scotland, and educated in Britain and during six years with the Merchant Navy. After settling in New Zealand in 1953, was an editor and feature writer for the Broadcasting Commission, attending Victoria University of Wellington part-time (B.A., 1957, M.A., First Class Honours in History, 1959). Awarded research scholarship at the Institute of Advanced

Studies, Australian National University, 1959–63, of which two years spent on research in Malaysia (Ph.D. 1965). Lecturer in South-East Asian History, Monash University, Melbourne, 1963–65; Senior Lecturer in History, University of Malaya, 1966–69; currently Professor of History, Columbia University, New York. His publications include *The Origins of Malay Nationalism* (New Haven & London, Yale University Press, 1967), recently translated into Malay for the University of Malaya Press; two collections of essays by Clifford and Swettenham published by Oxford University Press (1967 and 1968); *Sejarah Surat2 Khabar Melayu* (Penang, Sinaran Press, 1967); and (with David Joel Steinberg and others) *In Search of Southeast Asia: A Modern History* (New York, Praeger, 1971).

WINZELER, ROBERT L., born in 1940 at Canton, Ohio, and educated at Kent State University (B.A., 1963) and the University of Chicago (M.A., 1966, Ph.D. 1970). Did field research in Kelantan for fifteen months from August 1966, on a National Science Foundation Dissertation Research Grant, and in Kelantan and South Sulawesi on a University of Nevada Grant in the summer of 1971. Has taught at Northern Illinois University, and is currently Assistant Professor in the Department of Anthropology at the University of Nevada. He presented papers at the annual meetings of the American Anthropological Association in 1969, 1970, and 1971.

WYATT, DAVID K., born in 1937 in Massachusetts, and educated at Harvard University (B.A., 1959), Boston University (M.A., 1960), and Cornell University (Ph.D. 1966). Did research in Thailand on a Ford Foundation Area Training Fellowship in 1962–63, was Lecturer in South-East Asian History at the School of Oriental and African Studies, University of London, 1964–68; and for five months in 1966–67 was a Visiting Fulbright Lecturer at the University of Malaya. In 1968–69, he taught at the University of Michigan, and since then has been Associate Professor of History at Cornell University. His publications include *The Politics of Reform in Thailand: Education in the Reign of King Chulalongkorn* (New Haven & London, Yale University Press, 1969); (with A. Teeuw) *Hikayat Patani: The Story of Patani* (The Hague, Martinus Nijhoff, 1970); (with D.J. Steinberg and others) *In Search of Southeast Asia: A Modern History* (New York, Praeger, 1971); and he has edited the *Nan Chronicle* (Ithaca, Cornell University Southeast Asia Program, 1966).

1. The Malay Peninsula and Southern Thailand

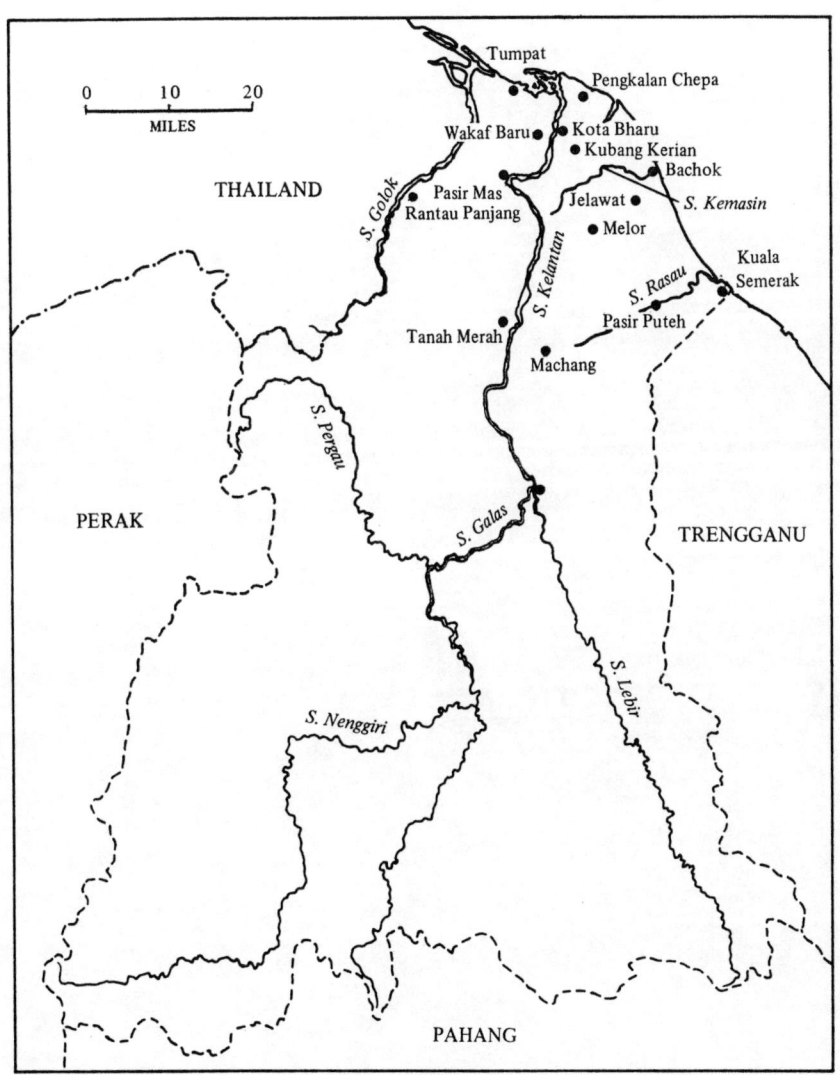

2. Kelantan

I
DAVID K. WYATT
Nineteenth Century Kelantan: A Thai View

IN modern times, neither Kelantan's role in Malay affairs nor its importance to the economic and political development of Malaya have been such as to commend its history to the attention of outsiders. The reasons for this neglect are in large measure natural. Kelantan was a late-comer to the predecessor of the modern state of Malaysia, being brought under the superintendence of the British High Commissioner for the Malay States in Singapore (but not within the Federation of Malaya) only after transfer from Siam in 1909; and it did not share in the rapid economic and social development of the states of the west coast of the Malay peninsula. The historiography of Malaysia has tended to look to the southern end of the peninsula for antecedents in the great Sultanate of Malacca and its successors; and to look to British rule in the federated states for the background of Malaysia's contemporary institutions. Neglected, and even overlooked, in this historiography is the rich past of the northern states of the peninsula, all of which have to some degree a strong and ancient connection with Siam.

Even if local, indigenous sources for the history of Kelantan are relatively sparse—and one is increasingly uncertain as to the justice of the severe judgment often made on this score—the difficulties of reconstructing the rich textures of Kelantan history are not necessarily insurmountable. Surely the keys to understanding Kelantan's past are the overlapping contexts within which it is set, for the immediately most obvious fact about Kelantan is that it has never stood apart from the currents of change and danger, chance and hope, which have swept past its advantageous position astride the trade routes of the South China Sea. To begin with, Chinese records locate a major state (*Ch'ih-t'u*) in Kelantan's neighbourhood as early as the seventh century, and the accounts of Chinese envoys, pilgrims and merchants reinforce their information through subsequent centuries, until Kelantan is met with in the form *Chi-lan-tan* in the thirteenth century (Wheatley, 1961, 26-36, 51-55, 68-71). This particular context of Chinese trade and maritime activity allows for at least the reconstruction of Kelantan's circumstances, location, and international economic activity in what, for South-East Asia, is deepest antiquity.

The succeeding period, from the thirteenth century to the sixteenth, may be approached by three different avenues. First, East Asian (including Chinese, Japanese, and Ryukyan) sources provide increasingly rich evidence of Kelantan's place in the trading system of the South China Sea. Second, the evidence of medieval Thai records places Kelantan within the context of a pre-Islamic Isthmian world of numerous small states sharing to some extent a common culture and mutually competing for power and prestige (Wyatt and Bastin, 1968, and Wyatt, 1972). This second context increasingly overlaps the new Muslim and Malacca environment of the southern reaches of the peninsula, which takes form in such historical sources as the *Sejarah Melayu*.

With the onset of aggressive European trading activities in the region and the fall of Malacca, coupled with the revival of Ayudhyan Siam's interest in the middle reaches of the peninsula, yet another combination of sources provides information on Kelantan and its neighbours in the sixteenth through eighteenth centuries. Portuguese, Dutch, English, and French materials in this period provide occasional glimpses of Kelantan viewed from a commercial and European perspective, taking over the function of earlier Chinese texts, while Thai and local Malay texts become increasingly useful. An example of the manner in which such disparate sources complement one another is perhaps the recently-discovered *Hikayat Patani* and the Dutch materials which so beautifully corroborate it (Teeuw and Wyatt, 1970).

Rentse asserts (1934, 44) that 'It is almost impossible to write an account of Kelantan's history without touching on that of Patani'. This is an understatement for the eighteenth and nineteenth centuries, for which one might rather say that the history of Patani *and* Kelantan cannot be written without reference to Siam, which so often involved itself, and became involved, in those states. Neither is Thailand absent in the record of the twentieth century. The kingdom was an active participant in the affairs of Trengganu, Kelantan and Kedah almost from the fall of the Kingdom of Ayudhya in 1767; it was recognized, and acted, as the paramount power in, and suzerain of, those states down to their transfer to Britain in 1909, and briefly occupied them again in 1943-45 under Japanese sponsorship.

The record of the relationship with Siam, in the form of historical documents, is considerable, and the work of tapping it has hardly begun. Walter Vella (1957, 59-77) has made use of printed Thai materials relating to the reign of King Rama III (reg. 1824-51) in his examination of Siamese relations with the 'Malay Vassal States' during that period. Cyril Skinner has utilized both Thai printed sources and Malay documents from Bangkok in studying *The Civil War in Kelantan in 1839* (1966). There is a great deal more material that remains untapped (Wyatt and Wilson, 1964; Wyatt, 1967a), which in its scope and continuity promises to be critical to an understanding of Kelantan's history during the nineteenth century.

The most frequently cited of Thai sources concerning Kelantan is a product of the period itself, the 'Phongsāwadān müang kalantan' (Chronicle of Kelantan, abbreviated *PMK*), first published in 1914 in the second volume of the monumental *Prachum phongsāwadān* (Collected Chronicles) series sponsored by the National Library. The *PMK* is an exceedingly curious document, explicitly identified in only two ways. Its subtitle—at least as printed—indicates that the original manuscript comes from the *Sālā Lūkkhun* (a Malay equivalent might be the *Balai Menteri*), the offices and audience hall in which Thai ministers of state conducted their common business with the king in the nineteenth century, which strongly suggests that the *PMK* is an administrative document, held for reference at the Court. The second explicit identification of the text comes at its end, where the last date mentioned—the date upon which a party of Thai envoys returned from an official visit to Kelantan—is 19 April 1877. A safe inference from this information is that the chronicle must have been written shortly after that date (and not in the Fourth Reign (1851-68) of the Chakri Dynasty as Vella (1957, 151) suggests). Had it been compiled much later, it surely would have made reference to significant events in Kelantan in the 'eighties.

If only for reasons of chronology, one might be tempted to associate the *PMK* with the Malay text published and translated by Marriott (1916) as 'A Fragment of the History of Trengganu and Kelantan', which was compiled in 1868 and recopied in 1876. Comparison of these two texts, however, reveals their wide divergence on interpretation, coverage, and emphasis. Both begin in roughly the same period, ca. 1770, but the Marriott 'Fragment' goes down only to the Civil War of 1839 while the *PMK* continues to 1877. Moreover, the *PMK* is clearly written from a Siamese point of view, biased in favour of Tengku 'Red Mouth' Senik, Sultan Mulut Merah; and it consistently writes '*came* to Siam' instead of '*went* to Siam'.

Taking account of the circumstances related in the closing paragraph of the chronicle, it seems reasonable to assume that the *PMK* was compiled by a Siamese officer in 1877 or thereabouts on the basis of Thai court records, and, perhaps, information procured in Kelantan during the visit of Thai envoys in March-April of that year. The occasion for its compilation probably was an expression of interest in Kelantan's history by the young King Chulalongkorn (reg. 1868–1910), an act completely characteristic of him, perhaps with a view to obtaining better information on which to base the decisions which he clearly was going to have to make with respect to Kelantan in the immediate future.

The translation of the *PMK* which follows is based upon the printed version of 1963, and in general is more literal than free. Romanization of Thai words and proper names is according to the General System of the Royal Institute of Thailand. Malay names have been rendered in their conventional forms as determined by reference to Marriott (1916), Rentse (1934 and 1936), and Skinner (1965).

CHRONICLE OF KELANTAN
According to a Manuscript in the Sālā Lūkkhun

We know that Kelantan once was only a small, petty country, beset by personal factions. When Tuan Maso[1] was the ruler of Trengganu and had established the country and become dignified, he sent an army to attack Kelantan and made it tributary to Trengganu. It is not known whether the family of the ruler of Kelantan at that time disappeared, but in Kelantan there is a cemetery, quite permanently and beautifully established, which appears to be the burial place of an important person. At the present day, however, no one goes there to salute the new year, as is the Malay custom. That locality is near the cemetery of the family of the present ruler of Kelantan, only 200 metres away, and the family of the ruler of Kelantan does not go there [to the old cemetery] to salute [the new year].

[1] Sultan Mansur Shah, reg. 1740–93.

[As for] the family of the present ruler of Kelantan, 'Red Mouth' Senik;[2] originally Raja Thawǫ[3] was the ruler of Kelantan when it was still a tributary of Trengganu. Raja Thawǫ was the governor for a long time. He had sons named Tuan Long Muhammad, Tuan Temenggong [Long Tan],[4] Tuan Banggul,[5] and Tuan Long Ismail,[6] each by a different mother. When Raja Thawǫ died,[7] his descendants and the assembly of chiefs[8] consulted together and conferred on Raja Thawǫ the posthumous name of Barahum[9] Long Yunus.

The [royal] descendents and assembly of chiefs together elevated Long Muhammad, the eldest son of Barahum Long Yunus, to be ruler of Kelantan; elevated Tuan Long Ismail to be Raja Muda, calling him *phrayā* Bān Thalē; elevated Tuan Temenggong to be *phrayā* Temenggong, and Tuan Banggul to be *phrayā* Banggul.[10] Kelantan was still a tributary state of Trengganu. The year [of this event] is not remembered.[11]

Later, the ruler of Kelantan became angry with the ruler of Trengganu. He consulted his seniors and juniors and the assembly of chiefs, and they decided to send the gold and silver trees of tribute[12] to His Majesty [the Siamese king], asking that Kelantan be separated from Trengganu. Having the gold and silver trees of tribute made, the ruler of Kelantan sent them to Songhklā to be forwarded for presentation to His Majesty, asking that [Kelantan be put] under the superintendence of Songkhlā like Trengganu. His Majesty King Rama I,[13] being informed, was pleased to state that, 'Kelantan and Trengganu are adjacent to each other. A quarrel having arisen, they cannot [remain] together. If [Kelantan] came under the superintendence of Songkhlā as well, and the ruler of Kelantan showed himself more favourably than Trengganu, the ruler of Trengganu would see that Bangkok supported Kelantan, and the ruler of Trengganu would feel humiliated. [We]

[2] The epithet 'Red Mouth' (*pāk dāēng*) of the Thai materials echoes the equivalent Malay phrase (*mulut merah*) mentioned by Rentse (1934, 58). He apparently chewed betel!
[3] Dewa? This man corresponds to the Long Bahar whom Rentse (1934, 52–3, 57) feels ruled ca. A.D. 1740.
[4] The Tuan Long Tan of Marriott (1916) and Rentse (1934, 58).
[5] The Chronicle writes *bā-ngōi* throughout. Rentse (1934 and 1936) also terms him Long Zainal.
[6] Chronicle writes *tuan lǫng salǫ*; put in this form by comparison with Marriott.
[7] Rentse (1934, 57) suggests, by implication, that Long Yunus may have died ca. 1800; but later (Rentse, 1936) gives a date of 1794.
[8] Text has *seri dewan kromkān*.
[9] I.e., *marhum*, Arabic 'the deceased.'
[10] These are Thai bureaucratic ranks, which are scaled from *khun* (lowest) and *luang* to *phra, phrayā,* and *čhaophrayā* (highest).
[11] According to Marriott (1916, 22), this was in A.H. 1216 (A.D. 1801); Rentse (1934) and (1936) has A.H. 1215 (A.D. 1800).
[12] I.e., the *bunga mas*.
[13] Reg. 1782–1809.

would never know the end of it'. So His Majesty was pleased to order that Kelantan be placed under the superintendence of Nakhǭn Sī Thammarāt, and so Kelantan was from that time forward separated from Trengganu.

Long Muhammad, the ruler of Kelantan, had no sons. *Phrayā* Temenggong had four sons, named Tuan Kota, Tuan Nik of Gagap, Tuan 'Red Mouth' Senik, and Tuan Busu.[14] *Phrayā* Banggul had a son named Tuan Tengah. Raja Muda *phrayā* Bān Thalē had two sons, named Tuan Besar and Tuan Busu. When *phrayā* Temenggong died, the ruler of Kelantan took Tuan Kota, Tuan Nik of Gagap, Tuan 'Red Mouth' Senik, and Tuan Busu in his care. The ruler of Kelantan had greater affection for Tuan 'Red Mouth' Senik than for all the others. Raja Muda *phrayā* Bān Thalē died before the ruler of Kelantan. In the Year of the Dog, tenth of the decade,[15] in the reign of His Majesty King Rama III [of Siam],[16] the ruler of Kelantan died at the age of 93. As governor he had ruled for 53 years. His relatives and siblings and the assembly of chiefs consulted together and posthumously named him Barahum Long Muhammad. [His Majesty the Siamese king] presented silver coins to make merit at his funeral in the amount of 3,200 *salyng*, the equivalent of 10 *chang* in silver.

In the Year of the Dog, tenth of the decade, all the relatives and siblings and the assembly of chiefs consulted, and together agreed that, as Tuan 'Red Mouth' Senik was a wise man and greatly beloved of Barahum Long Muhammad, he should be elevated to be ruler of Kelantan and govern the country thereafter.[17] Tuan 'Red Mouth' Senik therefore had the gold and silver trees of tribute made and appointed his younger brother Tuan Busu, *phrayā* Banggul, Tuan Besar— the son of Raja Muda *phrayā* Bān Thalē—and the assembly of chiefs to carry [his] report and take the gold and silver trees of tribute to Nakhǭn Sī Thammarāt. *Čhaophrayā* Nakhǭn Sī Thammarāt[18] conducted them into audience with His Majesty the King and presented the gold and silver trees in Bangkok.

His Majesty King Rama III, being informed, stated, 'The relatives, siblings, and assembly of chiefs have consulted together to nominate Tuan 'Red Mouth' Senik to be the ruler of Kelantan'. Therefore His Majesty was pleased to appoint Tuan 'Red Mouth' Senik to be the

[14] Names restored to Malay forms via Marriott (1916, 21–22) and Rentse (1936).
[15] A.D. 1838–9. Skinner (1966, 10, fn. 11) mistakenly converts this date as 1836–8, and in the same place outlines the problems surrounding it.
[16] Reg. 1824–51.
[17] As Skinner (1966, 11, fn. 16) points out, the chronicle here is silent concerning Raja Banggul's occupancy of the throne after the death of Long Muhammad.
[18] Personal name Nǭi, governor of Nakhǭn from 1811 to 1839.

ruler of Kelantan as they had together advised him. Then he appointed Tuan Kota, the elder brother of the ruler of Kelantan, to be *phrayā* Sunthǫnbodī Seri Sultan Dewa Maharaja, *phrayā* Čhāngwāng.[19] He appointed Tuan Senik of Gagap, the elder brother of the ruler of Kelantan, to be Tengku Seri Indera Perata Mahamenteri. He appointed Tuan Busu, the younger brother of the [new] ruler of Kelantan, to be Raja Muda. All the sons and nephews[20] of Barahum Long Muhammad were ordered called 'Tengku'. However, *phrayā* Banggul and Tengku Besar do not seem to have been appointed to any rank or position. *Phrayā* Banggul, Raja Muda [Tuan Busu], and Tengku Besar carried the royal appointments of the ruler of Kelantan, *phrayā* Čhāngwāng, the Raja Muda, and Tengku Seri Indera away and reached Nakhǫn Sī Thammarāt. The governor of Nakhǫn Sī Thammarāt appointed *luang* Chaiphonphak to take charge [of them] and go to Kelantan. *Phrayā* Banggul [,however,] did not land at Kelantan, but continued on to Pahang. Raja Muda and Tengku Besar landed at Kelantan. The ruler of Kelantan received the royal appointments in procession. Tengku Besar went to listen to [the reading of] the royal appointments that first day, and then never again called upon the ruler of Kelantan, because Tengku Besar was disappointed that when he went up to pay homage to His Majesty the King, who had honoured the ruler of Kelantan to the extent of appointing him ruler, he himself had received no rank, and so he was ashamed before his retainers and followers. Furthermore, Raja Muda and Tengku Seri Indera confiscated lands and orchards belonging to Tengku Besar and his group. Tengku Besar complained to the ruler of Kelantan, who ordered Raja Muda and Tengku Seri Indera to restore them, but they did not do so. Furthermore, the rice which he had bought and brought from Bangkok he could not sell, as the ruler of Kelantan and Raja Muda had issued a proclamation forbidding the people and merchants to buy the rice of Tengku Besar. Thus Tengku Besar was even more aggrieved.

On Friday, the seventh day of the waxing moon of the fourth month in the Year of the Dog, tenth of the decade [20 February 1839][21] Tengku Besar wrote a letter inviting *phrayā* Banggul, Tengku Tengah,[22]

[19] *Čhāngwāng* is a Thai term which can mean 'deputy' but also has vaguer connotations of independence and control. In both this case and that of Tuan Senik of Gagap, the Thais seem to have been recognizing their special status as elder brothers of the ruler with strong and unusual honorific titles.

[20] The word *lān* in Thai can mean either 'nephew' or 'grandson', but the former seems implied here.

[21] Dates converted by means of the tables in Khlǫi (1954).

[22] 1963 printed edition has only *ngǫ* where 1961 and earlier editions have *tangǫ* = Tengah. He is either the son of Raja Banggul (above, p. 6) or the son of Tengku Long Ismail (Rentse, 1936).

and Tengku Long Ahmad[23] to come and plot together with the sons of Tengku Seri Petera Maharaja.[24] They erected fortifications around the home of Tengku Besar and ten forts along the large river as far as the market. In the south, they erected forts up to Sungei Pinang, and they constructed forts to surround the residence of the ruler of Kelantan, [with] three groups [manning them], the group of Tengku Besar, one group of Tengku Long Ahmad, and one group of Tengku Seri Petera Maharaja. As for the ruler of Kelantan, *phrayā* Čhāngwāng, Raja Muda, and Tengku Seri Indera, they erected fortifications and fought, shooting guns large and small, but they were unable to defeat [the invaders].

The ruler of Kelantan sent a report to Nakhǭn Sī Thammarāt on Sunday the eighth day of the waxing moon of the sixth month in the Year of the Pig, first of the decade [21 April 1839]. However, at that time, *phrayā* Sī Phiphat[25] had taken command of an army sent from Bangkok to assist Kedah in fighting Tengku Massa-at,[26] the nephew/ grandson of the ruler of Kedah who was in revolt. *Phrayā* Sī Phiphat was stopping with his army in Songkhlā. Nakhǭn Sī Thammarāt therefore sent the report for the consideration of *phrayā* Sī Phiphat, the commander in Songkhlā. *Phrayā* Sī Phiphat sent *luang* Sǭnsēnī, a labour foreman,[27] to send a letter by ocean-going war boats to forbid the ruler of Kelantan and Tengku Besar to quarrel. *Luang* Sǭnsēnī reached Kelantan on Wednesday, the tenth day of the waning moon of the sixth month in the Year of the Pig, first of the decade [8 May 1839].

As for *phrayā* Banggul, knowing that *luang* Sǭnsēnī was coming to Kelantan with ocean-going war boats, he was fearful because he knew himself to be in the wrong. Therefore he induced Tengku Tengah and Tengku Long Ahmad and their followers, retainers, and troops to flee to the village of Salong in Trengganu, [so that] *luang* Sǭnsēnī would not be able to find and speak to him.

Luang Sǭnsēnī having forbade them, the ruler of Kelantan and Tengku Besar ceased fighting. Then *luang* Sǭnsēnī took Tengku Besar to go and see the commander, *phrayā* Sī Phiphat, in Songkhlā. *Phrayā* Sī Phiphat admonishing and instructing him, Tengku Besar became submissive, and gave his oath that he would not quarrel with the ruler of

[23] Text has Hāmad; amended by means of Skinner (1966).
[24] Who is this?
[25] That Bunnag, officially head of the Royal Warehouses Department (*krom phrakhlang sinkhā*), but much more active as the right-hand man of his brother, *čhaophrayā* Phra-Khlang (Dit Bunnag), who as minister in charge of the Kalāhom had responsibility for the southern provinces and tributary states. Cf. Wyatt (1968).
[26] Untraceable.
[27] *nāy phrai*, lit. (a man) in charge of *phrai*, freemen engaged in compulsory labour service.

Kelantan. *Phrayā* Sī Phiphat then had *luang* Sǫnsēnī bear his command and accompany Tengku Besar, together with his followers, in an ocean-going war boat to pay homage to His Majesty the King in Bangkok. Tengku Besar owned up to his faults and [promised] not to quarrel with the ruler of Kelantan in the future. He asked [to be allowed] to return to his original post with the ruler of Kelantan.

The officials took the testimony and oath of Tengku Besar and laid it before His Majesty and brought Tengku Besar in for an audience with His Majesty. His Majesty's greetings to Tengku Besar were many. Then His Majesty was pleased to issue an order to *phrayā* Sī Phiphat, and another to the ruler of Kelantan, *phrayā* Čhāngwāng, and Raja Muda. *Luang* Sǫnsēnī was instructed to accompany Tengku Besar back to *phrayā* Sī Phiphat at Songkhlā. *Phrayā* Sī Phiphat was given a letter to the ruler of Kelantan, and he was to have Tengku Besar take the royal command to Kelantan. Tengku Besar and his group reached Kelantan on Sunday, the eighth day of the waning moon in the first month of the Year of the Pig, first of the decade [29 December 1839]. Tengku Besar had men go to inform the ruler of Kelantan. *Phrayā* Čhāngwāng and Raja Muda had the assembly of chiefs and officers come and bear in procession the royal order and letter of *phrayā* Sī Phiphat to the residence of the ruler of Kelantan, as was customary. Tengku Besar went for discussions with the ruler of Kelantan, *phrayā* Čhāngwāng, and Raja Muda, and everything was settled. The ruler of Kelantan divided up the territory dependent on Kelantan and gave five localities (*tambon*) to Tengku Besar. The lands and people who belonged to them from earlier times were restored.[28] The people of the country all were in good order.

On Monday, the second day of the waxing moon of the eleventh month in the Year of the Rat, second of the decade [28 September 1840], the ruler of Kelantan sent a report to Nakhǫn Sī Thammarāt; and *luang* Seri Paduka Ali, who had gone 'to listen to government' in Kelantan [also] reported in a letter. The governor of Nakhǫn Sī Thammarāt passed these reports on to Bangkok. They reported that formerly the ruler of Kelantan had had a register compiled of those paying a head tax for the making of the gold and silver trees. He had employed men to go and report to *phrayā* Čhāngwāng, Raja Muda, and Tengku Seri Indera, that they should come and receive the register; but they did not come. Later, they replied that the districts should be divided up first. So the ruler of Kelantan divided up the districts so that

---

[28] Phrase not quite clear: *thī rai nā phū khon sǖng kiao khǭng yū tāē kǫn phrayā kalantan dai khün hai set lāēo.*

phrayā Čhāngwāng had as many as the ruler of Kelantan, and Raja Muda and Tengku Seri Indera each had a share. All the head taxes in the state were divided accordingly. Later, many evil men went in with *phrayā* Čhāngwāng, Raja Muda, and Tengku Seri Indera. They bullied and cut up the people, and there were many cases of complaints [against them]. The ruler of Kelantan could not settle [these complaints]. *Phrayā* Čhāngwāng put Raja Muda up to asking for his entitlement as *barahum*[29] from the ruler of Kelantan. The ruler of Kelantan told him that he would have to request it from the governor of Nakhǭn Sī Thammarāt. *Phrayā* Čhāngwāng said that if he were not given this seal, he would make trouble. *Phrayā* Čhāngwāng wrote a letter, attaching to it[30] the name 'Sultan of Kelantan.' The ruler of Kelantan and *phrayā* Čhāngwāng mistrusted each other. They each dug trenches three to four elbows deep around their homes; and the young braves of *phrayā* Čhāngwāng, Raja Muda, and Tengku Seri Indera constantly molested and cut up the young braves of the ruler of Kelantan. The ruler of Kelantan lost patience, and asked that the governor of Nakhǭn Sī Thammarāt call *phrayā* Čhāngwāng to Nakhǭn Sī Thammarāt and keep him there: then government in Kelantan could be orderly.

The [court] officials forwarded this report to His Majesty the King. Informed, His Majesty was pleased to state that, 'The ruler of Kelantan, *phrayā* Čhāngwāng, Raja Muda, and Tengku Seri Indera are brothers. Formerly it was stated that they were fond of one another and would cooperate in maintaining order in the country, so they were appointed and given rank and title. When such petty circumstances arise, they should not rush selfishly to grasp things. That this has occurred can only be seen to be the fault of the ruler of Kelantan. In future, it will be difficult to unite them.' Therefore, His Majesty was pleased to send an order to the governor of Nakhǭn Sī Thammarāt ordering the governor to write a strongly threatening letter. This the assembly of chiefs should first communicate to the ruler of Kelantan and *phrayā* Čhāngwāng. This should be sufficient to quiet matters. The governor of Nakhǭn Sī Thammarāt then wrote [such] a letter and had *luang* Prathētsongkhrām take it to the ruler of Kelantan, *phrayā* Čhāngwāng, Raja Muda, and Tengku Seri Indera. They were informed that, if *phrayā* Čhāngwāng were to take any action, he should first consult with the ruler of Kelantan. If any one broke this command, he would be punished. At that time, *phrayā* Čhāngwāng performed the Malay rice [ceremony].[31] The

---

[29] This does not really make sense: surely he did not wish to be called 'deceased' during his lifetime!

[30] Signing it so?

[31] *tham bun khāo khāēk*: a ceremony clearly is indicated, perhaps one which it was the

son(s) of *phrayā* Čhāngwāng regularly went to converse with him,[32] but the behaviour of *phrayā* Čhāngwāng and the ruler of Kelantan still was not marked by close trust.

On Sunday the twelfth day of the waxing moon in the ninth month of the Year of the Ox, third of the decade [30 July 1841], Tengku Besar came to Bangkok and laid accusations against *phrayā* Čhāngwāng, Raja Muda, Tengku Seri Indera and Ku Sarima,[33] stating that they had appropriated forest groves and lands that belonged to Tengku Besar and nineteen other proprietors in his group. Tengku Besar had reported this to the ruler of Kelantan, and the ruler of Kelantan had ordered [the lands] returned to Tengku Besar and his group; but *phrayā* Čhāngwāng, Raja Muda, Tengku Seri Indera, and Ku Sarima had not returned them. As for the ruler of Kelantan, he laid allegations against Tengku Besar, claiming that Tengku Besar had employed men to go and plot with *phrayā* Banggul, Tengku Long Ahmad, and Tengku Dareh[34] in Trengganu. Tengku Dareh had had men go and plot with the rajas in Lingga for assistance to Tengku Besar in doing ill against Kelantan. When challenged, Tengku Besar stated that when he had come to Bangkok, Tengku Long Ahmad had written a letter saying that he had asked only that Tengku Besar assist him in considering how he might return to Kelantan. [Thus,] Tengku Besar had not plotted [against] Kelantan as [alleged in] the letter of the ruler of Kelantan. The [court] officials forwarded the report of the ruler of Kelantan and the sworn testimony of Tengku Besar to the King, and His Majesty was fully informed [of their contents].

His Majesty the King, considering that the ruler of Kelantan and Tengku Besar were not in harmony with one another, and that their unity would be one in name only, while in their hearts they still would be antagonistic towards one another, [decided] that their country would have to be divided if the two sides were to have peace. [Just] at that time the ruler of Patani died. So His Majesty was pleased to elevate the ruler of Nǫngchik to be ruler of Patani; and [the new ruler of Patani] was induced to have Tengku Besar come with his followers to live in Nǫngchik, close to Songkhlā, in order that the enmity between them might be ended. Nǫngchik was a small state, and many of the group of Tengku Besar would come to live there. The state would become

---

prerogative of the ruler to perform. If, as the text suggests, it might have taken place in June, this may have been the *puja* ceremony.

[32] The implication here is that they were trying to moderate his behaviour.

[33] No such person appears in any of the literature; but possibly Tengku Seri Mas?

[34] Tengku Dareh is not identified: might he be a Trengganu figure? He might be = Tengku Teh, half-brother of Tengku (later Sultan) Umar of Trengganu, and later Sultan Muhammad of Lingga (Skinner, 1964, 187).

richer and more stable. Tengku Besar agreed to come and live in Nǫngchik. Therefore His Majesty the King issued orders to the governor of Nakhǫn Sī Thammarāt, the governor of Songkhlā, and the ruler of Kelantan. The governor of Chaiyā, *phrayā* Chaiyā Thāinām, was appointed commissioner to conduct Tengku Besar back to Kelantan. [There,] the family, followers, and group of Tengku Besar was divided up and brought to Nǫngchik. *Phrayā* Chaiyā Thāinām left Bangkok on Sunday, the third day of the waning moon of the eleventh month in the Year of the Ox, third of the decade [3 October 1841], and reached Kelantan on Saturday, the eleventh day of the waxing moon in the second month in the Year of the Ox, third of the decade [23 December 1841].

On Wednesday, the fourth day of the waning moon of the fifth month in the Year of the Tiger, fourth of the decade [30 March 1842], *phrayā* Chaiyā Thāinām sent[35] a report by *luang* Phiphitphakdī, which stated that he had admonished Tengku Besar to take his followers and group to Nǫngchik; but Tengku Besar had said that the people who would accompany him still were stuck to their land. In the sixth month, when they had harvested the rice from their fields, then they would come. Tengku Besar asked that *phrayā* Chaiyā Thāinām write a letter to *phrayā* Banggul and Tengku Long Ahmad in Trengganu to induce them to come to Kelantan. They arrived on Wednesday, the fifth day of the waxing moon of the fifth month in the Year of the Tiger, fourth of the decade [16 March 1842]. Their numbers included fourteen chiefs in charge of two hundred men, with twenty Trengganu Malays accompanying them, a total of 234 men. They stayed in front of the residence of Tengku Besar. *Phrayā* Chaiyā Thāinām had *phrayā* Banggul and Tengku Long Ahmad swear the oath of allegiance to His Majesty. Then he said that he would have *phrayā* Banggul and Tengku Long Ahmad come to live in Nǫngchik. They refrained from saying so, but it would appear that they did not wish to come. As for Tengku Besar, he made excuses and delayed going. [Furthermore,] Tengku Besar drew up a contract addressed to *phrayā* Chaiyā Thāinām in which he stated that if he were made ruler of Kelantan, he would give to *phrayā* Chaiyā Thāinām ten thousand dollars in silver, and to *khun* Samretphāsā, the interpreter, he would give five hundred dollars. The court officials presented the letter of *phrayā* Chaiyā Thāinām for His Majesty's consideration. His Majesty was pleased to issue an order to the governor of Nakhǫn Sī Thammarāt, and another to the governor of Songkhlā, stating that when Tengku Besar came to Bangkok, the ruler of Kelantan had made allegations against him. When faced with these,

[35] I.e., it arrived in Bangkok on this date.

Tengku Besar had not accepted them. Then Tengku Besar had stated that the ruler of Kelantan's accusations [against him], alleging capital crimes, were false. He could perform government service under the superintendence of the ruler of Kelantan no longer. He had asked to [be allowed] to take his followers and group to live in Nǫngchik. Therefore His Majesty had had *phrayā* Chaiyā Thāinām appointed commissioner to go and divide up his family in Kelantan and come and live in Nǫngchik. When [Tengku Besar] had reached Kelantan, he had asked *phrayā* Chaiyā Thāinām to write a letter to induce *phrayā* Banggul and Tengku Long Ahmad to come, and Tengku Besar had plotted to deviate from his agreement and not go to Nǫngchik. Furthermore, *phrayā* Čhāngwāng had quarrelled with the ruler of Kelantan. Whatever the collaboration between Tengku Besar and *phrayā* Čhāngwāng might yield, there was a commissioner in Kelantan, so that *phrayā* Čhāngwāng would act properly towards the ruler of Kelantan. If Tengku Besar were not separated from his followers and group, he would create a pretext to fight with the ruler of Kelantan again, and the affair would be prolonged. [The governors] were instructed to conscript the men of Nakhǫn and Songkhlā, two thousand men from each town. *Phrayā* Sanēhāmontrī[36] and *phra* Sunthǫnnurak[37] were to take charge of them and go down to join with *phrayā* Chaiyā Thāinām at Kelantan. When the ruler of Kelantan and *phrayā* Čhāngwāng and Tengku Besar saw this large force arriving, they would fear its power and matters could be settled. However, when they set out they were to spread a rumour that the festivities of the field shad ended, and the time had come when Tengku Besar should take his family, followers, and group up to Nǫngchik. The governor of Nakhǫn and the governor of Songkhlā had *phrayā* Sanēhāmontrī and *phra* Sunthǫnnurak go down to assist *phrayā* Chaiyā Thāinām receive the family of Tengku Besar and distribute food supplies to them, that they might not be in need.

Luang Phiphitphakdī received the royal order, and took leave of His Majesty to depart from Bangkok on Monday, the eighth day of the waning moon of the sixth month in the Year of the Tiger, fourth of the decade [2 May 1841]. He informed Nakhǫn Sī Thammarāt and Songkhlā of the [royal] order, and then went to Kelantan. *Phra* Sunthǫnnurak, in charge of men from Songkhlā, reached Kelantan on Wednesday [Monday?], the fourth day of the waxing moon in the second eighth month in the Year of the Tiger, fourth of the decade

[36] Deputy governor of Nakhǫn Sī Thammarāt, given name Nǫi Iat, the fourth child of *čhaophrayā* Nakhǫn (Nǫi), who was governor of Nakhǫn from 1811 to 1839.
[37] Apparently an officer on the Songkhlā establishment: see the third sentence of the following paragraph.

[11 July 1842]; and *phrayā* Sanēhāmontrī, in charge of men from Nakhǭn Sī Thammarāt, reached Kelantan on Saturday, the eighth day of the waning moon of the second eighth month in the Year of the Tiger, fourth of the decade [30 July 1842.] They consulted on public affairs in Kelantan with *phrayā* Chaiyā Thāinām and were told that Tengku Besar finally had yielded and had agreed to go to Nǭngchik. On Monday, the eighth day of the waxing moon of the tenth month in the Year of the Tiger, fourth of the decade [12 September 1842], Tengku Besar conducted his families away from Kelantan with a total of 1,388 families, comprising 6,863 men and women, old and young. In the transporting of Tengku Besar at this time, the ruler of Trengganu arranged for thirty boats to assist in transporting Tengku Besar. There were fifty elephants from Songkhlā and five belonging to Tengku Besar, all together fifty-five elephants. The *māēkǭng* Lamai of Sāi[38] took charge of one hundred men and went ahead. *Phrayā* Rangae[39] took charge of one hundred men and brought up the rear. *Phrayā* Chaiyā Thāinām went as far as the village of Tumpat to send them off, and had junior officers go with them as far as the borders of Kelantan. *Phrayā* Banggul and Tengku Long Ahmad returned to [fetch] their families in Trengganu and then followed Tengku Besar to live in Nǭngchik. *Phrayā* Banggul and Tengku Long Ahmad died in Nǭngchik. When Tengku Besar left Kelantan, it seems that the behaviour of *phrayā* Čhāngwāng, Raja Muda, and Tengku Seri Indera towards the ruler of Kelantan was softened. Therefore, *phrayā* Sanēhāmontrī sought out *phrayā* Čhāngwāng, Raja Muda, and Tengku Seri Indera and had them come to his fort. Then he arrested them saying that he would bring them with him to Bangkok. *Phrayā* Čhāngwāng, Raja Muda, and Tengku Seri Indera agreed to go with him. Then the ruler of Kelantan came to *phrayā* Sanēhāmontrī to beg that Raja Muda and Tengku Seri Indera [be allowed] to remain to assist the government of Kelantan. *Phrayā* Sanēhāmontrī, considering that Raja Muda and Tengku Seri Indera were but minor men, allowed the ruler of Kelantan to keep them. *Phrayā* Sanēhāmontrī took *phrayā* Čhāngwāng, Tengku Sulong,[40] Tengku Kaci,[41] and Tengku Senik,[42] together with five Malays and

---

[38] I.e., Sāiburī (Teluban), east of Patani on the coast.

[39] I.e., the governor or chief of Ra-ngae, an old town in the present-day province of Narāthiwāt, created a province on the seven-fold division of Patani in the first or second decade of the 19th century.

[40] Identified below as the eldest son of *phrayā* Čhāngwāng. Note that there is also a Tengku Tuan Sulong, another brother of 'Red Mouth' Senik, and others by the same name (Rentse 1936).

[41] Perhaps Kechil, brother of Tengku Besar, and son of Long Ismail (*phrayā Bān Thalē*) (Rentse 1936) or of Tuan Dagang (Marriott 1916, 22).

[42] There are many by this name in the sources.

thirty-three men—a total of forty-two men—with Wan Hanu and Che Wang, Malays in [the service of] the ruler of Kelantan, in charge of two *chang* weight of gold dust and Malay products, for presentations [to the King]. They reached Nakhọn Sī Thammarāt on Tuesday, the thirteenth day of the waning moon of the eleventh month in the Year of the Tiger, fourth of the decade [1 November 1842]. The governor of Nakhọn Sī Thammarāt then issued an order for *phrayā* Sanēhāmontrī to accompany *phrayā* Čhāngwāng and the forty-two officers and men, with Wan Hanu and Che Wang, to go in to be presented to His Majesty the King. Then His Majesty was pleased to have *phrayā* Čhāngwāng and his followers to go out and live in Nakhọn Sī Thammarāt.

Tengku Besar lived in Nọngchik for three years. In the year of the lesser dragon, seventh of the decade, 1207 of the lesser era [A.D. 1845–46], the ruler of Patani died.[43] His Majesty was pleased to appoint Tengku Besar as ruler of Patani. Tengku[44] was appointed *phra* Phiphitphakdī, assistant in the government. The ruler of Patani [Tengku Besar] then took some of his followers to live in Patani, while some still remained to live in Nọngchik. The ruler of Patani and the ruler of Kelantan returned to their mutual respect and affection for each other as before. The ruler of Patani requested Tengku Che'[45], the daughter of the ruler of Kelantan, to be the wife of Tengku Puteh, one of his sons. When they were married, Tengku Puteh agreed to come and live in Patani.

In the Year of the Ox, fifth of the decade, in 1215 of the lesser era [1853/54], in the reign of His Majesty King Mongkut, the governor of Yaring[46] died. His Majesty was pleased to appoint *phrayā* Čhāngwāng to act as governor of Yaring, and appointed Tengku Sulong, his eldest son, to be *luang* Sunthọn Raja, assistant in the government of Yaring. The governor of Yaring then took his son(s) and Malay chiefs and men to go and live in Yaring. When the governor of Yaring fell ill and died, *luang* Sunthọn Raja took his followers and went back to live with the ruler of Kelantan in Kelantan.

In the Year of the Greater Dragon, eighth of the decade, 1218 of the lesser era [1856–57], the ruler of Patani, Tengku Besar, fell ill and died. He had four sons, named Tengku Puteh, Tengku Madoh, Tengku Nidorahan, and Tengku Sabasu. They lived in Patani. His Majesty was pleased to appoint Tengku Puteh, his eldest son, to be ruler of Patani

---

[43] Agrees with the date given in the 'Prawat müang pattānī'. No date is given in *phrayā* Wichiankhiri (1964, 19).
[44] Text is deficient here: the proper name is omitted in the 1961 and 1963 printed editions.
[45] In Rentse (1936) she is listed as 'Tengku Raja (Engku Na Nik)'.
[46] Also written Jering.

and govern henceforth in the place of his father. The ruler of Patani and his wife constantly went to visit the ruler of Kelantan. The ruler of Kelantan took the son of the [new] ruler of Patani, [also] named Tengku Besar, who was his grandson, to live in Kelantan. The ruler of Patani took a daughter of *phra* Phiphitphakdī to be one of his wives.

In the Year of the Horse, first of the decade, 1221 of the lesser era [1859–60] His Majesty King Mongkut made a royal progress by water on his royal steamship to tour the coastal provinces of the south and went as far as Patani. When [His Majesty] was staying in the royal pavilion on the Son Peninsula at Songkhlā, the ruler of Kelantan took Tengku Besar,[47] his son, to be presented in audience to His Majesty the King. His Majesty then was pleased to bestow upon Tengku Besar[47] a title as *phra* Ratsadāthibǫdī Butburutphisēt, assistant in the government in Kelantan.

In the Year of the Greater Dragon, first of the decade, 1231 of the lesser era [1869–70], in the Fifth Reign [of the Chakrī Dynasty], His Excellency *čhaophrayā* Sī Suriyawong, Regent of the kingdom,[48] arranged for a steamboat named Prahphāt Udǫn Sayām, and appointed *luang* Kōchā Ishak to be a commissioner and go out to meet *phra* Ratsadāthibǫdī Butburutphisēt and bring him to be presented to His Majesty the King. The vessel Praphāt Udǫn Sayām left Bangkok on Thursday, the second day of the waxing moon of the seventh month in the Year of the Greater Dragon, first of the decade [12 May 1869], and returned to Bangkok on Sunday, the twelfth day of the waning moon of the seventh month in the Year of the Greater Dragon, first of the decade [6 June 1869]. [In the party which] came in for an audience with His Majesty the King, there were *phra* Ratsadāthibǫdī Butburutphisēt, four of his sons, thirty-two of the assembly of chiefs, the two Kapitan China, seven Chinese retainers, twenty Malay retainers, altogether seventy men.

On Monday, the sixth day of the waxing moon of the first eighth month[49] in the Year of the Lesser Dragon, first of the decade [14 June 1869], His Majesty was pleased to bestow upon *phra* Ratsadāthibǫdī Butburutphisēt a title as *phrayā* Ratsadāthibǫdī Butburutphisēt Prathētsarātchanarųbǫdin Surintharawiwangsā, governor acting for the ruler of Kelantan.[50] He presented to him a sword with a golden sheath. His

---

[47] This must be a mistake for Tengku Sulong (Tengku Ahmad), who in 1886 succeeded his father as ruler of Kelantan.

[48] During the minority of King Chulalongkorn (reg. 1868–1910), 1868–73. He was named Chuang Bunnag, and was the son of *čhaophrayā* Phrakhlang (Dit) mentioned in Note 25 above.

[49] Thai 'leap years' by the old luni-solar calendar had two eighth months.

[50] 'Red Mouth' Senik had ruled for 31 years, and by this time must have been quite elderly.

Majesty was pleased to have the vessel Praphāt Udǫn Sayām go and take *phrayā* Ratsadāthibǫdī Butburutphisēt [back]. It left Bangkok on Wednesday, the eighth day of the waxing moon of the first eighth month in the Year of the Lesser Dragon, first of the decade [16 June 1869], and returned to Bangkok on Saturday, the second day of the waxing moon of the second eighth month in the Year of the Lesser Dragon, first of the decade [10 July 1869].

In the Year of the Rat, eighth of the decade, 1238 of the lesser era [1876/77], was the time appointed for the Malay tributary states to send the gold and silver trees in tribute to His Majesty the King. The ruler of Kelantan appointed Wan Baja in charge of a party to take the gold and silver trees of tribute [to Bangkok]. A report arrived stating that the ruler of Kelantan was very old and asking that the government of the state be handed over to *phrayā* Ratsadāthibǫdī Butburutphisēt, and that he should present the gold and silver trees of tribute in place of the ruler of Kelantan thereafter.

When the state guests had taken their leave, His Majesty the King was pleased to issue an order bearing the seal of the *phra khotchasī*[51] in reply to the ruler of Kelantan stating that His Majesty the King, upon consideration, seeing that the ruler of Kelantan was aged, would be pleased to extend his royal grace and raise up *phrayā* Ratsadāthibǫdī Butburutphisēt to be the ruler. His Majesty would be pleased to raise the rank of the ruler of Kelantan to be the *čhāngwāng* of Kelantan and have the ruler of Kelantan consult with his senior and junior relatives and the assembly of chiefs; and if they together saw fit to do so, they should together report to His Majesty.

The ruler of Kelantan, Raja Muda, and *phrayā* Ratsadāthibǫdī Butburutphisēt wrote a letter and had Wan Muda, with officers and men, take it to Nakhǫn Sī Thammarāt, from whence it was forwarded to Bangkok. It stated that the ruler of Kelantan, Raja Muda, and *phrayā* Ratsadāthibǫdī Butburutphisēt had consulted with their senior and junior relatives and they had agreed. However, the ruler of Kelantan sent word with Wan Muda, apart from the letter, to be reported to His Excellency the *Kalāhom*[52] that he was gratified that His Majesty was pleased to increase his title and rank, for which His Majesty's mercy was to be complimented; but he asked that the title of *čhāngwāng* be changed to something else.[53]

[51] The seal of the Kalāhom Ministry, the ministry of the southern provinces.
[52] *Čhaophrayā* Surawong Waiyawat (Wōn Bunnag), son of *čhaophrayā* Sī Suriyawong (Chuang Bunnag).
[53] Consider the implications of this title, and the character of its holder, mentioned above, Note 19.

His Excellency the *Kalāhom*, being informed, reported to His Majesty the King. Informed, His Majesty the King was pleased to have the court officials of the department of the royal scribes inscribe the name on the title of appointment as, '*phrayā* Dēchānuchitmahitsarājānukūlawibūnlayaphakdī Seri Sultan Muhammad Rattanathādā Mahapathānāthikān', Superintendent of the Government of Kelantan. Then His Majesty was pleased to have *phra* Amǫrawisaisǫradet, head of the Artillery Department; *phrayā* Rātchawangsan, *čhāngwāng* of the Department of Cham Volunteers; and *phra* Sanēhāmontrī, assistant in the government of Nakhǫn Sī Thammarāt, go as commissioners with the warship named Phitthayam Ranayut to convey to Kelantan the titles of appointments and orders appointing the ruler of Kelantan as *phrayā* Dēchānuchit, and *phrayā* Ratsadāthibǫdī Butburutphisēt as ruler of Kelantan. Using its machinery, the warship left Bangkok on Sunday, the fifth day of the waning moon of the fourth month in the Year of the Rat, eighth of the decade [4 March 1877]. The appointment having been conferred, [the vessel] returned to Bangkok on Thursday, the seventh day of the waxing moon of the sixth month in the Year of the Ox, ninth of the decade [19 April 1877].

NINETEENTH CENTURY KELANTAN: A THAI VIEW

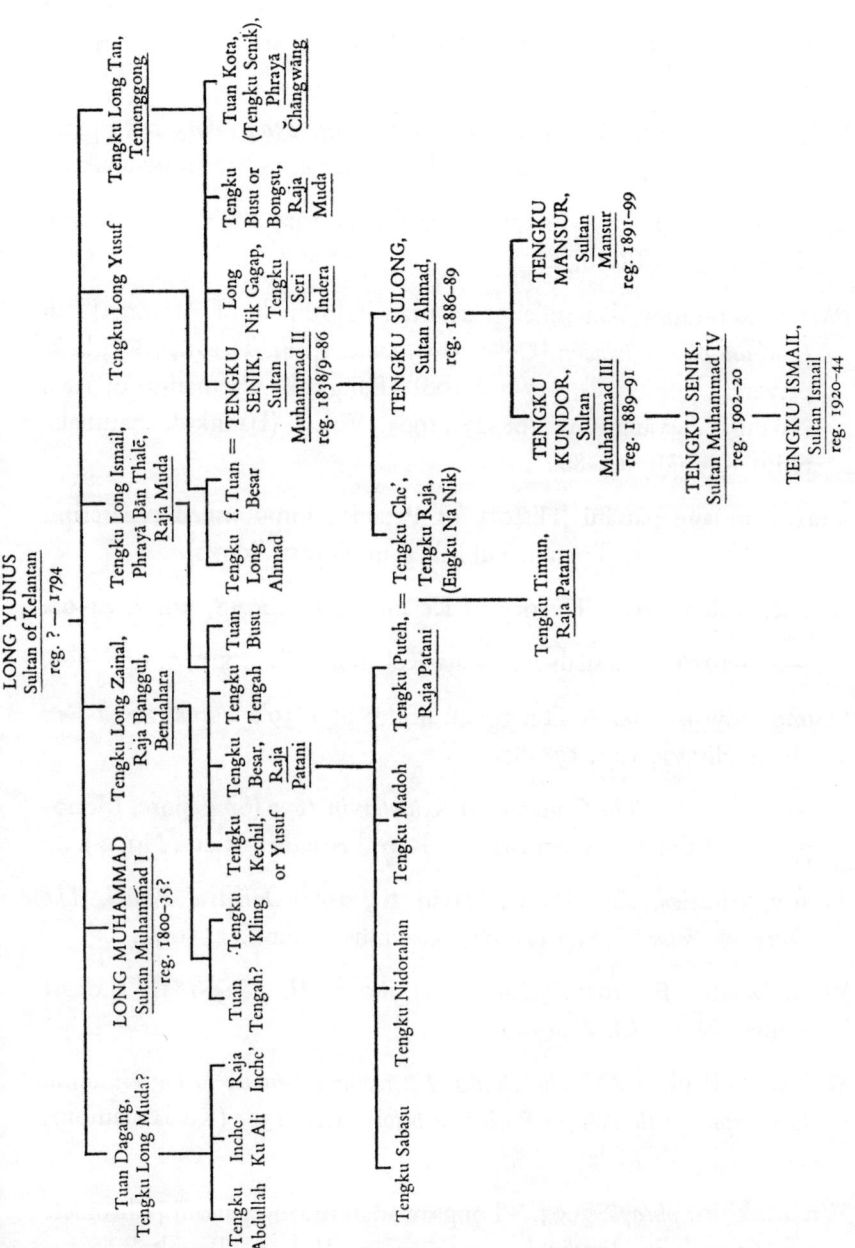

REFERENCES

Graham, Walter Armstrong, 1908. *Kelantan, a State of the Malay Peninsula. A Handbook of Information* (Glasgow, James Maclehose and Sons).

Khlọi Songbandit, 1954. *Patithin 250 pī, ph.s. 2304 thüng 2555 [250-Year Calendar, A.D. 1761-2012]* (Bangkok, S. Thammaphakdī).

Marriott, H., 1916. 'A Fragment of the History of Trengganu and Kelantan', *JSBRAS*, 72, 1-23.

PMK: 'Phongsāwadān müang kalantan [Chronicle of Kelantan]', in *Prachum phongsāwadān [Collected Chronicles]*, Pt. 2; 1914 (Bangkok. privately published), 117-33; 1961 (Bangkok. Cremation of *mọm* Nüang Chayāngkūn), 108-23; 1963. Vol. 1 (Bangkok. Samnakphim Kāonā), 563-80.

'Prawat müang pattānī [History of Patani]', unpublished typescript, n.p., n.d. (Portion published in Wyatt, 1967b).

Rentse, Anker, 1934. 'History of Kelantan', *JMBRAS*, XII, 2, 44-62.

——————1936. 'Salsilah Raja-raja Kelantan', *Ibid.*, XIV, 3, opp. 306.

Skinner, Cyril, 1964. 'A Trengganu leader of 1839', *Journal South-East Asian History*, V, 1, 178-87.

——————1966. *The Civil war in Kelantan in 1839* (Singapore, Monographs of the Malaysian Branch, Royal Asiatic Society, No. 2.).

Teeuw, Andries, and Wyatt, David K., 1970. *Hikayat Patani. The Story of Patani.* (The Hague. Martinus Nijhoff, 2 vols.).

Vella, Walter F., 1957. *Siam Under Rama III, 1824-1851.* (Locust Valley, N.Y., J.J. Augustin).

Wheatley, Paul., 1961. *The Golden Khersonese: Studies in the Historical Geography of the Malay Peninsula before A.D. 1500* (Kuala Lumpur, University of Malaya Press).

Wichiankhiri, *phrayā*, 1964. 'Phongsāwadān müang pattānī [Chronicle of Patani]', in *Prachum phongsāwadān*, Vol. 2. (Bangkok, Samnakphim Kāonā), 1-29 (First published in 1914; cf. *PMK*, above).

Wyatt, David K., 1967a. 'Thai Sources for the Study of Malaysias' History', *Peninjau Sejarah*, II, 1, 19-24.

———1967b. 'A Thai version of Newbold's "Hikayat Patani"', *JMBRAS*, XL, 2, 16–37.

———1968. 'Family Politics in Nineteenth Century Thailand', *Journal of Southeast Asian History*, IX, 2, 208–28.

———1972. *The Crystal Sands: Nagara Srī Dharrmarāja in Early Thai History*, Vol. I (Forthcoming).

Wyatt, David K., and Bastin, John S., 1968. 'Mainland Powers on the Malay Peninsula, A.D. 1000–1511', *International Conference on Asian History*, Kuala Lumpur. Paper no. 63.

Wyatt, David K., and Wilson, Constance M., 1965. 'Thai Historical Materials in Bangkok', *Journal of Asian Studies*, XXV, 1, 105–18.

2

MOHAMED B. NIK MOHD. SALLEH
Kelantan in Transition: 1891-1910

THE years between 1891 and 1910 constitute the most complex and crucial period in the history of modern Kelantan. The hitherto comparatively little known or obscure Malay state suddenly emerged to become a subject of controversy which involved two imperial governments—Siam and Britain. In fact the Kelantan affair became a matter of anxiety and concern for both Bangkok and London. The developments emanating from the dispute over Kelantan during this historic period determined and influenced not only the course of history and the fate of the state, but also changed or altered the future relations between Kelantan and Siam and Britain. During this period Kelantan was, in fact, caught up within the web of Siamese southward expansion and British forward policy in northern Malaya.

By 1900, while Siam was consolidating her influence and control over the Malay states of northern Malaya—Setul, Perlis, Kedah, Patani, Trengganu and Kelantan—over which she had previously exercised nominal control and influence,[1] Britain was also beginning to adopt a forward policy within the same area of the peninsula,[2] thus challenging

[1] For a brief account of the early history of Siamese-Malay relations, see above, Wyatt. Note that in the present paper, the spelling of Thai titles and names follows that given in the Malay sources.
[2] For a discussion of this, see Thio (1957, 6-17).

the Siamese claim to the Malay states north of Perak and Pahang. This inevitably brought Siam and Britain into direct confrontation in northern Malaya, and Kelantan became the victim.

Sultan Mansur (1891–1900)

During the last decade of the nineteenth century, Kelantan was ruled by Sultan Mansur,[3] who ascended the throne in 1891 following the sudden and unexpected death of Sultan Muhammad III,[4] his elder brother. In order better to understand the subsequent history of Kelantan, it is worth going back to the events of that year. When Sultan Muhammad III died in May 1891, the question of the succession to the throne arose yet again, for the second time in three years.[5] There were three principal claimants, Tuan Long Ja'afar (Tengku Petra),[6] Tuan (or Tengku) Long Senik,[7] and the brothers of the late Sultan Muhammad, notable among whom was Tuan Long Mansur, also known as Tengku Mansur.[8] Tuan Long Ja'afar seems to have been 'the popular candidate both with the Chiefs and people',[9] and according to one source an understanding had been reached with old Sultan Muhammad II when he died in 1886[10] that if his eldest son, Ahmad, should succeed him,[11] he in turn should be succeeded by the only remaining son,

[3] Tuan Long Mansor b. Tuan Long Ahmad, or Tengku or Engku Mansor as he was variously known. As far as may be ascertained from available sources, the Rajas of Kelantan prior to about 1900 were known by the title 'Tuan'. The titles 'Tengku' and 'Engku' became familiar only at the beginning of the twentieth century. A Chinese traveller who visited Kelantan in 1782, Hsieh Ching-kao, wrote that 'the Sultan... has his court daily attended by Wans and Tuans' (Tweedie, 1953, 216). Graham (1908a, 51) writes, '... the Rajas or Tengkus, as they now began to be called...', and Clifford (1961, 107) remarked in 1895 that 'the Kelantan ruling class belongs to the family of Wan'.

[4] Tuan Long Kundor b. Tuan Long Ahmad (reg. 1890–1). He was the Raja Bendahara when his father Sultan Ahmad died in 1890. The cause of his own sudden death in 1891 was unknown. Clifford (1961, 108) says that 'it was popularly rumoured that his death was the result of careful arrangements made to that end'. The persons responsible, were this the case, must have been from among his relatives, who included at that time Tuan Long Ja'afar or Tengku Petra (his uncle); his brothers Tuan Long Mansur, Tuan Long Mahmud, Tuan Long Idris, Tuan Long Yusof or Tengku Besar, and Tuan Long Salleh; and Tengku Chik Penambang (his cousin). See Clifford (1961, 108–9), and Mohd. Husin (1970, 81).

[5] Disputes over succession had apparently been a common feature of Kelantan history, at least since the death of Long Yunus (the founder of the present house) in 1794.

[6] Younger of the two sons of Sultan Muhammad II, brother of Sultan Ahmad, and only uncle of Sultan Muhammad III.

[7] Eldest son of Sultan Muhammad III.

[8] Sultan Muhammad III had eleven brothers and fourteen sisters by five or more different mothers.

[9] Clifford (1961, 109).

[10] Tuan Senik b. Long Tan was also commonly known as Sultan Mulut Merah (the Red-Mouthed Sultan).

[11] Tuan Sulong Ahmad b. Tuan Senik (reg. 1886–90) was also commonly known as Sultan Tengah (the In-Between Sultan).

Long Ja'afar.[12] Having been passed over once, however, Long Ja'afar was to be passed over again.[13]

Tuan Long Senik, though the eldest son of the late Muhammad III, and as a result having the right in normal circumstances to succeed his father, was also ignored in the succession struggle. It has been said that he was not only a weakling but a person of doubtful character, and thus considered unsuitable to hold the throne.[14] The third claimant, or group of claimants, comprised the brothers of the late Muhammad III, the most notable and strongest of whom was Tuan Long Mansur.[15] As events turned out it was Long Mansur, backed by the Dato' Maha Mentri and Dato' Sri Paduka,[16] the principal officers of state, who became the new ruler of Kelantan.

Tuan Long Mansur became ruler of Kelantan with the minor title of 'Raja Kelantan.' He did not assume the title 'Sultan' because he feared to raise trouble in the country if he attempted to do so, and also because he entertained a superstitious dread of doing so, based upon the short time that his immediate predecessor, Sultan Muhammad III, had lived on the throne.[17] His position as the new ruler of Kelantan was recognized by the Siamese Government in about 1894, when the latter conferred upon him the Siamese title of '*Phya Decha*.' It is not known why Bangkok recognized him as Raja Kelantan in preference to either Tuan Long Ja'afar, the oldest living member of the royal line at that time, or Tuan Long Senik, the eldest son of the late Sultan. One reason was probably that Long Mansur had paid much more in monetary tribute to the Siamese authorities than had the other candidates, in return for the recognition of his position. He was able to bribe the Siamese with large sums of money realized from the properties left by his late father (Sultan Ahmad) and brother (Sultan Muhammad III), including the shares due to his brothers, which he had not distributed to them.[18] It was also alleged that the person mainly responsible for procuring Bangkok's recognition of Tuan Long Mansur as the new

[12] Verbal communication from Tengku Khalid b. Tengku Chik Abdullah.
[13] This repeated neglect may have been due to the fact that he had a commoner mother (verbal communication from Tengku Khalid b. Tengku Chik Abdullah).
[14] Verbal communications from Tengku Khalid and Inche Mohd. Salleh b. Imam Haji Abdullah, in separate interviews. Asa'ad (1962, 81) says that after the death of Sultan Muhammad III there was a struggle for the throne, as a result of which Tengku Mansur was installed 'temporarily' (*sementara*), with the title of Sultan, pending the growth to maturity of Tengku Sri Indera (Tuan Long Senik), who was still young.
[15] Among the others were Tuan Long Mansur, Tuan Long Salleh, Tuan Long Mahmud, Tuan Long Idris, Tuan Long Sulaiman, and Tuan Long Yusof.
[16] Clifford (1961, 109). The personal name of Dato' Maha Mentri was Sa'ad (or Ha') b. Ngah (he was known also as Che' Ha'), and that of Dato' Sri Paduka was (Nik) Yusof b. Nik Abdul Majid (often known as Nik Soh b. Nik Jid, or as Nik Sri Paduka).
[17] Clifford (1961, 109).
[18] *Ibid.* Cf. Norman (1895, 580).

ruler of Kelantan, was Dato' Maha Mentri[19] who visited Bangkok in 1894[20] presumably for that purpose. It may well have been that Bangkok's ready recognition of Tuan Long Mansur as Raja Kelantan, was due to the latter's acceptance of a resident Siamese Commissioner in Kota Bharu and the hoisting in the capital of the Siamese flag. When Dato' Maha Mentri returned from Bangkok in 1894, he was in fact accompanied by this official.[21] No Siamese soldiers were however stationed in Kelantan.[22]

Tuan Long Mansur was recognized as 'Sultan' by Bangkok in about 1897, with the Siamese title of *Phya Phipit Pakdi*.[23] At the same time, Bangkok also recognized Tuan Long Senik (the Raja Muda) as Raja Kelantan (the heir to the throne), or *Phya Decha* in Siamese; and Tuan Long Zainal Abidin (the Tengku Sri Indera) as the Raja Muda, or *Phya Ratsada* in Siamese.[24]

The murder of Dato' Maha Mentri (1894)

Some time after his return from Bangkok in 1894, Dato' Maha Mentri was murdered in his house at Kampong Penambang.[25] Later investigation conducted by Siamese authorities in Kota Bahru revealed that at least three killers were involved in the shooting.[26] One of the killers, by the name of Tuan Kundor, who was later arrested, confessed that he and two others[27] namely Awang Chik and Ibrahim Chandu, were hired by the three brothers of Sultan Mansur, namely Tuan Long Mahmud, Tuan Long Sulaiman and Tuan Long Yusof, for a sum of two hundred dollars.[28] It appears that no action was taken by the Siamese authorities against either the killer or his hirers. Presumably the Siamese, having recognized Tuan Long Mansur as the new ruler of Kelantan and realizing the possible usefulness of his brothers to Bangkok in the near future, chose to do nothing to bring those involved in the murder to

[19] Verbal communications from Tengku Khalid and Inche Mohd. Salleh.
[20] Davies (1902, 3-4). [21] *Ibid*. The official was Phraya Tipakosa.
[22] *Ibid*.
[23] DRM. An additional mention occurs in OTHMAN.
[24] DRM.
[25] Davies (1902, 4), and HSK. Kampong Penambang is about two miles north of Kota Bharu. According to Mohd. Husin (1970, 88), he was shot dead by unknown persons at the house of his second wife, Hajjah Che' Wok. He was buried at Kampong Banggul cemetery.
[26] The enquiry took place only in 1901, almost seven years after the event, a delay perhaps explained by the fact that it was not until then that one of the killers, Tuan Kundor, was captured.
[27] DRM mentions only three killers, Tuan Kundor, Awang Chik, and Ibrahim Chandu. The name of a possible fourth, Tuan Yahya, or Tuan Ya, has also been mentioned (verbal communication from Wan Daud b. Wan Omar of Jalan To' Semian, Kota Bharu).
[28] DRM. Clifford (1961, 110) notes contemporaneously that Tuan Ja'afar or Tuan Long Ja'afar (Tengku Petra) was often said to have been implicated as well.

justice. Keeping his brothers alive to conspire against Tuan Long Mansur would make the latter so insecure that he would have no choice but to continue to depend on the Siamese, to the advantage of Bangkok.[29]

The motive behind the murder of Dato' Maha Mentri was not so clear. However, the fact that Maha Mentri was the chief backer and supporter of Tuan Long Mansur and mainly responsible for the recognition by Bangkok of the latter's position as the ruler of Kelantan, must have caused great disappointment amongst the brothers of Tuan Long Mansur, as well as arousing bitter hatred in them towards the Maha Mentri. Hence they probably decided to remove him from the scene.

Dato' Maha Mentri had also earned the ill feeling of Tengku Chik Penambang,[30] who ever since the death of Sultan Muhammad III in 1891 had been manoeuvring to regain the title of Raja Muda which had been held by his late father Tuan Bongsu. As a result of the machinations of Dato' Maha Mentri, it was believed, he was not given any title at all by Tuan Long Mansur, the new ruler of Kelantan.[31] Notwithstanding the above, there is no evidence to show that Tengku Chik Penambang had any hand in the murder of the Dato' Maha Mentri, despite the fact that, as will be seen later, he is known to have borne still other grudges against him.

With the death of Dato' Maha Mentri in 1894, Dato' Sri Paduka emerged as the sole prominent chief in Kelantan, as well as the most powerful, serving as chief minister of the state from 1894 to 1900.

Confrontation between Tuan Long Mansur and Tengku Chik Penambang (1893)

A year prior to the murder of Dato' Maha Mentri, there occurred a confrontation between Tuan Long Mansur (the Raja Kelantan) and Tengku Chik Penambang. Tengku Chik Penambang had no more liking for the Raja than for his chief minister and had been waiting for

---

[29] The Siamese Commissioner stationed in Kota Bharu from 1894 had apparently done nothing either to strengthen Tuan Long Mansor's position or to deal with the conspirators. Graham (1908a, 52) noted that Sultan Mansur 'had no sooner received his appointment from the Court of Siam than he found all his brothers arrayed against him and already scheming to compass his downfall'. Clifford (1961, 109) also remarked that not long after Tuan Long Mansur's accession his brothers contacted him and begged him to aid them against the Raja.

[30] Personal name Tengku Chik b. Tuan Bongsu, whose father established his court at Kampong Penambang, from which place the toponym descended. Tuan Bongsu was a younger brother of Sultan Muhammad II, the grandfather of the Raja, Tuan Long Mansur. Tuan Bongsu was given the title of Raja Muda by his elder brother, Sultan Muhammad. He died about 1887. Cf. OTHMAN, and Mahmud (1934, 40).

[31] OTHMAN.

an opportunity to move against him. The opportunity was provided by a minor incident which occurred round about the year 1893. The incident originated from a case of petty theft, which developed into violence which, had it not been for the tactfulness and diplomacy of Dato' Sri Paduka, would have sparked off a civil war in Kelantan.[32] A man named Ali, a henchman of Tengku Chik Penambang, one day stole a duck belonging to a Chinese, who had the matter reported to Raja Kelantan (Tuan Long Mansur). The Raja thereupon ordered one Penghulu Salleh and a man named Latif, along with two others, to go to Kampong Penambang and arrest Ali. Dato' Maha Mentri himself had advised the Raja to take this action,[33] but had already, on his own initiative, ordered his men to look for Ali and arrest him. Ali took refuge in the compound of the *Balai* of Tengku Chik Penambang. Further efforts by Dato' Maha Mentri's men to take Ali resulted in clashes with the followers of Tengku Chik Penambang.[34] Later the party sent by Raja Kelantan entered the Balai and had audience with Tengku Chik Penambang. No sooner had Penghulu Salleh indicated that he and his men had come to arrest Ali, than Tengku Chik Penambang, who was already upset with Raja Kelantan, burst into a rage which resulted in a commotion during which time Penghulu Salleh was stabbed in the chest and Latif slashed on the back, both being seriously wounded. When news of the incident reached the ears of the Raja, he was furious with anger, and quickly summoned Dato' Maha Mentri, Dato' Sri Paduka and To' Hakim Engku Sayyid[35] for audience and consultations. Soon afterwards, Raja Kelantan mobilized his chiefs[36] and men and had guns and ammunition prepared.

By next morning Raja Kelantan's followers had assembled at Kebun Mengseta[37] by the side of the Kelantan river about five hundred yards from the Raja's court or palace, waiting for the order to attack Kampong Penambang, the stronghold of Tengku Chik, who by then also

---

[32] *Ibid.*   [33] HSK.   [34] *Ibid.*

[35] To' Hakim, Sayyid Muhammad b. Sayyid Alwi, a judge and the third most powerful officer of state at the time (after Dato' Maha Mentri and Dato' Sri Paduka Raja), was either brother or cousin to the Sayyid Ja'afar who became *Hakim* during the reign of Sultan Muhammad II (1837–86). According to Sayyid Hassan b. Sayyid Yusof of Kampong Repek, Pasir Mas, a descendant of Sayyid Muhammad, Sayyid Ja'afar's father came originally from the Hadhramaut, by way of Trengganu (interview, November 1964). The seal used by Sayyid Muhammad (and inspected by the present writer) carried the legend: 'Al-Sayyid Muhammad bin Sayyid Alwi bin Sayyid Yahya, Hakim Negeri Kelantan '*afā-llāhu 'anhu* 1311' (1311 = 1893/94).

[36] OTHMAN mentions two particular chiefs, Dato' Kaya Hulubalang Kadok and Dato' Panglima Perang.

[37] Kebun Mengseta (lit., mangosteen garden) was from 1842 until about 1920 the main jetty and ceremonial ground of Kota Bharu. It had several wooden buildings within the compound where VIPs, mainly Siamese officials, stayed during visits to the capital. It was later badly eroded by flood-waters, and the remaining area is now occupied by the pier of the Malaysian Railways.

had his followers ready. Meanwhile Dato' Sri Paduka and To' Hakim Engku Sayyid tried their best to mediate in order to avoid bloodshed. Tengku Chik Penambang's chiefs or representatives, Nik Mat Besar and Wan Husin, refused to negotiate other than with Dato' Maha Mentri, who had been advised by Raja Kelantan not to go to Kampong Penambang along with Dato' Sri Paduka and To' Hakim Engku Sayyid for fear that he might be singled out and harmed, perhaps killed, by the followers of Tengku Chik. After a full day of negotiations, in which Dato' Sri Paduka played the chief role, a compromise was agreed upon. Tengku Chik Penambang agreed to pay one thousand dollars as compensation for the theft as well as for the wounding of two of Raja Kelantan's men, provided Ali, the alleged thief, was released. The compensation was paid in the form of four hundred dollars in cash with a further six hundred in kind, in the form of an elephant. Ali was soon released. Thus an incident which nearly brought civil war to Kelantan was amicably settled. Later Raja Kelantan returned the elephant to Tengku Chik Penambang as a gift, but retained the four hundred dollars.[38]

Conspiracy against Sultan Mansur

As already mentioned Tuan Long Mansur had succeeded to the throne of Kelantan in 1891, upon the death of his brother Sultan Muhammad III, without the unanimous approval of his brothers and other members of the royal family. Opposition to him, accordingly, was extremely prevalent among the disappointed. Hugh Clifford (1961, 109) recorded in 1895 that shortly after Long Mansur's accession his brothers had contacted him in his capacity as Acting British Resident of Pahang, begging him to aid them against the new Raja. They complained that the property which their late father and brother had bequeathed to them jointly had all been appropriated by him. They complained that the new Raja was not the proper ruler. They even invited Clifford to depose him and place Kelantan under British protection, arguing that Tuan Long Ja'afar (Tengku Petra) should have succeeded Sultan Muhammad III.

A British Member of Parliament, Henry Norman, who visited Kota Bharu in 1894 said (Norman, 1895, 580) that he was visited one night by four younger brothers of the Raja. During an almost four-hour interview with him they told him, amongst other things, that their brother the Raja had usurped the royal authority, and had used money which should belong to them to bribe Siamese recognition of his posi-

[38] OTHMAN.

tion. He was alleged to be very cruel to everybody, including his own brothers.[39] He had also issued orders forbiddng any white men from entering or visiting Kelantan and had given orders to expel white men from the state.[40] He was greatly hated, they said, even by most of his own people. The four brothers also told Norman that they were planning to rise against their brother, but had insufficient arms and money for the purpose. They enquired whether the British Governor at Singapore would sympathize with their cause and help them. Norman offered them little comfort.

In spite of the intrigues and internal instability, Kelantan during the reign of Sultan Mansur (as he became in or about 1897) continued to make slow but steady progress. Several reforms were introduced such as the building of a jail, the assessment of land revenue and land produce, and the creation of a state police force comprised mainly of Sikhs and Indians recruited from Singapore.

Death of Sultan Mansur (1900)

Towards the end of his reign, Sultan Mansur was often ill, and before the end of 1899 he was smitten by a feverish sickness from which he never recovered. He died on 10 February, 1900.[41] A local source (DRM) mentions that when, in early 1900, Sultan Mansur fell seriously ill, the then Raja Kelantan and heir apparent (Tuan Long Senik) and the Raja Muda (Tuan Long Zainal Abidin), probably sensing an outbreak of trouble in the event of his death, despatched two messengers to Bangkok, Wan Ya'acob and Wan Hassan,[42] to warn the Siamese authorities, who immediately sent a senior Siamese official named Phya Sukhum[43] along with two other Siamese, Kong Mirik and Kong Pha.

[39] The allegations of cruelty may have rested in part, as far as the brothers themselves were concerned, on their claim (Norman, 1895, 579) that the Raja kept them shut up in their houses and spied upon, so that they could sneak out only at night.
[40] Norman (1895, 582-3) refers to one unnamed white man who had earlier visited Kelantan, had run off with the wife of one of the Raja's men and behaved improperly to several other women, the latter being punished by the Raja by having their heads shaved and their ears nailed to trees. According to Davies (1902, 7), the Raja was also warned later by the Siamese 'to have nothing to do with the English'.
[41] According to available local histories, Sultan Mansor died at 6.30 p.m. on Thursday, 8 Shawal 1317, equivalent to 10 February 1900.
[42] The identities of these two men are unknown. Wan Hassan could have been Nik Hassan, the then Dato' Shahbandar of Sungei Pinang. He was a younger brother of Wan or Nik Yusof, the Dato' Sri Paduka.
[43] Phya Sukhum was at that time Siamese Commissioner for Singgora (Songkhla) and all the Malay states over which Siam claimed to exercise control. Phya Sukhum was one of the most intelligent and progressive Siamese officials of the period. He belonged to the group headed by Prince Damrong in Bangkok which believed that Siam should not only expand her territory as much as possible but also seek to tighten administrative control over her vassals, with a view to absorbing them into Siam proper. In pursuance of this policy, Siam had by this time already been attempting to take full control of the Malay state of Patani.

On arrival at Kota Bharu, Phya Sukhum had consultations with the Raja Kelantan and Raja Muda and then visited the ailing ruler. A week later Sultan Mansor died. He left no issue.

Struggle for the Throne

When Sultan Mansur died in February 1900, the question of the succession arose immediately. There appear to have been three major claimants or groups of claimants. They were Tuan Long Senik (Raja Kelantan), Tuan Long Ja'afar (Tengku Petra), or one of the brothers of the late Sultan who had since 1891 been conspiring against him.

By virtue of his title as Raja Kelantan, which was recognized by Bangkok in 1897, Tuan Long Senik, a nephew of the late Sultan, had a right to succeed to the throne. He was, however, opposed by his uncles, for they considered that they had a greater right to the throne on the grounds that they were the brothers of the late Sultan, and also because Tuan Long Senik had already been bypassed or 'disqualified' at the time of the death of his father, Sultan Muhammad III, in 1891.

As for Tuan Long Ja'afar or Tengku Petra, he must have felt that, being the oldest and hence most senior member of the Kelantan royal family, and the only surviving son of Sultan Muhammad II, he should be given the turn to ascend the throne. In fact, as we know, his candidature in 1891 had been approved or supported by his nephews, the brothers of the recently deceased Sultan Mansor (Clifford, 1961, 109). Moreover, he was popular amongst the chiefs and the people, and had it not been for Dato' Sri Paduka and Dato' Maha Mentri, who had backed and helped Tuan Long Mansor to ascend the throne in 1891, he could have been the Sultan of Kelantan in succession to Muhammad III. It was said (Clifford, 1961, 109) that 'the death of Dato' Maha Mentri in 1894' was 'approved if not actually ordered by Tengku Petra.' It has also been suggested that there was a plan to the effect that if Tengku Petra were to become the new ruler of Kelantan, Tengku Chik Penambang would be made the Raja Muda, and that Nik Mat Besar, the principal follower of the latter, would be appointed Dato' Mentri (chief minister).[44]

As events turned out, Tuan Long Senik was to become the new ruler with the minor title (as in the early years of Mansor) of 'Raja Kelantan'. It was said (Graham, 1904, 3) that his accession was 'in accordance with the dying wish' of the late Sultan Mansur.[45] But it is obvious that his

---

[44] Verbal communications from Tengku Khalid b. Tengku Chik Abdullah and Haji Nik Abdul Kadir of Jalan Merbau, Kota Bharu.

[45] It has not been possible to ascertain whether it really was the dying wish of Sultan Mansur that his nephew, Long Senik, should succeed him. Local sources differ on the point. For the fullest discussion, see Mohd. Husin (1970, 93-4).

accession was made possible by Siamese intervention or assistance. Had it not been for Phya Sukhum, Tuan Long Senik would not have become the new ruler of Kelantan. In fact, Tuan Long Senik owed 'his position to the Siamese, who installed him as such, in preference to the rightful heir, on the supposition that he would conform to their wishes and demands' (Waterstradt, 1902, 2). Having helped to install Tuan Long Senik on the Kelantan throne, Phya Sukhum returned to Singgora on 19 February 1900, but Kong Mirik and Kong Pha with twelve Siamese soldiers remained in Kota Bharu. However, the situation in Kelantan became so tense that Bangkok had to despatch another official, Luang Prong, to Kota Bharu on 26 February, by a Siamese gunboat called the *Muratha*.[46] Luang Prong ordered the Raja to summon all the brothers of the late Sultan Mansur before him. He told them that he had brought word from the King of Siam who, firstly, expressed his condolences over the death of Sultan Mansur; secondly, advised the Raja Kelantan, the Raja Muda and all the brothers of the late Sultan to be on friendly terms; thirdly, informed them that since there was going to be trouble in the state, Bangkok had to send and station Siamese soldiers in Kota Bharu, to keep the peace; and fourthly, wished to know whether the estate or properties left by the late Sultan Mansur had been distributed to the beneficiaries. Two days later Luang Prong went back to Singgora. Five weeks later, on 7 April, Phya Sukhum again visited Kota Bharu, to assess the situation in Kelantan and to prepare for a visit by the King of Siam. After spending eight days in Kelantan, Phya Sukhum returned to Singgora on 15 April.

The King of Siam arrived in Kota Bharu by a Siamese royal gunboat on 25 May. He was accompanied by, amongst others, Phya Sukhum, who had Raja Kelantan, Raja Muda, Tengku Temenggong, Tengku Petra and Tengku Chik Penambang introduced to the King. During an audience held on board the gunboat the King told the Kelantan rajas that he had come to see for himself the situation in the state and to find out how Raja Kelantan was faring, as he had heard talk of impending trouble in the state following the death of Sultan Mansur. However, he was happy to note that no serious trouble had occurred and that all the parties concerned had become reconciled. Thus was the succession 'settled'.

No sooner had Long Senik become ruler then he found his position to be one of extreme difficulty. In the first place, his accession to the throne, though backed and recognized by Bangkok, was not well received by his uncles and some other members of the Kelantan royal

[46] The following account is based on DRM.

family. The presence of the Siamese Commissioner and Siamese soldiers in Kota Bharu, however, deterred them from making any attempt either to depose Tuan Long Senik by force or do away with him. Under the circumstances, they had to resort to other means by which the new ruler, their own nephew, had to reckon with them. It appears that when Tuan Long Senik became ruler of Kelantan seven of the most powerful of his uncles and other relatives formed a league by the strength of which combination they extracted from him privileges to which, without such cohesion, they could never have aspired.[47] Prominent among these was the right to be consulted on all matters of state, and to veto the orders of their nephew-ruler if they thought fit; the power of disposing for their own benefit of certain revenue farms, heretofore the prerogative of the ruler only; and the promise of an income of $3,000 a year each from the general revenues of the state. (One local source (DRM) notes that six of the ruler's relatives demanded that the state revenue be divided among them.) Moreover, the new ruler being fearful of placing any restraint upon his uncles, they abrogated to themselves the right to use corvée labour whenever they pleased, to exercise the powers of Courts of Justice, and to imprison for indefinite periods, by mere verbal order, any person who might displease them. By nominally assisting the ruler in making the triennial *Bunga Mas* collection, they succeeded in attaching to themselves many thousands of the inhabitants of the state, who, paying the tax through them, were taught to consider their allegiance to the head of the state or ruler as quite secondary to that which they rendered to their overlord. The uncles also accumulated large estates in land by equivocal means, the taxes for which they systematically failed to pay, and they protected numbers of noted evil-doers from whose unconcealed crimes they derived pecuniary and other benefits (DRM). As a result of the foregoing, but owing chiefly to his inability to stem the tide of intrigue which his uncles and other relatives had set flowing in February 1900, the new ruler 'lost all but the outward semblance of power' (Graham, 1904, 2).

The second difficulty that had to be confronted by the new ruler related to the intrigue of foreign powers, namely Siam and Britain, both of whom were pursuing policies designed to gain control of the state of Kelantan. It was R.W. Duff and his Duff Syndicate which

[47] The seven consisted of five sons of Sultan Ahmad—Tuan Long Mahmud, Tuan Long Sulaiman, Tuan Long Idris, Tuan Long Yusof, and Tuan Chik Abdullah—together with Tuan Long Ja'afar (also known as Tuan Abdul Ghafar) b. Sultan Muhammad II (great-grandfather of Long Senik), and Tengku Chik b. Tuan Bongsu (a 'grand-cousin' of Long Senik). Cf. Graham (1904, 3).

sparked off and continued to influence the complicated series of events that now ensued.[48]

The Duff Development Company

The history of Kelantan during the period under study would be incomplete without an account of the Duff Development Company, for it was very closely related to the commercial and political development of the state of Kelantan. The company brought about difficulties and complications deeply affecting the political status of Kelantan, and led to confrontations between London and Bangkok on the one hand and between R.W. Duff and W.A. Graham on the other.[49] In the words of one historian (Emerson, 1937, 252), the company 'came to involve several of the imperial governments, vast sums of money, and two law-suits which ended only with their ultimate appearance before the House of Lords'. In short, the Duff Development Company brought to the surface the hitherto obscure position of the state of Kelantan, exposed the nature and extent of Siamese pretensions to or claims over the state, questioned the position and sovereignty of its ruler or Raja, and led to the signing of the Anglo-Siamese Treaty in 1902.

But before going further into the concerns of the Duff Development Company, it is necessary to explain briefly the historical position of Kelantan in relation to Siam and Britain. By the Treaty of Bangkok, signed by the English and the Siamese in 1826,[50] the Malay states of Kedah and Patani were described as provinces of Siam, while the status of Kelantan and Trengganu was left ambiguous. Article 12 of the Treaty merely defines the obligations of the contracting parties towards Kelantan and Trengganu as follows:

> Siam shall not go and obstruct or interrupt commerce in the two states of Tringganu and Calantan; English merchants and subjects shall have trade and intercourse in future with the same facility and freedom as they have heretofore had; and the English shall not go and molest, attack or disturb those states upon any pretence whatever.

This ambiguity gave rise to various interpretations of the position or status of Kelantan and Trengganu. The phraseology was so vague that two entirely opposite meanings could be drawn from it. The British

---

[48] Robert William Duff, then a police officer in Pahang, first visited Kelantan in 1895 with the Clifford Expedition, later resigned, and returned to Kelantan with commercial aims.
[49] William Armstrong Graham, an Englishman in the service of the Siamese Government, served as resident 'Siamese Adviser' in Kelantan from 1903 to 1909.
[50] Also known as the Burney Treaty, after Captain Henry Burney, who led the British mission to Ligor and Bangkok which resulted in the conclusion of the treaty, whose text is available in Maxwell & Gibson (1924, 77–82).

might argue that it did not admit the supremacy of Siam over the two Malay states; that it precluded Siam from any interference in the two states; that it conferred on Britain the right of opposing all forcible interference of the Siamese and also the right of direct negotiation with the states; and that the wording of the Article left the door open for extending British protection, and hence power and influence, to Kelantan and Trengganu, should the British ever consider it desirable to do so. The Siamese, however, might contend that the Article gave them the right of complete subjugation of the two Malay states so long as trade was not interrupted.[51]

Kelantan, and for that matter Trengganu, Kedah and Patani as well, were in theory generally regarded as tributary to Siam because they despatched triennially to Bangkok the *Bunga Mas* or ornamental flowers and leaves of gold and silver.[52] However, what this actually signified was a matter of dispute. Siam maintained that Kelantan and Trengganu were her dependencies,[53] whereas British officials in Malaya, obviously for good reason, usually insisted that the *Bunga Mas* was a token of friendship and alliance, and that Kelantan and Trengganu were practically independent Malay states (Thio, 1957, 7), and according to them also the Malay rulers or Sultans and their chiefs shared the same view, and denied the Siamese claim (Clifford, 1897, 13). The truth probably lies somewhere in between. But insofar as Kelantan is concerned, the significance of the *Bunga Mas* was clearly rather more than a matter of friendship and alliance; it was in addition a token of allegiance and an acknowledgement in some degree of dependence upon or even submission by Kelantan to Siam. In the early nineteenth century the Sultan of Kelantan looked upon the King of Siam with respect as well as with awe. It was the British officials in Malaya who propagated the idea that Kelantan (as well as other Malay states not under British 'protection') was an independent Malay state. Again and again in the

[51] For a discussion of these points, see Mills (1960, 177–8).
[52] Kelantan and Trengganu began sending the *Bunga Mas* to Bangkok triennially in 1812 (Wood, 1926, 275).
[53] Bangkok regarded Kelantan and Trengganu as vassal states. In theory, the two states (together with Kedah and Patani) were in a tributary relationship to Bangkok much as, for example, Annam and Korea were to Peking. They were not directly governed as an integral part of the Kingdom of Siam but were expected to send tribute to Bangkok (the *Bunga Mas*) once every three years. Presents and emissaries were also expected on special occasions such as the cremation of important Siamese officials and the installations of kings. They were expected to provide arms, men and supplies in time of war. Their foreign relations were (in theory) handled by Bangkok, and their rulers had to be confirmed in office by Bangkok. Their Malay rulers and their principal officials were given Siamese titles and insignia of office. All Sultans tributary to Siam were termed 'Governors' by the Siamese, and received the title *Phraya*. In return for assuming the responsibilities recognition of Siamese suzerainty imposed, vassal states were allowed to live under their own customs and rulers. Cf. Vella (1957, 60).

'eighties and 'nineties, the same British officials suggested that the 'independent' states of Kelantan and Trengganu should be brought under British control. London nevertheless rejected all proposals to draw the two Malay states into the British fold because of the 'cardinal principle of British foreign policy' that Siam should remain an independent and a friendly state. From the 1880s Siam was under threat from the French, who were already established in the Indo-Chinese states of Annam, Cochin-China, Cambodia and Laos. If the French were to succeed in establishing a predominant influence in Bangkok, not only would a profitable market be closed to British commerce but the British position in Burma would also be threatened by a strong military power. Hence the British Government persisted in the view that nothing should be done in the Malay peninsula to alienate Siam or give France an excuse for encroaching on her territory.

Nevertheless, Britain, for strategic and other reasons, concluded a Secret Convention with Siam in 1897, whereby the King of Siam promised not to cede or alienate to any other power any of his rights over any portion of the territories or islands lying to the south of Muang Ban Tapan, while Britain, on her part, undertook to support him in resisting attempts by any third power to acquire dominion or to establish its influence or protection in this specific area. The Siamese Government, moreover, agreed not to grant to foreigners any special privilege whether as regards land or trade in the peninsula without the written consent of the British. It was generally understood in London and Bangkok that the signature of the convention implied a recognition of Siamese claims to the northern part of the peninsula including Kelantan and Trengganu. Indeed in the subsequent Boundary Agreement of 1899 which defined the frontier between 'British' and 'Siamese' Malaya, it was formally admitted that Kelantan and Trengganu were 'dependencies' of Siam.

Meanwhile, at about the same time, the affairs of Kelantan took a serious turn. As Siam tightened her control over the Malay states in the Patani group, Kelantan began to feel the pinch of Siamese policy across the border. In Patani, Bangkok refused to confirm the succession of its new Raja until he had proved amenable to Siamese control. When Siamese officials appointed by Bangkok took over the collection of revenue and the exercise of civil jurisdiction in 1898, the Raja of Patani appealed to the British Governor in Singapore for protection. In 1899, the Raja of Saiburi, or Teluban, one of the seven states in the Patani group, similarly protested against Siamese encroachments and sought British support. In Kota Bharu, where a Siamese Commissioner had been stationed since 1894, similar attempts were made to bring Kelantan itself more directly under the control of Bangkok.

As has already been seen, the succession to the Kelantan throne of Tuan Long Senik, Raja Kelantan, in early 1900, had been hotly contested by his relatives, and become the occasion for a visit to the state in May by the Siamese king, and for the establishment in Kota Bharu of a force of Siamese soldiery in addition to the resident Commissioner. Though, shortly after this, the Raja of Kelantan requested the withdrawal of the Siamese force, the request was not acceded to. On the contrary, the Siamese set about making themselves as comfortable as possible, and the Commissioner proceeded to build himself a house and quarters for his men on the Kebun Mengseta, between the Raja's palace and the river. The land was at the time at least partially occupied by Malay houses but the Commissioner had 104 of them forcibly pulled down. No compensation was paid to the dispossessed owners either for their houses or the land on which they stood. No wages were given to the men engaged on the work nor were any payments made for the materials, which had to be provided free by the Malays. The conduct of the Siamese soldiers stationed in Kelantan was also bad and intolerable. They used to assault Malay women in the open streets almost daily, and many complaints were made to the Raja by the chiefs and the people concerning the crimes committed by the Siamese soldiers in Kelantan.[54] But nothing could be done. It looked as if before very long Kelantan would be for all intents and purposes, except in name, a Siamese province.

Such was the situation when Robert William Duff arrived in Kota Bharu in the middle of 1900 to obtain a concession. The Duff Development Company owed its origin primarily to the initiative and prowess of this single Englishman. Duff had been employed initially by the Public Works Department in Perak, but later volunteered to work in Pahang where he was given a police appointment (Hume, 1949, 148), and served as Chief Police Officer from 1894 to 1897.[55] Duff took an active part in the suppression of the Pahang rebellion and in 1895 participated in an expedition led by Hugh Clifford, which pursued the remnants of the rebels deep into Ulu Kelantan or the southern interior of the state. What Duff then saw of the state and the '... illimitable possibilities for development of all kinds inherent in its vast and largely

---

[54] The foregoing account of Siamese conduct in Kelantan in 1901-2 is drawn largely from Davies (1902, 7-8, 12), who was notably anti-Siamese, but who also includes the text of a letter of complaint said to have been addressed by the Raja to the Siamese King.

[55] W.J.P. Hume, *The Federation of Malaya and its Police Force, 1786-1952* (Government Printer, Kuala Lumpur, 1952), 8.

unoccupied expanses' (Wright and Reid, 1912, 152), led him to visualize a scheme for the exploitation of its potential riches. It could perhaps be added that Duff was among those Englishmen who believed that 'the flag follows trade'. After leaving the Federated Malay States service in January 1900, Duff returned to England where he formed the Duff Development Syndicate, registered in London in April 1900 (*SB*, 14 Jan. 1903). Having collected sufficient funds, the syndicate appointed Duff its representative to negotiate for a concession. When Duff approached the British Foreign Office for information regarding the question of who had the gift of land in Kelantan, he was advised to proceed to Bangkok and apply to the Siamese Government. In Bangkok Duff was told by the Siamese Minister of the Interior, Prince Damrong, that the gift of land in Kelantan was in the hands of the King of Siam (Wright and Reid, 1912, 154). After lengthy negotiations, Duff secured a letter from the Minister instructing the Raja of Kelantan to give him every assistance in travelling through the state for the purpose of trade. Duff, however, understood the letter to include permission to prospect.[56]

Accordingly, Duff, accompanied by Chappell, a mining engineer, and a Sayyid Hussin from Pahang,[57] arrived in Kota Bharu in August 1900. While in Kelantan, Duff discovered that he had been misled by the Siamese authorities in Bangkok, for the gift of land was indeed in the hands of the Raja of Kelantan and not in those of the King of Siam. He also learnt that a large tract of land had already been allocated to a number of Chinese who were in partnership with the Siamese officials in Kota Bharu, and that the leases were to be signed and sealed by the Raja on the day following his own arrival. Realizing that the granting of such concessions would eventually close the state of Kelantan to British enterprise, Duff succeeded in persuading the Raja not to complete the transaction. Instead, urging him to assert his independence of Siam, he asked for and obtained for his own syndicate a generous concession. After a brief secret meeting, the outlines of an agreement were drawn up, and the Agreement itself was finally signed on 10 October 1900, the contracting parties being the Raja of Kelantan on the one hand and R.W. Duff on behalf of the Duff Syndicate on the

[56] Memorandum, Duff Syndicate to Foreign Office, encl. in Colonial Office despatches, Series 273.

[57] Sayyid Hussin, a Pahang Malay of Arab extraction, served as Duff's interpreter with the Raja of Kelantan and is said to have been partly responsible for persuading the Raja to conclude the Duff-Kelantan Agreement or Partnership Deed of 1900, without the knowledge of the Siamese Commissioner in Kota Bharu. Sayyid Hussin himself later married a daughter of Tengku Petra Semerak (Tuan Long Idris), and became a prominent figure in the state.

other.[58] Under the Agreement, the syndicate was granted the right to form a company which would have exclusive commercial rights over some 3,000 square miles of land, in return for which the Raja was to receive $2,000 and 200 shares. In addition, the syndicate so formed was to have comprehensive administrative rights throughout the territory covered by the concession. In the result, the syndicate acquired not merely an area of land constituting practically one-third of the state of Kelantan, but also '... an absolute monopoly of all mineral, trading and other rights within the concession' (SB, 14 Jan. 1903).

The signing of the Agreement was immediately followed by serious political complications. The Duff Syndicate asserted the validity of the grant and their intention to ignore Siamese claims to suzerainty, claims which the British Government had formally recognized in the Boundary Agreement of 1899. This, the British Government saw, would create a dangerous precedent for the Germans, the Russians or the French. Should any of these powers defy Siamese authority in the Malay peninsula, Britain was bound by the Secret Convention of 1897 to assist Siam. In the face of Foreign Office reluctance to assist Duff, the syndicate adopted a policy of blackmail and warned the British Government that unless the latter protected them from Siamese interference in working the concession, they would seek the help of certain foreign governments who were anxious for a footing in the Malay peninsula, or else dispose of their rights to a German company. The Germans, the syndicate asserted, were working through the Danish and Chinese botanical expedition supposed to be then in Kelantan. If Britain did not take immediate action, Duff declared that the rich commercial advantages to be gained in the development of the state would fall to the Germans.[59]

After months of negotiations between London and Bangkok, the Siamese Government, following diplomatic pressure from Britain, finally ratified the Duff concession unconditionally in July 1901, the Duff Syndicate thereby obtaining at last full and undisputed possession of all the rights granted by the Raja of Kelantan in October 1900.

Meanwhile, the syndicate had been engaged in establishing itself in Kelantan. It opened its headquarters at Kuala Lebir, started the work of prospecting and mining, and began to administer the affairs of the con-

[58] Wright and Reid (1902, 157). The agreement was signed and sealed by the ruler and Duff in the presence of Sayyid Hussin and Nik Hassan (a younger brother of the Dato' Sri Paduka, Nik Yusof), together with the Raja Muda and the Council of Chiefs.
[59] Foreign Office Records, Series 69, vol. 224, Duff Syndicate to Foreign Office, 8 Feb. 1901, quoted in Thio (1957, 11).

cession. The poll-tax was abolished and administration of justice introduced. After the ratification of the grant by Siam, the syndicate was reorganized to become the Duff Development Company Limited, which was registered in London on 16 February 1903.

The Anglo-Siamese Treaty of 1902

While the Duff Syndicate was stepping up its activities in Kelantan, the Siamese were also trying to consolidate their position and influence in the state. From early 1900 onwards, especially after the accession of Tuan Long Senik as the Raja of Kelantan, Phya Sukhum and certain other Siamese officials made repeated visits to Kota Bharu trying to persuade the new ruler to submit completely to the demands of Bangkok and to hand over the administration of the state to them. Soon after the signing of the Agreement between Duff and the Raja in October 1900, Bangkok ordered the Raja on no account to grant land in the state to anyone except his own subjects, unless with the permission of the King of Siam, and Phya Sukhum later informed the Raja that the King of Siam wished to collect the revenues of the state, in return for which he would pay the Raja 'a certain monthly sum.'[60] In December 1900 the Siamese Commissioner in Kelantan, on instructions from Bangkok, ordered the Raja to replace the local currency with Siamese ticals or bahts (DRM). Siamese action in Kelantan was part of Bangkok's new policy of maximizing and expanding Siamese control in all the areas or states over which they claimed to exercise suzerainty. The Siamese were also compelled to adopt such a policy in response to the emergence of increasing British interest in the northern Malay states. Bangkok with good reason suspected that British officials in Malaya, in particular Frank Swettenham, had connived with Duff and other individual Englishmen, presumably with the blessing of London, to extend British influence and power not only in Kelantan but also in all the other northern Malay sultanates which had not yet been brought under British control or protection. Two weeks after the signing of the Agreement between Duff and the Raja of Kelantan, the Siamese Commissioner there, Phra Sastra Tarakit, heard rumours that the Raja of Kelantan and the Raja Muda were plotting against the Siamese and that the British would help them (DRM). It was also known to Bangkok that the Raja of Kelantan, and some of the Malay rulers of the seven states in the Patani group, were in secret contact with Swettenham with the objective of expelling the Siamese and bringing the states

[60] Translation of a letter, Raja of Kelantan to King of Siam, quoted in Davies (1902, 12).

under British protection.⁶¹ Indeed, early in 1901 the Raja of Kelantan was ordered to proceed to Bangkok to explain his position and conduct, and perhaps to hand over his state to formal Siamese administration. Duff and Swettenham managed to dissuade him from going.

Sir Frank Swettenham, from 1901 Governor of the Straits Settlements and High Commissioner for the Malay States, was at the forefront of British expansionism at this time and regularly engaged in persuading London of the advisability of a further forward movement. In his despatches he reported the deterioration of the political situation in the northern states, especially Kelantan, and pointed out the dangers for Britain inherent in the existing state of affairs. In particular, he said, other intervention, by Germany or the United States, was imminent.

To settle the problem, and to secure British interests, Swettenham put forward two proposals, in order of preference. Firstly, that the British Government should negotiate with Kelantan and Trengganu for the right to conduct their foreign relations and protect them from interference. Secondly, if the British Government still preferred to recognize Siamese authority over these states, he offered to assist Siam to obtain written agreements from Kelantan and Trengganu so as to give Bangkok a definite *de jure* status there. Such help however was to be conditional on the appointment of British officers to act as Residents. Under such an arrangement, Britain would enjoy some degree of control over the administration of Kelantan and Trengganu, while these states remained nominally under Siam.

The British Government considered Swettenham's proposals commendable and decided on immediate action. On 17 January 1902 the British Minister in Bangkok was instructed to start negotiations with the Siamese on the basis of the second of Swettenham's proposals. After some ten months of protracted negotiations in Bangkok, a Joint Declaration by Britain and Siam was concluded in London on 6 October. This agreement, known as the Anglo-Siamese Treaty of 1902, temporarily settled the 'Kelantan Question.' It is significant to note that the Raja of Kelantan was not consulted by either London or Bangkok about the negotiations or the Treaty. His place was merely to agree to what had been decided upon between Siam and Britain. Ten days after the conclusion of the agreement Swettenham visited Kota Bharu, to explain the terms of the Treaty and to persuade the Raja of Kelantan to sign it. The Raja, after raising a few points, accepted the Treaty and signed and sealed both the Malay and the English versions.

⁶¹ The Rajas of Kelantan and Patani were in correspondence with Swettenham in Singapore through couriers. As far as Kelantan was concerned, the couriers were Wan Muhammad Amin, Imam Haji Abdullah, Sayyid Hussin, and Duff himself.

Friction however arose with the Siamese, who objected to Swettenham's visit to Kelantan. While in Kota Bharu he was alleged to have persuaded the Raja of Kelantan to turn against Siam, though the Raja appears, in fact, to have opposed British intervention in the internal affairs of his state for fear this would invite additional Siamese pressure. Nor was he mistaken. A few days after Swettenham's departure a Siamese Commissioner arrived in Kota Bharu in a gunboat and forced the Raja to sign the Siamese version of the agreement, which was later found to be slightly different from the one concluded on 6 October.

The Anglo-Siamese Treaty of 1902 contained two vital clauses: one provided for Siamese control of Kelantan's foreign relations as well as limited mining and planting concessions to foreigners; the other for the appointment of an Adviser and Assistant Adviser, whose advice 'must be followed in all matters of administration other than those touching the Mohammedan religion and Malay custom.' In the secret notes exchanged by Britain and Siam at the same time, it was agreed that the Advisers should be of British nationality, and that their selection and removal, or renewal of their contracts, required the consent of the British Government. With the conclusion of the Treaty of 1902 the state of Kelantan thus came under a 'New Regime.'

The New Regime

The new administration now established in Kelantan lasted for six years, from July 1903 to July 1909. This was a transitional period during which time the terms of the Treaty were put to practical test. On the whole, the new regime brought considerable improvement in the internal administration of Kelantan. Nevertheless many difficulties were also experienced.

By common agreement between Siam and Britain, W.A. Graham and H.W. Thomson were appointed Adviser and Assistant Adviser respectively to the Raja of Kelantan,[62] and both arrived in Kota Bharu from Bangkok on 25 July 1903 by the Siamese gunboat *Muratha* accompanied by Chao Charoon, the Siamese Deputy Commissioner for the Monthon (Province) of Nakorn Si Thammarat. The next day, Charoon left Kelantan for Singgora (Songkhla) taking with him the small party of Siamese soldiers who had been quartered in Kota Bharu as guards to

[62] Graham had considerable administrative experience, first in British Burma and then with the Government of Siam, in whose Land Department in Bangkok he was then serving. Despite his British nationality, Graham may be regarded as having been 'pro-Siamese' in the situation in which he now found himself. H.W. Thomson was an officer of the Federated Malay States service, seconded to the Siamese Government for the purpose of the Kelantan appointment.

the former resident Siamese Commissioner, Phra Kucha.[63] Part of the Commissioner's staff left soon after Charoon's departure, while those few members who preferred to remain in Kelantan were soon enrolled in the service of the state to form the nucleus of the future Kelantan State Civil Service. Additional officials were from time to time recruited both locally and from the Federated Malay States or the Straits Settlements.

The condition of Kelantan at the time of Graham's arrival left something to be desired. The administration was incompetent and corrupt, while vice and crime flourished unchecked even in high places.[64] The previous Siamese Commissioners who had been stationed in Kelantan had obviously made no serious attempt to strengthen the Raja's position and improve his administration. The Raja, Graham wrote (1908a, 2), possessed only the 'outward semblance of power'. He was infirm of purpose, partly due to his fear of the Siamese, and because he was surrounded by seven or so of his powerful relatives who were conspiring against him. Being weak, he was 'unable to stem the tide of intrigue which his relatives had set flowing from the day... on which he became ruler'.

The prevailing conditions were such that it was necessary for Graham to initiate a series of reforms aimed at the basic essentials of organized government. Such reforms would also strengthen the Raja's power and prestige. Various departments of government were either reorganized or established, to streamline administration. Efforts were also made to preserve law and order in the state. Rural administration was looked into and restructured.

During the six years of the Graham administration many new measures or reforms were undertaken.[65] The existing but disorganized state police was transformed into a well-organized, responsible, and efficient force. Police barracks were built and new stations with living quarters were erected throughout the state. A new central police station at Kota Bharu was built in August 1904. By 1907 the Kelantan police had become a reliable instrument for the preservation of law and order, composed of about 250 men, half of whom were equipped with rifles.

[63] Phra Kucha's predecessors in office had been, successively, Phraya Tipakosa (appointed in 1894), Phra Ong Chao Sai, Phra Surarik, and Phra Sastra Tarakit, who was Commissioner at the time of the signing of the 1902 treaty. Other senior Siamese officials in Kelantan at that date were Luang Angsa (Military Commander) and Luang Nawang (Judge), the last-named remaining for some time in the new Kelantan administration.
[64] See Graham (1904, 2 and *passim*), and *SB*, 8 June 1905.
[65] The summary account of administrative change and reform that follows is drawn, for the most part, from the *Annual Reports* on Kelantan, 1903–09 (Graham, 1904, 1905, 1907, 1908b, and 1909).

The jail system was organized and placed on a more humane basis than in the past. A start was made in utilizing jail labour for more than coolie work. Convict labour was employed for cleaning the streets of the town and for public services, while some prisoners were given odd jobs about the Raja's palace. Convicts were also engaged in laundry work, carpentry, basket-weaving, and thatch-making, and jail manufactures sold to the public. A new main jail was built in Kota Bharu and occupied early in 1907, while a branch jail was later erected at Batu Mengkebang in Ulu Kelantan.

Judicial reforms were also effected. Penal, civil and revenue enactments were passed whenever necessary and duly enforced. The courts established by 1905 were the High Court of the Raja, the Central Court and the Small Court at Kota Bharu, and another Small Court at the headquarters of the southern district, Batu Mengkebang. A Court of Small Causes was also established at Pasir Puteh, which town became the headquarters of a new district. The Shari'a Court, which dealt mainly with breaches of morality, the settlement of matrimonial affairs, the distribution of inherited property, and other Muslim matters, was not interfered with substantially by the new administration at this stage.[66]

A Public Works Office was organized and the services of an engineer in the person of one Henry Richards secured (*SB*, 9 Mar. 1905). The office made substantial progress in the building of various government offices and the construction of roads in the state. In the field of education the new regime laid the foundation of a school system and of secular education in Kelantan. Hitherto, such secular education as was available in rural, peasant Kelantan was mostly elementary and little organized. Religious teaching was conducted by individual religious teachers, village *Imam* or *To' Guru*, who engaged in the teaching of Kuran reading and religious knowledge either in private houses or *pondok*, mosques and *surau*.[67]

One of the most difficult tasks facing the Graham administration was the creation of a State Treasury, hitherto unknown in Kelantan. In those days, the treasury, if such it could be called, was little more than a private purse for the Raja, his family and his immediate relatives. Under the reforms introduced by the new regime, the Raja agreed to content himself with what was apportioned to him by the State, and to leave the rest of the revenue in the keeping and management of the newly established Treasury, where proper registers of receipts and payments were kept, and regularly checked and audited. The Treasury

[66] Cf., however, Roff, below.
[67] *Pondok* are informal communities of students living in small huts (*pondok*) near the residence of well-known religious teachers; *surau* are small village prayer houses.

soon became an acknowledged institution, and the recognized repository of the state revenue. State revenues which, in any centralized sense, were practically nil in 1902, amounted to $320,000 by 1907.

The State Council, which was the advisory body to the Raja, was reorganized; its meetings were formalised and proceedings properly recorded. Membership consisted of the Raja (as President) and fourteen of the most influential persons in the state, including the Adviser and his Assistant.[68] From the time of its reorganization the Council passed numerous regulations, laws, orders, and rules 'providing for the administration of justice, for the control of the police, for the collection of revenue, and for various other matters' (Graham 1908a, 109).

The rural administration in existence prior to 1903 was greatly altered. Hitherto the state had been divided into several informal but recognized districts, held in fief by chiefs or Dato's who were in most cases members of the royal family. At the turn of the century the Galas district and the Lebir district, for example, were under the nominal charge of the Dato' Bentara and the Dato' Lela di-Raja respectively, but both lived in Kota Bharu, as did all the other chiefs (Clifford, 1961, 113). The chiefs in charge of the various districts had no right to the revenue of the districts concerned, save such sums as might be granted to them from time to time by the Raja (*ibid.*). The Chinese community in Kelantan, concentrated especially in the Galas district[69] and in Kampong China, a 'suburb' of Kota Bharu towards Penambang, had their own heads called Kapitan China, whose appointment had to be approved by the Raja. The Kapitan China were responsible to the Raja for the Chinese and for the collection of tax and royalty on the gold mined at the Pulai settlement in the Galas district. The general administration of the state, below the 'district' level, was for much of the nineteenth century in the hands of village *Imam*, who exercised delegated jurisdiction, partly religious and partly temporal, in areas known as *mukim*—essentially the 'parishes' of village *surau*. With the increase of Siamese influence in the state towards the end of the century, the Siamese system of *To' Kweng* ('circle' headmen, responsible for the temporal administration of groups of villages in areas known as *daerah*), and *To' Nebeng* (headmen of particular villages) was introduced. In theory, under this system, the Imam no longer exercised temporal authority, but confined himself to religious leadership, taxation and teaching within the area of his surau. Under the reforms introduced from 1903, the state was redivided by stages into five new districts,

[68] Graham (1908a, 126–7) gives a complete list of members.
[69] The Galas district included the Gua Musang and Pulai areas, where Chinese had lived for more than a hundred years.

namely Kota Bharu, Batu Mengkebang (later known as Ulu Kelantan), Pasir Puteh, Kuala Kelantan, and Kuala Lebir,[70] each of which was to be placed under a District Officer who also acted as Magistrate, Land Officer and Revenue Officer in his area. Immediately responsible to him were the To' Kweng, and below that the To' Nebeng, in direct line of administration. To' Kweng were commonly appointed by the Raja, usually after consultation with the people of the *daerah*.

The reforms introduced by the new regime evolved steadily and progressed without adverse reaction. Those relatives of the Raja who, in early 1900, had been so unhappy with the new ruler, and either individually or in groups had conspired against him, had to accept the new situation. Their general demeanour moved from aloofness and suspicion to a more promising disposition. In order to make them a peaceful, contented and useful element in the development of the state, Graham appointed them as heads of the newly established or reorganized government departments. They were assisted in the management of affairs by either British or Siamese officers who had been recruited to the State Civil Service from 1903. As time went on, they showed increasing interest in their work and rendered faithful service to the state.

Under the new regime, Kelantan, then, made considerable progress. The new administration had effected considerable alterations in the conduct of affairs. In six years, it had more or less brought order out of chaotic conditions; successfully checked the intrigues of the royal family and the nobility; resecured the state revenues from misappropriation and entrusted them to a newly created Treasury; passed numerous laws and regulations; brought justice within the reach of the populace; started many works of public utility; and organized or established numerous government departments for the proper administration of the state.[71] This state of affairs prevailed uninterrupted until 1909.

But the government conducted under Graham's advisership had also to face difficult times. The improved conditions brought about by administrative reform were threatened by dangerous irregularities which had crept into the tin currency of Kelantan, and by the prolonged conflict between the state and the Duff Development Company.

For many years, the locally manufactured tin money called *pitis*,[72]

---

[70] Only the first three became operative during the period under discussion.

[71] Cf. the account of his achievements given by Graham (1908a, 3).

[72] *Pitis* came in two denominations, the *puloh*, of which there were 48 to the Straits dollar, and the *keping*, of which there were ten to the *puloh*. The *keping* had a hole in the middle, and was usually carried strung on a length of cord. As Graham (1904, 24) remarked, ten dollars' worth of *keping* made a 'comfortable manload'. Tin *keping*

together with the Straits dollar, formed the ordinary currency in Kelantan. Prior to 1905, when the minting work was taken over by the state, the tin coins were manufactured by 'a sort of Company' whose shareholders were composed of the Raja and his relatives (Graham, 1905, 10). The profits, if any, were divided among them. During the year 1904 the company, wishing to improve the finances of the state, issued a subsidiary coinage called the *puloh*. But in their anxiety to take a greater profit the company produced the *puloh* at less than half its face value and with the worst possible workmanship. The new coin when first issued proved useful but was worthless outside Kelantan save for melting purposes or as a curio (*ST*, 23 Aug. 1905). About $160,000 worth of the coin passed into circulation (*SB*, 24 Aug. 1905), though about $50,000 worth of tin money sufficed for the needs of the state at the time (Graham, 1904, 24). The *puloh* were so plain and poorly designed that they simply asked to be counterfeited. As a result, false coins were manufactured in Singapore, Trengganu and elsewhere and shipped to Kelantan on an extensive and profitable scale (*ST*, 13 Dec. 1905), so much so that by July 1905 'the country had been flooded with a grossly debased coin and . . . the minting company was declining to redeem the coin under any circumstances' (Graham, 1907, 3). A serious situation arose, because Straits dollars were required for the purpose of trade with Singapore and elsewhere, and the absence of free convertibility hampered trade and commerce in Kelantan. The resulting financial crisis became so severe that the government decided to intervene.

In order to save the credit of the state and the country from financial chaos, the government took over the minting work at the end of 1905 and proceeded to redeem the coins.[73] The loss entailed by the redemption was so heavy, while the country was still flooded with coins, that the State Treasury was compelled to borrow some $60,000 from the Siamese Government. The Kelantan Government continued to call in the coin and managed to collect some 85 tons of coins, the metal content of which was worth only $40,000. In order to replace the money withdrawn from circulation, the coin collected was reminted into the old small *pitis* (*keping*) at about equal to face value. These replacement coins were issued in quantities sufficient only to meet local needs (*SB*, 14 Sept. 1905). Together with what remained of the former issue of small *pitis*, they constituted a local currency of some $55,000. Attempts to

---

had been in circulation in Kelantan for many years prior to 1903, but the *puloh* was first coined in 1904, as indicated below.

[73] The following details are based on Graham (1907, 3–5).

import spurious coins were discovered and dealt with, and the culprits caught were severely punished, thereby reducing counterfeiting to a negligible scale. The State Government also made arrangements with a London firm for supply of moulds or presses for the manufacture of zinc coins whenever it became necessary to make a new issue of small coin (Graham, 1908b, 1, 4).

Owing to the coinage trouble, the market became unstable, trade and commerce suffered and prices of commodities rose dramatically. The State Treasury became almost empty, while the annual budget showed a deficit. The financial situation was so acute in 1906 that Graham had to secure a further loan of $90,000 from the Siamese Government (Graham, 1909, 3). However in ensuing years the position changed for the better, and by 1911 the financial crisis had become, if not a thing of the past, a matter of rather less moment.

The '*pitis* affair,' throughout much of its course, had been greatly exacerbated by the British decision in 1903 to strike a new, standard, silver Straits dollar, and demonetize the old one of mixed (Mexican and other) parentage, a process accompanied, in the year following, by attempts on the part of the Straits Government to prohibit the flow of all dollar currency (old and new) into and out of the 'Siamese Malay States,' which of course included Kelantan. The Siamese Government, for its part, planned to take advantage of this situation by introducing into the state their own *tical*, news of this intention becoming known in Singapore early in 1904. Apart from fears concerning the effects such a move might have on trade, the British also mistrusted the political implications of any increased Siamese penetration of northern Malaya, and made it clear that the British Government would regard any attempt to introduce Siamese currency into Kelantan as an unfriendly act, in violation of Article V of the Anglo-Siamese Treaty of 1902. Bangkok was unwilling to accept this argument, holding instead that introduction of the *tical* to Kelantan was to be construed solely as a defensive measure against the dollar prohibitions of the Straits Government.

As a compromise, Bangkok assured London that if the Straits Settlements Government lifted the prohibition against import and export of old and new dollars, they would drop the plan to introduce Siamese currency into Kelantan. Negotiations, in turn, between Kelantan and the Straits Settlements Government resulted in an agreement by which the latter agreed to allow small importations of the new Straits dollar under special permits. It was later agreed further that in exchange for the abandonment of the Bangkok scheme to introduce Siamese currency into Kelantan, the Straits Settlements Government would allow free entry of old Straits dollars into the Straits Settlements and the Federated Malay States, as soon as the new currency regulations in those areas were enforced. Thus 'through the kindness of the Singapore Authorities, permits to import the old Dollar into Singapore for sale to the Banks were freely given', and as a result, 'considerable sums were got rid of at small loss' (Graham, 1905, 9). Meanwhile, the Kelantan Government banned the importation into the state of old Straits dollars, while the new ones were allowed to flow in. By the middle of 1905, the new dollar was in 'pretty general circulation' and was accepted as currency in Kelantan. Thus the financial crisis regarding the Straits dollar was eventually solved.

Kelantan-Duff Dispute

The Kelantan-Duff dispute was the direct result of the situational and personal conflict between Duff and Graham which started almost immediately upon the establishment of the new regime in Kelantan in July 1903. At the time of Graham's arrival in Kelantan on 25 July 1903, the Duff Development Company was in possession of extensive commercial and administrative rights within their concession, as well as a great deal of influence with the Raja, and in consequence played a very prominent role in the affairs of the state. In the opinion of Graham this situation was irregular and could only detract from his own position and dignity, not to say those of the Kelantan Government. He therefore began to question the rights of the company, and set out to put it in its proper place. On 12 August, not three weeks after Graham's arrival and on his advice, the Raja of Kelantan sealed an 'Explanatory Document', which was also signed by Duff on behalf of the company.[74] This document limited, in particular, the taxation rights enjoyed by the company within its concession. From this time forward the area of conflict between Kelantan and the company was to widen and develop. Graham and Duff both resorted to personal charges against the other; Graham was soon to accuse Duff of being a proud man enveloped in 'a cloud of allusions to Colonial Office influence through which he looms large, vague and threatening',[75] while Duff was in due course to accuse Graham of being a 'peculiar' man, engaged in intrigue against the Duff Development Company.[76] In March 1904 the Raja issued a decree defining exactly the boundaries of the Duff concession. By this time the company was beginning to feel the pinch and the effects of the

[74] Encl. in Desp., 3 Apr. 1907, CO 273/333.
[75] Encl. in Desp., 15 Jan. 1904, CO 273/304.
[76] Encl. in Desp., 3 Apr. 1907, CO 273/333.

policy adopted by Graham towards it. Application for a railway concession through the state had already been refused by the Raja on Graham's advice, on the ground that 'it is not at this moment ... considered necessary to the welfare of the State'.[77] Taxes that had been waived by the Raja in 1900 were again imposed within the company's territory, thus deterring the immigration of new settlers.[78]

The company, realizing that it would fail unless governmental interference was removed or a new agreement could be reached, decided to seek 'the intervention of the British Government in the Company's interests'. Since the establishment of the new regime in Kelantan, and more especially the arrival of Graham in July 1903, the Duff Company had been deprived of many of its original powers and privileges. The company charged that the Kelantan Government had either intentionally ignored the company's interests or had so designed their new administrative measures as to reduce the value of the company's commercial rights.[79] This had led the company into difficulties and involved it in a succession of defensive negotiations with the administration. Eventually, early in 1905, Duff, as representative of the company, went to Bangkok to obtain the assistance of the British Minister there, in an effort to settle the dispute through the Siamese Government. The negotiations which ensued resulted in the signing of a new Agreement, which was executed on 28 May 1905. This abrogated practically all the administrative rights held by the Duff Development Company, thereby reducing it to a purely commercial concern. The agreement was also intended to replace the vague and unsatisfactory document drawn up in 1900, when matters in Kelantan were in a state of uncertainty and the Raja in a difficult position.

Unfortunately the new arrangements arrived at in 1905 did not settle the conflict, which continued to develop in intensity. Constant representations were made by the company to the Siamese Government through the British Minister in Bangkok regarding Graham's unsatisfactory conduct and hostile attitude. The company also sought the intervention of the government in Britain to settle the dispute in Kelantan. A threat was made that unless Graham changed his hostile policy, the British Government would be compelled to insist on his removal.[80] But no satisfactory solution was found. Under the Anglo-Siamese Treaty of 1902, it was difficult for the Siamese Government to interfere in the internal affairs of Kelantan, and Prince Damrong, the

[77] Letter, Adviser to Duff, 3 Nov. 1903.
[78] Encl. in Desp., 3 Apr. 1907, CO 273/333.
[79] Encl. in Desp., 3 July 1907, CO 273/333.
[80] Letter encl. in Desp., 23 May 1908, CO 273/343.

Siamese Minister of the Interior, stated that if Graham's removal be insisted upon he would himself resign.[81]

By the end of 1907, the Duff Company felt it had failed in its endeavour to establish a commercial enterprise in Kelantan. The directors of the company concluded that under existing conditions they would have to consider closing down all work in the state.[82] Accordingly the company decided to proceed against the governments of Kelantan and Siam for the recovery of losses incurred, and for compensation for the loss of profits which they might have expected to make under different circumstances. Notifying the British Government of their intention, however, they learnt that certain negotiations were currently in progress between Britain and Siam. These negotiations, if concluded successfully, would *inter alia* bring Kelantan under British protection. Consequently, the company decided for the time being to defer taking legal action.[83]

The Anglo-Siamese Treaty of 1909

The 'new regime' established in Kelantan under the terms of the Anglo-Siamese Treaty of 1902 was not altogether satisfactory to either of the contracting parties. Though it brought about a marked improvement in the internal administration of Kelantan, the advisory system did not provide a fully satisfactory answer to the 'Kelantan question,' which continued to be a source of trouble, conflict and anxiety to Siam and Britain. Graham's appointment was also regarded in some quarters as unsatisfactory. His unfriendly attitude towards the Duff Development Company grew into serious antagonism which became the subject of continuous discussions in Kota Bharu, Bangkok, London and Singapore. The appointment of a Siamese Adviser of British nationality to the Raja of Kelantan was itself an anomaly which made the future position of the state still more uncertain. Was Kelantan ultimately to be a Siamese or a British dependency? A new settlement or arrangement was therefore inevitable.

The unsatisfactoriness of the existing position was accentuated by the Siamese plan to construct a peninsular railway connecting the Siamese provinces and dependencies in the far south with Bangkok. The plan,

[81] *Annual Report on Siam for 1907* (encl. in *ibid.*), p. 4.
[82] Encl. in Desp., 13 Dec. 1907, CO 273/343.
[83] The later history of the relations between the company and the Kelantan Government falls outside the scope of this paper, but was marked by some reduction in the size of the concession, and almost continual litigation on a variety of matters, culminating in appeals to the House of Lords. Matters were not finally settled until 1930. A narrative account of the whole complex affair, which greatly affected Kelantan's development, is given in Emerson (1937, 252-62).

as developed early in 1906, envisaged the construction of a railway from Trang, a port in the province of Phuket on the west coast of the Siamese part of the peninsula, to Pathalung on the east coast, which would then join the newly built line at Petchaburi. What alarmed the British was that construction and control of the proposed railway was to be entrusted to the Siamese Railway Department, whose Director-General and most of whose staff were German. For the British, the construction of the railway with German help—whether in personnel or material—constituted a threat to the paramountcy of their interests and influence in the Malay peninsula. For this reason, the British Government suggested to Bangkok that a separate railway department under a Siamese or British Director-General be created for the peninsular railway.

The Siamese Government, in rejecting the British proposal, argued that the establishment of a separate department would entail many problems, and much additional expense, while the exclusion of the German officials would be unjust because they were already in the service of the Siamese Government. Moreover, their exclusion would invite protests from the German Government. The Siamese, however, made a counter-proposal to the effect that the railway be constructed with a loan from the Federated Malay States Government, who should lend a sum of money at a low rate of interest, holding each section of the railway constructed as security for the loan.[84] Such an arrangement, the Siamese further proposed, should be 'on business and nonpolitical lines'.[85] The Siamese counter-proposal was welcomed by the Federated Malay States Government and London. Negotiations for a settlement of the railway question were about to begin, when it was learned by the British Legation in Bangkok that the Siamese Government was contemplating a general treaty with Britain.

Shortly after the signing of the Franco-Siamese Treaty in March 1907, Strobel, the General Adviser to the Siamese Government, threw out hints, during a conversation with Paget, the British Minister in Bangkok, to the effect that Siam was prepared to enter into general negotiations with Britain embracing several outstanding questions, and would be willing to cede Kelantan, Trengganu and Kedah to her, if Britain would make concessions to Siam in the matter of extraterritorial jurisdictions, similar to those made by France in the 1907 treaty. The proposal sounded promising to Paget, and in his despatch to London he wrote that the opportunity was now open to Britain to make 'an im-

---

[84] Encl. in Desp., 3 April 1907, CO 273/333. An earlier attempt to obtain loans from Germany or France had been dropped for fear of British opposition.
[85] Encl. in Desp., 18 May 1907, CO 273/333.

portant advance in the Malay Peninsula', if she so desired.[86] Consequently an inter-departmental conference was held in London on 28 May 1907, to consider and discuss the implications of the Siamese proposal. The conference, which was attended by representatives of the Foreign Office, the Colonial Office and the India Office, was in favour of the Siamese offer and agreed to open negotiations.

The Siamese wish for a new general treaty with Britain was prompted by their desire to settle all questions outstanding between them and the British, particularly as regards jurisdiction, for they wished 'to see the last of British extraterritoriality' in Siam (*SB*, 11 June 1908). In making the proposal for the cession of the Malay states of Kelantan, Trengganu and Kedah, the Siamese Government was of the opinion that these remote 'Siamese Malay States' were a source of trouble, weakness, danger and annoyance rather than of profit to Bangkok. Moreover, Kelantan and Trengganu had never formed an integral part of Siam. In spite of Bangkok's policy of strengthening Siam's administrative control by appointing royal commissioners in Kelantan and Trengganu from 1894 onward, and by extensive tours of the Siamese Malay states by the King of Siam in the 1890s, the loyalty of the Malay rulers was still in doubt. This uneasy and uncertain situation seemed to coincide with the desire of Britain to expand British influence in the north of the peninsula. The Siamese also realized that the appointment of a Siamese Adviser of British nationality to Kelantan in 1903, under the terms of the Anglo-Siamese Treaty of 1902, revealed ambitions to incorporate the state into 'British Malaya'. The activities of Duff and the company since 1900 were looked upon by Bangkok as part and parcel of a British scheme to wrest Kelantan, and possibly the other Siamese Malay states, from Siam and put them under the rule or protection of the Union Jack. Moreover, Swettenham's close connections and secret contacts with the Malay rulers of the Siamese Malay states had irritated Bangkok and undermined the relationship between the Straits Settlements and Siamese Governments. In view of these troubles, difficulties and irritations, especially with regard to Kelantan, Bangkok was prepared to see Siam retain only those territories over which she could exercise effective control.

There were several factors which induced the British Government to entertain the Siamese offer of a general treaty. In the first place, the transfer of the Siamese Malay states to Britain would advance the British sphere of influence in the peninsula. Secondly, the treaty would also safeguard British naval interests in Malayan waters, for the Siamese

[86] Encl. in Desp., 27 April 1907, CO 273/333.

Government was prepared to guarantee not to cede or lease, directly or indirectly, any territory situated in the peninsula south of the southern boundary of the province of Rajaburi, or in any of the islands adjacent to the above-mentioned region (*SB*, 15 July 1909). Another consideration was the desire of British subjects in Siam to acquire the right to hold land in the country—a right already acquired by French subjects under the Franco-Siamese Treaty of 1907. Furthermore, in the eyes of Straits and other commercial interests, the new territory gained by Britain would naturally enlarge the field for British trade and economic enterprise in the Malay peninsula (*MM*, 13 Mar. 1909).

Consequently, discussions between Siam and Britain were begun in Bangkok. During the negotiations that followed, the only serious hitches that occurred concerned the division between the regions where Siamese control was indeed effective and those where it was probably only nominal. Administrative, ethnological, and geographical considerations were applied in places, but these were subject to considerations of Siamese dignity. From the viewpoint of the British, or more especially that of the Federated Malay States Government, a frontier including all the Malay-speaking states or provinces in the northern Malay peninsula such as Legeh, Sai (Narathiwat), Raman, Jalor (Yala), Jering (Yaring), Patani (Pattani) and Nongchik, of the Patani group, and Setul (Satun) on the Kedah side, was more desirable. It had been the dream of Raffles, Braddell, Weld, Swettenham and Low and of certain Colonial Office officials that the line of division should be drawn so as to bring under British influence or control the predominantly Malay and Muslim states, leaving to Siam those mainly Siamese and Buddhist.[87] Moreover, it might well be assumed that the Malay rulers and peoples of the so-called 'Siamese Malay States' mentioned above, if given the choice, would prefer to be under British protection or control, for in such circumstances they would at least be joined with those other Malay states which had already come under British rule.

The Siamese Government, however, had different views. In the first place, the proposed cession was based entirely on the wish of Bangkok to disencumber itself of territory over which it exercised no effective control. As a result, the division, it was held, should be made from the standpoint of administrative rather than other considerations. Thus Siam named only the three Malay states, Kelantan, Trengganu and Kedah, over which it had the least hold.

Despite the divergent viewpoints, the British Government were at first determined to press for more territory. As a result, the negotiations

[87] For a British view at this time, see Blagden (1906, 109–10).

became difficult, and indeed for some time their outcome was in serious doubt. During informal talks with Strobel, the British chief negotiator, Paget, argued that from a racial standpoint, not only the states of Kelantan, Trengganu and Kedah, but also the other Malay states of Perlis, Setul and the Patani group should be transferred by Siam to Britain. Perlis and Setul were geographically, ethnically and culturally a part of Kedah.[88] As regards the Malay states of the Patani group, the situation had always been difficult. Their Malay Rajas had repeatedly rebelled against Siamese domination since the old Malay kingdom of Patani had been conquered and broken up by Bangkok in 1832. These rebellions were themselves clear proof that the Patani Malays did not like Siamese rule. As recently as 1902 the Siamese Government had arrested and deported the Malay ruler of Patani who, refusing to submit to Bangkok, had been alleged to be contemplating rebellion. From this time forward there had been other indications of dissatisfaction with the Siamese. Again, it was argued, the Malay states of the Patani group were geographically, ethnically, culturally and historically closely connected with Kelantan. The British Government therefore wanted to know whether the Siamese Government would be willing to relinquish those troublesome Malay states as well.

The request by Paget was ill-received by Strobel, who well knew that the British suggestion of the cession of more territory would meet with a strong reaction from the Siamese. He replied accordingly:

> If that is to be the game, I think we had better abandon the negotiations at once. I am having sufficient difficulty with the King about Kedah and am not prepared to go further than the three states I originally named. ... There are considerable settlements of Siamese in Setul, and it might not be possible to include that state. ... As for Patani it is out of the question, as the Siamese Government will never consent to its cession.[89]

Despite this intractability, it was agreed in subsequent talks between Strobel and Paget that Perlis should be included with Kedah, probably on political and geographical grounds.

The refusal of the Siamese Government to give up Setul and the Malay states in the Patani group had to be accepted, but early in 1908 Paget returned to the charge and claimed instead the southern part of the Malay state of Raman, and the Langkawi islands, leaving to Siam the Terutau and other small islands to the west of Langkawi (Thamsook, 233, 1967). This was agreed to by the Siamese.

[88] Perlis had become separated from Kedah, as a state in its own right, only in 1839.
[89] Encl. in Desp., 2 April 1908, CO 273/343.

During the latter half of 1907, as discussions proceeded between the representatives of the two Governments in Bangkok, the outlines of the resulting agreement were sketched in. A draft treaty was drawn up on the following lines:

i) The provinces of Kedah, Kelantan and Trengganu, the lower portions of Legeh and Raman, and the Langkawi Islands to be ceded by Siam to Britain.

ii) The Secret Convention of 1897 to be abrogated confidentially.

iii) Siam to make a public declaration to the effect that she will not cede or lease territory, coaling stations, or docks to any foreign power or company south of the limits agreed to under the 1897 Secret Convention (i.e. roughly south of the 11th parallel of latitude).

iv) Siam gradually to assume jurisdiction over British subjects resident in Siam. Effective safeguards to be given, in European judges and court advisers. The right to hold land and all other privileges enjoyed are to be given to British subjects resident in Siam.

v) A loan for constructing the Peninsula Railway to be raised from the Federated Malay States at 4%. Construction not to be undertaken by the F.M.S., but to be placed under a British engineer. The F.M.S. to have the right to inspect surveys, plans, specifications for rolling-stock, etc. A department for control to be organized in Bangkok (separate from the Siamese Railway Department and not staffed by German officials).[90]

Certain amendments were later made by the British Government to the draft treaty. The most notable, as far as Kelantan was concerned, related to the Boundary Protocol.[91] Sir John Anderson, Governor of the Straits Settlements and High Commissioner for the Federated Malay States, objected to the proposed Kelantan-Legeh boundary. As a result fresh arrangements were made with the Siamese Government for the cession of the lower part of Legeh including the headwaters of the Pergau River.[92] In return, a small corner in the northeast of Kelantan was to be given to Siam.[93] Eventually, on 10 March 1909, the final version of the treaty was formally signed in Bangkok by Paget and by Prince Devawongse Varoprakar, the Siamese Foreign Minister. It was duly ratified by both governments on 9 July the same year.

Meanwhile, a petition praying that the State of Kelantan be not transferred to Britain had been presented to the King of Siam in May 1908, by the Kelantan Government. A similar petition was about

[90] Quoted in Thamsook (1967, 233).
[91] Encl. in Desp., 27 April 1908, CO 273/343.
[92] The present day areas of Batu Melintang, Kampong Jeli, Kampong Jedok, Kampong Batang Merbau, and Kampong Ayer Lubok Bunga, in the Tanah Merah district.
[93] Including the present day Kampong Tanjong (south of Narathiwat), Kampong Che' Hel, Kampong Belawan (Ban Phrai Wan), Kampong Tabal (Ban Tak Bai), and Kampong Sungei Golok, as well as the areas watered by the Golok, Menara, Layar, Kayu Kelat, Padi, and Elong rivers.

to be forwarded to Bangkok by the Kedah Government. Paget, in his despatch to London dated 29 May 1908, commenting on the petition from Kelantan, wrote as follows:

> It is, I think, unnecessary to attach any importance to these documents as indications of the Malay preference for Siamese as opposed to British rule; they are more probably merely an expression of anxiety on the part of a few office-holders lest, in the change and under the more strict British regime, they should fall upon less easy and less lucrative days. The Siamese Government are, however, undoubtedly incurring some criticism, if not also ridicule, from various sources on account of the considerable cession of territory to Britain that they have in contemplation, and the petitions which they are now receiving from their Malay States do not tend to render the position easier or to reconcile them to the bargain. It would, therefore, be to the advantage of all parties that the present delay should come to an end, and that a decision regarding the new Treaty should be made in one sense or another as speedily as possible.[94]

Though the above represented the British view, it is undeniable that the Malay rulers, and the majority of Malays in the states concerned who had had dealings with Siam, had found Siamese control somewhat repugnant, and had they been given a free choice, would have preferred British rule. It is certainly true, however, that the uncles of the Raja of Kelantan, and some other interested parties in the state, were opposed to the contemplated change for reasons of their own (*UM*, 11 Apr. 1908). This minority group, with the backing and possibly at the instigation of Graham, was responsible for the petitions against the proposed transfer of Kelantan to Britain. The Raja of Kelantan was reported in the Malay press to have had discussions with his uncles, who tried to persuade him to go to Bangkok to appeal to the King of Siam not to agree to the transfer. This the Raja refused to do. It was likewise suggested in the same newspaper that the uncles of the Raja were opposed to the change as they wished to see Kelantan free from the interference of both Siam *and* Britain (*UM*, 30 Apr. 1908). As events turned out, the Siamese Government chose to ignore the petition from Kelantan, and negotiations continued uninterrupted to their conclusion.

The most important provision of the Anglo-Siamese Treaty of 1909, as far as Kelantan was concerned, was that the state (together with Kedah, Trengganu, Perlis and part of Lower Raman) was transferred directly from Siam to Britain. Under Article I, 'the Siamese Government [transferred] to the British Government all rights of suzerainty, protection, administration, and control whatsoever which they possess'

[94] Encl. in Desp., 29 May 1908, CO 273/343.

over the state of Kelantan. In return, Britain surrendered her extraterritorial rights in Siam. In addition, it was agreed that Siam should get a loan from the Federated Malay States, with which to build a railway linking the Siamese and Federated Malay States systems. The treaty marked the final stage in the extension of British political influence in northern Malaya.

The Transfer

Four months after the signing and ratification of the 1909 treaty Kelantan was officially transferred by Siam to Britain. The Raja of Kelantan, who was not even consulted, came to know officially about the new treaty through a letter from the King of Siam (*MM*, 17 July 1907). On 9 July, Phra Phisa, a Siamese official from Bangkok, arrived at Kota Bharu bringing the letter with him (Mohd. Yusof, 1953, 20). In a simple but colourful ceremony the Siamese envoy and party were received by the Raja of Kelantan at the Istana Balai Besar and the letter was read before the members of the State Council. It was said that the Siamese letter carried the title 'The End of Siamese Suzerainty Over Kelantan'. It explained the new treaty to the Raja and his Council, and informed them of the transfer. Two days later the Raja received a cable from Bangkok notifying him that with effect from 9 July 1909, the day when the treaty had been ratified by the Siamese and British Governments, the State of Kelantan was transferred by Siam to Britain. On the morning of 10 July the Raja ordered the white flag of Kelantan to be hoisted in place of the Siamese flag, which had been flown in Kota Bharu for the past fourteen years (Mohd. Yusof, 1953, 20).

James Scott Mason, the first British Adviser to the Raja of Kelantan arrived in Kota Bharu on 15 July to take over the administration of the state from Graham. The first phase of the actual transfer took place on the same day on which the 'handing over' ceremony was executed. Mason accepted responsibility for the state of Kelantan from Graham by a brief 'Document of Transfer' signed by the representatives of the respective governments at the Residency. Immediately after the signature of this document Graham and his party left Kota Bharu for Bangkok by a Siamese gunboat. With the transfer, and the departure of Graham, the period of Siamese advisory government, or the new regime, officially came to an end.

The second phase of the transfer of Kelantan occurred during the visit of Sir John Anderson, Governor of the Straits Settlements and High Commissioner for the Federated Malay States. Accompanied by Sir William Taylor, the Resident-General, and several others, Anderson arrived in Kota Bharu on 19 July 1909 to proclaim the formal assumption of British protection over the state. A guard of honour and a salute of 17 guns welcomed the Governor and his party. Next day they left Kota Bharu for Trengganu where a similar ceremony was held.

For over a year after the transfer nothing of significance took place to mark the change of status, beyond some changes in the staffing of the state civil service. The administration of the state continued smoothly and made quiet progress, very much on the lines already laid down by Graham.

The Anglo-Kelantan Treaty of 1910

The next important event in the history of modern Kelantan after the transfer was the signing of the Anglo-Kelantan Treaty of 1910. For this purpose Sir John Anderson made a second visit to Kelantan. Accompanied by Colonel Jackson, the Surveyor-General of the Federated Malay States, and R.E. Stubbs of the Colonial Office, he arrived in Kota Bharu on 22 October 1910 to conclude the treaty with the Raja of Kelantan. The treaty, prepared both in English and Malay, was signed by the Raja of Kelantan with Tengku Sri Indera Mahkota (Tengku Ismail b. Tuan Long Senik) and Tengku Chik Tuan Abdullah (an uncle of the Raja) as witnesses, while Sir John Anderson signed with Colonel Jackson and R.E. Stubbs as witnesses (SB, 3 Nov. 1910).[95]

By means of this treaty Britain formally assumed control of Kelantan's foreign relations. The treaty also established the right of the British Government to appoint an Adviser to the Raja of Kelantan, who undertook 'to follow and give effect to the advice of the Adviser ... in all matters of administration other than those touching the Mohammedan religion and Malay custom'. On the whole, the terms of the treaty had much in common with those of the Anglo-Siamese Treaty of 1902. The preamble described Kelantan as being 'recognised to be under the protection of Great Britain', but not a word was mentioned about suzerainty.

In conclusion it can be said that the Anglo-Siamese Treaty of 1909 brought to a close a period of inconvenient and ambiguous British and Siamese relations with Kelantan. It also marked the end of Siamese connection with and interference in the affairs of the state of Kelantan. By the Anglo-Kelantan Treaty of 1910, Kelantan was formally brought within the fold of British political and administrative influence as a protectorate. In spite of attempts in some quarters to incorporate Kelan-

---

[95] In the following year, 1911, the British formally recognized Tuan Long Senik, the Raja of Kelantan, as Sultan, and thenceforth he reigned as Sultan Muhammad IV.

tan into the Federated Malay States, the state preferred for its own good to remain 'unfederated', a status that was to persist until after the Second World War. For Kelantan, the period from 1900 to 1910 was indeed a period of transition.

REFERENCES

Monographs and Reports

Asa'ad b. Haji Muda, 1930–31. 'Riwayat Kelantan,' *Kenchana* (Kota Bharu), Apr. 1930—(? month) 1931, fifteen episodes.

Asa'ad Shukri b. Haji Muda, 1962. *Sejarah Kelantan* (Kota Bharu, Pustaka Aman Press).

Blagden, C.O., 1906. 'Siam and the Malay Peninsula', *Journal of the Royal Asiatic Society*, 107–19.

Clifford, H., 1897. *In Court and Kampong, being tales and sketches of native life in the Malay Peninsula* (London, Grant Richards).

———— 1961. 'Expedition to Trengganu and Kelantan, report by Hugh Clifford,' *JMBRAS*, XXXIV, 1, 1–162 (reprinted from the report written in 1895 and first published in 1938).

Davies, R.D., 1902. *Siam in the Malay Peninsula* (Singapore, Fraser and Neave).

Emerson, R., 1937. *Malaysia: A Study in Direct and Indirect Rule* (New York, Macmillan).

Graham, W.A., 1904. *Report on the State of Kelantan for the year August, 1903, to August, 1904* (Bangkok, Government Printer).

———— 1905. *Report on the State of Kelantan for the period 1st August, 1904, to 31st May, 1905* (Bangkok, Government Printer).

———— 1907. *Report on the State of Kelantan for the period 1st June, 1905, to 23rd February, 1906* (Bangkok, Government Printer).

———— 1908a. *Kelantan, A State of the Malay Peninsula. A Handbook of Information* (Glasgow, James Maclehose & Sons).

———— 1908b. *Report on the State of Kelantan for the period 24th February, 1906, to 14th February, 1907* (Bangkok, Government Printer).

———— 1909. *Report on the State of Kelantan for the period 15th February, 1907, to 4th Febraury, 1908* (Bangkok, Government Printer).

Hume, W.J.P., 1949. 'Malays on the Warpath', *British Malaya*, XXIII, 9.

———— 1952. *The Federation of Malaya and its Police Force, 1786–1952* (Kuala Lumpur, Government Printer).

Mahmud b. Ismail, Haji Nik, 1934. *Rengkasan Chetera Kelantan* (Kota Bharu, Matba'ah al-Asasiyah).

Maxwell, G. and Gibson, W.S., 1924. *Treaties and Engagements Affecting the Malay States and Borneo* (London, James Truscott).

Mills, L.A., 1960. 'British Malaya, 1824–67', *JMBRAS*, XXXIII, 3, 3–424 (edited and reprinted from the first edition of 1925).

Mohd. Husin Khali'i Haji Awang, 1970. *Kelantan dari Zaman ka-Zaman* (Kota Bharu, Sharikat Dian).

Mohd. Yusof b. Salleh al-Kelantani, 1953. *Penambah Ketahuan* (Kota Bharu, Mustafa Press).

Norman, H., 1895. *The Peoples and Politics of the Far East* (London, T. Fisher Unwin).

Thamsook Numnonda, 1967. 'Negotiations Regarding the Cession of the Siamese Malay States, 1907–1909', *Journal of the Siam Society*, LV, 2, 227–35.

Thio, E., 1957. 'A Turning Point in Britain's Malayan Policy', *Historical Annual, University of Singapore*.

Tweedie, M.W.F., 1953. 'An Early Chinese Account of Kelantan', *JMBRAS*, XXVI, 1, 216–19.

Vella, W.F., 1957. *Siam Under Rama III, 1824–1851* (Locust Valley, N.Y., J.J. Augustin).

Waterstradt, J., 1902. 'Kelantan and My Trip to Gunong Tahan', *JSBRAS*, 37, 1–27.

Wood, W.A.R., 1926. *A History of Siam* (London, T. Fisher Unwin)

Wright, A. and Reid, T.H., 1912. *The Malay Peninsula. A Record of British Progress in the Middle [sic] East* (London, T. Fisher Unwin).

Manuscript Material (as cited)

CO 273. Correspondence between Governor, Straits Settlements, and Secretary of State, Open, 1900–1909.

DRM. Diary of the Raja Muda, Tengku Zainal Abidin b. Tuan Long Kundor. (Manuscript diary of events occurring between 1896 and 1912. Untitled.) National Archives of Malaysia, Kuala Lumpur.

HKS. 'Hikayat Sri Kelantan'. (Author unknown, manuscript completed in 1914.)

OTHMAN. Othman b. Yusof, 'Rengkasan Tarikh Kelantan'. (Manuscript, undated but c. 1927–1941.)

Newspapers (as cited)

MM. *Malay Mail* (Kuala Lumpur), 1909.

SB. *Straits Budget* (Singapore), 1903–10.

ST. *Straits Times* (Singapore), 1905.

Interviews (conducted during 1963–65)

Tengku Khalid b. Tengku Chik Abdullah (Tengku Bendahara), Jalan Post Office Lama, Kota Bharu. (Died 1965)

Mohd. Salleh b. Imam Haji Abdullah, Kampong Che' Bakar, Jalan Sultanah Zainab, Kota Bharu. (Died 1964)

Wan Daud b. Wan Omar, J.P., Jalan To' Semian, Kota Bharu. (Died 1968)

Sayyid Hassan b. Sayyid Yusof, Kampong Repek, Pasir Mas

Haji Nik Abdul Kadir b. Nik Wan Ahmad, Jalan Merbau, Kota Bharu. (Died 1968)

3
IBRAHIM NIK MAHMOOD
The To' Janggut Rebellion of 1915

THE Pasir Puteh 'rebellion', like many other episodes in Kelantan history (and indeed in Malayan history generally) is still imperfectly understood.[1] The present paper is an attempt to look at the rebellion in the light of the sources available from Kelantan itself—both the oral memory that still remains and the written record, in particular the papers of the *Pejabat Balai* (broadly, Palace Office) and the office of the British Adviser in Kota Bharu.

Pasir Puteh is situated near the Kelantan-Trengganu border, about 27 miles from the state capital. The administrative district, centred on the town of Pasir Puteh itself, had been established a few years before Kelantan was transferred by the Siamese to the British. Its high revenue-yielding potential had very early been recognized (Graham, 1905, 18), and its fertility as a source of a variety of agricultural products known.

[1] Since this paper was first written in 1968, at a time when the Colonial Office records for the period were not available, J. de V. Allen has published an article entitled 'The Kelantan Rising of 1915: Some Thoughts on the Concept of Resistance in British Malayan History' (*JSEAH*, IX, 2, 241–57). This recites in some detail the speculations concerning the causes of the rebellion contained in the confidential reports furnished by the British officials W.G. Maxwell and R.J. Farrer to the High Commissioner, and transmitted by letter to the Colonial Office in two confidential despatches, dated respectively 2 June and 20 July 1915 (CO 273/426 and 427). The present discussion, based on the Kelantan state papers and other Malay material will, it is hoped, be usefully complementary.

On the coast stretch extensive coconut plantations, while further inland padi fields, rubber plantations, orchards and vegetable gardens have been characteristic features of the landscape. The livelihood of the rather dense population of the district is, therefore, based on agriculture.

In the past, apart from their legitimate preoccupations, the peasants of Pasir Puteh also indulged in illegal practices, some of which were attributed to the close proximity of the district to what was thought of as 'the lawless state of Trengganu'. Thus, thefts, assaults, brawls, house-breaking and so forth were common phenomena in their daily lives. Cattle thefts were particularly frequent because of their easy disposal across the border to Trengganu (Graham, 1905, 18). Gambling of a variety of forms was a popular pastime.[2]

This traditional way of life, however, was disrupted by the establishment of the District Office and its functionaries in 1905 (Graham, 1907, 11). The appointment of the District Officer, who combined the role of Magistrate, Revenue Collector and Land Officer, dislocated the power of the traditional territorial chief of Jeram, a sub-district of Pasir Puteh, and the enforcement of a new land system created misunderstanding among the uneducated and conservative peasantry. It was this socio-economic change that precipitated the rebellion.

On 12 May 1915, His Highness the Sultan of Kelantan, Sultan Muhammad IV, issued a Notice[3] declaring to his subjects that rebels had taken up arms against the State Government and, in fact, against his own person. The Notice stated that searches had been made for the rebels but they had yet to be arrested. His Highness therefore demanded that the leaders surrender themselves either to him or to His Excellency the British Adviser, within seven days of the date of the Notice, to answer charges levelled against them. Failing this, their houses would be burnt and their property confiscated. The leaders named were Engku Besar of Jeram, Haji Mat Hassan or To' Janggut of Nering, Penghulu Adam of Kelubi, Haji Sa'id of Cherang Tuli and Inche Sahak of Nering.

The Notice referred to the rising or riot which had broken out in Pasir Puteh district on Thurday 29 April. The Sultan, after consultation with the Malay members of his State Council and the British Adviser,[4] a few days later sent two of his leading officials to Singapore, bearing a letter from him reporting the incident to the Governor and Commander-in-Chief of the Straits Settlements and Labuan, and High Commis-

---

[2] Tweedie (1953, 218), quoting from a Chinese account of late 18th century Kelantan, provides evidence that gambling formed a prominent part of traditional royal festivals. More recently, an anti-gambling Notice of 1917 (encl. in Kel. M. 15/1917) listed no fewer than 33 different types of gambling games, most of which were proscribed.
[3] Encl. in Kel. PB. 531/1915.
[4] Sultan to BA, 28 Jamadal-akhir 1333 (12 May 1915), in Kel. PB. 126/1915.

sioner for the Federated Malay States and Brunei, Sir Arthur Young.[5] In Kelantan, the rising came to be known as '*Musoh To' Janggut*' that is, To' Janggut's rebellion, because To' Janggut appeared to be the most outstanding among the leaders.

Whether the rebellion was also aimed against the Sultan, as he claimed in the Notice, cannot be answered by a simple 'yes' or 'no'. In his official correspondence, His Highness always described himself as the sovereign ruler of Kelantan[6], and on this point alone any rebellion against the Kelantan Government could be said to be a rebellion against the Sultan. But it would be rash to jump to this conclusion merely on the strength of the Sultan's claim to sovereignty. For one thing, the impression is that the Sultan was not fully sovereign; also, it is necessary to consider the economic, political and social situation in the state prior to the outbreak, before reaching any final conclusion. In short, one needs first to analyse the causes of the rebellion.

Sultan Muhammad IV (or Tengku Long Senik, as he was then known) came to the throne of Kelantan on the death of Sultan Mansur, his uncle, in 1900, but he was formally installed only in 1911.[7] It must be noted in passing that between these dates two important events had taken place in the history of Kelantan. One was the signing of the Anglo-Siamese Treaty of 1902, by which Siam's suzerainty over Kelantan was recognized by the British and the Raja of Kelantan. The other was the Anglo-Siamese Treaty of 1909, by which the Siamese Government transferred to the British Government all rights of suzerainty, protection, administration and control whatsoever over Kelantan.[8] It is obvious, therefore, that while up to 1909 Kelantan had been under Siamese influence, from that year, or more particularly perhaps from 1910, when the Anglo-Kelantan Agreement was signed,[9] Kelantan was already under the influence of Britain. British influence was asserted through the Governor and High Commissioner in Singapore, whose 'advice' was channelled to the Sultan through the British Adviser or, in his absence, his Assistant, resident in Kelantan. Although the Anglo-Kelantan Agreement specifically stated that the Ruler had

---

[5] Sultan to Governor, undated, in Kel. PB. 108/1915 (the Governor's reply, in the same file, indicates that the Sultan's letter was dated 27 Jamadal-akhir 1333, or 11 May 1915).

[6] The preamble to all letters sent by the Sultan read: 'daripada kita al-Sultan Muhammad yang keempat, K.C.M.G., yang mempunyai takhta kerajaan negeri Kelantan serta daerah2 jajahan-nya' (from me, Sultan Muhammad IV . . . sovereign ruler of the state of Kelantan and all her territories).

[7] Bishop (1912, 11). The entry reads: 'The Coronation of His Majesty the King [of England] was celebrated in Kota Bharu. . . . At the reception the letters granting to His Highness the title of Sultan and recognizing his eldest son as his successor were read.'

[8] See above, Mohamed b. Nik Mohd. Salleh.

[9] Text in Maxwell and Gibson (1924, 111–112).

the right of internal administration, and although the laws of Kelantan were enacted by the Sultan-in-Council, in actual practice it was the Adviser, the only non-Malay member of the State Council, who was responsible for the bulk of the laws (Chan, 1965, 159, 170-1). Hence, it is clear that the sovereignty of the Sultan was merely 'an illusion' (ibid., 186). As such, the Sultan's claim that the rebellion had been launched against his person cannot be accepted at face value.

Apart from external influences on the internal administration of the state, past Sultans had apparently not been able to exercise power fully as rulers of their realm. The history of Kelantan, particularly before the establishment of the advisory system, had been marked by intrigue and near anarchy, in which the sultan either willingly delegated or helplessly lost part of his power to territorial chiefs. Engku Besar of Jeram was one of these. Before the opening of Pasir Puteh district under Graham's administration, Engku Besar had enjoyed the undivided loyalty of the people in and around Jeram, a settlement and surrounding area about three-and-a-half miles from Pasir Puteh town. It was in reaction to the dislocation of his power, after the District Office had been established, that Engku Besar instigated To' Janggut and others to stir the local inhabitants into defying the authorities.

Haji Mat Hassan, the most outstanding leader of the rebellion, was popularly known as To' Janggut because of his long white beard (*UM*, 10 June 1915), which he had sported ever since returning from the pilgrimage to Mecca (Yahya, 1955, 13). According to one source, To' Janggut possessed all the features of a brave and intelligent man. He was well-built and about six feet tall. He had sharp brown eyes which, it is believed, are a sign of bravery. His head was rather big and bald, and his forehead broad, with thick eyebrows; all these are supposed to signify intelligence, thoughtfulness and firmness. He is said to have been invulnerable and to have boasted that he was so (Abdullah, 1957, 1-2; *UM*, 10 June 1915).

According to tradition, at To' Janggut's birth the midwife had advised his mother to dry his caul, which was unusually thick, and later have it served to the boy in rice porridge. This, it is alleged, had been done by his mother when To' Janggut was in his teens and had completed Kuran-reading. This was how he had acquired invulnerability. Apart from this sanctity, other supernatural qualities were attributed to To' Janggut, acquired, it was said, through his teacher, a person of Minangkabau origin. The supernatural attributes conjured up in the popular mind with respect to To' Janggut, apart from his manifest bravery, help to explain how it became possible for him to command the allegiance of no fewer than two thousand followers against the authorities.

To' Janggut is believed to have been 62 years old when the rebellion occurred.[10] His father, Munas, had been one of the two most trusted bodyguards and warriors of one Tengku Sri Maharaja Tua who had been chief of Jeram from 1878, when Tengku Senik or Muhammad II was Raja of Kelantan (Yahya, 1955, 5-6). Whether Tengku Sri Maharaja Tua or each of his two predecessors had been an appointed chief or, alternatively, had ruled independently of the Raja, is difficult to ascertain.[11] According to one source (Yahya, 1955, 4), the first chief of Jeram, Long Ga'afar, had received the Raja's sanction. But it must be noted that while, throughout the peninsula, some territorial chiefs were given letters of appointment by the ruler of the state, it has also been held that few of the chiefs held any authority from the sovereign for their position.[12] And when the local government of Jeram was in the hands of Engku Besar, fifth in Long Ga'afar's lineage (Abdullah, 1957, 4), the treatment accorded him by the state authorities on the establishment of Pasir Puteh district cast further doubts on the legality of the position of the Jeram chief.

To' Janggut was a trader by profession. He used to travel, like other traders local and foreign, as far as Trengganu and even Patani to sell such local produce as rice, padi and coconut oil (Yahya, 1955, 13). In his spare time To' Janggut revelled in gambling, cock-fighting, fish-fighting and bull-fighting, which were then some of the most common and popular forms of entertainment in Kelantan. Though he was not a warrior of the territorial chief, like his father, To' Janggut was considered as belonging to the circle of aristocrats at Engku Besar's court. This was due to the connection between To' Janggut's father and Engku Besar's family in the previous generation, apart from the fact that To' Janggut was himself a native of Jeram. Moreover, as already remarked To' Janggut enjoyed a great reputation and popular respect not only for his bravery and similar attributes but also for his benevolence and altruism (Yahya, 1955, 13). Obviously, it was both an advantage and a necessity for Engku Besar to rally round him such supporters as To' Janggut, for even if he *had* been officially recognized by the Sultan as a chief, Engku Besar, like other traditional rural authority, controlled his

---

[10] Yahya (1955, 6) reads: 'Mat Hassan itu telah di-agakkan di-peranakkan pada tahun Masehi 1853 di-Jeram' (Mat Hassan is reckoned to have been born in 1853 A.D. at Jeram).

[11] A *kota*, or fort, had been built at Jeram near the river, though nothing is now left of it. The graves of Tengku Sri Maharaja Tua and other members of his family can be found about half a mile away from the site of the fort.

[12] See discussion and citations in Gullick (1958, 96).

district 'by his own strength rather than by the the backing of the Sultan' (Gullick, 1958, 97).

Like his predecessors, Engku Besar, as a territorial chief, and the aristocrats who surrounded him, enjoyed the allegiance of the people in and around Jeram. He drew his income mainly from taxes levied on the produce of and goods traded in the area. Right from the beginning, the district had been a source of personal revenue and benefit to a territorial chief, just as the state had been similarly regarded by the ruling class as a whole. This concept was not one easily surrendered. It was looked upon as a right hallowed by tradition, and any change which denied the chief this right would certainly provoke defiance.

The power of the Jeram chief began to be threatened immediately the new district of Pasir Puteh was opened. The district, embracing Jeram, was henceforth to be administered not by the chief but by a District Officer. No consideration, apparently, was given by the authorities in mitigation of the loss of traditional position suffered by Engku Besar on the appointment of this official. Presumably on the advice of Graham, the Siamese Adviser, the Raja appointed one Inche Ibrahim as the first District Officer in 1905. He had served as Chief Clerk in the Small Court in Kota Bharu (Graham, 1907, 11), and is believed to have come from Singapore.[13] The Kelantanese, particularly the uneducated and half-educated mass of the peasantry, would not as a rule take readily to an 'outsider' officiating over them.[14] Objection was, therefore, to be expected against the appointment of Inche Ibrahim. But his tact and initiative, and the interest that he showed towards the people, is said to have kept this objection to the minimum. The Adviser, in his annual report for 1905–06 (Graham, 1907, 11), commented that 'Inche Brahim' had justified his promotion from the comparatively humble post of a Court Clerk by serving very well as a District Officer. Certainly the criteria by which the Adviser had judged the District Officer's efficiency consisted of more than his ability to increase district revenue. In any case, he was popularly credited with increasing land alienation, and encouraging trade and farming in the district. As a result, it is said, within a few years after the district had been opened the new town was attracting practically all the trade that previously had gone to Jeram,

---

[13] Yahya (1955, 17) reads: 'Baginda pun menitahkan dan melantek Inche Yim [Ibrahim] dari Singapura tadi di-jadikan Ketua Jajahan' (His Highness then ordered and appointed Inche Yim, recently from Singapore, to be District Officer).

[14] The strictly exclusive organization of the present Kelantan State Civil Service, sometimes at the expense of efficiency, perhaps, bears this out. The term *'orang luar'*, i.e. 'outsider,' refers not only to a person who is from outside the state or the district but sometimes also to one locally born who is outside or has no acquaintance with the aristocratic circle.

much to the chagrin of Engku Besar and his retinue who were now deprived of their traditional income.

It is important to note that the opening of districts and the appointment of district officers to administer them were features of the enforcement of British policy in all the peninsular Malay states after 1872. In Kelantan, the British 'forward movement' may perhaps be said to have begun with Graham's appointment in 1903. The subjection of the ruler of the state to the advice of the Adviser in all matters except those pertaining to 'the Mohamedan religion and Malay custom' was stipulated in Article II of the Anglo-Siamese Agreement of 1902, and Article II of the Anglo-Kelantan Treaty of 1910 which followed the transfer of the state to Britain consequent upon the Anglo-Siamese Treaty of 1909. Whether the Raja of Kelantan was aware of the implications of this stipulation in the respective treaties, with reference to both himself and his subjects (or in a position to do much about it if he were), are moot points.

Although many of the administrative innovations which characterized the early period of increased Siamese/British control, during the years from 1903 to 1909, were slow to take effect (at least in part because of the need to take account of traditional authority), there was mounting interference in the patterns of the past. One of the first areas to feel the impact was the district. Among the most provocative aspects of reform and reorganization, as far as the territorial chief and his followers were concerned, was the introduction of a new system of public revenue collection, utilizing existing produce taxes, which was to hold sway for the best part of a decade from 1905. The implementation of this system, in so far as it was efficiently enforced, reduced the chief's power to nothing and subjected the taxpayer to strict rules of an unfamiliar kind. The system was based on a delegation of powers within an administrative hierarchy, and worked as follows:

> The circle headmen or Toh Kweng who are appointed by the Government with popular approval and who are in charge of the subdivisions of the district known as 'Kweng' draw up lists showing what each plot of padi should pay, and they also count the number of coconut trees etc., growing on lands other than padi land, and with the aid of certain Government rules on the subject, fix what must be paid for the given year. These details they forward to the Land Office, where assessment-rolls are prepared.... When the Land Office has completed the writing out of the assessment-rolls, these are sent to the Toh Kweng who are supposed to collect forthwith the ... sums mentioned in the lists.... The Toh Kweng, after making their collections, pay such collections into the Land Office in lump sums....[15]

[15] Land Office Annual Report for 1914, encl. in Kel. K. 44/1915.

Tax collection which had been traditionally the prerogative of the territorial chiefs was now entrusted to the To' Kweng. Taxes collected were channeled through the District Officer, who was both Magistrate and Land-Revenue Officer (Graham, 1905, 17), into the State Treasury. Thus, in each district, power now shifted from the chief to the District Officer, who became, in effect, the 'ruler' of the district and was in full command of it. Government rules on tax assessment and collection, as will be seen, constituted an encroachment on traditional practices.

Under the territorial chief, the extent to which the inhabitants of the district had been subjected to taxation was in proportion to the competence of the chief to collect and his income needs, and was also determined by the personal relationship between the people and their chief. The chief, in his heyday, as opposed to the District Officer who displaced him, did not have an elaborate hierarchy of subordinates. In fact this was not necessary as taxes collected were mainly for his own subsistence and that of his retinue. Only a nominal proportion of the taxes collected, if any, was remitted to the Sultan. In these circumstances, it may be said that taxation was neither severe nor extensive. Moreover, tax exemption, particularly among the chief's supporters, was common, for logically this constituted the surest means of ensuring support.

On the other hand, the District Officer was not at the apex of the administrative hierarchy as the chief was. He was but a central government agent, whose duty it was to fill the Treasury with as much revenue as possible and whose initiative in increasing revenue constituted one of the most important criteria in judging his efficiency. Moreover, his position was not markedly dependent on popular support; law and higher authority provided him with sanctions. In such circumstances, little flexibility could be expected in revenue collection.

This was the situation in which the inhabitants of Pasir Puteh found themselves when the District Officer displaced the territorial chief. With very few exceptions, there were no tax exemptions.[16] Neither

[16] Tax exemptions during the transitional period as stipulated in the 'Regulation to Provide for the Better Assessment and Collection of Hasil Paddi' and the 'Regulation to Provide for the Better Assessment and Collection of Hasil Nyior,' both of 1323 (1905), and dealing respectively with padi and coconuts (encl. in Kel. K. 949/1914 and Kel. K. 35/1915), were as follows:

	Padi Lands*	Coconut Trees†
To' Kweng	32 penjuru	100 trees
Nebeng (lesser headmen)	8 ,,	30 ,,
Clerk to To' Kweng	8 ,,	30 ,,
Imam	32 ,,	20 ,,
Khatib (surau officer)	24 ,,	15 ,,
Bilal (surau officer)	16 ,,	10 ,,

* wherever situated; † within the compounds of their own homes

A *penjuru* was equal to about four acres.

was there much possibility for tax evasion, as there was hardly any place in the district where the District Officer's 'arms' could not and did not reach. The simple rule was, pay the taxes or face the consequences. By the coconut and padi tax enactments of 1905, the inhabitants of the district were required not only to pay produce assessments on these commodities (as well as on the crop from betel leaf vines) but also to assist the To' Kweng in collection. Failure to comply with the requirements could mean imprisonment or fine or both. This applied to everyone in the district including the ex-territorial chief himself.[17]

Thus the opening of Pasir Puteh district and the appointment from Kota Bharu of an 'outsider' as the District Officer marked the beginning of a strained relationship between the chief of Jeram and the state authorities.

Although the first District Officer, Inche Ibrahim, was said to have got along quite well with the local people, and under him administrative measures were not imposed unduly strictly, there was general objection to the new system of revenue collection, which was relatively inflexible and comparatively more demanding than that of yore. Engku Besar, who suffered great humiliation not only by virtue of being deprived of his traditional power and income but also because he was forced to pay taxes like other people, resolved, therefore, to exploit the popular discontent to avenge himself. He secretly summoned to Kota Jeram To' Janggut and three other supporters who were respected in the community, and plotted with them against the district authority.

The ultimate objective was to stir up popular hatred towards the authorities. To' Janggut and his three colleagues, Haji Sa'id, Che' Sahak and Penghulu Adam, were to spread propaganda alleging that the authorities were out to oppress the people by taxation. The people were thus to be induced to boycott the taxes. As pointed out earlier, there was already a feeling of discontent among some sections of the district regarding the new system. To' Janggut and his colleagues, therefore, found a favourable response as they moved from village to village disseminating their propaganda.

[17] Section 7 of the Hasil Nyior Regulation, above, provides that anyone refusing to assist the To' Kweng in tax collection may be charged in court and, if found guilty, sentenced to one month in jail or a fine of $50, or both. Section 9 provides that anyone refusing to pay either of the taxes within two months from the date notified by the To' Kweng is to be regarded as being indebted, and if such debt is not paid at the next collection may be summoned. Section 12 provides that if an indebted person is neither present nor represented in court in accordance with such summons, he may be arrested and sentenced to two months' jail or a fine of $50, or both, in addition to incurring payment of the debt and the costs of the trial. Similar punitive measures are laid down in the Hasil Padi Regulation.

In 1910, Inche Ibrahim resigned his appointment as District Officer (Mason, 1911, 2), and the vacancy was temporarily filled by one Inche Leh, Head Clerk of the High Court.[18] Inche Leh's tenure of office lasted for perhaps a year, during which no unusual events were recorded. The continued peace in the district, in spite of To' Janggut's escapades, may be attributable to the fact that Inche Leh appears to have been local-born,[19] and therefore in a position to minister to local prejudices and habits. It may perhaps also be suggested that, aware that his was an interim appointment, Inche Leh saw no cause to be strict with the people and thereby earn their wrath.

But the situation changed when, in 1912, Che' Latiff, a Singaporean, replaced Inche Leh as District Officer. Abdul Latiff was well-built, full of initiative and a rather strict disciplinarian.[20] His appointment was, apparently, a well calculated one. Under his two predecessors, especially the last one, district administration had been wanting and tax collection, in particular, rather lax.[21] With him in office, general improvements were made (Langham-Carter, 1914, 4) and punitive measures as stipulated in the existing tax enactments were said to have been strictly enforced against irregularities in tax payment. From about 1913 onwards, the new District Officer seems also to have exploited possibilities for revenue collection to the full, even to the obvious disadvantage and indignation of the local people. An example is the auction of contracts to collect turtle eggs, and a type of grass called *kerchut*, in several places in the district, simply to increase revenue.[22] This measure naturally enraged those who had hitherto been collecting these products free.

[18] Graham (1909, 10) states that Ibrahim had gone on leave for five months in 1908, during which time Inche Leh, Head Clerk of the High Court, officiated for him. When Ibrahim resigned in 1910 no mention is made of who replaced him until Inche Abdul Latiff was appointed early in 1921. It is assumed here that Leh again acted as District Officer during this interval.

[19] The official reports do not state this, but Leh is a standard Kelantanese name, short for Salleh. Oral sources also claim that he was local-born.

[20] This information has been gathered from several elderly persons in the locality, and in addition from Tan Sri Nik Mustaffa Fadhil, now of Jelawat and previously in the Kelantan Civil Service, who remembers Che' Latiff well.

[21] Langham-Carter (1913, 3) notes that when Latiff took over as District Officer there was an increase in crime and a fall in revenue. The fall in revenue must be considered the product of the previous year's administration, for some of the taxes were required by regulation to be paid at the beginning of the year. For the following year, 1913, Langham-Carter (1914, 4) notes that there had been an increase in revenue, and that general improvements in road-making, building construction, and the like had been set in train. It is clear, likewise, from the statements of the local Small Court and Shari'a Court for the years 1912 and after, that the number of cases brought to trial increased tremendously (see Appendices 'D' in the *Administration Reports* on Kelantan for the years concerned). These are clear indications of the tightening up of the administration of justice in the district.

[22] DO to BA, 6 Jan. 1915, encl. in Kel. K. 54/1915, in which Latiff asked for permission to auction these contracts, the revenue from which, he said, would bring in an extra $50 to $60 a year. Permission was granted in BA to DO, 20 Jan. 1915, in *ibid*.

Furthermore, thefts (particularly of cattle), housebreaking, assaults, carrying of arms and other traditional indulgences and practices which had in the past continued with little interference from the authorities, seem to have been inhibited by Che' Latiff's efficiency.[23] The District Officer's efforts to crack down on crime and bring criminals to court are understandable. More cases tried meant more revenue from the judiciary; the number of court cases also constituted a measure of efficiency. It is said that one of the things that provoked the people most was the way Che' Latiff and his subordinates dealt with them, particularly in connection with taxation. A slight delay in payment, for example, often earned the payer insulting words and other forms of humiliation.[24]

In January 1915 a new land system was introduced in the state. Instead of the produce taxes imposed previously, a fixed land rent was to be levied, and simple titles were to be issued in due course for lands upon which rent was paid.[25] Though meant to be a substitute for the produce taxes, the land rent actually amounted to a new tax on landowners who had not previously worked their own land. Moreover, land rent was introduced precisely so that 'there should be a steady, if not very rapid, improvement in the land revenue' (Langham-Carter, 1915, 4). As such, the new system was, in the last analysis, an added burden on the people as a whole, although in some ways a marginal one. In particular, the land rent, which allowed for no significant exemptions, was seen to bear most heavily upon those who in the past, because of their status—as members either of the aristocracy or of the rural elite—had escaped much of the produce taxation.

The sudden implementation of the new system in Pasir Puteh by Che' Latiff obviously amounted to rubbing salt in the wound he had already inflicted on the people by his alleged harshness. It would cer-

[23] The *Administration Reports* on Kelantan show the following cases tried in the Small Court, Pasir Puteh:

Feb. 1906 — Feb. 1907
Thefts 5 cases, cattle theft nil, assaults 13 cases, housebreaking 2 cases, disobedience of orders 2 cases.

Feb. 1907 — Feb. 1908
Thefts nil, cattle theft nil, assaults 16 cases, housebreaking nil.
By contrast, the figures for 1914 (encl. in Kel. K. 249/1915) are:

Jan. 1914 — Dec. 1915
Thefts 28 cases, cattle thefts 54 cases, assaults 29 cases, housebreaking 9 cases, wearing kris in public places 20 cases.

[24] Several informants testified to this, including Haji Tuan Senik b. Tuan Muda, aged about eighty at time of interview. His late father had been a To' Kweng in To' Janggut's time, and his own son is now Penggawa (the title given subsequently to To' Kweng) of Limbongan, or Pasir Puteh.

[25] Notice 4/1914, Land Rules, encl. in Kel.K. 33/1915, reads: 'Pending the preparation of a complete Land Enactment, it has pleased His Highness in Council this day [19 March 1914] to order that (1) Fixed annual rents shall be substituted from 1st January, 1915, for the present produce taxes, these ceasing where fixed rents are collected.' Cf. also *UM*, 8 May 1915.

tainly invite opposition, as the then Acting British Adviser, R.J. Farrer (1916, 6), observed retrospectively:

> The local Malay is first and last an agriculturist. The land system is the framework about which are built his custom, his habit and his life itself. He shares with the peasantry of every other land on earth an affection for the ills he has in preference to others that he knows not of. It is obvious that any attempt to change in the twinkling of an eye the system to which he is accustomed into an entirely new system (whatever its theoretical excellence) would arouse sullen and determined opposition.

It is important to note that taxes in general were no new phenomena to the people. At least one of the produce taxes, the Padi Tax (*Hasil Padi*), had been introduced as early as 1892 (Graham, 1905, 7). The annual Poll Tax, locally termed *Hasil Kepala* and levied on every adult male who held no 'exemption ticket', had been introduced in 1904 (*ibid.*, 8). Similarly, the other produce taxes, namely those on coconuts, durian fruit, and betel vines, had been collected for many years before 1915. Logically, therefore, the substitution in 1915 of a fixed and limited land rent (the details of which are somewhat complex) in lieu of produce taxes would not necessarily amount to more than a marginal increase. As a completely new basis for taxation, however, it was bound, as the British Adviser remarked, to create misunderstanding and arouse opposition. Considering this, it is the less surprising that by April To' Janggut had no fewer than two thousand supporters willing to confront the government.[26]

With the success of the tax boycott, there was a corresponding deficit in revenue in the district. An investigation was undertaken and as a result the authorities discovered To' Janggut's plot. It was now no simple matter to undo what To' Janggut had done, for almost half of Pasir Puteh was behind him; the District Officer had to be very tactful.

On 29 April, Che' Latiff sent a police sergeant by the name of Che' Wan, and several escorts, to summon To' Janggut and his colleagues to the District Office to answer questions relating to the boycott. To' Janggut was at that time said to be in Kampong To' Akib about half an hour's walk from Pasir Puteh town. On arrival there, Sergeant Che' Wan saw a group of people, mostly armed with parang and kris, gathered in a clearing which in times of rejoicing and relaxation was presumably used for such pastimes as cock-fighting and *bersilat*, the Malay art of self-defence. The crowd were seemingly absorbed by the

---

[26] *UM*, 8 May 1915, estimated the number to be between 200 and 3,000. Yahya (1955, 19) says that they amounted to 'nearly 50% of the inhabitants of the district of Pasir Puteh,' and thus 'not fewer than 2,000 people'.

speech which was being delivered by an elderly man who was standing in their midst. From the distance, the sergeant could easily recognize, by the flowing beard, that the speaker was To' Janggut. He was armed with a kris which, it is said, had been made in Minangkabau and which To' Janggut carried with him wherever he went. Several people had on different occasions, or so it is alleged, fallen victims to the kris at To' Janggut's own hand when he got involved in quarrels, particularly while gambling.

At the sight of the approaching police sergeant, To' Janggut stopped his oration, and all turned their attention to the visitor. The sergeant explained why he had come. According to eye-witness accounts, transmitted by oral tradition, To' Janggut displayed no resentment when told that he was wanted at the District Office. But when the sergeant told him to walk in front and said that he would bring up the rear, To' Janggut insisted that Che' Wan walk first. He argued that he was not a convict, and that to be accompanied by a policeman from behind would imply that he was. At this juncture, the sergeant attempted to handcuff the defiant To' Janggut with the result that, in a split second, the latter flicked out his kris and plunged it into the sergeant's chest. Two or three other policemen who had been watching the incident from the beginning from a distance, presumably as a matter of precaution, took to their heels. The District Officer was duly informed of the tragedy.

Tradition has it that Che' Wan's body was later found to have been mutilated almost beyond recognition and thrown onto the sandy river bank at a place called Pasir Pa' Anor not far from where he had been stabbed by To' Janggut. The brutality was obviously intended both as an expression of defiance against the authorities and to heighten morale among the rebels themselves. Word of the incident soon spread, and bigger crowds gathered in the village ready to sack Pasir Puteh town.

Meanwhile, the District Officer had ordered six policemen to arrest To' Janggut. But seeing the formidable temper of the gathering crowd the policemen retreated (*UM*, 8 May 1915). The rising had started in earnest and the District Officer decided that he was not going to be a sitting duck. The following is Che' Latiff's own account of his escape from Pasir Puteh:

> ... at 2.30 p.m. I left Pasir Puteh owing to the disturbance as reported, with Toh Kweng Tuan Muda Jeram, Toh Kweng Awang Hamat Semerak, Ibrahim bin Haji Daud, ... several Clerks, five Police Constables, 1 Detective, one Warder and several kampong people escorting government money of about $10,200/- in a boat. At 7.30 a.m. on the next day we arrived at Bachok and the boat capsized and wrecked. At 9.00 a.m. we left Bachok in a

fresh boat. We arrived at Tumpat at 2.00 p.m. and thence proceeded to Kota Bharu at 5.00 p.m. At 7.00 p.m. I went to see the British Adviser, and at 8.00 p.m. attended State Treasury and deposited the above amount....[27]

According to a newspaper report (*UM*, 8 May 1915), when the boat carrying the District Officer and his party was passing Semerak some Malay villagers were seen running along the river bank trying to stop it. But before they could reach it the boat had made for the sea. If anything, this attempt throws some light on the extent of popular support for To' Janggut or the unpopularity of the District Officer.

After the killing of the police sergeant, the rebels descended on Pasir Puteh town; they were led by To' Janggut and Engku Besar (Farrer, 1916, 13). Their immediate objective was, it is alleged, to attack the District Officer. Finding that he had left, and that there was no resistance they broke into the local prison and released the twelve prisoners under detention there. They then burnt 'one row of Malay shops ... to the ground, and destroyed all the books and furniture of the Government and others ... and ... looted ... the contents of all the other shops. Besides this they also robbed the houses of Mr. Green and Mr. Jensen and burnt about twenty acres of ... coconut belonging to one Abdul Razak.'[28] A government Notice claimed that besides looting and causing damage to property belonging to Europeans, Chinese and Malays, the rebels also killed and injured a number of people.[29] No official statistics were provided.

After sacking the town, the rebels made for Semerak about ten miles away where several British planters lived on their coconut plantations. The exact movements of the rebels are not known, but the records report that anarchy reigned in the district for several days before the authorities took effective counter measures.

When news of the outbreak reached Kota Bharu, the state capital, the authorities sent Chief Inspector Jackson and thirty policemen to Gunong, about half way between Kota Bharu and Pasir Puteh. He was instructed to stand by in case the rebels made for Kota Bharu, as had been rumoured (*UM*, 8 May 1915). Two other British officers were sent in a small ship from Kota Bharu to Semerak on the second day of the outbreak to warn the planters about the rebellion. When the officers arrived at Semerak they found that the planters had already left. Many villagers were seen fleeing by boat to Besut, the nearest town on the other side of the Kelantan-Trengganu border.

[27] Monthly Report of the District Office, Pasir Puteh, for April 1915, encl. in Kel. K. Series.
[28] BA to Sultan, 8 May 1915, encl. in Kel. PB. 108/1915.
[29] Government Notice dated 8 June 1915, encl. in Kel. PB. 552/1915.

It was learned that soon after the planters had left, a group of rebels ransacked and burnt their quarters. The booty was carried away in sampans. All policemen in Semerak had fled, except two who went into hiding. This was probably a reaction to the excitement and fear caused by rumours that one of the District Officer's clerks and eleven others had been killed by the rebels (*UM*, 8 May 1915). Among the quarters robbed and burnt were those of Messrs. Markes and Owen, assistant managers of a coconut plantation of 3,000 acres in Semerak which was managed by one Mr. Morrison. Word then got round that two elephants had arrived in Pasir Puteh from Trengganu bringing arms and supplies to the rebels.

On 1 May, the Sultan issued a *titah* to the Dato' Mentri (Mohd. Hassan b. Mohd. Salleh) and Dato' Bentara Setia (Haji Nik Mahmud b. Haji Ismail) to proceed to Pasir Puteh and negotiate with the rebel leaders.[30] His Highness, the Dato' was empowered to say, would pardon them if the murderer of the police sergeant was handed over, and if the rebellion was discontinued. The British Adviser instructed the Chief Police Officer stationed at Bukit Jawa, $7\frac{1}{2}$ miles from Pasir Puteh, to assemble his men at Gunong and wait for the outcome of the Dato's mission. The British Adviser also suggested that all British women and children in Kota Bharu be evacuated. It was apparently feared that the rebels might advance to Kota Bharu; and as there were less than twenty Englishmen there it seemed likely to prove difficult to look to the safety of the women and children if the rebels came. They were finally transported to Simpang Kubang, a coconut plantation fifteen miles to the north of Tumpat and six miles from the Siamese border, where they were accommodated in the quarters of one Mr. Montgomery (*UM*, 8 May 1915).

The Dato' Bentara Setia reached Pasir Puteh at two the next morning. He had left Gunong at about ten that night and had to walk to Pasir Puteh as there was no road from Gunong. He spent the night at the house of one Haji Su at a place called Batu Sebutir where, coincidentally, he met the Imam of Cherang Tuli, Lebai Kadir, whom he had meant to employ as a go-between. As requested by the Dato', Imam Lebai Kadir undertook to get the five rebel leaders to meet the Dato' the next day; the venue was to be the Imam's house in Cherang Tuli on the outskirts of Pasir Puteh town.

While the Dato' and the Imam were in discussion that night, about fifty men armed with kris, spears, parangs and guns surrounded the house, but they soon disappeared, probably towards Pasir Puteh.[31]

[30] Manuscript report by Dato' Bentara Setia, encl. in Kel. PB. 108/1915.
[31] *Ibid.*

Next morning, 2 May, the Dato' continued to Cherang Tuli. The Imam had gone to consult the rebel leaders and came back at about ten to tell the Dato' that To' Janggut and his colleagues were reluctant to meet him. At that time, about sixty villagers came to the Imam's house. The Dato' asked them if they knew why To' Janggut and his followers defied the government. Most of them replied that it was apparently due to the heavy taxation imposed on them.[32] The villagers were apparently neutral; but to ensure that they remained loyal to the government the Dato' explained to them the new system of revenue.

Dato' Setia then sent fresh messengers to get To' Janggut and his fellow leaders to meet him. But before the messengers returned the Dato' received information from other sources that the rebel leaders refused to come; instead, they had requested two of the Dato's escorts, Nik Mat and Nik Mahmud b. Dato' Lundang, to meet them at Pasir Puteh. The Dato', however, did not permit the two to go as he suspected a trap; both of them had been involved, several years earlier, in the murder of a common relative of To' Janggut and Penghulu Adam.[33]

It appeared then to be futile to wait any longer. To' Janggut for his part apparently did not dare risk his life by coming forward to meet Dato' Setia. He had been warned, it is said, by some of the villagers not to come; they claimed that the Sultan's envoy had been sent to capture him. The Dato' himself felt it useless to wait because the people in the area, save for Imam Lebai Kadir and one or two others, seemed to be reluctant to do his bidding. Moreover, rumour had it that the rebels would be gathering between Cherang Tuli and Pasir Puteh town, at a place called Wakaf Berangan, at about noon to engage the government forces said to be arriving from Kota Bharu. However, before leaving for Kota Bharu the Dato' instructed the Imam to convey a letter to Engku Besar explaining why he had come and requesting that the wishes of the people of Pasir Puteh be clarified so that they could be conveyed to the Sultan.

What actually happened after Dato' Setia left is a matter of conjecture. One source records that next day, 3 May, the rebel leaders, after a lengthy deliberation among themselves, decided to send Engku Besar, with numerous escorts, to Cherang Tuli to discover what the government's proposals might be. To' Janggut did not accompany them. It is said

---

[32] *Ibid*. The report at this point reads: 'Maka jawab-nya bunyi fasal hasil2 terlalu berat ia-itu hasil sireh, tanah, durian, nyior, dan juga lesen2 satu pun tidak lepas....' (They replied that the reason was excessive taxation on betel vines, land, durian, coconut, and also licenses from which absolutely no one was exempt....)

[33] *Ibid*.

that Engku Besar and his men gave the same reasons for the rebellion as had been conveyed to Dato' Setia by the villagers the previous day (Yahya, 1955, 28–30).

To' Janggut's recalcitrant attitude was conveyed to the Sultan immediately; during the few days that followed, the Sultan issued warrants and instructions to various officers and headmen to arrest To' Janggut and his supporters.[34] Among those who received these *titah* were the To' Kweng and Inspector of Kweng of Bachok, Peringat, Semerak and Gaal—the four Kweng in the vicinity of Pasir Puteh—who were to enrol by corvée (*kerah*) all the peasants in their Kweng and proceed with them to Pasir Puteh to round up the rebels.[35] Each peasant participating in the raid was ordered to wear a red arm-band to distinguish him from a rebel. A *titah* was given to Imam Lebai Kadir and four other headmen (who were also armed with one of the warrants referred to in Note 34), to the effect that if they could not arrest To' Janggut and his followers by peaceful means they might use force.[36] Should they fail, they were to proceed with all speed to Kota Bharu and inform the Sultan immediately, so that the rebels might be subjected to bombardment.[37] British soldiers, equipped with big cannon, were merely awaiting the green light. They had left Singapore by sea on 2 May, under the command of Colonel Brownlow (*UM*, 22 May 1915). Early on the morning of 5 May, the British Adviser sent a telegram from Tumpat to his Assistant, W. Pryde, who was in Kota Bharu, instructing him to inform the Sultan that '230 British soldiers and a lot of Malays with two machine

---

[34] Several are encl. in Kel. PB. 126/1915, including the following two of special interest: (a) 'Waran bagi menangkap tuboh To' Janggut serta lain-lain-nya yang menyertai To' Janggut menderhaka di-Pasir Puteh itu: di-kurniakan waran ini kapada Imam Kadir, berlima dengan Haji Su, Penghulu Husin, Pa'da Awang Tukang dan Penghulu Adam.' (Warrant to arrest To' Janggut and his followers who have committed treason in Pasir Puteh: granted to Imam Kadir who will comprise a party of five with Haji Su, Penghulu Husin, Pa'da Awang Tukang and Penghulu Adam [b. Pa' Chik Bauk, as distinct from the Penghulu Adam who was one of the rebel leaders]); (b) 'Kuasa. Bahawa ada-lah kita, Sultan Muhammad IV, K.C.M.G., yang mempunyai kuatkuasa memerentah di-atas negeri Kelantan telah menjunjongkan titah ini kapada Tengku Besar Tuan Yusoff berikhtiar dengan sekelian ra'ayat2 jumlah Tengku Besar supaya pergi menangkap To' Janggut sa-hingga dapat-nya bawa turun kapada kita hidup atau mati ada-nya. Tengku Besar Tuan Yusoff; Tengku Sri Maharaja; Tengku Chik Penambang; Engku Setia; Dato' Megat Muda; Dato' Kaya Hulubalang; Dato' Panglima Perang; Tengku Muda Ja'afar.' (Authority. Be it known that we, Sultan Muhammad IV ... confer upon Tengku Besar this order, to organize all the villagers under his authority to go and arrest To' Janggut until such time as he may be brought before us, dead or alive. [Then following the names of other notables charged with Tengku Besar in carrying out the order])

[35] Sultan to To' Kweng and Inspector of Kweng, encl. in Kel. PB. 108/1915.

[36] Sultan to Imam Kadir and others (as named in the Warrant quoted in Note 34 above), undated, encl. in Kel. PB. 126/1915.

[37] Some time apparently lapsed before Imam Lebai Kadir and his colleagues reported the result of their mission, for in the meantime the impatient Sultan had ordered the To' Kweng of Peringat to find out about them (Sultan to To' Kweng, 21 Jamadal-akhir 1333 [5 May 1915], encl. in Kel. PB. 108/1915).

guns' had arrived in the warship *Cadmus* at Tumpat, and would be in Kota Bharu the same day.[38] Whether these reinforcements from Singapore had been asked for by the Sultan or whether they were sent on British initiative is not altogether clear.[39]

It is, however, significant to note that in the early months of the year, the people of Kelantan, particularly those in the remote areas, had come to believe that the British might be defeated in the European war then in progress and that, consequently, the Germans would overrun Kelantan. These rumours had alarmed the British authorities and led them to advise the Sultan to try to convince his subjects of the absurdity of the belief. In compliance with this advice, the Sultan had issued a Notice on 15 March referring to the superior strength of the Allies relative to that of the Germans. The notice also urged the people of Kelantan to have confidence in, and give their loyalty to, the British, claiming that a British victory was as certain 'as day succeeds night.'[40] Considering these circumstances, it is probable that the reinforcements from Singapore were despatched on British initiative. Presumably the outbreak in Pasir Puteh had been seen as a spark which might enkindle a state-wide rising, and the sending of soldiers from Singapore was a means of snuffing this out.

On 6 May, the British troops proceeded to Gunong and spent the night in the grounds of the Sultan's palace there. Dato' Bentara Setia informed the Sultan that, according to the morning's news, the rebels had advanced towards Kota Bharu and were waiting to engage the soldiers at Bukit Jawa. If this was true, trouble was likely to spread shortly to Kota Bharu. The Dato' therefore asked for permission to go to Gunong, and for a *surat kuasa* (letter of authority) authorizing him to enlist the assistance of the 'people of Gunong' for the soldiers. Permissision was given and the *surat kuasa* granted.[41] The plan was for the soldiers to advance, the next day, to Bukit Jawa and launch an attack from there. Meanwhile, one Tengku Muda Tuan Ja'afar had already assembled 200 local men at Bukit Jawa to assist the soldiers. Information was later received that the rebels had not actually reached Bukit Jawa but were waiting at Bukit Abal one-and-a-half miles away.[42]

[38] Encl. in Kel. PB. 126/1915.
[39] Cf., however, Pepys (1950, 1175), who states unequivocally that the decision to seek assistance from Singapore was the British Adviser's.
[40] Encl. in Kel. PB. 235/1915.
[41] Sultan to Dato' Bentara Setia, 22 Jamadal-akhir 1333 (6 May 1915), encl. in Kel. PB. 108/1915.
[42] Dato' Bentara Setia to Sultan, same date, in *ibid*.

On the next day, 7 May, the Sultan instructed several To' Kweng of the Kweng around Gunong and Pasir Puteh—Kemuning, Bengkelam, Tanjong Pauh and Banggu—to '*kerah*' the villagers and proceed with them to Gunong to help carry supplies for the British soldiers and others.[43] The villagers were permitted to carry arms, perhaps because some of them, especially those from Kemuning, had to pass through the strongholds of the rebels on their way to Gunong. Many peasants turned up but those from Tanjong Pauh and Banggu, according to reports by the respective To' Kweng, were frequently reluctant to leave their homes because thefts and robberies were rampant. In any case, those who did appear proved to be superfluous; no encounter with the rebels took place while the soldiers were advancing from Bukit Jawa to Pasir Puteh. The most that occurred seems to have been a certain amount of sabotage. One group of sappers from the Volunteer Engineers, under the command of Lieutenant Lamiswayer, extended telephone wires from Gunong for six miles towards Pasir Puteh by utilizing trees as posts. On the next day, it was found that the line had been cut at several places, presumably under cover of darkness (*UM*, 22 May 1915).

The British Adviser, who had by this time reached Pasir Puteh to supervise the search for the rebel leaders, informed the Sultan that the town was deserted except for a few souls. As he anticipated no fighting, he reported that he would send back the Dato' Setia and the villagers.[44] He and his men, however, would continue the search. In reply, the Sultan expressed regret that the rebel leaders were still at large and said that he would consider taking stronger measures to hasten their arrest.[45] On 13 May, the Sultan communicated to the British authorities his intention to place a reward on the head of each of the rebel leaders.[46] About a week later, a Notice was issued announcing the offer of a cash reward of five hundred dollars for the arrest of each leader, dead or alive.[47] It was later claimed that the measure proved quite effective, for not long after the offer had been announced, two of the leaders, Penghulu Adam and Ibrahim Teleng, were handed over to the authorities (*UM*, 7 Aug. 1915).

Meanwhile, the authorities had been informed that the rebels were now between Semerak and Pasir Puteh, keeping close to the sea. A gunboat was therefore sent to Kuala Semerak, and several rounds of four-

---

[43] Sultan to To' Kweng of Kemuning, Bengkelam, Tanjong Pauh, and Banggu, 23 Jamadal-akhir 1333 (7 May 1915), in *ibid*.
[44] BA to Sultan, 8 May 1915, encl. in Kel. PB. 108/1915.
[45] Sultan to BA, 28 Jamadal-akhir 1333 (12 May 1915), encl. in Kel.PB. 126/1915.
[46] Sultan to G.L. Ham (at British Adviser's office), 29 Jamadal-akhir 1333 (13 May 1915), in *ibid*.
[47] Notice dated 20 May 1915, encl. in Kel. PB. 552/1915.

inch shells were fired in what was taken to be the general direction of the rebels (*UM*, 22 May 1915). When searches were made immediately afterwards, however, no-one was to be found. According to the village elders the rebels were, at this juncture, taking refuge behind a tall ridge of earth or *batas besar* in Kampong Saring, about a mile from Pasir Puteh town. Apparently the authorities did not know of this hideout until much later, for no raids were made then. The British soldiers remained in Pasir Puteh for several days, during which time a reinforcement from the Malay States Guides arrived to assist them. With the arrival of this new force the rebels continued to keep low. This presumably led the authorities to believe that the rebels had broken up, and on 15 May the British soldiers were recalled. They sailed back to Singapore in the *Calypso* (*UM*, 22 May 1915). The Malay State Guides had with them two big cannon, or *meriam gunong*, and they were broken up into two units, one patrolling Pasir Puteh and the other the area between Kota Bharu and Tanah Merah. For the next week or so no incidents were reported in the Pasir Puteh district.

Back in Kota Bharu, and somewhat earlier, the British authorities had been alarmed when, on the night of 6 May, two groups of armed men were found loitering in the vicinity of the *Kota* or *Balai Besar*—the area in the vicinity of the Sultan's palace. One group was seen by G.L. Ham of the Residency personnel; the other, armed with spears, was found by another Englishman, Morkill, an hour later, that is, around nine o'clock.[48] With a few policemen from Penambang (about a mile-and-a-half from Kota Bharu) Mr. Morkill stopped them and confiscated their weapons. A brawl started but at that moment the Dato' Bentara Dalam and a fellow Malay official, who were on their night round, arrived and explained who the men were and why they were armed.[49] The confiscated weapons were thereupon returned to their owners. The armed men, including the group seen by G.L. Ham earlier, turned out to be from the 140 who had been ordered by the Sultan to guard the Balai Besar, and the palace of Tengku Sri Indera Mahkota close by, every night till the trouble was over.[50] The guards were identifiable by yellow arm-bands.

Another incident was also reported. At about one o'clock the same morning ten men went to the Mercantile Bank (the only one in Kota Bharu) and attempted to break in. The bank guard immediately informed the police, seeing whom the men made for their boat on the Kelantan river where a crowd of others was waiting. They numbered

[48] G.L. Ham to Sultan, 7 May 1915, in *ibid*.
[49] Dato' Bentara Dalam to Dato' Bentara Setia, 7 May 1915, encl. in Kel. PB. 108/1915.
[50] Sultan to G.L. Ham, 23 Jamadal-akahir 1333 (17 May 1915), encl. in Kel. PB. 127/1915.

about eighty in all, and escaped into the darkness.[51] Apart from these incidents, the situation in Kota Bharu was apparently normal. In Kuala Krai, however, some forty miles up-river, it was reported that the District Officer, Adams, had been threatened with a revolt by some 300 men (*UM*, 8 May 1915). With the help of the local police he managed to dispel them, the British Adviser later despatching a detachment of soldiers to the district as a precautionary measure.

Between the day of withdrawal of the British soldiers from Pasir Puteh on 15 May and 24 May, the district seems to have been enveloped in quietness. Those many villagers who had fled continued to stay away from their homes. The people who had deserted the district had done so, it has been suggested, for two reasons.[52] Firstly, when the disturbances first broke out, To' Janggut and his followers kept pestering reluctant villagers to support their cause and join them against the authorities; those who refused had their livestock seized and were threatened with more serious retribution. Secondly, some villagers were scared lest the authorities shoot them, mistaking them for To' Janggut's supporters, should they remain in their villages. Hence the desertion and quietness, which was broken only in the early hours of 24 May when the rebels launched a final attack on the Malay State Guides.

It is important to realize that the rebellion had been sparked off in connection with taxation. Now that it had been launched, nothing could have provoked its accentuation more definitely than further exactions on the people. Already, on 20 May, as has been noted, the Sultan had placed a substantial cash reward on the head of each of the rebel leaders. This merely served to increase their defiance of the authorities. Three days later another Notice had been issued, announcing that as a punishment for the outbreak the government demanded that each household in Pasir Puteh district pay a fine. The rate was ten dollars for a big house, five for a medium one and three for a small one. The fine was to be paid within fifteen days from the date of service of the Notice; otherwise the house with all its contents would be burned to the ground.[53] This exaction obviously constituted a further provocation, and with the British soldiers already withdrawn from Pasir Puteh the fresh assault on the 24th came as no surprise.

The following is a description of the incident and its outcome as given to the Sultan by the then British Adviser, W. Langham-Carter:

[51] Dato' Bentara Dalam to Dato' Bentara Setia, 7 May 1915, encl. in Kel. PB. 108/1915.
[52] Interview with Pa' Ngah Musa, an inhabitant of Kampong Sering, who himself fled to Besut.
[53] Notice dated 23 May 1915, encl. in Kel. PB. 562/1915.

At about 3.0 this morning the rebels descended on Pasir Puteh and attempted to attack us by sounding their guns, but later in the morning Mr. Maxwell and I, along with the other British Officers and the Sikh soldiers, pursued them.

When we reached Kampong Merbol, I found a group of men gathered in a house belonging to Khatib Abu Bakar, and the Sikh soldiers attempted to arrest him. But the house-owner slashed one of the soldiers with a parang. In retaliation the soldier stabbed Abu Bakar with the bayonet which was attached to his gun and Abu Bakar died there and then.

We then proceeded towards Kampong Pupoh. The moment we came to the edge of the padi field of Kampong Merbol, the rebels began to attack us by shooting from inside Kampong Pupoh. The soldiers retreated and dispersed.

We then entered Kampong Pupoh and I found that To' Janggut was already dead with only one bullet-wound. Two others were also dead but they could not be identified. And another, by the name of Deraman b. Diah of Kampong Telosan, was seriously wounded. Still another was also seriously wounded, but I think he had been carried away by his friends, for I found traces of blood along the route of escape. After that we searched for the rebels in other places but found none, and I think the rebels had dispersed and fled towards Kampong Kemuning. I shall pursue them further as soon as I receive information about their whereabouts.

I wish to inform Your Highness that I also burned the house of Pa' Nik Abas because it was in the compound of that house that Sergeant Che' Wan had been murdered.

Along with this letter, I send To' Janggut's body to Your Highness so that his death can be proclaimed in Kota Bharu.[54]

Thus died To' Janggut, the foremost leader of the rebellion. The two others who died with him on that fateful day were identified later by the villagers as To' Husein and To' Abas, staunch supporters throughout.[55]

At the suggestion of the then Acting Chief Police Officer, A.W. Hamilton, the Sultan and the British Adviser agreed that To' Janggut's body be displayed at the town *padang* (green), the present Padang Bank or Padang Merdeka, for the public to see.[56] The display was obviously intended as an example of the fate of a rebel. It lasted for several days (*UM*, 10 June 1915), during which the body was hung upside down. Thereafter it was buried at Pasir Pekan, on the river bank opposite Kota Bharu.

[54] BA to Sultan, 24 May 1915, encl. in Kel. PB. 126/1915. In Jawi manuscript, this appears to be a Malay translation of an English original, which the present writer has put back into English.
[55] The two were buried in a common grave in Kampong Sering.
[56] Memorandum from Dato' Bentara Dalam to Acting Chief Police Officer, 25 May 1915, encl. in Kel. PB. 126/1915.

With the fall of To' Janggut the rebellion came to an end. Other leaders fled to various places, particularly Siam[57] and Trengganu,[58] but most of them were later arrested and executed.[59] Engku Besar is said to have fled to Siam and to have died there a few years later.

The rebellion had lasted for hardly a month. It had caused neither much trauma nor the loss of many lives; only a handful had obviously perished or were later executed. In terms of its duration and its casualties therefore, it may be said to have had no great significance. But the incident typifies a very characteristic Malay reaction towards persistent and drastic interference from outside. Some may prefer to see in the rebellion a manifestation of 'nationalism'. In large degree this must depend on individual ideas of what nationalism is, and may require a line of reasoning rather different from that presented here. What is obvious from the evidence examined in this paper, however, is that the rebellion was not, preeminently, a revolt against the Sultan—though it is certainly possible that leading rivals for the throne may have been involved after the event—nor yet a nascent state-wide rising in expectation of a British defeat in the war, though as we have seen this last element was not altogether absent. Rather it was a concerted response to reforms which, in the eyes of peasants and many of the ruling class alike, constituted an unwarrantable intrusion into their traditional way of life. The seed-bed of the rebellion was clearly the dislocation of power of Engku Besar, the territorial chief of Jeram. More immediately instrumental were the changing tax structure and the attitude of the District Officer and his subordinates towards the inhabitants of the district, which together undoubtedly constituted the proximate cause. It is ironic that as a result of the administration's zeal to increase public revenues, they were to cause the state to incur additional liabilities of more than $87,000, the cost of putting the rebellion down (Farrer, 1916, 1).

[57] A handwritten report dated 31 July 1915 by one Haji Ahmad Penghulu (encl. in Kel. PB. 108/1915), states that the British Adviser had been asked to address a letter to the Siamese High Commissioner in Patani, requesting the arrest of Haji Sa'id and Che' Mamat at Gunong Telaga, Legeh; Pai, Engku Besar, and Nebeng Dutan at Tanjong Mas; and others in other parts of Siam. A draft letter, undated, from the British Adviser to the Siamese Deputy Commissioner at Bangnara, asking for his help obtaining these arrests, is in *ibid*.

[58] *UM*, 29 Sept. 1915, reported that two of the leaders, Penghulu Derahman and Pa' Mak Saman, had been arrested in Trengganu.

[59] *Ibid.*, where it is also stated that although Derahman and Mak Saman had been sentenced to death by firing squad, this was later commuted by the Sultan to life imprisonment. Cf. also *UM*, 27 Nov. 1915. On 4 October, *UM* reported that Ibrahim Teleng, another leader, had been sentenced to death; he was shot on the river bank opposite Kota Bharu. Penghulu Adam was fined $1,000 and sentenced to ten years in prison (BA to Sultan, 2 Aug. 1915, encl. in Kel. PB. 805/1915; and *UM*, 7 Aug. 1915).

On the occasion of the Sultan's visit to Pasir Puteh more than a year later, in June 1916, the then District Officer remarked (Farrer, 1917, 12):

Seeing the place *en fête* which a year ago had been a scene of anarchy, it was impossible not to reflect that had a few such visits occurred in the past, the dismal story of the Pasir Puteh riot might never have had to be written.

Considering the circumstances which had given rise to the rebellion, one wonders in just what way 'such visits in the past' could have rendered the history of Pasir Puteh district any different, or any less 'dismal'.

REFERENCES

Monographs and Reports

Abdullah b. Amirah Seling Kelantan, Haji, 1957. *Riwayat Hidup To' Janggut dan Peperangan-nya di-Kelantan* (Penang, Sinaran Brothers).

Bishop, J.E., 1912. *Kelantan Administration Report for the Year 1911* (Kuala Lumpur, Government Printing Office).

Chan Su-ming, 1965. 'Kelantan and Trengganu, 1900–1939,' *JMBRAS*, XXXVIII, 1, 159–98.

Farrer, R.J., 1916. *Kelantan Administration Report for the Year 1915* (Kuala Lumpur, Government Printing Office).

———— 1917. *Kelantan Administration Report for the Year 1916* (Kuala Lumpur, Government Printing Office).

Graham, W.A., 1905. *Report on the State of Kelantan for the period 1st August, 1904, to 31st May, 1905* (Bangkok, Government Printer).

———— 1907. *Report on the State of Kelantan for the period 1st June, 1905, to 23rd February, 1906* (Bangkok, Government Printer).

———— 1909. *Report on the State of Kelantan for the period 15th February, 1907, to 4th February, 1908* (Bangkok, Government Printer).

Gullick, J.M., 1958. *Indigenous Political Systems of Western Malaya* (London, University of London, Athlone Press).

Langham-Carter, W., 1913. *Kelantan Administration Report for the Year 1912* (Kuala Lumpur, Government Printing Office).

————— 1914. *Kelantan Administration Report for the Year 1913* (Kuala Lumpur, Government Printing Office).

————— 1915. *Kelantan Administration Report for the Year 1914* (Kuala Lumpur, Government Printing Office).

Mason, J.S., 1911. *Kelantan Administration Report for the Year 1328 A.H. (13th January, 1910—31st December, 1910)* (Kuala Lumpur, Government Printing Office).

Maxwell, W.G. and Gibson, W.S., 1924. *Treaties and Engagements Affecting the Malay States and Borneo* (London, James Truscott).

Pepys, W.E., 1950. 'A Malay Side-Show During the First World War', *Asiatic Review* (Oct. 1950), 1174–9.

Tweedie, M.W.F., 1953. 'An Early Chinese Account of Kelantan,' *JMBRAS*, XXVI, 2, 216–19.

Yahya Abdullah (Y'abdullah) Kelantan, 1955. *Peperangan To' Janggut, atau Balasan Derhaka* (Kota Bharu, Muslim Printing Press).

Manuscript Material (as cited)

Kel. K. Files of the British Adviser's Office, known as the 'K' series, 1915. National Archives of Malaysia, Kuala Lumpur.

Kel. PB. Files of the 'Pejabat Balai Kerajaan', or Palace Office, 1915. National Archives of Malaysia, Kuala Lumpur.

Interviews (conducted during 1968)

Tan Sri Nik Mustaffa Fadhil, Jelawat
Dato' Ariffin b. Abdul Ghani, District Officer, Pasir Puteh
Tuan Muhammad b. Tuan Senik, Penggawa, Limbongan (Pasir Puteh)
Haji Tuan Senik b. Tengku (Tuan) Muda, Kampong Saring
Pa' Ngah Musa b. Salleh, Kampong Saring
Haji Salleh b. Abu Bakar, Penghulu, Jeram

4
ABDULLAH AL-QARI B. HAJI SALLEH
To' Kenali: His Life and Influence

ANYONE studying the history of peninsular Malaya, and in particular that of Kelantan, however superficially, must encounter the name 'To' Kenali'. Looked at historically, To' Kenali revivified the religious thought of the Muslim community in this part of the world, by the teaching of pupils now scattered throughout Malaysia, and by his intellectual contributions to the founding and running of the Majlis Ugama journal *Pengasoh*, and later the journal *Al-Hedayah*, periodicals which among other things gave voice to the religious revival then taking place in the Middle East.[1]

It is of interest to us now to note that in his life and thought To' Kenali was clearly much influenced by the teachings of the philosopher al-Ghazzālī (1058–1111 A.D.), a renovator and purifier of Islamic thought in his own community and one responsible for many reforms in the elucidation of religious questions, based on a return to the teachings of the Holy Kuran and the Hadith and a new emphasis on *'ilm ladunī* (knowledge imparted directly by God through mystic intuition) from the past.

To expand on this, let us trace the record of To' Kenali's struggle and the outlines of his life.

---
[1] *Pengasoh* was published fortnightly from July 1918, and *Al-Hedayah* from June 1923. See Al-Ahmadi, below.

Origins and Background

He was born in Kampong Kenali, Kubang Kerian, some four miles outside Kota Bharu, in 1868, towards the end of the reign of Sultan Muhammad II (1837–86), and given the name Muhammad Yusof (though frequently referred to simply as 'Awang'). His father, a peasant farmer, was named Ahmad. Fatimah, his mother, was a woman of refinement, and a strong believer in the values of goodness and truth.

Muhammad Yusof was born into a poor family, possessed of very small means, a fact which helped form attributes of personality characteristically unassertive. His father was a rice farmer and his mother, as is usual among village folk, helped her husband in his work in addition to looking after the needs of the kitchen. The influence of his father on Muhammad Yusof's development was little felt, for he died when the boy was only five, after which he was entrusted to the care of his maternal grandfather. In the society within which To' Kenali was brought up, there was growing at the time a new awareness of the need to educate children, especially in the realms of Kuranic learning and of Islamic religious knowledge generally. As a result, Muhammad Yusof began his education with his grandfather, Che' Salleh (To' Leh), who taught him to read the Holy Kuran and to write. To' Leh was a pious man, possessed of sufficient religious knowledge to serve as a guide to life, aware of the imperatives of existence, obedient to the rules of Islam, and taking pleasure in the performance of his religious duties as a means of earning God's grace. At the same time, Muhammad Yusof's step-grandmother, To' Mek Ngah, impressed upon him other useful things, including the need to beware concerning the source of foodstuffs to be prepared for meals, for according to her the influence of forbidden foods could produce grave effects not just in this life but in the next.

Unusual Ability

To' Kenali's love of learning was evident from his earliest years. The desire to excel and continuously to improve his knowledge possessed him, and within a short time he had completed his reading of the Holy Kuran and was able to write well. It came as no surprise when the district *To' Kweng* (headman) engaged him, still aged only seven or eight, as a clerk to help with the figuring and other work associated with keeping tally of the padi, coconut and durian crops on which, at that time, produce taxes were assessed.[2]

---

[2] The then To' Kweng, Ahmad, died some time after To' Kenali's return from Mecca in 1908, and was succeeded by his son Ismail.

His Education Continued in the Capital

When he was about nine or ten years old (in 1878 or 1879), Muhammad Yusof decided to continue his education in Kota Bharu, walking the four miles each way twice a day. The focus of learning in the capital at this time was the Masjid Kota Bharu, the central mosque, where could be found a large number of religious teachers and some hundreds of students from every corner of Kelantan. The environs of the mosque were crowded with the *pondok* (small huts of bamboo and attap) of the students.[3] Many teachers also taught in their own homes, including, for example, at Kampong Banggul not far from the Masjid, Muhammad Yusof's first teacher, Haji Wan Ismail (father of Nik Mahmud, who many years later was to become chief minister of the state). One of Muhammad Yusof's fellow students with Haji Wan Ismail, and a close friend, was Idris b. Haji Hassan, who in 1921 was appointed State Mufti and held this post until his death six years later. Muhammad Yusof also studied in the early 1880's, it appears, with one Haji Ibrahim at the latter's *pondok* at Sungei Budur, Kota Bharu; with Haji Wan Muhammad Ali b. Abdul Rahman (better known as Wan Ali Kutan)[4]; and with a peripatetic teacher known as Tuan Guru Haji Taib, or Tuan Padang, originally from Padang in Sumatra (Abdullah, 1967, 21).

To the Holy Land

The Masjid al-Ḥarām in Mecca in the late nineteenth century, apart from being a place of worship, functioned also as a school or university, wherein selected teachers taught everything from the fundamentals of the Islamic religion to doctrine, law, Sufi mysticism, history, and the Arabic language. Teaching was done in small groups within the compound and cloisters of the Masjid, by means of recitation of texts in unison and individual recitation around the group. The school of the Masjid al-Ḥarām was second only (in the Hejaz) to that at the Masjid an-Nabawīy at Madina, and similar to that at the Masjid al-Azhar in Cairo, though the latter was to undergo substantial reformation in the 1890s. To all three came students and scholars drawn from every race and community and all degrees of society.

As a young student in his homeland To' Kenali longed to make his way to the centres of learning. In 1886, aged nearly eighteen, and after

---

[3] '*Pondok*' in northern Malaya was also the generic term for a community of students living in such huts, in these circumstances the term being qualified by either a place name or the name of the principal teacher. The community round the Kota Bharu mosque was known at this time as Pondok Kubang Pasu, after the name of the area.

[4] Born c. 1837, at Kutan, between Kota Bharu and Pasir Mas, Haji Wan Ali was noted as compiler of *Al-Jauhar al-mauhūb*, a collection of hadith published in Mecca in 1886, and other works. He died in Mecca in 1912. (Al-Ahmadi, 1966, 163–5).

a miserable six months' voyage in an ailing ship, he set foot on the holy soil of Mecca to pursue his education and to carry out the fifth obligation laid upon all able Muslims, the pilgrimage.

Life in the Holy Land

As has been noted, Muhammad Yusof came from a poor family. His journey to the Hejaz had been made possible only with the help of friends in Kota Bharu, who had collected on his behalf some $50.00, to which sum his mother was able to add only a further $22.00. The difficulties facing To' Kenali in a land of strangers cannot be adequately pictured. For nearly seven months he was without any proper place to live, and during this time camped out in the cloisters of the Masjid al-Ḥarām, where it was possible to rest only towards nightfall and eventually to sleep. His clothing was not much more than he stood up in, and he had little money for food with which to satisfy the pangs of hunger twice a day. Faced with this situation, he used to act from time to time as cook for picnics arranged by his friends, held in the surrounding valleys or bare foothills outside the town.[5]

Educational Development

Before leaving Kelantan, Muhammad Yusof had mastered the fundamentals of those subjects in whose study he had engaged. He had become a competent student of Arabic grammar and etymology in order to follow instruction in all branches of the Islamic religion. As a result he was well fitted to participate in and benefit from the teaching then available in Mecca. Unfortunately, it must be said that because of his poverty he was forced to learn from his teachers solely by listening, for he could afford to buy no books. When he wanted to study the texts he had to go to the bookshops and ask permission of the owners to use those they had on sale, examining them, as a result, with particular care and attention. Charitable collections of books, in the possession of the Masjid al-Ḥarām, were also consulted by To' Kenali to help him understand his teachers. And in addition he was sometimes able to borrow books from the teachers themselves. As a result of these pressures, perhaps, his very poverty carried To' Kenali through the depths of the sea of knowledge, and his progress exceeded that of his fellows.

It is clear that To' Kenali very frequently read and examined manuscript materials, written by various *'ulamā* and Islamic philosophers, in circulation in the Muslim world at that time. He also liked to question

---

[5] Among the friends assisting in this way were those known later, when teaching in Kelantan, as To' Bachok and To' Jelapang (Abdullah, 1967a, 26).

and examine what he was taught before it was repeated by the teacher, as a means of impressing upon himself the matter to be learnt, and in order to make his own comparisons and relate the material to his own experience. Voluminous reading and continuous critical study are, it may be said, the major factors in the development of any student's or scholar's knowledge.

Among the teachers at the Masjid al-Ḥarām whose names were most frequently mentioned by To' Kenali, one especially stands out—Tuan Guru Wan Ahmad, or to give him his full name, Ahmad b. Muhammad Zain b. Mustafa al-Patani. Apart from his fame as a teacher, he was well known also as a writer, second only to Shaykh Daud Patani.[6] To' Kenali came under the wing of this teacher not only where learning was concerned, but in his life too. The name of Wan Ahmad is still remembered throughout the Malay world, in Indonesia (especially Sumatra), Malaysia and Cambodia. In addition it is known that several other teachers from Patani and Indonesia probably attracted To' Kenali's interest, as well as a number of Arabs.

Visit to Egypt

In 1903, To' Kenali was taken to visit Egypt by his teacher Wan Ahmad. There were four in the party, To' Kenali, Wan Ahmad, Haji Nik Mahmud b. Haji Wan Ismail (son of his old teacher in Kota Bharu), and, it is thought, one Haji Ismail Patani. The brief record of this journey that is all we have indicates that the trip was at once one of general interest and sight-seeing and one directed to learning, especially concerning the development of Islamic education at the University of al-Azhar and at other institutions in Cairo. After a short time spent in meeting scholars in Cairo, and discussing matters of this sort with them, the group returned again to Mecca.[7]

Back to Kelantan

In 1908, after an absence of 22 years, To' Kenali came back to his homeland, Kelantan, and began to teach from his own house in Kampong Paya, still occupied by his mother, Hajjah Fatimah. Before long, however, students began to come to him not just from the nearby villages but from further afield, and to set up around his house, in traditional manner, the *pondok* in which they could live while learning from their teacher. By 1910 the first 'Pondok To' Kenali' was flourish-

[6] Shaykh Daud b. Abdullah b. Idris, of Patani, was the most eminent and prolific of peninsular Malay theologians in the early nineteenth century, during which time he lived and wrote in Mecca. For some details of his work, see Abdullah (1967b, 131–7).
[7] For one of To' Kenali's stories concerning this visit, see Abdullah (1969, 50–2).

ing, and as his fame spread he began to teach also once a week at the Masjid Kota Bharu. In 1915, at the urging in particular of his old friend Haji Nik Mahmud b. Wan Ismail (by this time Dato' Bentara Stia, and assistant to the chief minister of the state), he was persuaded to move his household into the capital, and for the next five years taught at the Masjid or at the Pondok Kubang Pasu. The Kota Bharu mosque was by this time a centre of Islamic learning not just for Kelantan but for the region as a whole, and frequented by many other notable teachers, among them Haji Nik Abdullah[8] and Haji Idris b. Haji Hassan.[9]

After five years teaching in Kota Bharu, during which he also made a notable contribution to the religious life of the state as a founder member of the Majlis Ugama Islam and as an editor of their fortnightly journal *Pengasoh*, To' Kenali returned once again to the kampong to live, this time to his birthplace, Kampong Kenali. His fame as a teacher again followed him, and within a short time a new Pondok Kenali had established itself around him. At its peak it formed a community of no fewer than 300 pupils, drawn from all over the peninsula, from Indonesia (especially Sumatra), Patani and Cambodia.

In carrying out his tasks as a teacher, To' Kenali prepared several graduated textbooks in a number of subjects relating both to Arabic language and religious knowledge. He himself played a considerable role in developing Arabic language teaching, and in the other areas made contributions fitting to the needs of the society in which he lived. Many of his more outstanding students were engaged by him as 'group teachers', and in addition some instruction in religious texts was afforded to local kampong children and adults. Where adult education was concerned, he invented a system of using popular moral tales (often humorous) as a means of drawing the attention of his hearers to the basic point he was trying to convey.[10] One of the more striking features of his teaching methods in general was that he himself always taught without the aid of books. Though his students might have the text in front of them, he never did. Besides emphasizing his prodigious powers of memory, this reflected the hard training which had been a part of his early and poverty-stricken years in Mecca.

The Death of To' Kenali

After 65 years on this earth, To' Kenali received the call of God on the morning of Sunday, 19 November, 1933, after an illness which had

[8] Haji Nik Abdullah, whose father's name is not known, died in 1354 (1935/36).
[9] Haji Idris b. Haji Hassan had been Assistant Mufti to Haji Wan Muhammad b. Haji Abdul Samad from about 1916, and followed him as Mufti early in 1921. He died in December 1927.
[10] Some two dozen of these tales are published in Abdullah (1969, 4–75).

affected his legs. The journal *Pengasoh*, on 11 December (vol. XVI, NO. 433), published on its front cover the only photograph of To' Kenali known (to this day) to exist, and wrote: 'Returned to the Land of Eternity, casting the whole of Kelantan into darkness and sorrow. *Fa-innā li'llāh wa innā ilaihi rāji'ūn* [We belong to God and to him we shall return],' adding that on the day of his death the house had been visited by no fewer than 2,500 people, and his funeral prayer attended by more than a thousand pious mourners.

To' Kenali was buried in what is today known as 'Kubor To' Kenali' (To' Kenali's Graveyard), 4½ miles down the Pasir Puteh road from Kota Bharu. His grave used frequently to be visited by the late Sultan Ibrahim (father of the present ruler), and is still so visited by large numbers of people, especially by his old pupils, now scattered throughout the length and breadth of Malaysia.

As one may express it in *pantun* form,

> From the village to the city,
>   Seeking friends who kindness give;
> His death bequeathes no worldly riches,
>   But saintly learning long to live.

Activities, Offices and Services Performed by To' Kenali

To' Kenali was at the forefront of those who took up the tasks, and held a variety of important offices, associated with the development of Islamic education and Malay cultural growth in Kelantan. He taught, of course, at the Masjid Kota Bharu from about 1910, and intensively from 1915, and acted for at least part of this time as a kind of head of Islamic education in the state, as assistant to the Mufti.[11] It was with his advice that Dato' Bentara Stia (Haji Nik Mahmud b. Ismail) proposed the formation of the *Majlis Ugama dan Isti'adat Melayu Kelantan* (Kelantan Council of Religion and Malay Custom), which came into being (with To' Kenali as one of the twelve foundation members) in December 1915, and is still extremely active today. Later, in January 1918, when the Majlis formed a *Meshuarat Ulama* (Conference of '*Ulama*') as a permanent body, To' Kenali was again one of its first members. When the Majlis began to publish its fortnightly journal *Pengasoh* in July 1918, To' Kenali became 'principal honorary editor',[12] and subsequently helped, through the Meshuarat Ulama, to run its popular 'Question and Answer' column on religious matters of the time. In addition, he

---

[11] Abdullah (1967a, 63, footnote 1), citing To' Kenali's son Haji Muhammad Salleh.
[12] 'Ketua pengarang yang kehormat' (*Pengasoh*, XVI, 433, 11 Dec. 1933). The actual editor during its early years was Haji Muhammad b. Khatib Haji Muhammad Said (Dato' Bentara Jaya, later entitled Dato' Laksamana).

was entrusted by the Majlis with the task of translating into Malay the *Tafsīr al-Khazīn* and *Tafsīr Ibn Kathīr*.[13] This exacting responsibility resulted in completion of part of the first of these works, but unfortunately the manuscript has to this day not been published. Also in the literary field it should not be forgotten that the monthly journal *Al-Hedayah* (first issued in July 1923), whose chief editor was Ahmad b. Ismail, frequently sought and obtained To' Kenali's advice and the benefit of his thought. The publisher's office was a place of constant resort for him, where he could regularly be seen reading the newspapers and periodicals of the day. In a more general way he was a great lover of learning, as evidenced by many features of his life, not least that among his collection of books was the manuscript 'Chetera Raja Muda', an important source of Kelantan history later given by him to the author of the well-known 'Hikayat Seri Kelantan' (Muhammad, 1964/65, 63). In the field of social change and development, he started in 1924 an Islamic society called *al-Jam'iyyat al-'Asriyyah* (The Contemporary Association) which often discussed controversial social and intellectual questions, as well as meeting for common prayer. In order to further its interests, the society erected premises in the centre of Kota Bharu, on Jalan Tengku Putera Semerak.

Extension of Influence

Observing the important offices filled by To' Kenali in his lifetime, and the energy and sense of dedicated service with which he fostered the growth of Islamic learning and culture in Kelantan in particular and Malaya in general, it is clear why his influence should have spread so rapidly and so thoroughly throughout the peninsula. The peak of his influence occurred towards the end of the reign of Sultan Muhammad IV (1900–20) and in the early part of the reign of Sultan Ismail (1920–44). Both rulers did much for the development of the state, especially in the field of religious development. This created ideal conditions for the extension of To' Kenali's influence, more especially as he was greatly respected by both men, and in addition had a close relationship with Haji Nik Mahmud b. Haji Wan Ismail (son of his old teacher), who as Dato' Stia and then as Dato' Perdana Mentri Paduka Raja (chief minister) wielded large powers in the governance of the state.

It would be no exaggeration to say that the spread of improved Arabic and religious education in the *pondok* and similar schools

---

[13] The second of these is the well-known *Tafsīr al-Qur'ān al-'azīm* by Imaduddin Abil Fida' Ismail b. Kathīr al-Qurashi (d. 774 A.H.). The first is a less familiar exegesis by Imam Khazīn.

throughout Malaya was due in part to the work of To' Kenali. He devised a system of graduated instruction in Arabic grammar and etymology which greatly aided his students in mastering the language. A well-known Kelantan teacher, Haji Ali Salahuddin b. Awang,[14] published these lessons of To' Kenali in 1945 in a volume entitled *Ad-Durūs al-Kenaliyyat al-Ibtidā'iyyah* (To' Kenali's Elementary Lessons). Another pupil of Kenali's, Shaykh Othman Jalaluddin al-Kelantani,[15] had earlier published a similar collection (2nd edition 1358 [1939/40]) under the title *Tasrīf al-'Arf* (a table of Arabic verb declensions). Both works enjoyed a wide circulation throughout the peninsula. In his *Tasrīf al-'Arf* Shaykh Othman wrote:

Truly, I have borrowed many morphological ideas of great value from my profound and learned teacher, one who has accumulated much valuable knowledge in the service of religion—that is to say, Muhammad Yusof, better known throughout Malaya by his Kelantan title, 'To' Kenali.'

Growth of Arabic/Religious Schools

The widespread fame of Pondok Kenali, already referred to, led, not surprisingly, to the production by this institution of many ulama, religious teachers, and writers, who had often come to Kelantan from many other parts of the peninsula (and overseas) and frequently returned there. Among the notable Arabic/Religious schools which, as a result, were subsequently started by pupils of To' Kenali, may be mentioned the following.

(1) Pondok Ahmadiyyah, at Bunut Payong, Kota Bharu, opened in 1931 by Tuan Guru Haji Abdullah Tahir b. Haji Ahmad.[16]

(2) Madrasah Manābi' al-'Ulūm wa Maṭāli'an-Nujūm, at Bukit Mertajam, Seberang Prai, Province Wellesley, opened in 1934 by Tuan Guru Shaykh Othman Jalaluddin al-Kelantani.

(3) Madrasah al-Falāh, at Pulau Pisang, near Kota Bharu, opened by Tuan Guru Haji Ali Salahuddin b. Awang.

---

[14] Born in 1902 Haji Ali Pulau Pisang (as he was later known from his place of residence and *madrasah*) taught for many years in Kota Bharu, was a long-time member of the Meshuarat Ulama of the Majlis Ugama, and the author of a number of works on the Arabic language. He died in 1968. (Abdullah, 1967a, 113–15; *Utusan Malaysia* [Kuala Lumpur], 5 Oct. 1968, where his date of birth is, however, given incorrectly).

[15] Born in 1867, Othman studied under To' Kenali when the latter returned from Mecca in 1908, and became an assistant teacher in the Pondok Kenali at Kampong Paya. He later wrote and translated prolifically, in 1934 opening the *madrasah* at Bukit Mertajam, Province Wellesley. He died in Mecca in 1952. For details of his work, see Abdullah (1967a, 118–19).

[16] Born at Kampong Sireh, Kota Bharu, in 1897, Haji Abdullah later taught at the Kota Bharu mosque, and spent some years in Mecca at the end of the 1920s, returning to live at Bunut Payong. He was a member of the Meshuarat Ulama from the 1930s, and died in 1961.

Many other schools, too, have been started or run by previous pupils of To' Kenali.

A Generation of Writers

Nor should it be forgotten that from among the students of To' Kenali there emerged a generation of writers of religious literature, many of whom still hold a high place in the Islamic community of this part of the world. Among these may be mentioned, in particular, the following.

(1) Shaykh Othman Jalaluddin al-Kelantani (1867–1952), founder of the Madrasah Manābi' al-'Ulūm at Bukit Mertajam, and author of the *Tasrīf al-'Arf* and other works.

(2) Haji Asa'ad b. Haji Daud (1886–1941), co-translator with Haji Ali Salahuddin b. Awang of the jurisprudential work *al-Umm* by Imam al-Shāfi'ī, influential in the development of religious education in Kelantan.

(3) Haji Ali Salahuddin b. Awang (1888–1968), founder of the Madrasah al-Falāh at Pulau Pisang, author of *Ad-Durūs al-Kenaliyyat al-Ibtidā'iyyah* and other works, including the translation referred to immediately above.

(4) Haji Ya'acob b. Haji Ahmad, known as Haji Ya'acob Lorong Gajah Mati, after the place where he lived and taught.[17]

(5) Shaykh Muhammad Idris al-Marbawi, an Islamic scholar who has made important contributions to the development of religious education by means of his several Arabic-Malay dictionaries (the first of which, *Qāmūs al-Marbawī*, was published in Cairo in 1927) and other works.[18]

(6) Haji Abdullah Tahir b. Haji Ahmad (1897–1961), founder of the Pondok Ahmadiyyah at Bunut Payong.

(7) Haji Ahmad b. Ismail, principal editor of *Al-Hedayah* (1923–26) and later founder and editor of *Al-Hikmah* (1934–41), translator and adaptor of numerous works from the Arabic.[19]

(8) Haji Hassan b. Haji Yunos, from Muar, (1907–), who studied under To' Kenali and later graduated with distinction from Al-Azhar University, becoming Assistant Mufti of Johore in 1940, and later Mufti.[20]

[17] Born in 1893, Haji Ya'acob studied with To' Kenali and then spent several years in Mecca from about 1911, returning to teach in Kota Bharu, where he also wrote numerous religious pamphlets (*risalah*). Two of his sons are also of literary note, Ustaz Haji Yusof Zaki, founder and owner of the Pustaka Dian press and its associated periodicals, and Haji Hassan, founder and owner of Pustaka Aman Press, now one of the largest Malay publishing houses in the peninsula.

[18] Muhammad Idris was born in Mecca of Perak Malay parents in 1895, and returned to the peninsula about 1910, later spending some four years in Kelantan studying with To' Kenali (during which time he also wrote for *Pengasoh*).

[19] Born in 1899, Ahmad Ismail spent a lifetime in the service of periodical journalism and the Islamic religion. After the Second World War he became a member of the Majlis Ugama, and was later entitled Dato' Lela Negara Kelantan. He died in 1969. For some account of his writings, see Abdullah (1967a, 120–1).

[20] Born in 1907, Haji Hassan has been a prolific writer on religious subjects (Abdullah, 1967a, 121), but more recently has principally been active in political life, serving as Chief Minister of Johore until 1967.

(9) Haji Ahmad Mahir b. Haji Ismail (1910-1968), Mufti of Kelantan for seventeen years until his death.

In addition to the pupils listed above (themselves constituting only a partial list of those who might have been included), To' Kenali's own sons continue to contribute to the furtherance of his work. He had four sons, all by the same wife, Rokiah bte Haji Mahmud (daughter of the Imam Muda of Kampong Kenali), whom he married shortly after his return to Kelantan in 1908. All four have devoted their lives to religious education in one form or another. The eldest, Haji Ahmad (b. 1909), is a teacher at the Pondok Kenali, and is much in demand for lectures and teaching in *surau* throughout the state. Haji Muhammad Salleh (b. 1911), has lived in Mecca since 1927 (apart from one return visit to Malaysia in 1962), where he is a teacher in the Madrasah al-'Arfiah, and author of a large number of religious books and texts.[21] Haji Muhammad (b. 1913) has also lived in Mecca for some years, where he is a pilgrimage agent (*shaykh haji*) working with Shaykh Muhammad Ali ar-Rashidi. Haji Abdullah Zawawi (b. 1926), To' Kenali's last son and youngest child, well-known for his talent as a *qari* (Kuran reader) and as an expert in *Qasidah* (Arabic verse), also lives in Mecca now, where, after graduating from the Kuliah Sharī'a (College of Muslim Law) in 1961, he is at present employed as an official of the Saudi Arabian Department of Education.[22]

Personality and Principles

To' Kenali was noted not just as a great religious teacher but as someone who lived by the highest personal standards in such a manner as to act as an exemplar to his fellow Muslims. Among his chief characteristics were that

(a) he honoured and respected his mother,

(b) he was kind hearted, and gave away personal possessions with readiness, especially to the poor and to children,

(c) he was patient, and slow to anger,

(d) he preferred to walk rather than ride, in order to discourage in himself feelings of superiority, pride, or haughtiness,

(e) he conducted his life in an independent manner, without relying on others to do things for him; for example, he did all his own marketing,

---

[21] A list of his publications is provided in Abdullah (1967a, 104-7). A brief account of Haji Muhammad Salleh's life, and of his return visit to Malaysia, may be found in Ahmad (1963).

[22] Further details concerning To' Kenali's sons, and their own offspring, are given in Abdullah (1967a, 100-10).

(f) he liked to read and to study, whether books or journals, and wherever he might find himself,

(g) he liked to sit and spend time in the mosque, sometimes sleeping there using his arm as a pillow,

(h) his clothing was simple and lowly.

There were those who looked upon To' Kenali as a 'saint' (*wali*) or Sufi mystic, because of his quiet and simple demeanour, his refusal to think of himself as important or to consider his own comfort, and his insistence upon regarding all men with equal love and as of equal status.

To' Kenali and Society

When he began his teaching career, To' Kenali is known to have delighted in discussing the political issues of the time, and sometimes questions of this sort were given more prominence than the usual sorts of lesson. For Kenali, this was one way to fit his teaching to those problems then confronting Kelantan Malay society. Because of this it was proper that in his discourse he should pose certain questions by means of realistic cautionary tales. The titles of many of these indicate their nature:[23]

> Honour thy father, but fear God
> Strengthen both religious and political knowledge
> Learning is what is inscribed on the heart
> Human knowledge is limited
> Admit you are wrong when you are wrong
> God's laws are always fitting
> Think before you promise
> Let custom die, but not religion[24]
> Where earth is trod there's sky above
> Ask those who know
> Wrongdoers are satisfied with their wrongdoing
> Prayer is the weapon of the faithful

To' Kenali and Poetry

In the course of his teaching, while naturally giving prominence to sayings from the Kuran and from the Hadith of the Prophet, To' Kenali sometimes scattered among them verses of his own composition or wise sayings, pearls from a string always in his possession. One of the verses often used by him was the following.

[23] The text of the tales is given in Abdullah (1969, *passim*).
[24] This is a play on one of the most familiar of traditional Malay sayings—'*Biar mati anak, jangan mati adat,*' 'Let the child die, but not the custom.'

THE DANGERS OF SMOKING

Smoking is nasty, stupid, wasteful and discreditable;
That it should demean its addicts is inevitable;
They fart foul air like the miasma of rotting vegetable;
Gusts of smoke from their lips smother character both visible and invisible.

Among his many sayings were these:

High or low, a government is dependent upon its officers; if the fox should become raja and the rat is permitted to be his minister, then there will be government, but in noisy disarray.

The honourable man is he who honours his mother.

Self-criticism is the root of progress in learning.

Influence of Imam al-Ghazzālī

Looking at the nature and characteristics of his life, it is evident that To' Kenali was influenced by the teaching of the Islamic philosopher Imam al-Ghazzālī, a Sufi mystic who had achieved '*ḥakīkat*' (truth) through knowledge of himself and of his God, and wished to spread the great joy and purity of this during the brief life that is afforded to us. The limited worldly prosperity he sought, and his rejection of self-importance, are manifest throughout his life.

These elements are contained in prayers collected and arranged by Imam al-Ghazzālī in his book *Ayyuha'l-walad* (Oh Son!) which became so much a part of the lives of To' Kenali and his pupils that they were known as '*Do'ā' To' Kenali*' (prayers to accompany the five daily rituals) In part they run,

Oh, my God, earnestly I beseech Thee for the gifts of perfection, everlasting health, infinite mercy, and useful energy. I pray to Thee to afford my life the summit of comfort, the summit of happiness in age, the perfection of goodness, and to extend to me gifts and graciousness which will benefit me. My God, help us and do not oppress us. My God, make our life in the hereafter pleasant, fulfil our desires for an increase in wisdom, follow us with strength when we go about our daily business morn and night.

My God, shed Thy mercy upon our place of return and in the hereafter, and give us Thy forgiveness for our sins, mend Thou our wickedness, and direct our endeavours towards Thy religion. To Thee we submit, and upon Thee we depend!

Looking back on the many aspects of his life raised and discussed in this paper, it is perhaps not too much to say that To' Kenali was an '*alīm* and Islamic revivalist of great note in this part of the Muslim world. One may also suggest, without much fear of contradiction, that as long as the journal *Pengasoh* still contributes to Malay letters, so long will To' Kenali live. And finally, it is certainly no exaggeration to say that while the Majlis Ugama Islam in Kelantan continues to exist, the name of To' Kenali will be remembered and spoken.

REFERENCES

Abdullah Al-Qari b. Haji Salleh, 1967a. *Sejarah Hidup To' Kenali* (Kota Bharu, Pustaka Aman Press).

────── 1967b. 'Pujangga Shaykh Daud Patani', *Majallah Dian* (Kota Bharu), 10, 131–8.

────── 1969. *Cherpen To' Kenali* (Kota Bharu, Pustaka Dian).

Ahmad b. Ismail, 1963. *Ilmu al-Huda* (Kota Bharu, al-Hikmah Press).

Al-Ahmadi, Abdul Rahman, 1966. *Pengantar Sastera* (Kota Bharu, Pustaka Aman Press).

Muhammad b. Muhammad Salleh, Nik, 1964/65. 'Chatetan Rengkas Tentang Sumber2 Tempatan Mengenai Sejarah Kelantan', *Journal Persatuan Sejarah Kelantan* (Kota Bharu), 1, 52–72.

5
WILLIAM R. ROFF
The Origin and Early Years of the Majlis Ugama

ON 7 December 1915, the Kelantan State Council, as recorded in Item 8 of the Minutes for that meeting, resolved upon the creation, 'for the people of the state', of a Council of Religion and Malay Custom (*Majlis Ugama dan Isti'adat Melayu*).¹ Twelve members were named to the Council, but the minutes report little more. A week or so later, on 24 December, the Sultan, Muhammad IV, at a large gathering of officials and prominent citizens, had read for him by his son, the Raja Kelantan, a speech formally inaugurating the *Majlis* and explaining his intentions for it. By '*ugama*', he said, was meant 'all matters pertaining to the Islamic religion which may bring benefit to the people of this Our state and increase the welfare of Kelantan', and by '*isti'adat Melayu*', 'all style and custom which may properly be preserved according to time-honoured usage'.² In passing it should be noted that though in this manner, as in the other peninsular Malay states of the time, '*adat* and *ugama*'—'custom and religion'—were spoken of in the same breath,³

---
[1] Extract from Minutes of the State Council, 7 December 1915, enclosed in Kel. M. 239/1916.

[2] 'Uchapan DYMM al-Sultan Muhammad IV . . . pada 17 Safar 1334 bersamaan dengan 24 December 1915' (Speech by Sultan Muhammad IV . . . etc.), mimeograph copy supplied in 1968 from the records of the Majlis Ugama, by courtesy of the Secretary, Inche Hussein b. Abdul Ghani.

[3] See, e.g., Roff (1967, 69–70). Though the implicit association between these twin facets

the Kelantan Majlis was, in the event, to concern itself solely with the latter. Continuing, the Sultan did little to define more exactly the duties of the *Majlis* (beyond stating that he would shortly promulgate an enactment or regulations), but made it plain, first that one of the hoped for results of the earnest endeavours of members would be to 'raise Kelantan to a status consonant with that of other advanced states', and secondly that members must recognize that they owed their position and their loyalty to himself, as sovereign of the state and by implication head of religion within it.

Lack of detail about the precise tasks of the Majlis did not prevent the holding of a series of extremely productive meetings during the early part of 1916, but several members were patently uneasy about the undefined nature of their responsibilities (perhaps principally, as we shall see, because they may have felt them to exceed what was proper according to the *Sharī'a*), and threatened to boycott the Majlis until a written constitution (*undang2 tuboh*) had been provided for it.[4] Though this behaviour produced a sharp rebuke from the Sultan (and an apology from the complainants), it resulted also in the passage by the State Council in October of Enactment No. 14 of 1916, entitled 'Undang2 bagi Anggota Majlis Ugama Islam dan Isti'adat Melayu Kelantan' (Rules for the Members of the Council of Islamic Religion and Malay Custom, Kelantan).[5] Much the greater part of this enactment was taken up (as its title may suggest) with the determination of procedural and similar matters—a number of them 'disciplinary'—concerning the members of the Majlis. Only four of its 28 chapters or sections dealt in any substance with the powers and duties of the Majlis itself, and then with considerable generality. Section 24 empowered the Majlis to regulate all matters concerning mosques and *surau* (prayer houses) in the state and their officers; Section 25 instructed the Majlis to 'guard, advise, arrange, give legal *fatwa* [opinions] concerning, originate, strengthen, implement, develop, and administer, all matters relating to the practice and performance of the Muslim religion and Islamic Law, for the benefit of the state and its people'; Section 26 required it to prepare annual estimates of expenditure; and Section 27 required annual

---

of Malay culture was of long standing, the exemption from British 'advisory' powers of matters concerning 'Malay religion and custom' set out in the Pangkor Engagement with Perak in 1874 crystallized the phrase, which was used with minor modifications in several later treaties of protection and advice, including those between Siam and Kelantan in 1902 and Britain and Kelantan in 1910.

[4] Kel. PB. 14/1916 contains a copy of the original complaint, and further correspondence.
[5] It should be noted that the full title of the Council—*Majlis Ugama Islam dan Isti'adat Melayu* (not simply *Majlis Ugama dan Isti'adat Melayu*)—dates from this enactment. Mackeen (1969, 39) is in error in this respect. It became usual to abbreviate the title to *Majlis Ugama*, the form that will be used in the remainder of this paper.

reports to be submitted to the State Council. As a general provision, it was stated that the exercise of executive authority by the Majlis required the approval of the Sultan in State Council, Section 21 reading (as nearly as may be translated): 'Implementation of decisions reached by the Majlis concerning aims, ideas, intentions or actions not previously intimated to Us require Our permission in Council'.

That the principal enactment establishing the Majlis, and the remarks of the Sultan at its inauguration, should lack specification or precision is less remarkable when one considers that, as an institution for the governance of Islam, it was without apparent models either in the remaining Malay states or in the Islamic world in general.[6] It is, in fact, the innovative character of the Majlis—both in itself as a central council of religion with sweeping administrative and coercive powers limited only by the final authority of the Sultan in State Council, and in the striking manner in which it elaborated and exercised these powers in its early years—that is of particular interest to the historian and to the student of modern Islam. Despite the tendency in those Malay states which had earlier fallen under British rule, towards the creation of hierarchically organized Islamic bureaucracies owing position and delegated authority to the Sultan and the traditional ruling class,[7] in no other state had there occurred anything approaching the kind of concentration of powers, the relative autonomy, and the financial independence which, from the first, the Majlis in Kelantan represented. Similarly, though in the Federated Malay States by the turn of the century there had taken place at Malay initiative considerable 'codification' of the *Shari'a* in the form of statutory enactments concerning the performance of religious duties and abstention from that which is forbidden, there had been independent developments of this sort in Kelantan itself, and the Majlis was subsequently to go much beyond the other states not merely in these respects but in the administrative regulation of 'parish' Islam, the provision of both religious and secular education, and a good deal else. Institutionally, indeed, it became itself a model for the rest of the peninsula, and in some measure remains so today. How, and why, then, did the Majlis come into being, and what structural changes did it promote in Kelantan Malay society?

R.J. Wilkinson once remarked (1908, 1) that 'of all branches of Malay research the study of jurisprudence is the one that presents the

---

[6] On this last point, see Mackeen, *loc. cit.*, where he appears to rely on a rather general remark by C. Snouck Hurgronje, *Mohammedanism* (New York, 1916), p. 84. But the present writer is likewise unaware of any precedent conciliar authority with powers analogous to those of the Majlis.

[7] For some discussion, see Roff (1967, 72–4); considerable detail is supplied by Sadka (1969, 265–71).

greatest difficulties'. Though one's aims may be more modest, and directed merely to the elucidation of early religious institutions, and the operation through them of the Shari'a, the difficulties remain formidable. In large part this is owing to the absence of even descriptive materials for the Shari'a in action for (say) most of the nineteenth century, but equally serious problems arise from the recognition that the Shari'a itself (the *hukum shara'*, as it was termed in Malay), and those institutions associated with it, formed one part only and that a changing and uncertain one, in the system of law and belief that characterized Malay peasant society. In the brief account of the organization of Islam in nineteenth and early twentieth century Kelantan that follows, these considerations may perhaps be borne in mind.

As has already been made clear in some of the preceding papers, nineteenth century Kelantan was only in a limited sense a centralized polity, though the long reign of Sultan Muhammad II in the mid-century (1837–86), following a bitter civil war for possession of the throne, saw some strengthening of administrative institutions. In the early part of the century authority outside the capital is said to have been exercised for all practical purposes largely by the *Imam* of village surau.[8] Institutionally, the surau was the ritual centre of rural Islam: the prayer house for congregational Friday prayers, the focus of all specifically Islamic religious ritual involving the community at large, some similitude of village school (where young boys were taught to recite the Kuran), and more generally a place of resort for the piously inclined, especially during the fasting month and at similar junctures in the religious calendar. Administratively, surau appear to have been of two kinds, *surau besar* (large) and *surau kechil* (small) the latter being effectively subdivisions or offshoots of the former, within a particular community or area, a relationship reflected especially in the relatively greater powers conferred upon the Imam of *surau besar*, especially concerning the right to receive *zakat* taxation and to perform marriages, though it is uncertain how far back this distinction dates.[9] All Imam, in addition to being responsible for the proper conduct of daily and Friday prayers, had an important role to play in ensuring that marriage and divorce were properly carried out according to the Shari'a, performing funeral rites, and assisting in the resolution of disputes relating to the interpretation

[8] Graham (1904, 16). The *Imam*, technically the leader of congregational prayer, was by extension religious leader of the community as a whole.

[9] It is possible that the formal distinction between *surau besar* and *surau kechil* developed in the later nineteenth century, as part of a more general process of administrative institutionalisation shortly to be described. The earliest known *kuasa* (written authorities) to Imam of the two sorts of surau (dating from the first years of the century) distinguish between them solely on administrative grounds.

of the law, most often in respect of the division of landed property. In addition, for much of the century, they appear to have had general administrative oversight of other matters arising in the *mukim*, or 'parish' area, including the alienation of land, supervision of produce taxes, and assessment and collection of the triennial *banchi* or poll-tax. With the introduction around the 1860s or '70s of district or 'circle' headmen on the Thai model, known as '*To' Kweng*', the mukim as defined by the *surau besar* (or larger surau) were retained as administrative units within the *Kweng*, and the two officials henceforth existed side by side, partitioning jurisdiction, it is assumed, along functional lines, though what little evidence there is suggests that the Imam retained greater authority in most situations.[10]

Physically, most surau buildings—relatively simple wooden structures on piles, thatch-roofed and partially mat-walled, with few or no internal divisions—appear to have been the result of *donum*, sometimes by the local nobility but more often by peasants with greater pretensions to wealth than their fellows and some predilection for learning or piety, who thereby acquired for themselves, and usually for their descendants, the position and prestige of Imam. Surau were accordingly frequently built upon the Imam's land and attached to, or at least contiguous to, his own house. Each surau—and especially the *surau besar*—had, nominally at least, a number of possible functionaries besides the Imam himself; in particular a *khatib*, the reciter of the Friday address, who commonly had some knowledge of Arabic, and a *bilal* to call the prayer times. Part of the subsistence of all surau functionaries, and some of the upkeep of surau buildings, was met by the surrender to the *Imam Besar* by the peasants of annual *zakat* and '*fitrah*' (*zakāt al-fiṭr*) taxes or alms.

Though the moral and spiritual authority of the Imam might well be shared with other figures of importance in Kelantan village life—in particular the *bomoh* or spirit-medium in any one of a number of forms, and the independent *To' Guru* (teacher) of a *pondok* school, should there be one in the mukim—and his civil authority with the To' Kweng the role of Imam was of great consequence and largely independent of external sanction. An Imam might or might not have his position warranted by a *Kuasa* (written authority) from the Sultan or from the local territorial chief but he seldom, in the mid-century, found himself answerable to central authority. It was less that the latter did not exist

[10] For example, after the introduction of a new system of land registration in 1881, measurement of holdings and authentication of plans lay first with the Imam in whose mukim the land lay. See the draft 'Memorandum on Land Tenure' produced by the British Adviser in 1923, encl. in Kel. K. 945/1923. Cf. also the remarks by Graham (1904, 17) on the inefficacy of the *To' Kweng*.

than that, in the circumstances of the time, its writ was not exercised beyond the environs of the capital, Kota Bharu, except in cases of judicial appeal or command when individuals might be brought into town for the purpose. There is evidence (HKS, 60 and 64) that at least by the 1830s (and presumably much earlier) there resided in Kota Bharu both a state *Mufti* and a *Hakim*—the former exercising judicial (rather than merely consultative) functions, assisted by a *Kathi*, in a Shari'a court restricted largely to Muslim personal law (especially marriage, divorce and property matters), but possibly concerning itself also with breaches of the moral law and ritual observance; while the latter acted as judge in what seems to have been primarily a criminal court, in which a mixture of Islamic and Malay customary (*adat*) law was administered.[11] The Mufti may also have kept a register of all Imam (and possibly other surau officials) in the state, over whom he had nominal jurisdiction, but it seems probable that this was an innovation of the late century.[12] The Kota Bharu area contained the only 'mosques' (in contradistinction to surau) in the state, the main mosque in Kota Bharu town (known simply as the *Masjid* Kota Bharu) and two older buildings with royal associations at Kampong Laut and Langgar. These mosques, and their officials, fell within the immediate administrative responsibility of the Mufti, and were supported both by *zakat* and *fitrah* collected directly from their parishioners, and by the proportion of these taxes which, theoretically at least, was delivered to the Sultan by the Imam of *surau besar* throughout the state for disbursement in this fashion and as alms for the other categories recognized as entitled to receive them.[13]

To summarize, the general picture one may derive of the mid-nineteenth century is one in which a significant segment of the rural elite in Kelantan peasant society, the Imam of village surau assisted by subordinates with some pretensions to learning and piety, formed the hinge of an attenuated if slowly strengthening religious administration, on the other side of which (somewhat removed in practical terms) functioned the nominally state-wide authority of the Mufti and Kathi, with their attendant officers of the Shari'a court. Throughout the society, spiritual authority was in some degree shared by the not specifically Islamic

---

[11] The Sultan in his *Balai* (audience hall) functioned as an appeal court, the *Mahkamah Balai*—certainly from the court of the *Hakim*, and possibly also from the Shari'a court.

[12] The earliest known mention of this occurs in a report by the Mufti in 1911, encl. in Kel. M. 18/1911, which refers to a list of '*pegawai surau*' (surau officials) kept by the then Mufti in 1311 (1893-4).

[13] It is difficult, indeed impossible, to determine the extent to which in nineteenth century Kelantan the treatment of *zakat* followed the outline given here, but later reference to the 'Sultan's share' of the tax, and to the use to which it should properly be put, make it clear that the system was ideally much as described. For Islamic precept concerning the disbursement of *zakat*, see, e.g., Gibb and Kramers (1961).

(though not, for that reason, necessarily 'un-Islamic') practitioners of folk religion as expressed in magic, in the traditional psycho-drama known as *main puteri* and in the shadow-play and similar forms, and also, and importantly, by the independent teachers of religion the To' Guru, most notably in the pondok schools in the countryside but also to some extent in the town. In the latter part of the century especially, partly because of the continuing exodus of Malay religious scholars from Siamese-dominated Patani, partly because of the growth in importance of the *haj*, the pilgrimage to Mecca, from around 1870, there were increasing numbers of individual teachers taking pupils both in the Kota Bharu *Masjid* and in their own homes throughout the town and its environs. Kelantan, and in particular Kota Bharu, which had been roundly castigated in the 1830s by the visiting Munshi Abdullah for its loose women and their ponces, its cockfighters and gamblers, and a population less than two percent of which (he alleged) was in the habit of performing its proper religious duties,[14] was, in some respects at least, suffering a change in reputation, despite Hugh Cliffords's complacent assurance in 1894 (1961, 17) that it was not a place in which one need ever fear 'serious religious prejudice or fanaticism'.

There can be no question but that many important changes took place, in the governance of Islam as in much else, in the quarter of a century that followed the death of Sultan Muhammad II in 1886. Concerning the general administration of the state, some measures of significance had been introduced a number of years earlier—particularly the establishment of the To' Kweng system of headmen around the 1870s, and, in 1881, the reorganization of the system of land tenure and registration—but it was principally in the 1890s, and largely under (or in reaction to) Siamese rather than British influence, that formal administrative change began to gather momentum. Oddly, it was a period marked by incoherence as much as order. Between 1886 and 1900 no fewer than four rulers came to the throne,[15] none enjoying any substantial security, all surrounded by intriguing relatives, all dependent on powerful ministers of state and to an increasing extent on Siamese favour, and all cons-

---

[14] Abdullah (1960, 87). Abdullah, who was fond of moralising from the superior vantage point of his association with the Straits Settlements and the British, was told by one Kelantan *raja* (and reports the fact without apparent irony) that as he was so good at preaching he'd get him a job as *kathi* and *khatib* if he cared to stay in Kelantan. *Ibid.*, 104.

[15] (1) Sultan Ahmad, 31 Oct. 1886–24 Feb. 1890; (2) Sultan Muhammad III (son of 1), 24 Feb. 1890–11 May 1891; (3) Raja (later Sultan) Mansur (bro. of 2), 11 May 1891–30 Jan. 1900; (4) Muhammad IV (son of 2), who became Raja of Kelantan on 30 January 1900, but took the title Sultan only in 1910. This list follows that given by Muhammad Yusof (1953). All other available lists have been collated and found either to confirm the foregoing or to be inaccurate, but cf. Mohamed, above, p. 29, Note 41.

cious of Kelantan as an arena not simply for local political struggle but for expansionist British and Thai rivalries. Out of this emerged, on the basis built by Muhammad II, the unitary state of Kelantan, shorn, where the monarchy was concerned, of some political independence (and ultimately of a great deal more), stripped to its nuclear territories, but increasingly drawn together by the administrative webbing of the modern state, however imperfectly this may have functioned at first.

Where Islam was concerned, the most noteworthy developments appear to have taken place under the influence of a rising minister of state of renowned puritanical passion, Che' Ha', who was made Dato' Laksamana in 1888 and some time later Maha Mentri, becoming in effect chief minister.[16] Though no direct connection can be established it seems likely that it was Che' Ha' who was responsible for the official concern for the better practise of Islam which began to manifest itself during Sultan Ahmad's brief reign (1886-90), a period that coincided with Che' Ha's rise to power. HKS (93) records that at this time the populace was instructed to obey more fully the injunctions of the Shari'a, and Imam Haji Wan Daud (who either then was, or shortly thereafter became, State Mufti)[17] was required to give public readings of *hadith* literature every Tuesday, which were attended by large numbers of people at the Sultan's order. At the same time, the *menora* and *Mak Yong* theatres, and other practices of the sort, were prohibited throughout the state as irreligious, together with such popular entertainments as cockfighting and the gambling associated with it (HKS, 90). By the early 1900s fresh regulations had been promulgated requiring regular attendance at Friday prayers in all surau, on pain of summons; penalising public breach of the fast during the month of Ramadhan; providing punishments (perhaps not for the first time, but with renewed force) for the offence of '*khalwat*' (impermissible consorting with members of the opposite sex);[18] and other matters of strict observance.[19] Adminis-

---

[16] His principal colleague (and also rival), Nik Yusof b. Nik Abdul Majid, Dato' Sri Paduka, had been chief minister in the last year of Sultan Muhammad II's reign (at which time Che' Ha' had been assistant to him), and was to become so again after Che' Ha's death in 1894. For a brief outline of these changes, see Ahmad b. Hassan (1964/65, 44-7), which follows HKS closely.

[17] Haji Wan Daud is known to have been Mufti by 1893-4.

[18] The term was not defined in the earliest extant Kelantan legislation on the subject (the *Undang2 Mahkamah Shari'a* [Shari'a Court Regulation], No. 5 of 1327 [1909], Section 11; and the *Notis* (?No. 4) of 1328 [1910] which re-enacted this Section; both measures being directed mainly against prostitution), but was subsequently understood to embrace the consorting in private of any Muslim with a person of the opposite sex, other than a spouse or those with whom, by reason of consanguinity as defined in the Shari'a, they were forbidden marriage. For a variety of later definitions in Kelantan and other states, see Ahmad Ibrahim (1965, 323-8).

[19] For a flippantly phrased list of matters dealt with, see Clifford (1898, 24). Cf. also Asa'ad (1962, 82), which describes in greater detail the restrictions upon dress referred to by Clifford.

THE ORIGIN AND EARLY YEARS OF THE MAJLIS UGAMA 109

tration of these regulations was assisted by a new emphasis on centralized control of Imam and other surau officials by the Mufti; by strengthening the membership of the Shari'a court; and possibly by the institution at this time of '*Pemereksa Jumaat*' (or '*Jemaah*,' for both terms were used)—inspectors who went round ensuring that surau were being properly run and Friday prayers fully observed.[20]

Though it is not to be supposed that these measures were in all cases effective, especially perhaps after the assassination (for political rather than other motives) of their principal author, Maha Mentri, in 1894—and visitors were accustomed to remarking on the fitfulness of their application[21]—it may be emphasized that their implementation took place in the context of, and were presumably much assisted by, increasing penetration of village society in the delta regions by the general administration. The details of this last process are still little known,[22] but at least from 1892, when the first of a series of Siamese Commissioners is understood to have taken up residence in the state and been successful in urging certain fiscal reorganization upon the ruler (in particular, the introduction of a new Padi Tax),[23] administrative reform made itself felt at the village level. Though many of the subsequent accomplishments of this reform seem to have affected primarily Kota Bharu—a public works department to develop town roads, the beginnings of a telephone service, a small printery for the issuance of government notices, a police force with two stations in town and four in outlying villages, and an enlarged judiciary with a newly built court house—'lower Kelantan' (the area of the plain) was drawn in also, especially with the opening of a central Land Office under competent

---

[20] Though '*Jumaah*' (or *Jumaat*) and '*jemaah*' (or *jemaat*) are in fact the same word (from the Arabic root *jm* [see Berger (1970, 4–5)]), they were frequently distinguished in Malay (as in the contemporary legislation in Kelantan), '*jemaah*' meaning merely 'assembly', and '*jumaat*' specifically 'Friday', from its association with Friday congregational prayers. A '*Mahkamah Jumaat*' was instituted in Kelantan at about this time, to deal with persistent absentees from Friday prayers. It appears to have been a division of the Shari'a court, and the post of judge in this division (though not the offence) was abolished in 1911, during a reorganization of the Shari'a court. See Kelantan Government Estimates for 1911, encl. in Kel. K. Conf. 14/1910.

[21] See Clifford (1898, 31), and the more considered remarks in Clifford (1961, 116–17). W.W. Skeat, visiting Kota Bharu in 1899, attended a performance of *main puteri*, 'conducted with a little more secrecy than I had expected, on the grounds that the Sultan disapproved of these rites, as not in strict accord with the Muslim faith', but he adds (1953, 115) that it seemed that everyone was aware that *main puteri* continued to flourish.

[22] It now seems clear that neither Malay nor British materials are likely to shed much additional light on this vital decade, especially where administrative growth is concerned. It is to be hoped that Thai sources in Bangkok may be more helpful.

[23] Graham (1910–11, 482) states, and in (1905, 7) implies, that the first Siamese Commissioner took up residence in Kota Bharu in 1892; Thamsook (1967), using Thai sources, gives 1894; and cf. also, Mohamed, above, p. 25.

management in 1896,[24] and the appointment of a Lands Commission to resurvey all lands, beginning in 1899—an activity in which both village Imam and To' Kweng were much involved.

It may also be suggested that the re-emphasis upon Islam that took place in the 1890s, and continued into the early century, was in some measure a response to the cultural as well as the political threat to Kelantan independence that existed at this time. It was scarcely unknown in Kota Bharu that the British had been successful in imposing their rule upon the western states and Pahang, with a marked diminution not merely in Malay authority of all kinds but in the Malay character of the states affected, nor that there was a real danger that they would wish to extend their influence to Kelantan. Siamese control of the neighbouring provinces into which Patani had been broken was notoriously unsympathetic to Islam, quite as much as to Malay sovereignty, even if the reports of British observers concerning the Siamese administration are recognized as having been partisan.[25] Internally, the political confusion and turmoil of the 1890s, with repeated changes of ruler and constant intrigue round the throne that threatened to tear the state apart, made it increasingly important to reassert whatever elements of stability and continuance were at hand. In these circumstances it is perhaps not surprising that for those Kelantanese to whom Islam was especially important as a component of Malay identity and integrity—as evidence, if properly held to, of the right to remain a unitary people, favoured by God, and as a means of social control—a pressing need to strengthen the faith should have been recognized.

British and Siamese struggles at the turn of the century over the fate of Kelantan, discussed in detail by Nik Mohamed b. Nik Mohd. Salleh, above, were resolved first by the Anglo-Siamese Declaration of 1902, which made provision for (among other things) the signing of an Agreement by the Raja of Kelantan accepting a Siamese 'Adviser' with powers much larger than those of earlier Commissioners,[26] and finally

[24] The office was run by Haji Che' Wok, a Kelantanese who had received some training in Johore.

[25] Davies (1902), in a series of articles originally published in the Singapore *Free Press*, refers frequently to alleged Siamese disregard for Islamic institutions (see, esp., pp. 11, 23 and 28); W.A.R. Wood, British Vice-Consul at Singgora, though more moderate in opinion and language, makes a strong point of Malay dislike of Siamese rule, and refers explicitly to the maladministration of Islam (see, esp., his reports of 22 September and 3 October encl. in Desp., Governor, Straits Settlements, to Colonial Office, 28 November 1908 and 2 January 1909, in CO 273/343). Neither of the anthropological expeditions to Patani, in 1899–1900 and 1901–2, though admittedly more concerned with religious belief and practice than with religious administration, makes similar strictures in its published acounts (see, e.g., Skeat and Laidlaw [1953]; and Annandale & Robinson [1903–4]).

[26] Text in Maxwell & Gibson (1924, 85 ff.). The Agreement was modelled on the earlier

by the conclusion of the Anglo-Siamese Treaty of March 1909, by which, concerning Kelantan, the Siamese transferred to the British 'all rights of suzerainty, protection, administration or control whatsoever they possess' (Maxwell and Gibson, 1924, 89). Under the 1902 Agreement, a 'Siamese Adviser' of British nationality, W.A. Graham, took up residence in Kelantan in July 1903, and proceeded to reorganize government along increasingly Western lines.

The record of Graham's administration is available from his annual reports to Bangkok, and in some measure from his published account of the state at this time (Graham, 1908a), but importantly also in the legislation of these years. It is clear that one of his first concerns, apart from trying to strengthen the finances of the state by improving revenue collection and controlling its disbursement, was to assert formal rights of administration over the two-fifths or more of the state—virtually the whole of the hinterland—that had been acquired as a commercial concession by R.W. Duff in October 1900 from a young and insecure ruler, new to the throne, anxious to avail himself of personal resources independent of internal and external enemies[27] In both respects Graham was at least partially successful, though the Duff Concession was to plague the Kelantan government for a further quarter of a century, and to play a large part in crippling its finances. From the point of view of the present paper, however, Graham may be said to have accomplished, between about 1905 and mid-1909, two things of importance. Continuing tendencies which had already begun he built a much stronger secular, and centrally controlled, administration at the village level, thus resolving the growing tension between Imam and To' Kweng in favour of the latter; and, despite the embargo on his interference in matters of 'religion and custom,' he succeeded in at one and the same time delimiting the powers of the Shari'a court (by separating it firmly from the remainder of the judicial process) and strengthening in legislative terms the authority of the court, and to some extent that of the Mufti, over religion in the state. It should be said that these accomplishments, except in so far as they reflect a concern for separation of 'church and state' such as was common to British administrators of the time, were less directly sought than the result of policies independently pursued.

Graham's recognition of the need to improve rural administration in the interests of maximising revenue from the produce and poll taxes, which still formed a substantial part of the state's income, led him to

---

British treaties of 'protection', requiring the Adviser's 'advice' to be accepted in all matters of administration save those relating to 'religion and custom'.
[27] See the discussion of the Duff Company in Mohamed, above.

develop plans (on the model of British administration in the FMS) for division of the state into five 'districts,' each under the charge of a District Officer who would be responsible for general administration, and especially for oversight of the To' Kweng. It was around the latter that rural administration increasingly centred, as by legislative regulation they were given the tasks of land, crop, and population assessment, revenue collection (under the supervision of four travelling Revenue Inspectors), police powers, authority to register and license fishing boats, and much else. Simultaneously, the secular authority of the village Imam waned, for though the Land Officers responsible for alienation of land and registration of title were still for the most part recruited from among the Imam, it was planned to train secular officials to supersede them, and Graham noted (1905, 18) that 'The duties of the local Imams have as far as possible been dissociated from those of Toh Kweng and are now almost entirely restricted to the spiritual control of their parishioners'. Though district organization proceeded only slowly, two were in existence (apart from Kota Bharu itself) by 1907—Batu Mengkebang (later called Ulu Kelantan) in the interior, and Pasir Puteh towards the Trengganu border—and Graham observed (1908b, 16) that those of the To' Kweng 'who were too weak to wield their authority with efficiency have found support in the arrangement', and no doubt also in the system of commission by which they were encouraged to surrender as well as collect revenue. In one respect only was it envisaged that the Imam be in any way drawn into the processes of modernization, Graham noting (1905, 34) that he had a scheme for assisting 'the Imam who conduct the local Koran schools', and for 'inducing them to introduce a certain amount of secular education into their curriculum'. No more was heard of this proposal, which in terms of teaching skills and materials (to say nothing of the essential nature of surau education) was unrealistic, and it appears not to have been pursued.

The actual administration of Islam in Kelantan, aside from being excluded from his competence by treaty, was not for Graham a matter of immediate concern, though he was markedly unsympathetic to the manner in which the Shari'a court functioned. In part this reflected a more general discontent with the operation of the judicial system as a whole, one of his first actions being to have a Courts Regulation passed by the new State Council, establishing in place of the old Kelantan Court a hierarchy of High Court, Central Court, and Court of Small Causes (all in Kota Bharu), following this with new Civil and Criminal Procedure Codes and a Police Regulation, all based on Western models. What he called the 'Ecclesiastical Court' was however, he said (1904,

30), 'managed exlusively by certain Imams and Hadjis learned in the law', and apart from persuading the ruler to agree to remove matters relating to morality and ritual observance from the jurisdiction of the police and the other courts and leave them solely within the jurisdiction of the 'ecclesiastical' court, he did nothing to interfere with its working. This last action was in itself, however, a departure of some significance, as Graham may have been aware,[28] for it had in the past been perfectly proper for the Shari'a court, and for the ruler of the state, to use the civil arm (if indeed that distinction were to be made) to apprehend and punish perpetrators of offences against Shari'a law. The change was, in due course, to lead to the development of alternative instruments for the enforcement of religious authority, and in particular to the bureaucratization of the Imam. Graham continued for a time to remain aloof from the Shari'a court, though he was moved to comment on the difficulties it had recently had in appointing and retaining *hakim* and *kathi* of ability,[29] and in 1906 he thought it proper to describe the court (1907, 15–16) as 'the last stronghold of the corruption and dishonesty formerly characteristic of the whole administration', while adding that in view of the stipulation against interference by the Adviser there did not seem to be 'much prospect of improving [its] condition'.

But his concern over the workings of the Shari'a court did not abate, and between early 1907 and his departure in mid-1909 he secured the passage of four successive Shari'a Court regulations which did much to set the court firmly within the context of Western-style procedure, and establish the boundaries of its jurisdiction. Copies of the first three (two passed in 1325, the first dated possibly 15 April and the second 7 December 1907, and the third passed in 1326 [1908]) cannot now be traced. The earliest extant, however, passed in 1327 (dated 24 May 1909),[30]

[28] There is a veiled reference by Graham (1904, 30), apparently to Davies' articles in the *Free Press*, to public criticism of Siamese restrictions in Patani on the right of the Raja to use the police and law officers in enforcement of the Shari'a.

[29] The terms *hakim* and *kathi* were both used at this time. There appear to have been three 'justices' in the Shari'a court—a *Hakim Mahkamah Shari'a*, an assistant (usually described as *Penolong Kathi*, or assistant kathi), and a *Hakim Mahkamah Jumaat*, or justice in the 'Friday court'. All three posts changed hands frequently in the early century. Graham (1905, 25; and 1907, 15) refers to two appointees from Mecca to the post of *Hakim Mahkamah Shari'a*, one who stayed for about a year and left in 1902, the other serving from some time later until 1905 when he also returned to Mecca. The *Penolong Kathi* seem to have been invariably Kelantanese, as were the *Hakim Mahkamah Shari'a* from about 1908, though the rate of turnover remained high in both posts. Early *Hakim Mahkamah Jumaat* are not known, but an appointment made in 1908 after the post had remained vacant for a year was terminated only in 1911, when the post itself was abolished (see Kel. M. 59/1911, which refers to the appointment, and cf. also Note 20 above). By at least 1900, the Mufti had ceased to exercise jurisdiction in the Shari'a court and was established as independent jurisconsult, and as court of appeal from the Shari'a court.

[30] In view of the fact that published collections of early Kelantan legislation are extremely incomplete, and individual measures often impossible to trace, reference will be made

explicitly repealed, amended and re-enacted the second in the series; and there is some evidence that the first dealt primarily with marriage and divorce. Only the third, then, remains a blank. But it is in any case abundantly clear that the cumulative intent of all four measures was to define the principal jurisdiction of the court as concerning (in the words of the 1909 regulation) 'cases affecting inheritance and matrimonial relations and matters connected therewith,' and to set out the procedures to be adopted by the court, especially relating to the rights of plaintiffs and defendants, the nature of testimony and rules of evidence, and the right of the court to set either discretionary (*ta'azīr*) or fixed penalties (the latter not always in agreement with the *ḥadd*, or fixed penalties, of Shari'a law), and award costs. The financial provisions in particular constituted an innovation, fines and costs being payable for the first time (by administrative fiat, not by law) into a public treasury, and the justices made salaried officers of the state; but in general there is no reason to suppose that the details of the Shari'a Court regulations departed radically from past practice in Kelantan, and certainly no means of proving this. What seems important is that the court was locked into Western forms of judicial procedure, and that the principle of having a separate 'religious court' was given a wholly different emphasis, it being established that the jurisdiction of this court was properly to be defined (perhaps even confined) by statutory enactment, a notion certainly foreign to Shari'a law, even in Kelantan.

During the same period, several additional legislative measures, in the form either of Regulations (*Undang2*) or Notices (*Notis* or *Perwawai*)[31] made provision for the further administration of Shari'a law relating to payment of zakat, attendance at Friday prayers and at compulsory religious instruction, the conduct of surau and duties of surau officials, and divorce. All seven of the measures known to have been passed at this time empowered the Shari'a court to try offenders and enforce statutory penalties, and the Mufti was charged with a variety of

---

where appropriate to the location of particular measures. A copy of the regulation at present under discussion is encl. in Kel. K. 20/1911, which also contains a manuscript translation into English. An incomplete English version in typescript is encl. in Kel. M. 218/1913.

[31] Legislation prior to mid-1909 was passed by the Raja in Council in the form either of *Undang2* (sometimes styled *Undang2 Peraturan*), or of *Notis* (sometimes styled *Perwawai* or *Notis Pemberitahu*). The former were known in English as 'Regulations,' and the latter as 'Notices'. Regulations seem always to have been printed; Notices were sometimes printed but more often were published in mimeograph manuscript form. Neither Regulations nor Notices appeared in numbered series, but both had the force of law, the distinction between them being largely one of weight and scope. After the introduction of the British regime, *Undang2* were known as 'Enactments', printed, and numbered annually in series; while *Notis* were published in cyclostyled typescript, but were not numbered in series until 1912.

specifically administrative responsibilities in connection with Imam and surau. It is probable that this legislation was largely repetitive of earlier disciplinary regulation, and that it was enacted at the instance of the Kelantanese rather than Graham, though he appears to have influenced drafting. The combined effect of the new measures was to strengthen the authority of central religious institutions, bound in important respects though these increasingly were by the restrictive explicitness of substantive law.

Under the first of the zakat notices, dated 9 September 1907 (which began by correcting the popular belief that the Padi Tax—introduced in 1892 but collected with increasing vigour under Graham—was a perversion of *padi zakat* to secular use), Imam were charged with supplying the names of defaulters to the Shari'a court in return for summons to serve upon offenders, the court being empowered in due course to require payment or distrain property in lieu. Further bureaucratizing this process, a later regulation, dated 8 March 1908, made it incumbent upon Imam to assemble lists of defaulters, signed by at least one other surau official, which were then subject to scrutiny by the *Hakim Mahkamah Shari'a* before issuance of summons. When cases came to trial, the Hakim was to require the accused to produce receipts for zakat surrendered, and only if these were not forthcoming, and after examination, to pass sentence—the statutory penalty now being increased to twice the amount of zakat due, together with a share of costs. A final notice, a week later, remedied an oversight in the preceding enactment by setting out the nature of a 'receipt', and requiring all Imam to use duplicate counterfoil receipt books.[32]

The Friday Prayer notice of 9 December 1907 made it obligatory upon surau officials to require all adult male inhabitants of the *mukim* to attend Friday prayers, except in cases of attested sickness or 'long journeys'. Persons unable to produce a certificate of sickness from a surau official were to have their names supplied to the *Mahkamah Jumaat* so that summons might be issued against them. On proof of guilt, the court was empowered to sentence the offender to the condign punishment of hard labour by carting sand.[33] Imam were instructed on no account to take it upon themselves to levy monetary fines locally. Imam were further required to ensure that by proper expenditure of their share of the zakat they maintained surau premises in a fit state for use. When additional wood was needed for repairs, application was to be

[32] All three zakat measures are encl. in manuscript form in Kel. PB. 10/1916.
[33] 'It is no uncommon thing to see a well-to-do citizen carrying a load of sand from the river to the Musjid compound in compulsory atonement for backsliding.' Graham (1908a, 32).

made to the Mufti, who would consult with the Revenue Office concerning the remission of lumber tax. The notice also required Imam to produce all adult males on occasion of a visit from the state's official travelling teacher of religion,[34] so that they might learn the fundamentals of prayer and the basic tenets of their faith. Failure to do this might be reported by the teacher to the Shari'a court, for appropriate action.[35]

Finally, the Surau Regulation of 1326 (dated 4 August 1908), which bears in many respects the marks of a consolidating enactment, set out in great detail a wide range of matters relating to the creation, territorial definition, and management of surau, together with the appointment, duties, and general responsibilities of their officials. Nothing serves to make clearer the manner in which the surau as the focal institution of rural Islam was in the process of being removed from the realm of the village and the rural elite to that of centralized authority in Kota Bharu. Though in some degree this was a matter of making *de facto* that which had previously been merely *de jure* (more accurately, perhaps, making *de jure* in terms of Western statute law that which had been *de jure* in terms of traditionally conceived Shari'a law, but was still very much in any case in the process of becoming *de facto*), administrative institutionalization tended to the specification and elaboration of altogether new areas of formal control.

The regulation is long, ill-organized, and somewhat repetitious, and it is not intended to discuss it in great detail. It is, however, useful to look at it briefly under three heads: matters concerning definition and delimitation of surau; matters concerning the duties of officials; and penal provisions. Some nine of the 23 sections deal with the first of these categories, laying it down (Section 2) that surau might be of the two kinds already referred to, *besar* and *kechil* (large and small), the former possessing (according, it was stated, to the dictates of Shari'a law) six officials—an *Imam Tua* and *Imam Muda* (senior and junior), two *khatib* and two *bilal*; the latter one only of each. It was stated (Section 4) to be within the competence of the Ruler in Council to create a *surau besar* from a small surau, or vice versa, and for the ruler acting alone (Section 21) to select from among the surau officials those best fitted to be Imam of both ranks, *khatib*, and *bilal*, and to make such changes from time to time as seemed to him necessary. Two sections (8 and 9) provided in detail for the creation of new *surau kechil* as a result of population growth or village partition, the procedure being for those wishing to

---

[34] It is not known when the post of *guru jajahan* was first created. There appears to have been one such for the whole state, at this time, certificated by and 'on the staff of' the Mufti.
[35] A copy of this *Notis* is encl. in Kel. M. 62/1914.

set up a new surau to apply to the ruler, who would then instruct the Mufti to examine the request in the light of the requirements of Shari'a law; it being also within the power of the ruler alone or when advised by the the Mufti to establish new surau at will. In addition, boundaries and disputes between *mukim surau* in terms of area, population, and taxation rights, were provided for (Sections 17 and 18) by a complex series of stipulations which envisaged the use of existing land registers and other records; and it was added (Section 19) that surau might be physically removed from one place to another only in accordance with population movement and with the approval of the ruler. As surau status and boundaries, inter- and intra-mukim divisions and loyalties, and the land and taxation rights that went along with them, were the stuff of village politics, it is clear that at least potentially the 'delimitation' provisions of the 1908 enactment sought to strengthen the political as well as the religious control of the centre over the village.

This is also evident in those sections of the regulation relating to the duties and responsibilities of surau officials. In the first place it was confirmed (Section 3) that while the principal duty of all Imam and other surau officials was to see to the proper conduct of Friday and congregational prayers, only officials of *surau besar* might collect zakat taxation or perform marriage contracts (for the regulation fee). Concerning marriage, *surau besar* officials were required (Sections 14 and 6) to provide those married with a *pas nikah* (marriage certificate) and while it was recognised that personal relationships or enmities might prompt some persons to have marriages conducted by other than officers of their own *surau besar*, the fees at least were to go to the latter. It was made obligatory for surau officials to ensure (Section 5) that all adult males attended Friday prayers or were reported to the Shari'a court in the terms laid down by the *Notis* on this subject. Concerning zakat, on which, as with Friday prayers, a previous notice existed, *Imam Tua* were merely exhorted (Section 11) to surrender the share of the *padi zakat* pertaining to the ruler and to the Kota Bharu mosques within two months of payment; and arrangements were made (Section 23) for the disbursement of the proper proportion of this zakat by the ruler to the officers of the mosques concerned.

The penal provisions of the regulation required (Section 7) all members of a mukim to obey the instructions of surau officials in all particulars relating to their *kuasa*, on pain of a fine of $5 or such other punishment as might be set out in the notices relating to Friday prayers and zakat. In addition (Section 22), anyone refusing to answer a summons properly served by a surau official, or guilty of other offences of this kind, could be sentenced by the Shari'a court to a fine of $50 or three months in jail. Surau officials themselves were forbidden (Section 11) to conceal the names of persons paying zakat, and on proof of guilt were to be obliged to pay double the amount improperly withheld. In general, surau officials were required to be of good behaviour and character, and anyone found lax in the performance of his duties, or guilty of taking part in bull-fighting or gambling, might, after two warnings, be fined or dismissed.

Graham's political control of public affairs in Kelantan had without doubt been resented by those male members of the royal family in particular (anathematized by the Adviser as 'the seven uncles', and later by the British High Commissioner as 'the wicked uncles'), and of the traditional ruling class in general, who were most affected by his insistence on the eradication of the arbitrary division of the state's resources that was reflected in the system of monopolies, concessions, individual rights of taxation, and personal administration of justice, which had been in some measure endemic in the state since the death of Muhammad II in 1886 but was much exacerbated by the accession of the young and inexperienced Muhammad IV in 1900. It is also evident that the principal beneficiary of effective centralization and bureaucratization was Muhammad IV himself, despite the irksome surrender of much day-to-day political authority to his 'Adviser'. In these circumstances it is clear that Muhammad IV was not averse to reassertion of his titular and proper authority over Islam, the one area in which, in the last resort, he was not obliged to seek or accept the Adviser's advice. It was, in addition, an area which promised very considerable control over the populace at large, by way of the institutions of Imam, surau, and Shari'a law. Notwithstanding the loss of secular authority by the Imam to the To' Kweng, and to the secular administration associated with them that was essentially the creation and creature of Graham, the Imam remained immeasurably important at the village level of society, in terms of relationships springing from kinship and land, in their intimate concern with an important segment of popular systems of belief, and in the ritual functions they performed, functions central to peasant life in a way that the more mundane responsibilities of the To' Kweng seldom could be. He who controlled the Imam, it might have been said, commanded the state. In the evolution of administrative machinery for Islam that took place in the middle of the first decade of the century, the authority of the ruler, as has been seen, was expressly invoked by all the statutory instruments then enacted, and with this the authority of the Shari'a court and the Mufti. Though, for the future, there were at least two possible areas of structural tension resulting— between ruler and court or ruler and Mufti—and though there was created an inherent and potentially dangerous problem of final authority, in permitting the Shari'a to be defined and limited by statutory enactment, the balance at the end of Graham's period as Adviser was one in which centralizing tendencies within Islamic institutions were already providing a counterweight to a secular state apparatus increasingly alien in content, personnel and ideology.

Final British authority over the affairs of Kelantan was achieved by the Anglo-Siamese Treaty of 1909, which resulted in the installation of the first 'British Adviser' in July of that year and was followed in October 1910 by a further Agreement, this time between Britain and the Raja of Kelantan, by which the latter undertook to 'follow and give effect to' the Adviser's advice in all matters of administration other than those 'touching upon the Mohammedan religion and Malay custom'.[36] Little immediate change resulted, the first British Adviser, J.S. Mason, following policies very similar to those initiated by Graham, based on similar assumptions concerning the desiderata for efficient, modern forms of government, and hampered to the same extent in carrying them out by the very limited revenues enjoyed by the state. Nevertheless, the fact that the Adviser was an official on secondment from the Malayan Civil Service of the FMS, subject to the General Orders of that service, and directly answerable, through the Federal Secretary, to the High Commissioner for the Malay States, led to increasing if gradual convergence in policy and practice between Kelantan and the rest of 'British Malaya', a process assisted by the appointment in 1910 of several additional MCS officers to key positions in the state.[37] Though the latter did not in all cases displace Malay departmental office holders, there was a marked tendency to emphasize the superior tutelary role of European officials, and a number of resigna-

[36] Maxwell & Gibson (1924, 109). Muhammad IV, who had merely styled himself 'Raja' in the early part of his reign, assumed the title of Sultan, and was formally recognized as such by the British, in 1910.

[37] The four European officials who had worked with Graham—the Assistant Adviser, Superintendent of Revenue, Superintendent of Lands, and Superintendent of Police—remained under the new administration for some months, being gradually replaced from the Straits or FMS services, with the addition of a new Residency Surgeon, Chief Police Officer, Supervisor of Customs, and Director of Works and Surveys. By 1914 there were seventeen European officials on the Kelantan establishment ('List of European Officers Employed in Kelantan, 1914', encl. in Kel. K. 114/1915).

tions took place of senior Malays who presumably did not take kindly to the new regime (Mason, 1910, 7; 1911, 2). A further cause of discontent among some members of the ruling class who had participated in government under Graham was the insistence of the British on the retrocession, even if for compensation, of large mining and other concessions obtained from the ruler in the early years of his reign (Mason, 1911, 5–6).

Like Graham before him, Mason's urge for administrative reform was directed initially towards the operation of the courts, which he thought compared very badly with those of the federated Malay states —largely, it would seem, because with the exception of one of the High Court judges who was Siamese (and who shortly resigned in favour of the Assistant Adviser), 'all Court officials are Malay' (Mason, 1910, 7). The Shari'a court he took particular exception to, describing it in his first annual report (which was otherwise cautious and non-contentious) as 'even less satisfactory' than the courts in general, and as the subject of numerous complaints concerning delay, corruption and misappropriation. Notwithstanding treaty restrictions upon interference in matters Islamic, Mason represented to Muhammad IV, shortly after his arrival, that 'in other states, it had not been necessary to establish [a Shari'a court], for if matters arose involving religion they could be adequately dealt with by a kathi, and where such matters concerned inheritance the kathi could divide the property according to Muslim law after determination by the judge of a customary-law court'. To this, the Sultan wrote later, he had replied that he would prefer to wait and see[38]; but this mild rebuff did not prevent Mason writing in his report for 1909 (1910, 7) that 'It will probably be necessary to take away the jurisdiction the Court at present holds in cases of inheritance of land', nor subsequently securing the passage of an enactment concerning 'Succession to Small Estates', which limited the jurisdiction of the Shari'a court in land inheritance cases to properties valued at $500 or more, removing all others (the great majority) to the jurisdiction of Land Officers.[39]

The British attitude to the Shari'a court (and it was true, as Mason had said, that in no previously protected Malay state in the peninsula did such a body exist) remained somewhat restrictive, though there is a

[38] Letter, Sultan Muhammad to BA, 22 November 1913, encl. in Kel. M. 218/1913, with a copy in Kel. PM. 348/1913. The passage in Mason's original reads, as quoted by the Sultan: '... darihal Mahkamah Shari'a itu di sebelah negeri2 luar tiada berkehendak diadakan kerana jika ada berthabit dengan perkara ugama memadai dengan kathi sahaja dan jika ada perkara berkenaan dengan pesaka2 boleh kathi itu membahagikan atas jalan hukum Muhammadiah kemudian telah dibicharakan oleh Hakim Mahkamah Adat.'

[39] Enactment No. 17 of 1910.

high probability that in the early years the motives for this related more to the pursuit of 'efficiency' and to general tendencies towards secularism, than to any fear of the burgeoning power of the court as an institution. The court itself, indeed, remained plagued throughout this time by instability of membership,[40] and came increasingly under the control of a new and powerful Mufti, Haji Wan Musa b. Haji Abdul Samad,[41] who, succeeding to this office late in 1908, was to hold it until 1916, benefitting for the first part of this period from the administrative reorganization set in train by successive British Advisers. Following Mason's reduction of the original jurisdiction of the Shari'a court in matters of Muslim land inheritance, his successor, J.E. Bishop (Adviser from October 1910 to March 1913), pursuing what was in essence Mason's first intention, reduced the size as well as the competence of the Shari'a court by abolishing in 1911 the post of *Hakim Mahkamah Jumaat* within it, and at the same time setting up separate kathi's courts in the two outer districts of the state, courts which were henceforth to be regarded as 'branches' of the Shari'a court in Kota Bharu, and of equal jurisdiction,[42] appeal from all three lying to the Mufti. In effect, the Shari'a court, it was intended, would become merely the kathi's court for Kota Bharu district—though it retained its old title in much official as well as common usage until around 1920 and was in fact of considerably greater size and importance than either the Pasir Puteh or Batu Mengkebang kathi's courts, in that it dealt with a greater volume of business, had a bench of two (the Hakim or Kathi, and an Assistant Kathi) and continued to be regarded by many if not most Kelantanese as the Shari'a court for the state. Bishop, reporting on his administrative changes in a letter to the Federal Secretary in December 1910, transmitting the state's annual Estimates for 1911, wrote that 'The powers of the

[40] Haji Nik Lah (or Leh?), who may have been Hakim in 1909, resigned in August 1910, and was succeeded by Haji Ahmad b. Haji Abdul Rahman, who resigned in turn at the end of December. Haji Wan Ismail b. Jamaluddin, an elderly man who appears to have been 'Kathi Kota Bharu' for some time from about 1900, came out of retirement to become *Penolong Kathi* in the Shari'a court in February 1909, and Hakim in January 1911, but was overtaken by illness, leaving the post early in 1912 and dying shortly after. He was succeeded by Haji Ahmad b. Haji Abdul Manan, who remained Hakim from 1912 until late 1915. During the same period, Haji Wan Ismail was succeeded as *Penolong Kathi* in January 1911 by Haji Ahmad b. Haji Abdul Rahman, and then early in 1912 by Haji Wan Hassan who lasted until late 1915. Haji Wan Sa'id was *Hakim Mahkamah Jumaat* in the Shari'a court until 1911, when the post was abolished.
[41] For Haji Wan Musa, see Muhammad Salleh, below. He had been preceded as Mufti by Haji Wan Daud b. Wan Suleiman, who died at an advanced age in November 1907, and by the interim (and seemingly not very dynamic) Haji Wan Ishak b. Abdul Rahman (? Abdul Manan), who resigned or was relieved of his appointment late in 1908.
[42] Save in one respect only—in that the district kathi's courts were not empowered to decide inheritance cases in which the value of the property (whether landed only, or personal as well, is not clear) exceeded $200.

Ecclesiastical Court... have now been more clearly defined and considerably reduced', and added that among other things it had lost its previous authority to deal with offences committed by 'Chinese and other non-Mohammedans'.[43] Though the next five years or so of British rule continued to see legislative provision made for the governance of Islam (in all some ten measures were passed between 1910 and 1915), most statutory instruments—with two important exceptions[44]—placed no additional powers in the hands of the Shari'a (or Kathi's) court, even if earlier legislation was in no way repealed. A certain halt, then, is evident in the accretion of powers to the Shari'a court, and it is worth noting that the Sultan himself, though clearly reluctant initially to agree to Mason's proposals for the Shari'a court, appears to have changed his mind by November 1913, when he wrote to the then British Adviser (W. Langham-Carter) that he had come round to Mason's views, because of the large number of petitions reaching him complaining of decisions of the court. For this reason, he said, 'We no longer wish to retain the Shari'a court, and such matters concerning religion as arise can be referred to the Mufti or Kathi for the determination of Muslim Law'.[45]

The Sultan's letter is hard to interpret, taken at its face value, for there is little other direct evidence to suggest what may have prompted it—though the Adviser, in a scribbled minute, comments that a recent Pasir Mas case decided by the Shari'a court, in which 'the Mhdn Court did not assist HH's witnesses in this matter, and there is money on deposit in favour of children which they would otherwise certainly not have [had?]', may have influenced the ruler's feelings.[46] Whether this

[43] Draft letter, BA to Federal Secretary, 6 December 1912, encl. in Kel. K. Conf. 4/1910. With the expansion of rubber cultivation on estates, Chinese were entering Kelantan in increasing numbers, the Adviser reporting in 1910 that 'Chinese labour now exceeds that of all other nationalities', adding that sanction had also been given to the importation of Tamil labour (Mason, 1911, 4).

[44] *Notis* 15/1914 (7 November 1914), 'Fasal Orang Islam Berkehendak Berbini Dua Tiga atau Empat', provided that anyone other than a member of the royal family wishing to take more than one wife must give a signed undertaking before the Shari'a court that he would be able to maintain and treat them equally, with fines of $100 or two months in jail for breach of the undertaking, or of $200 or three months for Imam and participants registering such a marriage without prior undertaking. (This is the first known attempt in the peninsula to restrict plural marriage among Muslims, and was met by sharp objections—see, e.g., the petition by some 118 inhabitants of Kota Bharu in Kel. PB. 285/1914—and seems not to have been enforced.) *Notis* 12/1915 (19 June 1915) laid down penalties for consumption of alcohol by Muslims, and for breach of the fast during Ramadhan, and was similar to earlier legislation in the FMS. Offenders could be arrested by the police and charged before the Shari'a court, sentences being in the form of parading the convicted through the town, together with terms in jail.

[45] Letter, Sultan Muhammad to BA, 22 November 1913, encl. in Kel. M. 218/1913. The Malay reads: '... tidaklah Kita berkehendak lagi diadakan Mahkamah Shari'a itu melainkan jika ada berthabit dengan ugama bolehlah ditanya akan Mufti atau kathi bagi hukom Muhammadiah'.

[46] Undated minute by BA on *ibid.*

was a proper inference or not, it is certainly possible, in the light of what has already been said concerning the structural tensions inherent in the division of religious authority between ruler and court, or ruler and Mufti, to see the Sultan's letter as acquiescence in a reduction of powers of the Shari'a court not merely in terms of its original jurisdiction, but in terms of its final jurisdiction, which added to it the Mufti as court of appeal; for the Mufti, as will be shown, had become increasingly powerful within the state apparatus, and is known in addition to have found himself in conflict with the ruler on points of law, especially concerning inheritance. Additional support is given to this view by the concluding sentence of the Sultan's letter which ran, 'And further, We shall select and appoint someone to oversee all surau in the state'. Up to this time, the Mufti alone had exercised direct responsibility for most aspects of surau organization and control.

The Mufti had been put on the government 'establishment', and provided with a fixed salary, early in Graham's period, at the same time as other members of the judiciary, all of whom had previously derived their remuneration from a share in fines and fees. The bureaucratization of the office—in terms of statutory responsibility (in conjunction with the ruler) for the delimitation of *mukim surau*, for oversight of surau maintenance, and less directly (through appointment and certification of such state officials as the *Pemereksa Jumaat* and *Guru Jajahan*) for general governance of the conduct of surau—turned the Mufti into an administrative as well as a judicial officer of state and gave him very considerable practical control over the affairs of village Islam, in so far as he cared to exercise it. This process was accelerated under the first British Advisers, who clearly sought above most other things administrative grasp and efficiency, and readily promoted the extension of bureaucratic organizational forms. Though the Imam and other surau personnel ultimately answerable to the Mufti continued to be 'unpaid', in that they derived material reward (in so far as it was institutionalized) from a combination of their share of the zakat taxes, a portion of marriage and divorce registration fees, and less clearly specified commissions on all land transactions within the mukim,[47] the Mufti's formal estab-

[47] It is clear that though steps had been taken by Graham to eliminate the Imam from official participation in land transactions, the practice continued, resulting (according to a description in 1910) in commission payments of several kinds, thus: (a) on new grants, two-thirds of 1/2% of the assessed value of the land was paid to Imam and Khatib jointly by the To' Kweng; (b) on transfers, from 50 cents to $2 was paid to the Imam and Khatib jointly by the Land Office, depending on the distance of the mukim from Kota Bharu, where testimony had to be given; and (c) a further 25 cents was paid by (both?) buyer and seller to Imam and Khatib jointly. Though at this time, when To' Kweng were being taken off commission and put on salary, administrative arrangements were made to regularize and reduce these payments to surau officials,

lishment—as represented under the heading '*Ugama*' in the annual Estimates—continued to multiply, and to seek, like all bureaucracies, to reproduce itself. In the year following the appointment of the two district kathi in 1911, both officials, supported by the Mufti, requested wage increases and additional clerical help, on grounds of pressure of work.[48] By 1914, the list of persons under the direct control of the *Pejabat Mufti* (Mufti's Office) and in receipt of government salaries had reached fifteen—the Kathi and Assistant Kathi of the Shari'a court, the two district kathi, the *Guru Jajahan*, seven clerks (one for the Mufti himself, three in the Shari'a court, two in the Pasir Puteh court, and one in the Ulu Kelantan—previously Batu Mengkebang—court), and three peons.[49] In addition, paid not by the government but from what was known as the 'Mohammedan Religious Fund', into which now went all fines from the Shari'a and kathi's courts, he had on his staff two *Pemereksa Jumaat*, and, from 1915, two *Juru Sukat Sempadan Mukim* (Demarcators of Mukim Boundaries).

Allied, then, to his judicial authority as court of appeal from the Shari'a and kathi's courts, and to his role as jurisconsult empowered *ex officio* to give *fatwa* on any matter of religious law referred to him, the administrative authority of the Mufti within the Western structure of government—penetrating at least in theory to all levels of society—resulted in conjoint powers of considerable magnitude. Though examination of the records makes it clear that the Mufti was careful to refer all appointments to establishment posts to the Sultan for consideration and approval (and subsequently to the British Adviser, in the case of personnel on government salaries), and though it is likewise clear that the Sultan took a close personal interest not merely in the Mufti's establishment but (as was provided in the Shari'a Court regulation of 1909) in the appointment of Imam and the settlement of disputes concerning surau demarcation, it is obvious also that the relationship was potentially one of strain and conflict. This, it will be suggested, was of some relevance to the founding of the Majlis Ugama at the end of 1915.

The year 1915 was, however, to be of considerable consequence in other ways, in particular as a result of what has since been known as the Pasir Puteh Rebellion (or as the 'To' Janggut' rebellion, after its peasant

---

especially where services were held not be to involved, it was some time before they became effective. See the memorandum, 'Commissions paid to Toh Kwengs and others by the Land Office', 27 March 1910, and further correspondence, encl. in Kelantan file No. 186 (no series designation), 1910.

[48] See corresp. encl. in Kel. M. 158/1912. Religious officials rapidly became accustomed to the ways of the bureaucracy, the kathi at Pasir Puteh applying in January 1915 for an 'overnight allowance' (or *per diem*) in addition to actual travelling expenses for himself and a clerk when visiting outlying parts of his district (Kel. K. 139/1915).

[49] List encl. in Kel. K. 108/1914.

leader). This was a complex affair, into which many strands were woven and from which, once it had begun, many individuals sought to profit, and its detailed history falls outside the scope of this paper.[50] Engku Besar, grandson of the last effective local ruler, certainly harboured irredentist ambitions, equally certainly encouraged To' Janggut to organize a peasant anti-tax and anti-foreigner movement, and may in addition (though this is much less clear) have received encouragement from fellow members of the ruling class close to the throne in Kota Bharu, in the interests (if this assumption were correct) at least of expelling the British and other foreigners, but also, perhaps, of aiming at the throne itself. Whatever the facts of the case, there appears to have been enough suspicion about the latter to lead Muhammad IV to see to the bases of his authority, whether in relation to possible contenders from within or in relation to the British, upon whom after the successful quelling of the revolt with aid from Singapore he was necessarily and visibly increasingly dependent.

One of the striking, if incidental, outcomes of the Pasir Puteh affair was the rise to prominence within the counsels of the ruler of a young man who now came to play a dominant role in the affairs of the state. Haji Nik Mahmud b. Haji Wan Ismail, son of the late Hakim of the Shari'a court,[51] had already spent several years in the ruler's service. After a brief period in Mecca in the early century he had returned to Kota Bharu around 1904, aged then about twenty, to become a clerk in the Balai Besar, the section of the palace housing the Malay administrative offices of state. He rose rapidly, being made 1st Clerk to the ruler in May 1908, Assistant Secretary in January 1909, and Assistant Private Secretary in December 1911, about which time he was also entitled Dato' Bentara Setia.[52] By late 1912 the aging Dato' Mentri (chief minister) was describing him as in effect his assistant, and said that he was doing most of the work in the Mentri's office.[53] At the time of the revolt, Dato' Setia and Dato' Mentri were together employed by the Sultan in a series of complicated diplomatic manoeuvres between Kota Bharu, Pasir Puteh, and the British, and then in mid-May were sent to Singapore to represent the state of affairs in Kelantan to the High Commissioner. There seems little doubt that Dato' Setia emerged during this period as the ruler's closest and most trusted adviser, bereft as Muhammad IV appears to have been of other counsel upon which he knew he could rely.

[50] For detailed discussion, see Ibrahim, above; and cf. Allen (1968).
[51] See Note 40 above. In addition to his service from time to time as a kathi, Haji Wan Ismail was an *alim* of some note, and taught many pupils at his house on Jalan Atas Banggul, Kota Bharu.
[52] See record of service encl. in Kel. M. 167/1915.
[53] Letter, Dato' Mentri to BA, 18 September 1912, encl. in Kel. M. 152/1912.

A second figure of importance to emerge at this time, and a close friend of Dato' Setia, was Haji Muhammad b. To' Khatib Haji Mohd. Said,[54] a man some seven years younger who had recently returned from ten years spent in the Middle East, mainly at Al-Azhar in Cairo. Finally, somewhat more behind the scenes, was Haji Muhammad Yusof b. Ahmad, better known as To' Kenali, contemporaneously the most influential of all Kelantan *ulama*,[55] who had taught and remained close to the young Dato' Setia and was possessed of many forward looking ideas regarding Islam and society. These ideas, allied to the more pragmatic arguments for institutional reform of which Dato' Setia was the chief proponent, seem together to have given birth to the Majlis Ugama, which was to be at once a means of restating the ruler's authority over his people and their welfare, principally by way of Islam; an assertion that Islam itself was not to be relegated to the subsidiary role envisaged for it by the British; and a vehicle for the modernization—indeed the transformation—of the state as a whole.

It should be said that the evidential bases for this supposed concatenation of impulses and motives are not in all respects immediately to hand, though to set them out in this way seems reasonable in light of all that for the present can be discovered. It is, however, possible to add yet one more quite straightforward *raison d'être* for the Majlis Ugama, perhaps the most straightforward of all, by steering a careful course through some of the mundane administrative problems which attended the governance of Islam during this year of 1915. The most pressing problem of the time concerned money—in particular payments into and out of the Muhammadan Religious Fund. As has been noted, this Fund —from which were paid such officials as the *Pemereksa Jumaat* and demarcators of mukim boundaries, the travelling expenses of kathis and their clerks, such sums for mosque construction as were not met by zakat, and contributions to the thrice-yearly festival obligations of the Kota Bharu Mosque—was made up of fines exacted in the Shari'a and kathi's courts, a large proportion of which, until 1914, came from fines for non-attendance at Friday prayers.[56] In March of that year the State

[54] Born in 1888, the son of the senior khatib of the Kota Bharu Mosque (who was also in charge of the Land Office in Kota Bharu from early in the British period), Muhammad studied under Haji Omar b. Ismail, a noted *alim* and teacher in Kota Bharu (for a brief biography of Omar, see Al-Ahmadi [1966, 165–9]) from about 1896 to about 1903, and then briefly in the newly opened government vernacular school, before going to Mecca about 1905, and thence to Al-Azhar. He returned to Kota Bharu towards the end of 1914.

[55] For an account of To' Kenali's life and influence, see Abdullah, above.

[56] As neither the December 1907 *Notis* nor the Shari'a Court regulation of 1909 prescribed monetary fines (in lieu of or in addition to the older punishment of carting sand), it is unclear when these were introduced. They were certainly being levied by 1910, and were possibly an administrative innovation under the British.

Council had been asked to consider a proposal by the Sultan prohibiting Imam of *surau kechil* from enforcing attendance, and establishing exemptions for non-attendance at *surau besar* during rice planting and harvesting, during the floods of the rainy season, during the fasting month, and on public holidays.[57] A *Notis* to this effect (No. 9 of 1914) was passed on 30 August, despite protests by the Mufti, who objected especially to the relaxation of *surau kechil* regulations, on the ground that it was lawful, and indeed enjoined by the Shari'a, that people should pray in their own *surau*.[58] The immediate effect of the promulgation of this notice was drastically to reduce the amount taken in fines by the Shari'a and kathi's courts, and consequently the income of the Muhammadan Religious Fund.[59]

In April 1915, the Mufti found it necessary to ask the British Adviser for permission to transfer $100 from the account of the Muhammadan Religious Fund in the Pasir Puteh district treasury to that in Kota Bharu in order to pay the salaries of officials.[60] On inquiry by the Adviser, the State Treasurer confirmed that the amount standing to the credit of the Fund in Kota Bharu had fallen to a mere $29 after payment of $460 towards the Ramadhan, Prophet's Birthday, and *Mi'rāj* feasts in the Kota Bharu Mosque.[61] At the same time, the Mufti wrote also to the Sultan, complaining that 'Friday fines' had greatly fallen off, as indeed had attendance at the surau. It was clear, he said, that 'Friday fines' could no longer adequately supply the Muhammadan Religious Fund, and he

---

[57] Extract from Minutes of the State Council, 14 March 1914, Item 6, encl. in Kel. M. 62/1914; and cf. also the Adviser's minute dated 26 March, on *ibid.*, which records a conversation with Dato' Setia concerning the Sultan's wishes in the matter.

[58] The Mufti is said by the BA (minute dated 17 November, on *ibid.*) to have felt in addition that there would be popular resentment in some areas if people were forced to pray in the *surau besar* rather than in their more immediately local *surau kechil*. The view of the Sultan, on the other hand, was said to be that too many people attended only the small surau, leaving the larger without adequate congregations. One result of the dispute over this point (rather than over the interpretation of the Shari'a as such) was that while the new *Notis* continued to stand, the Sultan decided to get a more accurate measure taken of the population of individual *mukim surau*, a decision which led to the appointment of the first *Juru Sukat Sempadan Mukim* in 1915, as referred to above. The Mufti continued to press for stricter attendance regulations, as witnessed by his further correspondence with the BA, encl. in Kel. M. 184/1914.

[59] The amount on deposit to the credit of the Fund from 1910 to 1915, and the expenditure from 1912 to 1914, were as follows:

		On Deposit	Expended
As at December 31,	1910	$ 429	N.A.
	1911	283	N.A.
	1912	943	$1,763
	1913	1,069	1,368
	1914	715	1,030
	1915	18	N.A.

Source: *Kelantan Administration Reports*, 1911–1916, Appendix 'A'; and letter, Mufti to Office of BA, 20 July 1915, encl. in Kel. M. 71/1915.

[60] Letter, Mufti to Office of BA, 10 March 1915, encl. in Kel. M. 48/1915.

[61] Minuted on *ibid.*, 12 March.

suggested that if the ruler wished to increase the money available for expenditure on religious purposes there were two alternatives; either the old Friday prayer *Notis* should be revived (with exemptions solely for periods of flood), or the income from marriage and divorce registration fees should be used for religious purposes, as was the case in the FMS.[62] The Sultan forwarded this letter to the Adviser, supporting the latter proposal. The Pasir Puteh affair then intervened, but by late May the question had been raised again, this time by Dato' Setia, who merely sent to the office of the Adviser a bill for $60 for expenses in connection with *Mi'rāj* at the Kota Bharu Mosque, and asked that it be paid.[63] After some prevarication on the part of the British, who pointed out that expenses of this kind had not fallen on state funds in the past, payment was agreed to on the insistence of the Sultan. A month later Dato' Setia sent a second bill, for expenses incurred during the current period of Ramadhan.[64] Again the bill was paid, but the Adviser wrote to inform His Highness that this was not a charge that the state would in future be prepared to meet.[65] To this the Sultan replied, in unmistakably magisterial tones, that 'expenses for obligatory religious purposes in the Mosque are of great importance, concerning which it is proper that the Government make fixed provision in the annual Estimates of expenditure', and he suggested again that revenue derived from Muslim marriage and divorce fees be applied to this purpose.[66] Faced with this intransigence concerning a matter in which he himself was forbidden by treaty to interfere, the Adviser discovered upon inquiry that Muslim marriage and divorce registration brought in close to $12,000 a year,[67] and agreed henceforth to set aside the sum of $1,500 annually for the Muhammadan Religious Fund, on condition that all Shari'a and kathi's court fees and fines—including those for non-attendance at Friday prayers—be paid into the general revenue.[68] So, for the moment, was

[62] Letter, Mufti to Sultan Muhammad, 13 March 1915, encl. in Kel. PB. 108/1915.
[63] Letter, Dato' Bentara Setia to Office of BA, 29 May 1915, encl. in Kel. M. 71/1915.
[64] Letter, Dato' Bentara Setia to Office of BA, 26 June 1915, in *ibid*.
[65] Letter, BA to Sultan Muhammad, 29 June 1915, in *ibid*.
[66] Letter, Sultan Muhammad to BA, 24 Sha'ban 1333 (7 July 1915), in *ibid*. There is some reason to suppose that this letter may have been drafted by Dato' Setia.
[67] The exact figures, as supplied in a letter from the Mufti to the office of the Adviser, 20 July 1915, in *ibid*., were:

	1913	1914
Kota Bharu	$ 8,654	$10,298
Ulu Kelantan	527	528
Pasir Puteh	[1,881]	1,642
	$11,062	$12,468

In Pasir Puteh in 1913, total court revenues of $2,377 did not distinguish between fees and fines, but according to Langham-Carter (1914, Appendix 'A') the latter amounted to only $486.

[68] Minute by BA, 2 August 1915, on Kel. M. 71/1915. A fortnight later the Adviser went

the matter settled, though not without much irritation and frustration for the Malays involved, and a new recognition of the extent to which the governance of Islam, and the furtherance of specifically Islamic ends, had become dependent on largesse distributed by alien and non-Muslim officials.

Towards the end of 1915, a number of processes had come together to prompt a re-evaluation of the role of Islam in the state. These it is possible to review. In the most general way there was rising anxiety about the effects on Kelantan society of the incursion of outsiders of all kinds into the state. Though the movement of Chinese and Indians into Kelantan had been miniscule compared to the deluge that had afflicted the western states of the peninsula,[69] it was not negligible and had brought problems in its train. Attention is focussed upon some of these by certain of the *Notis* concerning religion and morality, of which eight were passed between March 1914 and December 1915 (out of a total of ten from 1910–15), at least five pertaining directly to the effects of increased contact with aliens. Notices prohibiting Malay participation in Chinese gambling by means of the card game known as '*daun cheki*' or '*daun sekopong*' were passed between March 1914 and November 1915; others forbidding for Malays the Chinese '*hua-hui*' lottery were promulgated in November 1914 and January 1915.[70] The *Notis* of 16 June 1915 already referred to, forbidding the consumption of alcohol by Malays as an offence against Shari'a law, testified to a cultural importation enjoyed by Europeans, Indians and Chinese alike; and similarly a notice forbidding the purchase or consumption of *chandu* (opium)

---

home on leave, being replaced by R. J. Farrer as Acting Adviser. The Sultan subsequently made it clear that on no account would he have Langham-Carter back in the state, writing to the High Commissioner in February 1916 that when he heard of this possibility, 'dire dismay seized me. . . . I look on such an idea with utter dislike'. (English translation of letter, Sultan Muhammad to High Commissioner, 8 February 1916, encl. in Desp., Conf., High Commissioner to Colonial Office, 25 February 1916, in CO 273/444).

[69] No figures are available prior to 1911, by which time a certain influx into the state had already begun. In that year, 9,844 Chinese were enumerated (7,225 men and 2,619 women), and 731 Indians (648 men and 83 women). By 1921, there were 12,755 Chinese (an increase of 30%) and no fewer than 3,575 Indians (an increase of some 400%); in both cases, but particularly in that of the Chinese, the sex ratio had deteriorated. While these figures have to be interpreted carefully, and Kelantan's population of 286,751 in 1911 and 309,300 in 1921 remained overwhelmingly Malay, there is no question but that some social effects were felt.

[70] No copy can be traced of the first '*daun cheki*' Notis (2/1914), but a copy of the second, which increased penalties for members of the Malay ruling class ('Tungkus, Ungkus or Datohs') (22/1915), is encl. in Kel. M. 184/1915 (and cf. also the letter requesting this, Sultan Muhammad to BA, 23 Zulhijah 1333 (31 October 1915), encl. in Kel. PB. 281/1915). A copy of the first '*hua-hui*' Notis (14/1914) is encl. in Kel. K. 88/1913, and of the second (unnumbered/1915) in Kel. K. 1265/1914.

by Malays outlawed for Muslims what was essentially a Chinese practice.[71] While it could scarcely be argued that Kelantan Malays were not at the best of times inveterate gamblers[72] (though there is little or no previous evidence for the use of opium or alcohol), it is clear that for the morally minded the new forms of gambling introduced by the Chinese constituted an added threat. At the same time, there was evidence of growing concern for the virtue of Kelantan girls at the hands of Indians and Chinese, adding a new and objectionable dimension to the old problem of prostitution. The Sultan himself, in September 1915, drew the attention of the British Adviser to complaints of 'Hindus and Chinese misusing Mulsim girls' and suggested a *Notis* proscribing this.[73] Later it was to be argued that the growing problem at this time of Malay girls disavowing Islam and turning apostate in order to avoid penalty for contracting Chinese marriages was the result of the lax enforcement of Shari'a law which, it was felt, characterised the first decade or so of British rule.[74]

In one sense or another, indeed, many if not most of the ills of the time might have been claimed to spring not just from British rule in general but from the way in which the British chose to comport themselves towards Islam—nominally unpartisan but in fact limiting (most of all when assisting in defining) and interfering. The problem of British rule *per se* had, of course, been drawn attention to by the Pasir Puteh revolt, for whether or not this was from the first and at all times directed at expulsion of the British from the state as a whole, the ease with which the British had put down the revolt and reasserted their authority, formally speaking in the name of the Sultan, had made it clear to all that if Kelantan independence was in any real sense to be maintained, this had to be done within the framework of a persisting British presence. The implications for Islam—which for many epitomised the essence of the Malay state, as opposed to the Western administrative forms that had been superimposed upon it—were brought home by the difficulties experienced throughout 1915 in carrying out everyday reli-

[71] A copy of the 'alcohol' *Notis* (12/1915) is encl. in Kel. M. 83/1915, and a copy of the '*chandu*' *Notis* (28/1915) in Kel. K. 1130/1915.
[72] A later anti-gambling notice, No. 5 of 1917 (copy encl. in Kel. M. 15/1917) listed by name no fewer than 33 different varieties of gambling game, by no means all of which appear to have been of Chinese inspiration. As early as 1910 the BA (Mason, 1910, 8) had remarked, perhaps over-complacently, 'Since British protection has been extended to Kelantan the practice of gambling in the Raja's Balai has been stopped'.
[73] Letter, Sultan Muhammad to BA, 6 Zulkaedah 1333 (14 September 1915), encl. in Kel. M. 139/1915 (copy also in Kel. PB. 237/1915). In response the Adviser minuted that 'we should try to do something to decrease the immorality that distinguishes Kota Bharu', and noted that he was enquiring of Johore and Kedah what measures were taken there.
[74] Secretary, Majlis Ugama, to Sultan Muhammad, 10 February 1920, encl. in Kel. PM. 63/1920.

gious administration in the face of tight British control of the purse strings. In other respects, too, it had become clear, especially perhaps to the ruler—who in May 1915 had been made aware at one and the same time of his political instability in relation to a section of his own family and ruling class and of his virtually unavoidable future reliance upon British support—that the institutional forms assumed by Islamic administration since the early century, though in some respects stating unmistakably the right of the ruler to act and arbitrate as defender of the faith, had also reared alternative bureaucratic and judicial sources of authority within the Muslim community to challenge his own. If the growth of powers vested explicitly in the Shari'a court had been arrested as the result of the course followed by the first British Advisers (and more recently by the Sultan himself), that of the Mufti had not. And it was with the Mufti acting as the apex of Shari'a court authority and as the administrator of an Islamic bureaucracy that the ruler now found himself increasingly in conflict. Though the crucial area of difference related to interpretation of the law concerning *harta pesaka* (inheritance) and *bayt ul-māl*,[75] it is evident that more general tensions existed affecting such matters as the organization of surau, the powers of Imam, and similar concerns at the village or 'constituency' level.

Finally, Kelantan Islam, as we have seen, had reacted before to cultural assault and social upheaval by a self-strengthening of its moral foundations and a renewed insistence on Shari'a law. In the present crisis Islam again appeared to many of the concerned to offer, indeed to command, the only positive solution. In the meantime, however, between 1890 and 1915, a new generation of *ulama* had been reared which increasingly saw Islam not merely as a way of reviving or reasserting the past but as a means of determining the future. It is from the general ambience of this generation that the creative response to the problems of the time that the Majlis Ugama represented may be said to have emerged. It was no accident that in his first public pronouncement concerning the Majlis the Sultan was moved to describe as one of its principal tasks that of raising Kelantan 'to a status consonant with that of other advanced states'. This was not a merely theological, doctri-

[75] '*Bayt ul-māl*' (Ar., public treasury) was used in the Malay states to denote the repository for wealth accruing to the Muslim community as a whole as a result of operation of Shari'a law, especially in relation either to succession without heirs, or to division of property upon death where canonically prescribed heirs were insufficient to exhaust the property. Cases of the latter sort, in particular, had been at issue between the Sultan and the Mufti, the Sultan arguing that where heirs existed the estate should be divided fully among them, the Mufti that in specific cases this should not be done and the resulting balance paid into *bayt ul-māl* (see, e.g., the case dealt with at some length in Kel. PB. 60/1915, which began in February 1915, and also Note 98, below, which refers to some of the outcome).

nal or ethical argument. Nor, though reformist ideologies played some part and will repay study in this context as they have in others, was it much related to the classical *kaum muda—kaum tua* debates of the time.[76] The British, in six years of rule, had failed miserably (in part, certainly, because they were constricted by budgetary difficulties of inordinate magnitude)[77] visibly to advance the fortunes of the state and its people, the one thing which, arguably, might have been expected of them in their self-imposed role. A handful of government schools (only three in government-provided buildings) all with small enrolments, poorly equipped and teaching at best the three R's; a few roads and public buildings, principally in Kota Bharu; administrative departments which employed at the top too great a proportion of non-Kelantanese; these things scarcely constituted a social revolution. The failure underscored the belief that if modernization were to come, it had best come at the hands of the Kelantanese themselves, using the cultural forms at their disposal.

When Dato' Setia and Haji Muhammad b. Khatib Haji Mohd. Said took their proposal for the creation of the Majlis Ugama to the Sultan sometime towards the end of 1915, as it is understood they did,[78] there is no knowing how many of these diverse ends they had in mind or presented to the ruler. The appearance that the Majlis tends to present in retrospect—of a clever and calculated attempt to kill a covey of birds with one stone—is almost certainly misleading. Nevertheless, as a prelude to more detailed discussion one may perhaps be forgiven for phrasing it in this way. By putting the future of Islam and of Islamic institutions into committee, a committee in which, by definition, no one man could expect to become all-powerful, and by in addition making the committee dependent on the ruler for its being, its continued existence, and in a measure its revenues, it greatly strengthened the position of the Sultan (and his immediate advisers) vis-à-vis both secular and sacerdotal rivals—at once demonstrating his continued concern to function as the

[76] For a discussion of some of these in Malaya, see, e.g., Roff (1962, 162 ff).
[77] Without embarking on a lengthly excursus concerning public finance in Kelantan, it may be noted that while the revenues of the state had risen from just under $400,000 in 1909 to nearly $700,000 in 1915, this did not constitute a remarkably rapid rate of growth, and in addition the state had become indebted to the FMS in 1912 to the amount of some $2½ million, for cancellation of part of the Duff Concession. Annual expenditures invariably exceeded revenue (except in 1913), and the costs of the Pasir Puteh revolt in 1915 added further problems. By the end of 1915 the state had an excess of liabilities over assets of some $3½ million. For a summary presentation, see, e.g., Farrer (1918, 1).
[78] Accounts by numerous informants suggest this, though no details are available and nothing appears in the written records. To' Kenali's association with the scheme at this point is also unclear.

religious leader of his people and acting to provide him with a secure base for the exercise of power. At the same time (and here the crux of the Majlis really lay) it was made financially independent by allocating to it on a systematic basis some two-thirds of 'the ruler's share' of the compulsory zakat tax, giving it a regular and assured income which, while freeing it from direct reliance upon the British, made it possible for the Majlis itself to act as an agent for growth.

Aside from its organizational coherence and financial independence, the most striking difference between the Kelantan Majlis and those *ad hoc* committees of State Council and the like which, in the other Malay states, served roughly similar if unintegrated functions with respect to Islam, was its composition. In Selangor, Perak or Johore for example, such bodies as existed to oversee the administration of Islam were conceived strictly within the framework of the traditional aristocratic society, and of those formulae which specified dual attention to 'religion and Malay custom.'[79] In consequence they were heavily dominated by non-*alim* members of the ruling house and the hereditary aristocracy. In Kelantan, by contrast, though the Majlis was nominally made responsible for matters of 'custom' as well as religion, the circumstances under which it came into being dictated both a very different composition and different tasks. Of the twelve members named by the Sultan to the State Council early in December 1915 there were, in order of mention (an order not to be supposed accidental, and almost certainly drawn up with some care by Dato' Setia), the following: four recognised *ulama*—To' Kenali; Haji Wan Muhammad b. Abdul Samad, senior imam of the Kota Bharu Mosque and brother to the then Mufti;[80] and the two khatib of the Mosque, Haji Mohd. Said b. Jamaluddin, currently also in charge of the Land Office, and Haji Wan Abdullah b. Abdul Samad, another brother of the Mufti; five appointive civil servants, two of commoner origin (Mohd. Ghazali b. Arifin, a Singaporean and governments upervisor of schools, entitled Dato' Bentara Luar,[81] and Mohd. Daud b. Salim, previously 'Che' Wok' of the Land Office and shortly to be made Dato' Isti'adat, or palace cham-

---

[79] See, e.g., Roff (1967, 72-4), and Sadka (1969, 265-71).

[80] From 31 December 1915 Haji Wan Muhammad was also Hakim of the Shari'a Court, succeeding Haji Ahmad b. Haji Abdul Manan, who, having expressed a wish to resign in 1912 had it acceded to by the Sultan, at somewhat short notice, in December 1915 (letter, Sultan Muhammad to Haji Ahmad, 12 Safar 1334 [20 December 1915], encl. in Kel. PB. 330/1915). It seems clear, especially in view of later developments, that the Sultan wished to advance Wan Muhammad.

[81] Mohd. Ghazali had come to Kelantan in 1900 as a clerk to Muhammad IV and teacher to the latter's son Ismail (later Sultan). In January 1905 he was appointed head teacher of the government vernacular school in Kota Bharu, in 1911 being made 'Visiting Teacher' for the state. He was created Dato' Bentara Luar in 1911.

berlain), two from middle-rank old families loyal to the throne (Nik Ja'afar b. Haji Nik Abdul Kadir, a palace official recently entitled Dato' Bentara Dalam, and Nik Wan Mohd. Amin b. Wan Musa, Hakim of the *Mahkamah Adat* [customary-law court], a largely ceremonial office), and the sole member of royal blood initially appointed, Tengku Abdul Rahman b. Sultan Muhammad III, who was government superintendent of To' Kweng and a younger brother of the ruler; one 'businessman', Tambi Omar b. Tambi Kechik, a Malay of Indian extraction from Penang who owned a rubber estate and some town property; and the twin official progenitors of the Majlis, Dato' Bentara Setia (effectively, by this time, chief minister of the state)[82] and, as a fifth *alim*, Haji Muhammad b. Khatib Haji Mohd. Said, who at first held no other appointment but in March 1916 became 2nd Assistant Secretary to the ruler and was then, or shortly thereafter, created Dato' Bentara Jaya. Haji Muhammad was named Secretary to the Majlis, but it was left to the members to elect their own President (*Yang di-Pertuan*). Diplomatically, perhaps, they went outside their own ranks to the Sultan's son-in-law, Tengku Muda Hassan b. Tengku Muhammad, at that time a judge of the High Court.

Much of the politics of the Majlis, it may be suggested, is immediately clear from its membership. Those excluded were precisely those by whom the Sultan at the time felt himself most threatened—the members of the royal family with whom he had had political differences during the Pasir Puteh revolt, and most notably the Mufti, Haji Wan Musa, whose absence from a council of religion that was about to assume a large number of his existing functions is striking. Equally, most of those included were manifestly the ruler's own men, and in some cases (especially the civil servants) his own creations. Much of the functional bias given to the Majlis is also clear, from the very high proportion of *ulama* within it (five of the original twelve), who could be expected to give some real Islamic content to its deliberations and the imprimatur of theological respectability—though it should be noted that it was not, in the cant term, markedly *kaum muda* in composition, the most radical member probably being the secretary, Haji Muhammad.

All members of the Majlis served without remuneration, though all except To' Kenali, it may be observed, were then or shortly thereafter in receipt of regular salaries for other services. Forced, to begin with, to

[82] The old Dato' Mentri, whether for reasons of age or ill-health (he died in 1921, aged over 70) or because of residual doubts as to his loyalty to the throne during the Pasir Puteh revolt (see the British Adviser's comments on the Maxwell and Farrer reports, *op. cit.*), had become ineffective, though he did not resign officially until 1917 (see Kel. K. 611/1911).

conduct their business in entirely unsatisfactory quarters—the house of Dato' Setia, and then, for the rest of 1916, three cramped rooms in the upper storey of the Land Office building—they nevertheless entered into their work with great energy and enthusiasm. In the course of the first year, 37 formal meetings were held, and it is clear from the attendance record that an inner cabal rapidly emerged, which was to be the real driving force behind the council—Dato' Setia (in November 1916 made Vice-President because of the persistent illness of Tengku Muda Hassan), Haji Muhammad, Khatib Mohd. Said, Imam (and Hakim) Wan Muhammad, and Tengku Abdul Rahman.[83]

Islam in Kelantan, as we have seen, had already been bureaucratized in considerable degree, by a variety of statutory enactments and administrative regulations and practices. All that the Majlis now had to do, to establish its authority, was to take the machinery over and adapt it to its own ends and ideals. This process occupied much of the early and middle part of 1916, bringing in its train a structural revolution of some consequence. The first step, and that which in the long run made all the others possible, was the assumption of control over the collection and disbursement of zakat. By a *Notis* (3/1916) drafted by the Majlis and passed in State Council on 25 January 1916, the Majlis became, in effect, the recipient of some two-fifths of all zakat levied in the state.[84] In substance the measure was not very dissimilar to previous notices on the subject, in that the *nisab* was fixed at 400 *gantang* (Malay gallons) of padi (unhusked rice), anyone harvesting more than this being obliged to deliver 25 gantang to the Imam of his *surau besar*, in return for the proper receipt. As before, of the total amount taken by the Imam two-fifths was to be devoted to the needs of the surau and its officials.[85] Provision for the remaining three-fifths was, however, somewhat altered, for whereas by the requirements then in force (principally the surau regulation of August 1908, Sections 11 and 23), Imam had merely

---

[83] Khatib Haji Mohd. Said and Haji Muhammad were, of course, father and son, and Dato' Setia had married Haji Muhammad's elder sister Eshah. The two families—and in particular Dato' Setia and Haji Muhammad and their descendants—continued to dominate Kelantan politics for many years, and remain powerful today. The Majlis played a not unimportant role in ensuring this, especially through its command of (secular) educational and other resources.

[84] In the event the proportion was somewhat larger, at least for the early years. See, e.g., the first *Kenyataan* (Annual Report) of the Majlis (manuscript, encl. in Kel. PM. 8/1917 and Kel. M. 133/1917), p. 1, which details the year's finances. Note that by the amending *Notis* No. 8 of 1916 (18 April 1916) most of Ulu Kelantan was excluded from zakat collection, because of difficulties of administration. A copy of this last *Notis* is encl. in Kel. M. 173/1913.

[85] Of the two-fifths, half was to be retained by the senior Imam for upkeep of the surau, and the other half to be divided into sixths, 3/6 going jointly to the two Imam, 2/6 to the two khatib, and 1/6 to the two bilal. Imam were also given small commissions for prompt remittance of zakat to Kota Bharu.

to deliver the proceeds of this portion of the zakat to Kota Bharu for proper distribution by the the ruler (on the basis of one-third of the amount for the poor and needy and similar categories, and the remaining two-thirds for the three central mosques), it was now determined that after retention of the surau two-fifths Imam should sell the remainder of the padi (at a price to be fixed annually by the Majlis) and the whole of the proceeds be deposited in the government treasury. Of this sum, one-third was to be paid out again to the ruler, for the charitable purposes referred to, and the remainder to stand to the account of the Majlis Ugama, to pay its own staff and after that to disburse as it should think fit, for the upkeep and improvement of the central mosques or 'for such other religious purposes as it may decide upon'. In fact what the Majlis did was to put all officials of the central mosques on fixed salaries (for the first time), provide a certain amount for celebration of the three main festivals in the Kota Bharu Mosque and elsewhere, and, at the end of its first year, emerge with a credit balance of some $7,000.[86]

With this success behind it, the Majlis decided in the following year, 1917, to put collection of the *fitrah*[87] on a similar footing, something that had never been done successfully before,[88] the fitrah being generally regarded as Shari'a enjoined alms which might be distributed at will to recipients selected by the giver. Though in practice fitrah, when paid, was often given at least in part to surau officials, it was also customary to reward in this way religious teachers, midwives, and others who had performed practical or ritual services during the year. The long preamble to the first *Notis* concerning fitrah, passed by the State Council on 17 April 1917 (11/1917), suggests recognition of the fact that while systematic collection of zakat and application of the surplus, especially to mosque and surau maintenance, had long been accepted, any attempt to centralize and make fitrah collection compulsory was likely to meet with some resentment. Fitrah was, however, said the preamble, to be

[86] This was reached much as follows (discrepancies in totals accounted for by rounding off):

	Income		Expenditure
Zakat, 21 May–24 Dec.	$12,264	Salaries, 3 Mosques	$3,295
Bayt ul-māl	111	Majlis staff & exps.	168
Other	94	Commissions to Imams	31
		Payment to Sultan	2,000
		Miscellaneous	102
	$12,469		$5,596
		Balance	$6,873

Source: *Kenyataan* Majlis Ugama for 1916, op. cit., p. 1.

[87] Fitrah (*zakāt al-fiṭr*) is the annual gift of alms, made in the Malay states in the form of husked rice and hence known as '*beras fitrah*', payable at the end of the fasting month.

[88] The only reference to any earlier collection occurs in the preamble to the 1917 '*fitrah*' *Notis*, which suggests that around 1902 some attempt was made to legislate for this. No trace of the legislation survives, and it was not repeated or referred to in the interim.

devoted to quite specific ends, it being the desire of the Sultan not only to spread the influence of Islam by provision of places suitable for the proper performance of all religious obligations, but to seek means of advancing the state and enabling all its sons to reach the heights of worldly achievement as well as favour in the hereafter by providing schools for the teaching of all kinds of knowledge and skill, in every mukim and district of Kelantan. The regulations that followed used complex formulae, but in essence required all households in the state to pay approximately half the customary fitrah of one gantang of husked rice per person to the Imam of their surau. Of this amount, one-eighth (later amended to one-fifth)[89] was to be retained by the surau for its own purposes, and the remainder sold and the proceeds sent to the treasury account of the Majlis Ugama, which would use the money to build mosques and schools. In the first year of operation of both zakat and fitrah collection, 1917, the Majlis found itself in receipt of no less than $29,000—$10,515 in zakat and $18,712 in fitrah—and at the end of the year had a credit balance of more than $20,000 after expenditure.

So much, for the moment, for the financial resources with which the Majlis was able to provide itself, remedying all the purely fiscal problems of the past. Returning to the early part of 1916, the structural revolution in the administration of Islam wrought at this time was achieved primarily by stripping the Mufti of most of the executive and administrative authority (and eventually much of the judicial authority) that had accrued to this office during the previous decade, and substituting for it the authority of the committee, the Majlis Ugama. It has already been noted that the Mufti was not a member of the Majlis. By a brief *Notis* of 18 April 1916 (10/1916)[90] the Surau regulation of 1908 was repealed, and it was provided that henceforth the Majlis Ugama should be the sole *Nazir* (supervisor) of all mosques and surau and their personnel in the state, in terms to be set out shortly in a further enactment. It was expressly forbidden for anyone other than the Majlis or the Sultan to interfere in such supervision, and surau officials were instructed to refer all matters for decision to the Majlis Ugama. Given that the village surau (there were 261 in the state at this time)[91] constituted the irreducible basis of Islamic administration throughout Kelantan, it was clear that the Mufti's authority in this respect had been undercut com-

[89] By *Notis* 25/1919 of 9 September 1919.
[90] Copy encl. in Kel. M. 192/1916.
[91] *Kenyataan* Majlis Ugama for 1916 (encl. in Kel. PB. 8/1917 and Kel. K. 133/1917), para 12. Of these 235 were *surau besar* and 26 *surau kechil*.

pletely. Haji Wan Musa reacted by asking (be it noted) the British Adviser, firstly whether the then Travelling Teacher might be appointed *Penolong Mufti* (Assistant Mufti),[92] and secondly for a ruling upon whether the Demarcators of Mukim Boundaries were to remain under the Mufti's control.[93] The first enquiry was referred to the Sultan, who replied that as the duties of the Mufti had now been much reduced there was no case for the appointment of an assistant.[94] Concerning the second enquiry, which had been raised also by the Majlis in connection not just with the demarcators but with the *Pemereksa Jumaat* (Friday inspectors), the Adviser minuted that all matters, and all state officials, connected with mosques and surau had been transferred entirely to the Majlis.[95] It is clear that at this time there may have been some misgivings on the part of certain members of the Majlis about the all-embracing powers it was taking unto itself, and the letter addressed by four of them to the president (and forwarded to the Sultan) on or about 13 May, complaining that the Majlis had as yet no constitution, and asking for its powers to be defined in consultation with the members,[96] certainly represented anxieties of some sort—though whether in the interests of what was proper according to Shari'a law or because of residual concern about the position of the Mufti is not apparent. In either event, the processes now in train were not arrested.

Sometime probably in late June 1916, Mufti Haji Wan Musa b. Abdul Samad resigned, and was replaced on 21 August by his brother, Haji Wan Muhammad, who was already Hakim of the Shari'a court[97] —though ironically the departure of Wan Musa did not give victory

[92] Minute by BA, 29 April 1916, on Kel. K. 303/1916.
[93] Minute by BA, 29 April 1916, on Kel. K. 304/1916.
[94] Minute by BA, 16 May 1916, on Kel. K. 303/1916.
[95] Minute by BA, 11 May 1916, on Kel. K. 304/1916. Cf. also, letter, Secretary Majlis Ugama to Dato' Bentara Setia, 10 May 1916, encl. in Kel. PB. 113/1916.
[96] Letter from To' Kenali, Nik Min [Nik Wan Mohd. Amin], Khatib Haji Wan Abdullah, and Imam Haji Wan Muhammad, to Yang di-Pertuan Majlis Ugama, date illegible, in letter, Secretary Majlis Ugama to Dato' Bentara Setia, 13 May 1916, encl. in Kel. PB. 114/1916. It may be noted that two of the signatories, Wan Abdullah and Wan Muhammad, were brothers of the Mufti, but it is not clear whether this was relevant. Wan Muhammad was to succeed his brother as Mufti some three months later, upon the latter's resignation. Cf. Muhammad Salleh, below, for divergent views on zakat, which may also have been to the point.
[97] Sultan Muhammad to Haji Wan Muhammad, 21 August 1916, encl. in Kel. PB. 204/1916. The posts of Mufti and Hakim Mahkamah Shari'a were held concurrently until December 1919, when at the suggestion of Dato' Setia (by this time Dato' Sri Paduka Raja) Wan Muhammad was made a member of the State Council, and his recently appointed Assistant Mufti, Wan Hassan b. Haji Wan Muhammad, succeeded him as Hakim—a post which was henceforth, however, styled merely *Kathi Besar* (Chief Kathi) of Kelantan, the term 'Shari'a court' at long last being dropped for good (Kel. PM. 239/1919). The apparent judicial impropriety of acting at one and the same time as Hakim of the Shari'a court and as Mufti was lessened in view of the fact that from the date of Haji Wan Muhammad's appointment as Mufti appeals from the Shari'a court were heard not by the Mufti alone but by the Majlis Ugama.

to the Sultan in the *Bayt ul-māl* question which had been such a source of discord between them.⁹⁸ His resignation, however, removed the last powerful functionary of the pre-Majlis regime, and it was presumably no accident that Wan Muhammad's appointment as Mufti was followed a day later by the passage through the State Council of a new Shari'a Court *Notis* and a new and full Mosques and Surau enactment elaborating the brief *Notis* passed earlier in April. The Shari'a Court *Notis* (19/1916), aside from continuing the process of restricting the powers of the court to deal with inheritance cases,⁹⁹ listed fourteen matters in which the court had original jurisdiction, from questions relating to marriage, divorce and maintenance, to *khalwat*, breach of the fast, absenteeism from Friday prayers, wrongful teachings, and other specified offences against Shari'a law, appeal in all cases lying not, as before, to the Mufti, but to the Majlis Ugama. The mosques enactment, 'Undang2 dan Peraturan bagi Masjid dan Surau' (Enactment No. 10 of 1916), though introducing little of substance that was new, beyond formalizing even further all processes connected with village surau and with the duties of their Imam and other officials, was principally important for the fact that it gave the Majlis Ugama, as Nazir of all mosques and surau, the right to appoint, promote or dismiss all mosque or surau officials (subject only to the approval of the Sultan), to issue Imam with written *kuasa* (appended as schedules to the enactment) setting out their responsibilities to the Majlis as well as to the inhabitants of their mukim, to settle disputes and to use the To' Kweng to investi-

---

⁹⁸ The Sultan's position on this was clear in principle (see Note 75, above), and appears to be evidenced further by an extract from the Minutes of the State Council for 16 June 1915, recording that the Sultan did not agree that heirs should (in all cases?) inherit according to Shari'a law (minute by British Adviser, undated, on Kel. K. 639/1916). After continued differences of opinion between Sultan and Mufti it was decided by the State Council on 30 June 1916 (arguably in favour of the Sultan, and apparently shortly after the resignation of Wan Musa as Mufti) that where heirs existed the estate might be divided fully among them, although the words 'according to Shari'a law' appear to have been added. The Adviser minuted finally, however (on *ibid.*, and also undated), that on 17 October 1916 the State Council agreed to rescind its resolution of 15 June 1915, with the result that the right of *Bayt ul-māl* to receive residual portions of estates was upheld (thus seemingly supporting the ex-Mufti's views), the Majlis Ugama to act as administrator on behalf of the *Bayt ul-māl*. Cf. also the letter, Dato' Bentara Setia to High Court and eight others, 6 November 1916, which confirms this interpretation. Adequate assessment of this complex question, which was undoubtedly of political importance, is hampered by the relative absence of case materials, but cf. also Muhammad Salleh, below, p. 156, and Note 11.

⁹⁹ For the original British action in this respect, resulting in the removal from the jurisdiction of the court in 1910 of all land inheritance cases below $500 in value, see above, Note 39, and the text at that point. In 1914, the Adviser obtained the further agreement of the Sultan to exclude from the jurisdiction of the court all inheritance cases where the property was over $500 in value and in dispute, subject only to the possibility that the Mufti might sit as assessor in the civil court hearing the case. Now, in 1916, the competence of the Shari'a court was limited in inheritance cases to property valued at less than $100.

gate surau affairs, and to be consulted on all *fatwa* other than those issued in strict accordance with the Shāfi'ī school or in highly special circumstances. Finally, in October 1916, the capstone was set on the legal, judicial, administrative, doctrinal and other powers of the Majlis Ugama, by the passage, already referred to at the beginning of this article, of the 'Rules for the Members of the Council' (Enactment No. 14 of 1916), which instructed them, among other things, to 'guard, advise, arrange, give legal *fatwa* concerning, originate, strengthen, implement, develop, and administer all matters relating to the practice and performance of the Muslim religion and Islamic law, for the benefit of the state and its people'.[100]

How, then, did the Majlis actually use the resources of power and money now at its disposal? Part of its custodial function related to the maintenance of morality, good behaviour, and the proper practice of Islam in the state, but even in this area of interest (which it pursued, it must be confessed, with some vigour) it showed for the most part a spirit of innovation and reform which had been absent during previous periods in Kelantan of chastisement of backsliders. Few of the measures it prompted were entirely negative, save perhaps for the sabbatarian impulse reflected in the *Notis* of 18 April 1916 (11/1916) which forbade performance of 'noisy' entertainments (such as the *Mak Yong*, *menora* and *wayang kulit* theatres) on Thursday evenings, on the eve of other holy days, and during the fasting month, and the *Notis* of 23 September 1917 (32/1917) which forbade the comic or irreverent use of religious terms, references or quotations in theatrical performances. It is true, also, that the Majlis shared the concern of its predecessors to ensure regular attendance at Friday prayers (*Notis* 27/1916 of 7 November 1916), and that in 1917 two measures were passed, one prohibiting the 'excesses' of religious enthusiasm associated with some of the Sufi orders of mysticism and requiring all persons wishing to teach any *ilmu* impliedly of a Sufistic sort to obtain authority from the Majlis Ugama (*Notis* 18/1917 of 15 May 1917);[101] the other (*Notis* 45/1917 of 18

[100] See above, p. 102. There remains some confusion over whether this was technically a Notice or an Enactment, though the available copy is entitled 'Undang2'. Farrer (1917, 6) refers to it as a Notice, and the subsequent Adviser minuted on 15 March 1919 (on Kel. M. 239/1916, in which a Malay typescript of the document is enclosed) that it was apparently not numbered as an Enactment.

[101] This *Notis* was prompted by agitation arising from the presence of one Shaykh Abu Hassan al-Azahari, a Sufi *shaykh* of the Ahmadiyyah *tarekat*, who came to Kelantan from Mecca at about this time, and was allegedly taken up by, among others, the ex-Mufti, Haji Wan Musa. The Kota Bharu religious establishment, represented by the Majlis, was hostile to Shaykh Azahari, and following an appeal to the Sultan in early May (letter, Secretary Majlis Ugama to Sultan Muhammad, 8 May 1917, encl. in Kel. PM. 79/1917) the State Council issued an expulsion order on 15 May. He was subsequently allowed to return to Kelantan in 1922 (see Kel. M. 14/1922 and Kel. PM. 28/1922).

December 1917) forbidding the issuance of any *fatwa* without prior approval of the Majlis, and establishing *fatwa* so issued or approved as the final word on the question concerned.[102]

In some respects, however, even in relation to the control of public behaviour, the Majlis may be said to have been ahead of its time. Where the old and intractable problem of prostitution was concerned, there was some recognition of it as a social and not merely a moral problem, and though initially the rather draconian legislation of the past was merely revived,[103] the Majlis empowered itself to order the removal of 'notorious' prostitutes (and pimps) from Kota Bharu and other towns (where the trade was mainly plied), not merely as a form of banishment but in the hope of reasserting the stronger social controls of village society.[104] In November 1916 it was proposed, even more imaginatively, that a financial inducement of $20 be offered to any man prepared to marry a prostitute on the Majlis 'list', on condition that there be no divorce for at least a year.[105] A quite specific problem for Kelantan women was taken under consideration early in 1919 (though the Majlis' share in this is not altogether clear), with discussion in the State Council concerning the number of Kelantan women married by Indian merchants (known generally as '*orang Kabuli*' or Afghans) and subsequently deserted when their husbands moved on. A *Notis* of 23 September 1919 (27/1919) laid down extremely stringent undertakings about maintenance and other matters required in writing from all 'Indians' before marriage to Kelantan women was permitted.[106] In the field of penology, the Majlis proposed in November 1916 to appoint teachers of religion to the police force, and, more importantly, to the jail,

---

[102] On 24 January 1918 the Majlis established a '*Meshuarat Ulama*' (Conference of '*Ulamā*') 'to answer all disputed questions and all enquiries concerning Shari'a law', and in effect to assume the Majlis' responsibility for issuing and approving *fatwa* (*Kenyataan Majlis Ugama* for 1918 [encl. in Kel. K. 510/1919], para 13(2)). This council or committee appears to have been composed of the *ulama* members of the Majlis, with some additions, but its composition at this time is vague. Most of the *Meshuarat Ulama*'s decisions were publicized in *Pengasoh*, after that journal's inauguration later in the year, and many of them appear to have been written by To' Kenali, who was prominent in the Meshuarat (cf. Abdullah, above).

[103] See, e.g., *Notis* 5/1916 of 1 February 1916, which was drafted by the Majlis in response to a petition from eleven Kota Bharu residents, dated 29 December 1915 (Kel. PB. 3/1916).

[104] This legislation (*Notis* 26/1916 of 7 February 1916) was later amended by *Notis* 3/1919 and 7/1919 (14 January and 25 February 1919) to require prior approval of the State Council and a court order issued by either the Shari'a or a kathi's court before such removal was legally enforceable.

[105] See letter, Yang di-Pertuan Majlis Ugama to Sultan Muhammad, 6 November 1916, encl. in Kel. PB. 266/1916. The Sultan, while approving in general, reduced the sum payable to $10. It is not known how well the scheme worked subsequently, but four such marriages took place in the two months up to the end of 1916 (see *Kenyataan Majlis Ugama* for 1916, *op. cit.*, p. 1).

[106] See Kel. PM. 115/1919. An additional copy of the *Notis* is encl. in Kel. M. 148/1919.

arguing that most people in jail were there as a result of ignorance and that religious teaching should help to make them better citizens.[107] Rather similarly, referring in 1917 to the large number of convictions for petty theft, it thought the root cause was gambling, especially by young people, and regretted that there was no juvenile court able to deal with the problem, nor adequate facilities for education.[108] The Majlis even turned its attention to public health, making a series of recommendations involving the systematic removal of night soil (preferably by convicts, thus acting as a deterrent to crime!), and its subsequent incineration, and for the installation of state-provided latrines in villages where no latrines existed, a small charge to be made per household.[109]

The most striking evidence, however, of the Majlis' forward-looking characteristics, and concern for the modernization and material progress of the state, is seen in its plans for education and for the associated activities of translation and publishing. Though, as we shall see, some conflict of demand developed between the claims of education, as recognized by the Majlis itself, and those of mosque provision and maintenance, accepted as a prime responsibility both in terms of its original mandate and in relationship especially to its zakat income,[110] the forces of education proved for the time being the stronger. In November 1916 the president of the Majlis reported to the ruler that it had decided at a recent meeting to ask to be permitted to appoint someone to translate from the Arabic books containing knowledge useful for the administration and conduct of affairs of state, and secondly for permission to open a school in Kota Bharu at Majlis expense,[111] and to prepare text-books

[107] Letter, Yang di-Pertuan Majlis Ugama to Sultan Muhammad, 6 November 1916, encl. in Kel. PB. 265/1916. The proposal was approved by the ruler on condition that costs were met by the Majlis, and appointments were made in 1917.

[108] Letter, Secretary Majlis Ugama to Sultan Muhammad, 8 January 1917, encl. in Kel. PM. 18/1917. As one result of the lengthy consideration clearly given to this matter, the anti-gambling *Notis* 5/1917, of 24 January 1917, was passed by the State Council, providing differential penalties for youths and older men.

[109] See the minuted discussion between the British Adviser (to whom the Majlis had addressed its recommendations) and the Residency Surgeon, on Kel. K. 91/1917. The Adviser commented (24 January 1917) that, 'As things are most of the night soil goes into the river—where it does no harm?', but the Surgeon replied (31 January) that incineration was by far the best way of getting rid of human faeces, and supported the Majlis' proposal for Kota Bharu. In due course—that is to say, by July 1919—an incinerator was installed.

[110] The *Kenyataan* Majlis Ugama for 1916, *op. cit.*, para 14, in addition to making general remarks in this context, had drawn attention to the very poor state of repair of the Kota Bharu Mosque in particular, and to interim measures that would be undertaken to remedy something of this. For some, however, expectations were larger, including apparently the British Adviser, who wrote (Farrer, 1917, 11) that as a result of the efforts of the Majlis, 'it is hoped that in a very few years the Kota Bharu mosque will be rebuilt and be a credit instead of a disgrace to the country'.

[111] At Majlis expense, except that the government was to be asked to restore the $300 p.a. paid as salary to a teacher in the Kota Bharu Mosque from 1903 until the post was abolished at the request of the Sultan in 1913 (see corresp. encl. in Kel. K. 596/1913). This was agreed to.

for the use of students. Such a proposal, it was felt, would result in the establishment of an educational institution which would become a seed-bed for progress among the young of the state.[112] Referring again to the project in its first annual report, the Majlis emphasized that the proposed school would concern itself with 'all forms' of education, not just the teaching of Islam.[113]

The idea was developed further in a second letter to the ruler the following April, in the context of a discussion concerning the necessary premises for the school, for which it was proposed that the Majlis purchase the house of the recently retired Dato' Mentri at a price of $15,000.[114] By this time the decision had been taken to institutionalize *fitrah* as well as zakat collection, and to devote the proceeds from the former specifically to education as well as mosque development, and the Majlis felt itself on surer ground both financially and morally. The education to be provided in the Majlis school, it explained to the ruler, would, in so far as it was religious education, be directed to the production of kathis, imams, and similar learned officials. In addition, however, tuition would be provided in the many subjects then so necessary, it was suggested, such as English and (Western) law, so that within five or six years the government service would be able to draw most of its recruits from this source. Further, a proportion of graduates would themselves become teachers in other schools throughout the state, which would in turn improve these schools and thus benefit the whole of Kelantan and make famous the name of the ruler.[115] The plan was a sweeping, even an exciting one and on 5 August 1917 the new 'Madrasah Muhammadi', named after the Sultan, was formally opened by him in the presence of the British Adviser and a large gathering of notables.[116]

[112] Letter, Yang di-Pertuan Majlis Ugama to Sultan Muhammad, 6 November 1916, encl. in Kel. PB. 264/1916. The terms used in this last sentence were those normally used with reference to rice cultivation.
[113] *Kenyataan* Majlis Ugama for 1916, *op. cit.*, para 14.
[114] The house, facing the main *Padang* (town green) and close by the Kota Bharu Mosque, was in an ideal situation, and had been valued six years previously by the Director of Works, at $13,000, though the Adviser, when approached for the government loan needed by the Majlis thought a more suitable location might be found, 'some way away from the Padang—*and the ladies who frequent it*' (italics in original). The secretary of the Majlis replied that in order to get away from 'the ladies' it would be necessary leave town altogether, that the Majlis had for long wished to open a 'College', and that this seemed an excellent and reasonably priced building. The loan was made (corresp. and minutes in Kel. M. 87/1917). The building, in addition to housing the school, also housed the offices of the Majlis, which last it continues to do today.
[115] Letter, Secretary Majlis Ugama to Sultan Muhammad, 23 April 1917, encl. in Kel. PM. 68/1917.
[116] On 15 August the Madrasah Muhammadi was visited by the High Commissioner, in the course of an official visit to the state. The Adviser reported later (Farrer, 1918, 10) that His Excellency had 'addressed a few words of advice for the boys, which words are recorded and preserved with the utmost pride by the managers of the school'. Tact was ever a Malay virtue.

It had, in effect, three divisions, though one was for the moment separate: a Malay vernacular school, with some eight teachers; an English school, with two teachers; and the older 'Arabic' or traditional religious school, which was now conducted under Majlis auspices, but situated as before in the Kota Bharu Mosque, next door to the Madrasah Muhammadi. From the start, the Madrasah was an enormous success, enrolment in the vernacular division rising to 310 by the end of 1917, including thirty boys who left the government vernacular school in Kota Bharu to join.[117] The following year the Majlis opened new vernacular schools in Pasir Puteh and Pasir Mas, and some time later in Kampong Kutan; total enrolments continued to rise, reaching nearly 500 by the end of the decade. In September 1918, the British Adviser (Farrer) proposed that in view of the educational accomplishments of the Majlis, all government vernacular schools in the state be transferred to its supervision, and he drafted the annual Estimates for 1919 accordingly, only to have the proposal disallowed by the High Commissioner's staff in Singapore.[118] Where its English division was concerned, with an enrolment of some thirty boys at first, rising to 58 by 1921,[119] the Majlis decided in addition to bear the cost of sending some of the more promising pupils to Singapore or to the Malay College at Kuala Kangsar (Perak) for more advanced English education, four boys being so supported from mid-1920, with another five put up the following year.[120]

In addition to and in some measure supporting the educational work of the Madrasah Muhammadi and its district schools, the Majlis acquired sometime in 1917 a printing press, known as the Matba'ah Majlis Ugama, and began production of a variety of literature, using the translation and other writings of its officials, of whom there were now several engaged in work of this sort. Its first publication, so far as is known, was *Jambangan Melayu*, translated and compiled by Haji Omar

[117] State 'Annual Report on Education for 1917', encl. in Kel. K. 181/1918.
[118] See the lengthy correspondence and minutes in Kel. K. 1142/1918, and Kel. K. 623/1918. Government expenditure on education throughout the state at this time amounted to only $4,000 per annum. The objection to supervision of government schools by the Majlis seems to have come originally from W.G. Maxwell, Secretary to the High Commissioner, though the latter supported him.
[119] Letter, Secretary Majlis Ugama to BA, 4 April 1921, encl. in Kel. K. 224/1921. A photograph of nine graduates of the English division of the Madrasah in 1920 appeared in *Al-Hikmah* (Kota Bharu), IV, 145 (June 1937)—many of them by this last date having achieved positions of considerable distinction in their own and other states. Though the Madrasah school was not the first to provide English education in Kelantan (there had been sporadic government night classes in Kota Bharu and elsewhere from about 1911), it was the only one of any substance, and trained a generation of Kelantan civil servants.
[120] See correspondence between the Majlis Ugama and Sultan Muhammad in May 1920, encl. in Kel. PM. 226/1920, and correspondence between the Adviser's Office and Dato' Perdana Mentri in May 1921, encl. in Kel. PM. 189/1921. Of the nine boys named therein, only six appear to have remained at the College.

b. Ismail, which appeared in August 1917, a collection of pieces dealing with the proper use of language.[121] Numbers of others followed in the next few years, most relating to the principles and precepts of Islam, including one compiled by Dato' Setia (by now Dato' Sri Paduka Raja) himself, *Kitab Chahaya Pernama*, published in June 1918. Also in 1918, the Majlis began publication of a fortnightly journal, *Pengasoh*, edited by the secretary, Haji Muhammad (by now Dato' Bentara Jaya), and containing articles of wide general and educational as well as specifically religious interest. Within a short time, *Pengasoh* became one of the most influential and widely circulated journals in the peninsula, contributed to by all Malay writers of importance of the time.[122]

By 1920, then, the Majlis had become a large and flourishing organization, employing a staff of more than fifty clerks, accountants, teachers, compositors, writers, translators, book-binders, and others—not to mention the central mosque officials also on its payroll—and managing several schools, a press, and a leading journal, and handling a budget of some $60,000 annually.[123] In addition, it was already beginning, with some financial acumen, to seek fresh sources of income, recognizing both that there was an inevitable ceiling to the amount that could be taken in zakat and fitrah taxes, and that these revenues themselves were bound to fluctuate with the seasonal uncertainties of the rice harvest. Though forbidden by Shari'a law, certainly as understood in Kelantan at the time, from the taking of interest, and hence from many of the safer and more obvious forms of investment,[124] it is possible nevertheless that the Majlis might, in other circumstances, have become a major economic entrepreneur in the state. Only the caution of the British officials, for whom speculation with public funds was by regulation disapproved, prevented it early in 1920 from acquiring 500 acres of state land with the intention of developing a rubber estate to produce alternative income.[125]

---

[121] Haji Omar, who had taught *fikh* at the Kota Bharu Mosque for many years, was an accomplished scholar in Arabic, and a prolific writer. A brief account of some of his works (which places his *Jalan Sejahtera* prior in time to *Jambangan Melayu*) is given in Al-Ahmadi (1966, 165-9).

[122] *Pengasoh* began to make a profit in 1920, and by the middle of the decade was making in the neighbourhood of $1,500 a year. The Matba'ah was also profitable, doing much of Kota Bharu's job-printing and clearing $1,332 by 1920, together with $219 from the sale of publications.

[123] The annual estimates of the Majlis for 1921 (encl. in Kel. PM. 434/1920), which appear to have been the first formally prepared, list revenue and expenditure for 1920. The figure of $60,000 is somewhat inflated by inclusion of some $9,500 of the 'surau share' of zakat and fitrah. The wages bill for employees, excluding officials of the central mosques and menials, came to $14,042.

[124] This effectively ruled out the 5% Victory Bonds suggested by the British Adviser.

[125] It was the intention of the Majlis to spend any additional income on, among other things, sending to Europe 'promising students, when available, to prosecute useful studies such as Medicine, Law, Engineering etc., etc., at the English Universities and

But the Majlis was not without its problems and its critics. There was a good deal of feeling against centralized collection of the fitrah, which prompted recalcitrance followed by punitive legal action.[126] There were many complaints about the energy with which the Majlis appears to have prosecuted all laxness in collection or remittance of zakat and fitrah, despite circumstances in which Imam still laboured under conditions of inadequate clerical help, problems of handling and storing large sums of money, and hazards of theft and fire.[127] There was feeling at the local level about the allegedly inequitable division of the zakat and fitrah proceeds, and somewhat more pointed criticism from some quarters, both about the priorities set by the Majlis and the actual handling of its financial affairs. In July 1919, for example, Haji Wan Abdullah b. Abdul Samad (brother of both the ex-Mufti and the then Mufti, and previously a member of the Majlis, replaced in 1917 for reasons of 'ill-health' by another Kota Bharu khatib, Haji Wan Daud) addressed to the British Adviser a long and strongly argued petition signed by no fewer than 526 other people, complaining in detail about everything from the price-fixing of *beras fitrah*; to the Majlis' expenditure of its income 'as it pleases'; the question of whether, according to Shari'a law, payment of the taxes might be compulsorily directed at all; the Majlis' failure to build mosques; its assumption of the right to issue *fatwa* for the whole state, principally through the columns of its journal *Pengasoh*; and a number of other quite specific matters of considerable interest in the context of the time.[128]

Out of all this, it was the question of priorities that emerged as the central problem for the Majlis, not least because it was a question in which the Sultan himself took a close personal interest. The Majlis had never denied that one of its principal responsibilities was to attend to the repair and maintenance of mosques, nor that the condition of the Kota Bharu Mosque in particular was such as to warrant its replacement in due course. As early as April 1917, in a letter to the Sultan already

---

Colleges' (Memorandum, 'Planting Scheme of the Majlis Ugama and Istiadat Melayu, Kelantan', encl. in Kel. K. 425/1920). This file, and Kel. PM. 178/1920, contain lengthy correspondence and minutes on the Majlis' scheme, which was prompted in part by its recent commitment to find a large sum of money to fund a new mosque for Kota Bharu (see below).

[126] The records contain references to numerous instances. See, e.g., Kel. M. 191/1918; though in some respects this was a special case, involving also disputed mukim boundaries.

[127] See, e.g., the cases dealt with in Kel. M. 64/1919 and Kel. K. 359/1919, and cf., also, discussion of the general question of relations between Imam and the Majlis in Kel. PM. 264/1922.

[128] The petition is encl. in Kel. M. 120/1919. A more extensive study of the religious politics of the time, which examines some of the issues raised here, is at present in progress and will be published later.

quoted, concerning the expenditure of $15,000 on the proposed school, the Majlis said it was anxious to proceed with construction of a new mosque in Kota Bharu, but that cost of materials was high because of the war and to embark on such a project at present would cost at least $200,000, a sum the Majlis could not command, and it recommended postponement.[129] In July 1917, obviously a little under pressure, especially now that fitrah collection had started, the Majlis wrote again to the Sultan, arguing for continued postponement on the same grounds, and adding that in view of the fact that money was being collected from everybody it seemed necessary, if the Majlis was to avoid criticism, to lay some of it out again as rapidly as possible for the benefit of all, and that the most useful way of doing this would be to make education widely available.[130] Again the Sultan agreed.

As far as the records reveal, little more was heard of the mosque question until mid-1919, by which time it is evident that the ruler himself had become directly interested—possibly in response to the current public criticism of the Majlis, though certainly also as a result of his own desire to see Kota Bharu equipped with a state mosque worthy of Kelantan, a desire the more pressing with the advance of old age and infirmity. In July 1919 he informed the British Adviser that he would like to see plans of the mosques in Kuala Lumpur and Kuala Kangsar (the Adviser minuting that His Highness intended the new mosque to be a building 'of some pretensions'), and further enquiry was made, also at the ruler's request, for the plans of the mosques in Langkat and Deli, in Sumatra, 'which are regarded with special admiration in Kelantan'.[131] Faced, perhaps, with the inevitable, and unquestionably with a growing need to 'clear up misunderstandings concerning the actions of the Majlis',[132] the Dato' Sri Paduka, whose brain-child the Majlis had principally been, drew up in the name of the Sultan a document setting out afresh the purposes for which the Majlis had been created, and shortly thereafter went on sick leave, instructing his principal ally (and now deputy) Dato' Bentara Jaya to present this document to the Sultan for approval, and if this were forthcoming for its promulgation to the people of Kelantan.[133] It was a kind of surrender. The document, en-

[129] Letter, Yang di-Pertuan Majlis Ugama to Sultan Muhammad, 23 April 1917, encl. in Kel. PM. 68/1917.
[130] Letter, Yang di-Pertuan Majlis Ugama to Sultan Muhammad, 10 July 1917, encl. in Kel. PM. 109/1917.
[131] Minutes by the Adviser, and correspondence, contained in Kel. K. 660/1919. The Kuala Kangsar mosque, then the newest and architecturally most striking in the peninsula, had been completed in 1917, at a cost of some $221,000.
[132] Draft letter, Dato' Bentara Jaya to Sultan Muhammad, minuted, 24 August 1919, on Kel. PM. 206/1919.
[133] *Ibid.* Dato' Jaya explicitly states that before the Dato' Sri Paduka went on leave he asked him to submit the document to the Sultan for approval. The ruler is said to have tho-

titled 'Pemberitahu Berkenaan Dengan Tujuan di-Himpunkan Wang Majlis Ugama Islam dan Jalan Membelanjakan-nya' (A Notice Concerning the Aim of Majlis Ugama Collections and their Disbursement), began by listing in order of priority the Majlis' tasks. First, to construct a large and strongly built mosque in Kota Bharu, estimated to cost not less than $300,000; secondly, to organize religious and other schools and to extend such education to the rural areas and into every mukim; thirdly, to further the advancement of knowledge by such means as operating a printing press, translating materials from Arabic or English into Malay, and running a journal like *Pengasoh*; fourthly, to build mosques in those towns needing them; fifthly, to pay the salaries of teachers in its schools and mosques, of the travelling religious teachers in the countryside, and of the Majlis' staff; sixthly, having satisfactorily carried out the above, to seek other ways to improve the welfare of the state and its people, especially in relation to Islam; seventhly, not to interfere with the expenditure of the share of the zakat and fitrah employed by local Imam to repair and maintain their surau, except as already provided by regulation; and eighthly, to deposit all sums accruing to the Majlis in the government treasury, and to ask the Adviser to conduct an audit of the accounts every six months.[134] Finally, in a somewhat emotional peroration, it was stated by Dato' Sri Paduka, in the voice of the Sultan, that it must be recognized that since the setting up of the Majlis it had grown from strength to strength, and all its endeavours with it. It was proper that everyone should know that the progress that had been achieved had been due to the faithful and unremitting work of its members in pursuit of the ideals originally laid down for it, loyalty that would not be forgotten while the name of Kelantan continued to live.[135]

The Kota Bharu Mosque, then, was to cost at least $300,000, and with that decision the troubles of the Majlis Ugama began, and its

---

roughly agreed with its contents, and to have presented it to the State Council, which gave it its imprimatur on 27 August, 400 copies then being printed for distribution. A certain coolness between Dato' Sri Paduka and the Sultan is noticeable at this time.

[134] In this context it should be noted that although the Majlis had initially, early in 1919, reacted strongly to a suggestion that the State Auditor examine its accounts regularly (the Majlis' own auditor, as it happened, was a brother of Dato' Jaya and brother-in-law to Dato' Sri Paduka), this appears to have been the result of pride and a strong insistence on its non-governmental status rather than of peculation, for a proposal that they themselves *request* a six-monthly audit, by someone to be nominated by the Adviser but not a member of the Audit Office staff, was readily agreed to. The first audit was in fact carried out by the Adviser himself, covering the period from 1916 to July 1919, when he reported the accounts in error by only half a cent, and recommended a raise for the chief clerk who was responsible for keeping them (see corresp. and minutes in Kel. K. 105/1919 and Kel. K. 560/1919).

[135] Sultan Muhammad himself lived only until December 1920, and so did not see the laying of the foundation stone for the new mosque, named after him, in May 1922.

pioneering work in education and modernization, while by no means ceasing, came increasingly to falter. Within a few years, as the result of a combination of circumstances, of which the debt incurred for the construction of the new mosque was by far the most important, the Majlis was in trouble financially and was to remain so for the better part of two decades. But it had wrought the beginnings of an indigenous social revolution, and though this was to be in some respects deflected in the years that followed, the Majlis as an organization continued to wield great power. It was the culmination of and inheritor to a complex process of bureaucratization of Islam that had been under way for some decades and had never been completely dissociated from the politics of the state. It provided institutional support not merely to the ruler (who certainly found himself in a stronger position vis-à-vis both the British and internal forces of discord in 1920 than in 1915), but also for the 'new men' who were henceforth to dominate Kelantan political life. Its relevance to the political history of Kelantan in no way ceased with the deflections of course that occurred after 1920. It has been discussed here, however, primarily as an indigenous agent of directed social change, utilizing the institutions of Islam, wedded to Western bureaucratic forms, to further what appears to have been genuinely perceived by its progenitors as the interests of the state as a whole despite the undoubted fact that, on the one hand, it was the peasantry alone who provided the financial basis of its power, and on the other that it was a relatively small group among the 'new men' who were to benefit most from the processes set in train.

Beyond trying to analyze the intricacies of administrative change and development during the crucial 'contact years' of Kelantan's modern history, and in particular to trace the strain of insistent self-determination that ran throughout, based on a clear if not always commonly shared vision of the essential elements of their own society, I have been concerned, by implication, to suggest two general points. The first, and the more obvious, is precisely that elements of institutional continuity in the modernization of traditional societies should not be underrated, and certainly cannot be ignored. The second is prompted by the reflection that perhaps too much attention has been paid in the past, where study of the modernization of specifically Islamic traditional societies has been concerned, to the dramatic clash of rival ideologies and the rubrics of 'reformism', and too little to the more mundane but often sinewy detail of administrative institutionalization and bureaucratization, which must lie at the root, if not at the heart, of much social change.

REFERENCES

Monographs and Reports

Abdullah b. Abdul Kadir, Munshi, 1960. *Kisah Pelayaran Abdullah* (new ed'n, ed. by Kassim Ahmad, Kuala Lumpur, Oxford University Press).

Al-Ahmadi, Abdul Rahman, 1966. *Pengantar Sastera* (Kota Bharu, Pustaka Aman Press).

Allen, J. de V., 1968. 'The Kelantan Rising of 1915: Some Thoughts on the Concept of Resistance in British Malayan History', *Journal South-east Asian History*, IX, 2, 241–57.

Ahmad b. Haji Nik Hassan, Nik, 1964/65. 'Kajian Rengkas Mengenai Keturunan Long Yunus Kelantan dari tahun 1756 hingga tahun 1920', *Journal Persatuan Sejarah Kelantan* (Kota Bharu), I, 39–51.

Ahmad Ibrahim, 1965. *Islamic Law in Malaya* (Singapore, Malaysian Sociological Research Institute).

Annandale, N. & Robinson, H.C., 1903. *Fasciculi Malayenses. Anthropological and Zoological Results of an Expedition to Perak and the Siamese Malay States, 1901–1902. Anthropology, Parts I & II(a)* (Liverpool, University Press).

Asa'ad Shukri b. Haji Muda, 1962. *Sejarah Kelantan* (Kota Bharu, Pustaka Aman Press).

Berger, M., 1970. *Islam in Egypt Today: Social and Political Aspects of Popular Religion* (Cambridge, Cambridge University Press).

Bishop, J.E., 1912. *Kelantan Administration Report for the Year 1911* (Kuala Lumpur, Government Printing Office).

Clifford, H., 1898. *Studies in Brown Humanity, being Scrawls and Smudges in Sepia, White, and Yellow* (London, Grant Richards).

―――――― 1961. 'Expedition to Trengganu and Kelantan, report by Hugh Clifford', *JMBRAS*, XXXIV, 1, 1–162 (reprinted from the report written in 1895 and first published in 1938).

Davies, R.D., 1902. *Siam in the Malay Peninsula* (Singapore, Fraser and Neave).

Farrer, R.J., 1916. *Kelantan Administration Report for the Year 1915* (Kuala Lumpur, Government Printing Office).

―――――― 1917. *Kelantan Administration Report for the Year 1916* (Kuala Lumpur, Government Printing Office).

——— 1918. *Kelantan Administration Report for the Year 1917* (Kuala Lumpur, Government Printing Office).

Gibb, H.A.R. & Kramers, J.H., 1961. *Shorter Encyclopaedia of Islam* (Leiden, E.J. Brill, and London, Luzac & Co.).

Graham, W.A., 1904. *Report on the State of Kelantan for the year August, 1903, to August, 1904* (Bangkok, Government Printer).

——— 1905. *Report on the State of Kelantan for the period 1st August, 1904, to 31st May, 1905* (Bangkok, Government Printer).

——— 1907. *Report on the State of Kelantan for the period 1st June, 1905, to 23rd February, 1906* (Bangkok, Government Printer).

——— 1908a. *Kelantan. A State of the Malay Peninsula. A Handbook of Information* (Glasgow, James Maclehose & Sons).

——— 1908b. *Report on the State of Kelantan for the period 24th February, 1906, to 14th February, 1907* (Bangkok, Government Printer).

——— 1909. *Report on the State of Kelantan for the period 15th February, 1907, to 4th February, 1908* (Bangkok, Government Printer).

——— 1910–11. 'Malay States. II—Non-Federated States', *Encyclopaedia Britannica* (11th ed., London, 1910–11).

Langham-Carter, W., 1913. *Kelantan Administration Report for the Year 1912* (Kuala Lumpur, Government Printing Office).

——— 1914. *Kelantan Administration Report for the Year 1913* (Kuala Lumpur, Government Printing Office).

——— 1915. *Kelantan Administration Report for the Year 1914* (Kuala Lumpur, Government Printing Office).

Mackeen, A.M.M., 1969. *Contemporary Islamic Legal Organization in Malaya* (New Haven, Conn., Yale University Southeast Asia Studies).

Mason, J.S., 1910. *Kelantan Administration Report for the Year 1327 A.H. (23 January, 1909—12 January 1910)* (Kuala Lumpur, Government Printing Office).

——— 1911. *Kelantan Administration Report for the Year 1328 A.H. (13th January, 1910—31st December 1910)* (Kuala Lumpur, Government Printing Office).

Maxwell, W.G. & Gibson, W.S., 1924. *Treaties and Engagements Affecting the Malay States and Borneo* (London, James Truscott).

Muhammad Yusup b. Salleh al-Kelantani, 1953. *Penerangan Masa* (Kota Bharu, Mustafa Press).

Roff, W.R., 1962. 'Kaum Muda—Kaum Tua: Innovation and Reaction Amongst the Malays, 1900–1941', in K.G. Tregonning (ed.), *Papers on Malayan History* (Singapore, Journal South-East Asian History), 162–92.

──────── 1967. *The Origins of Malay Nationalism* (New Haven, Conn. & London, Yale University Press).

Sadka, E., 1969. *The Protected Malay States, 1874–1895* (Kuala Lumpur, University of Malaya Press).

Skeat, W.W. & Laidlaw, F.F., 1963. 'The Cambridge University Expedition to Parts of the Malay Peninsula, 1899–1900. Personal Accounts by the late W.W. Skeat & Dr. F.F. Laidlaw', *JMBRAS*, XXVI, 4, 9–174.

Wilkinson, R.J., 1908. *Law. Part I. Introductory Sketch*, in R.J. Wilkinson (gen. ed.), *Papers on Malay Subjects* (First Series) (Kuala Lumpur, Government Printing Office).

Manuscript Material (as cited)

CO 273. Correspondence between Governor, Straits Settlements, and Secretary of State, Open and Confidential, 1900–1920. Public Records Office, London.

HKS. 'Hikayat Sri Kelantan' (author unknown, manuscript completed in 1914). Page references are to the MS held by the National Archives of Malaysia, Kuala Lumpur.

Kel. K. Files of the British Adviser's Office, known as the 'K' series, Open and Confidential, 1910–1920. National Archives of Malaysia, Kuala Lumpur.

Kel. M. [Administrative] Files of the 'Mahkamah' ([High] Court), 1911–1920 (all extant to 1920). National Archives of Malaysia, Kuala Lumpur (listed therein under the code D/MH 1).

Kel. PB. Files of the 'Pejabat Balai' (initially Pejabat Balai Besar, from 1914 Pejabat Balai Kerajaan) or Palace Office, 1913–1916 (all extant). National Archives of Malaysia, Kuala Lumpur.

Kel. PM. Files of the 'Pejabat Mentri' (also known as the Opis Mentri) or [Chief] Minister's Office, 1913, 1916–1917, 1919–1920 (all extant to 1920). National Archives of Malaysia, Kuala Lumpur. [Note. Though the term 'Opis Mentri' predominated in the early part of the period, and files were superscribed 'OM', 'Pejabat Mentri' gradually displaced it, and the present writer, for reasons of eventual consistency, has thought it best to standardize on the latter.]

6

MUHAMMAD SALLEH B. WAN MUSA
(*with* S. OTHMAN KELANTAN)
Theological Debates: Wan Musa b. Haji Abdul Samad and His Family

KELANTAN, a state which may be regarded as unique in peninsular Malaya, has a history unusually productive of well-known figures in the fields of politics, literature, the arts, and most of all, perhaps, religion. Its *ulama* have attracted the interest of most historians concerned to investigate and describe the development of Malay thought, religion and society across the years.

Studying the history of learning and religion in Kelantan presents some difficulties, for one can know little with certainty about the past in the absence of written materials of some reliability and substance. For the purposes of the present article we have divided the growth of religious thought in Kelantan into three stages. The first we may call the transitional stage, beginning with the establishment of Islam in Kelantan around the thirteenth or fourteenth centuries. With this early period and its intellectual struggles, from the arrival of Islam until the end of the eighteenth century, we shall not here be concerned. It was a stage largely taken up with the acceptance of Islam by the people of the state, and the strengthening of the elements of the faith.

The second stage we may call the pioneering stage, that is to say, the period of the development of Islamic learning in Patani (at that time culturally a part of the state of Kelantan), beginning in the early nineteenth century. There then emerged several famous *ulama* and translators of scholarly works from Arabic into Malay, such as Shaykh Daud b. Abdullah al-Patani.[1] In Kota Bharu too, the capital of Kelantan, during these years, Islam became more firmly established, as we may note from the endeavours of Haji Abdul Samad b. Mohd. Salleh (1816–91), better known as Tuan Tabal. Tuan Tabal was born in Kampong Tabal Tempoyak (now in southern Thailand), and later, as his fame as a pious and learned *alim* spread, became son-in-law to To' Semian Wan Abdul Rahman, one of the chief ministers of the state, marrying the latter's only daughter, Wan Kalthum. As a result of this marriage he settled in Kota Bharu, and taught in a surau in Kampong To' Semian Tua. He later died at this place, and his grave in Kampong Banggul is still visited by pilgrims today.

Haji Wan Abdul Samad, or Tuan Tabal, left a large number of students who became *ulama* of note, among them his sons Wan Musa and Wan Abdullah, Haji Daud b. Che' Husain,[2] and Hakim Haji Nik Abdullah b. Raja Zainal,[3] all of whom strove to strengthen the pursuit of truth and promote the faith. Tuan Tabal, like Shaykh Daud Patani before him, left numerous writings, translations into Malay from the Arabic of the *ulama*. The fruits of his own pen, too, found expression in many books, such as the *Minhat al-Qarīb, Kifāyat al-'Awām, Jalā' al-qulūb bi-dhikr Allāh,* and others. In his writings he was especially concerned with the harmonization of jurisprudence (*fikh*) with mystical truths as represented by the notion of *iḥsān*, here implying purity of intention and sincerity in thought, word and deed. In this, his researches reveal considerable differences in approach from those of Shaykh Daud Patani, who was for the most part concerned solely with *fikh*.[4]

Throughout the nineteenth century the development of Islam and Islamic learning in Kelantan proceeded apace, through contributions of the *ulama*, both oral and written, pertaining to various subjects, thanks to the serious efforts of these scholars. The developments described made Kota Bharu a centre for study and a fount of learning second only

---

[1] See above, Abdullah, p. 91, Note 6.
[2] Haji Daud Kechik, as he was widely known, studied with Tuan Tabal from the age of thirteen, later going to Mecca where he himself had many pupils of note. He died in 1925.
[3] Haji Nik Abdullah was Hakim of the *Mahkamah Kelantan* (the then High Court) at the close of the nineteenth century, and died in 1927. He was grandfather (mother's father) to S. Othman Kelantan, author of the concluding part of the present article.
[4] For additional information on Tuan Tabal, see Al-Ahmadi (1966, 158–63).

to Patani for those seeking to advance their knowledge and understanding of the Shari'a. Students came not merely from the rest of peninsular Malaya but from Siak and Palembang in Sumatra, and even from Cambodia. Formal education and learning at this time were based mainly on the *pondok* system; the texts studied were not arranged according to any fixed syllabus, nor learning otherwise organized as it is today. Similarly, students' ages were of no account, and the length of time spent in study was not limited; as a result, sixty-year-olds might find themselves sitting in the same circle as twelve-year-olds. At this time, too, there was little or no debate about what might be regarded as errors of opinion in religious law. If there was debate at all, it was likely to be over relatively small matters such as the precise interpretation of *niat*, certain *hadith*, or *kadim*.[5] This was because, as a result of the condition of the state at this juncture, there was no recognition of wider necessities of thought. Active propagation of ideas may sometimes give rise to recriminations directed against those who have transgressed the limits of religious law.

The developments in Islam and Islamic learning of the late nineteenth century gave way directly to what we may call the third stage, which set in as the turn of the century approached, at the hands of Tuan Tabal's pupils and the new generation they represented.

Already a well-known *alim* in Kota Bharu, Haji Wan Musa b. Haji Abdul Samad (1874–1939) may be regarded as heading this third generation, along with Muhammad Yusuf b. Ahmad (1868–1933)—better known as To' Kenali—Mufti Haji Wan Daud, and Hakim Haji Nik Abdullah. Apart from being educated at home by his father, Tuan Tabal, Wan Musa had been taken by him to Mecca, along with his brothers Wan Muhammad, Wan Omar, and Wan Abdullah. While still a youngster he was able to study with several teachers in Mecca, among them the renowned Haji Wan Ahmad Patani.[6] As a result, he was inducted into a number of important fields of knowledge, such as the Sufism of the monistic (*wahdat al-wujūd*) school of Imam Mahyuddin ibn al-'Arabi and (through his own father) the practices of the Sufi *tarekat* of Abu'l-Hasan ash-Shādhilī. In the realm of jurisprudence, scholastic theology, and other subjects, he learnt from a number of other teachers, notably Haji Wan Ahmad Patani himself, who implanted in him a new spirit and filled him with an enthusiasm

---

[5] *Niat* (Ar., *niyyah*), in this context, refers to the formulation of intention before prayer, and the question of whether this should be made aloud or inwardly. *Hadith* refers to the corpus of 'tradition' emanating from the Prophet, and *kadim* (Ar., *qādīm*) to certain Sufistic interpretations of the attributes of God inherent in Him.

[6] See above, Abdullah.

for the study of society (what today would be called sociology) and politics.

Haji Wan Musa went to and from Mecca several times in his youth. In the course of this period, he married a girl named Nik Jah from the family of Nik Wan Zainab (later to become Sultanah Zainab, consort to Muhammad IV) of Kampong Atas Banggul in Kota Bharu. The marriage ended in divorce, as did a later marriage with another Kampong Banggul girl, Wan Embung.[7] He returned finally to Kelantan to settle down in July 1908, aged 24. His grandfather Haji Wan Ishak b. Abdul Kadir[8] thereupon betrothed him to another young girl of good family from Kampong Atas Banggul, Nik Zainab bte Nik Yahya.[9] This third marriage lasted, and was blessed with twelve issue, six boys and six girls.[10]

Haji Wan Musa was well known to be an *alim* possessed of sound knowledge of the religious sciences, and despite his short temper was always willing to retract his opinions in the interests of establishing truth. Along with such characteristics of modesty and piety, went a refusal ever to follow the instructions or bidding of another, even of a ruling Sultan, if these should appear to him to conflict with the law of God and the teachings of His Prophet—an intransigence which was later to lead to one of the major turning points of his life.[11]

[7] He had two children by Nik Jah and one by Wan Embung, all of whom died in infancy.
[8] Haji Wan Ishak b. Abdul Kadir, from Patani, had married Nik Wan Lebar, sister to Nik Wan Zainab, wife of To' Semian Wan Abdul Rahman, the minister whose daughter, as indicated above, married Tuan Tabal. Ishak died in 1924, aged ninety.
[9] Daughter of Nik Yahya b. Wan Endut, Nik Zainab was born in 1883 and died in 1958.
[10] In order of birth, Nik Fatimah, Nik Abdullah (b. 1900, d. 1936), Nik A'isyah, Nik Muhammad Nur ul-Din (b. 1325 [1907/08]), Nik Khadijah, Nik Mahmud (b. 1333 [1914/15]), Nik Abdul Rahman (b. and d. 1335 [1916/17]), Nik Kalthum, Nik Muhammad Salleh, the present writer (b. 1920), and Nik Muhammad Mahyuddin. Nik Muhammad Nur ul-Din studied under To' Kenali and To' Khorasani (for the latter, see below, Note 19), and in 1926 went to Mecca, where he studied with Shaykh Omar Hamdan, Sayyid Yamani, Shaykh Ali Maliki, and Shaykh Hamzah Masri. He returned to Kelantan in 1934, and in 1936 was made Inspector of Majlis Ugama schools until the Japanese occupation. In 1970 he became a teacher at the Masjid Muhammadi, Kota Bharu. Nik Mahmud also studied with To' Kenali and To' Khorasani, and went to Mecca in 1930, continuing to India in 1937, where he attended the Darul-'Ulum at Deoband under Maulana 'Ubayd-Ullāh as-Sindhī (see below) until the outbreak of war. He returned to Kelantan in 1945, and from then until 1948 was a member of the Majlis Ugama. He now teaches at the Islah school, Padang Bongor, Kota Bharu, and is Imam to the present Sultan of Kelantan. Nik Muhammad Mahyuddin (b. 1342 [1923–24]) is currently principal of the Muslim College, Klang, Selangor. The career of Wan Musa's eldest son, Nik Abdullah, and the writer's own, are given in some detail below.
[11] The occasion related to a complex inheritance case which came to a head in 1915 and concerned the disposition of a royal *istana* (palace), and the land associated with it, near the then Istana Jahar (now Istana Tengku Puteri). The disputants were Tengku Kembang Meriam, a daughter of Sultan Ahmad (d. 1889) and granddaughter of Sultan Muhammad II (d. 1886), who held, supported by her sisters, that the istana had been the property of her father, who had given it to her before his death; and, on the other side, Tengku Embung, also a granddaughter of Muhammad II (through her mother, Engku Nanik, the late Sultan Ahmad's sister), who held that the istana had been given

In 1908, at the age of 34, he was appointed to the post of Mufti of Kelantan, the highest office in the religious administration of the state. His *fatwa* in the years that followed were often at variance with the views of many *ulama* of the time. One such pointed difference concerned the attitude of the Majlis Ugama Islam (founded late in 1915) in its decision to centralize the collection of zakat and fitrah taxes and use a substantial proportion of these for the purpose of building a large and expensive stone mosque in Kota Bharu, to replace the old wooden Masjid. This intention of the Majlis Ugama was supported by most Kelantan *ulama*, but violently opposed by Haji Wan Musa (who had ceased to be Mufti in mid-1916, after his dispute with the Sultan over the handling of inheritance matters). For Haji Wan Musa, zakat and fitrah monies were the right of the poor. If this right were to be taken from them, or used for needs of other kinds, nothing at all would remain to them. This, he argued, would be unjust and oppressive. His views on the subject prompted furious debate, and a state of enmity developed between him and the state officials in power at the time. True to his principles, however, he continued to refuse to accept the Majlis Ugama's position, despite the fact that construction of the Masjid Muhammadi was begun in 1922. To the day of his death, in 1939, he declined to set foot inside the completed building.

His steadfastness in pursuing what he saw to be the law of God is clearly evidenced in his earlier disagreement with Sultan Muhammad over the property division between Tengku Embung and Tengku Kembang Meriam. Despite influence of many kinds brought to bear on him to alter that decision, he continued to abide by the saying of the Prophet Muhammad, '*Lā ṭā'ata limakhlūq fī ma'ṣiyat al-khāliq*' (Obedience to men ceases when it involves disobedience to the Creator). Although as a result he was forced to resign the post of Mufti, and went back to living as a free and independent individual, pursuing the fight for religious education and advancement in other ways, he continued to be harassed by some of the officers of state, with allegations that he was a traitor and the like. The style of government in Kelantan at that time, aristocratic and without a proper constitution that could guarantee the liberty of the subject, exposed him to perpetual danger. As a result he was forced eventually to leave the state. He did not settle

---

to Engku Nanik by Muhammad II. Sultan Muhammad IV supported the claim of Tengku Embung, who had previously been married to his father, Muhammad III (d. 1890), When the case came to court, Haji Wan Musa, as Mufti, was asked by the Sultan to give a decision according to the Shari'a law, and on the evidence presented to him found in favour of Tengku Kembang Meriam. Sultan Muhammad IV thereupon endeavoured by argument and other means to persuade him to reverse his decision, but failed to do so, Haji Wan Musa resigning as Mufti in mid-1916. (Cf. above, Roff, p. 131.)

in one place, as had been his custom, but went back and forth, mainly to Trengganu where he received a warm welcome from the chief minister, Haji Ngah, Dato' Amar di-Raja, spreading religious education and the teachings of the Ahmadiyyah-Shadhiliyyah *tarekat*. His life remained unsettled in this fashion until the death of Sultan Muhammad IV in December 1920, when he returned to Kota Bharu and lived there as before.

Sultan Ismail, who succeeded Sultan Muhammad IV, differed from his father in greatly respecting Haji Wan Musa. The same was true of the new Sultan's younger brother, Tengku Ibrahim (officially known as the Raja Kelantan)[12] and other members of the royal family. Despite this he continued to be strongly opposed by a section of the notabilities living in Kampong Atas Banggul, and in particular by the Dato' Perdana Menteri Paduka Raja, Haji Nik Mahmud b. Ismail. He was regarded by this group not just as a singularly stubborn *alim*, but as a serious foe.

One particular distinction of Haji Wan Musa was that he always acted as a straightforward and honest adviser to many members of the royal family, not least because he wished to ensure that the younger sons were properly educated. He advised the Tengku Bendahara (Tengku Chik Abdullah b. Sultan Ahmad, d. 1927) to send his son, Tengku Khalid, to study overseas, and did the same for the Tengku Besar Indera (Tengku Mohd. Yusof b. Sultan Ahmad, d. 1940)and Tengku Muda Hasan b. Tengku Mahmud (d. 1936), with their sons Tengku Abdul Majid and Tengku Abdullah respectively. He frequently reminded the royal family that if they did not take pains over the education of their children, their authority would gradually wane, and before long be assumed by other groups. His advice was much heeded by the family, especially by Tengku Muda Hasan, who sent Tengku Abdullah to study law in England, where he qualified in 1937.[13] His admonitions to royalty were prompted by recognition of the fact that many of the aristocracy in Kelantan at this time were engaged in giving them contrary advice, to the effect that if they lived like royalty, educated or not, they would remain royalty, drawing a comparison with the fact of the greatness of the Prophet Muhammad despite his alleged illiteracy.[14]

---

[12] Tengku Ibrahim was later to succeed his brother as Sultan, on the latter's death in 1944, reigning until his own death in 1960.

[13] Tengku Abdullah returned to Kelantan in September of that year, and took up service in the judiciary. He died suddenly in May 1941, at the age of 33, while a judge of the High Court.

[14] This relates to a disputed passage in the Kuran, Verse 2 of Sura 62 (*al-Jumu'a*), one of several in which the word '*ummī* occurs. The Arabic reads, '*Huwa'lladhī ba'atha fi'l-ummiyīna rasūlan minhum yatlū* ...' (which may be rendered, 'It is He who has sent amongst the Unlettered an apostle from among themselves ...'; trans. A. Yusuf Ali). Many *ulama* hold that '*ummī* here indicates that the Prophet was illiterate. According to others (including the present writer) it is clear that it refers, rather, to a community of people—just as the term *Nasara* referred to Christians, or *Yahudi* to Jews—and that

The Kelantan *ulama* of the day, save for friends such as Hakim Haji Nik Abdullah b. Raja Zainal, all disagreed with Haji Wan Musa in contesting this and other points, influenced as they were by the current authorities, led by the Majlis Ugama. Their hostility, however, was not fully expressed because Haji Wan Musa was much loved by the royal family, especially Sultan Ismail.

Apart from the special advisory role referred to, Haji Wan Musa's intimate knowledge of religious law led to the introduction of many changes based upon the views of Egyptian *ulama* such as Shaykh Muhammad Abduh, Rashid Ridha, and other well-known Azhar theologians. He raised repeatedly the question of *niat*, regarded by him as an inward matter of expressing in the heart a purpose and intention which then became the essence on the basis of which the validity or otherwise of a religious act (in this case, prayer) might be ascertained. His views on this were opposed by most Kelantan *ulama*, for whom the *niat* meant only the verbal utterance of prescribed formulae, such as the '*uṣallī fard adh-dhur*' for the *Zuhr* (mid-day) prayer, or the '*nawaitu*' for the religious duties of fasting, and so on. Tengku Mahmud Zohdi of Patani (later to become *Shaykh al-Islām* in Selangor) offered systematic argument against Haji Wan Musa's views in a pamphlet published in Mecca in 1341 (1922–23), but the former's contentions failed to disprove Haji Wan Musa's opinions, which were cogent and convincing.

He also promoted reform of several customary religious practices, such as utterance of the *talkin* over the dead after burial;[15] recitation of *tahlil* in the house of the deceased at intervals of seven, forty and one hundred days after death, and the feasts connected with these occasions;[16] ritual processions to celebrate the Prophet's Birthday (*Maulud Nabi*); staying to read the Kuran (usually for some nights) at the graveside of a deceased *alim*; or sleeping in the grave before burial, in order to symbolize the witnessing of blessings which accrue to the deceased; all of which practices he adjudged to be innovations (*bid'ah*) and forbidden. As a result, he was accused by most *ulama* of his time as a bearer of new or false teachings. But their criticisms and attacks did not worry him. At that time the term '*kaum muda*' was still unknown in Kelantan.

---

the '*Ummī* were those who fought shoulder to shoulder with the Prophet Muhammad. According to the Islamic scholar Imam Shah Waliyullāh al-Dihlawī, the meaning of '*ummī* is 'a chosen people who elevate experience or practice above theory'.

[15] Talkin (Ar., *talqīn*, lit. act of instruction or dication), refers to the practice of giving instructions to the deceased, intended to help him answer correctly the questions of the 'Interrogators of the Dead', the angels Munkar and Nakīr, pertaining to the principles of the faith.

[16] Mal. *bertahlil* (from the Arabic), refers to the recitation or repetition, usually for a set number of times, of the first part of the Islamic creed, '*lā ilāha illa Allāh*' (there is no god but Allah).

Haji Wan Musa gave great importance to Sufi mysticism (*taṣawwuf*), as much as to the clarification of questions of law (*fikh*), for to him no practice could be wholesome if it were not accomplished in the proper spirit of purity of heart. He brought to life Sufi mystical knowledge and the way of the *tarekat*, but not by blind acquiescence (*taklid*) in the traditional practices of the past, as was the fashion with most *ulama* in Kelantan and elsewhere in the peninsula, for *tarekat* of this sort, he felt, led mankind only to stagnation in the teaching of a religion ideally based on an understanding of the three elements of intellect, intuition, and emotion (*akal*, *hati* and *nafsu*).

In the year 1937, he gave a ruling concerning dogs, which said that dogs were ritually clean, could be kept as pets, and that contact with their saliva did not require subsequent ceremonial purification. This ruling was issued in reply to a question put by the Raja Kelantan, Tengku Ibrahim. It was hotly opposed by a great many *ulama*, especially the Mufti, Haji Ibrahim b. Haji Yusoff, and the Chief Kathi, Haji Ahmad Mahir b. Haji Ismail. Discussion waxed furious until, upon the wise suggestion of the Raja Kelantan, a full-scale Council of Debate (*Majlis Muzakarah*) was arranged, the largest ever held in Kelantan. On one side were arrayed the Mufti and Chief Kathi, on the other Haji Wan Musa and a well-known *alim*, then Kathi of Singapore, Haji Abbas b. Muhammad Tahir, assisted by the young Dr. Burhanuddin Al-Helmi.[17]

The Council was held in the Istana Chemerlang in the centre of Kota Bharu, and attended by all the notables of state, including Sultan Ismail himself and the Raja Kelantan. The disputants addressed themselves with great seriousness to questions of *talfiq*—the elucidation of the rulings of all the great Imams or jurists of the Schools of Law concerning matters which, at a particular time, need to be clarified in the light of actuality and experience. On this historic occasion, Haji Wan Musa and his fellows put forward a series of arguments which could not be answered or explained away in any learned fashion by the Mufti and other *ulama* of his persuasion. As a result of the debate, though no final

---

[17] Later well-known as a Malay nationalist leader, and often spoken of as 'the father of Malay nationalism'. Several times jailed for his political activities, he was a member of Parliament for many years, and until his death in 1969 was President of the Pan-Malayan Islamic Party. His best known writings are *Perjuangan Kita* (Penang, United Press, 1955), and *Asas Falsafah Kebangsaan Melayu* (Djakarta, Tekad, 1963). A *pantun* delivered by him at the Malay Nationalist Party general conference in Malacca in 1946 has since been regarded as *keramat* (sacred):
    On the ruins of Malacca Fort,
        We erect the spirit of Freedom;
    Unite! Malays of every sort,
        Assert the just rights of our Kingdom.

decision was agreed upon, Haji Abbas Taha published a book of some 115 pages entitled *Risalah Penting, pada Masalah Jilat Anjing diatas Empat2 Mazhab* (A Treatise of Importance, on the Question of Dog Saliva according to the Four Schools of Law), published by the Ahmadiyya Press, Singapore, in 1937.

In short, throughout his life (he died in 1939), Haji Wan Musa always aroused opposition. But as an *alim* of true uprightness, and of great authority, he strove only for the heights, and with his learning, broadened by a variety of experience, he brought up his sons to become meticulous and juristically well-versed scholars of the Shari'a, capable of responding to the challenges of modern times. In addition, it was his great desire to see the royal family become leaders among the educated so that their regal attributes might be firmly entrenched and become a model to the people, especially the young, of Kelantan. This idea of his, and these desires, conflicted markedly with those of the aristocratic group associated with Kampong Atas Banggul, who, for their part, conducted a psychological struggle to weaken the position of those rulers and their families who, still reigning at present, descend from the famous Long Yunus.[18]

Throughout this account it has been made clear that Haji Wan Musa was the very first person in Kelantan among the *ulama* to work for major change in the direction of a dynamic society that would fight the obscurantism, religious accretions (*bid'ah*), and decadent traditionalism still stoutly defended by members of the feudal class. The feudalists who defended these traditions paid little attention to the education and the welfare of the common people. Haji Wan Musa took as direct models the life-style of the Egyptian people under their leader Mustafa Kamil. The reforms proposed by him to the *ulama* and to the people had no great success, though they raised the level of consciousness in some quarters, for the holders of power in the state were drawn from the feudal class and remained passive. Despite this he continued his struggle until he had breathed his last.

This righteous struggle was carried on also by his first-born son and great hope, Haji Nik Abdullah (born in 1900, sadly he predeceased his father in 1936), who began his work in 1934 after finishing his education in Mecca. Haji Nik Abdullah had received his early schooling from his father, and had also had the opportunity to study for some years with

[18] Long Yunus was the founder of the present Kelantan ruling house, which has occupied the throne since 1756, after the defeat of the last Raja of Kubang Labu, Long Muhammad (in some versions, Long Pandak). Long Yunus, son of Long Sulaiman and grandson of the Raja of Patani, died in 1794. Since his death twelve Sultans of his line have ruled Kelantan.

Haji Awang Kenali (To' Kenali). Following this, he had studied *hadith*, philosophy and logic, and other subjects, with Abu Abdullah Sa'īd Hasan b. Nur Hasan al-Khorasani of Deoband (India), who took up residence in Kelantan around the time of the first world war.[19] As a result of his friendship with the last-named *alim*, hope grew within him for a (local) similitude of the Deoband school. In 1926, Haji Nik Abdullah went to Mecca to continue his education, learning from such well-known teachers as Shaykh Omar Hamdan, Shaykh Ali Maliki, and Abu al-Samah al-Zahiri. But the most eminently pious teacher with whom he studied was Hakim al-Islam Maulana 'Ubayd-Ullah as-Sindhī (1872–1944), who happened to be in Mecca at that time.

It was the teachings of 'Ubayd-Ullāh as-Sindhī that brought him to a fuller and more correct understanding of all branches of the Shari'a, until he was spoken of as *waliyy al-hay'ah* (possessing the attributes of *wali*, or saint) with reference to Hahdhrat al-Imam al-Shah Waliyullah al-Dihlawī.[20] The certificate given to him by 'Ubayd-Ullāh on 29 Zulkaedah 1351 (3 July 1933) described his studies of the Shari'a as having reached the standard or level of *al-'Ulamā' ar-Rāsikhūn* (scholars who have attained a profound expertise in the religious sciences), and as well-versed in Islamic knowledge, a standard not previously conferred upon anyone from either Kelantan or anywhere else in the Malay peninsula. His father, Haji Wan Musa, received an intimation from the Prophet Muhammad in the form of a dream on the night of Sunday 22 Sha'ban 1352 (10 December 1934) concerning that which had been taught to Haji Nik Abdullah within the Shari'a.[21] From this dream stem-

---

[19] Known as To' Khorasani, Sa'īd Hasan was of Afghani descent. He died in his sixties in 1943.

[20] Shah Waliyullāh of Delhi (1703–62) was one of the most influential renovative Islamic thinkers in India, his ideas giving rise to what became known as the Waliyullāhi Movement, within which tradition the Darul-'Ulum school in Deoband was founded in 1867.

[21] Dream can be one of the sources of revealed truth, and may be so understood when occurring to painstaking *ulama* (*para ulama yang muhaqqiq*). In a verified hadith from the Prophet Muhammad, he is recorded as saying that 'The good dream is one of the forty-six perfect attributes of prophets'. And he said further, 'After the Prophet Muhammad there will be no man with revelations of the miraculous, save that among men of holiness there will appear unto them special dreams.' This is referred to in Ibn Khaldun's *Muqaddimah* (1967, 397). Haji Wan Musa's dream was as follows. The Prophet Muhammad said to him, 'Oh Musa, you must be wise and follow the Book of Allah and my *sunna* [customary practice]. Strengthen the teaching of your children and of others. God will appoint you and your children to be among those who are *muqarrabīn* [i.e., those brought close to God by virtue of their piety and unexcelled devotion]. The way of Shah Waliyullāh that has been learnt by your son is my way and according to my true *sunna*.' Upon which Haji Wan Musa replied, 'Oh Prophet, how can that be, for I have listened to many experts in the *hadith* following many different ways, all saying that these are your *sunna*?' The Prophet replied, 'The way of Shah Waliyullāh is my *sunna*, that which I taught to my Companions and to one *Tā'bīn* (Successor) after another. Later, understanding became confused and content unclear, until Allah enlightened the way of Shah Waliyullāh with my testament.'

med a continuing 'familial' connection with the group of *waliyy al-hay'ah* among his sons in particular and his pupils in general. This was similar to the connection with the *ahl al-bayt* (members of the house of the Prophet) ordained by the Prophet Muhammad for his friend Salmān al-Farisi when he said '*Salmān minnā ahl al-bayt*', which is to say, 'Salmān too is one of us, a member of the house'. *Ahl al-bayt* refers to those who possess the tradition inherited within the lineage of the patriarch Abraham, Friend of God, in striving to establish the true religion for humanity.

As with the example of the Prophet Muhammad and his Companions, the ties of *waliyy al-hay'ah* were handed on to the children of Haji Wan Musa and their followers, to fight to create a society inspired by the ideals of the Caliphate, for the strengthening of the spirit of justice and good works for all mankind throughout the world, as was laid down by Imam Shah Waliyullāh al-Dihlawī in '*al-jāddat al-qawiyyat al-Muḥammadiyya*' (the mighty highway of Muhammad),[22] to attain that which is desired by Allah.

Haji Nik Abdullah's reputation as an *alim* of note gave rise to some reaction in Kelantan even while he was still in Mecca. Opponents of Haji Wan Musa's struggle felt that here was yet another and stronger challenge emerging. Anxiety about the post of Mufti, which at that time was the centre of some dissension, was being pressed in certain quarters. Haji Nik Abdullah's reputation made him a possible candidate for this most important job. At the same time, two graduates from Egypt also had expectations. They were Haji Nik Mustaffa Fadhil b. Haji Nik Mahmud (son of the Dato' Perdana Mentri or chief minister), and Haji Ahmad b. Haji Ismail, better known as To' Kemuning. Between October 1929 and June 1930 the Dato' Perdana Mentri visited his son in Egypt, and made the pilgrimage to Mecca. In the course of this journey, some misunderstanding arose concerning Haji Nik Abdullah, in which it was alleged that he had been in receipt of incorrect education and knowledge, and was frequently in dispute with his teachers. These calumnies were ignored by the people and the nobility of Kelantan, and especially by Sultan Ismail.

Haji Nik Abdullah returned to Kelantan in 1934, and received an extraordinary welcome from the royal family. He taught Bukhārī at the Raja Muda's palace to thousands of listeners from all over the state. Particular honour was paid to him by the Raja Kelantan, Tengku Ibrahim, who repeatedly asked his advice on religious matters. He

---

[22] That is to say, the teaching policy of the Prophet Muhammad and his followers for the strengthening of the Caliphate. See Shah Waliyullāh, *Tafhīmat-i Ilahīyya* (various editions).

taught the major works of Shah Waliyullāh al-Dihlawī, such as *Fauz al-kabīr fī uṣūl at-tafsīr; al-Musawwā;* the *Hujjat Allāh al-Bālighah; al-Inṣāf fī bayān sabab al-ikhtilāf;* general Kuranic exegesis, and the like. He was, however, given little time to realize his desires, for not much more than a year after returning to Kelantan death overtook him, on 21 Safar 1355 (13 May 1936), when he was still only 35 years old. He was buried in Kampong Banggul.

The death of this young and learned *alim* brought about a lessening in the conflict that some had wished to stir up concerning the office of Mufti. The group that had been in opposition to Haji Wan Musa's ideas felt assuaged, for they knew that others of his sons and pupils, also learned—such as Haji Nik Muhammad al-Sidqi, who became Inspector of Majlis Ugama Schools after the death of his father, and Haji Muhammad b. Haji Ibrahim Kota[23]—were not in a position to further the aims of Haji Wan Musa, because they had not been influenced in the same way by the work of Shah Waliyullāh al-Dihlawī.

The hopes and desires of Haji Wan Musa, implanted also in his son Nik Abdullah, were thus left unrealized at the time of their death. Though other *ulama* have since replaced them, it was as though the wave of renewal in the development of Islamic thought in Kelantan had spent itself. The highway for confronting the modern world, laid out in Shah Waliyullāh's *Hujjat Allāh al-Bālighah*, seemed to have been blocked.

Haji Wan Musa brought up his children in a radical-progressive way. He did not lose all hope with the death of his son Haji Nik Abdullah, but transferred these hopes rather to the present writer, to further the causes in which he believed. Because this struggle is still being fought, and the writer is engaged, with God's help, in pursuing the ends that have been described, facing a future that is full of challenge, it is best that the present account of the development of religious thought in Kelantan come to an end at this point, to be continued by one rather more removed from the field of battle.

*   *   *   *

The period of greatest importance in the Islamic reform movement in Kelantan after 1946 dates from the return of Haji Nik Muhammad Salleh (writer of the preceding section of this article, and widely known as Haji Nik 'Leh) from India, where he had been studying at the Jāmi'a

[23] The latter now lives in Tabal, southern Thailand, from whence Haji Wan Musa's father originated.

Milliyya-i Islamiyya in Delhi, headed then by Dr. Zakir Husayn.[24] Before entering the Jāmi'a Milliyya at the end of 1939, Haji Nik 'Leh had studied from 1937 at the Darul-'Ulum in Deoband, which was at that time under the direction of Maulana Sa'īd Husain Ahmad Madani.

As had been desired by his late father Haji Wan Musa, based on the concept *al-jāddat al-qawiyyat al-Muḥammadiyya* (see above) developed by Shah Waliyullāh al-Dihlawī in his book *Tafhīmat-i Ilāhiyya*, Haji Nik 'Leh from the moment of setting foot again on Kelantan soil until early death in 1972 pursued the truth in religious teaching. In forwarding his struggle he had no assistance either from friends of his youth or from his brothers, nor did he work on behalf of any organization or other concern that might have lost him his freedom to speak, act, and choose without duress. He stood on his own, as a truly independent *alim*—*al-ḥurr*—tied to no-one.

Born at Merbau, Kota Bharu, in March 1920, Nik 'Leh was taught Arabic and Malay by his father until the age of fourteen. He was reared in the religious discipline that had become a tradition in his family. Before his brother Nik Abdullah left for Mecca in 1926 he studied with him such major works as Shah Waliyullāh's *Fauz al-kabīr*, *al-Inṣaf*, and the *Hujjat Allāh al-Bālighah*, and Ibn Khaldun's *Muqaddimah*. Other teachers were Haji Asa'ad b. Haji Daud, Haji Husain Pulau Pinang, Haji Ayub b. Haji Husain Kamboja, and other well-known *ulama* of the day.[25]

After receiving his basic education in Kelantan, he was sent by his father to Mecca in 1936. There he met Maulana 'Ubayd-Ullāh as-Sindhī, his brother's teacher. On the advice of the Maulana he went to India to continue his education at Deoband. In his own opinion, too, the teaching available in Mecca was insufficient. He was convinced that religion there was shrouded in Arabic custom. From 1936 to 1939, accordingly, he lived and worked in Deoband. There he studied most aspects of Islamic learning in a philosophical way—*hadith*, the Hanafi school of *fikh*, pure philosophy and logic, astronomy, and so on.

---

[24] Zakir Husayn (1897–1969), noted Indian educator, was Vice-Chancellor of the Jāmi'a Milliyya from 1926 to 1948, and Vice-Chancellor of Aligarh Muslim University from 1948 to 1956. Appointed Vice President of India in 1962, he became President in 1967 until his death.

[25] Haji Asa'ad (1886–1941) of Kampong Kangkung, Pasir Mas, studied with To' Kenali and Haji Nik Abdullah b. Wan Musa, and was co-translator with To' Kenali of al-Shāfi'ī's *al-Umm*. He became a member of the Majlis Ugama in the 1930s, and taught at the Masjid Muhammadi and the Jami'a Merbau (the latter founded in 1939). Haji Husain came to Kelantan from Penang in 1914, and studied under both Haji Wan Musa and the latter's son Haji Nik Abdullah. From 1916 he taught at the Majlis Ugama school in Kota Bharu. He retired in 1945, and died later the same year. Haji Ayub came to Kelantan from Cambodia in 1925, and studied with Haji Wan Musa's brother, Haji Wan Abdullah b. Haji Abdul Samad, and with To' Kenali. He later went to Mecca, returning to Kelantan in 1934. He died only in 1970.

Among his teachers were Maulana Shamsul Haqq Fashawar, Maulana Shafik Deoband, and Maulana Husain Ahmad al-Madani.

Then he began to feel unhappy about the education in Deoband itself. At that time there emerged among certain Deoband *ulama* an attitude that regarded obvious externals, such as beard wearing or the use of short clothing, as in themselves holy. He viewed this as a symptom of fanaticism, likely to damage Islam, and recalled that he had seen similar phenomena in Mecca. Observing this growth, he went off to Delhi, to study at the Jāmi'a Milliyya.

He remained there from 1939 until 1943. The head teacher at the time was Maulana 'Ubayd-Ullāh as-Sindhī, who had just been permitted to return to India after 25 years of enforced exile, a sentence imposed upon him by the British as an 'undesirable person' for the crime of fighting against them during the First World War. The Vice-Chancellor of the Jāmi'a Milliyya was Dr. Zakir Husayn, who became Haji Nik 'Leh's friend and teacher.[26]

Among all his teachers, 'Ubayd-Ullāh as-Sindhī left the strongest impression. From him he obtained ideas relating to all aspects of life, of a kind that continued to influence him to his last days. From his formal teaching he gained true knowledge and understanding concerning the reconciliation of Kuranic philosophy with all world religions and philosophies. At the same time he studied the philosophy of history and civilization.

One section of the Jāmi'a Milliyya was known as the *Bayt al-hikmah* (House of Philosophy). In the *Bayt al-hikmah* Haji Nik 'Leh extended his knowledge of all branches of Islamic learning by deep study. The *Bayt al-hikmah* was a place of research for students, among whom he was recognized as one of great promise, assured of a bright future. In the final examinations of 1943 he graduated with the title '*Ulama Besar*', an honour unprecedented in modern Kelantan history since his brother's death.

Haji Nik 'Leh was unable to pursue satisfaction of his thirst for further learning because of the worsening condition of the Second World War. At the end of 1943, supported by the spirit implanted in him by 'Ubayd-Ullāh as-Sindhī, he embarked upon a career in the army. He served first as a publicity officer, newspaper translator and the like with the British Information Service in Calcutta. Towards the end of 1944 he entered the Security Service of the United States Army in Ceylon. With the end of the war in 1945 he left the ranks of the military, and on 14 April

[26] He had a final opportunity to meet Dr. Zakir Husayn in 1968, the year before the latter's death, when, as President of India, he paid a state visit to Malaysia and went also to Kelantan.

1946 returned to Kelantan, to continue the historic movement for the reformation of Islam with renewed organization and vigour.

When he arrived back in 1946, Kelantan Malays had great expectations of him. In June of that year he proposed the formation of a school to be called Al-Islah, as a means of spreading knowledge of Islam, and the formation of 'people's classes' and educational scholarships for the study of philosophy in both its theoretical and its practical aspects. The proposals were well received, save that his wish to introduce the teachings of the school of Shah Waliyullāh al-Dihlawī were to be frustrated. Members of his own family opposed him on this question, until finally he was ousted from the school. All his work in the interests of teaching Islam at Al-Islah went for nought.[27]

The most striking element of this situation lies in the fact that he was never given a *tauliah* (certificate of permission) from the Majlis Ugama Islam, such as is required by law of all teachers of religion in Kelantan. He asked that he be examined upon his knowledge, but no-one in the Majlis was prepared to administer an examination, not even the Mufti himself, Haji Ahmad Mahir b. Haji Ismail. Haji Nik 'Leh's letter to the Majlis in 1948 asking for permission to teach was answered only in 1951, when the Majlis informed him that a *tauliah* had been refused. He did not, however, cease teaching, without a *tauliah*, until his death. The final attempt to interfere with his teaching occurred in 1968, when his father's old *surau* was pulled down by his brothers, in order to put up a new one with the financial assistance of the Majlis Ugama. From that time he was forced to teach only in his own house.

As an *alim*, he did not allow his hopes and ambitions to be eroded. Early in 1970 he opened, in his house, a new place of education, the 'Kuliah Pengajian al-Kuran' (College for the Study of the Kuran). From this institution have appeared numerous religious publications of a general kind, Kuranic exegeses, and considerations of such questions as bank interest, lotteries, life insurance, and the like.

The principal points at issue between the Majlis Ugama authorities and Haji Nik 'Leh concerned the matter of zakat and fitrah taxation. In 1947 he published a booklet entitled *Risalah Masalah Fitrah dan Fitrah Kanak2 yang belum Baligh* (On the Question of Fitrah, and Fitrah for Children not yet of Age) (Kota Bharu, Al-Kamaliah Press). In this he argued that according to the opinion of all four schools of law, including the Shāfi'ī school itself, fitrah is payable by all persons able to fast during the fasting month, and that as a result children and slaves are

---

[27] The school still exists, on Jalan Chepa, Kota Bharu, but has been turned over entirely to English education, except for a few Islamic lessons, mainly in elementary *fikh*.

exempt.[28] This contention was hotly opposed by *ulama* of the Majlis Ugama, who recognized that this would reduce the income of the Majlis, dependent annually on collection of the zakat and fitrah paid by the populace. Rejecting Haji Nik 'Leh's arguments, an *alim* from Besut, Trengganu, Haji Abbas b. Haji Muhammad, published shortly after a pamphlet entitled *al-Qaul al-haqq* (Statement of Truth) (Kota Bharu, Mustafa Press), and a second rebuttal appeared, also in 1947, entitled *al-Qaul al-Jamīl* (Elegant Opinion) (Kota Bharu, Al-Hikmah Press) and written by Haji Mukhtar b. Haji Ahmad, younger brother of the Haji Tahir who in the 1930s had founded the Pondok Bunut Payong.[29]

From another work published by Haji Nik 'Leh in 1947, *Filsafat Berumahtangga* (Philosophy of the Family) (Kota Bharu, Mustafa Press), arose a particularly acerbic dispute, prompting no fewer than three state Muftis—of Johore, Pahang and Trengganu—to attack him. Together they spoke of him as '*kufr*' (*kafir*, or unbeliever), and the Mufti of Johore (Sayyid Aluwi b. Tahir al-Haddad) termed him also '*zindik*' and '*mulḥid*'—a heretic, pretender to the faith, and one disloyal to God.[30] In his *Filsafat Berumahtangga* Haji Nik 'Leh had argued that, from the point of view of Islam, the purpose or end of the family was the formation of human society and human civilization. The Islamic conception of the need for the family, he claimed, was validated in the Kuran, and by several comparisons with the philosophies taught by Western scholars. Because of his wide-ranging and scientific style of analysis, Haji Nik 'Leh's intentions were misunderstood by a large number of *ulama*, and the book was banned by the Kelantan Majlis Ugama.

The work of Haji Nik 'Leh which has attracted most attention is his *Sinaran I'tiqād* (Illumination of Belief), published originally in 1938 before his return to Kelantan, and explaining the question of the *Isrā'* and *Mi'rāj* of the Prophet Muhammad by means of intellectual elucidation.[31] This, together with his *Rahsia Kelahiran Nabi Muhammad* (Secret of the Birth of the Prophet Muhammad), published (Kota Bharu, Al-Ahliyah Press) in two volumes in 1947, provoked very considerable controversy. In the latter work, apart from dealing with the actual birth, Haji Nik 'Leh argued that the Prophet was given the task of uniting all

[28] For a discussion of the development of fitrah legislation by statute in Kelantan, see above, Roff.
[29] See above, Abdullah.
[30] These views were conveyed to all Imam and officially appointed Majlis Ugama teachers by the then Mufti of Kelantan, Haji Ahmad Mahir b. Haji Ismail, in the form of an 'unofficial notice' (*peringatan yang tidak resmi*).
[31] '*Isrā*', the miraculous nocturnal journey of the Prophet from Mecca to Jerusalem (*Kuran*, Sura 17, Verse 1); '*Mi'rāj*', the ascension of the Prophet from the Masjid al-Aqsā (in Jerusalem) to heaven. *Sinaran I'tiqād* was published under the auspices of Haji Nik 'Leh's brother Nik Muhammad, and printed at the Majlis Ugama Press, Kota Bharu.

men 'of God's Book' (thus including the scriptural Jews and Christians), or of similar intellectual beliefs, under the appeal of the Kuran. He added, further, that the prayers received by the Prophet on the night of his Mi'rāj were a means of preparation for acquisition of the status of God's Caliph. These arguments seemed to imply an interpretative movement such as had not previously been suggested by any other *alim* in Kelantan.

Apart from the four publications mentioned above, Haji Nik 'Leh produced some hundreds of other pamphlets and similar works on other subjects. In a series of lectures published (in cyclostyled form) by the Kuliah Pengajian al-Kuran, beginning in early 1970, there have so far appeared 24 exegetic pieces, thousands of copies of which, in bound form, have been distributed throughout Malaysia, southern Thailand and Brunei. These lectures have given rise to new hope in Malay society, for throughout them Haji Nik 'Leh stressed that an Islamic '*hukumah*,' or government, must be brought into being, especially in the circumstances of the present, in order to give birth to lasting justice and peace.

In addition, there are in manuscript, but not yet published, commentaries on two of the important works of Shah Waliyullāh al-Dihlawī, entitled respectively 'Asas Kebenaran antara Filsafat Shah Waliyullāh dengan Filsafat2 Dunia' (Foundations of Truth between the Philosophy of Shah Waliyullāh and World Philosophies), and 'Tafsir atas Kitab *Fauz al-kabīr*' (Exegesis of the *Fauz al-kabīr*), as well as a work on the abbreviated letters found at the beginning of some chapters of the Kuran,'Muqatta'āt al-Qur'ān', and a commentary on parts of Ibn Khaldun's *Muqaddimah*, entitled 'Kritik Filsafat Kemasharakatan Ibn Khaldun' (Social Philosophical Critique of Ibn Khaldun).

What Haji Nik Muhammad Salleh's final effect on Kelantan society and Islam will be is hard to say, and there is no question of his continued controversiality. Like those who went before him, however—like Tuan Tabal, Haji Wan Musa, and Haji Nik Abdullah, and indeed like generations of Kelantan scholars of many shades of opinion—he was deeply dedicated to the advancement of his people and the strengthening of what he saw as their principal source of strength, the religion of Islam.

REFERENCES

Al-Ahmadi, Abdul Rahman, 1966. *Pengantar Sastera* (Kota Bharu, Pustaka Aman Press).

Ibn Khaldun, 1967. *The Muqaddimah. An Introduction to History* (transl. by Franz Rosenthal, abr. and ed. by N.J. Dawood) (London, Routledge & Kegan Paul).

7

ABDUL RAHMAN AL-AHMADI

Notes Towards a History of Malay Periodicals in Kelantan

As part of its long and creative historical tradition, Kelantan has been the source of numerous writings in a variety of literary forms, from religious works and narrative poems to tales of the past. This tradition has been continued from early in the twentieth century to the present by way of mass media such as newspapers and journals, as well as religious and general literature of a new kind. If we examine the remarkable quantity of writing emanating from the state (whether in the form of books or other materials), it is clear that Kelantan emerges as the centre of Malay literary activity for the whole East Coast of the peninsula, from Patani to Pahang and from before the Second World War until today. Literary enterprise in Kelantan in the field of periodical journalism, especially, is evidenced by the large numbers of serial publications produced, more than thirty having appeared between 1918 and 1970.[1]

[1] Though the relationship between periodical (or other) publication and functional literacy is a complex (and not always a relevant) one, and most Kelantan publications have circulated outside as well as inside the state, it may be helpful to give what literacy statistics are available for two strategic years from within the period covered by this paper, 1931 and 1947, derived respectively from Vlieland (1932) and Tufo (1949). In 1931, 8 per cent of all Malay males aged over fifteen were recorded as literate in Malay, giving an absolute figure of some 8,000 persons (for women the rate was 0.4 per cent). In 1947, 18.6 per cent of all Malay males aged over fifteen were recorded as literate in any language (necessarily implying Malay), giving an absolute figure of 30,270 (while for women the rate had risen to 2 per cent).

The oldest and longest lived of these journals, founded over fifty years ago and still appearing today, is *Pengasoh*, which published its first fortnightly issue on 11 July 1918 (1 Shawal 1336), under the auspices of the then recently formed Majlis Ugama Islam.

Although *Pengasoh* appeared on the scene a little late if compared, for example, with the first ever Malay-language newspaper, *Jawi Peranakan* (Singapore, weekly, 1876–95); with *Seri Perak*, the first paper to be published in any of the peninsular states (Taiping, weekly, 1893–?); or indeed with *Al-Imam*, the first Malay journal in South-East Asia to concern itself principally with Islamic matters (Singapore, monthly, 1906–8); we should not forget that the publication of any journal depends largely on the availability of the printing press. The introduction of the press to the Straits Settlements and the west coast Malay states, with their British connections, obviously preceded its introduction to Kelantan. The latter state was at this time still associated mainly with Siam, and in the nineteenth century 'publications' in Kelantan still appeared entirely in manuscript form. Abdullah Munshi, who visited the state in 1838, commented (Abdullah, 1860, 83) on the number of manuscripts available in Kota Bharu, among them religious texts, and *hikayat* such as the Hikayat Isma Dewa Pekerma Raja and the Kitab Khoja Maimun. At this time, too, a woman writer known as Neng Rumek produced an account of the Kelantan civil war known as the Sha'er Musoh Kelantan, and other texts dealt with the political events of the later century.[2]

The introduction of the printing press to Kelantan may perhaps date from the time of Sultan Mansur (1891–1900), when he opened the first Land Office in Kota Bharu in 1896, itself the product of a visit to, among other places, Johore and Singapore.[3] Though the grants issued as a result of the work of the Lands Commission set up in 1899 to resurvey all lands were certainly in manuscript, it is possible that early in the new century some printing of grants or register books had begun. The most persuasive evidence, however, suggests that the first press was installed in Kota Bharu in September or October 1901, during the early reign of Muhammad IV, and owned by the Orang Kaya Seri Akar Raja, Nik Hasan b. Pa' Nik Jid, a younger brother of Nik Seri Paduka Raja, the then chief minister of the state.[4] It is also sometimes suggested that however this first press was come by, the ruler himself had a share in its

---

[2] For a discussion of these materials, see Muhammad (1964/65, 59ff). For the 'Sha'er Musoh Kelantan' in particular, see the unpublished M.A. thesis by Kassim b. Ahmad, University of Malaya, Kuala Lumpur, 1961.

[3] Personal communication from Sa'ad Shukri b. Haji Muda, Kota Bharu.

[4] Muhammad Yusof (1953, 40), where the site is given as a building owned by Nik Seri Paduka Raja on Jalan Sultan (near the present-day Mercantile Bank).

ownership and operation. Whatever the circumstances, it was sold in due course to one Haji Nik Mat b. Haji Wan Daud, then to Dato' Kaya Bakti (Haji Muhammad b. Salleh) and Haji Wan Ali Kutan,[5] and finally in 1917 to Engku Abdul Kadir (Engku Dir), who thenceforth operated with it the firm known as The Kelantan Printing Press.[6] Also in 1917, in November, the Majlis Ugama Islam purchased a press for $1,000 from one Inche Ja'afar b. Haji Muhammad, and with this started its Matba'ah Majlis Ugama (Religious Council Press), from which *Pengasoh* began to appear the following year.

Pengasoh is still today the Malay journal with the longest continuous (or virtually continuous) history in Malaysia, and has seen many changes of editorship. Its first honorary editor was Haji Muhammad Yusof b. Ahmad (To' Kenali),[7] though the early editorials were written by Haji Nik Mahmud b. Ismail (then Dato' Bentara Setia, and principal originator of the Majlis Ugama, shortly to become Dato' Seri Paduka Raja, or chief minister), and before long the effective working editor was Haji Muhammad b. To' Khatib Haji Muhammad Said (associated with Dato' Setia in founding the Majlis, and shortly to be entitled Dato' Bentara Jaya).[8] Articles were contributed by To' Kenali himself, by Haji Hassan b. Idris, Muhammad Daud b. Salim,[9] To' Khatib Haji Muhammad Said b. Jamaluddin,[10] and the Dato' Bentara Luar, Muhammad Ghazali b. Mohd. Arifin.[11] Its contents were wide ranging, for apart

---

[5] Haji Nik Mat was of the family of Wan Ahmad Patani. Haji Muhammad is said to have had his own printing press in 1905, and the Haji Wan Ali Kutan with whom he was then (or later) in partnership was Wan Ali b. Wan Yusof, probable author of the Hikayat Seri Kelantan (see Muhammad, 1964/65, 64), not Wan Ali b. Abdul Rahman, compiler of the *hadith* collection *Al-Jauhar al-mauhūb* (see Al-Ahmadi, 1966, 163), who was also known as Wan Ali Kutan.

[6] Engku Abdul Kadir, originally from Patani, was related to the Raja Muda of Kelantan, Tengku Zainal Abidin b. Sultan Muhammad III.

[7] See above, Abdullah. Since this volume first went to press, publication of *Pengasoh* has been temporarily suspended.

[8] Born 1888 in Kota Bharu, Haji Muhammad had studied religion there before spending some ten years in the Middle East, mainly at Al-Azhar in Cairo, returning to Kelantan in 1914. He became Dato' Laksamana and State Secretary during the 1920s, but resigned in 1933, and died in 1939. Cf. above, Roff.

[9] Better known as Che' Wok Johor, Muhammad Daud came originally from Manir Tendung, Pasir Mas, but had had administrative experience in Johore. He was in charge of the Kelantan Land Office from its inception in 1896 until 1904, later became one of the foundation members of the Majlis Ugama Islam dan Isti'adat Melayu, and in 1917 became first *Nazir* (Supervisor) of the Madrasah Muhammadi, the school set up by the Majlis that year. He was subsequently entitled Dato' Isti'adat.

[10] Father of Haji Muhammad (Note 8, above), Haji Muhammad Said had been born in Kota Bharu c. 1856, and was at this time senior *khatib* in the Kota Bharu Mosque. During the early years of British rule he was in charge of the Land Office, and was the first Kelantan Malay to be awarded the I.S.O. He died as Dato' Seri di-Raja in 1938, aged 82. See obituary in *Al-Hikmah*, v, 212 (6 Oct. 1938), p. 20.

[11] A Singaporean, Muhammad Ghazali had come to Kelantan around 1900, as secretary to Muhammad IV and teacher to his young son Ismail (Sultan of Kelantan from 1920). Appointed head teacher of the government school in Kota Bharu, he was for many years in charge of education throughout the state.

from articles on religion (and a *fatwa*, or question and answer, section on religious topics run by To' Kenali), it published articles on general knowledge, the history of Malaya, British law and government, political science, economics, a column on the Malay language, and news about events both inside and outside Kelantan.

In its second and third years new writers began to appear in *Pengasoh*, including men such as Megat Othman b. Ali,[12] who translated many articles from the *Encyclopaedia Britannica*, and the critical historian Muhammad al-Jauhari, whose analyses were both sharply argued and scholarly. During 1919, apart from a few months between June and October when the journal was looked after by Muhammad Daud b. Salim, supervisor of the recently established Madrasah Muhammadi, the school associated with the Majlis Ugama, *Pengasoh* came under the full editorial and literary control of Dato' Bentara Jaya, honorary secretary of the Majlis and right hand man to the chief minister, Haji Nik Mahmud. Dato' Jaya wrote voluminously for the journal (and elsewhere), especially on topics relating to history and the science of Western government. When he relinquished the editorship in 1922, his place was taken by Hassan b. Haji Omar for more than ten years until March 1933,[13] the latter being succeeded in turn by Haji Ahmad Mahir b. Haji Ismail.[14] Following Haji Ahmad, Haji Muhammad Adnan b. Mohd. Arifin (younger brother of the Dato' Bentara Luar) and Haji Wan Mahmud b. Haji Wan Daud[15] took over the journal from early in 1935 until the invasion of Kelantan by the Japanese in 1941 stopped publication for a time.

Production of *Pengasoh* was resumed after the war, with Haji Muhammad Adnan continuing as editor from 1947 until 1953, when he was succeeded by Hassan b. Haji Muhammad until mid-1960. A break in publication followed, but the journal was restarted in November 1964 under the editorship of Ismail Yusoff, printed for the first time not by the Majlis' own press but by a newcomer to the Kota

[12] Originally from Perak, Othman came to Kelantan in 1917 as head teacher in the English division of the Majlis Ugama school. He became secretary of the Majlis itself in 1920, and was later entitled Dato' Megat di-Raja. He returned to Perak towards the end of his life, and died there.

[13] Born at Kampong Penambang in 1901, Hassan was one of the first pupils at the Majlis Ugama's Madrasah Muhammadi in 1917. He was later on the staff of the Majlis (and from 1933 a Member) until his death in 1935.

[14] Haji Ahmad, Secretary of the *Meshuarat Ulama* (Conference of 'Ulamā) of the Majlis Ugama in the 1930s, was appointed Chief Kathi for Kelantan in 1937, and after the war became Mufti, dying in 1968.

[15] Of Patani descent, Haji Wan Mahmud became a teacher at the Kota Bharu religious school Jami'a Merbau (opened in 1939) during the Japanese occupation. Prior to the war he had been politically active in the local branch of the Kesatuan Melayu Muda (KMM, Young Malay Union), and on the return of the British he was jailed for some six months.

Bharu scene, Pustaka Aman Press, founded early in 1959. This arrangement lasted for only twelve months, but in 1967 *Pengasoh* was revived yet again, with Inche Hassan b. Haji Ya'acub and Drs. Abdul Ghani Azmi as joint editors, and printed by Al-Ahliyah Press.

As may be seen, through its long life *Pengasoh* has experienced many varieties of editorial impress. What has not changed, however, based on the ideals that originally inspired it, is its role as a religious journal with the capacity to make a major contribution not just to Kelantan but to the wider Islamic society of the peninsula.

In September 1920, two years after the founding of *Pengasoh*, a second periodical was started in Kota Bharu, the monthly *Al-Kitab*. *Al-Kitab* was owned and run (and sold at a subscription of $10 annually) by Dato' Bentara Jaya and Megat Othman, both at this time still closely associated with the Majlis Ugama and *Pengasoh*. Although Roff (1961, 8) described *Al-Kitab* as less a periodical proper than the serial publication of a translation of the Kuran with commentary (and it did in fact publish parts of such an exegesis, translated from the English of Maulvi Muhammad Ali), it had wider aims, styling itself 'a journal of miscellaneous knowledge', and contained in addition (as had been forecast by *Pengasoh* in its issue of 16 July 1920), contributions to an (Arabic-) Malay dictionary, articles on politics and Islamic history, a Muslim calendar, and monthly stories for the delectation and improvement of its readers. The first of these stories, 'Anchuman Kekaseh', published from the second issue of the journal onwards, concerned mainly the heroes of current Middle Eastern nationalism, Amir Faisal, Mustafa Kamal, and others.

Much of the importance of *Al-Kitab* in the eyes of its audience, however, stemmed from its publication in Malay of a translation of and commentary upon the Kuran, a want much felt at the time (the translation of al-Baiḍāwī into Malay by an Achehnese scholar in the late nineteenth century—and published in Istanbul—being as yet unknown in Kelantan), and though this particular version did not altogether satisfy the thirst for guidance to the Kuran, it did not go unpraised. Despite this, *Al-Kitab* lasted for only four issues, largely because of controversy arising out of Muhammad Ali's translation, regarded by many as very naive in its views, and irresponsible. Publication was followed by a storm of argument, over such matters as the question of the division of the traditional parts of the Kuran, the *sura* or 'chapters' of the original being rearranged in the Muhammad Ali text. Though publication of the translation was defended, especially, it appears, by Dato' Bentara Jaya, who discussed the whole matter in *Pengasoh*, the older and more conservative section of the readership refused to relent. Dato' Jaya's view was that there was no compulsion to follow Muhammad Ali, that the version was not in all respects incorrect, and that such errors as there were could be corrected. To which the conservatives replied that this might be all very well while Dato' Jaya was alive, but should the call of Allah come, what price then *Al-Kitab's* exegesis? (*Pengasoh*, 20 Nov. 1920).

After the demise of *Al-Kitab* (in December 1920), the next Kelantan journal to appear was *Al-Hedayah*, published monthly from June 1923 for nearly three years. It was declared by its founders to be a journal of 'dissemination, demonstration, directive, and delight'. Among those on the editorial board were Ahmad b. Ismail,[16] the Dato' Bentara Luar (Muhammad Ghazali b. Mohd. Arifin) and his brother Muhammad Adnan, Haji Abdul Rahman b. Daud al-Makki,[17] Hassan b. Haji Omar, Mahmud b. Khatib Haji Mohd. Said,[18] and Muhammad b. Haji Sulong. It was printed at Al-Asasiyah Press (founded by Ahmad Ismail) in Kota Bharu.

A large part of *Al-Hedayah* was taken up with the discussion of all manner of things from household affairs, private obligations and public duties, matters of opinion such as those raised by the daily press, scientific questions, and the art of organization, to original tales, detective stories such as those about the American 'Nicholas Carter', and serialized novels like *Jogan Setia* that told of the national struggle of the Turks,[19] in addition to news and views concerning Kelantan. The journal also dealt with religious questions, the issue of Malay-language education, and (especially useful) published notices and reviews of

[16] Ahmad Ismail was born in Kota Bharu in 1899, and attended the Malay school there from 1912–15, later learning Arabic from To' Kenali. In addition to being principal editor of *Al-Hedayah* he himself started and edited the weekly *Al-Hikmah* (1934–41, see below), founded a press of this name in 1939, and throughout the late 1920s and the 1930s published numerous translations from the Arabic (for some account of these, see Li, 1966, 161–71). After the Second World War he was made a member of the Majlis Ugama and created Dato' Lela Negara. He died in 1969.

[17] Haji Abdul Rahman was born in 1900 in Mecca (hence the toponym al-Makki), grandson of Shaykh Nik Mat Kechil, a pilgrimage shaykh from Patani, and came to Kelantan about 1918. After a brief return visit to Mecca he worked for the Majlis Ugama Islam in Kota Bharu, later (in the 1930s?) becoming principal of the Madrasah Zainal Abidin in Kuala Trengganu. After the war he came back to Kota Bharu to teach at the Jami'a Merbau, retiring as principal only in 1968.

[18] Brother of Muhammad (Dato' Bentara Jaya) and son of the Superintendant of the Land Office, Mahmud had served in the Kelantan civil service from 1904 to 1914 (when he resigned for a period) and again from 1918, when he was appointed Collector of Town Revenues for Kota Bharu, becoming Assistant District Officer of Pasir Mas sub-district in 1920, and later a Magistrate. He was entitled Dato' Andika Raja during the reign of Sultan Ismail.

[19] Translated from Nakula Afandi Haddad's *Fir' aunat al-'Arab 'indat-Turk*, set in Istanbul at the beginning of the First World War. For an introduction and the first instalment, see *Al-Hedayah*, I, 1 (Jun. 1923), 14 and 23–4.

books and periodicals appearing in the Malay peninsula and Indonesia.[20] A list of some of the latter as they appeared in *Al-Hedayah* for two years from mid-1923 may be of interest:

1. *Sha'er Merak Emas*, by Muhammad Yusup b. Salleh, published by Wan Muhammad Hanafi, Kota Bharu.
2. *Sha'er Haluan Pelayaran*, by Zainal Abidin, published in Singapore.
3. *Sha'er Pemimpin Nazam*, Singapore.
4. *Medan Muslimin*, published in Java.
5. *Warta Islam Bergerak*, quarterly journal partly in Indonesian and partly in Javanese, published in Java.
6. *Seri Poestaka*, published by the Balai Pustaka in Betawi (Batavia, now Djakarta).
7. *Bintang Hindia*, published in Betawi.
8. *Djauhara*, a monthly magazine from Ampat Angkat, Bukit Tinggi, Sumatra, edited by Sa'adiah Shukor, Khatijah, and Rasmin, and published by Haji Abdul Latiff Shukor.
9. *Adh-Dhakirat al-Islamiyyah*, published by the Jabatan Baru, Betawi. A journal for the discussion of Kuranic exegesis, religion in general, and *adat*.
10. *Djaga* (*Suara Merdeka*), published thrice-monthly by the International Debating Club (so named) of Padang Panjang, Sumatra.
11. *Pemandangan Islam*, published by the organization Sumatera Thawalib, in Padang Panjang.
12. *Persatuan*, published weekly in Samarinda, Kalimantan (Indonesian Borneo), containing world news and material concerning the advancement of Islam.
13. *Al-Islam*, a journal published in Javanese. This was returned to the publisher by *Al-Hedayah* (whose staff could not read Javanese), with the hope that no offence would be taken.
14. *Semaian*, the thrice-yearly journal of the Kuala Kangsar Malay College, Perak.
15. *Warta al-Wafq*, a weekly in Arabic, published by Muhammad Sa'id al-Fatat (al-Makki), at Banten, Java, containing politics, social comment and literature.
16. *Chendera Mata*, published half-yearly by the Sultan Idris Training College, Tanjong Malim, Perak.
17. *Tetauan Muda*, published quarterly by the Persekutuan Rembau Ternakkan, Seremban, Negri Sembilan.
18. *Istri Susila* (Solo, Java), an Islamic magazine intended especially for women.

[20] This practice had been initiated by *Pengasoh*, and was followed also by *Majallah al-Kamaliah* (1930), the resulting information providing a useful bibliographical tool for early Malay and Indonesian publications.

The easiest way to discuss Kelantan's numerous periodicals from this point on is probably to take them one by one, and give what information one can about them and those connected with them. Between the publication of *Al-Hedayah* (which ceased in February 1926) and the Second World War, a further eight periodicals appeared during this 'first phase', to be followed after the war by some twenty others. They may be listed and commented on as follows.

Terok

A monthly magazine published from March 1927 by Tengku Ismail Pekerma b. Tengku Pekerma Raja of Kelantan, Assistant District Officer of Pasir Puteh, who had been educated first in the English-language division of the Majlis Ugama school in Kota Bharu, and then at Kuala Kangsar Malay College. His assistant editor (and also his chief clerk in the district office) was Muhammad Daud b. Haji Muhammad Salleh. *Terok* was the organ of the Persekutuan New Club (so named) in Pasir Puteh, and the two issues which are all that are thought to have appeared contain articles of general interest and some relating to Islam. The journal was printed by Al-Kamaliah Press, founded in Kota Bharu in 1926 by Umar b. Haji Taib. The title *Terok*, in the Kelantan dialect, refers to a purse or bag made from the flower sheaths of certain sorts of palms and creepers, and used as a carry-all.

Torch

Possibly entitled *The Torch*, this journal, which was published, apparently in 1928, by the Old Majlisian Society, consisting of former pupils of the English-language division of the Majlis Ugama school in Kota Bharu, may have been written in either English or Malay, or both. It is thought to have been, at least in intent, a monthly, but few issues seem to have appeared and none are known to exist today.

Petra

A fortnightly paper serving as the voice of the Petra Kelab, a club founded in Kota Bharu in November 1928[21] to foster cultural interests and to give a lead to the young in pursuit of change and development, *Petra* began publication in October 1929 and ran for six issues (and/or—if irregular—six months). It was edited by Abdul Kadir b. Ahmad, assisted by Muhammad Asa'ad b. Haji Muda, who also acted as manager.[22] *Petra* was an eight-page, large format paper, costing fifteen cents

---

[21] An article entitled 'Tarikh [sic] perdirian Petra Kelab dengan rengkas', concerning the origins of the club, appeared in the first issue of the journal, p. 6.

[22] Abdul Kadir b. Ahmad (d. 1943) has been better known subsequently as Abdul Kadir Adabi, and Muhammad Asa'ad b. Haji Muda (d. 1971) as Asa'ad (or Sa'ad) Shukri b.

a copy and printing an edition of about 500 at Al-Kamaliah Press. It contained articles attacking injustice and oppression, and published also Kelantan news of interest, including crime reportage. On one notable occasion it publicly contested the advertised plans of a foreign company to plant oil palm for the first time in Pahang. In general it acquired a radical and 'nationalist' reputation.

Petra stopped publication as the result of an article entitled 'Ulama Mana Mengganti Nabi?' (What *ulama* [could possibly] take the place of the Prophet [Muhammad]?), written not by the editorial staff but by an outsider. The article criticized the old-fashioned Kelantan *ulama* of the day, leading those *ulama* who disagreed with its views to seek ways of having publication of *Petra* stopped. As most members of the Petra Kelab were junior government servants, the government issued instructions that its officials be prohibited from joining. In consequence, many members resigned, the journal lost support, and finally ceased publication.

During its lifetime *Petra* acquired something of a following outside Kelantan, especially in Indonesia, where copies were sent on an exchange basis—for example, to the Balai Pustaka in Djakarta. Many readers' letters from Indonesia appeared in *Petra* in the form of articles, to be responded to in turn by articles written by the *Petra* staff. One correspondent of Asa'ad Shukri should be noted—Hassan Bandung, who sent to Kota Bharu copies of his own books and other writings[23]

Majallah al-Kamaliah

A fortnightly journal published in Kota Bharu for some months from January 1930. It was managed by Umar b. Haji Taib, a cousin of Asa'ad Shukri and owner of Al-Kamaliah Press. The principal editor was Haji Nuh b. Ali, a teacher in the Madrasah Muhammadi, who also practised as an advocate and was widely known in the town as 'Haji Nuh Lawyer'. He was assisted by one Shaykh Ali b. Kassim, apparently a Kelantan Malay of Indian extraction.

Haji Muda, the Arabic appellations 'Adabi' and 'Shukri' being assumed in company with others of the radical young Kota Bharu intelligentsia in the 1930s (among the best known being Ishak 'Lutfi' Omar, later Mentri Besar of the state, and Yusof 'Zaki' Ya'acub, founder of Pustaka Dian press). Because the more recent form of the name is now that by which they are best known, it will be used henceforth in the present article, if occasionally anachronistically.

[23] Ahmad Hassan was born in Singapore in 1887 of a Tamil father and Javanese mother, and later taught at several religious schools in Singapore and Johore, writing also for the early Malay newspaper *Utusan Melayu* (founded in Singapore in 1907). He moved to Bandung in Indonesia in the early 1920s, and became a leading figure in the modernist Islamic movement Persatuan Islam. He published extensively, his best known work perhaps being *Al-Furqān (Tafsir Qu'rān)* (Surabaya, Salim Nabhan, 3rd ed. 1957), a translation of the Kuran into Indonesian, with exegesis, which was for some time banned in parts of the Malay peninsula for its alleged *kaum muda* tendencies.

Many of the articles in the *Majallah al-Kamaliah* appear to have been contributed by the editor himself, but it contained also material in translation from the Arabic, news of local events, and, like *Pengasoh* and *Al-Kitab* before it, notices and reviews of current books and periodicals from elsewhere. The main interest of the journal was unquestionably religious, and the articles, often of a homiletic kind, were regarded at the time as representing '*kaum muda*' or modernist thought.

Kenchana

This journal appeared monthly for a year from April 1930, and then fortnightly until its demise shortly thereafter. It was printed at Al-Kamaliah Press in Kota Bharu, and edited by the indefatigable Asaʻad Shukri b. Haji Muda, who also wrote in its columns a fifteen-part history of Kelantan which was later to appear in revised form as a separate publication (Asaʻad, 1962). Though it contained many articles of a current affairs and general kind, *Kenchana* is also of some interest as being the first periodical in Kelantan to cater especially for women, most issues containing at least one article by or about women, reflecting both the increasing prominence of the '*kaum ibu*' (women's group) in modern Kelantan and peninsular Malay life and the slowly increasing literacy of this section of the community.[24] *Kenchana* was unique, as well, in sponsoring a 'Kenchana Library', in which books translated by the editor, and by Abdul Kadir Adabi and Yusup Helmi, were published.[25]

Kenchana was eventually discontinued as a result of a government legislative requirement that all publishers and editors of periodicals register with the authorities under the 'Printing Presses and Seditious Publications Enactment' (No. 5 of 1931). Asaʻad Shukri was at this time holding an official post, as a clerk in the High Court, Kota Bharu, and felt intimidated by the passage of this enactment, as he was no doubt intended to be.

Suara

A weekly journal which was published, apparently only briefly, in Kota Bharu from March 1931. Edited by Nuh b. Ali Bafdzal, with Ahmad b. Isa Banjari as manager, it seems to have emanated from a

---

[24] The first Malay journal in the peninsula to be published explicitly by and for women, *Bulan Melayu*, began publication in Johore Bharu in June 1930 as the journal of the Persekutuan Guru2 Perempuan Melayu, Johor (Association of Malay Women Teachers, Johore) edited by Hajjah Zin bte Suleiman.

[25] The first publications in this series, as advertised in Vol. 1, No. 10 of *Kenchana* (Jan. 1931), were *Huriah, atau Tukang Nyanyi Awazul* (2 vols.), and *Pergerakan Perjuangan Kaum Ibu, atau Rahsia Kaki Dayan Kesaktian*, the latter again displaying emphasis on the emancipation of women.

trading company known as the Sharikat al-Ittihad al-Islamiah. Nothing is known to the present writer about either this body or the journal.[26]

Al-Hikmah

A weekly journal (thrice-monthly originally) published between April 1934 and the end of 1941, and edited by Ahmad b. Ismail, previously the leading member of the editorial board of *Al-Hedayah* and an active translator and adaptor of Arabic-language novels and other works.[27] Many of these were published in serial form in the journal, as were the original novels *Achuman Mahkota* and *Melati Kota Bharu* by Abdul Kadir Adabi, who often acted as Ahmad Ismail's assistant editor. *Al-Hikmah* was a well produced magazine, popular throughout the peninsula and particularly noted for the interest and high quality of its photographic illustrations, prepared from its own blocks, a technique not previously employed in Kelantan. For the first five years it was printed by Al-Asasiyah Press in Kota Bharu, but from 1939 had its own press (Al-Hikmah), which also published some general literature.

The content of *Al-Hikmah* was a blend of popular and educational articles and current weekly news and report from the peninsula and Kelantan, and from overseas (especially after the start of the war in Europe), and reached a high standard of presentation, comparable to that anywhere else in the country. Both Ahmad Ismail and his assistant Abdul Kadir Adabi were often outspoken on local affairs, and had several encounters with the Malay and British authorities as a result.[28] The journal also participated from time to time in peninsula-wide controversy. During the visit to Malaya in mid-1938 of the McLean Commission on Higher Education, *Al-Hikmah* was alone among the Malay press in advocating the establishment of a university in the country, the burden of Malay opinion being that such a step would not be in the Malay interest in view of their already disadvantaged educational status.[29]

Majallah al-Riwayat

A fortnightly published from November 1938 for about a year, edited by Ishak Lutfi Omar,[30] and published at the latter's newly form-

[26] It is possible that Nuh b. Ali Bafdzal originated from Salor, across the river from Pasir Mas, which used to be inhabited by a number of Arab and Parsi merchants and others, and was also the site of a well known *pondok*.
[27] For some account of these, see Li (1966, 167–71).
[28] See, e.g., the dispute with the Majlis Ugama in 1938/39 in *Al-Hikmah*, 220 & 221 (1 & 8 Dec.), 226 (12 Jan.), and 232 (23 Feb.); and with the government (over alleged misreporting) in late 1940, in 322 & 323 (14 & 21 Nov.)
[29] See, especially, virtually every issue appearing in June and July 1937.
[30] Born 1918 in Kota Bharu, educated locally and for ten years in Mecca, he became Secretary-General of the Persekutuan Persetiaan Melayu Kelantan (League of Malay

ed Al-Ma'arif Press in Kota Bharu. As its name suggests, the journal published mainly short stories, most of them translated from the Arabic, though sometimes from English or other originals. The titles of a few of the most popular were 'Cherita pertelingkahan enggan2 antara orang2 makan gaji dengan orang2 berniaga' (A dispute between wage-earners and employers), 'Cherita Monte Carlo', and 'Cherita Sexton Blake'. In addition the journal contained some locally written tales, of which 'Kawin segera' (Hasty marriage) may be cited as an example. About half way through its relatively short life (from issue No. 14), *Majallah al-Riwayat* began to publish also articles of general topical interest.

* * * *

Matahari

The coming of the Japanese to Kelantan in early December 1941 did not put an immediate end to literary activity, though normal publication came to a halt. Kelantan was the first state on the East Coast (and indeed in the peninsula) to be invaded (in the morning hours of 8 December), and from the very beginning of the occupation the propaganda section of the Japanese army was ready to launch a campaign on behalf of the Greater East Asia war and to urge the Malays to rise against the British who had for so long kept them in chains. On 29 December[31] there appeared in Kota Bharu the first issue of a weekly paper entitled *Matahari*. The editors were listed as Abdullah A., Sidi, Sanusi, and Ilias. Only seven issues were published. The contents consisted of appeals to the Malays to fight against the British and help the Japanese army to achieve a shared peace in Greater East Asia. With the imminent fall of Singapore towards mid-February, no doubt this task was regarded as having been achieved.

* * * *

With the end of the war, and of the Japanese occupation, life in Kelantan, as elsewhere in Malaya, was slow to resume its normal

---

Loyalists, Kelantan) on his return from Mecca after the war, and served as an official of the Majlis Ugama. Resigned from the latter to contest the 1959 state elections as a Pan-Malayan Islamic Party candidate, and when successful became the first elected Mentri Besar of Kelantan, relinquishing the post in 1964 but remaining in the Assembly. He became Mentri Besar again in 1973, when Dato' Muhammad Asri entered the federal cabinet.

[31] The legend on the cover of the first issue gives 'Ahad, 10 Zulhijah 1360'. This date corresponds to 29 December 1941, which was a Monday, but as 'Ahad' signifies Sunday there is clearly a minor discrepancy here.

energy, caught up as many people were with the struggle for economic rehabilitation—and of course with new political demands upon their time. Between 1947 and the present, however, some 21 periodicals have been published, the details being as follows.

Penyedar

A journal published twice-monthly in Kota Bharu by Muhammad Asri b. Haji Muda[32] on behalf of the Penyiaran Jabatan Sosial, Persekutuan Persetiaan Melayu Kelantan (Publications of the Social Division, League of Malay Loyalists, Kelantan),[33] from 13 June 1947. Printed by Al-Kamaliah Press, it appeared for only a few issues. Largely political in content, it dealt especially with political movements in the peninsula and the revolutionary nationalist struggle in Indonesia, and with related ideological questions. In addition, it contained a series of articles on the history of Patani,[34] a special column on the affairs of the League, notes on religious questions such as zakat taxation, short stories and poems. Among the contributors were those writing under the names Tan Busu Setia, Abdul Rab Attamini,[35] Ibnu Khatib,[36] Kelana Jayaputera, and Keris Mas.[37] Two advertisements run by *Penyedar* at this time may also

[32] Born 1923 at Kampong Masjid, Kota Bharu, and educated at Padang Garong Malay school and the Majlis Ugama school. After the war taught (from 1948) at the Madrasah Ma'ahad Ihya al-Sharif, Gunong Semanggol, Perak, becoming also Assistant Secretary-General of the Persekutuan Persetiaan Melayu, Kelantan (1945-6), and Secretary of the radical Muslim movement Hizbul Muslimin, formed at Gunong Semanggol. A founder-member of the Pan-Malayan Islamic Party, he was Acting Secretary-General until 1954, and then Vice-President. He became President in 1970 on the death of Dr. Burhanuddin Al-Helmi, but had been already effectively so for some years during the latter's detention and subsequent political restraint. Dato' Muhammad Asri (as he now is) has been a member of both the Kelantan State Assembly and the national Parliament since 1959, and was Mentri Besar of Kelantan from 1964, until entering the federal cabinet in 1973.

[33] The Persekutuan, led by members of the Kota Bharu journalistic intelligentsia who before the war had been active in such organizations as the Kuala Lumpur based Kesatuan Melayu Muda (Young Malay Union), was actively anti-colonialist and populist-nationalist in sentiment, was formed in 1945, and was one of the associations represented at the 1946 Malay Congress at which UMNO was formed.

[34] During late 1947 and early 1948 there was a strong irredentist movement in the ethnically Malay and Muslim areas of southern Thailand, reflected in peninsular Malay politics principally through the Gabongan Melayu Patani Raya (GEMPAR), which was strongly represented in Kelantan.

[35] Originally from Ambon, Abdul Rab came to Kelantan and joined the teaching staff of the Majlis Ugama Islam before the Japanese occupation, taught at the Jami'a Merbau during the occupation, and after the war was active in the Hizbul Muslimin movement (cf. Note 32, above). Arrested by the British about 1949, he was deported to Indonesia and now lives in Bandung.

[36] This appears to have been a pen-name of Khaidir Khatib, long political secretary to Dato' Asri when Mentri Besar of Kelantan. Originally from Minangkabau, Sumatra, he taught for some years from 1942 at the Madrasah al-Ahmadiah, Pasir Mas.

[37] 'Keris Mas' (Kamaludin Muhammad), born near Bentong, Pahang, in 1923, has been one of the leading writers (especially of short stories) in post-war Malaysia, and is Chief Editor of the Dewan Bahasa dan Pustaka in Kuala Lumpur.

be noticed, one for a volume entitled *Polikatan*,[38] written by Sa'ad Shukri and Muhammad Asri b. Haji Muda and published by 'Duantara' at Al-Kamaliah Press, and a novel, *Pahlawan Rimba*, by Keris Mas, published by Pustaka Permai.

Berita Pertanian Kelantan

An official journal published three or four times a year from February 1956 to the present by the Department of Agriculture. It gives agricultural news and information concerning, for example, the care of crops, use of fertilizers, and the like. It has been printed as a rule by the Muslim Press, the latter founded about 1955 by Shaykh Muhammad Abdullah, an Arabic and Malay bookseller.

Suara Islam

A monthly journal published from early in 1957 until 1959, run by Muhammad Asri b. Haji Muda for the Persatuan Islam Sa-Malaya (Pan-Malayan Islamic Party),[39] and printed at the Majlis Ugama Press in Kota Bharu. It published articles relating to Islam and statehood, political theory, and current social issues, as well as reporting Malayan and overseas news of interest to its members. The assistant editor, Amaluddin Darus,[40] had a team of writers working for him, among them Osman Abdullah, Hassan Adli, Baharuddin Latif, and Khaidir Khatib.

Taman Wanita

Published by the Perkumpulan Wanita Kelantan (Kelantan Women's Association), Kota Bharu, this appeared first in December 1958, but lapsed and was not revived until September 1968, ceasing publication again during 1969. It was edited by Nik Fatimah Haji Karim,[41] assisted by Zainab Yusof Idris, and Zahrah Ibrahim Haji Omar. Others taking part were Karimah Zainab, Nik Faridah, Umi Salmah, Nik Latifah bte Haji Daud, and Siti Aspah bte Haji Wan Omar. The final issue to appear also included an article by one of the best known women scholars

---

[38] The title is compounded from '*politik*' (politics) and '*perkataan*' (word), and the book is thought to have been a kind of political dictionary.

[39] The PMIP (Malaya) came into being in 1951/52 (the first Kelantan branch, at Pasir Mas, was started in 1953), and contesting the first national elections in 1955 won the only non-Alliance seat in the Federal Legislative Assembly. In 1959 it became the principal opposition party in the nation's Parliament, and captured both the Kelantan and Trengganu State Assemblies, the former of which it has continued to hold. For discussion, see below, Kessler.

[40] Amaluddin Darus, originally from Kedah, was with the Pasir Mas fire brigade for some years, and active in Islamic politics. He was appointed a Kelantan state senator by the PMIP government in 1959, an office he continues to hold.

[41] Headmistress for some years of the Sekolah Menengah Zainab (Zainab Middle [i.e High] School) in Kota Bharu.

in Malaysia, the Kelantan-born Nik Safiah Haji Karim, now lecturing at the University of Malaya, who contributed an article entitled 'Mengenai Kebudayaan Melayu' (Concerning Malay culture).

Suloh Pelajar

Published in cyclostyled form, this was a 24-page journal produced especially for students, starting in 1960. Only two issues appeared, with S. Othman Kelantan as editor and Tajul Ariffin as publisher.[42] It contained articles on Malay literature, short stories, poems, and brief articles on other subjects.

Timur

Like *Suloh Pelajar*, this was published only in cyclostyled form, by an organization known as Asmupati (Angkatan Sasterawan Muda Pantai Timur, or Generation of Young East Coast Writers).[43] The sole issue to appear was dated December 1960. It was devoted to questions concerning the struggle for Malay as the national language, and was contributed to by (among others) Abdullah Muhammad, S. Othman Kelantan, Anwar Halim, and Hashim Ahmad. It contained in addition poems by Tajul Ariffin.

Majallah Dian

The first journal in the peninsula of the 'digest' type to be published in Malay (and perhaps in any other language), *Majallah Dian* began publication at approximately two-monthly intervals in August 1961, and still comes out regularly. It is edited by Yusof Zaki Ya'acob, the owner and manager of Dian Press in Kota Bharu, which has also published a variety of other literature.[44] A large part of the content of the *Dian* digest consists of articles translated from Middle Eastern periodicals (with a few written locally), concerning psychology, science and technology, sociology, and history. Short stories, both in translation and original, are also included from time to time.

---

[42] Sayyid Othman b. Sayyid Omar, who writes under the name S. Othman Kelantan, is a Malay school-teacher and a nationally known short-story writer and novelist. Tajul Ariffin, whose literary activities have lain mainly in the field of poetry, comes originally from Negri Sembilan.

[43] The president of Asmupati was Abdullah Muhammad, and the secretary Tajul Ariffin.

[44] Son of a well-known Kota Bharu religious teacher Haji Ya'acub b. Haji Ahmad (popularly known as To' Guru Haji Ya'acub Gajah Mati, after the lane in which he lived), Yusof Zaki (b. 1928) has been one of the major literary and cultural forces in post-war Kelantan, principally through the Dian Press and associated activities (cf. also below, *Santajiwa* and *Mingguan Kota Bharu*). Educated in Kelantan and then at the University of Al-Azhar in Cairo (1949) and the American University in Beirut (1950–4), he returned to Kelantan in 1955 and in 1957 founded the Dian Press (Pustaka Dian, now Sharikat Dian). His own writings include a number of works (in Malay) on sociology and psychology. His brother, Haji Hassan, is founder and owner of the Pustaka Aman Press in Kota Bharu, one of the largest publishers of Malay books in Malaysia.

Pantai Timur

Published monthly from October 1962 to August 1963, edited by Ismail Shauki b. Haji Ahmad with the assistance of several well known writers from throughout West Malaysia, and published by Pustaka Aman Press, Kota Bharu. The importance of this journal lay in its publication of articles on the history, culture, and traditional tales (*dongeng*) of Kelantan, among the latter being 'Awang Selamat' and 'Dewa Muda', arranged by Abdullah 'Aqhas.[45] It also included photographs of historical places in the state. Among other local contributors were Ahmadi Asmara and S. Othman Kelantan.

Bakti

Published by the Kesatuan Guru2 Melayu Kelantan (Kelantan Malay Teachers' Association)[46] in 1963, and edited by Yusof Mustafa[47] with the assistance of S. Othman Kelantan. Others on the editorial committee were Wan Ibrahim, Nik Zainab Karim, and Wan Ismail.

Rumaja Pantai Timur

A magazine of entertainment for young people, published for one issue only, at Bunut Payong, Kota Bharu, in August 1963, though it had no connection with the well-known *pondok* there. The editors were Noor Sabia, Shamsulnaeem, and Ruhusna.

Purnama

A monthly general knowledge journal published initially in 1964, with a second issue appearing in January/February 1965, and none thereafter. The editor and manager was Ismail Shauki b. Haji Ahmad, and the journal was printed at Al-Ahliyah Press, Kota Bharu.

Majallah Kelantan

A monthly journal originally, which began publication probably in 1964 and ran for about a year until 1965, produced by the Jama'ah Penerbit (Publications Committee) of the Kelantan State Government and printed at the Muslim Press, Kota Bharu. It dealt in a general way with Kelantan society and the development of the state. From the end of 1965 until the end of 1967 the task of editing and producing the journal was given to Abdullah b. Muhammad (Nakula), a noted antiquarian

---

[45] Otherwise known as Abdullah Al-Qari b. Haji Salleh, author of the article on To' Kenali in the present volume.

[46] Founded in 1960.

[47] Born 1919, Yusof graduated from the Sultan Idris Teachers' Training College in 1938, and has written numerous books and articles, the best known of the former being *Mestika Bahasa* (Kuala Lumpur, Dewan Bahasa & Pustaka, 1959).

and owner of the Bintang Emas Press.[48] Under his editorship, *Majallah Kelantan*, in addition to publishing news of official state interest, included a regular religious column entitled 'Kenali-lah Diri Saudara' and a long series of articles on the history of Kelantan written by Nakula himself that attracted much attention among local historians. During the period of Nakula's editorship the journal appeared at first fortnightly and then monthly again. Plans are at present being made to revive the journal, under Salehuddin Abdullah.[49]

Journal Persatuan Sejarah Kelantan

Published by the Persatuan Sejarah Kelantan (Kelantan Historical Society), and intended to appear annually, there has in fact been only one issue of this journal, dated 1964/65. The editorial committee consisted of Abdullah b. Muhammad (Nakula), Nik Muhammad b. Haji Nik Muhammad Salleh, and Nik Ahmad b. Haji Nik Hassan, who were also the only contributors to this issue. Their articles covered Kelantan prehistory, the period of Long Yunus, a survey of Kelantan history from the mid-eighteenth century to 1920, and a detailed discussion of local source materials for Kelantan history.

Santajiwa

Published by Dian Press, Kota Bharu, as a roman-script companion to its jawi-script *Majallah Dian* (and in fact containing much of the same material), this appeared for eight issues before ceasing publication in late 1966. It was edited by Yusof Zaki Ya'acub, assisted by M.S. Razim, A. Sabri, and Nabilah Rushdi.

Siaran PAS Kelantan

An ostensibly monthly (though latterly somewhat irregular) journal published from April 1966 by the Jabatan Penerangan (Information Section) of the Pan-Malayan Islamic Party's Badan Perhubongan (Liaison Division), in Kelantan. Numbering among its editors Salehuddin Abdullah, Khaidir Khatib, and Amaluddin Darus, it was printed until the end of 1966 by Al-Kamaliah Press, and thereafter by Al-Ahliyah until publication was stopped in May 1969 (as with all other party political organs), as a result of the national emergency then declared.

---

[48] Abdullah Nakula (as he is best known) was born in Kota Bharu in 1931, and educated at the Majlis Ugama school and the Jami'a Merbau. He founded the Bintang Emas Press (since renamed Penerbitan Mahligai) in 1962.

[49] Born in Pasir Puteh in 1937, Salehuddin was educated locally and attended the Institut Islam Negeri in Jogjakarta, Indonesia, in 1955. He is at present Liaison Secretary (Setiausaha Perhubongan) with the Kelantan branch of the PMIP.

The journal presented the views of the Pan-Malayan Islamic Party (PAS, Persatuan Islam Sa-Malaya), and contained articles on the Islamic struggle in Malaysia and on political developments in Kelantan. Of particular importance was the column written under the pseudonym 'To' Janggut's Grandson'.[50]

Mingguan Kota Bharu

This weekly newspaper, started in May 1966, was both popular and influential among a considerable body of readers in Kelantan. The first weekly to appear since the pre-war *Al-Hikmah*, it was published by Dian Press and edited by Muhammad Zain b. Salleh.[51] In its twenty or so pages weekly it published both local and national news of importance and a wide variety of articles on politics, society, culture, religion and history, as well as short stories, poems and letters to the editor. It suspended publication in March 1970, for mainly financial reasons arising in part from distribution difficulties outside the state.

Pedoman Masharakat Islam

An annual journal (of which only one issue appeared, in 1966), published by the Madrasah Diniah Bakariah Terusan, a major religious school at Pasir Tumboh, near Kota Bharu. Edited by Muhammad al-Ghazali Kartosuwirjo (the last name adopted from that of the Indonesian nationalist hero), the sole issue published had 72 pages, and contained an account of the school's history and articles on religious matters, many of contemporary interest.

Pelopor

Published monthly from June 1967 by the Jabatan Penerangan (Information Section) of the UMNO Jawatankuasa Perhubongan (Liaison Committee) in Kelantan. It was edited by Dasuki Ahmad,[52] and printed at the Muslim Press. Publication was stopped in May 1969, as a result of the national emergency.

As a party organ it was chiefly concerned to present the UMNO point of view, introduce Kelantan UMNO figures to its readers, stimulate local political activity, and draw attention to the national developmental aims and achievements of the central Alliance government.

---

[50] To' Janggut, who led the ill-fated rising of 1915, is today regarded as a nationalist hero. For an account of the rising, see above, Ibrahim.

[51] Born at Salor in 1947, Muhammad Zain has been on the staff of the Dian Press since 1970.

[52] Originally from Batu Tiga, Pasir Mas, Dasuki was educated locally and at the university of Al-Azhar in Cairo, where he graduated in Shari'a law. He was UMNO candidate for the parliamentary constituency of Pasir Mas Hulu in the 1969 general elections, but was unsuccessful.

Pendukong

A journal produced by the Persatuan Penulis Kelantan (Writers' Association of Kelantan)[53] from December 1968, concerned with literature, the arts and society. It contained short stories, poems, and dramatic pieces, and some articles on Kelantanese culture and associated matters. Among those principally concerned with it were S. Othman Kelantan, Ashari Muhammad, and a number of the younger Kelantan writers in particular.

Nilam

Published by the Persatuan Pelajar Pusat Pengajian Tinggi Nilam Puri, the students' association of the Nilam Puri Centre of Higher Islamic Studies, Kota Bharu,[54] this journal appeared twice during the academic year 1967/68, and contained mainly articles on the Islamic religion.

Deru

A cyclostyled journal produced by the same association as *Nilam*. Four monthly issues appeared between March and June 1968, containing news of Nilam Puri activities and articles by students.

*   *   *   *

In addition to the journals listed above, many others (roughly thirty or so) have been published by various schools in Kelantan — some emanating from religious institutions, some from Malay schools and some from English. These cannot be listed here. Nor does the present brief outline take into account the commemorative '*majallah*', not strictly periodicals or serials, which from time to time have been published in Kelantan—for example, *Ilham*, produced by the Persatuan Guru2 Ugama Sa-Malaya (All-Malayan Association of Religious Teachers) in 1968, edited by Abdul Aziz b. Omar, Muhammad Radhi b. Puteh, and Khuzaimah Kesmani, and the '*majallah*' *Chenderamata* published in February 1969 by the Kongres Pemuda Kelantan (Kelantan Youth Economic Congress), which contained many of the papers read at that meeting.

---

[53] Formed in May 1966, with Don Madhi as president and Alias Harun as secretary.
[54] Founded in September 1965, Nilam Puri is housed in one of the old royal palaces, donated for the purpose. It has become one of the major centres of Islamic teaching in the country.

REFERENCES

Abdullah b. Abdul Kadir, Munshi, 1960. *Kisah Pelayaran Abdullah* (introd. and notes by Kassim Ahmad) (Kuala Lumpur, Oxford University Press).

Al-Ahmadi, Abdul Rahman, 1966. *Pengantar Sastera* (Kota Bharu, Pustaka Aman Press).

Asa'ad Shukri b. Haji Muda, 1962. *Sejarah Kelantan* (Kota Bharu, Pustaka Aman Press).

Li Chuan Siu, 1966. *Ikhtisar Sejarah Kesusasteraan Melayu Baru, 1830–1945* (Kuala Lumpur, Pustaka Antara).

Muhammad b. Haji Nik Muhammad Salleh, Nik, 1964/65. 'Chatetan Rengkas Tentang Sumber2 Tempatan Mengenai Sejarah Kelantan,' *Journal Persatuan Sejarah Kelantan* (Kota Bharu), 1, 52–72.

Muhammad Yusup b. Salleh al-Kelantani, 1953. *Risalah Penambah Ketahuan* (Kota Bharu, Mustafa Press).

Roff, W.R., 1961. *Guide to Malay Periodicals, 1876–1941. With details of known holdings in Malaya* (Singapore, Eastern Universities Press).

Tufo, M.V. Del, 1959. *Malaya, comprising the Federation of Malaya and the Colony of Singapore. A Report on the 1957 Census of Population* (Kuala Lumpur, Government Printer).

Vlieland, C.A., 1932. *British Malaya. A Report on the 1931 Census* (London, Crown Agents for the Colonies).

8

RAYMOND FIRTH

Faith and Scepticism in Kelantan Village Magic

THIS paper has two aims: ethnographically, to give data on Kelantan Malay magic in the coastal area near Bachok, mainly from 1939-40, before modern education reached the people; and more theoretically, to explore the problem of local beliefs in magic, and to challenge monolithic views of Malay magic as a unitary self-sufficient system of general credence. Even in recent publications one may read of 'the Malay world-view' or 'Malay magical thought' as if all Malays, even nowadays, shared the same concepts. My argument to the contrary is that certainly nowadays, and even a generation ago, in a part of Malaya which has been recognized as a stronghold of magical practices, Malays have been more pragmatic, shown more variation in their beliefs, been more experimental in their attitudes, than could be inferred from the literature.

From a body of material collected by my wife and me during two periods in Kelantan I examine briefly here some aspects of the magic of agriculture, of fishing, of personal protection and healing, with a gloss relating the art of a conjurer to beliefs in superhuman power. Much of my argument revolves around the interpretation of specific incidents in which particular magicians and an audience took part, because so much discussion of Malay magic has been couched in general terms which obscure significant elements in the social setting. Certainly I agree that Malay folk beliefs used—and to some degree still use—a general conceptual framework expressed in such terms as *ilmu*, *tuntut*, *ubat*, *semangat*, *hantu*, *keramat*, which may be crudely translated as knowledge, revelation, medicine, soul, spirit, superhuman power. These and many other concepts can be integrated at an abstract level into a system, but it is a system with much variation in different sectors of Malay society and with different individuals; inferences from it alone may give a very false idea of what any actual person believes and does. Some people integrate such notions with their Muslim theological concepts, others reject a great part of them. The more magical aspect of them may not be denied, but depending upon the age, sex, occupation and education of a person they may be utilized more or less; their validity may be not so much questioned as ignored. On the other hand, obscure factors in a person's history—such as illness or other misfortune—may incline him more than others to belief in the greater immediacy and truth of such folk resources. So, in the same community, faith and scepticism in magical concepts and practices may appear side by side in different people, or even alternate in the same person at different periods.

By magic in this context I mean action, primarily ritual action, based on belief in superhuman power, and directed to a specific aim. (Anthropologists will recognize in this statement that I have taken position on some classical theoretical issues, but do not feel it necessary to defend this here.) The notion of faith has its own complexities. When it is said that a person believes in or has faith in a certain set of magical concepts and practices, there are several possibilities. He may think the concept is a true one, and be prepared to implement his belief by appropriate action. He may think the concept is true, but not think that it applies to his particular situation and therefore not be willing to do anything concrete about it. He may think that the concept is true in general, but that it is untrue as a description of the particular item before him. Or he may doubt the truth of the concept in general but think that in particular cases there may be 'something in it', so that he takes the precaution of acting as if it were true. From consideration of the Kelantan situations we observed, I would argue that instances of all this occurred, as well as more radical scepticism which would deny the validity of much that was put forward as magical knowledge and action. Insofar as faith is regarded as a confident expectation of a given result, it will be seen that this was often lacking among our Malay friends, whose attitude towards magical practices tended to be much more dubious, even experimental. And if, as sometimes is said, faith constitutes a defence against surprise, here too weaknesses in belief were revealed. On the other hand, magical practitioners often operated with assurance, displayed considerable authority, and were ingenious in reinterpreting untoward events in terms of their own system of extrahuman concepts.

Magic of the 'Rice Soul'

I begin with consideration of agricultural magic, especially in regard to the *semangat padi*, the so-called 'rice soul'. Consideration of the concept of *semangat padi* shows definite variation here from the conventional ideas of the homogeneity of the treatment of the 'rice soul' throughout Malaya (Skeat, 1900, 250n; Shaw, 1926, 20; Winstedt, 1951, 39, 55; Endicott, 1970, 23). In fields immediately inland from the Bachok coast, on the seaward side of the Kemasin river, a fair amount of rice was grown, by both 'dry' and 'wet' methods. The cultivators recognized the validity of the notion of *semangat padi* as the vital principle of rice, but tended to regard it as contextually determined for ritual purposes. Some did celebrate rites in connection with it, but to a limited degree; others did not celebrate it at all. The reasons given were pragmatic. It was said that more rites were performed elsewhere, in places nearer forest—as in Besut, where, it was said, offerings were formally set out. But locally, it was argued, offerings to the 'rice soul' were not generally made since the fields were 'in the middle of the land' with no 'ailments' such as pigs or other forest animals to destroy the rice (cf. Downs, 1967, 171). Again, it was stated that only if a person cultivated a lot of padi (i.e. many hundred *gantang*) did he *buat semangat padi*; and as I saw, many ordinary cultivators with small crops did not do so. Even if the cultivator was himself a magical practitioner in other matters he might not do so. One man, a line-fisherman who produced also 100–150 gantang of padi per season, practised as a *bomoh* with *siup* technique (see later); but though a ritual specialist for healing, using traditional concepts of soul and of magical protection, he saw no need to practise magic for his rice. And owners of fields which yielded large crops, but who had leased out these fields to other cultivators, took no pains to see that any *semangat padi* rites were carried out; they regarded this as entirely an affair of their tenants.

There were traditional ideas of a magical order about the local agriculture: a scheme of lucky and unlucky days; notions of a 'fruitful hand' akin to the 'green thumb' of English gardening. One man kept to hoeing and left all planting to his wife because the Lord didn't give him bounty, but what she planted grew. The concept of *semangat padi* was used at times in a concrete way, equivalent to the notion of quality of a rice—as having a 'harsh essence' (*semangat keras, padi dia keras nasi*) or a 'pleasant essence' (*bau bangin, bau sedap, semangat ini*). But there were also traditional ideas of the *semangat padi* as a being of a more personal order, highly sensitive to rough treatment, so that it would enter the dreams of a cultivator at night, weeping, to complain. Yet despite such ideas, I could not get any informant to admit the correctness of statements by Wilkinson and others (Wilkinson, 1906, 50; 1932, 604; Skeat, 1900, 227; Endicott, 1970, 149) that the small harvest knife (*tuai*, in Kelantan *ketaman*) was used because otherwise the *semangat padi* would be angry. One man (a fisherman) said it might be true of the country of the person who alleged this, but it was not true of Kelantan. Another (a rice cultivator) denied that it made any difference to the *semangat padi* whether the knife or the sickle was used; he argued that the farmers of the west coast used the slashing sickle method, and their rice was better than that of Kelantan.

This last man did actually perform some rites over the *semangat padi*, though they were relatively simple. Awang-Meh Sari, though he used to go to sea before he had children, had spent most of his life as a cultivator. When I knew him in 1940 he had 15 fields of rice, yielding between 400 and 700 gantang of padi a year. He grew vegetables extensively; he owned 4 cattle. Awang said that he himself did not actually *buat semangat* with full rites; he simply took a small sheaf (handful) of padi and put it away 'in the place' in the granary attached to his house. I asked if I might see the place and he became embarrassed; he said one could not go in at midday; that the old people said that if one goes in at midday the padi gets 'chilled' (*sejuk*, a common term in magical vocabulary to indicate lowered resistance). He added that in the early morning it would be all right, and when I asked again he invited me for the next day when the sun should be only a little above the horizon. At 7.30 a.m. I went to his house. He warned me not to speak when we entered the granary, and told me that children were not allowed there at all. I put out my cigarette as a sign of respect but noticed that Awang himself went in smoking. He took a lamp and held it down for me to see. In a large basket of the type used for storing rice or salt lay two sheaves of padi, together with a dry coconut, a working adze, and a small basket tray containing water in a shell, oil in the bottom of a china cup, bananas and sugar cane. There appeared also to be earth in the bottom of the basket, but Awang said this was not significant.

That there were two sheaves of padi was not particularly relevant; Awang said it didn't matter if there were one or two. But the dry coconut and the materials on the tray were significant, and were described in traditional classificatory rhythm: *nyior sa buteh*; *ayer (ai) sa chawan*; *minyak sa titek*; *pisang sa buteh*; *tebu sa ruah*: a coconut; a cup of water; a drop of oil; a banana bunch; a sugar cane node. All these were components of magical offerings. The working adze had caught my attention. I thought it might represent the sacralization of a working tool. No, said Awang, it was there only for security—he was afraid people might otherwise want to borrow it; it had no connection with the *semangat padi*. (This was a cautionary lesson to the anthropologist not to jump to conclusions!) The large basket was used as an ordinary rice store as well as a ritual repository, the tray of offerings and the sheaves of *semangat padi* being simply lifted up on top. The remainder of the rice crop was stored in a separate shed. At the end of each ritual season the old ritual sheaves were not thrown away but left at the bottom of the basket; only after ten years or so might the oldest ones be thrown out. There was thus a continuous succession in the *semangat padi*, since each heap had sheaves of successive years. (What I had taken to be earth at the bottom of the basket was probably the residue of former sheaves.)

Awang described his procedure in taking the ritual sheaves. He selected grain heads that 'look towards the house', that is, which curved that way. The idea of this was that the *semangat padi* should 'return to the house'. After these particular sheaves had been taken and deposited, the owner does not visit his fields for two days following; he may do so only on the third day. Why? 'The *semangat padi* doesn't like it.' The concept of the *semangat padi*, as described by Awang, was that it was like a child, easily disturbed, pleasured by simple things. He said that the sheaves of *semangat padi* were cut by himself alone, in the very early morning, when it was truly dark. He could speak to no one, and he had to return at once. The *semangat padi* would become 'chilled' if these observances were not kept, and would 'flee to the west', which was its origin. And 'if the *semangat* is lacking, we will hunger, what will we do?' As for the offerings, the *semangat padi*, like a child, likes these things, but does not eat them.

According to local tradition it is good to complete all critical operations concerned with padi in the morning. With planting of either 'dry' or 'wet' rice it is good to finish and return in the morning, and it is good also to finish the padi harvest in the morning. The elders say it is not good to finish and bring back the last sheaves of padi in the afternoon—'the *semangat padi* likes to return in the morning'. When the padi was harvested, said Awang, according to the elders, a little should be left standing for the birds, and the old people had an instruction (*pesan*) for this, in the form of a chant:

He! Semangat semangin	Hey! Spirit
Mu berusong berdola	You're carried in a litter
Beripung bertambun ka rumah aku	Heaped up to my house
Hampar-hampar	Spread out there
Tinggal ka burong berian	Leave a gift for the birds
Sedekah ka dia lah![1]	As charity for them!

So, said Awang, merit will go to a man who works padi.

But despite such views about the sensitivity of the rice soul and the possibility of loss if it were not ritualized, most rice cultivators to whom I spoke seemed tough-minded on the practical issue. So a woman rice cultivator confirmed the saying of the elders about bringing in the last of the padi at harvest in the morning; but she attributed it to prudence—otherwise it would be eaten by the chickens! When I asked about the custom of leaving a little for the wild birds she seemed indifferent—when they are hungry they come and eat anyway, she commented.

In general I had the impression that the attitude towards agricultural magic in this area, even among rice planters, was rather informal and casual. It was not so much sceptical as pragmatic: people who carried out the rites did so as precaution because of the scale of their operations, and from respect to tradition, not because they regarded these rites as obligatory in themselves. The rites were not of *pars pro toto* kind, done on behalf of the total harvest of the community. They were individual, often modified and curtailed, and small operators totally ignored them. There was some belief, some suspension of judgement, in their validity, and a general disinclination to implement ideology by ritual activity.

Tradition and Novelty in Fishing Magic

The situation was very different with fishing. Earlier I have dealt very briefly (Raymond Firth, 1966, 122-5) with the part played by magic in the Kelantan fishing industry, particularly in placating sea spirits and in enabling master fishermen to 'meet with fish'. Whereas rice cultivators who celebrated the 'rice soul' tended to rely on their own resources, and master fishermen might perform some magic rites, Kelantan fishing has often been supplemented by magical aids of other kinds. Apart from general belief in the over-riding concept of the bounty of Allah, which might be granted or withheld at the will of the All-Mighty, help was sought from men of learning or holiness in the

[1] Difficulties in rendering spoken Kelantan Malay into writing have been indicated by C.C. Brown in his classic study (1927), and are appreciated by Malay linguists to whose competence I cannot lay claim. But I would note here that the richness of Kelantan dialect offers a problem in the theory of communication which is not solved in written Malay by simply converting it into standard romanized form (cf. Raymond Firth, 1966, 388-91) even though Malays in Kelantan write in this form.

Muslim religious field, and from professional magicians (*bomoh*),[2] some of whom had no direct knowledge of the sea and fishing.

To illustrate local beliefs in fishing magic, including beliefs in its relation to Islam, I describe here a particular type of rite performed by a religious man (*orang lebai*), and its effect upon the local circle of fishermen. To set this in perspective I outline the general course of events in the fishing season of 1940, especially as seen by several master fishermen closely connected with this ritual. (For convenience I indicate the magical practitioner as B, and the master fishermen as L, M and P—cf. Firth, 1966, 109–111, 383, for some details of the fishing season and the receipts of L and M.)

I first consider the position of M. He was an intelligent man of long fishing experience who combined a rather self-consciously pious attitude towards Islam with a firm belief in spirits of the sea. With his dry, often subtle sense of humour and whimsical realism in discussing human relationships, his comments were among the most revealing offered to us. As the fishing season developed I noted several fairly distinct elements in his interpretation of success or failure. (The account is much compressed from my notebooks). Early in 1940 he like other fishermen was complaining about lack of success, and he had gone to a local holy man, To' Wali Awang of Bukit Merbau, to bless some rice he had taken, by stirring a finger in it. M spoke also of a net magician (*bomoh pukat*) living inland, whom local fishermen used. This man did not 'use *hantu*' but only the Kuran; he too uttered formulae over rice. M said he had called in this man a year or so before but without 'agreement'—he got no good catches as a result.

When M began to get good catches his first statement was in orthodox Muslim terms, for the bounty of Allah, expressed particularly through prayer and the blessing of the holy man. Early in February M got his new net ready and on his first day out he brought in the best catch of his village. I chaffed him about this, because the day before he had been very vague about making the traditional net offerings, and I thought he had not done these magic rites. I said 'But you didn't make the offerings!' He answered with a twinkle 'Made them—last night!' He had nine 'pious men' to perform the 'prayers of hope'

---

[2] Variance in spelling and in meaning have been given to this term in the literature. Howison (1801, 100) has *boomo* (as doctor); Wilkinson (1903, 134) has *bomor* and *bomo*; and *bomoh* (1932, 150); Swettenham, (1905, 30) has *bomo*. Favre (1875, II, 226) gives only *bumu*, as elephant-hunter. Pak Che Mat once gave me *bo'omor* in what he seemed to think was high-class pronunciation. Like Gimlette (1913, 29; 1915, 2 *et seq.*; 1929, 18 *et seq.*; and Cuisinier (1936, 31 *et seq.*; 1957, 89) I have tended to favour *bomor* (1966, 122–4), which has also had official authority (State of Kelantan: Estimates, 1938, 23—'Bomor for H.H.') (cf. Gimlette, 1913, 31). I here follow the recent *Kamus Dewan* (1970).

(Firth, 1966, plate IIb) and one afterwards to make the offerings. For about a week he was very successful, and was elated, saying that other master fishermen would be very 'sick' at this outstanding performance; he likened their competition to cocks fighting and giving peck for peck. To draw him I said I supposed his success was due to his having had the fishing ground very much to himself, and to luck; he agreed, but added 'Tuhan Allah'. 'There it is—I think Tuhan Allah gives to me.' On another occasion he said 'Tomorrow, if Tuhan Allah grants, I shall get fish.' When he got a phenomenal catch, while many other nets got nothing, he said, obviously very pleased, that he was 'in agreement'— equivalent to being 'in luck'. He said that his success was due to To' Wali, the holy man, and hence to God. He added that six or seven fishing experts had gone to the holy man, but that he 'agreed' usually with only one or two. I asked why? He replied 'I don't know' but added with a laugh 'perhaps because if with all, they would all become rich, would all build tile houses, and the price of large boats would go up to $300!' But this idea that magical discrimination was necessary to avoid inflation was not meant very seriously. He said however that the arts of the holy man were often effective for only a week or so, instancing examples. (Note the pragmatic aspect of this: the chances are that one or two fishermen will have success, but that their success will not continue for very long unless they have exceptional skill. What success that occurs can then be attributed to the immediate selective virtue of the holy man's blessing.)

Traditional folk ideas also played a considerable part in M's thinking about fishing. Towards the end of February I met him one evening with a ritual smear of rice paste on his forehead—he had just been dyeing his net according to his usual practice, weekly, with appropriate rites asking for blessing and the goodwill of sea spirits. As an instance of his magical belief, he said he had just met another expert who had just put ropes on his new net. 'I told him that he will probably get fish; a new net gets fish.' I asked if offerings would be made over it. He answered 'One must; if it is a new net, one must make offerings.' He went on to say that if it had been him he would not have put ropes on the net that day. Why, because it was Friday, the day one goes to mosque? No, because it was the 14th day of the 4th month (by local Malay reckoning). On the 4th, 14th, and 24th of the 4th month one should not do work on the net—nor also on the 3rd, 13th and 23rd of the 3rd month, and so on. The net would foul the lure, and break. 'But would you not go to sea?' I asked. 'Going to sea, that doesn't matter.' he replied. But he added that if it were for (ordinarily) the first time in a season, the opening day, he wouldn't. He quoted a colloquial saying which may be rendered as 'An ill-starred day, 'twill tear the net'—so old people said. Then he went on 'but if a *juru selam* has knowledge, a bit of revelation, it doesn't matter'. M was convinced that boat measurements could express relationships of good and bad fortune in fishing (Raymond Firth, 1966, 145), and inclined to believe that there were ways of injuring another man's net so that it wouldn't get fish. He told me that an *ubat* could be prepared by mixing hair of pig or tiger (both animals unmentionable at sea) with an infusion of *larak salah* (a medicinal plant, unidentified); if this were put in a kind of Siamese pot for keeping rice warm and secreted in the boat carrying the net, it would be prevented from getting fish. Such an *ubat* could cost $5 to $10—a vast sum in 1940. He said that one fisherman alleged such magical interference with his net and so had not gone out to sea for a month; that a *bomoh* to whom he had gone for help refused to come, saying, 'That is a net to which people have done evil'. Yet M was doubtful about the efficacy of much-vaunted talismans such as ambergris (Raymond Firth, 1966, 125). He distinguished between 'true' ambergris, which he described as the vomit of a large fish, and alleged ambergris from Mecca, which he had already used to no avail, and he held sceptically that while real ambergris was very dear that which people sold as such probably wasn't true anyway. Certain traditional taboos he categorically denied. I had been told that umbrellas should not be carried on a fishing boat. M argued that this was not correct. He said he took an umbrella himself in the rainy season, and suggested that I take one on my own boat; he said he had seen umbrellas occasionally on boats at Beserah in Pahang, and that when parties including women travelled to Semerak, Besut and other places they must have umbrellas against the midday sun. He added that people of the Perhentian islands, who were wise in all sea lore, brought umbrellas and even shoes with them when they came to the mainland. He certainly did not subscribe rigidly to a rule against mixing terrestrial with marine categories of objects. He was not without magical reservations. He said that one thing was prohibited on a boat, a certain kind of pandanus mat; if this was taken aboard a sailing boat there would be no wind. Yet even here he commented shrewdly, 'I think this is not true either—if it is taken in the season when there is plenty of wind, how will a mat stop it'?

With this critical intelligence and pious tendency, he might have been expected to reject the more purely magical rites connected with traditional *hantu*. Yet here he displayed an uncertainty, a swing in opinion, which showed his more orthodox and more sophisticated views to some extent at war with the strength of his involvement in his daily striving for fish and for reputation. He was no blind adherent of magic. Towards the end of the season, when fish were very scarce, P said 'There are no fish, so people are using *bomoh*.' Commented M caustically, 'When fish are plentiful *bomoh* don't matter; all men get fish'. But he also held that if fish were not in season then it was no good making offerings; the object of the offerings was to get men to 'meet with fish', not to conjure up fish out of nowhere. He said 'If I don't get fish for several days, and all other men are getting fish, *then* I make the offerings, so that the sea spirits will be pleased, and I will meet with fish.'

The critical elements in M's judgement of the validity of magical performance emerged especially in his attitudes towards the practices of B, who while generally a minor scholar and teacher of religion, also served on occasion as *bomoh*. At an early stage in the 1940 season M had employed B to make the offerings for his net, and continued to give him alms as a kind of retaining fee. But M was clearly ambivalent about B's powers. He said at the start 'B is only a little skilled; he's not a man of the sea', and attributed his own net's success as much to the blessing of the holy man (who, however, was not a 'man of the sea' either!) When M heard that another fisherman, L, whom he did not rate highly, was going to have B also make net offerings he was scornful—'all the same, I think he won't get any fish; he is not skilled; if he makes the offerings today, tomorrow, he won't get above other people. You will be able to see; he's not skilled.' And he laughed and said 'We shall see'.

Now M's general estimate of L was about right, but in fact, whether through a spurt of enthusiasm generated by knowledge of the offerings or not, L's net did actually get a bumper catch the next day. This was generally attributed to the efforts of B. When next evening I asked M what he thought he replied 'I think B has magic power (*ada keramat*).' He said he thought that B was 'true' and skilled. Some days before, P, an old fishing expert and *bomoh*, had said to him that in making offerings to land spirits B was wrong; that one should invoke only sea spirits for fishing, and on the beach, not beside a house. Yet, M now thought, B was right: 'inland spirits can reach out to sea; sea spirits can reach inland.' However, M was much indebted to P, to whom he had been like an adopted son, and he added diplomatically 'when I am with P I follow him; when I am with B I follow him; I don't want to fight with them. But I think B is cleverer than P; I think B is *keramat*.'

Now this was a switch of opinion, as others too realized. Our servant Mamat, who had known B's father as a *bomoh besar*, and thought B himself was a clever *bomoh*, told me that four days previously M had said that he didn't trust B's performance. 'Now, he trusts!' (But P, with whom I discussed the matter, was still sceptical. His view was, let us wait and see; other nets for which B made offerings have got nothing as yet.)

A couple of days later M and I returned to the subject of fishing success. He held that only those master fishermen whose fathers had also been experts got fish. He quoted cases of men without ancestral heritage whose lack of success proved this. I asked why—do the dead watch over the sea? 'No, they don't come back,' he replied, but went on, 'I think they ask over there'—meaning that they intercede with Allah on behalf of their sons. He said that he himself went every Friday to the cemetery to ask his father, his mother and his dead child to make him rich and give him fish—he prayed to them. Their bones are in the grave, he said, but their spirits (he used the term *nyawa*) are yonder and have the shape of men. 'But do they hear?' I asked. 'People say they hear; if not, what is the good of going? It is simply work thrown away!' Then he came back to the subject of B. He said that about ten years before B had made offerings for one net, but no fish resulted, so he stopped. The net of M himself recently was the first net for which he had performed ritual since then. M then revealed that misleadingly he had told P—as indeed he had virtually told me too—that B had *not* made the offerings for him. He said he had told P, 'What is the good of getting him, a man of prayer, who doesn't go to sea . . . ?' He said that he had talked in this vein, but then towards midnight, when all men were inside their houses, he had the rites performed. Afraid that if it were generally known that he had had the magic done, but got no fish, people would chaff him and he would be ashamed, he had given a false impression.

M continued to oscillate in his attitude towards the validity of B's magical technique. When other master fishermen were successful and he himself was not he said 'It is not that I am unskilled, no; I think that no fish have been given to me'. He had lost confidence in B. Retrospectively, he thought that on the days when L got large catches it was because Tuhan Allah had wished to give him fish; even if B had not acted as *bomoh*, L could easily have got the fish. M backed this up by pointing to two other expert fishermen for whom B had made offerings, and who had caught no fish. In order to draw him my wife commented 'It is as Tuhan Allah wills'. He replied rather sharply 'As Tuhan Allah wills—but the men of Perupok [his competitors] get the bulk of the cash'. He admitted that some people might have special powers: one fisherman, previously markedly successful, had lost his wife by death, and had had few good catches since. M commented 'I think his wife was *keramat*.' But thinking of the non-success of others beside himself he said in resignation 'Tuhan Allah gives to all the same.' He hoped that people would speak of himself as good-omened, of blessed mouth, and then he would continue to get fish. About *bomoh* he said that people went from one to another, seeking success, and if they couldn't go themselves they sent their womenfolk far afield, as far as Ketereh or Pasir Mas, to get rice or water that had been blessed. However, though M himself got no further large catches, when some fishermen for whom B had made the offerings did very well he reverted to his opinion that B was *keramat*. He also pointed out that P had formerly acted as local *bomoh* for the nets, and was probably ashamed to see that another had been successful where he had not. He said 'perhaps the sea spirits like the offerings of B; perhaps they don't like the offerings of P.' And he added rather unfeelingly that P was an old man and perhaps he would die. M's belief in B's powers was further demonstrated when his eyes became very bloodshot from his work at sea. We put drops of acriflavin in them but he also consulted B, who said that he had been afflicted by sea spirits and recited a formula over them; he then refused more medicine, saying that he would see the effects of the formula first—though he consented to wear dark glasses which we gave him, saying that B had also advised them.

So here was an expert fisherman who, having a great amount of empirical knowledge of his craft, had also a set of beliefs of a mystical order, mingling Islamic concepts of the bounty of Allah with concepts of the power of sea spirits and the efficacy of human ritual to placate them. But he did not have a simple blind faith. He did not operate 'in obedience to the rules which the superstitious people have followed for ages' (Clifford, 1897, 148; also Skeat, 1900, 193). Doubt, suspension of judgement and even scepticism were mingled with his belief. A constant theme in his whole situation was his faith in the control exercised by the will of Allah over the destinies of men—this he never questioned. But a variable factor, in his judgement, was the degree to which the bounty of Allah was being accorded to him personally. Yet this was cross-cut by two other elements. One was the pragmatic nature of the situation: if it was the season when fish were normally absent, or if fish were present but the interference of another fisherman spoiled the shooting of his net, then he attributed his poor catch to these empirical factors and not to lack of Allah's favour. Nor were the rituals of magic, in his view, designed for such situations; they were for situations where fish were available but he was not getting them. The test in particular was where other fishermen were getting catches but he was not. This was where in his view offerings to spirits could be useful. But offerings in themselves could not remedy lack of fishing skill—hence his protests in the case of L. Yet if a *bomoh* were powerful enough (*keramat*) then he might overcome even relative lack of fishing skill, though only for a short time. Hence his concession that after all the performances of B *did* seem to give results. Note that his position was not quite that which anthropologists have generally recognized—where the efficacy of the ritual in general is not questioned but only the proficiency of individual practitioners. The position of M was more complex. The efficacy of the will of Allah was not questioned, but the efficacy of the arts of *bomoh* was subject to continual scrutiny—not just individual *bomoh*, but all *bomoh*. Only when empirical evidence seemed to indicate that they had produced results was he willing to concede their validity. But his alternation of faith and scepticism about the performances of *bomoh* did not mean that he lacked a general belief in the significance of magical forces. Apart from his free use of the concepts of *hantu* and of *keramat*, for instance, he recognized various rules of a mystical order, especially when backed by the authority of the elders. What he questioned was not so much the operation of mystical forces as the ability of men to cope with them. What did emerge very clearly with M was his tendency to retreat from faith in *bomoh* to faith in Allah —not at all the conventional picture of 'Malay first and Muhammedan afterwards' which is often offered in the older literature (e.g. Clifford, *loc. cit.*).

Another complicating element in M's attitudes was the problem of the extent to which modern changes had rendered old concepts and practices invalid. However, he did not seem as much bothered by this as did P, who as a *bomoh* of long standing had more of a vested interest in traditional matters. On one occasion P admitted with a laugh that while nets should be ritually sprinkled in order to get fish, as tradition dictated, nets which had not been sprinkled also took fish. He added, with a twist of his mouth, wryly, 'They don't understand, they haven't learnt, they don't know'— a kind of rather bitter 'ignorance is bliss' view.

The position of the *bomoh* B was also very interesting. He was a producer, not a consumer, of fishing magic; yet, a professedly religious man, he was operating with traditional local concepts of *hantu*. I was impressed by his apparent modesty and sincerity. He took the line that his role was to aid fishermen, not to substitute for them. 'Just to help', was his slogan. When L got his first phenomenal catch of fish B was sitting near by on the sand when the carrier boat came in. After the fish had been sold he asked me how much it fetched. When I told him he said 'Good!' So I asked him 'What if it had been a poor catch?'

'What about it, Tuan, I would help again.' His view was that his rites, if effective, helped to stop the fish from bolting the net, so that the fisherman had a fair chance to catch them.

B allowed me to be present when he performed his rites over the net of L; they began about 9 p.m. at the house where the net was kept, on the verandah. The master fisherman, who was also the major net owner, and four members of his crew constituted the group, apart from a few children on the outskirts. First the *bomoh* laid a cotton thread of three strands in the middle of some soft wax and moulded it to candle shape. A tray of conventional offerings had been prepared, and from it B took an egg, examined it close to his eye and then stuck the candle upright against it. He called for *beras kunyit*—rice with some shavings of turmeric root in it. Holding this in his hands and facing towards the sea (away from Mecca, in itself significant for a ritual address by a man of religious learning) he recited a long formula. From time to time he stirred the rice with his finger. (He was rocking slowly from side to side, a movement which I had noted he made also in ordinary conversation.) Most of the formula was inaudible, but occasionally he spoke more loudly, enabling me to hear what seemed to be characteristic phrases of the kind used by *bomoh*, addressed to *jinn* and *hantu* by name, and asserting that the reciter knew their origins. One of the principal spirits I heard addressed was Jinn Kuning, generally believed in Kelantan peasant circles to be very powerful. Then the *bomoh* passed the tray of offerings through incense smoke and recited another long formula.

The group then adjourned outside the house, on the earth below. A sail had been put up as a windbreak; the net remained on the verandah. I asked if I could see exactly what was to be done. B said 'Yes, but it is good if you keep ten feet away,' and I noted that part way through the rite he ordered one man who had inched forward to within about six feet to get back. At this stage the offerings were divided into three portions: i, for consultation; ii, for placing at the boats; iii, for throwing into the sea.

i. Consultation. The *bomoh* took a *parang* (short chopper) and with it dug a rectangular hole in the earth behind the sail screen. He stuck the parang in the soil at the side, then carefully slid the first portion of offerings on a banana leaf off the plate into the bottom of the hole. The top of the egg was broken with the parang and the egg added again to the offerings—having been opened for the spirits. The candle was lit from a lamp used hitherto to illuminate the scene, the lamp was extinguished, and the candle too was lowered into the hole. Then B, with knees apart, recited another formula, observing the flame the while. He sprinkled turmeric rice upon it, and also threw some of the rice up on to the net above, twice, part way through and at the end. Several times while the formula was being recited the flame died down, seeming as if it might go out, but then revived again.

ii. Boat offering. Immediately after, the rite over the boat took place. B sat in the boat, held rice paste in a brass bowl and recited a formula—a picturesque sight in the moonlight. The boat owner then sprinkled his boat with *ayer beluru* (medicated water, *beluru* being a large climbing plant, *Entada* sp., of which the bark has a pungent odour). B then sprinkled rice paste and burnt incense first under the bow and then under the stern of the boat. A similar rite was then performed for the carrier boat, used to bring catches of fish to shore. Each boat captain sprinkled his own boat with medicated water, one saying 'I just dare to do my own', as an indication of the awe with which the rite was viewed. The second portion of offerings was put by the sternpost of each boat.

iii. Then the *bomoh* went down to the sea and stood in the water up to his shins; there he cast away the third set of offerings, and so completed the rite.

The formulae used, and most of the offerings, seemed to be part of the common stock of *bomoh*'s invocations and rites. But an idiosyncratic element, which was novel to the fishermen and which they did not pretend to understand, was the procedure with egg and candle, which seemed to involve very powerful spirits, needing special knowledge and confidence to control. Great interest was taken in the display and several fishermen came to discuss it with me. P emphasized that the results depended upon Allah and said 'I have had no teacher for this; I don't understand the meaning of it. The people who use it know.' But he and the others thought that the candle flame gave sign of the advent of *jinn* of various kinds. He contrasted with this the procedures of *juru selam* who used only excerpts from the Kuran as formulae, combined with smearing on rice paste. B himself took a very tentative attitude towards the efficacy of his rites. He was not sceptical about them, or cynical as M tended to be—it was rather that he seemed honestly to think that their outcome was uncertain. He said that he was the only man in the Perupok area to perform rites in this way—which was confirmed by the fishermen. He said also that he used the same technique in cases of sickness, but only a little—if a patient was crazy or had swollen limbs. His knowledge of what to do did not go far.

In accounting for the validity of his performance B explained that his grandfather and his father had been *bomoh*, but that while he had had a little instruction from his father his *guru* had been To' Mamat of Kota Bharu and Sungei Besar, who had been a pupil of his grandfather. B said that he used primarily Jinn Tanah, the Earth Spirit, in his rites (hence the adjournment to the ground outside the house, and the pit dug in the ground). As against the opinion of P he held that according to the teaching of his own guru, the spirits of the sea could ascend on to the shore, and spirits of the inland could be effective at sea. Hence he performed his rite inland, with the earth as location, instead of on the seashore—though he also invoked Anah, Manah, Ganah (see p. 211) as spirits of the strand. He said that he had been told by his teacher not to invoke 'Sang Gano' (Sang Gana, cf. Cuisinier, 1936, 163n), lest being always present but called upon only occasionally he be angry and make people ill. But he did use Semar, (who, he said, originated in Mecca and was the first to become Haji—so in his view was obviously legitimate to invoke; this bears out Cuisinier [1936, 182n]). Of the candle rite B said that he judged by the flame whether the *jinn* were 'in agreement', whether they desired the appeal. He obviously felt that in invoking these *jinn* he was dealing with dangerous forces. So he refused to recite his formula to me; he said that without the flame he was afraid—he couldn't tell what their attitude was. With the flame one could tell 'a little' about how the spirits would be likely to react: if the flame was small and red, it was Jinn Merah; if small and white, then Jinn Puteh; if clear, then Jinn Kuning. When the flame burned up brightly this was a good sign; if it died down, this was a bad sign. As for egg offerings (to Jinn Tanah) he used these according to the stage of the rite. On the first night he used only one egg, on the second night he used two; should his efforts still be unsuccessful he continued, adding an egg each night until he reached a total of seven. There he stopped—if no results had been obtained by then he would hand the case over to another *bomoh*, since it would be an indication that the *jinn* were not willing to cooperate with him. He explained the unique nature of his rites locally by pointing out that his teacher gave his *ilmu* to only one son, and to himself, B, who was like a son to him, and that he had no other pupil to whom he handed it on.

Though I did not challenge his religious orthodoxy directly I am sure that he regarded himself as doing a morally and theologically respectable job, controlling and directing the *jinn* in the interests of hungry and suffering humanity. I did question him on the general issue. He said quite definitely that an *orang lebai* might be a *bomoh*. Those with 'knowledge' might have it of two kinds—of the Kuran and of the *bomoh*—and it was legitimate to use both if one had them. A religious man might 'blow' and make offerings. But he might not play the violin. Why not? Because the Prophet Muhammad didn't like it. Hence such a man couldn't conduct a *main puteri*. He himself could go into trance (*lupa*) but was embarrassed to do so. When I questioned whether the Imam and other dignitaries approved of religious men being *bomoh* he replied 'How can they be angry, when the Imam himself calls me in? When his son or his wife is sick, he calls me; he has been two or three times to do so.' He said also that To' Guru Bachok, a highly respected Muslim teacher, had the attitude, if a person is sick the thing is to clear it up—implying that the end justified the means. B said too that even *main puteri* was tolerated by Islamic dignitaries, provided it was held for one of their relatives in another house than their own. I emphasize that what I am giving here is essentially the viewpoint of a local man justifying himself, and a viewpoint in 1940; it is not necessarily a 'correct' view from the standpoint of the religious authorities, and it is not necessarily a modern view. But it was certainly widely held in the Bachok area thirty years ago, with sincerity and a sense of moral commitment.

The admitted uncertainty as to his results which B showed was the very antithesis of a common stereotype of a magician, often represented as boldly confident in the validity of his rites. Some Kelantan *bomoh*, such as my old teacher To' Mamat Mindok, were quietly and firmly convinced of their powers. This was perhaps partly temperamental, partly a matter of field—for, in the end, sick people probably get well more often than mediocre fishermen catch fish! But B behaved as a man who had in his possession a powerful but dangerous tool of the accuracy of which he was not certain, but with which he was willing to experiment, convinced of the propriety of his intentions. He might almost be described as a 'reluctant magician'. He certainly seemed very far from wanting to claim the quality of being possessed of supernatural power, as had sometimes been said of him. Gimlette, one of the most careful students of Kelantan magic, wrote of 'the self-reliance of the *bomoh* and his sublime belief in his calling' (1929, 52). As a general statement this can pass, but it must not be taken as applying to every instance, and it is important to realize this in order to understand the interplay between the producer and the consumer of magic, and the nature of interpretations given to it.

The Concept of Keramat

Though belief in Malay magic does not rest on the notion of *keramat* they are closely associated. The concept of *keramat* has often been discussed, and translations ranging from saint, shrine, venerable, sacred, miraculous, to prohibited, taboo, haunted have been suggested. It has been thought to apply basically to places and only secondarily to persons and things; it has been interpreted as representing a high concentration of *semangat*, of wonder-working power ... and so on (Marsden, 1812, 255; Favre, 1875, I, 354; Skeat, 1900, 673–4; Wilkinson, 1903, 509; Cuisinier, 1936, 31–33; Endicott, 1970, 90–95). Many examples of the use of the term *keramat* were given to us in 1940. A *jitong* (*Gluta* sp.), a large tree growing near the seashore, was pointed out as *keramat*. According to Gimlette (1939, 97–8) such trees can yield an irritant juice used by 'vindictive natives of Kelantan' against their victims. We were not told this, but it was said that *hantu* liked such trees and were liable to strike people who passed beneath. A man of Kubang Golok who defecated beneath one could not rise from his crouching position until a *bomoh* was summoned, came and 'blew' upon him and hit him on the back. The *hantu* clawing at his posterior released their hold, and off he ran. When a *bomoh* neighbour of ours cut down a *jitong* tree he first made offerings near by; no one could take the wood for fires. An elephant by name Berma Sakti (the female principle of Brahma) was said by peasants to be *keramat*, and to be called every month to clear one of the Sultan's residences of evil. If a person was ill, and the elephant was called and given an offering of turmeric rice and bananas to eat, the evil was lifted. The animal was possessed by a *hantu*—'If there's no *hantu*, there's no *keramat*; if there's a *hantu*, *keramat*'—but the name of the *hantu* was not known. The shadow play figures Pak Dogol and Wak Long were *keramat*, as shown by the raw cotton threads round their necks. When a *dalang* presented me with a set of figures and asked me to choose which I would like, he courteously refused to give me the current Pak Dogol, and gave me the current Wak Long with a request that I would let him take it away to his house for an hour or so (to be rendered innocuous). Other people told me that all Pak Dogol figures, even old disused ones, were *keramat*, and that if a woman were giving birth they should be kept under a platform or high on the wall where they could not be walked on, as they were dangerous. The *dalang* said that certain illnesses such as headache could be diagnosed as caused by Pak Dogol and consequently could be relieved only by his agency (cf. Cuisinier, 1957, 83–90).

These examples are of objects regarded as possessing special powers which can be harmful to men but which may also be used to relieve illness. These powers are usually associated with *hantu*, and contact with them tends to be cautious, with elements of taboo. When the term *keramat* is applied to persons, especially to living persons, the associations are apt to be different. The taboo aspect tends to be subordinated to the creative power aspect; it is benefit rather than harm to people that tends to be emphasized. I think the best translation for *keramat* is usually extraordinary or superhuman power, with positive or negative aspects uppermost according to circumstances.[3] When the *bomoh* B was said by M to be *keramat*, elements of taboo were almost entirely lacking; it was the positive theme of recognition of his success that was expressed, success to an unexpected, seemingly superhuman degree. His success was thought to be due to his control of powerful *hantu*, but this putative control in itself implied that he had qualities lacking in ordinary people, and so worthy of respect. This positive aspect of the *keramat* quality that might attach to a living person came out very strongly in some of M's other remarks. When I asked him formally what the term meant he replied 'it's like the fever of a child—if To' Wali is *keramat*, he stops it' and he added significantly 'if the fever does not stop, perhaps he is not *keramat*.' This conditional attribution of *keramat* is a factor which I think should be strongly emphasized. It is essentially judgement by results. 'If a child loses a gold plaque, its parents may promise rice and bananas to To' Wali if they find it. If he is *keramat*, perhaps they will come across it.' The notion of *keramat* has a strong inferential aspect; it is an invisible power the presence of which is inferred from concrete events which are taken to be evidence. As an illustration of such power greater than normal M cited the behaviour of To' Wali Ismail, near Ketereh. To fishing experts with whom he was in good relations he gave blessed rice, passed his hands over their faces and said 'go to sea, tomorrow you will get fish.' But when M went to visit him he didn't appear—not that he was not present, but one could be quite close to him and not see him if he wished to be invisible, even if he was in the same room. On this occasion the Wali's son said he was in the room, but M could only hear his voice—the Wali announced that he was going to Mecca to pray, but would be back that afternoon!

Though to be *keramat* can connote sainthood, it was understood that a person who became *keramat* was not necessarily a man of great learning in religious matters. One of my friends said rather unkindly that the Wali of Bukit Merbau, who was *keramat*, would take thirty years of teaching before he could be the equal in learning of To' Guru Bachok, who was held in great esteem as a teacher. To be *keramat* could be the result of searching, a matter of obtaining special knowledge—*ilmu keramat*, it was stated, was different from other knowledge—and my

---

[3] The concept of *keramat* seems to me to be very similar to that of *mana* in Oceania, as I noted in 1940 (Raymond Firth, 1967a, 192n).

informant said that he himself could ask for it. It was implied that in becoming *keramat* one came into the possession of a secret, and that one need not grow gradually into it. The Wali of Bukit Merbau was said, in 1940, to have been *keramat* for only a year, and he 'had become *keramat* at once' (I think, after the death of a predecessor). It was alleged that if To' Guru Bachok wished it, he could be ten times as *keramat* as the Wali of Bukit Merbau![4] In all this, there was no suggestion of *keramat* being associated with any particular 'concentration of *semangat*' (Endicott, 1970, 93) which I think is a mistaken notion; *keramat* is an active, often offensive power, whereas *semangat* is a rather passive, sensitive, life principle.

In the local fishing magic, then, though there were recognized traditional procedures for seeking success, the attitude towards them tended to be exploratory, choosing between alternatives, testing by results, assigning or rejecting attributes of special powers to particular individuals. The fishermen by no means accepted and practised a completely unchallenged integral ritual system. The attitude to healing magic had much in common with this.

Role of Bomoh *in Personal Protection*

Concern for bodily health was a major field for exercise of a *bomoh*'s arts, since while agriculture or fishing were actually carried on by only a fraction of the coastal population, every member of it was liable to be afflicted by illness. While there was room for interpretation, illness commonly involved some concepts of spiritual attack and defence. Apart from any other specialism he might have, then, each *bomoh* usually had a set of magical (and putatively medical) procedures not only for healing, but also for protecting people against spirit harm. (For this reason some translations of *bomoh* have taken the medical/magical aspect of his work as primary). Although there was considerable variation in individual procedures, in the Perupok area the protective and healing techniques of *bomoh* in 1940 fell into three main classes: *siup* (*tiup*); *bageh* (*berbageh*); and *main puteri* (*peteri*, *putri*) (Gimlette, 1929, 73, 77 *et seq.*, 100; 1939, 186; Cuisinier, 1936, 93–112; 1957, 89). I have already dealt briefly with the more dramatic aspects of *main puteri* (Raymond Firth, 1967b) and hope later to examine further symbolic aspects of those healing rites which use spirit mediums. Here I illustrate the theme of faith and scepticism by examples of simple protective and healing rites of *siup* and *bageh*.

---

[4] To' Guru seems to have had a contempt for the local Wali. He was alleged to have said that to claim to be a saint while sitting in a kampong (and eating in luxury) was no good—it was known from the Kuran that saints sat on hills and ate green shoots!

In 1939–40 a local *bomoh*, P, as a neighbour and senior man of influence, had made himself responsible for much of our comfort until we became familiar with our surroundings. In his prime he had been an expert fisherman, and also a circumciser at Muslim initiations. His long experience, his many local kin contacts, and a client relationship with a sister of the Sultan, sometimes inclined him to dogmatic pronouncement, but his force of character, his esoteric knowledge, his shrewdness and his rough good humour, coupled with his age, meant that people gave him a good deal of respect and often accepted his views. Soon after we arrived P made it his business to see that I was instructed about the spiritual as well as the physical dangers of the place. An occasion arose from the illness of the wife of our servant Mamat (Che' Mat), due, so P alleged, to a breach of respect behaviour to a local *hantu* living in a depression near our house. He dealt with the illness by formula and offering, in a rite he termed *tiup* (blowing). He dictated the formula to me:

> He! Nenek, Surubang Kuning
> Mu dudok pegang Kuala Daromain
> Mu jangan buat kerenah, datang Che' Mat duadua laki bini
> Jangan buat kerenah, Tuan punya Me' sendiri.

The symptoms were outlined by P as dizziness and pain in the stomach after evacuation, which apparently had occurred too near the *hantu's* dwelling. The *hantu*, Yellow Turban by name, commanded the area in the immediate vicinity so that no alien spirit could enter, and the depression, his 'house', was *keramat*. But P affirmed that he could control the spirit by formula and offerings, with 'blowing'. The formula, addressing the *hantu* as ancestor, and by name, cited his 'domain', the *kuala* or little estuary near by, and requested him not to do harm to the inhabitants of our house. P dramatized the situation saying, 'I speak as you have written. When I blow, he goes; I chivvy him; he gets angry; says 'You want to make war on me, you speak strongly'. But he can't do anything. I say 'You get back there, go to sleep again.' 'P spoke without reserve, not at all shy of admitting that he was a *bomoh*, and gave a lot of this information quite unsolicited. He added that I too could use this formula: 'If you speak like this yourself the spirit won't stay.' And he went over the recital three times to ensure that it was correct. (As commonly in such cases, it was in use of the name of the *hantu* that the power of the formula was thought essentially to lie). P then led me to a dark hole in the watercourse about twenty yards from our house and showed me the remnants of offerings that, unasked, he had laid the night before at the base of a coconut palm. He said that the *hantu* was of ancient residence; that at the time when the estuary was formed the spirit had taken up his abode. He also said that the spot where our house had been built was one feared by local Malays as a dwelling place since it was the abode of Surubang Kuning; that the government officer responsible for our accomodation had known of this, but had said it didn't matter!

Later, as we were walking along the beach at the water's edge P suddenly remarked, 'This edge here has three spirits. If there are many people they get angry; one shouldn't do it.' He refused to give me the names of these spirits on the spot. He said, 'Let's go and find a comfortable place by ourselves, you and me; if there are other people present I can't speak of the spirits, they would be angry.' When we were seated above the beach he went on, 'There are three *hantu* at the border of the sea—it is true. One is Anah, another Ganah, another Janah.'[5] Then he gave a brief formula for coping with them, beginning:

I know your names, Anah, Ganah, Janah
Don't you do evil
To people walking along the edge of the strand
Don't you do evil
You dwell equably
Another time I will give you a mass of *pulut* rice
An egg, a handful of parched rice,
A plate of pancake, a cigarette, and a bunch of betel and areca.

P said that such *hantu* were continually walking about, in the night and even by day. He also said that out on the sea were other *hantu*, in the areas where men caught fish, and he gave me a formula of similar type to deal with one of these, Jinn Kuning, whose dominion was the current line or tide-rip.[6] He explained that Jinn Kuning was apt to hinder progress of a boat at sea, making noises 'bu—ow, ow . . .' in an adverse current, but when spoken to in an appeasing way he would disappear and the way would be open. Parallel to Jinn Kuning, the Yellow Jinn, were Jinn Hitam, the Black Jinn, who lived 'on top of the skin of the earth', and Jinn Merah, the Red Jinn, who lived on the tops of tall mountains. These caused illness—for instance, Jinn Merah affected people with pains and convulsions—'he eats men; when he is angry, people die.'

[5] According to To' Mamat Mindok, independently, these three, or alternatively Anah, Janah, Manah, were siblings, *hantu* of the water's edge, responsible for overturning boats as they came in; their father was Usemain Pari (cf. Cuisinier, 1936, 183) and their mother Mak Sengaroh (see Note 6).

[6] *Tali harus* (coll. *tali aroh*) = scum-line of meeting tides, tide-rip. (Cf. *Mambang tali harus*, spirit of tide-rips, as 'the most feared of the demons of the sea'—Wilkinson, 1932, I, 400; also 1906, 68).

Material of this kind illustrated the belief of an old *bomoh* in his role of expositor, protector and healer, through his knowledge of magic. It was part of his job, as he saw it, as a functioning member of the village community, to safeguard people from the effects of spirits who might be around. He expected remuneration from me for some of his more formally given information—but so he would have done from a fellow-villager; and he was always willing to warn people of dangers from spirit forces. His beliefs in the immanence of such forces were not always shared. This discussion took place about midday, before the first fishing boats came in with their catch. When we had strolled down to the beach to see them come in P explained to a curious crowd, of mainly fish dealers, how he had been tutoring me in the knowledge of *hantu*. The crowd was grinning, and as I noted at the time there was clearly a large element of apparent unbelief in what he was saying. On the other hand, there was a respect for the old man's sincerity, and one fish dealer commented reassuringly on P's affirmations about the presence of spirits 'Oh! they must be there.' These were people who were not directly concerned with catching fish, but with hard bargaining and movement from one urban centre to another. While they probably were quite ready to accept ideas of spirits involved in illness, they seemed to feel no immediate need of protection, and to regard these tales of *hantu* along the beach with indifference if not scepticism.

The question of faith or scepticism in the healing procedures of the *bomoh*, as with fishing magic, is bound up with their apparent success or failure. Yet the issue is often not clear-cut. As we were going one evening to a *main puteri* performance P was called to come and *siup*—a man who had been fishing in the surf had returned with a bad stomach pain, and was lying immobile in his house. P said to us that he would take only a little while. He laid hands on the man's stomach, and repeated a long formula, invoking Anah, Ganah, Janah, Jinn Kuning Tali Harus, and Jinn Hitam—*hantu* (as already mentioned) of the water's edge and of the tide-rip, especially—who were thought to be responsible for afflicting the sick man. P massaged the patient's belly, pressing down; the man rolled on his side, and was massaged lightly there also. The *bomoh* called for rice, repeated a 'release' (*pelepas*) formula, 'blew' and threw two handfuls of rice in four separate motions each at the waist, thighs, knees and feet of the patient. Then we went on.

As we went P commented that the patient had said he felt better after the proceedings, and added that the *hantu* had gone. 'But perhaps they may return' he said calmly. This was evidently the *bomoh*'s conventional way of escape from the dilemma of non-success. Instead of having to interpret the failure of his healing technique in sceptical terms he could justify the technique while admitting its temporary ineffectiveness. The situation was conceived as one of competing forces—the exorcising *bomoh* and his tutelary spirit, and the afflicting *hantu*. In a temporary illness the *hantu* are expelled and do not return; in a chronic illness even if they are expelled they may return, and the result may be fatal. Lest we may be inclined to sneer, Europeans should remember the grim joke sometimes made in Western medicine—'the operation was successful, but the patient died'.

By 1963 P had been dead about twenty years. In August of that year I went with L to the house of a son of P, to see a *bageh* performance. The patient was the son himself (call him Q) who complained of pain in the lower left ribs, which had begun with fever, and which he had had for some time. Nevertheless he was mobile, trotting round in a rather agitated way, doing the honours of his house and attending to his guests. In effect the performance was to be a trance rite without orchestra. This was cheaper than a *main puteri*, partly because no license fee was needed to get permission from the District Office. The rite began with the preparation of the *nasi guru*, the offering to the presiding genius Nenek Batara Guru, and with the censing of the ritual paraphernalia, including a cushion and two orange cloths for the medium. An areca palm branch was prepared by cutting off its top, stripping it of its lower pinnules, and tying it into a whisk shape. The medium changed his sarong and took post in front of the chief *bomoh*, and each recited a long invocation, sometimes antiphonally. There was much calling on Tuhan Allah and on Nabi Muhammad, and later on the Four Shaykhs, the Seven Dewa, and on Jinns and Hulubalang. The medium, sitting with the areca branch in his hand, began to quiver slightly, but as the chanting proceeded his quivering became more violent. At last he gave a shriek, his shoulder muscles began to work, and he appeared to undergo a personality transformation.

The chief magician then began to question the medium, and there was also consultation of the significance of rice grains set out on the cushion, as oracles to identify the *hantu* responsible for the illness. A more senior medium also joined in the proceedings, and after much exploration and rejection of spirit forces of different kinds the afflicting agency was finally pinned down. It was the *penggawa* of the dead *bomoh* P, the patient's father—'control' spirits whom he had been alleged to foster. Then came a dramatic turn in the proceedings—though not an unusual one. The patient Q, who had been submitting to the ministrations of the medium, now in turn became possessed by the spirits, i.e.

went into trance. He engaged in violent contortions—a kind of hypnotic frenzy, threshing about with arms and legs and throwing himself around in an apparently uncontrollable seizure. (But I noted that he retained *some* measure of control, since at no point did he collide with us or other participants, though he looked as if he might do so at any moment). Then he collapsed, completely exhausted, at the edge of the raised part of the room. The audience, which had been following these events tensely, in contrast to the nonchalant way in which they had viewed the medium's performance, were now very concerned, and the medium too was anxious. The medium clearly dropped back from his 'other personality' role into his ordinary state, and with solicitude asked the patient 'Are you all right? Do you want any more?' The patient, who had been revived with ritual water, weakly said he wished to continue, and the seance went on, with the medium now in renewed trance. Having previously worked over the patient from the toes upwards, he was now shaking him at the neck, though not very violently. As a more peaceful phase now seemed well on its way, and it was midnight, we left the house; I gathered later that the seance had a normal ending, including making offerings and other placatory acts.

I saw several points of significance in this performance. In the long invocations of the trance medium, lasting almost half an hour, and uttered in a brassy, commanding voice, I recognized much of the material given me by my own teacher To' Mamat Mindok more than twenty years before. There was clearly a great deal of common ground not only between *bageh* and *main puteri*, but also between performances of a generation apart. At the same time the arrangement of the material —titles of *hantu*, phrases of invocation—showed personal idiosyncratic elements, though it was noticeable that the phraseology of the junior *orang lupa* (or *to' bageh*) was very similar to that of the senior, his teacher. Belief in and practice of many magical rites had obviously strong continuity in the area, reinforced by a pedagogic tradition of magic which had endured.

The impressive 'patient participation' also followed tradition though the *lupa* of the patient at both periods usually took a quieter trance form. But by this particular violent participation the patient not only accepted but confirmed the identification of the cause of illness presented to him. One may interpret his trance also as being in effect a statement revealing some of his own fears and emotions, possibly hitherto hidden from him, about the aetiology of his illness. The physical aspects of his crisis may have given him a kind of catharsis—through muscular tension and release of an almost organismic kind. The psychological aspects may have given him an emotional release, a 'coming clean' of his own attitudes, perhaps an open acknowledgement of some dereliction of duty felt towards his dead father. While the diagnosis was couched in the form of a complaint or justification by a spirit, basically the patient's response implied a recognition of powerful forces within himself which had previously not come to full expression—and perhaps including an admission of some shortcoming or fear. What amounted to a public 'confession' of direct involvement in a residual relationship with his dead father could however be interpreted as avoidance of an explicit declaration of an embarrassing kind, since it was not as his ordinary personality but in another form that the patient made his demonstration. But it seems a fair inference that the emergence to the surface of these other aspects of his personality in a cooperative context could be psychosomatically of benefit to him.

A question of some interest to me was why the *penggawa* of my old *bomoh* friend P should have been thought to have emerged into activity only at that point, about twenty years after the death of their putative controller. At first I thought there was a possibility that our arrival in the village after so long might have stirred some old memories. But it did not appear so. I was told that the patient had been ill for some time before our coming, and that for a long while his wife had wanted him to undergo a *bageh* performance, but that he had refused. (After seeing his reaction I was not surprised; it must have been a traumatic, even physically painful experience, like shock treatment, even apart from any emotional disturbance caused to him, and he may well have been afraid. Moreover, it appeared that all along it had been thought that it was his father's control spirits which had been afflicting him— and indeed I was actually told this before the night's performance took place.)

The general setting of this particular diagnosis is interesting. It was an article of local faith that a fisherman might foster or look after a *hantu* to get protection at sea, as an agriculturalist might for his own purposes. This was believed to be not common, except with *bomoh*, since it involved some knowledge of magical formulae and other controls, as well as occasional offerings, especially when a service was required. And if a man ceased to look after the spirit and provide the offerings he was in danger—the spirit, unfed, could turn on him and make him ill. I asked did my old teacher To' Mamat Mindok foster a *hantu*? No, was the answer, he fostered a *penggawa*, tiny, but more powerful. People of old used to employ *penggawa* for many purposes: in competitive top spinning, to block the top of an opponent; to prevent theft from one's house; to help in raising poultry; to help one to return when in difficulties out at sea. A *penggawa* is not the spirit of a dead person, or of an ancestor; it is rather of the quality of *angin* ('wind', humour, temperament)—though there was some dispute about this. *Penggawa* are not commonly kept by people as spirit familiars—only sporadically. They are more powerful than ordinary *hantu*: they can be commanded to go and fetch things from distant places (see below, p. 218) whereas *hantu* cannot be so used; they are superior to *hantu*, who are afraid of them and can be gripped by them. In a broad sense, *penggawa* can be classed as a kind of *hantu*, but they differ from ordinary *hantu* in that they do not consume blood, and so are given offerings of eggs—though even this distinction has its complications.

Now, on the death of a person his *penggawa* could pass to his descendants. To' Mamat Mindok had no son, but the *bomoh* P did, and it was alleged that his *penggawa* wished to dwell with his son Q. But Q didn't want them. Why did he not wish to look after his father's familiar spirits? Because this was onerous; he didn't want the trouble of travelling about, performing *bageh* and other rites over sick people, as would have been demanded as a public service when his fostering of *penggawa* became known. So, since the spirits wished to descend and be fostered by him, and he refused, he became ill.

This explanation put a different complexion on the case. In concrete material terms one can see some part of his personal history as a conflict within himself. After his father's death Q may have recognized a tendency, which he thought to be inherited, to instability and trance behaviour. This he suppressed because he didn't want the effort which any public display of this would entail, as in trances of healing rites. This suppression by itself may not have made him ill, but any physical illness tended to be interpreted by others if not by himself as a manifestation of his denial of his inner tendencies. Only as the years went by would he consent to a formal confrontation with these elements of his personality, a process of a painful kind, however cathartic. What the ritual did was to isolate and personalize these elements, and give them some form of overt expression in a generally recognized cultural convention, and to suggest some displacement activities. (Cf. also an interesting case in Rosemary Firth, 1966, 195).

In 1963, as in 1940, there was clear evidence of much firm belief in magical ideas and practices in fields where mental and physical elements of the personality were closely associated, and orthodox medicine was still far from secure in its therapy. On the other hand, much of the treatment of simple physical illnesses had passed, over the generation, from *bomoh* to dispensary. It was not so much that scepticism had replaced faith in magic in these spheres, but that the area of magical operations had become more circumscribed.

Kelantan magical concepts tend also to be strengthened by their interrelation with concepts in other fields. In this particular case the *penggawa* of the dead *bomoh* P were identified as figures known from the shadow play; they included Arjuna, and Hanuman (Anomeng Gerop Puteh, perhaps to be rendered as White-Fanged Hanuman). These spirits were said to be very bold, and violent. So the first trance medium dared to deal only with lesser spirits (*main hantu*) and it was the second, the senior man, in whom the familiar spirits finally appeared (*main penggawa*). Even then, it was explained to me, not all the familiar spirits were 'cleared' in the night's performance—'if Hanuman had come out last night, ah! perhaps I should have run away', commented my guide. There seemed obviously a very sincere belief in the force of these spirits and a real fear of their damaging power if they should actually succeed in freeing themselves from the restraints imposed upon them by the *bomoh*.

Yet even though all such matters were seriously discussed, and firm assertions were made about afflicting and controlling spirits, participants in the discussion, as the audience at the seance, were not averse to making jokes about them. It was suggested semi-seriously that I myself might like to use a *penggawa* also; this I refused, saying that a Malay familiar spirit was of no use to me. As we were talking I began to put my shoes on and found a frog in the toe of one. As I shook it out our landlady, Che' Minah, laughed and said '*penggawa*, a *penggawa* seeks you.' But then seriously she denied that such a spirit would enter a frog, though she agreed it might enter a bird. Her sister-in-law fled from the frog but Minah pushed it out with her toe, saying that a pair of them lived in a hole in the timber of the house, and added laughing, 'my familiar!' But after this joking there was solemn debate about where these spirits lived, some saying they lived in the ground, others that they lived on the mountain tops, in places that were *keramat*.

Magic, Conjuring and Unbelief

Some of these issues came up in a dramatic way in a case which arose from a summons for healing but spilled over into a conjuring performance.

Early in 1940 the wife of our neighbour P became seriously ill (she died not long after). A Malay *bomoh* from Siam came to attend her, introduced by To' Mamat Mindok. I was told that perhaps he was *keramat*; he could produce sugar from a bowl of ashes; he had thrown away a young girl's earring and then made it appear again in her ear; he had torn a cloth in two and it was afterwards seen to be whole. But there was also scepticism. The *bomoh* wanted $5 (then a large sum) for *ubat*, and one man said 'if it were me I'd engage with my thumbprint before the D.O. [District Officer] to pay him $20 *after* the cure.'

Two days later, on the initiative of P and of Mamat our servant, the *bomoh* gave a demonstration of his powers in our house—this locale being chosen partly because we wanted to see him at work and partly because we would pay. The conjurer, Che' Mamat, known as To' Bomoh, the curer and also as To' Haji (though he had not been to Mecca), came late, and was rather silent. He wound a black cloth round his waist, above his black shirt. First he rattled a pencil against his nose septum to show that there was no hole there, then apparently passed a thread on which there was a large knot through the septum, winding the ends of the thread round his head, where they stayed during the performance. Then he took some of our newspaper, made a little ball of it, put it on a tray and put a food cover over it—tray and food cover being from our household. A little later, to the astonishment of the audience, he produced from under the cover biscuits and sugar—about half a pound of each. Then he ordered a bird to be made of paper. One of the audience cut it out, but he said it had to be folded, and since no one else could do this properly he did it himself—a small figure about 3 inches high and 2 inches broad. He covered the paper bird with another food cover—actually a fisherman's pandanus hat which I happened to have at hand. After some manipulation he produced from under the cover a proper bird, a dove—but it was dead. Finally he swallowed a mouthful of black cotton and produced it from his navel.

The powers of the *bomoh* had been explained as due to his control over Jinn Islam—his *penggawa*, his familiar spirit, went and brought back from outside the objects he produced. The spirit was not evil; he did not take gold or cash, but only small things. These were edible or otherwise usable—if sugar, it could be eaten; if a dove, it could be kept as a pet. It is of critical significance to note that in general local view if the arts of the *bomoh* had been sorcery (*seher*) then the sugar would not have been edible, and the bird would disappear again when we tried to keep it in a cage. In other words, the test of the morality of magic was empirical: 'good' magic yielded useful results; 'bad' magic yielded results which were illusory. I asked where did the things come from which the *bomoh* produced? The answer was ingenious, and again empirical—from Chinese shops, and the Chinese had so much property that they did not miss them! The *bomoh*'s *penggawa* did not take things from Malay shops. (This was a good way of getting round two difficulties: that Malay shopkeepers might protest at the idea of spirits thieving from their shelves; on the other hand, no Malay shopkeepers reported such losses.) Such explanation helped the *bomoh* in allowing him to buy his goods in Chinese shops, where he was less likely to be detected.

There were certain significant points about the magician's performance. He brought no visible 'properties' with him, such as wand or screen. He wore the nail of the little finger of his left hand very long. He had voluminous trousers. He was unwillingly induced to come a little forward to perform—in the end, P measured a fathom by arm-length and he rigorously stayed at that distance. As far as I could observe he used no formula of any kind in his performance, either aloud or quietly muttered. Hence I concluded that what he did meant to him simple conjuring and was not a ritual performance. I could not observe any obvious manipulation or 'passing' of objects, but he took a long while in preparing the folded ball of paper from which he later produced the biscuits and sugar. I took it that the production of the bird dead was an accident—that the bird had suffered too much in transit and concealment.

But the audience reaction was different. When the bird was discovered to be dead the *bomoh* was asked to bring it alive. Both Mamat and P, it appeared, had hoped that the bird (in effect acquired through our money) would fall to him to keep; when it seemed to be dead their hopes were dashed. But the magician, embarrassed, did not pay very much attention to it. He rapped around it on the floor, and finally said he couldn't revive it. He was drawing the black thread from his navel at the time, and (in an ingenious piece of ad-libbing) called attention to the fact that the thread had broken—hence, he said, the bird could not live. The attitude of his original sponsor, To' Mindok, was one of rather curt dismissal: 'Oh! you can't bring the bird alive; come along; let's go home.' So he and the magician went almost at once.

Then the storm broke. Our neighbour P was very disgruntled. He said angrily, 'He has deceived me; I believe he brought the bird with him.' The master fisherman M said, 'How could that be? The bird is newly dead; and he has been here three or four days; it would have been rotten.' He added logically, 'if he brought the bird, he brought the sugar and biscuits. If he fetched these (i.e. his *penggawa* did) then he fetched also the bird.' (In this discussion *bawa* was used for the idea of the magician personally bringing the objects, and *ambil* for the idea of his familiar spirits fetching them for him). For this rather credulous view there was some support. But P was not appeased. He cried 'I wanted a live bird, and here is a dead one. I am fed up.' He went over to the window, looked out over the inevitable crowd assembled on such an occasion and harangued them, holding out the bird with its wings spread. 'I have been deceived; I wanted a live bird, and he has brought this dead one; I believe that he had it with him. What do you think?' Various voices answered from the darkness outside, the general view being that the *penggawa* of the *bomoh* had indeed 'fetched' the bird, but had grasped it too tightly for it to survive. P returned to the centre of the room—'I am the only person who doesn't believe; they all believe it was his *penggawa*; I don't believe.' (My wife, sympathetically, not to isolate him, agreed, while at first I took the other side). He then said 'Mem [my wife] and I are the only two who don't believe.' Then M asked again, 'How could he have brought a dead bird and kept it with him all this time?' I commented that perhaps he had brought a live one and it ate from the biscuits and sugar—a suggestion received with much laughter. Again P said 'I think he brought the lot himself.' As the argument went on there seemed to be some move towards this view. But while P declared in his disappointment that he was sceptical of the *bomoh*'s abilities, Mamat, as he confirmed later, still believed that the *bomoh* could produce a live bird through his familiar spirit. Finally it was arranged that since I was willing to pay $1 for the *bomoh*'s performance, even though it only resulted in a dead bird, P and Mamat would offer him another dollar to produce a live bird the following night.

One of the aspects of such an affair was undoubtedly the desire of some participants to get the goods produced—very evidently this was behind the disgust of P and Mamat. But M commented shrewdly, 'How can you expect a bird worth $5 for $1?' But willing to take advantage of the situation should it turn out favourable he himself said 'We'll ask him to produce ten bottles of scent tomorrow!' His attitude obviously was to be much more interested in what goods the *bomoh* could produce than in the manner in which he produced them. It was the presence of the dead bird that couldn't be kept as a pet that precipitated all this discussion—in a way the magician had presented the audience with an object out of category. It was not that he had not produced a result—he had produced a *wrong* result—not an illusory object, but a useless object. This could be accounted for neither by the notion of familiar spirit nor that of sorcery. The residual view of his performance, that of sleight of hand, probably from a special pocket in his trousers, was one to which people came only slowly, and much later.

The next day we had further opinions. A general view was now that the production of the dead bird had not been 'correct', and that this meant that the *bomoh* had probably brought it with him to the scene and conjured it up. But if he would produce a live bird this next evening it would be 'correct' and his claims would be justified; the power of his familiar would be admitted. Parallel instances of other marvels were given in support of this view.

The performance of the second evening was a complete success. The *bomoh* produced in sequence: a live dove; cotton thread from his navel; beans; and coarse local lump sugar. (He said that a large lump of sugar was *ubat*, but did not specify what kind). He was then asked for scent, in line with a previous suggestion. Over this there was a haggle, mainly in terms of what those who had asked for it were willing to pay. The *bomoh* said that there was no scent locally or in Bachok that his familiar spirit could lay hands on; that he would have to go to Kota Bharu for it; that this was 'difficult', and would cost $2.50. In this setting of magical ideas it seemed that payment by the consumer was intended to cover two elements: a contribution for witnessing the production of articles in this wonderful way; and a compensation for the 'trouble' taken by the familiar spirit in fetching them. But the economic factor was evident. I inferred that the high price asked by the *bomoh* for production of a bottle of scent was really intended by him as a deterrent. He had come prepared to produce bird and sugar, but not scent, so set the price at a figure which he knew the consumers would not pay. The dove he did produce was worth only about 20 cents; one with a melodious note would have cost him many dollars.

Finally, the magician did a vanishing ring trick. With a fine display of bravado, stimulated by his success, he said openly that this *was* conjuring (*silap mata*). But he also stated quite solemnly that the dove had been brought from the hills by his familiar spirit, a *penggawa* by the name of Makar. This admitted conjunction of conjuring and spirit aid in the same evening's performance was very striking; it indicated that the *bomoh* felt very sure of himself, and of the reactions of his audience in terms of the local conventions of belief in spirit capacity and spirit control. If he had gone into trance during any part of his performance, I might have thought that like many other *bomoh* he did have a sincere belief in his own powers and in the spirit forces he claimed to control. I have no reason to think he did not believe in spirit forces, but it was clear that in this instance his production of objects was knowingly based upon sleight of hand conjuring. He was therefore consciously using techniques of deception, which I thought rare with Kelantan *bomoh*.

But the case did indicate a kind of calculating scepticism in at least one practitioner of the magic art.

On this second occasion his audience appeared quite satisfied. In particular, P held that the bird was a genuine product of the *bomoh*'s art of spirit control, while another prominent participator said 'It is correct; it is his *penggawa*.' Mamat was enthusiastic and had more ambitious plans for the *bomoh*, which, however, we were not prepared to support financially.

Four days later came the denouement. It was established that the *bomoh* had actually bought his biscuits and sugar in a local shop after all; then an old man from a nearby hamlet revealed that the *bomoh* had obtained a live dove from his sister's child. Reactions of people to this discovery of the *bomoh*'s unmistakable trickery were, not unexpectedly, self-justification. Mamat said he had challenged the *bomoh* to greater feats, whereupon he had run away. M said he didn't attend the second performance because a travelling pedlar had identified the *bomoh* as a swindler who had got money from his village by inducing people to put cash in a bowl and bury it, with promise of turning it into large sums—when they went to fetch it in the morning the bowl was empty and the *bomoh* gone. To' Mamat Mindok explained how the *bomoh* had cheated on the nose trick, and how when he found out about the larger deception he had sent the man away lest the people be angry with him. But he did add that the *bomoh* had an *ubat* which had prevented the audience from seeing what he did—after all, to his fellow professional, one could understand how he might think that success was due not to technical skill but to magic art.

Summary

In a way this analysis is a small contribution to the intellectual history of a part of Kelantan a generation ago, showing the kind of compound of mystical and pragmatic ideas then current about some important sectors of social affairs. If faith be the acceptance of the witness of things seen to things unseen, then there was much strong faith in magic. A strongly integrated framework of ideas expressed in terms such as *semangat*, *hantu*, *keramat*, and in actions such as use of *ubat*, *tiup*, *bageh*, etc., symbolized forces responsible for success and failure, health and sickness, ease or disturbance of mind. Yet this was not the only possible framework, and the magical one was challenged at times, and interwoven at times, by the religious framework of Islam and the quasi-scientific framework of empiricism. However much inclined to respect for traditional norms, the Kelantan coastal Malays were apt to view their magic in a relatively sceptical, flexible way, which in its own particular setting at that period probably had distinct functional advantages for them. Advances in mechanization, medical care, education in the area over the last generation have tended to reduce belief if not in the validity at least in the necessity of magic. The broadening of interests since Independence may have drawn off some of the interest formerly focussed upon magical practices. However much this may be seen as a gain in social and intellectual maturity, the traditional magical ideology should not be despised but regarded as worthy of understanding as part of the attempt to provide an intelligible framework for dealing with human problems.

REFERENCES

Brown, C.C., 1927. *Kelantan Malay*, in *Papers on Malay Subjects* (Second Series) (Singapore, Government Printer).

Clifford, Hugh, 1897. *In Court and Kampong* (London, Grant Richards).

Cuisinier, Jeanne, 1936. *Danses Magiques de Kelantan*. (Travaux et Mémoires de l'Institut d'Ethnologie, XXII, Paris, Institut d'Ethnologie).

——— 1957. *Le Théatre d'Ombres à Kelantan* (Paris, Gallimard).

Downs, R.E., 1967. 'A Kelantanese Village of Malaya', in Julian H. Steward (ed.), *Contemporary Change in Traditional Societies*, Vol. II, *Asian Rural Societies*, 105–86 (Urbana, University of Illinois).

Endicott, Kirk Michael, 1970. *An Analysis of Malay Magic* (Oxford, Clarendon Press).

Favre, P., 1875. *Dictionnaire Malais-Français*. 2 vols. (Paris, Maisonneuve et Cie).

Firth, Raymond, 1966. *Malay Fishermen: Their Peasant Economy* (2nd ed., London, Routledge & Kegan Paul).

——— 1967a. *Tikopia Ritual and Belief* (London, George Allen & Unwin).

——— 1967b. 'Ritual and Drama in Malay Spirit Mediumship', *Comparative Studies in Society and History*, IX, 190–207.

Firth, Rosemary, 1966. *Housekeeping among Malay Peasants* (London School of Economics Monographs on Social Anthropology, No. 7, 2nd ed. London, Athlone Press).

Gimlette, J.D., 1913. 'Some Superstitious Beliefs Occurring in the Theory and Practice of Malay Medicine,' *JSBRAS*, 65, 29–35.

——— 1915. *Malay Poisons and Charm Cures* (London, J. & A. Churchill) (3rd ed. 1929.)

——— 1939. *A Dictionary of Malayan Medicine* (ed. and completed by H.W. Thomson). (London, Oxford University Press).

Howison, James, 1801. *A Dictionary of the Malay Tongue* (London, Arabic and Persian Press).

Marsden, William, 1812. *A Dictionary of the Malayan Language* (London, Cox & Baylis).

Shaw, G.E., 1926. *Malay Industries. Part III, Rice Planting*, in *Papers on Malay Subjects* (First Series, reprinted) (Kuala Lumpur, Government Printer).

Skeat, W.W., 1900. *Malay Magic* (London, Macmillan & Co).

State of Kelantan, 1937. *Estimates of the Revenue and Expenditure for the Year 1938* (Singapore, Printers Ltd).

Swettenham, *Sir* Frank A., 1905. *Vocabulary of the English and Malay Languages* (5th ed., Vol. I) (Shanghai, Kelly & Walsh).

Wilkinson, R.J., 1903. *A Malay-English Dictionary* (Singapore, Kelly & Walsh).

——— 1906. *Malay Beliefs* (London, Luzac & Co).

——— 1932. *A Malay-English Dictionary (Romanized)*, 2 vols. (Mytilene, Salavopoulos & Kinderlis).

Winstedt, R.O., 1951. *The Malay Magician* (London, Routledge & Kegan Paul).

9
DOUGLAS A. RAYBECK
Social Stress and Social Structure in Kelantan Village Life

SOCIAL stress is a problem that all societies must deal with. It is always present to some extent as it is a natural concomitant of social change. Stress results from any situation that tends to create an imbalance in or a strain on the existing social order and it is psychologically discomforting to individuals.

Kelantanese society is subject to numerous stresses, but the means for dealing with them are limited. Two of the common means of relieving psychological and social stress described in anthropological literature are, respectively, alcohol and physical mobility (Horton, 1943; Savishinsky, 1970). However in Kelantan, where alcohol is forbidden by Islam and where most villagers are tied by economics and values to their rice lands, neither means is practical.

In addition to these limitations there are aspects of Kelantan village social organization which contribute to the difficulty of resolving social stress. One problem is the unformalized nature of Kelantanese social controls which, unlike the regulation of many societies, do not impose clearly defined penalties for stress-producing behaviour. Another difficulty is the existence of strong social pressures which inhibit the acknowledgement of conflict situations. Without this initial step the resolution of such conflicts is made even more difficult. Consequently, a study of stress and its management can provide interesting insights into Kelantan village society and the manner in which it strives to maintain its integrity.

Village Social Structure

Space limitations do not permit me to give a detailed description of Kelantanese social organization.[1] However, before considering the problem of stress in Kelantan village life I want to describe briefly some elements of the social structure, emphasizing their relation to village life and to the socialization of the individual.

The family is both the most basic and the most important social institution in any culture. The family is the socializing unit into which an individual is born and with which he is most intimately involved until its members die or he marries and moves away. In Kampong Purapura households range in size from two to fourteen individuals, although both of these sizes are atypical.[2] Household composition is often limited to the nuclear family, but the presence of one or two grandparents and/ or other close relatives is not uncommon. Living quarters are frequently crowded and children often sleep in the same room with their parents.

The responsibility for raising a child to become a proper adult is one that is very keenly felt. The Kelantanese attitude toward child rearing is that children are malleable and educable, and what they become is a reflection on their parents and, to a lesser extent, their other relatives. As a result of this attitude, and an extremely close emotional bond between parents and children, children are carefully looked after. They experience a great deal of emotional warmth, and should a child cry there is always someone there to pick it up and comfort it.

As in other parts of the peninsula, while a child is young, few demands are made upon him, save that he avoid both fighting and revealing to outsiders occurrences that take place among the family and kin (cf. Djamour, 1965, 105). From the ages of 5 to 12 a child is gradually taught to respect the rules of courtesy (*budi bahasa*) which are an important element of Kelantanese culture.[3]

The father is frequently absent from the house during the day and a young child receives most of his socialization from his mother, his siblings, and from grandparents, if they live nearby. As in other areas of Malaysia, young children are rarely struck. When punishment is

---
[1] Existing sources which describe Kelantan's social structure include Downs (1967); Raymond Firth (1966); and Rosemary Firth (1966).
[2] My field work, on which this paper is partly based, was supported by a grant (MH 11486) from the National Institute of Mental Health. This support is gratefully acknowledged.
[3] The term 'Kelantanese' refers only to Malays born and raised in Kelantan.

necessary, it usually takes the form of threats based on the supernatural (*hantu, orang minyak*, etc.) or derision (*maki*). On the rare occasion when a child is struck for an offence, it is usually the mother who does so. A father will strike a child only in the most serious instances and should he do so too often he must fear public opinion.[4] An older child (6 to 12 years of age) will be told he is acting stupidly or otherwise insulted. However, after a child, particularly a boy, passes the age of 12 he is hardly ever struck. Should a youth prove unresponsive to his father's remonstrances, first his relatives and then important members of his village will come forward to advise and warn him. If a youth persists in behaviour that is disruptive of village life, such as fighting and petty theft, he will be warned that he will be turned over to the police if he doesn't cease such behaviour. In extreme instances, this threat is carried out. I have recorded four examples from the Kampong Pura-pura area, and it is usually the father who reports the youth since it is viewed as his responsibility. Such occurrences, while very rare, serve to emphasize the importance attached to public opinion and village harmony.

Within a family, the most grievous offence a youth can commit is to be disobedient and to strike a parent. Significantly, such behaviour is termed *derhaka*, a word which can mean 'disobedient' but which also means 'treachery' and is the common term for state treason, an offence which all Malays feel to be very repugnant. A youth known to be guilty of such an offence will be shunned by adults and youths as well, and should he persist in such behaviour his actions will probably be reported to the police.

Status change from youth to adult is gradual and is only truly complete after marriage when an individual becomes a parent. It was felt that boys should marry as soon as they could support a family and that girls should marry soon after puberty (Smith, 1963, 302). The increasing importance of obtaining an education is beginning to result in marriages at a later age, especially for boys. Traditionally marriages were arranged by the parents who often, but not always, took the desires of their children into account. This is largely true even today, but now most youths can usually veto a marriage proposal to which they are strongly opposed. Nonetheless, it is not unusual for a youth to marry having only glimpsed his wife once or twice prior to the ceremony.

After marriage both parties are expected to fulfill adult role expectations. For the man this means that he should work regularly enough to support his family without borrowing money, that he should support his kin in all matters, that he should fulfill his religious duties, such as the

[4] Construction of village houses is such that full privacy is difficult to maintain.

paying of the yearly *zakat* and *fitrah* taxes, that he should take an active part in village life, assisting his friends and neighbours when called upon, and finally that he should avoid personal or public behaviour that would disrupt the harmony of the village. A woman's role consists of bearing children, being a good parent, being industrious around the house and treating her husband with respect in private life as well as public.

According to Muslim law and *adat temenggong*, a patrilineally oriented code, a woman has an inferior status in comparison to her husband; however, in Kelantan, and to a lesser extent in other states of West Malaysia, most women gradually assume a status which is equal to their husband's for all practical purposes save some jural rights. This is particularly apparent in the economic sphere, where women own property and also take an active part contributing to the family income through the sale of produce or handicrafts. Usually it is the wife who handles the family money. She is free to make minor purchases on her own but she will not usually make a major expenditure without first consulting her husband.[5] A woman also has a powerful voice in important family affairs, such as determining the choice of a suitable spouse for her child. In cases where they disagree the wife should, and usually does, concede to her husband. Some women, however, have been known to enlist the aid of their relatives to put pressure on their husbands. Such practices are rare because they lead to divisions between in-laws, and dissension of any kind is strongly disapproved of.

Despite the large amount of money involved, and other factors such as public opinion, Kelantanese marriages are notoriously brittle. Over a ten year period from 1948 to 1957 the percentage of divorces against marriages in Kelantan was 70.96, though it fell somewhat to 65.9 in the following decade to 1966 (Gordon, 1965, 26; Roff, 1968, 290). This figure is by far the highest in the peninsula, followed closely only by Trengganu and Perlis. Smith attributes Kelantan's significantly higher divorce rate to the fact that marriage ages in Kelantan are lower than for other states (1963, 304). I agree with this argument but would also maintain that other social factors, such as the marked sensitivity of the Kelantanese to social affronts, are contributing causes.

The commonest reasons for divorce the Malays give are incompatibility and barrenness. Muslim law makes it quite easy for a husband to get a divorce, but a wife can obtain one only in those cases where she can prove abandonment or maltreatment. However, women can and do

---
[5] Wives who act too independently are referred to pejoratively as *bengkeng*, meaning fierce, bullying, or strong-willed.

frequently engineer their own divorce. One of the most common means of accomplishing this is for the wife to be insolent to her husband in public and thus expose him to the village as a man unable to control his wife. Divorce is then his only practical solution.

Kelantanese, and Malay, kinship is characterized by bilateral kindred and a modified Eskimo kinship terminology. A Kelantanese kindred usually extends horizontally to embrace third cousins on either side of ego. Frequently, however, individuals with more peripheral kin ties are known and their inclusion within the kindred usually depends on variables such as social prominence, the strength of particularistic emotional bonds, residential proximity, etc. Vertically the kindred includes relatives to the third ascending generation. The extent of vertical reckoning is hindered by the absence of enduring family names. Each individual is referred to by his or her father's name, e.g. Abdullah bin Yusof, or Abdullah son of Yusof. Thus there is no common designation linking an individual with his grandparents or great grandparents. Kelantanese, as other Malays, divide their kindred into two gross categories. Near relatives (*waris dekat*) and distant relatives (*waris jauh*). This terminological distinction reflects not only kinship proximity, but also closer emotional ties, and, as I shall shortly describe, greater responsibilities toward ego. The *waris dekat* usually includes ego's direct ancestors and his descendants, his parents' siblings and their children, and his own siblings and their children (cf. Djamour, 1965; Wilson, 1967; Downs, 1967). More distant relatives may be included depending on considerations such as those mentioned above for kinship reckoning.

The members of ego's kindred, although not a corporate descent group, still perform a few functions. Foremost among these is support for ego. Such support consists in part of providing ego with emotional warmth and a sense of security. This is the most basic expectation of all kinsmen, especially *waris dekat*. The degree of emotional closeness is ideally related to kinship proximity, but, in reality, it is equally dependent upon the personalities involved and other social circumstances.

While ego is young, members of his kindred share part of the responsibility for socializing him, and when he is older they continue to support him in his endeavours and in conflicts with non-kin. Thus, when a youth is old enough to marry, if his parents are unable to raise the necessary brideprice, members of the *waris dekat* usually supply the funds but will expect repayment at a later date. An individual turns first to his kindred for loans and for assistance in co-operative efforts (*gotong royong*) such as house moving (cf. Raymond Firth, 1966, 105). Ego can expect to be invited by his *waris* to their feasts and ceremonies, and in return he is expected to invite members of his kindred, especially those living close to him, to his ceremonies. Such mutual obligations are well remembered and people are quick to feel slighted if their invitations are not reciprocated. Such slights are a good indication of friction within a kindred.

The personal and social importance of a kindred to an individual is difficult to over-emphasize.[6] Attitudes toward kin are formed early and modified only slightly through time. The warm personal relationship ideally existing among kin forms a model for other social relations whether in the realm of economics, politics, or simply village affairs (cf. Wilson, 1967, 125). This, quite naturally, has important implications for the wider social network.

After the family and the kindred the village or *kampong* is the most significant element of the Kelantanese social matrix. It is the largest unit in which a Kelantanese is involved in daily social interaction. Geographical village boundaries exist and are recognized but village membership is more realistically determined by patterns of interaction. Villages serve as centres for a number of activities, and people who regularly participate in these are often functionally, even if not geographically, members of the village.

The village is important to the peasant because it is the milieu in which his identity is established and maintained. In a sense the village acts as a social anchor for the individual's personality. Within the village most face-to-face interaction occurs, most friendships are formed, and it is here that a person is socialized—he learns what to expect of others and what is expected of him. Thus the village unit is largely responsible for giving an individual the feeling of security so important to the Kelantanese.[7]

The significance of village affiliation is often emphasized by a dichotomy made between residents and non-residents. Co-residents are *orang sini*, people of here, while non-residents are *orang luar*, people from outside. Initially, all *orang luar* are viewed with suspicion and villagers are reluctant to discuss all but the most trivial village affairs with them (cf. Downs, 1967, 132). This dichotomy is muted when the outsider is either a close relative of a village resident or lives in the same general area, and it is most apparent when the outsider is from a state other than Kelantan. When a stranger identifies himself he often uses the name of his village

[6] As an illustration, one resident of Kampong Pura-pura who was childless after 15 years of marriage and perhaps more sensitive to kin relations than average, knew the names, occupations, residences, and approximate ages of 317 people to whom he could trace a kinship bond.

[7] The emphasis on village importance conflicts with Swift's description of village life among the matrilineal Malays of Negri Sembilan (1965, 143–5).

(e.g., '*Hamba orang Semut Api*' or 'I am a man of Semut Api'). If he has no kinship links with members of the village he is visiting then this designation will be a primary means of defining his relationship to that village.

Social relations within the village are often on a personal level, especially in villages where most of the members are kin to one another. However, while status differences are seldom large enough to inhibit social interaction they do exist and the Kelantanese are very sensitive to them. This sensitivity is reflected by courtesy behaviour (*budi bahasa*), some of it very subtle.

Status within the village depends on a number of variables. Assuming an individual possesses valued Kelantanese personality traits, his status usually depends on wealth, the existence of a large kindred on which he can call for support, religious training, the respect of other villagers, and education. Persons who are wealthy and powerful should nonetheless avoid ostentatious displays. Such exhibitions are viewed as a breach of manners and normally result in a loss of prestige. Exceptions are made for important ceremonies, especially marriages. At such times wealthy families may spend large amounts of money without fearing public disapproval.

Traditionally villages served as the centres for a number of activities which promoted social interaction, but the members of a village seldom acted as a functioning unit to achieve a particular goal. This situation is still largely the case today although increasing pressures for modernization sometimes force villagers to act concertedly.

Except for local councils such as Kampong Pura-pura, most villages are administered by a *penghulu* who may have jurisdiction over as many as three villages. He is appointed by the District Officer and his duties include the collection of certain taxes, keeping records and acting as an official link with the District Office. As Downs has pointed out, such appointees are generally not well regarded in Kelantan villages and people have as little to do with them as possible (1967, 131). Instead, whatever real political power there is in a village rests with an unofficial leader termed the *ketua kampong*. The ketua is not elected but gradually accepted over time until his position is 'understood'. He is usually a man of high status, as described above, well versed in *adat* and possessed of a strong personality. His power and its application are not formal. Instead, he achieves his ends mainly through persuasion, working unobtrusively and often enlisting the assistance and moral support of other important villagers such as the Imam. One of his principal functions is to maintain the harmony of the village, resolving local conflicts within the village without calling in outside officials. In this respect his responsibilities sometimes conflict with those of the penghulu who is obliged to report legal offences to the police. Should such a situation arise the penghulu will usually await the outcome of the ketua's efforts before informing outside authorities.[8]

In those instances where the matter under consideration involves the whole village or a major portion of it no action will be taken unless the influential men (*orang besar*) of the village are in agreement (cf. Downs, 1967, 132–233). This is partly to protect the harmony of the village and also because of the manner in which decisions are carried out. Each *orang besar* activates his network of kin ties to realize a given decision. Should one influential man dissent then a sizeable portion of the village, his kindred, will not support the proposed action. Thus, depending on the size of his kindred and his status within it, each villager is involved to a greater or lesser degree in the government of the village. This weak authority structure helps to explain why villages seldom function as integrated units.

Villages are also the centres of religious worship in that each has a centrally located building at which people can pray. In small villages this is often a simple structure called a *madrasah*, *balaisah*, or *surau* and may even form part of a regular dwelling. In larger villages such as Kampong Pura-pura there is a full sized mosque and on Fridays people from neighbouring villages without mosques will often journey in for the noon-day prayer. Larger villages have a resident Imam and usually several religious teachers who earn their living by instructing children in Kuran reading, but a small village may have only one or two religious teachers.

Religious occasions such as the celebration commemorating the end of the pilgrimage to Mecca (*Hari Raya Haji*) and the end of the fasting month (*Hari Raya Puasa*) often involve inter-village travel since it is the custom at such times to visit relatives and friends. Intra-village visits are also important at these times since they provide occasions to resolve conflicts that may exist between relatives and friends. Throughout the year village social pressure and the general lack of privacy also insure a fairly rigorous observance of the five daily prayers, as well as fasting during the month of Ramadhan.

Larger villages have a weekly or daily market which provides a centre for petty trading and the circulation of village gossip. The selling and buying of goods, however small the quantity, is always accom-

---

[8] In Kampong Pura-pura, governed by a local council with nine elected and three appointed officials, it was the ketua who was most active in resolving local interpersonal problems.

panied by strenuous bargaining. The motivation for this haggling is partly economic but more importantly it demonstrates to his opponent and to other villagers an individual's skill in obtaining a good price. Despite this competition, however, people seldom try to drive a hard bargain with fellow villagers. To do so consistently would result in adverse public opinion and loss of business (cf. Raymond Firth, 1966, 201). It is felt that economic and work relations within the village should approximate the social relationships between kin (cf. Wilson, 1967, 106; Raymond Firth, 1966, 6–7).

Finally, the village is the centre for various traditional competitions such as top spinning and kite flying and numerous forms of entertainment. In Kampong Pura-pura as in many other large villages there is a centrally located field which is the site for such activities. Most forms of entertainment are inexpensive, seldom costing more than 20 cents and are always accompanied by food stalls which spring up overnight to take advantage of the crowds.[9] Such occasions provide yet another opportunity for socializing with fellow villagers.

Almost all the above mentioned village functions serve in part to emphasize and promote the unity and cohesiveness of village members. This is understandable when it is remembered that there is little reliance on an effective formal authority structure or on jural sanctions and, as in all societies, there exist centrifugal pressures working against social unity.

Village Social Values

As the foregoing indicates, the loose bilateral nature of kin relations and the informal authority structure do not provide a structure which rigidly defines behaviour patterns. Instead, cooperation and harmony which are necessary for the maintenance of the social system remain largely voluntary. This is not to say that there are not social pressures encouraging village unity but only that these pressures are not jurally defined and thus lack the force of formal sanctions.

There exist a number of institutions in Kelantan village society which have a centripetal social function, that is, they promote cohesion and harmony. A number of these have already been mentioned and include reciprocal feasting, holiday (*Hari Raya*) visiting, and occasions of cooperative effort (*gotong royong*). Behaviour associated with these institutions can also serve as a sensitive indicator of social stress.

In addition to these institutions there are sets of strong social values which reflect the importance of interpersonal harmony and help to

[9] Traditionally, such entertainments were provided free at celebrations such as weddings and in some areas this is still the case.

maintain it. These values can also contribute to a better understanding of some aspects of social stress in Kelantan society. Thus before proceeding further I wish to describe briefly the most relevant of these social values.[10]

One of the most significant of the central or focal Kelantanese values is the importance and dignity of the individual. Each person must be treated with appropriate respect and care should be taken to avoid giving offence. To this end there exists a fairly elaborate system of courtesy behaviour, *budi bahasa*, which helps to pattern many forms of interaction. *Budi bahasa* literally means the 'language of character' and it is through this language that an individual communicates his breeding and his sensitivity to those with whom he interacts more formally. A person who through his words and actions displays an insensitivity to the dignity of others is often referred to as *kasar*, or coarse, unrefined and impolite. This is contrasted with ideal, *halus*, behaviour which is polite, refined, and carries connotations of social delicacy and tact. Should an individual persist in *kasar* behaviour he will be described as 'insufficiently educated' (*kurang ajar*) and may even be likened to an animal, a great insult.

Individual dignity can best be maintained in an atmosphere of interpersonal harmony. The Kelantanese have two terms for this value concept, *patut* and *sesuai*. Both mean that which is fitting, proper and harmonious. To be *patut* or harmonious with others a Kelantanese should accurately perceive his status in relation to the status of those he comes in contact with and this perception should be reflected in appropriate words and actions. Ideally this behaviour should be slightly more deferential than a relationship actually calls for. In this way an individual not only displays respect for the other person but he demonstrates that he is an innately *halus* person, well educated in *budi bahasa* and, therefore, also worthy of respect.

Subscription to these values and behaviour is encouraged by a desire to avoid feeling *malu*. For a Kelantanese to be *malu* is to be shy, humble, embarrassed. For the individual this can be an affectively charged state of marked discomfort. It can result from inappropriate, that is non-*patut*, behaviour of his own, or through the *kasar* behaviour of others which reflects on him, or simply through associating with a status that is markedly higher than his. Most Kelantanese avoid *malu* and the discomfort associated with it as much as possible.

Malu and the other concepts described above reflect an inordinate sensitivity to interpersonal relations in Kelantanese social life. Affront

[10] Malay values have been treated more extensively by Wilson (1967).

is easily taken and resolved only with difficulty. Furthermore, the closer the relationship between two people, the stronger is the affront if *patut* behaviour is not observed and the greater is the resulting feeling of *malu*. For example, a husband will find the disrespectful behaviour of his wife far more *malu*-producing and disharmonious than similar behaviour on the part of a friend.[11]

Overt Social Stress

The centrifugal pressures alluded to earlier can be viewed as foci of social stress. In Kelantan, as elsewhere, the most common sources of social stress derive from conflicts of interest between individuals and, by extension, between kindreds. Briefly, social situations in which stress often arises include new marriages, polygynous marriages, inheritance and, less often, politics and economic activities. A secondary source of stress may be termed role stress, where an individual is dissatisfied with his status within the social system. This dissatisfaction may stem from a personal inability to realize the potential of a status or it may be due to adverse changes in a status through time that are beyond the individual's control. (Common examples would include widowhood, old age, etc.) Frequently these two sources of stress occur together and thus this separation of them is in part artificial.

Both stress situations can generate anger, dissension and dissatisfaction. However, the expression of these emotions in a society where individuals are so sensitive to interpersonal relations can jeopardize the highly valued but tenuous harmony of village life. Thus the very values and institutions that foster harmony are also capable of magnifying stressful situations and making their resolution more difficult.

This presents Kelantan village society with a serious problem. Unless situations of stress are acknowledged, it is difficult to resolve them, but the acknowledgement should be of such a nature that it does not increase the existing problem or contribute to a new one.

The existence of a stressful problem is, if possible, seldom referred to publicly by the parties immediately involved, even though the entire village may be well aware of the situation. Instead, unsatisfactory relationships are usually subtly, or not so subtly, hinted at. This, however, is not always possible.

Some stress situations are so overt and entail such disruptive consequences that they must be openly acknowledged and resolved as quickly as possible. The most disturbing situation of this type involves open

[11] As mentioned earlier, since it is difficult for a woman to initiate a divorce, she may take advantage of this sensitivity and purposely create a *malu* situation for her husband in order to force him to divorce her.

disputes between members of the same kindred (*waris*) or between affines. Such a case occured in Kampong Pura-pura during my field work.

A quarrel had been going on covertly between Ali and Ismail for three years.[12] The two men were brothers-in-law, Ismail having married Ali's sister, and part of the friction between them stemmed from the sister's inheriting land that, according to Muslim law, should have gone to Ali. The friction was increased when Ali asked Ismail, who worked as a carpenter, to build him a house and then declined to make full payment for the work.

This unsatisfactory situation had existed for some time when the two men became embroiled in a misunderstanding regarding the disciplining of Ismail's son, Ali's nephew. Ismail lost his temper and struck Ali several times with a *parang*. Ali suffered cuts on the left thigh and shoulder but was able to walk a mile to the nearest police post where he reported the incident and was then taken to the hospital, where he remained for two weeks. Ismail surrendered himself to the police and after a day in jail was released on a bail of $300 which was raised by his *waris*. Ali had brought assault charges against Ismail and was determined to take the matter to court.

This situation was potentially hazardous for Kampong Pura-pura since the dispute involved both men's *waris*, which were large and connected through a number of marriages. If the dispute continued other relatives would be pressured to take sides and in so doing would increase the likelihood of further friction. The situation could have become especially difficult for those villagers who were related to both Ali and Ismail.

Thus one evening the imam, the ketua kampong, and a wealthy, respected friend of both Ali and Ismail visited the two men. To both they stressed the desirability of protecting the welfare of the village and pointed out the danger and unseemliness of an open dispute between 'brothers'. They requested Ismail to pay Ali $200 as a consolation (*sagu hati*) and they asked Ali to discontinue the court case. Both men agreed to these conditions and together submitted a letter of explanation to the court stressing that it was improper for two brothers (*adik-beradik*) to go to court over a personal dispute and requesting that the charges against Ismail be dismissed.

Ismail's portion of the letter had stated that he was not fully responsible for his actions as he had been invaded by the spirit of Satan in a moment of weakness. He meant this to be taken quite literally since

[12] For obvious reasons these names, as well as the name of the village, are fictitious.

it is common knowledge in Kelantan that spirits (*hantu, jinn*, etc.,) can in certain circumstances possess a man's body and direct his actions The court ignored this argument and fined Ismail $500 but did not impose a jail sentence.

Although the court found it irrelevant, Ismail's excuse provided a means for Kampong Pura-pura villagers, especially members of Ali's *waris*, to rationalize his actions. It also facilitated his reacceptance and the reestablishment of harmonious relations between the parties involved. A portion of the blame, and responsibility for a normally unacceptable act, was displaced to the spirit world.

Naturally, this excuse and the payment of consolation money did not completely remove the tension between Ali and Ismail. For the next two months the two men largely avoided one another. Other villagers took care to invite both men to feasts and ceremonies so that neither would be made *malu*. In time, partly due to social pressure from influential *waris* members, they began inviting one another to feasts, and their interaction approached the village norm. Although the friction between them probably still existed, it no longer openly threatened the welfare and harmony of the village.

Covert Social Stress

In circumstances where social stress exists but is less intense it will often be expressed and even resolved covertly. That is, there will be no open confrontation between the concerned parties nor will any grievances be aired: in short, the stress situation may be resolved without its existence being publicly acknowledged.

There are two general ways in which stress can be subtly manifested. The first makes use of social indicators. In such cases an individual will frequently indicate his displeasure by the way in which he participates in traditional village social life. If angry at his parents-in-law, a man may not pay them an expected visit on *Hari Raya Puasa*, or he may 'forget' to invite them to a *makan Maulud*, a feast celebrating the Prophet's birthday. Such instances indicate to the other party that something is amiss and also stimulate village gossip. The gossip may persuade the offending party to reduce the stress through a friendly overture, often a little gift or an invitation to a small *makan*. If this does not occur in a reasonable period of time other relatives may intervene and encourage a reconciliation, often through the same traditional social occasions that first indicated the existence of a problem.

The second means of indicating stress is even less direct than the first since it tends to occur in somewhat more serious situations and involves recourse to the supernatural world. Kelantanese recognize that susceptibility to certain illnesses, especially some forms of mental disorder, can be related to problems of social stress.[13] However, many of these illnesses are attributed to spirit intervention rather than directly to a stress situation. People who are worried (*susah hati*) or disturbed (*kachau*) are more apt to be invaded by a mischievous spirit.

Kelantan society has an institution which exists ostensibly to treat these disorders but which also covertly helps to resolve the stress that often underlies them. This institution is *main puteri*, a ritual healing ceremony which has been described at some length by Gimlette (1915) and by Raymond Firth (1967) and thus will be described here only in brief.

When a person complains of feeling ill, initial treatment will in part depend on the symptoms. When the illness appears severe the patient may receive Western medical treatment. More commonly a *bomoh*, or medicine man, is called in to investigate the nature and cause of the illness. The illness may be attributed to a particular spirit, *hantu*, and a cure may be attempted at the patient's home. If the patient shows no favourable response to the treatment, the *bomoh* will, after a few days, usually recommend a *main puteri* performance.

The performance will be arranged and paid for by several members of the patient's family and kindred. The cost by Kelantanese standards is quite high and can seldom be borne by one individual. The performance may run from one to three nights and involve an expenditure of between $50 and $120. Arrangements for the performance include construction of a special shelter without walls, preparation of special foods to be used as offerings to the spirits, and occasionally the purchase of special clothing.

The personnel involved in a *main puteri* include the *bomoh*, who will enter a trance and be inhabited by various spirits, the *mindok*, who helps to guide the *bomoh* through his trance and interrogates the spirits as they appear, and five to seven musicians. Present also in the shelter are the patient and his or her attendants and just outside is the audience composed of interested villagers, relatives and friends.

The *main puteri* usually begins around 9 p.m. and during the performance it is common for a large audience to assemble. The *bomoh* opens the performance with a prayer to his teacher. Usually, even if the particular illness has been diagnosed earlier, he proceeds to investigate the general cause of the disease through a process of divination. At this time he discusses in a loud voice the symptoms of the illness with the

[13] For a recent treatment of this topic see Resner and Hartog (1970).

patient's relatives and with other bystanders. These symptoms may range from vomiting and diarrhoea to less serious complaints, such as the inability to sleep properly or a general lack of appetite.

Next the *bomoh* enters a trance in which he is visited by a series of spirits and attempts to determine which one of them is responsible for the patient's illness. He is led through this procedure by the *mindok*, who interrogates each spirit to determine its identity. The spirits frequently vary in character, ranging from fierce and dangerous, to comic and obscene. Much of this is regarded as good entertainment, but an element of tension is always present. For example, when a dangerous spirit appears the children present are jostled to ensure they remain awake, for a sleeping child is thought to be quite susceptible to such spirits.

Throughout the evening the *bomoh* will come out of trance several times. During these breaks he and some other players may sing and perform comic skits. During the trance, each time he is inhabited by a different spirit he will touch the patient, not directly but with a cloth. The theory is that if the spirit which inhabits him at that time is responsible for the illness, the patient will be 'moved' (*gerak angin*) and respond.

Once it has been determined which spirit is to blame, the *mindok* will interview him as to why he has caused the trouble. Once this is ascertained the *mindok* then promises the spirit a reward (*pelepas niat*) if the spirit will leave the patient in peace. Later there will be a ritual to facilitate this and if the patient shows improvement, an offering of food is given to the spirit. This action concludes the healing ceremony.

I have indicated earlier that illnesses treated in a *main puteri* can range from the obviously serious and physical such as cholera to those characterized by symptoms which are more likely psychosomatic, such as an inability to sleep. The Kelantanese have numerous terms for these latter illnesses; some of the more common are *lemah semangat*, or weakness of spirit, *sakit angin* and *sakit jiwa*, both of which mean sickness of the soul or spirit. Such illnesses, while seemingly diffuse and nebulous to the outsider, are very real to the Kelantanese and are generally taken quite seriously.

Such illnesses provide a mechanism for calling attention to a stressful social problem which the individual is unable to solve himself. This inability is largely due to the social values mentioned earlier which mitigate against the direct recognition of a conflict situation and/or one of role dissatisfaction. If an individual were to point out such a situation, he would very likely increase the *malu*-ness of the people involved and add to the stress of the situation rather than reduce it. Although other villagers are often aware of an individual's problem, especially if it is the result of a conflict situation, they are subject to the same social inhibitions and will not openly mention the problem to the parties involved.

Of 80 observed *main puteri* performances, 44 were judged to treat primarily psychosomatic or psychological complaints and 75 per cent of these involved female patients.[14] This sexual bias is not surprising in a peasant level Islamic society where a woman's role is frequently less meaningful and satisfying than a man's and where she can do less to alter it. Women are also frequently involved in conflict situations arising from problems of adjustment to a new marriage and from polygynous marriages. Of these 33 cases involving women, and on the basis of social evidence, 18 were judged to have elements of conflict situations and 15 appeared to be cases of role dissatisfaction. These last were frequently women in late middle age, post menopause, widowed and whose children were married and living neolocally. Additional supportive evidence is supplied by Rosemary Firth (1966, 195), who describes an instance where the female *main puteri* patient resented her husband's attentions to his newly acquired second wife; and by Gimlette, who mentions two instances where female patients benefited from a *main puteri* performance. One case was a woman who had just had an abortion and the other an old lady seeking attention who liked 'to take medicine' (1923, 89). The remaining 11 performances involved males experiencing problems with their relatives or in fulfilling their culturally defined roles.

Once a patient's complaints of 'illness' result in a *main puteri* performance he has succeeded in placing himself and his problem before village society in a manner that avoids further interpersonal stress. Furthermore, Raymond Firth (1967) has noted that the 'spirit' speaking through the *bomoh* frequently points out the nature of the stressful situation and, sometimes, which parties are to blame and what their faults are. Firth refers to *main puteri* in this regard as a 'cathartic mechanism' (1967, 212). The spirit standing outside Kelantan society can articulate its problems in a manner that a typical villager dare not.

Besides calling attention to the stressful situation, *main puteri* can also help to resolve it. For example, in a conflict situation such as that of a woman who feels her husband and her affines are treating her poorly, the

[14] I want to express my indebtedness to Clive Kessler, who observed most of these performances and generously made his data available to me. Since neither Mr. Kessler nor I is a qualified physician there is some question regarding the accuracy of case classifications. Consequently these cases should be taken as suggestive rather than conclusive.

fact that they contribute to the considerable expense involved in a *main puteri* performance publicly demonstrates their solidarity with and responsibility for her. In those instances where the stress derives primarily from role dissatisfaction the patient, through *main puteri*, becomes socially more visible and important. In some forms of *main puteri* the patient may take an active part in the proceedings and, within the bounds of the performance, may assume the status of royalty. Also, as in the other example, the fact that a patient's relatives find him or her important enough to warrant the expense involved in a *main puteri* performance should reduce role dissatisfaction even if only temporarily.

In addition to the circumspect negotiations carried out by informal village leaders, and institutions such as feasting and holiday visiting which function in part to relieve social stress, it is apparent that stress management in a Kelantan village frequently involves the spirit world. This involvement may mean displacing the blame for deviant behaviour to a spirit as in the case of Ismail. It may also lead to the projection of social problems into the spirit world through an appropriate 'illness' as described above. In both circumstances recourse to the supernatural world is necessitated by a social system which inhibits a candid treatment of stress.

The result of this situation is that villagers are often required to maintain a social fiction, placing the responsibility for stressful circumstances outside the social sphere, while at the same time being perfectly aware of the 'real' state of affairs. Obviously such a means of managing social stress, depending as it must upon largely voluntary village cooperation, is hardly ideal or infallible. While these methods of stress management seem to work well enough in traditional Kelantanese villages, there are already indications that they are not adequate for dealing with the stresses generated by modernization. As new political, economic, and educational influences gradually erode traditional social organization and its attendent social values there will very likely be an increasing reliance on formal sanctions, many of which will be imposed from outside the village.

REFERENCES

Djamour, J., 1965. *Malay Kinship and Marriage in Singapore* (New York, Humanities Press Inc.).

Downs, R.E., 1967. 'A Kelantanese Village of Malaya', in J.H. Steward (ed.), *Contemporary Change in Traditional Societies* (Urbana, University of Illinois), vol. II, 105–86.

Firth, Raymond, 1966. *Malay Fishermen: Their Peasant Economy* (London, Routledge and Kegan Paul).

────── 1967. 'Ritual and Drama in Malay Spirit Mediumship', *Comparative Studies in Society and History*, IX, 190–207.

Firth, Rosemary, 1966. *Housekeeping among Malay Peasants* (New York, Humanities Press Inc.).

Gimlette, J.D., 1923. *Malay Poisons and Charm Cures* (2nd. ed., London, J. & A. Churchill).

Gordon, S., 1965. 'Malay Marriage-Divorce in the 11 States of Malaya and Singapore', *Intisari*, II, 2, 23–32.

Horton, D., 1943. 'The Function of Alcohol in Primitive Societies: A Cross-Cultural Study', *Quarterly Journal of Studies on Alcohol*, IV, 199–320.

Resner, G. and Hartog, J., 1970. 'Concepts and Terminology of Mental Disorder Among Malays', *Journal of Cross-Cultural Psychology*, 1, 369–81.

Roff, W.R., 1968. 'Judith Djamour, *The Muslim Matrimonial Court in Singapore*. London School of Economics Monographs on Social Anthropology, No. 31, London, Athlone Press ...', *Bijdragent ot de Taal-, Land- en Volkenkunde*, 124, 286–91.

Savishinshky, J., 1970. Stress and Mobility in an Arctic Community: The Hare Indians of Colville Lake, Northwest Territories (Unpublished PhD. Thesis, Cornell University).

Smith, T.E., 1963. 'Marriage, Widowhood and Divorce in the Federation of Malaya', *International Population Conference*, V, 2, 302–9.

Swift, M.G., 1965. *Malay Peasant Society in Jelebu* (New York, Humanities Press Inc.).

Wilson, P., 1967. *A Malay Village and Malaysia* (New Haven, HRAF Press).

10

MANNING NASH
Ethnicity, Centrality and Education in Pasir Mas[1]

KELANTAN, for historical reasons, has been a hinterland on the Malay peninsula. A hinterland in a rapidly modernizing nation has special tensions, problems, and promises. The Kelantan hinterland has a cultural cast, an economic pattern, a social organization, and a political stance that differentiates it from the larger society and political system of which it is a part.

Kelantan is overwhelmingly Malay—more than 90 per cent of the population meet the ethnic definition of Malay; one whose first (often only) language is Malay, a believer in Islam, and descent from people who had the foregoing two cultural features. Kelantan is overwhelmingly rural, and the people who live in the kampongs are predominately engaged in agriculture—padi rice growing and rubber tapping. Most of the older Malay arts and crafts are still alive—silversmithing, ironmaking, batek dyeing and weaving, keris making. And there are numerous Malays engaged in commerce as small merchants and market traders, and, of course, the coastal population are fishermen. In short, it is an economy of the peasant variety—basically subsistence,

[1] The research on which this paper is based was supported by the National Science Foundation. I am indebted to Belinda Burley, my field assistant, for the administration of the tests. She was supported by the Committee on Southern Asian Studies, University of Chicago.

but with many acts of exchange and cash transfer for the artisan skills needed by peasants and for some of the services needed by urban dwellers. Socially Kelantan has the Sultanate and its aristocratic outliers, but these are chiefly symbolic, guardians of Malay custom and Islam. The major social divisions, in the Malay world, are first between the town based bureaucrats (which I have elsewhere called a salariat) and the peasantry. The bureaucrats are Westernized, Anglicized, and in government hierarchies engaged in one aspect or another of the administrative process.

They form a category in the status system clearly defined in contrast to the peasantry. The peasantry, broadly on economic grounds, are in three categories: *orang kaya* (the rich), *ada harta* (some land and wealth, sometimes called *boleh makan*, can eat, or make ends meet), and the *miskin*, the poor, who are tenants or labourers who just eke out a precarious living. To an outsider the distances between the categories of peasant are not large, but add to them the differences in local power and respect, clothing and gold display, feast and ritual expenditure that go with them and they get magnified into status differences, if not true social classes.

One important fact of Kelantan social organization lies in the ways the peasants are tied into different hierarchies through sets of broker roles, i.e. those roles that have loci and activities both with the kampong and at other, more complex levels of social organization. The *imam* (the leader of a religious congregation) ties the kampong to the State Council of Religious Affairs (*Majlis Ugama*), and to the Council's *ulama* who grant teaching certificates. The *penggawa* ties the peasant to the State government; and there are many representatives of the Federal government engaged in projects, not to mention the police, who tie the peasant directly into the national level. A fuller analysis is given in my forthcoming book, but any idea of isolated, autonomous kampongs must fall in the face of the actual organization of Kelantan. And if to that is added the travel the peasants do to other parts of the peninsula, to Mecca, and to Thailand, plus the presence of radio and television communication and several newspapers in both *rumi* (Latin script) and *jawi* (Arabic script), the notion of kampong isolation vanishes completely.

On the cultural side, Kelantan has some peculiar features (Downs 1967; Firth, 1966). The *bersilat* (a form of Malay defence) is still regularly practised in its display aspects, the shadow play is going strong, tops are still spun by adults, and the practices of the trance shamans are still fairly intact and used widely by Kelantanese. There is a Kelantan claim that in some sense they are the 'bastion' of Malay culture and custom. But the bastion is embattled. There is unease as the pressures of modernization wear on the Kelantanese. There is economic and political pressure from other parts of Malaya, and there is also the internal pressure generated by different interpretations of Islam by modernists, fundamentalists, and the indifferents of the cities and salariat. What I have called the 'kampong ideology' still exists among the peasantry, but it is a tradition in tension (Nash, 1966). The kampong ideology holds that a Malay should live in the sweet shade of his own *dusun* (where garden and tree crops grow), engaged primarily in padi farming, among a group of co-religionists and many kinsmen. In this setting he is to exhibit the grace and charm of relaxed primitive sufficiency as he orders his life according to Islam and treats his neighbours with the 'soft and gentle' manners involved in face to face social interaction.

One final, important and constantly visible fact of Kelantan life has been political competition between the United Malays National Organization and the Pan-Malayan Islamic Party. Kelantan is the stronghold of the PMIP, and the PMIP flourishes in other parts of the peninsula having similar demographic, ethnic, and cultural composition. The PMIP has as its slogan *bangsa* (race, lineage) *ugama* (religion) and *tanah ayer* (our native land). These powerful symbols condense for the peasantry of Kelantan the major points of conflict in the social, cultural, and economic aspects of their daily lives. These symbols enable them to think, without great analytical apparatus, about the salient facts: they may be dispossessed by people of a different ethnic group; the people of that ethnic group are not co-religionists; and their patrimony may slip away. The overwhelming political and economic fact of life in the peninsula is the contradiction between the distribution of economic power and the distribution of political power. And that these two distributions are coincident with the major ethnic differences results in a communal competition which in 1969 finally broke the fragile bonds of co-operation resulting in a suspension for a time of the political process.

This brief background sets the context of the analysis of the educational system in Pasir Mas, one of the eight districts in the state. Pasir Mas, just across the Kelantan river from Kota Bharu is the second largest settlement in the state. The district has about 90,000 persons, and the town itself, Pasir Mas, has about 12,000. The town is the administrative focus of the district, and the market centre. It houses the agencies of state and federal government—courts, police, land records, medical and dental services, rubber replanting board, district office, and agricultural extension services. It is also the educational centre of the district. There are four primary schools: Yoke Eng, Chinese; Sultan Ibrahim, English; a Malay Sekolah Kebangsaan ('National School') for boys; and one for girls. At the secondary level there is the Sultan Ibrahim Secondary English School, which also has an upper secondary Malay stream. In addition there is an Arabic secondary school and seven *pondok* (religious boarding schools) in and around Pasir Mas. Education in an economic sense is one of the chief industries of Pasir Mas. More than 4,500 students are engaged in the educational processes of the town.

In general, the aims of education in post-independence Malaya were very clear, at least to the political elite. The Razak report (1956), the Rahman Talib report (1960), other government reports and enquiries (Ministry of Education, 1965a and 1968b), and the University attitude (Wong, 1964) stressed that education must have as a major component the building of Malaysian national consciousness, on the one hand, and the development of the skills and knowledge to support the technological and economic bases of a developing and modernizing nation. At this general level there is no debate, and the 17.6 per cent of total public expenditure that goes to keep 91 per cent of the primary school population in school, or the 52 per cent of the lower secondary in school, is generally thought to be an unquestioned social good.

But below the aims of the government are the hopes, values, tensions, and social organization of the concrete local and regional societies who provide the human material for the educational process. For them, education has other meanings, other ends, and other perils. One expectation among the adults of Pasir Mas is that education be instrumental—conduce to the social mobility of their children. Another common expectation is that education increase the Islamic knowledge and piety of their children; another is that education place the Malay child in competitive advantage with the Chinese; another is that education promote pride in Malay culture and language; and finally that education provide the means for Malay political and economic dominance. These expectations are widespread. They are a contrary, if not contradictory, bundle of hopes, and they become more contrary when the Malay perils of education are included. Malay adults fear that the most effective economic or technological education will alienate their offspring from piety, family, and Malay culture. They fear that education will load the heads of the young with perverse ideas leading to the loss of Malay dominance, Islamic purity, and political weight. The Arabic schools and the pondoks are obviously the choice of those who feel this most strongly, but the uneasiness is widespread even in those who support their children for the upper secondary in the English medium.

What is abundantly clear is that ethnicity, as that symbol expresses and condenses the position and aspirations of Malays, is at the heart of the meaning of education in Pasir Mas. Education for the control of the central institutions of the society in a particular cultural mode is what education means in Pasir Mas. And all the fuss over language, medium of instruction, content of curricula, finance and school organization can be understood only by recalling that it is ethnically organized groups struggling to dominate a set of central institutions which are truly at the core of the conflict, and not the symbols alone.

What the research problem is, and a problem that seems to have little empirical underwriting in Malaysia (or elsewhere for that matter), is just what is it that schools do, and in what real ways do they transmit what sorts of aspirations, allegiances, identities, as well as skills and knowledge? To get at this problem in Pasir Mas, it was necessary to use some of the tools of social science.

Two sorts of tests were given to various segments of the school population. First a modified version of the Cantril 'self-anchoring' test was given to forms 5 and 6 of the secondary schools. The self-anchoring test, briefly, is a ladder with ten rungs. The person who adminsters the test runs his finger up and down the rungs, and he says imagine the bottom rung to be the lowest level you can reach in life and the top rung the highest. Place yourself as you feel you are on the ladder today; now place yourself where you were five years ago; and finally place yourself where you expect to be in five years' time. After this was done, the students were asked to write an essay about the content of positions A, B, and C. From these essays the chief nouns of aspiration, value, goodness, merit, and worth were extracted. Arbitrarily 12 such values or concepts of value were extracted, and, for control, three which did not appear at all were added. This 15 item list was presented to form 3 of the secondary and to standard 6 of the primary school. They were asked to rank order the values.

The logic of these tests is straightforward. They allow a person to estimate his own life chances, to describe the content of those life chances, and to indicate what sort of hope and momentum there is to his career. The list of values of the older school children is then given to younger school children for ranking. It is thus empirically possible to see what happens in schooling to the shape of values, and, since these tests were given in Chinese medium, Malay medium, and Arabic medium as well as pondok schools, to see what effect the different kinds of schools systems have on the content and development of values and aspirations.

248 KELANTAN: RELIGION, SOCIETY AND POLITICS IN A MALAY STATE

TABLE

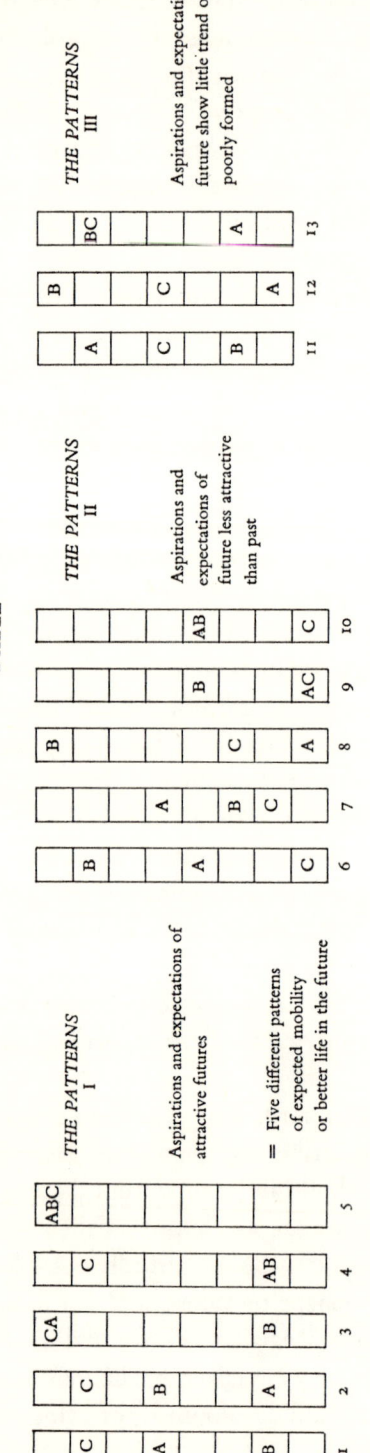

THE PATTERNS I

Aspirations and expectations of attractive futures

= Five different patterns of expected mobility or better life in the future

THE PATTERNS II

Aspirations and expectations of future less attractive than past

THE PATTERNS III

Aspirations and expectations of future show little trend or are poorly formed

Pattern 1 = The 'home' (point B) was less desirable than the school (point A) and the future (point C) will be even more attractive than either the school or the home.

Pattern 2 = The home more desirable than the school, future more attractive than home or school.

Pattern 3 = The home is least attractive, and the school is a high point; matched by expectations of the future.

Pattern 4 = Both the home and school are on the same level and both less attractive than the future.

Pattern 5 = Always at maximum, home, school, and future are equally highly attractive.

Pattern 6 = Home was best, school is worse, and the future is even more bleak.

Pattern 7 = School is high point, home and past are better than the future.

Pattern 8 = Home was best, school is low point, future better than school.

Pattern 9 = Home was best, school and future equally dismal.

Pattern 10 = Home and school are equally better than dismal future.

Pattern 11 = School is high point with future little better than past.

Pattern 12 = School is low point with future somewhat worse than past.

Pattern 13 = School is low point, home and future at some high point.

ETHNICITY, CENTRALITY AND EDUCATION IN PASIR MAS

School, Grade Medium of Instruction	No. 1	Per Cent	No. 2	Per Cent	No. 3	Per Cent	No. 4	Per Cent	No. 5	Per Cent	No. 6	Per Cent	No. 7	Per Cent	No. 8	Per Cent	No. 9	Per Cent	No. 10	Per Cent	No. 11	Per Cent	No. 12	Per Cent	No. 13	Per Cent	TOTAL
Arabic School Form 3. All Malay	128	94	1	1							3	2	1	1							1	1	1	1			135
Sultan Ibrahim School Form 5 D (Eng.)	129	85	1	1											21	14									1	1	152
Sultan Ibrahim School Upper 6 (Eng.)	27	100																									27
Sultan Ibrahim School Lower 6 (Eng.)	25	81									2	6	1	3	2	6					1	3					31
Sultan Ibrahim School 5 B (Eng.) All Malay	40	100																									40
Sultan Ibrahim School 5 C (Eng.)	27	69	5	13	1	2					1	2			1	2			1	2					3	8	39
Sultan Ibrahim School 5 A (Eng.)	17	71	4	17																	2	8	1	4			24
Sultan Ismail College Lower 6 (Arts, Eng.)	24	96																			1	4					25
Sultan Ismail College Lower 6 (Sci., Eng.)	13	68					3	16	1	5					2	10											19
Sultan Ismail College Lower 6 (Engrg., Eng.)	25	89			2	7							1	3													28
Sultan Ismail College Upper 6 (Arts, Eng.)	15	100																									15
Sultan Ismail College Upper 6 (Engrg., Eng.)	17	71			1		4	16			1	4			1	4	1	4									24
Sultan Ismail College Upper 6 (Sci., Eng.)							1	4			1	1	1	4			1	3	1	4			1	1			24
Chung Hwa 5 (Arts)	19	50	13	34	2	5											1	3			2	5	1	3			38
Chung Hwa 5 (Sci.)	11	39	5	18			2	7									1	4	1	4	3	11	3	1			28
Pondok Lubok Tapah	12	100																									12
TOTALS	529	80	50	8	6	1	10	2	1 / 596 90%		9	1.3	4	1	27	4	3		2 / 45 7%		10	2	6	1	4 / 20 3%		661

Sultan Ibrahim School = 338   Arabic School = 135   Chung Hwa = 66   Pondok = 12   Sultan Ismail = 100

As a control, family background data in so far as this was available and accurate was used for each student to control for variability in primary socialization and family experience. The body of empirical material resulting from these tests permits testing of the hypothesis that school experience is crucial in shaping aspirations and values; that variations in the school system produce variations in the aspirations and value content; and that schooling does affect national loyalties, ethnic self-definitions, and conceptions of the desirable.

The tests themselves, it must be noted, were an unusual experience for the students of Pasir Mas, and those in the Chinese secondary school in Kota Bharu included in the sample. The open-endedness of the test nonplussed many of the respondents. They are used to taking tests with 'right' answers, and they are accustomed to pleasing authority. But even though they sought to find the correct or acceptable answers, I believe the administration of the tests largely overcame the usual school testing context. Tests like these are only reliable when an extensive ethnographic understanding of the general social and cultural context, as well as the school, has been achieved. These tests were given on my third visit to Pasir Mas, and with the help of a field assistant who had more than two years experience in Malaya, most of that in the school system.

An inspection of the 13 empirically derived patterns of expectation and aspiration (see Table) shows interesting social data about the *vector* of mobility in regard to the future. The first five patterns are various forms of upward mobility; patterns 6 through 10 are various forms of downward mobility, and patterns 11 through 13 are essentially trendless. School attenders in the secondary school system are overwhelmingly optimistic about their futures. Of the 661 respondents, 596 chose vectors of increasing expectation and bright futures. This 90 per cent optimism reached 100 per cent in the pondok religious boarding school, in the upper sixth form of the English medium of the Sultan Ibrahim School, chiefly Malay in ethnic composition, and in the fifth form of the same school in English medium, all Malay in ethnic composition.

On the whole, secondary schooling is an achievement in the minds of students (and their families and in the society at large). With a secondary school completion certificate the student can reasonably expect to work at an occupation outside of the kampong roster (the rural rice growing, artisan, and petty trader occupations). In Kelantan, to *makan gaji* (earn a salary) at a desk job, as a civil servant or as a teacher, confers not only economic well-being but deference and status. The vectors of mobility beyond the status and economic components which are common to all the secondary students, irrespective of ethnic group, language, medium and content of instruction, of course have different specific components, to be elaborated further on.

While it is true that secondary school students are overwhelmingly positive about their futures, the greatest amount of downward mobility expectation is found in fifth form students, irrespective of language of instruction, content of curriculum, or ethnic background. This is first of all to be explained by the life cycle in the school system. Unless a student is planning to go on to university, his secondary school education normally ends in the fifth form. Thus the fifth form is the end of the line in schooling, and the terminus is not a station for embarking upon new directions. Given this cycle in the school system, pattern 8 (school is the low point, home was best, future must be better than school), is to be expected, and indeed it is. In the fifth form of the Malay secondary school, Sultan Ibrahim, 14 per cent of the students chose that pattern.

In the urban (Kota Bharu) Chinese secondary school Chung Hwa form five, 16 per cent of the students expected one kind or another of downward mobility. In the arts form five of Chung Hwa, only 3 per cent expected downward mobility, showing some differences between those in science where the going is tough and those in arts where generalized literacy is usually enough to make it to the sixth form.

As part of the cycle, lower sixth form students are under great pressure, many will be weeded out. At Sultan Ibrahim School in the lower sixth English medium, 15 per cent of the students had expectations of downward mobility. There is some difference between the expectations of students at Sultan Ibrahim and Sultan Ismail College in their downward expectations. Sultan Ismail is in Kota Bharu, has more Chinese, Indian and urban Malay students than its equivalent Sultan Ibrahim in Pasir Mas.

The most interesting single finding about the vector of mobility is that place in the rhythm of school is most determinative of expectations as to the future. This variable swamps all others—including curriculum content, language of instruction, ethnicity, family background, rural or urban residence, and type of school. Overwhelmingly, secondary students are optimistic—the more successful of them, as in the upper sixth form, are nearly 100 per cent hopeful for the future, and in the most traditional pondok they are the same, and in the Arabic school nearly so, reaching 94 per cent expectations of upward mobility.

The mobility patterns not only have deference and aspiration vectors. They have content. The content was derived from essays. Each student in the upper forms was asked to write an essay saying what the differences between points A,B, and C were. From these essays major themes or values were excerpted. The essays were written either in Malay or English, no Chinese language was used even in the Chinese medium schools. These values could be studied against the individual student's aspiration profile, or against his family's economic and social background, but we choose the path of characterization by ethnic group, school type, and level of education. Obviously this manner of grouping the values places emphasis on social and cultural variables rather than on individual or family background. At some future date, in some future paper, a comparison of the two patterns, the individual and the cultural will probably yield further insight into the dynamics of education in Pasir Mas.

The values embedded in the essays of the upper school children in Kelantan in the order of their frequency were:

1. to help your country
2. to help your race
3. to have a lot of wealth
4. to be independent
5. to be hard working
6. to be free from worry
7. to be respected by society
8. to help your religion
9. to be mature
10. to mix well in society
11. to have power over people

These values (expressed here in the form they were given as rank choices to the lower school attenders) are summaries of ways of expressing these ideas in the students' essays. The first five values were expressed in more than 90 per cent of the essays, the next three in more than 75 per cent, and the last three in under 50 per cent. Taken, then, as the values profile of all secondary students in the sample, they show a value cluster or profile that is overall achievement oriented, individualistic but oriented to the collectivities of nation, ethnic group, and religion. By whatever criteria modernization is judged on the psychological or attitudinal sides, this value profile indicates secondary school children are indeed overwhelmingly modern in value structure. They have an aspiration and expectation direction coupled with concrete hopes that are not well fitted to the rural, agricultural, ethnically intense, kampong and family context that characterizes contemporary Kelantan.

It is, at least, a strong inference that the values have been nurtured and fostered by the educational process itself. That making it to secondary education, irrespective of ethnic background or religious affiliation, creates hopes of social mobility and a value system congruent with those aspirations.

This holds despite the fact that 'to help your religion' has a differential rank if the sample is broken Malay/non-Malay. For the Malay sample this value is the fourth most frequent, appearing in 90 per cent of the essays. For the non-Malay it is in last place, appearing in fewer than 30 per cent of the essays. Religion in the context of Kelantan is an interesting cognitive item. For Malays it is not separable from ethnic identity or cultural heritage. In Kelantan, Malay equals Muslim, *bahasa Melayu*, and *isti'adat Melayu*, That is, a Malay means someone who follows Islam, speaks Malay and takes the customary codes of law and behaviour to be binding. For Kelantan Chinese, religion is a much more diffuse thing or set of ideas. Chiefly, religion is the familial ancestral cult expressed in the home altar. Beyond this there are various local temples mixing forms of Taoism and Buddhism and spirit mediumship. The worship in these temples is also mainly geared to personal and familial fortunes and only as an aside to the commemoration or veneration of particular members of the pantheon. For Indians, who are Hindus chiefly, religion is also diffuse and concerned chiefly with domestic arrangements of marriage, burial, and initiation and the states of impurity and purity.

Given these different meanings of everyday religion in Kelantan, the value 'to help religion' can have meaning only to Malays. The Chinese do not conceive of missionizing, rationalizing or improving relations with the supernatural; nor do the Indians. And even if they did there is no clear secular manner for doing that. Malays see religion and culture as indistinguishable and many of them do have programmes for the spread, the intensification, the purification of Islamic belief and doctrine. On the face of it then, religion must be a value with completely different sense in the three major idioms of supernatural discourse in Kelantan. With this caveat, the next sentence is adequate. Clearly it is centrality that overwhelms ethnicity for these secondary school children.

Centrality needs explanation, even as does ethnicity. In their simplest sense 'central' institutions and 'central' values refer to those values held by persons and groups who are the legitimate elite of the society and who occupy the commanding heights of political and economic power, controlling through a set of institutions (politics, schools, communication media, religious codes etc.) the macro levels of the society (Shils, 1961). As a logical and empirical corollary societies have peripheries not merely in spatial or ecological terms, but in the sense of having values other than, or different from the centre, and the institutions in which those values are embedded are local and regional rather than at the macrosociological level of structure, taking the peninsula as a whole. The content of the Kelantan values has been sketched in an earlier paper (Nash, 1967) and will be spelled out at greater length in a forthcoming book of mine. Suffice it to say that local, regional, or from the analytical point of view, the peripheral values of Kelantan are not those predominately expressed by the secondary school children in Pasir Mas and Kota Bharu. They are the central values, closely in accord with values of UMNO, the cosmopolitan Malay, or the west coast urbanized populations.

These values have been part of the public policy of the Alliance government, and hence part of the radio and television systems, and more importantly the ethos of the national school system—out to make citizens who are economically fit, achievers, loyal to their ethnic group but not hostile to others, and having decent levels of piety. Apparently the schools have, at least in the secondary levels, communicated these values. Or to put it another way, children who are successful to the secondary level are those who have absorbed the values. Perhaps, indeed, one could not *get* to the secondary level without assent to and internalization of these values. At any rate, whatever the fine grained dynamics, the centre in terms of values and institutions has won over the periphery. For clearly Kelantan is PMIP country, and the Pan-Malayan Islamic Party has a different profile of values: race, religion, and Malay ownership are the chief features, set in a society of cooperative people expressing the fine (*halus*) behaviour of well-bred kampong Malays.

If centrality swamps ethnicity in the aggregate reply of students, periphery is strong enough. The value systems of students in the Arabic school and in the pondok school express, as would be expected, a shape much closer to that of the local and regional culture. Religion, respect in society, and helping the race, move up. Helping the country moves down, and having lots of wealth almost disappears. There is overlap in the first five values, but the orders are different, and below these the order is much more varied among Arabic and pondok students, who therefore may be said to have either a shortened, or a more intense, value focus, staying close to religion, race, social respect, and nation, followed by high value on being free from worry.

Outside of the Arabic and pondok schools there is little variation by medium of instruction, sex, or ethnic background. Statistical manipulation leads to results of no social significance. Hence it is not ethnicity that counts: Malays, Chinese, and the few Indians in the secondary schools show similar value clusters. It is the Malays in the Arabic and pondok schools who show different patterning of values (albeit with an important overlap). The hypothesis that values are formed by the school experience is thus reinforced. Those in schools where the central values are inculcated have those values: those in schools espousing the peripheral values (from the point of the macro system) internalize the local and regional values.

From the values expressed in the essays of the secondary school students a list of values (the eleven named above) plus three others were given to lower school students, who were asked to rank these values. The added values never appeared in the essays of the secondary students. These added values were:

1. to be adventurous
2. to have magic power
3. to have a knowledge of sex

To seek adventure is not a desire often expressed in adult Kelantan conversation, but getting magical power and possessing sexual knowledge are frequently the chief topics of coffee house conversation among males of all ages. That they do not appear in the student essays is probably due to the school environment. Secondary school students are all aimed at the difficult task of entering the university. It is a serious business, requiring diligence, sacrifice, and near total orientation to the task of passing examinations. There are, outside of the formal team competitions, which they hardly ever play, few elements of free, playful or joyous behaviour. In addition writing an essay is no place to freely express deep feelings, but accentuates the social and cultural rather than the psychological or personal levels.

The ranking of the eleven values, and the three added, by lower school children is an attempt to get longitudinal information bearing on the contention that value clusters are shaped by the educational experience itself. Evidence has already been presented to indicate that the secondary school students have an aggregate value profile; that this profile is only modified by Arabic school and pondok school attendance; and that this profile stems from the values and policies of central values as expressed in the centrally governed organization of the national schools; and finally that the central values are patterned differently from the local and regional values as expressed in the kampong ideology and the politics of the periphery. If lower school children are somewhat different from secondary school students, then added strength is given to the hypothesis that educational experience shapes the value profile.

It is not germane to this paper to analyse fully the more than 600 responses of lower school children. What is relevant is the shape and pattern of the ranking of values by those respondents. The aggregate profile of the lower school children shows a greater scatter of value rankings, a greater emphasis on maturity, independence, respect, and mixing well. The chief match with the secondary school is the emphasis on hard work. This clearly indicates that the value profile of the secondary school students is formed in the educational matrix, while the lower school children are somewhere between the kampong ideology or Chinese commercial familism (to erect a shorthand for the chief value syndromes in Kelantan) from which they came and the Westernized achievement orientation they will arrive at if they make it to secondary school.

From the hypothesis and its accompanying evidence that centrality swamps ethnicity in the educational process stem two stubborn and seemingly irreducible observations. First, the major axis of political and economic organization in Kelantan is communal and ethnic; second, the school inculcated value systems do not find the economic and social contexts appropriate for their implementation or realization. To understand the implications of these observations requires the correct apprehension of ethnicity and its relation to social mobility in the Kelantan context.

The major ethnic groups of Kelantan are held apart by several simple social mechanisms. Endogamy, based on Islamic writ in the Malay community and on life style in the Chinese community, keeps biological or cultural assimilation to a minimum. Residence, with Chinese chiefly in the urban centers and Malays in the kampong, is a further isolating device. And the lack of commensuality, of religious community, of cross-ethnic voluntary associations and contexts for intimate interaction, further define boundaries between the ethnic groups. The Chinese and Malays do interact in the impersonal arenas of politics and economics, and it is here they stress their ethnicity. In a situation of relative scarcity of economic goods and limited routes of social mobility, ethnicity becomes a resource in the arenas of competition. As the competition becomes fiercer, ethnicity becomes more and more of a counter in the battle. It is clear that as modernization has spread throughout the Malay peninsula ethnic groups have become more and more defined and bounded. The Bugis, the Minangkabau, the Kelantanese have over time become the Malays, an ethnic group; while the six or seven language and culture groups from China have similarly become the Chinese.

Ethnicity is, then, a means of rallying persons and resources in a struggle for goods and social place. Ethnicity becomes dominant in that struggle when two conditions obtain: great disparity between the ethnic groups (and in Malaysia the disparity is doubly compounded by Chinese economic dominance and Malay political dominance); and few channels for non-ethnic competition (and again the political life of

Malaysia is communally organized, while the modern market sector is Chinese and European dominated, with all that that implies in terms of credit, trust, and communication).

In this context, the values inculcated in the school system may lead to sharpened, rather than diminished, ethnic friction. The paradox is this: in secondary school a relatively modern value system is both taught and internalized. Chinese and Malays share the same dominant values and hence will compete for the same things, but the competition involves ethnic and primordial resources. Hence as the value systems become more and more congruent, as Malays get more and more modernized, the ethnic hostility will continue to rise. It is not values which are in conflict; it is social groups coming more and more to share the same values which are in political and economic competition in the context of ethnic disparity and absence of civil channels for the expression and regulation of economic and political conflict.

Without a prescription for ethnic harmony, this paper can end on a cautionary note. Schools promote value consensus when they are effectively tied to the central values and institutions, but it is the organization of political and economic life that provides integration in a modernizing society. Therefore, it is the reconstruction of politics and economics that reduces the ethnic component in competition, not the mere establishment of common values, aims and orientation. In a modern society it is as much procedure as culture that holds it together in the fragile and instrumental manner that complex societies are held together.

REFERENCES

Downs, R.E., 1967. 'A Kelantanese Village of Malaya', in Julian H. Steward (ed.), *Contemporary Change in Traditional Societies* (Urbana, University of Illinois), vol. II, 105–86.

Firth, Raymond, 1966. *Malay Fishermen: Their Peasant Economy*. (2nd ed., London, Routledge & Kegan Paul).

Ministry of Education, 1968a. *Education in Malaysia* (Kuala Lumpur, Dewan Bahasa & Pustaka).

―――― 1968b. *Educational Statistics of Malaysia, 1938 to 1967* (Kuala Lumpur, Dewan Bahasa & Pustaka).

Nash, Manning, 1967. 'Tradition in Tension in Kelantan', *Journal of Asian and African Studies*, I, 310–14.

Rahman Talib, 1960. *Report of the Education Review Committee, 1960* (Chairman, Inche Abdul Rahman b. Haji Talib) (Kuala Lumpur, Government Printing Office).

Razak, 1956. *Report of the Education Committee, 1956* (Chairman, Dato' Abdul Razak b. Hussein) (Kuala Lumpur, Government Printing Office).

Shils, Edward, 1961. 'Centre and Periphery', in *The Logic of Personal Knowledge* (London, Routledge & Kegan Paul), 117–21.

Wong, R.H.K., 1964. 'Education and Problems of Nationhood', in Wang Gungwu (ed.), *Malaysia: A Survey* (New York, Praeger), 199–209.

11

ROBERT L. WINZELER

The Social Organization of Islam in Kelantan

Introduction

By the social organization of Islam I mean not so much higher legal organization or the bureaucracy as the more important sorts of religious institution, religious leadership, and the specialist roles with which the Malay populace has vital and generally recurrent interaction, in particular as I observed these in and around the town of Pasir Mas for a fourteen month period in 1966–67.[1] My subject is both the 'traditional' side of Islamic social organization and the effects that various processes of change have had, particularly the effects of the rise of modern party politics. Several features of the Pasir Mas area have special significance for the present analysis. First, there is a concentration of traditional religious schools, including several prominent ones located on the edge of town. Second, the Pasir Mas area is widely known as one of the strongholds of the Pan-Malayan Islamic Party (PMIP). While there is, indeed, one sub-district where this party has in the past had the support of over 90 per cent of the population, in most sub-districts support is somewhat more evenly divided between the PMIP and the

[1] My research was sponsored through an N.S.F. Dissertation Research grant (GS1306) for which grateful acknowledgement is made. The material presented here is drawn mainly from several chapters of my doctoral dissertation ('Malay Religion, Society and Politics in Kelantan', Department of Anthropology, University of Chicago, 1970).

United Malays National Organization (UMNO), as was the case with regard to the town Malay population itself and with the village area in which much of my rural research was concentrated. This state of affairs afforded a view of religion and religious organization from both sides of the political fence—a matter of some consequence since religion and politics have become so importantly intertwined in Kelantan.

Development of Islam in Kelantan

What Islam was like in the broad, open, presently densely populated wet-rice plain of northern Kelantan before change began to occur, presumably in the closing decades of the nineteenth century, is a topic which eludes precise if not satisfactory delineation. It is however quite possible that the character of religion in this region was formed at a fairly early period, perhaps as early as the seventeenth century or before, when the Patani region to the north—with which northern Kelantan has strong cultural and linguistic ties—still flourished as one of the major centres of long distance trade in South-East Asia. In any case towards the second half of the seventeenth century Patani declined as a major centre of South-East Asian trade as the main lines of international commerce shifted southward, though it never totally lost its place of importance in the world of South-East Asian Islam. In Kelantan, with its large agrarian heartland, religion and culture probably developed at least until around the middle of the nineteenth century as much or more in response to the internal character of the Kelantanese countryside as to external trade-linked influences, in this way acquiring the rather distinctive cast that was noted by earlier observers and is still so strongly evident today.

The patterns of change which have characterized or affected the growth of Islam in the Kelantan plain since the waning decades of the nineteenth century are, at least in broad terms, better understood. Here as elsewhere in the peninsula Islam entered a new phase of growth after the onset of the colonial period, partly as a result of the impact of wider, more or less contemporary, developments in Southeast Asia and world Islam and partly as a result of changes brought about by colonial intrusion and its political and economic effects upon Malay society. The former sources of change—the stepped up contact between South-East Asians and the centres of Islam in the Middle East, above all via the pilgrimage, the increasing importance of cosmopolitan urbanism, and the greater potential for contact among diverse Muslim ethnic groups that was associated with such developments and with the 'opening up' of the Malay peninsula and new regions of Indonesia—have all been discussed, at least in general terms, as have the reform movements with which they are associated.

As for the latter type of source of religious change, Roff (1967) has shown at some length how the introduction of British rule stimulated the elaboration of centralized religious legal apparatus, religious councils and bureaucracies and Western type religious schools in the Malay states generally. And while in Kelantan the course of these developments may not have been brought about by an entirely analogous set of influences they followed the same general course. On the other hand an at least equally significant set of changes induced at the village level, above all in the realm of land tenure and social stratification, has had important implications for religious development.

Raymond Firth (1966, 269) has summarized in broad terms the general nature of such changes as of 1940:

> There is little doubt that during the last thirty years the position of the peasant in Kelantan has tended to change, particularly in the direction of greater differentiation in levels of wealth. Under the old system, with a large degree of arbitrary control by the ruler and the nobles and territorial chiefs, and much closer dependence of 'their people' upon them, the wealth of the peasant was always subject to distraint on the part of his superior. With the introduction of effective British administration, with its system of land registration, moderately impartial Courts, regular salaries to officials paid out of State revenue, and substitution of fixed annual dues with centralized exchequer control for the more local, variable and arbitrary produce taxes, 'farms' and other levies, the personal, social and economic ties between peasant and his feudal lord have tended to disappear. While this has meant greater freedom, security and individuality for the peasants as a whole, it has also facilitated economic differentiation between classes of peasants.
>
> In agriculture the security of land tenure, the comparatively low quit-rents for non-cultivating as well as for cultivating owners, the entry of rubber as a commercial crop and probably the growth of population also, have promoted the existence of *petits rentiers* living largely on the shares of the produce of their lands worked by others. Definite information on the situation is lacking, but I am inclined to think that the practices of share-cropping rice lands and of leasing the produce of orchards have increased considerably in recent years, perhaps to an extent hardly realized by the Government.

These changes, the differentiation of levels of wealth and the emergence of a class of better-off peasantry living upon their shares of produce and upon returns from such investments as rural coffee- and provision-shops or, more recently, rice mills, affected the social organization of Islam in the region in several ways. For one thing, partly at least in conjunction with developments and influences originating elsewhere, they facilitated the elaboration of the institutional and role structure of rural Islam by encouraging or permitting increased religious status assumption.[2]

The *haj* is important in this respect. It represents a religious achievement which is more or less directly arrived at through a large expenditure of funds. Malays who can afford it go, and for decades now have gone, on the *haj* in substantial numbers.[3] And while not all *haji* become active religious functionaries on return, they do play a religious role. Equally importantly, in the past they often took along a child or grandchild and remained for a period of years in Mecca so that today it is not uncommon to meet Malays in rural society as well as in more urban elite sectors who have spent many years in Mecca. The establishment of religious trusts (*wakaf*) which commonly consist of a shelter built along a road or in a cemetery, but may also take the form of prayer house (*surau*), is also strongly encouraged from those who can afford it, as an act of piety for which one receives merit or reward (*pahala*). Religious schooling, too, is an important means of enhancing religious status and role. Villagers who in the past could afford it sent their sons to study at traditional religious schools, just as they have in more recent times sent them to the modern Malay or Arabic religious schools which have become much more widely available since the war. In such cases a strong Islamic orientation has thus been maintained or initiated in the family, and expressed in the attempted attainment of religious status—as teacher, community leader or at least pious man—roles sometimes filled by a father or elder brother as well.

Traditional Religious Roles and Institutions

Leaving aside for the moment consideration of the most important such religious functionary, the religious scholar-teacher or *guru pondok*, there are in the Pasir Mas area a series of types of religious leader or functionary who devote some portion of their time to religious matters, as well as others who may or may not perform religious duties but who receive prestige and are apt to be objects of a certain amount of communal or individual ritual attention.[4] Among the more important

---

[2] Poverty of course has its place in Islam. Saintly ascetics (*wali*), for example, are said to be poor and to have no need for money—indeed it is commonly held that they will freely give money (which appears from nowhere) to those who are truly in need. Nor are all other sorts of religious figures men of wealth. However, where an important religious figure is wealthy it may well be that religious achievement has generated wealth, through a marriage or through gifts or the returns of office. In any case access to religious status for either oneself or others is facilitated by wealth.

[3] There were 167 pilgrims from Pasir Mas district (pop. 90,000) in 1966-67, mostly older folks travelling in couples who traveled on any one of three ships. The total cost per head was about $1,700.

[4] Islam as is frequently noted knows no clergy. There are, however, throughout Islam

of the former are local imam who are affiliated, commonly by inheritance, with a neighbourhood surau or prayer house, as well as district imam who head the larger official mosque congregations. There are also men and women in most neighbourhoods who instruct children in elementary Kuranic study, and finally those called *lebai* who are credited with piety (*beribadat*) and some degree of sacred knowledge and ritual skill. *Haji* even if they do not seek an active instrumental religious role such as teacher or imam are attributed some measure of religious (and social) prestige. Finally there are much more occasional extraordinary religious figures such as *wali* (saints), who today are either suspect or are disdained in more religiously learned circles but who are still sought out by many people, particularly women, who either accept them or are apt to say at least that they are curious to see if the powers (soothsaying, divination, cursing, blessing, etc.) they are reputed to possess, or to be able to invoke, can be used to solve some personal problem.

The outwardly significant aspect of a role, that which governs the relationship between the incumbent and those with whom he is interacting, consists of its attributes—a set of shared perceptions and valuations concerning what the role-incumbent 'is' and 'does' and which define his moral worth. Broadly speaking, then, these religious roles have two general sorts of attributes, the provision of ritual or other religious services and/or the exemplification of religious virtue—piety, religious learning and in some cases possession of 'blessings' or 'powers' (*berkat*).

Traditional piety (*beribadat*) consists of the faithful and diligent performance of religious duties (*ibadat*), the prayers, the fast, the pilgrimage if possible; the notably pious are also apt to be pointed out as individuals who pray more often, particularly during the fast, or who fast extra days following the close of the fasting month (when others are celebrating).[5] The pious man is also marked by his dress and his moral behav-

---

generally, religious functionaries whose services are vital to the religious life of the community as well as those who occupy positions of prestige which they have attained through meritorious achievements such as the completion of the pilgrimage or scholarly study, or which they enjoy because of some respected link of descent—most importantly with the family of the Prophet. In addition, particularly in those cultures which occupy marginal positions in the Islamic world, and where among other things literacy in Arabic is restricted, there is a strong tendency for individuals who possess (or are reputed to possess) the ability to read the language of the Kuran, or who are attributed some other special link with divinity, to play an especially vital role. Here also religion is particularly apt to constitute the basis for a very important prestige-authority hierarchy (Goody, 1968).

[5] Devoutness, piety and religious knowledge are of course not characteristic only of those individuals who occupy one or another special religious status. Where the broader populace is concerned these characteristics are linked to differences in sex and age. Broadly speaking boys receive more religious training than girls and men are expected to be more devout and involved in religious matters than women—though women are not completely excluded from Islamic affairs since they do in some cases go on the

iour. The most ubiquitous item of dress which serves to differentiate those who occupy some special religious status from those who do not is the white skull cap (*kupiah*). This is the mark of the religious student and the returned *haji*, but the wearing of it, rather than the dark felt *songkok* or, in the case of many villagers, the coloured head scarf, serves to signify religious status in general. In the case of at least the more important religious figures the *kupiah* is supplemented by other items, most importantly the white head scarf (*serban*) which is wrapped into a turban or draped about the neck. Correct morality is also a very important facet of the traditional image of piety. This is expressed both through the avoidance of those things which are known to be forbidden (*haram*)—pork and alcohol, for example—as well as those which are regarded as undesirable (*makroh*), such as smoking, or eating fermented fish sauce (*budu*). Moderation in eating and other personal habits is also important. Beyond this the conservative sense of correct morality may find expression in speculation about the possible or probable *haram*-ness of a variety of things, particularly today those things associated with Westernization.[6]

The services or assistance provided vary according to the role in question. Kuran teachers provide instruction in elementary religious study. Pious men (*lebai*), even if they do nothing else (such as Kuran teaching) are called to pray at feasts in general and may be engaged to read prayers over a grave for a night or so following a burial. Also any of the foregoing may also be called upon to make charms (*azimat*), mainly by writing Kuranic verses on slips of paper which are then carried on the person, or to prepare the all-purpose and ritually ubiquitous sacred water or *ayer tawar*, generally by reciting Kuranic verses over a container of water which is then drunk, or used in a special bath, by the person in need, particularly if the practitioner has gained a reputation for efficacy in such things. Similarly, although curing and exorcism are primarily in the hands of another set of specialists, *bomoh*, they may occasionally engage in these activities.

The role of imam or designated community religious leader varies according to whether or not the person concerned is affiliated with a district mosque where Friday prayers are held, and which may serve several or more villages, or with the local prayer house or *surau* which is commonly used only by a neighbourhood or hamlet. Today the

---

haj, teach religion and go to the prayer house to listen to religious teaching—and older men are generally more wrapped up in religion than younger ones.

[6] Such notions of piety are attacked by younger, more Western-oriented Malays and to some extent by the religiously modernist but for others they are still the prevailing religious norms.

THE SOCIAL ORGANIZATION OF ISLAM IN KELANTAN 265

mosque district (*mukim*) is the basic unit in the official religious administrative structure and the imam is the leading officer of this district. His duties include leading the Friday prayer, the collection of religious taxes, the solemnization of marriages, and supervision of matters relating to the mosque. He is also required to deal with breaches of religious law and is authorized to arrest and take to court violators of religious statutes. The imam of a local surau, which he or his father may have built themselves, serves a much more limited community in fewer ways: directing the preparation of corpses for burial, leading prayers for the dead, perhaps providing religious instruction, and so forth. The surau of the religious community which centres upon it is however an important focus for village religious life, involving people in ways that the larger mosque may not. Certain village Islamic celebrations such as *Maulud Nabi* (the Birth of the Prophet) as well as prayer readings during the fasting month will be held there under direction of the mosque imam. Moreover the community surrounding the surau, the neighborhood or hamlet of several dozen households (called a kampong, as is a larger village) is apt to possess a distinctive place name and represent the social unit on which notions of solidarity and cooperativeness are primarily focused, and therefore to be the locus of some of the most important traditional religious activities—the ritual feasts which are sponsored by individual households or organized communally.

Pondok

The religious roles and institutions discussed up to this point are aspects of local religious organization; most local communities contain Islamic religious specialists of one sort or another and have access to either a surau or a mosque. Religious education on the other hand entails a number of religious leadership roles and attendant structures which in some instances at least have a regional rather than local or district importance. This is particularly true in the case of traditional religious teachers (*guru*), the leading religious figures in the Pasir Mas area, and the schools they head. In addition to modern religious schools which concentrate upon teaching Arabic and both religious and non-religious subjects, there are several other types of religious school. The term *madrasah* is today commonly applied to a school held in a simple prayer house or mosque type structure. The sort of religious instruction offered may be elementary Kuranic instruction provided for local children but it may also include more advanced religious instruction or religious instruction for adults, often offered on Friday morning by a more noted religious teacher. The most important such religious schools are those at which students come to live and study on a full-time daily basis, supporting at least one and sometimes several full-time teachers. These schools or *pondok*[7] draw students from wider areas as well as local surroundings—in some cases from the other Malay states and southern Thailand and beyond.

Boys who go to pondok traditionally do so after they have completed elementary religious study. Students live in ones, twos and threes in small individual or double huts—called *pondok*—or in similar fashion in sections of longhouses. Among other things, students occupy themselves with the lessons given by the teacher on one or another subject or with practising reading and chanting, studying texts or commentaries, helping one another, or in some cases teaching younger children. In earlier decades pondok were for the Pasir Mas area an important part of a limited range of opportunities for schooling. In the village in which I worked it was formerly not uncommon for boys of families who could afford it to spend a year or two in a pondok, those serious in pursuing advanced religious study remaining or going on to a different school, the rest leaving. More recently increased availability of other forms of education, namely elementary 'people's schools' (*sekolah ra'ayat*), government primary and secondary schools and modern religious or 'Arabic' schools (*sekolah Arab*) has largely done away with this tendency. Also, in Pasir Mas, where the major government Malay and Arabic schools of the district are located, many of the students who live in the several large pondok are in fact attending the other schools, particularly the Arabic school, and use the pondok mainly as a place to stay. It is also common to find students who in addition to pursuing religious studies are in the process of trying to pass examinations for government school certificates.

The physical structure of a typical pondok includes a central building where prayers and teaching are conducted (a mosque or a surau, which may be called a madrasah) plus perhaps several lesser prayer houses, a residence for the guru and the living quarters for the students. The layout

---

[7] *Pondok* have been attributed a vital role in the organization and development of Islam in Indonesia and occupy a prominent place in the historical and ethnographic literature of the region (generally under the more common name of *pesantren* [Snouck Hurgronje, 1906; Drewes, 1955; Geertz, 1960a, b]) but there has been little or nothing written about their role in the peninsular Malay states. They appear to be particularly characteristic of Kelantan and the Patani area—the Malay region just to the north, in present day Thailand—and perhaps to a lesser degree of the rice growing regions of the north-western states. Patani, presumably because of its ancient importance as a trading centre, was perhaps the most important region in the peninsula for such traditional religious scholarship and education and has some of the largest and most famous pondok, but the Kelantan plain has, at least over the course of this century, been a centre in its own right. Their continuing presence also tells one a good deal about the strength conservative Islam has achieved and maintained in Kelantanese society.

varies; in some cases the students' quarters are grouped in a circle but in most cases there are several rows of longhouse arrangements plus single huts erected where there is room. The pondok in Pasir Mas are all densely packed and occupy up to several acres. In some cases in rural areas pondok are located away from other residential areas and in others they occupy a part of a village complex which in some cases has grown up around it. In Pasir Mas two of the still flourishing pondok, and the remnants of an earlier one, constituted the nucleus of several different distinct quarters or neighbourhoods, known in each case as 'the pondok'. The inhabitants of these communities, several hundred or so in some instances, regarded themselves with varying degrees of explicitness as followers or students of the guru and were generally so regarded. A part of this community lives in the pondok itself, in houses built wherever there is room, or on the borders of it. Such people may be old folk who find it a good place to spend their last years, surrounded by the more intensive religious activity and the haze of piety and spirituality that is thought to pervade it. Some of the men, younger as well as older, are not uncommonly former students who continue to identify strongly with the guru and with the milieu generally. Such individuals typically work as traders, carpenters, tailors, small shop-keepers and drivers— though some are school-teachers, particularly religious school-teachers.

The influence of a guru and the significance of the pondok does not stop with this immediate community. A frequent sight around pondok is a procession of men and boys in white skull caps and scarves on foot or riding bicycles on their way to pray at a feast or conduct a burial. Similarly the advice of a guru in particular is sought about a variety of spiritual matters of concern to many Malays.

The status of guru in local Malay society rests upon a complex set of beliefs and values. In particular they are traditionally viewed as the religious figures who most clearly embody in their learning and modest and devout personal life styles the virtues, wisdom and power of Islam. In some cases gurus have the popular reputation of being *berkat* or blessed. There is a considerable amount of popular folklore about the mystical powers of such figures, particularly about those of earlier times—about how people who spoke against them were suddenly affected by invisible forces or about how some sinful activity such as animal fighting was prevented because the animals were brought too near the presence of the guru. At least one prominent guru in the rural Pasir Mas area about whom such beliefs were held, received and dealt with a large number of visitors seeking curing or other sorts of assistance. On the other hand a number of gurus in the area were known strongly to advocate strictly reformist or fundamentalist Islamic practices and to discourage customary pursuits which were in conflict with these. One such guru for example employed only the Islamic marriage ritual (*nikah*) for his daughter, avoiding the costly and elaborate Malay *bersanding* ceremony.

Modern Developments: Politics and Religion

The Second World War brought in its aftermath of general modernization and independence a set of developments which have affected the organization of religion as they have most other facets of Malay life.[8] But it is with the growth of modern party and governmental politics—partly a matter of national developments and partly a reflection of local circumstances in Kelantan—the formative phase of which occurred during the 1950's, that I shall be concerned here.

With the rise of the PMIP, and its electoral victories in the 1959 elections—which brought control of the state government and all but a couple of national parliamentary seats in Kelantan—religion became a major ingredient in and focus of politics. The PMIP of course organized itself in part as a religious movement, seeking not only to protect and further the position of the Malays but also to enhance the practice of Islam and define an Islamic version of modernity. Aside from campaigns and other purely 'political' activities the party sponsors religious programmes, the celebration of Muslim holidays, and talks by prominent religious leaders; on one occasion in 1967 several came from Indonesia. It has also attempted upon occasion to provide temporary religious teachers for villages which lacked them (in some cases such teachers were refused permission to enter UMNO kampongs) and through its direction the state government has made a considerable effort to aid religious education, particularly modern religious (*sekolah Arab*) education. But UMNO and the national government, not to be entirely outdone, took up the cause of religion as well, attempting to recruit its own set of religious notables and to disseminate its own propaganda about the proper relationship of Islam to government, arguing that the PMIP does not 'follow' religion but merely uses it to 'confuse people.' The national government's religious buildings programme has

[8] The growth of modern forms of education has been particularly significant. These include both the extension of secular primary vernacular education to rural areas, initially in the form of communally initiated 'people's schools' (*sekolah ra'ayat*), and of primary and secondary government schools, to towns such as Pasir Mas. There has been a similar expansion of modern-type religious schools. The Arabic schools are modelled on the lines of Western-type schools in that they provide day schooling for large numbers of both boys and girls, organized into a yearly graded curriculum. Such schooling is oriented first to the study and mastery of Arabic and the use of Arabic as a medium of study of both religious subjects—Kuran, commentaries, law, grammar, etc.—and secular ones. There are a large number of these schools, the biggest and most important of which are operated by the Majlis Ugama Islam.

been a cornerstone in UMNO's Kelantan struggle; gleaming new mosques and newly refurbished prayer houses, each dedicated by a prominent national UMNO leader, dot the Kelantan countryside.

Because politics are partially based upon and strongly oriented to religion they have obviously had a considerable impact upon religious roles and the organization of religious life. What the long-term effects of politicization will be is difficult to say at this point—but immediately apparent effects have been to place considerable pressure upon religious relationships, roles and institutions. These pressures are not so apt to be present or apparent in situations where common political loyalty to one or the other of the parties happens to obtain in a given area. But where political loyalties are divided they are quite evident. Religious leaders are in effect faced with the decision to take sides, thereby probably alienating adherents of the opposite party, or to remain neutral, thereby relinquishing influence in an extremely important field of mass concern.

In the Pasir Mas area religious leaders responded to the coming of politics in a variety of ways; becoming in some cases active political leaders, in others partisan supporters and advisers, in yet others hanging back or remaining publicly neutral. In those instances where religious leaders had become involved as party activists they and the institutions with which they were affiliated had become local centres of partisan hostility. In the Pasir Mas town area for example the main lines of political factionalism were drawn between several of the pondok neighbourhoods and some of the core residential areas of town. The former were centres of PMIP strength, a number of the more important party leaders living in one or another of the pondok and many of the resident men and youths serving as party organizers and workers. In the town, on the other hand, particularly in areas with a strong middle class of school-teachers, officials and office workers, a goodly portion of whom—particularly the school-teachers—tended to be politically active, UMNO was well entrenched. As a result, political involvement of several of the *guru pondok* in the PMIP was to become one of the main issues, and probably the most emotional one, of the struggle. Specifically, during the 1964 election campaign one PMIP guru who had run a small pondok located a short way out of town and who had previously stood as a party candidate and won a seat in the State Assembly was arrested and detained, along with several other party leaders, for violating internal security enactments by using 'overly inflammatory rhetoric' in advocating support for the PMIP. The arrests had provoked among PMIP people a mixture of outrage, a deeper distrust of the national government and, with some reason, concern over the possibility of more such arrests. On the other hand, politically concerned UMNO townspeople, who in some cases had come to view the several important PMIP gurus with about as much animosity as their followers did reverence, held that this is what happens when religious leaders go too far in mixing religion with politics. By 1966-67 the emotional intensity of the campaign had receded—though it was revived by several incidents, one of which involved the murder in the state capital of the PMIP member of Parliament from a Pasir Mas constituency and the subsequent by-election to replace him—but a considerable amount of animosity remained. Several families in my own neighborhood, which was located near to one of the pondok areas, maintained that they no longer had anything to do with the pondok or went to visit in the area.

The intrusion of party politics also had some effect upon the organization of religious leadership in the rural village where I conducted research over a nine-month period. A part of this village, including the imam of the district mosque, supported the PMIP; a somewhat smaller, though well organized and in their own view more progressive, segment, located in several contiguous hamlets, supported UMNO. When I first visited this village one of the first things I noticed was a half finished mosque upon which no work appeared to be in progress. This turned out to be the case, and to have been so for some time. Work had begun some five years before under the direction of a part-time carpenter who as a popular leader and effective organizer was instrumental in gathering materials and mobilizing a cooperative work force. He and a number of the active participants of the project were from several adjacent hamlets and were UMNO supporters whose intention it had been to seek funds from the national government's religious buildings construction programme to bring it to completion. This however was blocked by the district imam who was backed by the PMIP faction. Their objection was that such funds came from the national welfare lottery and were therefore *haram*. After this the carpenter and the other UMNO partisans withdrew their efforts, further work ceased, and the mosque was left to stand as I found it. Enough had been done so that Friday prayers could be held, but these were mainly avoided by the UMNO villagers. Finally, during the latter part of my stay, the imam announced that proper funds had been obtained from the PMIP state government and work started once again, this time however with hired labour.

There were effects in the opposite political direction as well. Social and ritual life in the hamlet of the village where UMNO support was concentrated centred around a neighbourhood surau and a coffee shop, both of which were located adjacent to the home of the UMNO carpenter. The imam of the surau was a *haji* and an UMNO sympathizer, as was one other religious figure, a *lebai* who lived down the lane a bit, both of them close relatives of a number of the local UMNO leaders. Two other *haji* in the immediate area, however, were PMIP adherents and had as a consequence of the mosque incident stopped using the surau for occasional prayers—as some of the villagers did—and one for a while had refused to speak to the UMNO imam of the surau, though he had subsequently got over this.

Not all religious figures had been drawn into the hostilities as partisan advocates or adherents, or remained so if they had been. One of the other officers of the mosque, for example, who had originally organized the building in his front yard of a local PMIP chapter house, closed it down, explaining to me later that people in the village had become too upset over politics and thus that it was better just to have a coffee shop, which he hoped to open whenever he could raise some money. Similarly the guru of the small pondok that was also located in this part of the village had, people agreed, remained discreetly silent throughout the controversy and continued to be admired by all groups, though he was not in any case much involved in village matters.

REFERENCES

Drewes, G.W.J., 1955. 'Indonesia: Mysticism and Activism', in G.E. von Grunebaum (ed.), *Unity and Variety in Muslim Civilization Civilization* (Chicago, University of Chicago Press), 284-310.

Firth, Raymond, 1966. *Malay Fisherman: Their Peasant Economy* (2nd ed., London, Routledge & Kegan Paul).

Geertz, Clifford, 1960a. 'The Javanese Kijaji: the Changing Role of a Cultural Broker', *Comparative Studies in Society and History*, II, 2, 228-49.

———— 1960b. *The Religion of Java* (Glencoe Ill., Free Press).

Goody, Jack, 1968. 'Introduction' to his *Literacy in Traditional Societies* (Cambridge, University Press).

Roff, William R., 1967. *The Origins of Malay Nationalism* (New Haven, Conn. & London, Yale University Press).

Snouck Hurgronje, C., 1931. *Mekka in the Latter Part of the Nineteenth Century* (transl. J.H. Monahan) (Leyden, Brill).

12

CLIVE S. KESSLER

Muslim Identity and Political Behaviour in Kelantan[1]

THE aim of this essay is twofold. It seeks to provide an explanation, in the context of the overall development of Kelantanese society from precolonial times, of the electoral successes of the Pan-Malayan Islamic Party, or PMIP, in Kelantan since 1959. It also seeks to examine the nature of the PMIP's appeal among the state's predominantly peasant population. On the one hand, it seeks to locate the PMIP within an antecedent pattern of relations between religion and elite politics in Kelantan; on the other, it attempts to indicate the manner in which the PMIP has succeeded in articulating widespread peasant grievances by means of a largely implicit Islamic theory of society and politics. Both dimensions of the argument are directed towards indicating the complexity, both historical and contemporary, of the sources of support for the PMIP. To indicate that complexity serves to call into question some

[1] This article is based upon research conducted in Malaysia, principally in Kelantan, from August 1967 to October 1968 and from January to July 1969. I wish to acknowledge my gratitude to the London Committee of the London-Cornell Project for East and Southeast Asian Studies (financed jointly by the Carnegie Corporation of New York and by the Nuffield Foundation) and to the Senate and Faculty of Arts of the University of Sydney (for the award of the Hannah Fullerton Post-graduate Travelling Research Scholarship). Both these sources supported me in Malaysia and during periods of library research before and after fieldwork. I also bear an immeasurable debt towards those Kelantanese into whose lives I intruded, impelled by a curiosity to find out things which quite clearly it may not have been in their interest to divulge.

existing accounts of the PMIP's successes in the state—accounts which, lacking both the historical and anthropological dimensions, have crudely characterized the PMIP as but the manifestation of an archaic religious fanaticism and of an ethnically narrow xenophobia.

I

The half century before the outbreak of the Pacific War witnessed the hesitant beginnings of Malay nationalism, propounded serially in three variants—the Islamic, the radical nationalist and the elitist-administrative—each of which was associated with a particular elite engendered by British colonial rule (Roff, 1967). It was the Japanese occupation, however, which burst asunder the strands of that exaggerated and rather artificial continuity aimed at in Britain's paternalistically custodial policy towards the Malays and which created the preconditions for mass support of Malay nationalist politics. As a political force Malay nationalism was called into fruition as a response to British proposals for Malayan Union in 1946,[2] when, under the aegis of the English-educated nobility who in the 1930s had created the third variant of Malay nationalism in the Malay Political Associations of the various states (Roff, 1967, 237–47, & 1968), the United Malays National Organization was formed. As it set about the pursuit of independence, the UMNO joined into an Alliance with Chinese and Indian parties; in response, some Malay politicians of varying inclination (radical, religious and nationalist) broke away from the Malay popular front which had come together as the UMNO in 1946. Thus, in their modern forms, the dissenting Malay parties were created —the Party Negara, the Partai Rakyat Malaya and the Persatuan Islam Sa-Tanah Melayu or PMIP—and the UMNO rump which remained as senior partner in the Alliance was very much a union of the old Malay Political Associations. Led by the UMNO, whose core perpetuated the ascendancy of that third pre-war variant of Malay nationalism (cf. Scott, 1968, 314–43), the Alliance all but swept the field in the pre-independence elections of 1955, and in 1957, as the party of independence and the constitution, provided the government of the new sovereign Federation of Malaya.

In 1959, the Alliance went back to the electorate to secure a renewed mandate, but suffered a number of setbacks. The most serious of them, both at the time and in its subsequent implications, was the success of the PMIP in the East Coast states of Kelantan and Trengganu: thirteen

[2] A fully documented account of that central episode awaits the opening of archives. For a preliminary account see Allen (1967).

out of sixteen federal seats, and forty-one out of fifty-four state assembly seats, fell into its hands—enough to enable the PMIP to form the state government in both cases. Within three years the PMIP government of Trengganu was to be toppled, but in Kelantan it held on, precariously at times, over the next decade and through two subsequent elections. Returned to power in Kelantan in 1959 with twenty-eight out of thirty seats in the State Assembly, the PMIP had received such extensive support that a decade of its diminution (determinedly sought by the UMNO) failed to undermine the PMIP's status as the majority party in the state.

The PMIP's victory in Kelantan in 1959, and its success in retaining control of the state thereafter, betokened the revival and coalescence of those two earlier variants of Malay nationalism—the Islamic and the populist or radical nationalist—which had historically preceded the elitist-administrative variant now employing the UMNO as the vehicle of its political ascendancy. The PMIP's successes in Kelantan (and beyond it in 1969) signalled the challenge of those revived and reorganized forces to the UMNO's claims to be the sole embodiment of the national hopes of the Malays and the only effective protector of their popular interests. How, it may be asked, did this merger of rejuvenated forces as a challenge to the UMNO ascendancy take place, and why in Kelantan? That question raises, by implication, another: what has been the role of Islam in mobilizing in Kelantan a peasant-based political rejection of the UMNO, its leaders and its policies?

Scholars, working in disciplines often ill-equipped to deal with the complex nature of peasant-based populist movements,[3] have attempted to explain the nature of the PMIP's support.[4] These explanations, made often only *en passant*, have tended to be partial in both senses of the word. They have grasped only a small part of the truth and, mistaking that part for the whole and finding it unsubtle, they have often been pejorative if not indeed hostile. Their commitment to their somewhat simplistic explanations has led a succession of writers to characterize the political objectives and appeals of the PMIP as crude and simplistic, and the primitive nature of much social-scientific theory has been projected instead onto one of its recalcitrant objects of study. I have elsewhere (Kessler, 1972), by extensive quotation, summarized the more commonly held explanations of the PMIP's successes in Kelantan and

[3] The essays in Ionescu & Gellner (eds.), (1969) are illustrative of the problem.
[4] See Gallagher (1966), Gullick (1964, 138–9, & 1969, 213), Maryanov (1967), McGee (1962, 79–80), Means (1969 & 1970), von der Mehden (1963 & 1964), Milne (1964), Nash (1966), Ratnam (1965 & 1969), Ratnam and Milne (1967 & 1970), Rudner (1970), Smith (1960), Tinker (1956) and Vasil (1965). For general accounts of Malaysian politics see Milne (1967), Ratnam (1965) and Means (1970).

briefly indicated some of their deficiencies. Until 1969 the problem, as it posed itself to scholars, was to explain why support for the PMIP was largely confined to the East Coast of the peninsula, and for the most part they have sought answers in the special characteristics, alleged and real, of East Coast Malay society—in its isolation, its alleged backwardness and in its 'strongly and traditionally Islamic character' (von der Mehden 1963, 611). Since the PMIP's successes in the northwest states in 1969 such a strategy is no longer viable, and the problem would now seem to be that of explaining why the Kelantanese peasantry anticipated by a decade the political response of the Malay peasantry elsewhere in the peninsula. This new perspective would seem to require, but in a more sophisticated fashion than has hitherto been the case, a consideration of the special characteristics of Kelantanese society. Only the outlines of such an analysis can be given in an article of this scope. That outline will point to the distinctive circumstances of Malay political awakening in Kelantan during the colonial period and to the manner in which national politics were subsequently woven (through the activities of those groups in Kelantanese society who have represented the contending parties) into the social fabric of a Malay state of unique complexity.

A further, and central, shortcoming of the existing accounts of the PMIP's successes has been that all of them have assumed, without attempting to explain, the existence of a crucially important religious dimension to the PMIP's political appeal. Indeed, it may be said that insofar as they have been content to assert the importance of the religious appeal without attempting to find what underlies it, scholars, by that concentration, have tended to exaggerate the influence of a seemingly noumenal and disembodied 'religious factor'. Moreover, inasmuch as they have usually been content to characterize Kelantanese society as 'backward' and the PMIP's successes therein as the survival of pre-modern styles of political activity, scholars have accommodated that elusive factor of the Islamic political appeal unanalysed into their accounts as the purportedly natural residue of a waning traditionalism. The PMIP's resurgence, and successes beyond the East Coast, in 1969 no longer allow the party and its appeals to be characterized as some deviant, paradoxical, even atavistic and strictly local East Coast phenomenon. One must look instead at the predicament of the modern Malay peasant and examine how Islam speaks to the popular experience of that predicament.

This account, then, expanding upon my previous discussions, will attempt to analyse in some depth the nature of the Islamic political appeal in Kelantan. It seeks to show how that appeal is generated by the tension between the implicit social theory of Islam and the social experience of the Kelantanese peasant. It attempts to show how the strength of that appeal derives from the ability of an Islamic idiom of political discourse to transform the nature of political demands: to allow the presentation of sectional interests in a universalistic, and thus morally sanctioned, fashion. Through its ability to effect that translation, the Islamic idiom permits one of the contending parties, in a politically divided and conflict-ridden situation, to present itself as the vehicle of popular interests and the 'general will'; in consequence, it also facilitates the casting of the other party into the role of the protector of sectional, unpopular, and hence also immoral, interests—those which reject, by cutting themselves loose from, the purported general interest. The Islamic idiom may thus provide the cement of collectivist solidarity for the party which, by appealing to popular interests, succeeds in presenting itself as the vehicle of a morally sanctioned general interest.

★ ★ ★ ★

Before embarking, however, upon an analysis of how the Islamic appeal is generated and operates in Kelantan, it is necessary first to give some account of the social and political circumstances which lie behind it, lending to it its rich resonances. To omit such a consideration would be merely to repeat the error of regarding that appeal as a given factor, separate (and on a different level) from the more mundane and tangible sources of the PMIP's support.

The religious appeal, however, cannot be so neatly separated, since it is the means whereby those other factors are organized in relation to each other and given coherent expression. This outline of the circumstances underlying the political appeals of Islam in Kelantan therefore attempts briefly to indicate some of the more salient 'special characteristics' of Kelantanese society—those which, after some half a century of colonial rule and more than a decade of independence, have acquired an immediate political relevance. Such an account involves a consideration of the distinctive effects of colonial rule upon Kelantanese society, at both the elite and peasant levels, and of the manner in which modern party politics have been grafted onto Kelantanese society through the shifting association of various elites in Kelantan with parties at the national level. It is only from such a perspective that the PMIP's electoral seizure of power in Kelantan in 1959, and its subsequent retention of control in the state, may be understood. For the parties which contested the 1955 elections in Kelantan, and which in modified form have contested three subsequent elections in the state, did not suddenly emerge from a social and political vacuum but had their origins in political trends which had slowly emerged in the state during the period of colonial rule. Post-independence Kelantanese politics, centering upon the PMIP's efforts to capture and retain power in the state, are but a continuation (from one point of view) of the main theme of Kelantanese politics during the colonial period: the rivalry of the established nobility and aristocracy of the state with emerging non-traditional elites for control over the state and for influence upon higher centres of power with which the state's affairs were bound up. The basis of modern politics in Kelantan lies in a kaleidoscopic reshuffling of the affiliations of traditional and non-traditional urban elites in Kelantan with parties at the national level and of their connections through rural elites with the peasant electorate in the countryside. It involves, on the one hand, the rivalry of the core of the state's established aristocracy with newer elites for control of Kelantan through control of a modern and electorally successful political party; and, on the other hand, the thwarting of the aristocracy's hopes by the PMIP, popular support for which came more clearly (as a shift took place in the class basis of political affiliation in the countryside) to represent the reluctance of the middle and lower peasantry to accept again the hegemony of a traditional elite representing interests regarded as opposed to their own.

II

The complexities of dynastic politics provided both the occasion and the pretext for British intervention in most of the Malay states, and Kelantan was no exception. Following the long reign of Sultan Muhammad II (1837–1886) the throne was briefly held by Sultan Ahmad (until 1890). Over the next decade the internal politics of Kelantan centred upon the rivalries of Ahmad's royal relatives. These royal rivalries were played out with shifting alliances of support from among the state's aristocracy, itself divided behind its leading strongmen. In 1900 Raja Muhammad, a grandson of Sultan Ahmad, came to the throne, backed alike by R.W. Duff, later by W.A. Graham and finally, after the imposition of the British protectorate, by the weight of the system of indirect rule under a British Adviser with its attendant constitutional fictions.[5] Subsequently, the recognition of the Raja as Sultan Muhammad IV was arranged by the British. Thereafter, the failure of To'

[5] See Mohamed, above.

Janggut's uprising—whatever its original nature[6]—confirmed both Muhammad's tenure of the throne and his dependence upon the British as guarantors of his position. Confirmation of Muhammad's position removed from dispute the succession question and thereby moderated the severity of royal politics. The British presence, however, did not automatically place the same kind of brake upon the aristocratic politics of manoeuvre around the throne (and now the Residency as well). The emergence, in the wake of the Pasir Puteh uprising, of Haji Nik Mahmud bin Haji Ismail[7] to a position of influence in Kelantan is part of that pattern of aristocratic manoeuvre, and the foundation of the *Majlis Ugama Islam dan Isti'adat Melayu Kelantan* (complex as are its origins[8]) was thus in part the product of aristocratic political rivalries. This fact has constituted part of the very nature of the *Majlis* in the eyes of some Kelantanese, and continues to do so with effects into modern times. In time, however, the British presence had its effect upon aristocratic politics as well: Haji Nik Mahmud's pre-eminence among the aristocracy was confirmed by the usefulness of his services to a succession of Advisers during his lengthy tenure of the Chief Ministership until 1942.

British colonial rule in Kelantan, as Emerson remarked (1937, 248ff) closely approximated to the ideal model of an indirectly ruled protectorate wherein the ostensible object of policy was the reform, rather than any fundamental transformation, of local society. Considerable use was made in local affairs of local talents, and opportunities for government employment (both at the administrative and at the lower clerical and technical levels) were opened to the more fortunate Kelantanese. One of the tasks which from the outset the Majlis set itself was the provision of educational facilities, in both English and Malay, for local Malay youths.[9] Thus, in addition to the considerable autonomous power which the Majlis (and those who controlled it) exercised under colonial rule over large areas of traditional Malay life, it also controlled access to the educational avenue out of traditional life and into modern salaried employment, together with its prestige and security.

Thus, even after the more immediate controversies surrounding the creation of the Majlis abated,[10] that body continued for some to be the object of intermittent criticism. For though, as it set zealously about discharging its new duties for the comprehensive administration of Islam, it became an impressive focus of religious life in the state, the

[6] See Ibrahim, above, and Allen (1968).
[7] Biographical details concerning Haji Nik Mahmud are given in Roff, above.
[8] Ibid.
[9] Ibid.
[10] Ibid.

Majlis nevertheless continued to present a dual nature—on the one hand as the formal instrument giving expression to the Sultan's leadership of the Faithful in his state, and on the other as both the product of, and as an instrument in, the pursuit of power by the leaders of the state's aristocracy. Whereas earlier critics, from among the former Mufti's supporters, had criticized the Majlis on somewhat parochial grounds, the criticisms which arose in the late 1920s and 1930s came from new directions and were aimed at the contemporary role of the Majlis. On the one hand, Islamic modernists criticized the religious bureaucracies in Malaya as strongholds of an outdated, erroneous and retarding version of Islam (Roff 1962; & 1967, 56–90); on the other, the creation of a system of Malay vernacular education in the state had given rise to a small but vociferous local intelligentsia in Kelantan. This intelligentsia created and supported a series of periodicals in which, often with guarded indirection, they gave expression to their views.[11] They attacked the state establishment as 'feudal' and criticized its privileges as benefits enjoyed at the expense of the Kelantanese people as a whole. By the end of the 1930s many of the intelligentsia, giving expression to that embryonic populist and radical nationalism which had characterized their journalistic efforts, had joined the semi-secret *Kesatuan Melayu Muda* or KMM (cf. Roff, 1967, 221–34), in which, ceasing to be exclusively concerned with parochial Kelantanese issues, they became involved in a widespread Japanese-sponsored web of pan-Malay and anti-colonial activity.

Meanwhile, however, the controversy between the Islamic modernists and traditionalists, centering upon the Majlis and reaching up to the highest levels in Kelantanese society, continued, reaching its climax in 1937 in a dispute over the cleanliness of dogs in which Dr. Burhanuddin (later to become President of the PMIP) played a small part on the modernists' side.[12] And while adjudication in that case favoured the modernists, such victories had meaning only at the elite level of the participants themselves and among their urban followings. In the countryside, where the overwhelming majority of the Kelantanese still lived as peasant agriculturalists, the general effect of the protracted argument seems to have been only to consolidate the allegiance of the peasantry to the traditionalist spokesmen and functionaries, both urban and rural. These traditionalists, in the face of modernist calls to purge Islam and restore its pristine purity, were far more tolerant of those local accretions to formal Islamic belief which were an inseparable part of rural folk Islam in the eyes of its adherents. Like the traditionalists, the peas-

[11] See Al-Ahmadi, above.
[12] See Muhammad Salleh, above.

antry and their village religious leaders found no use for subtle distinctions between an alleged core of Islam and local accretions of belief and practice, and the modernists thus made little headway in mobilizing a mass following with arguments which branded as un-Islamic practices which, for most of the peasantry, were the very stuff of Islam. At the same time the arguments and style of the traditionalist scholars (deriving from the *pondok* schools which remained in close contact with rural life) were familiar and acceptable to peasants separated by a wide social gulf from the contentions of the urban Cairo-oriented modernist elite.

The political and religious disputes of the 1930s in Kelantan thus saw the Majlis as the central target of the attacks of both the radical intelligentsia and the Islamic modernists. Neither of these groups made any great headway, either in urban society (where they collided with the superior weight of the state establishment) or among the rural peasantry, from whom they were separated by an unbridged social gulf. The peasantry, for their part, were strengthened in their allegiance to their rural spokesmen and leaders who, for the meantime, enlisted their politically still irrelevant sympathies, in the name of Malay tradition, behind the Majlis and the state establishment. Thus far, then, popular allegiance was to the side identified with the Majlis but not, it seems, to the Majlis itself: it was the lesser functionaries of that body (and the traditionalist teachers of independent position) rather than the office-holding aristocrats who enjoyed the primary loyalty of the peasants.

British policy in Kelantan in the 1920s and 1930s was a gradualist one, aiming at the preservation of continuity in local society rather than at any fundamental transformation of it. It looked to the emergence in the state of a British-sponsored model Malay monarchy: the Sultan at its head, its sinews a tutored gentry, while the whole superstructure was to be held up by the strong 'backbone' of a 'thrifty, prosperous and loyal peasantry' (Haynes 1932, 56–7). There thus survived in Kelantan, to a far greater extent than elsewhere in Malaya, a functioning Malay polity in a state which remained predominantly Malay and agricultural. Little European commercial development took place, while official policy and established local Chinese interests (as well as nascent Malay political sentiment) discouraged any influx of Chinese who might have engulfed the Malay population and undermined, by their commercial activities, the Malay peasant economy. In the 1930s, moreover, the politically influential aristocracy, remarking upon the fate of Malay society in the face of such disruptive changes elsewhere in the peninsula, exerted their influence that the same consequences should not follow in Kelantan, and a quite rigorous and effective Malay Reservations Act, consolidating measures going back to pre-colonial times to control the acquisition of land by outsiders, was enacted in 1930. This, of course, could only be achieved with British co-operation, but they, by this time, as their colonial custodianship in Malaya came to be questioned by non-Malays, happily rediscovered their treaty obligations to protect Malay interests. In the Unfederated Malay States, and especially in Kelantan, this turn in policy was taken to its logical conclusion by administrative officers who, identifying strongly with local interests, embarked upon a paternalistic programme which they believed would enable a traditional Malay society, based upon a rice-growing peasantry, to develop from within on its own resources and in its own direction, free from undesirable 'alien' influences.

The joint consequence of all these trends was to preserve in Kelantan a functioning and predominantly agricultural Malay society, the lives of the majority of whose members continued in many respects to be more directly affected by traditional patterns of peasant/gentry relationships than by the colonial administration itself or by new commercial interests and activities. Indeed, the result seems to have been markedly to strengthen many traditional features of Kelantanese society, but most especially the position of the established traditional elite and its hegemony over local life even in the remoter villages of the state. Such a paternalistic nurturing of what was fondly believed to be a traditional Malay society did not, of course, leave Kelantan unaffected.[13] But the survival under British protection of a Malay sultanate guarded by the colonial authority from all outside influences other than itself created the conditions wherein, from the outset, modern politics were intra-Malay politics centering upon divisions within Malay society rather than (as elsewhere in the peninsula) being dominated, as Malay society collapsed under the impact of an alien commercial revolution, by interethnic issues. It is not surprising then, given the nature of indirect rule, that the established state aristocracy so easily withstood the faint challenges to its position mounted during the colonial period by newer elites. That same pattern of elite rivalry was to survive as the major axis of Kelantanese politics in the post-colonial situation. The question would be that of the changes wrought in that pattern by an electoral democratic system wherein the previously unheeded voices of the peasantry, expressed at the ballot, would intermittently become an important factor in the state's political life.

★ ★ ★ ★

[13] This is made clear in my comments below, pp. 289-90.

In Kelantan, as elsewhere in Malaya, Britain's post-war proposals for Malayan Union provoked massive counter-demonstrations from the Malays. In Kota Bharu the demonstrators called for the preservation of the state's separate identity, for the continued recognition of Malay pre-eminence in the peninsula, and, symbolically encapsulating those two claims, for the retention of the Sultan to protect his people and head their religion in Kelantan. These anti-British demonstrations were supported by the two main political associations in the state at that time; by the *Persekutuan Persetiaan Melayu Kelantan* (PPMK) and the *Persatuan Melayu Kelantan* (PMK). Both were predominantly urban organizations and neither was particularly large or elaborate in formal apparatus. But there the similarity ends.

The PPMK aspired to be a popular association. For its membership it drew upon the Malay-educated of Kota Bharu and the district towns, while its leaders were the veterans of the KMM—that is to say, the same radical core who had constituted the journalistic intelligentsia in the 1930s. In addition to its more specifically focused political activities, such as the Malayan Union proposals called for, the PPMK maintained those wider social and educational interests which had characterized the previous journalistic preoccupations of its leaders. In *Penyedar*[14] they again attempted to create a journal as the vehicle for their critical activities; they also conducted surveys seeking to expose the neglectful deficiencies of colonial education in the state. Implied in such activities was a quite fundamental opposition, informed by populist nationalist sentiment, to colonial rule. For that reason the association and its leaders were considered suspect by the British authorities, and at the beginning of the Emergency in 1948 most of its leaders were detained. The PMK, on the other hand, was an elite association whose limited membership consisted mainly of the upper echelons of the indigenous, English-educated and aristocratic civil servants of the state. Efforts to found such an association had been made shortly before the war in Kelantan, but little had come of those efforts; now, however, from those origins, such an organization was resuscitated to face the exigency of the Malayan Union proposals.

Both these organizations were represented at the Malaya-wide congress, called in Kuala Lumpur, to oppose Malayan Union, as a result of whose deliberations the UMNO was founded under Dato' Onn bin Ja'afar. Heading the PMK delegation to the congress was Dato' Nik Ahmed Kamil, elder son of Dato' Haji Nik Mahmud who during the Japanese occupation had resigned from the position of Chief Minister

[14] See Al-Ahmadi, above.

of Kelantan which he had so powerfully held for some quarter of a century. Educated at the Majlis school and later at the Inns of Court in London, Dato' Nik Kamil had returned to Kelantan to succeed his uncle, Dato' Haji Muhammad bin To' Khatib Haji Mohd. Said,[15] as State Secretary at the age of 23. Within several years he was elevated to act as his father's Deputy Chief Minister, and in that capacity had played a prominent part in the revision and codification of Kelantanese laws (including those pertaining to the Majlis Ugama) in the late 1930s. Subsequently, Dato' Nik Kamil succeeded his father as Chief Minister in 1942.

After the foundation of the UMNO, national politics increasingly occupied Dato' Nik Kamil's attentions as he worked in close concert with Dato' Onn, and he was therefore succeeded as Chief Minister by Tengku Hamzah bin Tengku Zainal Abidin. Hitherto Tengku Hamzah, another graduate of the Majlis English school, had been State Secretary; his father, Tengku Zainal Abidin bin Sultan Muhammad III, was the former Raja Muda whose title had been changed to Raja Dewa when the British, shortly after the imposition of their protection upon Kelantan, had secured his assent which permitted the installation of Muhammad IV as Sultan and the recognition of the right of Muhammad's son, Tengku Ismail, to succeed him. Meanwhile, at the national political level, Dato' Onn was to leave the UMNO, founding in opposition to it first the Independence of Malaya Party and thereafter the Party Negara. Throughout this period, which also saw the defection from the UMNO of its religious wing to form the PMIP,[16] Dato' Nik Kamil remained loyal to Dato' Onn and to his new creation, the Party Negara, which, by the time of the 1955 elections, constituted the main focus of what Malay opposition there was to the still overwhelmingly powerful rump of the UMNO.

Kelantanese politics of the colonial period up to the 1955 elections evidence a single theme: the failure of new, emergent elites to gain any mass following or to make any dent in the hegemony exercised over Kelantanese life by the traditional nobility and aristocracy who had been co-opted into the system of indirect rule; and the consequent survival, as the fulcrum of Kelantanese politics, of a traditional elite who had monopolistically mediated the state's relations with the colonial authority. That elite now sought to play the same role for the state

---

[15] For details of the earlier career of Haji Muhammad bin To' Khatib Haji Muhammad Said see Roff, above.

[16] A clear account of the origins of PMIP has yet to be written. John Funston is currently engaged in writing a thesis on the subject for Monash University. I am grateful to Mr. Funston for allowing me to see an unpublished paper of his on the subject (Funston, n.d.).

in the emerging national political system; the 1955 elections in Kelantan thus came as a test of the old elite's ability to gain a popular mandate to continue playing its accustomed role under changed, and changing, circumstances.

★   ★   ★   ★

One issue was dominant, to the exclusion of all others, in the 1955 elections in Malaya—that of independence. The party which could most clearly and unambiguously claim to be for independence was the Alliance, which achieved a resounding victory throughout the country, including Kelantan where (in terms of candidates) it was represented almost exclusively by the UMNO. But those who represented the UMNO in Kelantan were a very different group from those who led it nationally and in the other states. When the broad Malay front of 1946 began to fragment, the UMNO rump which remained was very much a confederation of the old Malay political associations of the Malay administrative elites of the various states. In Kelantan, however, apart from a few notables of rather marginal status, control of a rather weak UMNO organization lay primarily with a politically inexperienced group of Malay-educated leaders, sons of petty traders and lesser wage-earning functionaries in the state's administrative apparatus. This new group was for the most part younger than the old radical intelligentsia, and though to a large extent they shared the latter's general outlook they were largely uncontaminated by the disfavour which the radicals had earlier called upon themselves. The reason for this somewhat peculiar complexion of the Kelantan UMNO leadership has already been suggested: that group in Kelantan which most closely approximated to the UMNO leadership in the other states was already committed to another party; Dato' Nik Kamil had remained faithful to Dato' Onn and his Party Negara, and had attached to that party the support of the quite cohesive core of the state's traditional aristocratic elite. In Kelantan in 1955 Party Negara was, and was also seen to be, the party of that core of the state's traditional elite who, by virtue of their fortunate birth and English education, constituted the upper echelons of the Kelantan Civil Service. In other words, it was the old PMK of 1946, now attempting to become a mass party by reaching down for support from a popular base. Party Negara was thus seen as the party of the old elite in Kota Bharu and of their large network of kin and clients in the capital and those rural areas where their influence was strong. To what extent this was an electoral disadvantage is unclear, but certainly the equivocal stance adopted by Party Negara towards the prospect of independence under the aegis of the Alliance Party was not a vote-winning one.

Similarly, the position adopted by the PMIP in the 1955 elections—calling uncompromisingly for independence on terms other than those which the Alliance was presenting, while expressing dissatisfaction with the terms and implications of the Alliance's constitutional proposals—was not one capable of being effectively presented in competition with the Alliance's readily appealing demand for a mandate for virtually immediate independence. Like the two other parties, the PMIP in Kelantan in 1955 lacked a developed organizational apparatus reaching out into the countryside where most of the voters lived. Moreover, as a party which had not yet elaborated or made fully clear its ideology and programme, it had no readily identifiable constituency of support, and a similar lack of social definition also characterized its leadership. Its public personalities tended to be traditionalistic *ulama*, behind whom stood a small group of radical, indeed in some cases somewhat secular, Malay nationalists whose earlier involvement in the Malay Nationalist Party (the post-war outgrowth of the KMM) had directed their attention to Indonesia as the fount of pan-Malay politics and as the repository of political strategies and experiences to be emulated. In addition to the traditionalistic *ulama* and the young radicals (many of whom served their apprenticeship in radical Islamic Malay politics in Perak before returning to Kelantan in expectation of the elections) some former members of the old intelligentsia joined or were sympathetic to the PMIP; others of the pre-war intelligentsia remained privately committed to the socialistic Partai Rakyat (which enjoyed miniscule support in the state) or else became sympathizers and supporters of the UMNO, with which at that time they could still feel a certain degree of ideological compatibility and social affinity.

The resounding Alliance victory in 1955 signalled the end of Party Negara as a real force in Malayan politics. Its defeat in Kelantan left the old elite three alternatives: the unlikely one of desisting altogether from involvement in modern party politics; the unpromising one of attempting to revive Party Negara; and the realistic one of attempting to find for themselves in an existing and successful party an instrument whereby they might reassert their control over the state's affairs. In time they came to choose the third. For the defeated PMIP, which had met with even less support in Kelantan than had the Party Negara, the choice was otherwise. Convinced that their time had not yet come and that their espousal in an Islamic idiom of the claims of a populist Malay nationalism would receive a more enthusiastic response after the implications of Alliance-sponsored independence had become clear, the PMIP leaders turned their attentions to the elaboration of the party's ideology and programme, and to the task of consolidating its leadership and its organizational arm reaching into the Kelantanese countryside. As the gentry and the PMIP leaders set about their chosen tasks they set in motion a process which was to take a decade to complete. For in Kelantan in 1955 the only case of an unambiguous identification of a national party with a local elite had been that of the Party Negara, which had sustained a mortal blow, whereas members of the contending non-traditional elites had been fragmented in their allegiances between the other parties. In the wake of the UMNO's victory in 1955 a process was set in motion which entailed the reshuffling of the political allegiances and party connections of the various urban elites in Kelantan, and of their connections through rural elites with the peasant electorate in the countryside. By 1969 that reconstitution of the same elements into a new configuration had been completed.

★   ★   ★   ★

The victory of the PMIP in Kelantan in 1959 (when the Alliance managed only to retain constituencies consisting of the commercial heart of Kota Bharu and part of the state's vast *ulu* hinterland, and when the PMIP carried the whole of the state in between those two extremes) came as a surprise, and bewildered observers chose to explain that outcome as the product of some mysterious tidal wave of archaic religious fervour. There is no doubt that the PMIP was swept into office on a massive wave of enthusiasm, but the sources of that enthusiasm need to be examined. Its origins lay in a complex concatenation of diverse facts, only some of which can be noted here.

The UMNO's defeat was in part a rejection of the politically inexperienced representatives elected in 1955, who after their election became entangled in bureaucratic politics in the capital and lost contact with their supporters in the countryside. But the UMNO cohort of 1955 faced special problems. Under the arrangements providing for a transition from colonial rule to independence (and combining elements of both) the members elected to the State Council in 1955 did not constitute a majority on that body, which continued to be dominated by appointed members from among the tutored and office-holding aristocracy. Moreover, the position of Chief Minister (still held by Tengku Hamzah) continued to be appointive, and its incumbent from among the majority of appointed members. Power in the Council, and state, thus remained in the hands of an elite whose recent attempt, in the Party Negara episode, to re-establish its political pre-eminence on a modern and popular foundation had been thwarted by the success of the UMNO candidates now confronting them as a minority in the Council. The election did not end their rivalry, which continued to be waged in a smaller arena not commanded by the winners at the election. In quite practical terms the UMNO representatives were stymied. Having no great influence upon the state's affairs, they were in no position to initiate, or become identified with, measures which might redound to their advantage in subsequent elections. It was only towards the end of this period, with the 1959 elections in view, that a new Chief Minister was belatedly appointed who might work more effectively with the elected members.

That new appointment was part of a larger shift in tactics. The approach of the 1959 elections intensified the rivalries between the various UMNO leaders (who looked to the expanded and wholly elective State Assembly to be chosen as the means of finally giving recognition to popular feeling and power to its representatives). These rivalries not only divided the party and weakened it in its approach to the electorate; those internal divisions also provided the opening for various members of the Party Negara to begin working their way to influence within what they believed would certainly be the winning party again. In going back to its supporters in 1959, the UMNO was thus riven with division, amongst its old guard and between the old and the new, all of whom, in the belief that that party would again prevail, were less concerned with the power of popular votes than with the powers which would accrue to the party after its expected victory.

The confidence that the UMNO would again win was, from one point of view, a natural one. It had kept faith with its supporters: it had promised in 1955 to bring about independence and to preserve Malay pre-eminence in the independent multi-racial state to emerge, and it had delivered on that promise. This expectation of continued Malay support, however, was focused exclusively at the level of national issues. It neglected important local dimensions of the political situation.

The UMNO leaders failed to note the gulf which had begun to separate their party from the Kelantan people, and, preoccupied with internal rivalries, they failed to detect a note of disappointment, even disillusion, which seems to have spread among the predominantly rural electorate. That disappointment, and resentment at the failure of the politically hamstrung UMNO representatives to acknowledge or alleviate the sources of peasant discontent, produced a disillusionment, not so much with party politics as such as with the Alliance and the independence which it had provided. Their experience of independence since 1957 did not match the peasantry's hopes which had been raised in 1955. Independence, for many of the Kelantanese, had connoted not merely a constitutional transfer of power but also a radical redress of a neglect of Malay peasant life which, they had been encouraged to believe, would necessarily follow from such a transfer of sovereignty from an alien power to the leaders of their own people. The UMNO victory in Kelantan had produced no such redress, while the Alliance's victory at the national level and a post-independence Alliance federal government had only served to deliver power of decision over Kelantanese peasant lives into the hands of those remoter from them (geographically, if not always socially and culturally) than had been the Advisers of the pre-independence period. Experience provoked a new, and more realistic, assessment of the nature of independence, but one which saw power and the benefits of the new order concentrated in the west coast states with their large non-Malay populations. This view carried with it a resentment against those who enjoyed power in the new national system, remote from Malay life as lived by its humbler adherents, and an extreme distrust of the motives of those Malays who worked within (and profited from) such an arrangement without showing any great concern for popular interests and hopes in the benefits of independence.

The popular, if inchoate, hope had been that independence would somehow redress a longstanding neglect of Malay rural society and of the interests of those who had increasingly to struggle for subsistence in it. Far from these hopes being fulfilled, a minor economic slump and a continuing fall in rubber prices (which most severely affected the wealthier and more influential villagers) seem to have persuaded the majority of the Kelantan electorate that the age of improvement for which they had voted in 1955 was receding rather than drawing nearer, and that the political promoters and constitutional provisions of independence were responsible. They had been made receptive to the appeals of a party which could successfully respond to their sense of grievance and which was prepared, in a fundamental critique, to lay the blame for those grievances upon the Alliance Party and the constitutional provisions of the independence it had attained.

*   *   *   *

What, it may be asked, were the sources of popular discontent in Kelantan? I argue that, whether or not the conditions of peasant life were objectively worse in Kelantan than in the other states, the distinctive pattern of development of Kelantanese society facilitated a clearer and earlier perception in Kelantan of the sources of rural grievance; and that the distinctive pattern of Kelantanese intra-Malay politics, unaffected by communal complications, facilitated the expression of class-based conflicts of interest within Malay society. I argue, then, that given the absence of ethnic pressures blurring the perception of class differences, Malay politics in Kelantan could give earlier expression to modern political differences within Malay society; and that, contrary to some commonly held views, Kelantanese support for the PMIP evidences not so much an obsessive xenophobia as an uninhibited intra-Malay rivalry often unmindful of any Sino-Malay political antagonism.

The Kelantanese coastal plain had long been densely populated. In 1921 it was, after the Kuala Lumpur urban area, the second most densely populated area of British Malaya (Thomson, 1921, 20). Population growth in Kelantan during the colonial period was slow, in part because of the steady migration out of the state which may attest to a shortage of land even at that time. The failure of Kelantan to be self-sufficient in rice throughout most of the colonial period may also attest to the same fact. British colonial rule, while strengthening certain traditional features of Kelantanese society, did not insulate the state entirely from modern changes (some of them hardly noticed by the British). British policy in Kelantan was much concerned with grandiose plans to survey and register all village lands in the state. This task, it was felt, was necessary to provide security to the yeoman peasantry which needed to be brought into being as the basis for a stable British-sponsored Malay monarchy. But just as happened earlier in England and France,[17] the very measures which released the peasants from their traditional obligations to a feudal aristocracy quickly became the means whereby encroaching market forces undermined the security of peasant smallholdings and placed control of the peasant sector increasingly within the grasp of those with more ready access than peasants to cash. Security of title benefits the cash buyer of land; it does so at the expense of the peasant's security of traditional tenure. His release from feudal obligation only prepares the means for his entrapment by capitalist mortgage. In the absence of a substantial Chinese middle class, and with a quite rigorously implemented Malay Reservations Act inhibiting the purchase of land by all save Kelantanese Malays, these new forces worked to the

[17] See Tawney (1912) and Marx (1958, 305–6).

advantage of four classes of local Malays: the wealthy aristocracy; those with salaried employment; the merchants; and the richer peasants, capable of producing surpluses for cash, in the countryside.

Thus, in circumstances where avenues of upward mobility out of peasant society were few, pressure of population on land exacerbated the difficulties of the lowest levels of a peasantry struggling to eke out subsistence. Such peasants, when forced to mortgage and sell their land, were generally bought out in Kelantan not by Chinese (as usually happened elsewhere in Malaya) but by local Malays. The rate at which this process has taken place in Kelantan has been influenced by the fact that, unlike some other areas of Malaya where peasants indulge in mixed farming or combine the subsistence cultivation of rice with the small-holder production of rubber for cash,[18] the Kelantanese peasant economy in most areas of the coastal plain has been overwhelmingly a single-crop economy. This affords the poorer rice-growers little scope to augment their income from other sources and thus to diminish their dependence upon (and the precariousness of their tenure of) their padi-fields. The purchase of small-holder land primarily by local Malays in Kelantan thus led to a less inhibited development of class differences within Kelantan Malay society, and, in the absence of numerous non-Malay landowners, to a clearer and earlier perception by the peasantry in Kelantan than elsewhere in Malaya of those economic divisions and conflicts of interest within Malay society. Already before the Japanese occupation Raymond Firth (1946, 296–7) noted the emergence of a new land-owner class in Kelantanese society as a result of British land policy.

These tendencies were accentuated in the post-war period. Not only did population increase, putting added pressure on the land; at the same time, changes at the macro-level in the Malayan economy (following the devastation of the occupation and reconstruction thereafter) would appear to have altered the condition of the surviving peasant sector. The increasing industrialization and commercialization inherent in the reconstruction policy diminished the overall significance of the peasant sector, and made it increasingly subject to the impact of the expanding modern sector. Thus, as the peasant population increased, and as people beyond the peasant sector increasingly gained access to cash which enabled them to buy up village lands, external pricing mechanisms more forcefully intruded into the rural economy. Given, at the same time, the importation from Thailand of superior but cheaper rice, there began an increasing discrepancy between the market value

[18] A detailed analysis of such a mixed peasant economy is provided by Swift (1965).

of land and the price commanded by any surplus from agricultural production which reached the market. A dislocation of the traditional village economy took place, caused by the impingement of external factors and expressing itself in a growing disparity between the increasing price and scarcity of land, on the one hand, and the more stagnant padi price on the other.

The effect of such trends, and most markedly in a predominantly one-crop rice economy, are clear. Security of title, and the readier access of non-peasants to cash, makes for insecurity of peasant tenure and thereby for loss of peasant control over the rural economy. A single-crop economy accentuates those trends discussed by Swift (1967) whereby marginal subsistence in times of crisis leads to mortgage and forced sale. In a mixed peasant economy, where risks are spread and where in addition to rice there are alternative (and more ready) sources of cash, the peasant whose tenure of his padi-lands is threatened may, unrealistically even, hope for some cash windfall, or may sell his rubber small-holding and thereby hope to redeem a mortgage or buy other padi-land. In a single-crop economy there is no basis for this perhaps illusory belief, and peasants in Kelantan have realized the irrevocable nature of the loss of village land. In consequence there has developed in Kelantan a quite fundamental and widespread anxiety over land, and over the prospects for a people and a whole way of life dependent upon land. There has followed an inchoate, but quite real, perception of the effects of increasing population, of the declining profitability of rice-growing and of the increasing purchase of village lands by those outside the peasant sector. In the 1950s Wilson's survey of the economics of padi production revealed a greater rate of tenancy and mortgage, and other symptoms of long-standing rural impoverishment, in Kelantan than in the northwest rice-bowl areas (1958, 30–1). Whether or not it was the case that in absolute terms the rural situation was worse in Kelantan than elsewhere, the ethnic homogeneity of Kelantan permitted a keener perception of the rural situation by the peasantry, and a rudimentary awareness of fundamental conflicts between peasant and non-peasant, between landlord and tenant, and between town and countryside.

The new independent political order in Malaya did not alleviate those anxieties over land. Rather, it increased them. Independence, and Alliance rule from Kuala Lumpur, entailed a new input of cash into rural society through the hands of a whole new class of salaried officials and of government and party functionaries. They did not merely aggravate the economic situation in the countryside; manifestly, the very loyalty of these new men to the UMNO (from whom their positions derived) led that party to be seen as the party of 'the comfortable people'—the new salariat and townspeople, and those in rural society who had some affinity of interest, and prospered by association, with them. The rejection by the electorate of the UMNO candidates in 1959 was thus part of a wider phenomenon—a rejection of the whole new order and those associated with it. As a group the assemblymen and bureaucrats and party functionaries had hoped to supplant in popular esteem the traditional leaders of rural society—headmen, *imam*, religious teachers and the pious men of the villages—who had hitherto enjoyed the immediate allegiance of the peasantry. These village leaders, who lived among the peasantry and fully shared their anxieties, saw the challenge to their own position which the new men represented. They saw that challenge as an assault upon village life as a whole: upon Malay peasant culture and upon Islam, which were the pillars of Malay village life, and of their position at its head. Their influence in rural society converted peasant land anxieties into a generalized concern at the prospects of traditional Malay culture and of an independent Malay peasantry in the new independent nation. These headmen and religious leaders found a special resonance in the PMIP's message, as the party voiced its doubts about the fate under the Alliance regime of Islam and traditional Malay values. In the months preceding the 1959 elections the PMIP had quietly gone about securing the committed support of the village leaders, and, through them, of the majority of the peasantry of Kelantan.

This linkage between traditional village leaders and the leaders of a party with whom they could identify created that wave of enthusiasm upon which the PMIP was swept into office. That victory brought into office, as the first elected chief minister of Kelantan, Ishak Lutfi Omar,[19] a former inspector of schools for the Majlis, who had been the representative of the PPMK at the national congress of the Malays in 1946. Together with him twenty-seven other PMIP candidates assumed their seats in the State Assembly, the overwhelming majority of them religious teachers, former *imam* and headmen from the countryside. Direction of the state's affairs thus fell into the hands of a group of men characterized equally by their unfamiliarity with bureaucratic procedures for the exercise of power and by their continuing close connections with village life and its traditional underpinnings.

★ ★ ★ ★

Thus, both in Kelantan and at the national level, the PMIP's victory represented the revival of the Islamic and radical populist forms of

[19] See Al-Ahmadi, above, Note 30.

Malay nationalism. Its success in Kelantan had been attained through the ability of Islamic and radical nationalist leaders, working upon the distinctive tensions within Kelantanese society, to effect a linkage with the mass of the electors through traditional rural leaders whose position was threatened by the new political apparatus of the centralizing state and its dominant party. The PMIP's success further complicated the lot of the traditional elite of Kelantan, who now faced two tasks: that of capturing full control of the Kelantan UMNO and of defeating the PMIP by it. Kelantan politics of the ensuing decade display those gentry objectives as their main theme. That period, and those efforts, were again to bring the Majlis into the forefront of Kelantanese politics. The Kelantanese peasantry in the 1960s, as in the 1930s, stood behind their traditional leaders in what they saw as a stand for Islam and Malay culture; but in the 1960s those leaders enlisted their support not to the cause of the Majlis but in opposition to the old elite's efforts, through the UMNO and the Majlis, to reassert its dominance over the state.

In its efforts to unseat the PMIP from power in the state, the UMNO attacked the PMIP as a party merely of rhetoric. Only the UMNO, it declared, could bring real benefits to the Malays; moreover, it claimed that in practical terms it was just as Islamic as the PMIP, which, it charged, merely exploited religion for its own ends without attempting to advance the cause of Kelantanese Islam. To press home that point the UMNO dwelt heavily upon the question of federal grants which might enable the building of modern mosques, built of stone and cement, to replace dilapidated mosques and prayer-houses built in traditional fashion of timber and thatch. The PMIP was reluctant to see such new mosques, erected by the UMNO, built in Kelantan, and the party averred that it was not bricks and mortar but faith which made prayer acceptable unto Allah. They cast back at the UMNO its own allegation that Islam was being used for political gain, and claimed that for the true Muslim prayer was more meaningful in a humble prayer-house, built by poor villagers with their own efforts and materials, than in an elegant mosque, provided as a facility by others but in which the congregants felt themselves as strangers.

Behind these claims lay more intricate, and worldly, issues. The UMNO's hopes of demonstrating its political effectiveness and goodwill towards the Kelantanese were obstructed by an impasse. The PMIP would co-operate in federal development projects provided it had a say in their location, but the Alliance would not accede to such conditions, which might allow the PMIP to point out to its supporters that they need not fear deprivation of federal government projects as a result of returning a PMIP state assemblyman to represent their constituency; on the other hand the PMIP would not allow the Alliance to put federal projects only into areas where the UMNO found strong support since this would be to the direct political advantage of the UMNO and would undermine PMIP support. Because of this impasse direct channels to the electors of Kelantan through the PMIP-controlled state government were closed to the Alliance and federal authority. The UMNO therefore put forward plans for the building of mosques which might remove the obstacle of state government intransigence. It sought a way to the electors through the Sultan and Majlis. Its victory in 1959, however, had given the PMIP access to channels of advice to the Sultan, and thereby a measure of control over the composition and policy of the Majlis Ugama. The Majlis was therefore susceptible to PMIP influence, and the PMIP was able temporarily to discredit the UMNO's mosque-building plans on the grounds that they were to be financed from the proceeds of the Social Welfare lottery, which, as gambling, was forbidden as a source of funds, if not for all purposes then at least for the building of places of Muslim worship.

In the heat of the 1964 election campaign, as the UMNO sought to discredit the PMIP for its alleged manipulation of Islam, its attacks came to be directed at the Majlis itself, where the PMIP was thwarting the mosque-building plans of the Alliance. The Sultan thereupon became unwilling to see the Majlis, which gave expression to his leadership of all the Faithful in his state, embroiled in partisan vituperation, and expressed his desire that legislation governing the Majlis Ugama be revised so as to raise that organization, and himself, above political dispute. New and comprehensive legislation was introduced in 1966. Among other things it revised Majlis appointment procedures so as to allow representation of both parties and to leave the balance of power and administrative competence in the hands of the personal appointees of the Sultan himself. Furthermore, the new legislation, whether by oversight or intent, failed to answer the hopes of the *imam* in the parishes of the state (about 75 per cent of whom had voted PMIP) for more adequate financial remuneration, thereby prompting, during the fasting month in 1967, a strike wherein all the *imam* of the state threatened not to collect the *fitrah* dues, payable at the end of the month, from which the Majlis derived a substantial portion of its revenue. The difficulties which the *imam* experienced in extracting any concession from the Majlis embittered them, and many of the PMIP's village *imam* were convinced that the UMNO was using the Majlis to strike through them at their party.

The Majlis, as suggested earlier, had from its very inception been implicated in Kelantanese politics, but the new measures, in popular opinion, did little to extricate it from such involvement. Under the new legislation Tengku Abdul Aziz—son of the former chief minister Tengku Hamzah, grandson of the Raja Dewa, and the current Sultan's senior son-in-law—was appointed President of the Majlis Ugama. At the same time, culminating the return of the Kelantanese elite to take over the UMNO in the state, Tengku Aziz's brother, Tengku Razaleigh, after studying economics and law in Britain, emerged (in concert with Dato' Nik Ahmed Kamil) as the effective head of the Kelantan UMNO; and thereafter the Crown Prince and only son of the Sultan married a niece of Tengku Aziz and Tengku Razaleigh. At about the same time federal funds for the construction of mosques began to flow through the Majlis (and a number of imposing structures were completed by the time of the 1969 elections). Thus, in popular estimation, the Majlis, far from being extricated from compromising political entanglements, was by the new legislation made into an explicit instrument of the old elite's bid, backed from Kuala Lumpur and in UMNO garb, to reassert its control over the state. When, shortly before the 1969 elections, the Majlis issued instructions to the predominantly PMIP-inclining *imam* of the state not to mention politics in their weekly sermons and circulated authorized sermons to be read, these popular suspicions were reinforced.

With the formal apparatus for the administration of Islam in the state thus (in their eyes) compromised and tainted, popular village Islam, as expounded by religious teachers and *imam* sympathetic to the PMIP, came increasingly to represent the focus of the religious allegiance of the peasantry, and thereby to provide the idiom and motivation for the expression of popular interests—interests centering upon the PMIP and in opposition to the elite, town and federal interests which, in popular eyes, the UMNO had come to embody and promote. And as the UMNO, by the weight of its superior organizational force, began its strenuous campaign activity, the rich Islamic repertoire of belief, going back to the tribulations endured by the Prophet Muhammad himself—beliefs which allow the force wielded by powerful opponents to be presented both as a test of the true believer's commitment and as the proof of the essential correctness of the cause espoused by the weak and the vulnerable—came to play an important part in validating, in their own eyes, the actions of the PMIP's supporters and in cementing their allegiance to their party.

During the 1960s the UMNO succeeded in making substantial inroads into the PMIP's support. The defections to the UMNO were not without their significant implications. In 1959 the villagers of Kelantan had voted overwhelmingly for the PMIP; the diminution in PMIP support over the decade was to reveal where the real strength of the party lay and which interests it most effectively articulated.

The UMNO made itself increasingly acceptable in Kelantan in the 1960s because of the lack of any seemingly viable alternative to the Alliance at the national level; it thus won a kind of resigned, even grudging, loyalty in Kelantan. Some villagers, furthermore, wearied of the ineffectuality of PMIP rule and of the stymied relations between federal and state authority and, eager for change, came to accept that an UMNO government in the state was the only means to secure federal funds which might lift Kelantan out of its neglect and stagnation. Most converts who allowed themselves to be persuaded by these arguments were villagers who, because they were not fundamentally dissatisfied with their position in rural society, had some affinity of interest with the UMNO and its rural representatives and who recognized that they stood to prosper under an UMNO state government. These converts consisted principally of wealthier landlords, often those who engaged in petty trade and money-lending and who were thereby acquiring village lands through mortgage and forced sale. They were those who saw that they might prosper individually, without having to throw in their lot with a movement collectively to defend what were regarded as popular and common interests. The poorer villagers, on the other hand, quite realistically saw that the rich were prospering at the expense of the poor, whose land they were buying; they also saw that the Alliance's Kemubu Irrigation Project would work far more to the advantage of the rentier landlords than of the small-holders and tenants. Conversions to the UMNO thus only accentuated for the lower peasants the fact that the UMNO was the party which appealed to and represented the interests of those against whom in local terms their own interests stood opposed. In other words, the diminution of PMIP support through the defections of the wealthy and comfortable shifted the axes of political allegiance towards those of class interest and, in not altogether inchoate form, was popularly seen to do so. Stripped bare, a clearer structure emerged. Villagers spoke of the UMNO as the party 'of the blue-bloods, of the townsfolk and of the wage-earners, and of their friends who sit comfortably, lending money and buying land, while others labour in the fields'.

The emerging class-lines of support for the PMIP became increasingly clear. It drew its support from among a middle and lower peasantry whose anxieties over land were expressed in the idiom of the protection of a traditional village way of life based upon the small-holder's relation to his land. For example, the UMNO, to underline its claim that the PMIP had no monopoly on Islam, gave place of honour at its party rallies to UMNO-supporting village hajis who at the same time en bloc were the local traders, larger landowners and money-lenders. The duality of their role did not escape the poorer villagers, nor did tenant farmers fail to appreciate the irony involved when landlords, one day after haggling with their share-croppers over the division of the year's harvest, returned next day urging the view that the UMNO was the best protector of the security of the Malay people as a whole. Thus generalized resentments against the UMNO and more specific resentments against its beneficiaries and representatives in rural society reinforced each other, and, in response to internal developments within the UMNO, that party had by 1969 come to be seen by many villagers as the party serving the interests of those, in village society and beyond, who showed no great concern over the survival of an independent Malay peasantry. It had come to be seen as the federally-backed instrument of the old elite and its rural retainers in the elite's bid to reassert its control over, and against the interests of, the peasantry of Kelantan.

When the UMNO candidates for the 1969 election were declared, one local observer, upon looking at the list, remarked upon the lack of subtlety with which the old Party Negara was making 'a scarce-disguised comeback in UMNO garb'. And when the PMIP won its third election in 1969, and the Kelantan electorate rejected the 'special offer' of $546 million of projects should the Alliance be returned to power in the state, one village lady metaphorically remarked that 'There'll be no fine cow given away free, but whose would it have been anyway?'

* * * *

Underlying the political division in the Kelantanese countryside, therefore, were socioeconomic factors of some importance. Given that fact, it is no longer possible to depict support for the PMIP as simply the outbreak of an archaic religious fanaticism. On the contrary, it constitutes a response to real issues and contemporary predicaments. To assert, however, that support for the PMIP reflects underlying class tensions in the countryside and that it is based upon a not unrealistic assessment of the nature of antagonistic interests in rural society does not mean that the PMIP supporters see (or that outside observers may see) that political stance as an explicit act of class-conscious strategy. But while such a long-term and analytical assessment of the peasant predicament may be lacking in Kelantan, support for the PMIP does nevertheless represent an effective and realistic, if short-term, response to some of the more pressing problems of the poorer peasants—the small-holders, and those who, combining work on their small-holdings with share-cropping, still try to think of themselves as members of an independent peasantry. The realistic and practical nature of support for the PMIP may be illustrated.

Quite apart from the many small favours done by the PMIP to many Kelantan electors during its decade of rule in the state, the federal constitution did leave land matters entirely in the hands of the state governments, and when the failure of political co-operation between federal and state authority deprived Kelantan of federally funded land development schemes, the PMIP state government began to make available vast areas of upriver Kelantan as small-holdings to be opened up by the individual efforts of landless grantees from the densely populated areas of the Kelantan delta. But even in cases where it did not make land available in this fashion, the PMIP state government's exclusive control over land matters was of considerable political importance. Most Kelantan peasants, insofar as it is possible to make the distinction, cared less about large questions of national political principle than about their own immediate interests and preoccupations in Kelantanese village society. These centred primarily upon land, and often involved complex bureaucratic problems of taxes, titles and transfers. What primarily they wanted was some effective means of dealing with those very complex, and for them difficult, matters, and irrespective of whether in national terms the UMNO was the dominant Malay party, so long as the PMIP held state power it was most often more immediately in their interests to side with those who had effective control over village land matters.

Furthermore, for such purposes it was more in their interest to elect a PMIP than an UMNO local assemblyman, not only because the PMIP was (and seemed likely to continue to be) the governing party at the state level, but also because with great insight they saw that they had greater control over a PMIP than an UMNO assemblyman and could therefore work more effectively for their own ends through him. The electors remembered that in the past UMNO assemblymen had often neglected their constituents, and they had seen that the self-interest of

UMNO assemblymen did not require them to keep in close contact with their electors. For if they were professionals, they might, after five neglectful years of office and subsequent defeat, revert back, for example, to a legal career; and even if they had no such independent position or resources to fall back upon, defeated UMNO candidates (the electors had seen) would be well looked after by their party—for example, with a job in the party machine or in the federal government's rural adult education programme. PMIP candidates, on the other hand, were usually men of lesser means more closely tied to village life in their constituencies. They had no soft cushion to fall on, and their party's resources to provide for them after defeat were limited. Thus, if they wanted to continue enjoying their elected position and avoid rebuff at the end of their term, they had to keep in close contact with their electors and deal seriously and sympathetically with the varied problems brought before them. PMIP assemblymen were thus significantly dependent upon their voters and this, the voters saw, enabled popular opinion appreciably to influence the actions of elected PMIP representatives. Their representatives' dependence gave the voters the effective leverage to have their often quite minor but complicated problems adequately seen to at the District Office and at the state government level. One percipient UMNO leader, despairing of his party's ability ever to get the Kelantanese peasantry to accept his party's view of politics, exclaimed: 'These people don't elect a representative or policy-making assemblyman—they elect themselves a welfare officer!' For such purposes Western-educated professionals of independent position from outside the constituency were of little use, and unlike local PMIP representatives, were subject to few controls on the part of the voters.

Thus on one occasion an UMNO official was berating the peasantry for their refusal to elect professionally competent UMNO candidates who might be, in his terms, really effective in state government, and for preferring their own 'village nobodies' of no training and little experience in the high art of administration. The object of his remarks was a PMIP state assemblyman, and member of the State Executive Council, who, before becoming a PMIP candidate, had been a petition-writer in one of the district towns. The UMNO official could not see that his background—the man's intimate knowledge of the kind of administrative complications which peasants wish to have sorted out, and his vast experience of the ways in which redress could effectively be secured by intercession with the District Office or State Land Office—was in many ways an ideal training for a state assemblyman, and certainly one which, in his constituents' eyes, made him not only accessible but also most useful. That same assemblyman—who took a personal and sympathetic interest in his constituents' problems, and who would often stop his car by the road in order to help a constituent bring his goods to market—exemplified the care which most PMIP assemblymen took (and had to take) over their supporters. The same man, in a village speech, once declared that the PMIP state government had made over a nearby area of common grazing land (dating back to colonial times) to village agricultural use because his party, unlike others, gave priority to the needs of people over those of cattle. The argument may have been specious, but it resonantly articulated the state government's style and the reasons why the PMIP was able to retain the support of so large a part of the Kelantan electorate despite its inability to implement any great projects for change.

III

In conclusion, I return to consider the nature of the Islamic political appeal in Kelantan, and to show how in Eric Wolf's terms (1969, xi) the idiom of village Islam has lent a 'transcendental' dimension to mundane village life and to the political response of the villagers of Kelantan.

In my earlier discussions (1972 & n.d.) of how, in Kelantan at least, the Islamic political appeal works I pointed out that there is, almost inevitably, a tension between religiously inspired world-views and the social experience of the believer. In Islam this tension is particularly acute since, of all the world religions, Islam alone claims to possess an adequate and comprehensive social theory. In the eyes of its adherents it is consciously seen as *the* sociological religion. But the social theory of Islam is in some respects problematic. Its very idealism, and the circumstances of its elaboration, make that social theory a potent weapon for the criticism of almost any existing social and political order, but most especially by a solitary group of people who share a common and fundamental belief that they live in a far from ideal society articulated in accordance with narrow interests not their own. Islam thus provides an idiom for the presentation of moral claims upon unresponsive authority. It not only provides an idiom, or vehicle, for the expression of neglected popular interests and for a demand that justice be done by those interests; it also provides a means of translating those sectional demands into a morally sanctioned and universalistic form. It facilitates the presentation of a demand for redressive justice as a general social interest and casts those at whom the popular demand is directed into the role of protectors of sectional and immoral interests selfishly hostile or unresponsive to the demands of the 'general will'. How is this transformation brought about?

The political impact of Islam is generated by the tension between the purportedly complete, but nevertheless problematic, social theory of Islam and the social experience of the believer. The problematic part of the theory, and thus also the tension, are engendered by the effort to reconcile idealized Islamic views of the nature of man and society with the inescapable facts of political life. For politics is about social division and sectional interest, about antagonism and rivalry, and it is just these facets of social life which the highly idealistic social theory implicit in Islam finds difficult to acknowledge. As I have argued, Islamic social theory is overwhelmingly ethical and individualistic. Its focus is upon the individual, and it looks to the possibility of his behaviour being actuated by higher principle rather than being conditioned by baser interests and actual social circumstances. The means by which it attempts to realize that possibility are almost exclusively hortatory. Consistent with the egalitarian ethos of its Kuranic foundations, this theory construes the nature of social obligations in a special way. By and large, obligations attach themselves to men in virtue of their common, and divinely created, humanity rather than inhering in particular social statuses. More than a theory, then, the Islamic view is a vision of the kind of society which would, or presumptively should, emerge quite automatically if men would only act in accordance with those higher principles of personally disinterested motivation which the religion urges. It is thus an individualistic theory in the sense that it is largely blind to the existence and role in society of organized groups, intermediate between the individual and the total community, and to their sectional interests. Its stress is upon the nexus of mutual obligations subsisting between, on the one hand, a total community and, on the other, a morally depicted individual who is conceived of atomistically, stripped of any particular social status, as the major constitutent component of a society and its theory. This unmediated polarity of individual and community sets up the key terms and problems of Islamic social theory, and generates the main points of tension, as manifested in individual behaviour, between social theory and social reality. Thus a social theory which portrays social relations between the public and private domains in moral and idealistic terms both enables and requires sectional interests to be advanced as overall social needs; and a theory of society which makes no clear distinction between the political regime and the community (and which validates the former by allowing it to masquerade as the latter) translates the advancement of neglected sectional interests into a legitimate rejection of a political authority morally disqualified by its unresponsiveness.

The key terms, and problematic points, of Islamic social theory focus upon the tension between personal interests and the common interest, and between privately interested action and moral and personally disinterested commitment. These antinomies are presented in Islam as the opposition between sincerity and reason, on the one hand, and deceit and personal desire, on the other. (The same problems, of course, are those of all social theory, but, as I have suggested, they are highlighted with an unparallelled sharpness in Islamic social thought). Inherent in such a position is a grave distrust of private ends, a suspicion that they are the product of baser desires which threaten to seduce men away from the reasoned recognition of their joint interests with, and obligations towards, their fellow men.

For the Kelantanese, just as James Siegel has pointed out (1969, 102–4) for the Achehnese, this opposition is expressed in terms of the opposition between *nafsu* (the animal desires of the flesh and the temptations towards a morally unregulated pursuit of private ends) and *akal* (the intelligent and reflective control whereby the individual, weighing his own motives and interests with a degree of detachment, holds his desires in check to the extent that they are subversive of his moral bonds to his fellow man and community). Anything which would seem to be prompted by the attempt of *nafsu* to subvert the tenuous dominance of *akal* is therefore to be deplored and resisted. For example, the more orthodox Kelantanese villagers who revile the shadow-play as un-Islamic do not revile it so much, as is sometimes suggested, because it involves invocations to godlings from a non-Islamic pantheon whose existence might detract from the Unity of the one true God, but rather because the insistent and reverberating tunes of the shadow-play orchestra, which make people spin their heads and tap out rhythms, thereby agitate and activate their *nafsu*, perhaps to the extent that they will forget themselves and act beyond the constraints of a moral and morality-supporting *akal*. The same argument applies to the *main puteri*, or healing seance, and, to a lesser extent, to more modern forms of entertainment. Similarly, one PMIP *alim*, aware of the precariousness of the command of *akal* over *nafsu* and seeking to argue why Islamic law should be mandatory upon all the citizens of a country which was but 50 per cent Muslim, claimed the law of Islam and Allah to be *hukum akal* whereas secular law and the law of other religions were *hukum nafsu*. The two, he averred, could not co-exist side by side, because, necessarily, the tolerated operation of base *hukum nafsu* would subvert the operation of the higher *hukum akal*. Again, old villagers have remarked to me that this world is a prison for the faithful because, unlike the infidels, they are enjoined to desist from the temptations of *nafsu*; in heaven, on the other hand, the virtuous who have resisted the insistent temptations of *nafsu* in this life will be richly rewarded with all the pleasures of personal and bodily enjoyment which in that realm will no longer be tainted with Satanic *nafsu*.

In this context of ideas the notion of 'sincerity' takes on a particular meaning which merges with that of disinterest. Sincerity does not connote a brutally honest recognition, and explicit declaration, of where one's interests and inclinations lead one, but rather refers to an unburdened state of mind in which one may properly approach one's fellow man. That state of mind is one of equanimity and lack of tension, attained by one's own already successful efforts to bring self-regarding inclinations under control. It comes from the conscious and successful subordination of *nafsu* to *akal*. Only then, in the recognition that one's own inordinate and insistent interests may cause disharmony and conflict, can one approach others in that moral and mutually regarding fashion which prevents one from doing violence to them.[20]

This notion of sincerity may be contrasted with the English usage, which suggests an even crudely forthright frankness—not the renunciation of private interests and ends, but the explicit acknowledgement of their irresistibility. It was this latter notion which seemed, to many Kelantanese, to be manifested in the UMNO's approach to them. The UMNO claimed to be sincere, but made itself morally unacceptable by the very terms in which it proclaimed its sincerity. In a speech at the laying of the foundation-stone of a mosque during a Kelantan by-election, the then Deputy Prime Minister, Tun Abdul Razak, made the following forthright declaration to the electors of the district:

> It is said that we of the UMNO harbour ill-will against the people of Kelantan, and that we refuse to help this state to progress from its backward condition. This is not true. We have only the best of intentions towards all the people of Kelantan and all the Malay people. There is nothing that we would like more than to be able to help you. But, alas, as things now stand we cannot. I shall be completely frank and sincere (*ikhlas dan jujor*) with you. We cannot help you until you turn the PMIP out of power in this state and elect an UMNO government in its place. The reason is simple: we cannot help you until you enable us to help you. We can only help those who help

[20] Geertz's discussion (1960, 72–6 & 238–41) of the term *ikhlas* in the Javanese context is relevant here, as are Jay's allied remarks (1969, 66–7 & 177) on the concept of *rukun*.

us. We can only provide projects to those who vote for us. This is sincere talk. Those are our terms and that is our offer.

Such a position was incomprehensible to the Kelantan electors, or rather, in terms of what they understood by it, Tun Razak's protestation was self-contradictory. In coming with his own terms and in attempting to drive a bargain, Tun Razak was seen as being not merely intransigent but also violent. By his refusal to acknowledge the kind of people and commitment he was confronting, and by refusing to admit that there were fundamental differences of interest and allegiance separating his listeners from him, Tun Razak was seen as committing some kind of moral and social violence. He was, in his listeners' terms, being anything but sincere. With an undisguised measure of inflexible self-interest he was offering them a mosque, and other benefits, provided they forgot about their fundamental principles and simply concentrated upon the undeniable attractions of what he offered them. In short, Tun Razak's appeal was seen by his listeners as an appeal to *nafsu*. To them his behaviour was that of *nafsu*, and his appeal was that others should relate to him on that same basis.

The same view characterized the popular reaction to the special offer of $546 million of projects during the 1969 election. That offer, too, was seen as an appeal to *nafsu*. It was not that the projects and their benefits were unwanted, but precisely because they were wanted the inclination to seek them was to be distrusted and resisted. For so lavish an offer was construed as an appeal to the worst inclinations, that men must seek to suppress, and anyone who might come with such temptations was, in quite a real sense, an ally of the devil—whose protestations of generosity, goodwill and sincerity are not to be taken at face value. The special offer was thus seen as an attempt to subvert a moral stance which had withstood a variety of assaults for a decade:

'Why,' asked the leader of the PMIP at a village rally, 'do they make a special offer only to the people of Kelantan, when for years they have scorned and abused us? When for years they have failed in their bids to seize control over us? Why have they made no special offers to the Malays in other states who have supported them faithfully over the years? Why have they put this price of $546 million on us alone? Because their own people have no price! Why do they approach us with inducements of money? Because of *nafsu*!'

Dato' Muhammad Asri, in this explanation, was not only calling into question the sincerity and good faith of the Alliance, and suggesting that the UMNO was attempting to do a deal between its own *nafsu* for power and the ever-present and tenuously controlled *nafsu* of the

Kelantanese for worldly goods. He was also saying that those who might succumb, and who had in the past succumbed, to the Alliance's tempting offers had a price but no value; the Kelantanese supporters of the PMIP, on the other hand, precisely because they prized themselves and their own commitments in far more than material terms, could not be won over through *nafsu* by the price of money. He who acknowledges his own *nafsu* has already all but succeeded in overcoming it; those who do not acknowledge, but act upon, their own *nafsu*, are thwarted in the pursuit of their private ends by the refusal of others to act impulsively upon unregulated *nafsu* alone.

The UMNO's repeated blindness to the limits of its own notion of sincerity led to an inability to see that the terms in which it presented itself to the Kelantanese peasantry served only to alienate them from the UMNO and strengthen the terms of their allegiance to the PMIP. It therefore brought into disrepute the whole Alliance effort to persuade the Kelantanese of the advantages of modernity. It served morally to discredit the UMNO itself and all its promises and declarations. All the claims of miles of roads built by the Alliance federal government, of mosques erected, of land projects opened, and of the value in money of all these efforts—the naked statistics of its quantified claims, suggested that the UMNO was a party of *nafsu* which appealed to *nafsu*. On the other hand the PMIP repeatedly denied that it was against progress; it was opposed only to the kind of progress the Alliance offered and the way it was offered. A PMIP candidate declared:

> The UMNO claims that we are against progress. We are not. But we are against their kind of progress. Theirs is a progress of bricks and mortar only, superficial and materialistic. That is not the kind of progress which is either desirable or necessary. What is required is that sort of progress which is sought by, and which will benefit, the people as a whole—not display projects but projects directed at the needs of all the people, most especially the ordinary people who, for all the years of Alliance rule, are still ground down in hardship and poverty. For us the concept of progress is not simply an economic concept, measurable in terms of the number of factories or land schemes which have been opened. For us progress consists of uplifting a society and a people from material poverty, social oppression and a crippling backwardness. Its goal is moral, not just material. It is directed to the people and its own dignity. That, back to the time of the Prophet Muhammad, is the Muslim meaning of progress.

The Kelantanese were not the first to choose what they regarded as justice' over material concepts of progress, and it is difficult to assert that their choice was a wrong one. In making that choice they were voting in accordance with what they saw as their own interests. But the terms in which their demands were cast transformed the appearance of those interests from being the sectional interest of a group in society to a moral imperative of society as a whole. Once questions of interest have been cast into the mould of *nafsu* and sincerity, an antagonism between two sectional interests is transformed into a conflict between the moral requirements of social life itself and those who seemingly choose not to acknowledge them. The unmediated polarity of public and private interest permits one of the contending sides to pre-empt, and present itself as, the claims of the public good. The antagonism is transmuted into an apparent conflict between legitimate social imperatives and illicit private interests. And since it is the political authority of the community which is identified with the latter, that authority is morally disqualified from legitimacy.

The PMIP has thus tapped some profound and fundamental Islamic appeals in order to mobilize a committed rejection of the Alliance government's plans for the creation of a new modernizing society in Malaysia. Far from being otherworldly in its appeals, the PMIP has called forth from its supporters an energetic stance towards the life of this world and towards the actual political circumstances within whose constraints peasant life is lived. Far from eliciting support by threatening to deny the attractions of the afterlife to recalcitrants among a devout peasantry, the PMIP has mobilized support by the more than merely rhetorical appeal of the Islamic themes of commitment and of the significance of hardship not as a punishment but as a trial for true believers. In this fashion the Kelantanese peasantry, aware of their own shortcomings of knowledge and observance as Muslims and of the limited opportunities available to them for continual and practical political activity would, on special occasions and at the party's call, take a stand on principle, asserting the value to themselves of their own self-respect in the more widely recognized currency of the price of their own votes. In such moments—by their commitment and through their refusal to place a purely material price on themselves and by means of the party's ability to endow their endurance of hardship with meaning and dignity—the Kelantanese peasantry would, in an exemplary act made in admittedly extraordinary circumstances, approximate momentarily to those ideal standards of principled and 'disinterested' Muslim behaviour which, as worldly and of necessity materialistic peasants, they are in their mundane lives so far (even in their own estimation) from attaining. Thus to many Kelantanese, Islam represents their own potential but generally unactualized ideal selves; and the PMIP represents Islam, not because of any irresponsibly purveyed short-cuts to salvation but because the party has the ability (and hence in their eyes also the right) to call forth their unfulfilled selves, albeit transiently and sporadically, in the name of Islam.

In other words, the Kelantanese affirm to themselves in terms of periodic devoutness a standard of Muslim behaviour which they do not (and know they do not) equally attain in their daily lives in terms of knowledge and orthodoxy and formal observance. Thus for many Kelantanese who are either unable or disinclined to act in continual conformity to the letter of religious obligation, periodical opportunities for evidencing a transitory but exemplary commitment come to be seen as opportunities to offset, in their profit-and-loss accounts for salvation, their deficiencies in formal observance. For a meticulous attention to such formal requirements is commonly regarded by them as ideally a mode of religiosity appropriate only to learned teachers and aged villagers preoccupied with approaching death; it is also seen as a mode in practice often affected by those of UMNO-inclination and dubious 'sincerity' who, abstaining from committed Islamic action in those moral and political contexts where they themselves regard such behaviour as mandatory, are seen as giving but the lip-service of 'praying with the mouth but not the heart'.

In Kelantan, then, idealized Islamic notions of the nature of man and society have come to constitute a form of 'inverted world consciousness' (Marx, 1964, 41) providing illusory or temporary fulfillment to the unfulfilled and immaterial recompense to the materially unrewarded. This has been possible precisely because of the very tensions between social experience and Islamically-inspired social theory. The Islamic vision of the just society, articulated by the PMIP, has been the moral touchstone of a rejection of the UMNO and Alliance. That vision of the just society, consisting of individuals motivated by principle rather than immediate interest, has provided the behavioural rhetoric in which a peasantry (whose mundane lives are far from being uniformly principled and unmaterialistic) become momentarily in their own eyes the kind of people who would populate the envisaged just society of Islam. Thus in a perhaps somewhat ritualized gesture, when the normal social order and its familiar motivational considerations are suspended, the Kelantanese attain in their own eyes that perfection they are enjoined unto, and thereby also exempt themselves from attempting to live the exemplary lives of the just in what they regard (by ideal standards) as an unjust society.[21]

[21] This argument concerning the nature of the Islamic political appeal is a version of the

Here a further point becomes important. For some of the PMIP leaders, and for many of its supporters in the countryside, the argument between the UMNO and the PMIP is, at some fundamental level but in an ill-defined way, an argument about the feasibility and desirability of implementing Islamic social theory—of building a society on the basis of the Kuran and Islamic law and of the practice of the Prophet Muhammad himself when he created and led the first Islamic society in Madina. Certain of the PMIP's *ulama* strongly maintained that the implementation of Islamic theory was not only desirable and possible but also necessary and obligatory, and these claims were enthusiastically received by many of the PMIP's supporters. The UMNO, on the other hand, without rejecting Islam, would maintain that the modern world was too complex to be governed by the shackles of so limited and traditional a view, and while approving of a society governed by general 'Islamic principles' would maintain that it was no longer possible to organize a society in detail, or live a life in the modern world, in strict conformity to traditional legal-religious principles. Their claim, then, was that Islamic theory was no longer applicable to, and could not alone govern, many areas of modern life, most especially the realm of politics.

The UMNO thus appealed to the voters not to attempt what was in its view the impossibility of living, and acting politically, in accordance with what was imagined to be Islamic theory. This appeal, however, presented itself as a challenge to voters who believed that such a theory existed and was capable of being acted upon. And when the UMNO appealed to voters to act instead in accordance with what it regarded as a sensible and realistic assessment of where their interests lay, they chose to act in accordance with their own rather than the UMNO's implicit theory of political behaviour. In so doing, they acted in the real world in accordance with a theory which the UMNO claimed could not be acted upon in the real world. Thereby, and paradoxically perhaps, they produced real political consequences which repeatedly reconfirmed and revalidated for them a view of man and society which the UMNO asserted was politically inapplicable. Their response, then, was to prove the UMNO wrong by enacting that theory in both a symbolic and

---

anthropological analysis of 'ritual reversals,' wherein certain features of an unideal but inescapable reality are in ritual temporarily denied while, in a ritual assertion, what ideally should be is given expressive ascendancy over what is. Such ritual statements not directly but inversely reflect social reality: the ideal counterpoints the real. Thus Beidelman (1966, 465) similarly argues that for the Nuer sacrifice 'is both a symbolic model ... of the social processes of their society and also a kind of pledge ... that Nuer remain aware of moral order, even though they cannot and do not wish to conform to it entirely in all states of their everyday lives.'

practical assertion of its applicability. And while in general they could not accept the UMNO's pragmatism, whereby actions were to be judged in terms of practical results, but rather chose to evaluate actions by the meanings attached to them, they would, by repeatedly giving the PMIP their support, vindicate their allegiances and themselves in the UMNO's own terms—in the PMIP's quite tangible electoral successes which denied the UMNO the power it so ardently sought. It is little wonder, then, that the UMNO made such small headway in its efforts to convince the PMIP supporters of the irrelevance of 'Islamic social theory' to their own lives.

IV

In this account I have attempted to indicate the depth and complexity of the sources of popular support for the PMIP in Kelantan. In so doing I have sought to highlight the deficiencies of other accounts of the same phenomenon which in facile fashion and with neat but crude typologies speak of religious fanaticism, peasant traditionalism and of the survival of archaic political responses. I have attempted to show how factors from quite diverse realms—from traditional and elite politics of the colonial period in Kelantan and from the changing conditions of peasant life—have meshed together to produce a rich and complex outcome whose true nature has not hitherto been adequately recognized. Above all, I have sought to indicate the central role of popular Islam in welding together those diverse trends and galvanizing the political response of the Kelantanese peasantry to their present predicament. I have sought to show how the elusive strength of the PMIP in large measure rests upon the fact that popular Islam is at one and the same time both the object and instrument of a movement to defend what are regarded as peasant allegiances and interests. I have also sought to indicate what political linkages bind the peasants to allies beyond rural society, how those linkages relate to divisions within rural society, and how also the multiple role of Islam binds the peasants to each other and to the party which is the vehicle of their demands. I have sought to demonstrate that a crucial part of that rearguard action by the peasantry is the defence of such elusive things as their sense of their own worth and dignity and of the culturally given terms which they employ to validate to themselves their own existence. Popular Kelantanese Islam, in other words, is not only an idiom for the perception and discussion of grievances. It is also a way of apprehending the world which carries with it ways of acting in the world. Popular Islam provides the Kelantanese with an implied grammar of motives and a rhetoric of political action. It provides them with a repertoire of techniques for fashioning the world and themselves in it.

Islam, as Ibn Khaldun remarked (1958, I, 323) may be the cement of the solidarity of the common people in political action, or, as Engels (1958, 399) later put it, where all social and political and philosophical theory is tied into theology the masses may find it necessary 'to put forward their own interests in a religious guise in order to produce an impetuous movement'. And while Engels (1958, 400) may also have been right when he asserted that 'the transformations which this material [of traditional religion] undergoes spring from class relations, that is to say, out of the economic relations of the people who execute these transformations', that is only half of the truth. The other half is that though there may be underlying reasons for religious innovations, these changes are made in order that religion may continue meaningfully to validate his existence to the believer. Thus Eric Wolf (1969, xi) is also only half right when he remarks that transcendental issues may appear in very prosaic and mundane guise among the peasantry, for it is also true that in peasant society, certainly in Kelantan, mundane issues may be invested by religion with rich transcendental undertones. Religion, not entirely divorced from social and political concerns, may insinuate the bearing of the transcendental upon, and thereby spiritualize, the mundane lives of peasants. That is one of the strengths of Kelantanese Islam and Kelantanese society—a strength which the PMIP has recognized and to which it has also given expression.

REFERENCES

Allen, J. de V., 1967. *The Malayan Union* (New Haven, Conn., Yale University Southeast Asia Studies).

——— 1968. 'The Kelantan Rising of 1915: Some Thoughts on the Concept of Resistance in British Malayan History', *Journal South-East Asian History*, IX, 241–57.

Beidelman, T.O., 1966. 'The Ox and Nuer Sacrifice: Some Freudian Hypotheses about Nuer Symbolism', *Man*, n.s., 1, 453–67.

Emerson, R., 1937. *Malaysia: a Study in Direct and Indirect Rule* (London, Macmillan).

Engels, F., 1958. 'Ludwig Feuerbach and the End of Classical German Philosophy' in *Karl Marx and Frederick Engels: Selected Works* (2 vols.) (Moscow, Foreign Languages Publishing House), vol. II, 360–402.

Firth, R.W., 1946. *Malay Fishermen: Their Peasant Economy* (London, Routledge & Kegan Paul).

Funston, J., n.d. 'The Early Development of UMNO and PMIP'. (Unpublished MS.)

Gallagher, C.F., 1966. *Contemporary Islam: a Frontier of Communalism* (American Universities' Field Staff Reports Service, Southeast Asian Series, Malaysia 14, No. 10).

Geertz, C., 1960. *The Religion of Java* (Glencoe, Ill., The Free Press).

Gullick, J.M., 1964. *Malaya* (London, Benn, 2nd ed.).

────── 1969. *Malaysia* (3rd ed. of Gullick 1964) (London, Benn).

Haynes, A.S., 1932. *Annual Report on the Social and Economic Progress of the People of Kelantan* (Kota Bharu, Al-asasiyah Press).

Ionescu, G. & E. Gellner (eds.), 1969. *Populism: its Meaning and National Characteristics* (London, Weidenfeld & Nicolson).

Jay, R.R., 1969. *Javanese Villagers: Social Relations in Rural Modjokuto* (Cambridge, Mass., M.I.T. Press).

Kessler, C.S., 1972. 'Islam, Society and Political Behaviour: Some Comparative Implications of the Malay Case', *British Journal of Sociology*, XXIII, 33–50.

────── n.d. 'Islam, the Protestant Ethnic and the Malay Peasantry', in *Proceedings of the 28th International Congress of Orientalists* (forthcoming).

Ibn Khaldun, 1958. *The Muqaddimah: An Introduction to History* (trans. by F. Rosenthal) (London, Routledge & Kegan Paul, 3 vols.).

Marx, K., 1958. 'The Eighteenth Brumaire of Louis Bonaparte', in *Karl Marx and Frederick Engels: Selected Works* (Moscow, Foreign Languages Publishing House), vol. I, 221–331.

────── 1964. 'Contribution to the Critique of Hegel's Philosophy of Right: Introduction', in R. Niebuhr (ed.), *Marx and Engels on Religion* (New York, Schocken), 41–58.

Maryanov, G.S., 1967. 'Political Parties in Mainland Malaya', *Journal South-East Asian History*, VIII, 99–110.

McGee, T.G., 1962. 'The Malayan Elections of 1959', *Malayan Journal of Tropical Geography*, XVI, 70–99.

Means, G.P., 1969. 'The Role of Islam in the Political Development of Malaysia', *Comparative Politics*, I, 264–84.

────── 1970. *Malaysian Politics* (New York, New York University Press).

von der Mehden, F., 1963. 'Religion and Politics in Malaya', *Asian Survey*, III, 609–15.

────── 1964. 'Some Aspects of Political Ideology in Malaysia'. In R.K. Sakai (ed.), *Studies on Asia*, 5 (Lincoln, University of Nebraska), 95–104.

Milne, R.S., 1964. 'Politics and Government', in Wang Gungwu (ed.), *Malaysia* (London, Pall Mall), 323–35.

────── 1967. *Government and Politics in Malaysia* (Boston, Houghton Mifflin).

Nash, M., 1966. 'Tradition in Tension in Kelantan', *Journal of Asian and African Studies*, I, 310–14.

Ratnam, K.J., 1965. *Communalism and the Political Process in Malaya* (Singapore, University of Malaya Press).

────── 1969. 'Religion and Politics in Malaya', in R.O. Tilman (ed.), *Man, State and Society in Contemporary Southeast Asia* (London, Pall Mall), 351–61.

Ratnam, K.J. & R.S. Milne, 1967. *The Malayan Parliamentary Election of 1964* (Singapore, University of Malaya Press).

────── 1970. 'The 1969 Parliamentary Election in West Malaysia', *Pacific Affairs*, XLIII, 203–26.

Roff, W.R., 1962. 'Kaum Muda—Kaum Tua: Innovation and Reaction amongst the Malays, 1900–41, in K.G. Tregonning (ed.), *Papers on Malayan History* (Singapore, Journal South-East Asian History), 162–92.

────── 1967. *The Origins of Malay Nationalism* (New Haven, Conn. & London, Yale University Press).

────── 1968. 'The Persatuan Melayu Selangor: An Early Malay Political Association, *Journal South-East Asian History*, IX, 117–46.

Rudner, M., 1970. 'The Malaysian General Election of 1969', *Modern Asian Studies*, IV, 1–21.

Scott, J.C., 1968. *Political Ideology in Malaysia: Reality and Beliefs of an Elite* (New Haven, Conn., Yale University Press).

Siegel, J., 1969. *The Rope of God* (Berkeley, University of California Press).

Smith, T.E., 1960. 'The Malayan Elections of 1959', *Pacific Affairs*, XXXIII, 38–47.

Swift, M.G., 1965. *Malay Peasant Society in Jelebu* (London, Athlone Press).

———— 1967. 'Economic Concentration and Malay Peasant Society', in M. Freedman (ed.), *Social Organization: Essays Presented to Raymond Firth* (London, Cass), 241–69.

Tawney, R.H., 1912. *The Agrarian Problem in the Sixteenth Century* (London, Longmans).

Thomson, H.W., 1921. *Kelantan Administration Report for the year 1921* (Kuala Lumpur, Government Printing Office).

Tinker, I., 1956. 'Malayan Elections: Electoral Pattern for Plural Societies?', *Western Political Quarterly*, IX, 258–82.

Vasil, R.K., 1965. 'The 1964 General Elections in Malaya', *International Studies*, VII, 20–65.

Wolf, E.R., 1969. *Peasant Wars of the Twentieth Century* (New York, Harper & Row).

Wilson, T.B., 1958. *The Economics of Padi Production in North Malaya* (Part I) (Kuala Lumpur, Ministry of Agriculture, Federation of Malaya).

GLOSSARY

adat	custom, customary law
akal	intelligence, the faculty of reason
alim	one learned in religion (pl. *ulama*)
attap	palm-leaf thatch
Balai Besar	large audience hall of the palace
bahasa	language
bangsa	race, ethnic community, people
bayt ul-māl	treasury (for religious purposes)
beras	husked rice
bersilat	the Malay art of self-defence
besar	adjective indicating large, important, or powerful
bilal	caller of prayer times, minor official of mosque or *surau*
bomoh	spirit doctor
budi bahasa	courtesy
daerah	district
dusun	orchard, orchard land surrounding a village house
fatwa	legal ruling by an Islamic jurisconsult
fitrah	religious tax (or alms) enjoined by Islam, paid (in Kelantan) in husked rice at the end of the fasting month (Ar. *zakāt al-fiṭr*)
gaji	wage, salary
gantang	the Malay gallon measure for grain
guru Jajahan	travelling (religious) teacher

Hadith	the corpus of traditional acts and sayings of the Prophet Muhammad
haj	the pilgrimage to Mecca
haji	one who has made the pilgrimage to Mecca
hakim	judge, usually in a secular court
halus	fine, refined
hantu	ghost, evil spirit
haram	forbidden in Islamic law
Hari Raya Haji	holiday for the time of the pilgrimage
Hari Raya Puasa	holiday for the end of the fasting month (Ramadhan) (Note: The term '*Hari Raya*' used alone ordinarily denotes the Ramadhan holiday.)
hasil	tax (as in *hasil kepala*, poll tax; *hasil padi*, padi tax)
harta pesaka	inherited property or wealth
hikayat	story, history
hukum	law
hukum shara'	Sharī'a (Islamic) law
ilmu	knowledge, general or esoteric
imam	leader of mosque or *surau* congregation
istana	palace
isti'adat	custom, customary ceremonial
jinn	a supernatural being, not necessarily evil (cf. *hantu*)
juru selam	one especially skilled in detecting the presence of shoals of fish; literally, an expert in diving.
kampong	village
kasar	rough, coarse
kathi	religious magistrate
kaum ibu	the 'women-folk'
kaum muda	of the 'young group' or 'new persuasion', in contradistinction to *kaum tua*
kaum tua	the old group, 'old-fashioned'
kerah	corvée, tribute labour
keramat	sacred, (*ada keramat*, to possess magical power)
keris	Malay dagger
ketua kampong	village headman
khatib	reciter of the Friday address in mosque or *surau*
kuala	river-mouth
kuasa	authority (as in *surat kuasa*, letter of authority, warrant)

kupiah	cap, ordinarily the white skull cap worn by the religious
lebai	man of piety
madrasah	religious school of a modern type
main puteri	dance-drama healing ceremony
Mak Yong	traditional theatrical performance
majallah	journal, magazine
majlis	council
makan	food
malu	shy, embarrassed, ashamed
masjid	mosque
matba'ah	printing press
menora	theatrical performance deriving from Thailand
menteri	minister (of state)
Menteri Besar	Chief Minister
mufti	Islamic jurisconsult
mukim	'parish' of a *surau* or mosque
nafsu	the animal side of human nature, base desire
nazir	inspector, superintendent
nisab	the portion of the *padi* harvest above which *zakat* tax is payable
padang	field, more especially the 'town green'
padi	unhusked rice (also, generically, on the stalk)
pantun	traditional, four-line, verse form, rhyming abab
parang	machete
pas nikah	marriage certificate
patut	proper, fitting
pejabat	office
Pejabat Balai	Palace Office
penggawa	1. district headman (elsewhere in the peninsula, *penghulu*); also, 2. familiar spirit
pitis	low denomination tin coin
pondok	religious school, from the 'huts' in which students live
Puasa	the Fast, used synonymously with *bulan puasa*, the fasting month, or Ramadhan
puloh	Kelantan coin of the early twentieth century (lit. 'ten')
sakit	sickness

selampit	the art of reciting folk tales, usually to the accompaniment of a spike fiddle
semangat	spirit, vitality (as in the spirit or virtue inherent in 'inanimate' things of value, e.g. padi, *semangat padi*)
Sharīʿa	Islamic law
shaykh haji	agent for, or on, the Mecca pilgrimage
songkok	the black, slightly fore-and-aft 'pill-box' hat customarily worn by Malays
surat kuasa	letter of authority or appointment
surau	building used for purposes of religious worship
tanah ayer	homeland
tarekat	Sufi mystic order
To' Kweng	district (circle) headman (from the Thai)
To' Nebeng	village headman (from the Thai)
ubat	medicine
ugama	religion
ulama	those learned in religion (pl. of *alim*)
ulu	up-river, the 'interior'
undang2 tuboh	constitution
wakaf	religious endowment (usually of land or immovable property)
wali	saint
waris	kindred
wayang kulit	puppet shadow play
zakat	religious tax (or alms) enjoined by Islam, paid (in Kelantan) in unhusked rice at the end of the harvest

A BIBLIOGRAPHY OF KELANTAN

An alphabetically arranged list of books and articles published in Western languages, Malay, or Thai, dealing in whole or in part with Kelantan.

Certain features should be noted. With a few exceptions official publications have been excluded, as have all serial titles as such. Most of the articles are cited from learned journals, though a number of particular interest or importance are cited from more ephemeral publications. No attempt has been made to search popular literature published in Malaysia, though publications within this category (especially the Malay daily and periodical press) have contained material of much current and often of more lasting interest to scholars. A full list of newspapers and periodicals published within Kelantan itself may be found in the article by Al-Ahmadi in the present volume.

Although the bibliography (which has been made as comprehensive as possible within the limits described) concerns primarily Kelantan, material relating to Patani and the other Malay areas of southern Thailand, which have had such close historical and cultural links with Kelantan, have also been included in some number. No attempt has been made, however, to provide full coverage either of pre-nineteenth century southern Thailand (but see A. Teeuw & D.K. Wyatt, *Hikayat Patani. The Story of Patani*, The Hague, Martinus Nijhoff, 1970, pp. 298–306), or of the diplomatic relationships between Britain, France, and Thailand at the turn of the nineteenth century, except, in the latter case, where Kelantan is specifically discussed.

Compilation of the bibliography has been assisted by all contributors to the present volume, and gratitude is due in addition to Dr. Amin Sweeney, who supplied a number of references concerning the Kelantan shadow play and related subjects, and Dr. Geoffrey Benjamin, who supplied references to the Temiar and other aboriginal peoples of the area. Errors and omissions are the responsibility of the editor.

Abbreviations used

JMBRAS: Journal of the Malayan (from 1964, Malaysian) Branch of the Royal Asiatic Society
JSBRAS : Journal of the Straits Branch of the Royal Asiatic Society
b. : *bin* = son of
bte : *binte* = daughter of
Mohd. : Muhammad (used in all cases where Muhammad is the *entry* name).

À travers le monde. 'L'incident de Kelantan. L'Angleterre et le Siam dans la Peninsule Malaise'. À Travers le Monde, n.s. VIII (1902), 317–18.

Abbas *b*. Taha. Risalah penting pada mas'alah jilat anjing di-atas empat2 madzhab. Singapore, Ahmadiyah Press, 1937.

Abd. Ghani *b*. Abbas. 'Wayang kulit'. Dewan Bahasa, III (1959), 563–8.

Abdul Hamid, A. Puteri Sa'adong. Cherita sejarah yang mashhor dalam negeri Kelantan. Penang, Sinaran Press, n.d. (? 1963). [Children's book].

A[bdul] Jalil *Haji* Noor. Tok Janggut pahlawan Kelantan. Singapore, Pustaka Nasional, 1966. [Children's book].

'Abdul Kadir Adabi' (pseud.) See Abdul Kadir *b*. Muhammad.

Abdul Kadir *b*. Muhammad. 'Achuman mahkota'. Published serially in the journal Al-Hikmah (Kota Bharu) in the 1930s, but not known to have appeared separately. [Historical fiction].

——— 'Melati Kota Bharu'. Published serially in the journal Al-Hikmah in the 1930s, but not known to have appeared separately. [Fiction].

——— 'Saya ka-Patani'. Al-Hikmah, Nos. 251–6, 258–60 (6 Jul.–7 Sept. 1939). [A series of nine descriptive articles, based on a visit.]

Abdul Malek, *Dato'*. 'The Kelantan coat of arms'. Malaya in History, VI, 1 (1960), 44.

Abdullah, *Haji*. 'A fragment of the history of Trengganu and Kelantan' (ed. and transl. by H. Marriott). JSBRAS, 72 (1916), 3–23.

Abdullah b. Abdul Kadir, *Munshi*. Kisah pelayaran Abdullah. Edisi baru dengan pengenalan dan anotasi di-selenggarakan oleh Kassim Ahmad. Kuala Lumpur, Oxford University Press, 1960.

─────── The voyage of Abdullah [from Singapore to Kelantan in 1838]. A translation from the Malay, by A.E. Coope, with notes and appendices. Singapore, Malaysia Publishing House, 1949.

─────── Kesah pelayaran Abdullah, terkarang oleh Abdullah b. Abdul-Kadir munshi (ed. by R.J. Wilkinson). Singapore, Methodist Publishing House, 1907 (and frequently reprinted).

─────── 'The journal of a voyage from Singapore to Kelantan' (transl., by B.P. Keasberry, part of an intended complete version never continued). Journal of Eastern Asia (Singapore), 1, 1 (1875), 104–9.

─────── Kesah pelajaran Abdoellah b. Abdel-Kadir moensji, dari Singapoera sampai ka negeri Kelantan (ed. by R. Brons Middel). Leiden, E.J. Brill, 1893.

─────── Tjarijosipun Abdullah bin Abdulkadir munsji saking Singapura lajar dateng Kelantan (transl. into Javanese by Djaka Mubtadi). Batavia, 1893.

─────── Voyage... de Singapore a Kalantan... entreprise en l'année 1838 (transl. with notes by Ed. Dulaurier). Paris, 1850.

[Note. No attempt has been made here to list completely the many editions of this famous work. The foregoing are the principal Malay and English versions, with some translations.]

Abdullah Al-Qari b. *Haji* Salleh. Sejarah hidup To' Kenali. Kota Bharu, Pustaka Aman Press, 1967.

─────── 'Pujangga Shaykh Daud Patani'. Majallah Dian (Kota Bharu), 10 (1967), 131–8.

─────── Cherpen2 To' Kenali. Kota Bharu, Pustaka Dian, 1969.

Abdullah b. Amirah, *Haji*. Riwayat hidup To' Janggut dan peperangan-nya di-Kelantan. Penang, Sinaran Press, 1963.

Abdullah b. Muhammad ('Nakula'). 'Kelantan dalam zaman Long Yunus'. Journal Persatuan Sejarah Kelantan, 1, 1 (1964/65), 73–81.

─────── 'Kelantan dari zaman pra-sejarah hingga zaman permulaan Srivijaya'. Ibid., 15–38.

────── 'Peristiwa penting dalam sejarah Kelantan hingga tahun 1909'. Majallah Kelantan (Kota Bharu), I, 11 (Jul. 1966), 10; 12 (Aug. 1966), 5–6; ? 13 or 14 (? date); 15 (Sept. 1966), 5, 8; 17 (Oct. 1966), 5, 8; 20 (Dec. 1966), 5, 8–9; II, 1/2 (Jan. 1967), 5, 8–10; 5 (Mar. 1967), 5, 8–9; 9 (Oct. 1967), 5, 8–10; 10 (Nov. 1967), 5, 8–9. [Thirteen instalments; not known whether completed, as journal stopped publication for uncertain period.]

'Abiha' (pseud.) 24 jam di-Sungei Golok. Dungun (Trengganu), Timor Press, n.d. [Fiction].

Adams, T.S. 'Vocabulary of Pangan'. JSBRAS, 85 (1922), 97–123. [The language is actually Temiar, collected on the Sungei Nenggiri, Kelantan.]

Agus Salim. Puteri Sa'dong (Puteri Kelantan). Singapore, Pustaka Nasional, 1968. [Children's book].

Ahmad b. Ismail. Ilmu al-huda. Kota Bharu, Al-Hikmah Press, 1963.

Ahmad b. *Haji Nik* Hassan, *Nik*. 'Kajian rengkas mengenai keturunan Long Yunus Kelantan'. Journal Persatuan Sejarah Kelantan, I, 1 (1964/65), 39–51.

Al-Ahmadi, Abdul Rahman. 'Chorak khusus Islam dalam kesusasteraan'. In his Pengantar Sastera (Kota Bharu, Pustaka Aman Press, 1966), 157–168.

────── 'Mesjid tua Kampong Laut perlu di-pelihara dan di-rawat'. Mingguan Kota Bharu, 106 (27 July 1968), 5–8.

────── 'Kenangan sa-pintas lalu kepada Allah-yarham Enche Sa'ad Shukri'. Majallah Kelantan, III, 2 (1971), 11–13.

Allen, James de V. 'The Kelantan rising of 1915: some thoughts on the concept of resistance in British Malayan history'. Journal of Southeast Asian History, IX (1968), 241–57.

Anika N.S. 'Ungkapan daerah: sumbangan dari daerah Kelantan'. Santajiwa (Kota Bharu), 1 (1965), 116–17.

Annandale, Nelson. 'The Siamese Malay states'. Scottish Geographical Magazine, XVI (1900), 505–23.

────── 'The zoological names and theories of the Malays'. Proceedings of the Royal Physical Society of Edinburgh, XIV (1900–1904), 446–61.

―――― 'Human souls and ghosts among the Malays of Patani'. Report of the British Association for the Advancement of Science, 72 (1902), 752–3. [Abstract only].

―――― 'Religion and magic among the Malays of the Patani states'. In Annandale, N. & Robinson, H.C., Fasciculi Malayenses .... Anthropology, Parts I (89–104) and IIa (21–57). Liverpool, University Press, 1903.

―――― 'Primitive beliefs and customs of the Patani fishermen'. In *ibid.*, Anthropology, Part I (73–68).

―――― 'Customs of the Malayo-Siamese'. In *ibid.*, Anthropology, Part IIa (61–89).

―――― 'Notes on the popular religion of the Patani Malay'. Man, III (1903), 27–8.

―――― 'The peoples of the Malay Peninsula'. Scottish Geographical Magazine, XX (1904), 337–48.

―――― 'The theory of souls among the Malays of the Malay Peninsula'. Asiatic Society of Bengal, Journal, n.s. V (1909), 59–66.

Annandale, Nelson & Robinson, Herbert C. 'Some preliminary results of an expedition to the Malay Peninsula'. Journal of the Royal Anthropological Institute, XXXII (1902), 401–17.

―――― 'On the wild and civilized races of the Malay Peninsula'. Report of the British Association for the Advancement of Science, 72 (1902), 766. [Abstract only].

―――― 'Anthropological notes on Sai Kau, a Siamo-Malayan village in the state of Nawnchik (Tojan)'. Man, II (1902), Art. 86 (3 pp.)

―――― 'Contributions to the ethnography of the Malay Peninsula.... Part II, Coastal people of Trang'. In their Fasciculi Malayenses.... Anthropology, Part I (53–65). Liverpool, University Press, 1903.

―――― Fasciculi Malayenses. Anthropological and zoological results of an expedition to Perak and the Siamese Malay states, 1901–2. Anthropology, Parts I and IIa, and Supplement (with map and itinerary). Liverpool, University Press, 1903.

Arifin b. Abdul Rashid. Rengkasan sejarah Kelantan. Kota Bharu, Pustaka Aman Press, 1962.

Asa'ad [Shukri] b. *Haji* Muda. 'Kilatan, atau riwayat Kelantan'. Kenchana (Kota Bharu), I, 1–12, II, 13–15 (April 1930–? May 1931).

———— Bahasa beradat. Kuala Lumpur, Federal Publications, 1960.

———— Sejarah Kelantan. Kota Bharu, Pustaka Aman Press, 1962.

———— Detik2 sejarah Kelantan. Kota Bharu, Pustaka Aman Press, 1971. [Note. Based on the same author's Sejarah Kelantan, this has been revised and amplified with the assistance of Abdullah Al-Qari b. Haji Salleh and Abdul Rahman Al-Ahmadi.]

Ashby, H.K. 'Off-season padi trials in the Salor irrigation area, Kelantan, in 1953'. Malayan Agricultural Journal, XXXVII (1954), 3–11.

L'asie française. 'L'Angleterre et le Malacca Siamoise'. Bulletin Mensuel du Comité de l'Asie Française, III, 38 (1904), 258.

———— 'L'Angleterre et la Siam dans la Peninsule Malaise. La question de Kelantan'. Ibid., VII, 70 (1907), 17–21.

Baharon b. Azhar Raffiei. "Engku'—spirit of thunder'. Federation Museums Journal, n.s. XI (1966), 34–7. [Concerns the Temiar].

Baker, A.C. 'A journey from the Cameron Highlands to the East Coast railway'. JMBRAS, XI, 2 (1933), 288–95.

B.[aker], A.C. Review of Raymond Firth, Malay Fishermen: Their Peasant Economy. British Malaya, XXIII, 11 (1949), 192–3. [Baker had been British Adviser in Kelantan.]

Balfour, Henry. 'Report on a collection of musical instruments from the Siamese Malay states and Perak.' In Annandale, N. & Robinson, H.C., Fasciculi Malayenses.... Anthropology, Part IIa (1–18). Liverpool, University Press, 1903.

Bee, R.J. 'Some Kelantan place names'. JMBRAS, XI, 2 (1933), 138.

Benjamin, Geoffrey. 'Temiar social groupings'. Federation Museums Journal, n.s. XI (1966), 1–25.

———— 'Temiar kinship'. Ibid., XII (1967), 1–26.

———— 'Temiar personal names'. Bijdragen tot de Taal-, Land- en Volkenkunde, 124, 1 (1968), 99–134.

———— 'Headmanship and leadership in Temiar society'. Federation Museums Journal, n.s. XIII (1968), 1–43.

Berwick, E.J.H. 'Wet padi mechanical cultivation experiments, Kelantan, season 1950–51'. Malayan Agricultural Journal, XXXIV (1951), 166–84.

———— 'Dry padi mechanical cultivation experiments, Kelantan, season 1950–51'. *Ibid.*, 185–206.

———— 'Some Kelantan bird names'. JMBRAS, XXVI, 1 (1953), 140–4.

Biles, H.F. 'A Kelantan myth'. Malayan Historical Journal, III, 1 (1956), 40.

Birch, E.W. 'The taking over from Siam of part of Reman or Rahman'. JSBRAS, 54 (1910), 145–55.

Blagden, C.O. 'Siam and the Malay Peninsula'. Journal of the Royal Asiatic Society (1906), 107–19.

Bowen, John. 'Note on 'Patani guns and foundry' site'. Journal of the Siam Society, XV, 2 (1922), 103–4.

Braddell, Roland. The legal status of the Malay states. Singapore, Malaya Publishing House, 1931.

———— Taraf Negeri2 Melayu pada sisi undang2 (transl. of the foregoing by Mohammad Zain b. Ayob). Singapore, Ahmadiyah Press, 1935.

Brandt, J.H. 'The Negrito of peninsular Thailand'. Journal of the Siam Society, XLIX (1961), 123–60, with 11 unnumbered plates.

———— 'The Southeast Asian Negrito'. *Ibid.*, LIII (1965), 27–44.

Bridges, W.F.N. 'Surveys for title in the F.M.S., with notes on the surveys in the U.M.S.' Report of Proceedings, Conference of Empire Survey Officers, 1932. London, H.M.S.O., 1933, 262–8.

Brown, C.C. Kelantan Malay. In Papers on Malay Subjects, 2nd series. Kuala Lumpur, Government Printer, 1927.

———— 'Kelantan bull-fighting'. JMBRAS, VI, 1 (1928), 74–83.

———— Studies in country Malay. London, Luzac & Co., 1956.

Bucknill, J.A.S. 'Observations upon some coins obtained in Malaya and particularly from Trengganu, Kelantan, and southern Siam'. JMBRAS, I, 1 (1923), 194–217.

Bulletin économique Indochine. 'Les moutons de Kelantan au Thanh-hoa'. Bulletin Économique Indochine (1910), 258–9.

Burgess, Anthony. The enemy in the blanket. London, Heinemann, 1958; reprinted in his Malayan Trilogy (London, Pan Books, 1964), and in The Long Day Wanes (New York, W.W. Norton & Co., 1964). [Fiction].

———— Beds in the east. London, Heinemann, 1959; reprinted as above. [Fiction].

Cameron, William. 'On the Patani'. JSBRAS, 11 (1883), 121–42.

Carey, Iskandar. Tengleq kui serok. A study of the Temiar language, with an ethnographical summary. Kuala Lumpur, Dewan Bahasa dan Pustaka, 1961.

———— 'Mendrik kinship terminology'. Federation Museums Journal, n.s. XIII (1968), 49–56.

Chan Su-ming. 'Kelantan and Trengganu, 1909–1939'. JMBRAS, XXXVIII, 1 (1965), 159–98.

Chandran, J. 'Three agreements relating to the northern Malay states concluded in 1896, 1897 and 1899'. Peninjau Sejarah (Kuala Lumpur), III, 2 (1968), 52–62.

———— 'The British foreign office and the Siamese Malay states, 1890–97'. Modern Asian Studies, V (1971), 143–59.

Čharat Kamphlāsīri (ed.) 'Phrabǫrommarāchāthibāi nai pharabāt somdet phra čhunlačhǫmklao rüang bāēp krāp bangkhom thūn phrakarunā nam khāēk müang thawāi khrüang rātchabannākān lae kān thūn bōēk krāp thawāi bangkhom lā [Comments of His Majesty King Chulalongkorn concerning forms for the presentation of tribute by foreign rulers and forms for taking leave]'. Sinlapākǫn, VIII, 2 (2507/1964), 53–60. [Concerning tribute ceremonies from such states as Kelantan; from correspondence between Chulalongkorn and Ministry of the Interior, 1900.]

Chulalongkorn, King of Siam. Čhotmāihēt raya thāng sadet praphāt nai ratchakān thī 5, sadet praphāt huamüang nai lāēm malāyū, rattanakōsin sok 117, 118, 119, rūam 3 khrāo [Documents concerning royal travels in the Fifth Reign; travels in the provinces of the Malay Peninsula, 1898/99, 1899/1900, 1900/01, together three occasions.] Bangkok, Funeral rites of Queen Saowaphā, 2462 (1919). [Notes on visits to Kelantan, 29 Jun. 1898 (pp. 5–7) and 23 May 1900 (pp. 32–4).]

———— Čhotmāihēt phrabāt somdet phra čhunlačhǫmklao čhaoyūhua sadet praphāt lāēm malāyū khrāo r.s. 109, r.s. 117, r.s. 119, r.s. 124, r.s. 128 [Documents concerning King Chulalongkorn's travels in the Malay Peninsula in 1890/91, 1898/99, 1900/01, 1905/06, and 1909/10.] Bangkok, Funeral rites of Prince Nakhǫn Rātchasimā, 30 March 2467 (1925). [Notes on visits to Kelantan 13 Jun. 1890

(p. 53), 29 Jun. 1898 (pp. 61–3), 23 May 1900 (pp. 82–3), and 28 Jun. 1905 (pp. 98–9).]

———— Čhotmāihēt phrabāt somdet phra čhunlačhǫmklao čhaoyuhūa sadet praphāt lāēm malāyū khrāo r.s. 107 lae 108 [Documents concerning King Chulalongkorn's travels in the Malay Peninsula in 1888/89 and 1889/90.] Bangkok, Funeral rites of Prince Nakhǫn Rātchasimā, 15 February 2467 (1925). [Note on a visit to Kelantan, 5 Sept. 1888 (pp. 5–6).]

———— Phrarātchahatlēkhā nai phrabāt somdet phra čhunlačhǫmklao čhaoyūhua rµang sadet praphāt lāēm malāyū mµa 108, 109, 117, 120, rūam 4 khrāo [Royal letters of King Chulalongkorn on four of his visits to the Malay Peninsula in 1889/90, 1890/91, 1898/99, and 1901/02.] Bangkok, Funeral rites of Princess Sīsatchanālai, 2468 (1925). [Reference to Kelantan, visit of 29 Jun. 1898 (pp. 207–8).]

———— Raya thāng thīao chawā kwā sǫng dµan [More-than-two-months' tour of Java.] Bangkok, Funeral rites of Prince Nakhǫn Rātchasimā, 2468 (1925). [Diary includes reference to a visit to Kelantan, 7 Aug. 1896 (pp. 417–19).]

———— Phrarātchaniphon phrabāt somdet phra čhunlačhǫmklao čhaoyūhua raya thāng sadet phrarātchadamnoen praphāt thāng bok thāng rµa rǫp lāēm malāyū r.s. 109 [Royal writings of King Chulalongkorn on his royal progress by land and sea around the Malay Peninsula in 1890/91]. Bangkok, Funeral rites of Prince Lopburi Ramēt, 2475 (1932). [Includes a short diary account (pp. 335–41) of a visit to Kelantan on 13 June 1890, with some political references.]

———— Čhotmāihēt sadet praphāt ko chawā nai ratchakān thī 5 thāng 3 khrāo [Documents on the three visits to Java in the Fifth Reign.] Bangkok, Ceremonies honouring Princess Suchitraphāranī, 2463 (1920); reprinted, Bangkok, Funeral rites of Phrayā Phitakthēpaksǫn, 2509 (1966). [Note on a visit to Kelantan, 7 Aug. 1896 (pp. 79–80).]

———— Pramūan phrarātchahatlēkhā ratchakān thī 5 thī kīaokap phārakit khǫng krasūang mahātthai [Collected letters of the Fifth Reign concerning the responsibilities of the Ministry of the Interior.] Bangkok, 2 vols., Ministry of Interior, 1970. [Kelantan affairs extensively detailed in a series of letters from the King to Prince Damrong Rajanubhab, 2 Apr. 1902–30 May 1908, (pp. 491–557).]

Clark, Kathleen. 'The great drums of Kelantan'. Straits Times Annual (1963), 78–9.

Clarke, W.B. 'The incantation and sacrifice of the pawang Ma'Yong'. JMBRAS, III, 3 (1925), 106.

Clifford, Hugh. 'Expedition to Trengganu and Kelantan, report by Hugh Clifford'. JMBRAS, XXXIV, 1 (1961), 1–162; reprinted from the edition first published in Kuala Lumpur, Government Printer, 1938. [Report originally written in 1895.]

―――― 'A journey through the Malay states of Trengganu and Kelantan'. Geographical Journal, IX (1897), 1–37.

―――― 'The East Coast'. In his In Court and Kampong, being Tales and Sketches of Native Life in the Malay Peninsula (London, Grant Richards, 1897), 1–16; reprinted in Stories by Sir Hugh Clifford, selected and edited by William R. Roff (Kuala Lumpur, Oxford University Press, 1966), 10–22.

―――― 'The people of the East Coast'. In his In Court and Kampong, op. cit., 17–29.

―――― 'The fate of Leh the strolling player'. In his Studies in Brown Humanity, being Scrawls and Smudges in Sepia, White and Yellow (London, Grant Richards, 1898), 22–35; reprinted with some alterations under the title 'A Malayan actor-manager' in his The Further Side of Silence (Garden City, N.Y., Doubleday, 2nd. ed. 1927), 341–57; original version also reprinted in Stories by Sir Hugh Clifford, op. cit., 143–54.

―――― 'British and Siamese Malaya'. Proceedings of the Royal Colonial Society, XXXIV (1902), 45–75; also published in the Journal of the Royal Colonial Institute, XXXIV (1903), 75–105.

Cole. R. 'Temiar Senoi agriculture. A note on aboriginal shifting cultivation in Ulu Kelantan, Malaya'. The Malayan Forester, XXII (1959), 191–207, 260–71.

Colonial office journal. 'Kedah, Perlis and Kelantan'. Colonial Office Journal, IV (1911), 200–7.

Coulson, N. 'System of land tenure in Kelantan'. Malayan Agricultural Journal, XVI (1929), 118–26.

Craig, J.A. 'Dry padi in Kelantan'. Ibid., XXI (1933), 664–6.

―――― 'Agriculture in Kelantan'. Ibid., XXIII (1935), 369–74.

Crawford, Hunter A. 'The birth of the Duff development company in Kelantan, 1900-1912. A note prepared from documents kindly made available by Hunter A. Crawford . . . .' Malaysia in History, XIII, 2 (1970), 2-10.

Crosby, Sir Josiah. Siam: the crossroads. London, Hollis and Carter, 1945. [Crosby was British Ambassador to Siam, and reflects on British-Thai relations, inter alia as they affected or were affected by Kelantan.]

Cuisinier, Jeanne. 'The sacred books of India and the Malay and Siamese theatres in Kelantan'. Indian Art and Letters (London), n.s. VIII, 1 (1934), 43-50.

——— 'L'âme et les mots qui l'expriment en Malais'. Bulletin de l'Association Française des Amis de l'Orient (Paris), VIII (1930), 25-35.

——— Danses magiques de Kelantan. Travaux et Mémoires de l'Institut d'Ethnologie, Université de Paris, No. XXII, Paris, 1936.

——— Sumangat. L'âme et son culte en Indochine et en Indonesie. Paris, Gallimard, 1951.

——— Le théatre d'ombres à Kelantan. Paris, Gallimard, 2nd ed. 1957.

Darus Ahmad. 'Pahlawan bangsa. To' Janggut'. In his Orang Besar Tanah Ayer (Penang, Sinaran Press, 1958), 26.

Daud b. Haji Nik Mat, Nik (Dato' Aria di-Raja). 'The legend of Sungei Lubok Jong, in the district of Pasir Mas, Kelantan'. JMBRAS, XXV, 1 (1952), 155-7.

Davies, R.D. Siam in the Malay Peninsula. Singapore, Fraser & Neave, 1902. [An anti-Siamese polemic originally published as newspaper articles.]

Davison, William. 'Journal of a trip to Pahang with H.E. the Governor, August 17th to 28th, 1889'. JSBRAS, 20 (1889), 83-90. [Includes notes on a day in Kelantan, 23/24 Aug.]

De indische gids. 'De Maleische staatjes Trengganoe en Kelantan'. De Indische Gids, XIX (1897), 1370-86.

Dennys, N.B. 'Patani'. In his A Descriptive Dictionary of British Malaya (London, London & China Telegraph Office, 1894), 273-5. [Substantially from A.M. Skinner, A Geography of the Malay

Peninsula and Surrounding Countries (Singapore, Mission Press, 1884).]

Dentan, Robert K. 'Senoi-Semang'. In F.M. LeBar et al (eds.) Ethnic Groups of Mainland Southeast Asia (New Haven, Conn., Human Relations Area Files Press, 1964), 176–86.

Dewan bahasa dan pustaka. Cherita selampit. Kuala Lumpur, Dewan Bahasa & Pustaka, 1959.

Dobby, E.H.G. 'The Kelantan delta'. Geographical Review, XLI (1951), 226–55.

Dobby, E.H.G. et al. 'Padi landscapes of Malaya. Daerah Tanjong Pauh, Kelantan'. Malayan Journal of Tropical Geography, X (1957), 3–42.

Downs, R.E. 'A rural community in Kelantan, Malaya'. In R.K. Sakai (ed.), Studies on Asia (Lincoln, Neb., University of Nebraska Press), 1 (1960), 51–62.

――― 'A Kelantanese village of Malaya'. In Julian H. Steward (ed.), Contemporary Change in Traditional Societies (Urbana, Ill., University of Illinois Press, 1967), vol. 1, 105–86.

Dubois de Jancigny, A.P. Japon, Indo-Chine, Empire Birman (ou Ava), Siam, Annam (ou Cochinchine), Peninsule Malaise, etc., Ceylan. Paris, Firman Didot Frères, 1850.

Duckworth, W.L.H. 'Malaya: physical anthropology. Notes on the anthropological observations made by Mr. F. Laidlaw in the Skeat expedition to the Malay Peninsula'. Journal of the Royal Anthropological Institute, XXX (1900), Anthropological Reviews, Miscellaneous, No. 75.

――― 'Results of Skeat's expedition to the Malay Peninsula'. Ibid., XXXII (1902), 142–52.

Duff development company. The Duff development company's territory, 1910. London, Duff Development Co., 1910. [Consists of sixty plates illustrative of the Kelantan of the time, and of the company's activities.]

Endicott, K.M. An analysis of Malay magic. Oxford, Clarendon Press, 1970.

Evans, I.H.N. 'On a coin mould from Kelantan'. Journal, Federated States Museums, XII, 1 (1924), 7–8, and plate IV.

―――― 'An ethnological expedition to south Siam'. *Ibid.*, XII, 2 (1926), 35–7.

―――― 'On a stone spearhead from Kelantan'. *Ibid.*, XV (1930), 1–3.

―――― 'On a pictured stone from Kelantan'. *Ibid.*, 37.

―――― The Negritos of Malaya. Cambridge, University Press, 1937.

―――― 'Danses magiques de Kelantan. By Jeanne Cuisinier'. Man, XXXVIII (1938), Art. 151 (2 pp.) [Review by 'E.I.H.N.']

Eastern world. 'Siam's concern for her Islamic population'. Eastern World, III, 4 (1949), 15. [Official Siamese reply to an article by Barbara Whittingham-Jones, *q.v.*].

Far eastern review. 'Construction work on the Federated Malay States railways'. Far Eastern Review, XXI (1925), 723–5.

Farrer, R.J. 'A Buddhist purification ceremony'. JMBRAS, XI (1933), 261–3.

Federated Malay States. Report of the rice cultivation committee. Kuala Lumpur, Government Printer, 1931 (Federal Council Paper No. 31 of 1932, printed separately from the Proceedings).

―――― 'Tamil immigration into Kedah, Perlis and Kelantan'. Federal Council Paper No. 8 of 1910, printed in Proceedings of the Federal Council for 1910 (Kuala Lumpur, Government Printer, 1910), pp. C26–35.

Federation of Malaya. Report of the rice production committee. Volume one. Kuala Lumpur, Government Printer, 1953.

Firth, Raymond. 'Economics of a Malayan fishing industry'. Man, XLI (1941), Art. 58 (5 pp.)

―――― 'The coastal people of Kelantan and Trengganu, Malaya'. Geographical Journal, CI (1943), 193–205.

―――― Malay fishermen: their peasant economy. London, Routledge & Kegan Paul, 1946; 2nd ed., revised, 1966.

―――― 'Ritual and drama in Malay spirit mediumship'. Comparative Studies in Society and History, IX (1967), 190–207.

Firth, Rosemary, 'Housekeeping among Malay peasant women. Summary of communication. . . .' Man, XLII (1942), Art. 33 (2 pp.)

―――― Housekeeping among Malay peasants. London, Athlone Press, 1943; 2nd ed., revised, 1966.

Fisk, E.K. 'The economics of the handloom industry of the northeastern Malay states'. JMBRAS, XXXII, 4 (1959), 1–70.

Fraser, T.M. Rusembilan, a Malay fishing village in southern Thailand. Ithaca, N.Y., Cornell University Press, 1960.

——— Fishermen of south Thailand: the Malay villagers. New York, Holt, Rinehart & Winston, 1966.

Geographical journal. 'The new British-protected Malay states: Kelantan, Trengganu and Kedah'. Geographical Journal, XXXIII (1909), 478–85.

Gibson-Hill, C.A. 'Cargo boats of the East Coast of Malaya'. JMBRAS, XXII (1949), 106–25.

——— 'Malay hats and dish-covers'. Ibid., XXIV, 1 (1951), 133–58.

Gimlette, J.D. 'Some superstitious beliefs occurring in the theory and practice of Malay medicine'. JSBRAS, 65 (1913), 29–35.

——— Malay poisons and charm cures. London, J. & A. Churchill, 1915; 3rd ed., revised, 1929; reprinted, Kuala Lumpur, Oxford University Press, 1971.

——— 'A curious Kelantan charm'. JSBRAS, 82 (1920), 116–18.

——— 'Smoking over a fire to drive out an evil spirit'. Man, XXIV, (1924), Art. 3 (2 pp.)

——— 'A bee bomor'. JMBRAS, IX, 3 (1926), 421–2.

——— A dictionary of Malay medicine (ed. and completed by H.W. Thomson). London, Oxford University Press, 1939; reprinted 1971.

——— 'Incidents in the life of a residency surgeon', British Malaya, II (1927), 146–9, 158.

Glaskin, G.M. The beach of passionate love. London, Barrie & Rockliff, 1961. [Fiction].

Gnewoesjewa, E.I. 'De levengeschiedenis van W.P. Mamalyga (Malygin): 'rustverstoorder' in Nederland-Indie' (transl. from the Russian of Elizaveta Gnevusheva by L.E.L. Sluimers). Bijdragen tot de Taal-, Land- en Volkenkunde, 121 (1965), 303–49.

Goss, P.H. 'The penggawas' roads of Kelantan'. Empire Survey Review, V (1939), 89–92.

Graham, W.A. Kelantan, a state of the Malay Peninsula. A handbook of information. Glasgow, James MacLehose & Sons, 1908.

―――― 'Malay states. II.—Non-federated states'. Encyclopaedia Brittanica, 11th ed., London, 1910-11.

Gullick, J.M. 'A survey of Malay weavers and silversmiths in Kelantan in 1951'. JMBRAS, xxv, 1 (1952), 134-48.

Haron Yusof. Kota Bharu: shorga atau neraka. Ipoh, Ra'ayat Trading Co., 1966. [Fiction].

Hill, A.H. 'Kelantan padi planting'. JMBRAS, xxiv, 1 (1951), 56-76.

―――― 'Kelantan silver work'. Ibid., 99-108.

―――― 'Some Kelantan games and entertainments'. Ibid., xxv, 1 (1952), 20-34.

Holman, Dennis. Noone of the Ulu. London, Heinemann, 1958.

―――― The green torture. The ordeal of Robert Chrystal. London, Robert Hale, 1962. [Contains information on the Communist 'Emergency' as it affected the Gua Musang area.]

Hooijer, D.A. 'Rhinoceros sondaicus desmarest from the Hoabinhian of Gua Cha rock shelter, Kelantan'. Federation Museums Journal, n.s. VII (1962), 23-4.

Hsu Yun Ts'iao [Hsu Yun-ch'iao]. Pei-ta-nien shih [History of Patani]. Singapore, 1964.

―――― 'Notes on Tan-Tan'. JMBRAS, xx, 1 (1947), 47-63. [The Chinese text of this article may be found in the Journal of the South Seas Society (Singapore), 1, 1(1940).]

Husein Ahmad. Che' Siti Wan Kembang. Penang, Sinaran Press, 1964. [Children's book].

'Ibhy' (pseud.) Melihat tanah ayer. Kota Bharu, Ismailiyah Press, Vol. I (all published), n.d. (1941).

'Ibrahim Shukri' (pseud.) Sejarah kerajaan Melayu Patani. Pasir Puteh, Tengku Zainab bte Tengku Abdul Muttalib, n.d. (1961).

Ibrahim b. Haji Yaacub. See 'Ibhy'.

Inder Singh s/o Sgt. Ram Singh. 'The Kelantan disturbances (1915)'. In his History of the Malay States Guides, 1872-1919 (Penang, privately published, n.d. [?1965]), 121-2.

Ishak b. Haji Muhammad. Anak Mat Lela Gila. Kuala Lumpur, Federal Publications, 1960; first publ. 1941. [Fiction. Chap. 8 deals with a religious school in Kelantan.]

―――― Jalan ke Kota Bharu. Singapore, Qalam Press, 1956. [Fiction]

Ismail *Munshi, Inche*. 'The medical book of Malayan medicine' (transl. by I.I., with medical notes by J.D. Gimlette and determinations of drugs by I.H. Burkill.) Gardens' Bulletin (Singapore), VI (1930), 333–499. [Referred to by R.O. Winstedt in his obituary of Gimlette, *q.v.*, where Gimlette is wrongly given as editor. The original Malay work is of west coast origin, and contains references to Kelantan only in Gimlette's notes.]

Ismail Bakti. "Bunga mas', golden flowers: gift or tribute'. Malaya in History, VI, 1 (1960), 40–2.

Jack, H.W. 'Brief notes on agricultural conditions on the East Coast of Malaya'. Malayan Agricultural Journal, XVI (1928), 88–91.

Jawatankuasa penghebaan dan barang2 peringatan kenangan kemahkotaan. Chenderamata perayaan kemahkotaan . . . Tuanku Yahya Petra ibni Almerhum Sultan Ibrahim . . . etc. Kota Bharu, Kerajaan Kelantan, 1961.

Jawi peranakan. 'Patani'. Jawi Peranakan (Singapore), Nos. 515 and 516 (31 Jan. and 7 Feb. 1887). [Two long descriptive articles, under this or a similar title.]

Jimin *b*. Idris. 'Distribution of orang asli in West Malaysia'. Federation Museums Journal, n.s. XIII (1968), 44–8, map.

Jones, L.W. 'Kelantan section of the East Coast railway, Federated Malay States'. Royal Engineers Journal, XLIV (1930), 647–56.

Keith, A. 'Account of a journey across the Malay Peninsula from Koh Lak to Mergui'. JSBRAS, 24 (1891), 63–78.

Kelantan government and Duff development company. Arbitration proceedings (Sir A.G. Lascelles, arbitrator). Kuala Lumpur, Government Printer, 1917. [Cited from H.R. Cheeseman, Bibliography of Malaya (London, Longmans Green, 1959), 83]

Kesatuan pelajar2 Melayu Kelantan. Chenderamata konggeres ekonomi pemuda Kelantan. Kota Bharu, Kesatuan Pelajar2 Melayu Kelantan, n.d. (1969).

Khasnor Johan. 'The bunga emas in Malay-Siamese relations'. Journal of the Historical Society, University of Malaya, IV (1965/66), 11–15.

Kiernan, V.G. 'Britain, Siam and Malaya, 1875–1885'. Journal of Modern History, XXVIII (1956), 1–20.

'Kijang Puteh' (pseud.) See Sheppard, Mubin.

Koh, Natalie. 'The voyage of the Gypsy. An account of an archeological survey carried out in south Thailand in August, 1960, by a team from the University of Malaya in Kuala Lumpur ... etc.' Journal of the Historical Society, University of Malaya, 1 (1960), 35–48.

Laidlaw, F.F. 'Note on the invocation of akuan'. JMBRAS, I, 2 (1923), 376–7.

——— 'Travels in Kelantan, Trengganu and Upper Perak, a personal narrative'. Ibid., XXVI, 4 (1953), 148–64.

Leach, E.R. 'A Melanau (Sarawak) twine-making device, with notes on related apparatus from N.E. Malaya'. Journal of the Royal Anthropological Institute, LXXIX (1949), 79–85.

Life magazine. 'Life visits the beach of passionate love'. Life, 31 (31 Dec. 1951), 84–7.

Linehan, W. 'Coins of Kelantan'. JMBRAS, XII, 2 (1934), 63–9.

——— 'A note on Sai'. Ibid., XX, 2 (1947), 104.

——— Memorandum on the relations between Thailand and the southern states of the Malay Peninsula. Singapore, Government Printer, 1941. [H.R. Cheeseman, Bibliography of Malaya (London, 1959), 90. Beda Lim, 'Malaya, a background bibliography', JMBRAS, XXXV, 2 & 3 (1962), 50, omits the words 'Memorandum on' but otherwise appears to have taken the entry from Cheeseman. In view of the supposed date of publication, and of the fact that Cheeseman describes the work as 'originally...confidential', it may have referred to the *northern* states of the peninsula, for the southern would not make much sense. It has not been found possible to trace a copy in either Britain or Malaysia, and the entry must be regarded as suspect.]

Long, Edward E. 'In and around Kelantan'. British Malaya, IV, 6 (1929), 181–3.

Low, V.F.S. 'Kelantan and its natural resources'. Mining Magazine, XXIV, 1 (1921), 11–20; reprinted in the Far Eastern Review (Jul. 1921), 426–31.

——— 'Little known Malay'. Mid-Pacific Magazine, XXIV (1922), 351–4.

MacDonald, Simon. The geology and mineral resources of north Kelantan and north Trengganu. Ipoh, Government Printer, 1967. [Geological Survey, West Malaysia, District Memoir No. 10.]

Mahmud b. Haji Ismail, Haji Nik. Rengkasaan chetera Kelantan. Kota Bharu, Majlis Ugama Press, 1934.

Majallah kelantan. 'Ini-lah Kelantan. Ra'ayat Kelantan dengan perayaan puja umor'. Majallah Kelantan, I, 12 (1966), 7, 10.

―――― 'Penternakkan lembu-kerbau di Kelantan'. Ibid., I, 21 (1966), 3-4.

―――― 'Mesjid tua Kampong Laut'. Majallah Kelantan, II, 6 (1967), 9.

―――― 'Tuan guru Haji Husin Rahimi dalam kenangan'. Ibid., III, 10 (1971), 9.

Malaya in history. 'Malay tengkolok'. Malaya in History, VIII, 1 (1962), 32-5.

Malayan historical journal. 'Obituary of Major [Tengku] Haji Mahmud Mahyiddeen b. Tengku Abdul Kadir Kamaruddin'. Malayan Historical Journal, I, 1 (1954), 60-1.

Malm, William P. 'Music of the Ma'Yong'. Tenggara (Kuala Lumpur) 5 (1969), 114-20.

―――― 'Malaysian Ma'Yong theatre'. TDR/The Drama Review, XV 3 (T50) (Spring, 1971), 108-14, plates.

Marre, Aristide. Malais et Siamois; de l'esclavage dans la presq'île, malaise au XIXe siècle. Louvain, J.B. Istas, 1894; Orleans, Pigelet, 1894.

Maxwell, C.H. 'Some Malay words and derivations'. JMBRAS, XII, 2 (1934), 182-3.

Maxwell, W.E. 'A journey on foot to the Patani frontier'. JSBRAS, 9 (1882), 1-67.

Maxwell, W.G. & Gibson, W.S. Treaties and engagements affecting the Malay states and Borneo. London, James Truscott, 1924.

Medhurst, W. A voyage to the East Coast of Malaya. Singapore, 1828.

Middlebrook, S.M. 'Pulai: an early Chinese settlement in Kelantan'. JMBRAS, XI, 2 (1933), 151-6.

Mohd. Adnan b. Muhammad Arifin. Kitab tikaman bahasa. Kota Bharu, Al-Hikmah Press, 3rd ed. 1963; first publ. 1934.

Mohd. Affandi Hassan. 'Dari kelab keritik pena. Pertentangan, karya S. Othman'. Dewan Bahasa, XII (1968), 243-51.

Mohd. Daud Jamil. Tawarikh Gunong Reng. Kota Bharu, Al-Ahliyah Press, 1959.

Mohd. Ghazali.' Court language and etiquette of the Malays'. JMBRAS, XI, 2 (1933), 273-87. [Dato' Mohd. Ghazali was Dato' Bentara Luar of Kelantan.]

Mohd. Hussin Khali'i, *Haji Awang*. Kelantan dari zaman ka-zaman. Kota Bharu, Dian Press, 1970.

Mohd. b. *Haji Nik* Muhammad Salleh, *Nik*. 'Chatetan rengkas tentang sumber2 tempatan mengenai sejarah Kelantan'. Journal Persatuan Sejarah Kelantan, I, 1 (1964/65), 52-72.

────── 'Negeri Kelantan dari segi sejarah'. Mastika (Kuala Lumpur), XXVI, 12(1966), 10-13, 42-4.

────── 'Bunga mas dalam sejarah Kelantan'. Ibid., XXVII, 3 (1967), 23-8.

Mohd. Taib b. Osman. 'Naskah tulisan tangan Hikayat Seri Kelantan'. Bahasa (Kuala Lumpur), III (1962-63), 2-17.

────── 'A note on Abdullah's account of the Kelantan civil war in his Kesah Pelayaran Abdullah'. Bijdragen tot de Taal-, Land- en Volkenkunde, 120 (1964), 342-9.

────── 'A text on the rules of the Kelantan bull-fight'. JMBRAS, XXXVII, 2 (1964), 1-10.

────── 'Mythic elements in Malay historiography'. Tenggara, II, 2 (1968), 80-9.

Mohd. 'Uthman El-Muhammady. 'Ajaran tasawwuf Tuan Tabal dalam Jala' al-Qulub'. Nusantara (Kuala Lumpur), I (1972), 114-33

Mohd. b. *Haji* Yaacob, *Haji*. 'Dry season cultivation of vegetables and food crops on islands and river banks in Kelantan'. Malayan Agricultural Journal, XV (1958), 156-62.

Mohd. Yusup b. Saleh al-Kelantani. Risalah pechahan empat. Kota Bharu, 2 vols., 1935.

────── Risalah sinaran Kelantan. Kota Bharu, 2 vols., 1937.

────── Risalah penambah ketahuan. Kota Bharu, Mustafa Press, 1953.

―――― Risalah zaman-zaman kejadian. Kota Bharu, Mustafa Press, 1953.

―――― Risalah penerangan masa. Kota Bharu, Mustafa Press, 1953.

―――― Risalah laksana sahidangan. Kota Bharu, Mustafa Press, 1953.

Mustaffa Fadhil Mahmud (Dato' Seri Amar Diraja, Kelantan). 'Ringkasan, pandangan dan ulasan berkenaan dengan selapit atau ahli nyanyi bagi cherita2 lama di-dalam Kelantan'. Dewan Bahasa, II (1958), 223–5.

―――― 'Ringkasan asul usul manora.' Dewan Bahasa, II (1958), 462–7.

'Nakula' (pseud.) See Abdullah b. Muhammad.

Nash, Manning. 'Tradition in tension in Kelantan'. Journal of Asian & African Studies, I (1967), 310–14.

―――― 'The market as an arena for change in Kelantan, Malaysia'. American Anthropologist, LXX (1968), 944–9.

Needham, Rodney. 'Temer names'. JMBRAS, XXXVII, 1 (1964), 121–5.

Noone, H.D. 'Report on the settlement and welfare of the Ple-Temiar Senoi of the Perak-Kelantan watershed'. Journal, Federated States Museums, XIX, 1 (1936), 1–85.

―――― Report on a new neolithic site in Ulu Kelantan'. Ibid., XV (1939), 170–174, map, plates.

―――― 'New neolithic site in Ulu Kelantan, Malaya'. Nature, CXLV (Jan. 20, 1940), 112. [Note only].

Noone, R.O. 'Notes on the kampong, compounds and houses of the Patani Malay villages of Banggul Ara, in the mukim of Batu Kurau, northern Perak'. JMBRAS, XXI, 1 (1948), 124–47.

―――― 'Nutritional aspects of the preparation of hill paddy among the Temiar Senoi'. Bulletin of Raffles Museum, Ser. B, IV (1949), 8–10.

―――― 'Notes on the trade in blowpipes and blowpipe bamboo in north Malaya'. Federation Museums Journal, n.s. I/II (1954/55), 1–18.

―――― 'The distribution of the Malayan aborigines'. Ibid., III (1956), 1–30.

Norman, Henry. The people and politics of the Far East. Travels and studies in the British, French, Spanish and Portuguese colonies, Siberia, China, Japan, Korea, Siam and Malaya. London, T. Fisher Unwin, 1895. [Esp. chap. 33, 'On a raft through a forbidden state'.]

Office internationale d'hygeine publique. 'Statistique. États Malais non-fédérés. 2. État de Kelantan'. Bulletin Mensuel, Office Internationale d'Hygeine Publique (Paris), XXX, 2 (1938), 385–6. [Vital statistics 1931–5.]

Ommaney, F.D. 'The fishermen of Kelantan and Trengganu'. Geographical Magazine, XXVI (1963–64), 8–13.

Othman Kelantan, S. Pengertian. Machang (Kelantan), Pustaka Murni, 1966. [Fiction].

—— Pertentangan. Kuala Lumpur, Pustaka Antara, 1967. [Fiction]

—— Angin timor laut. Kuala Lumpur, Utusan Melayu Press, 1969. [Fiction].

—— 'Pahlawan lembu'. Dewan Bahasa, XIII (1969), 232–8. [Fiction].

—— 13 cherpen. Kota Bharu, Pustaka Dian, 1970. [Fiction].

Parry, M.L. 'The fishing methods of Kelantan and Trengganu'. JMBRAS, XXVII, 2 (1954), 77–144.

Peacock, B.V. & Dunn, F.L. 'Recent archeological discoveries in Malaysia, 1967'. Ibid., XLI, 1 (1968), 171–8.

Pepys, W.E. 'Kelantan glossary'. JSBRAS, 74 (1916), 303–21.

—— 'A Malayan side-show during the first world war'. Asiatic Review (Oct. 1950), 1174–9. [The To' Janggut rebellion.]

—— 'Kelantan during world war I'. Malaya in History, VI, 1 (1960) 36–9.

Pertubohan kebudayaan kebangsaan Melayu. Chenderamata malam seni asli Kelantan (29 dan 30 October 1965). Kota Bharu, Pertubohan Kebudayaan Kebangsaan Melayu, 1965.

'Phongsāwadān müang kalantan' [Chronicle of Kelantan]. In the Prachum phongsāwadān [Collected chronicles], Part 2. Bangkok, privately published, 1914, pp. 117–33; reprinted, Bangkok, Funeral rites of mōm Nüang Chayāngkūn, 1961, pp. 108–23; reprinted, Bangkok, Samanakphim Kāonā, 1963, pp. 563–80.

Pickering, W.A. 'The Mekong treaty and the Malay Peninsula'. Asiatic Quarterly Review, 3rd ser., I, 2 (1896), 241–7. [This issue of the Review contains several other articles on the 1896 Anglo-Siamese treaty and its effects.]

Pinkerton, W.J.D. Report on investigations into the possibilities of irrigation in Kelantan. Kuala Lumpur, Kyle, Palmer & Co., 1934.

Railway gazette. 'Reconstruction of the Malayan East Coast line. Work done in 1947–53'. Railway Gazette (Oct. 15, 1954), 435–6.

Ratnam, K.J. & Milne, R.S. 'Constituency studies: (a) Pasir Puteh'. In their The Malayan Parliamentary Election of 1964 (Singapore, University of Malaya Press, 1967), 225–42.

Ray, S.H. Review of S.V.D. von P.W. Schmidt, 'Die sprachen der Sakei und Semang auf Malacca etc.' Man, II (1902), Art. 47 (2 pp.)

Reid, A.J.S. 'A Russian in Kelantan?' Peninjau Sejarah, I, 2 (1966), 42–7.

Rentse, Anker. 'Notes on Kelantan rejang'. JMBRAS, IX, 1 (1931), 139–40.

——— 'Two folktales of Kelantan'. Ibid., 141–2.

——— 'Kelantan names for bullocks according to their colour'. Ibid., 143–5.

——— 'Kelantan Malay charms'. Ibid., 146–57.

——— 'Gantang of Kelantan'. Ibid., XI, 2 (1933), 242–4.

——— 'Notes on Malay beliefs'. Ibid., 245–51.

——— 'The points of the compass in Kelantan'. Ibid., 252.

——— 'History of Kelantan'. Ibid., XII, 2 (1934), 44–62.

——— 'The Kelantan shadow play'. Ibid., XIV, 3 (1936), 284–301.

——— 'Majapahit amulets in Kelantan'. Ibid., 302–4.

——— 'A note on Kelantan gold coins'. Ibid., 305.

——— 'Corrigenda [to his history of Kelantan].' Ibid., 306, and genealogy opposite.

——— 'Panganerne: Malayas jungledvoorge.' Geografisk Tidskrift, XL (1937), 110–36. [On Kelantan Negritos; in Danish.]

——— Gold coins of the north-eastern Malay States'. JMBRAS XVIII, 1 (1939), 88–97

―――― 'The origin of the wayang theatre (shadow play)'. *Ibid.*, xx, 1 (1947), 12–15.

―――― 'Some further notes on coins from the north-eastern Malay states'. *Ibid.*, 16–22.

―――― 'An historical note on the north-eastern Malay states'. *Ibid.*, 23–40.

Rentse, Anker & Mahmud, Dato' Haji Nik. 'Silsilah raja-raja Kelantan'. *Ibid.*, xiv, 3 (1936), opposite 306.

Rubber industry. 'The state of Kelantan'. *Rubber Industry* (1914), 162–4.

Rudie, Inge. 'Modernisering, vendidebatt, og lokalt ledershap' [Modernization, value debate, and local leadership] Tidsskrift för Samfurnforskning, ix, (1968), 89–102. [With brief abstract in English.]

Sa'ad Shukry. See Asa'ad [Shukri] *b. Haji* Muda.

Safiah *bte Haji* A. Karim, *Nik.* 'Loghat Kelantan—huraian fonoloji dan chatetan pendek mengenai sifat2 umum-nya'. Dewan Bahasa, x (1966), 258–64.

―――― 'Meninjau beberapa aspek fonoloji loghat Kelantan'. *Ibid.*, xi (1967), 357–62.

―――― 'Penyelidekan bahasa2 orang2 asli tanah Melayu'. *Ibid.*, xii (1968), 399–404.

Samad Ismail, A. 'Dari kelab keritik pena. Pertentangan, karya S. Othman'. *Ibid.*, 307–9.

Savage, H.E. 'A preliminary account of the geology of Kelantan'. JMBRAS, iii, 1 (1925), 61–75.

―――― 'A Pangan vocabulary'. *Ibid.*, iv, 1 (1926), 147–53.

Savage, H.E. (transl.) 'Two Malay tales'. *Ibid.*, 138–47.

Schebesta, Paul. Orang-utan. Leipzig, Brockhaus, 1928. [Esp. chap. 4.]

―――― 'Grammatical sketch of the Jahaij dialect, spoken by a Negrito tribe of Ulu Perak and Ulu Kelantan, Malay Peninsula' (transl. by C.O. Blagden). Bulletin of the School of Oriental & African Studies (London), iv, 4 (1928), 803–26.

―――― Among the forest dwarfs of Malaya (transl. by Arthur Chambers). London, Hutchinson, n.d. (1929). [Esp. chap. 5].

―――― 'Grammatical sketch of the Ple-Temer language' (transl. by C.O. Blagden). Journal of the Royal Asiatic Society (1931), 641–52.

―――― Les pygmées. Paris, Gallimard, 1940. [Esp. chaps. 6–9.]

―――― Die Negrito Asiens. Studia Instituti Anthropos, Wien-Modling, St. Gabriel Verlag, 1952–1957. Vol. 6, Band I, 'Geschichte, geographie, umwelt, demographie, und anthropologie der Negrito' (1952); Vol. 12, Band II, 'Ethnographie der Negrito', 1 Halbband, 'Wirtschaft und soziologie' (1954); Vol. 13, Band II, 'Ethnographie der Negrito', 2 Halbband, 'Religion und mythologie' (1957).[HRAF translations of (1954) and (1957) are available at member institutions, or at the Human Relations Area Files Office, New Haven, Conn., U.S.A.]

―――― Tanah Melayu; wanderungen und forschungen in den dschungeln Malayas. Wien-Modling, St. Gabriel Verlag, 1960.

[Note: It is possible that others of the numerous articles in German by Schebesta, listed in Karl J. Pelzer (comp.), West Malaysia and Singapore: A Selected Bibliography (New Haven, Conn., Human Relations Area Files Inc., 1971), 155–8, may contain references to Kelantan.]

Schmidt, S.V.D. von P.W. 'Die sprachen der Sakei und Semang auf Malacca und ihr verhaltnis zu den Mon-Khmer-sprachen'. Bijdragen tot de Taal-, Land- en Volkenkunde, Ser. 6, VIII (1901), 399–583.

Scott-Kemball, Jeune. 'The Kelantan *Wayang Siam* shadow puppets 'Rama' and 'Hanuman'. A comparative study of their structure.' Man, LIX (1959), Art. 108 (6 pp.)

Scrivenor, J.B. The economic geology of Kelantan and Trengganu. Kuala Lumpur, Government Printer, 1971.

Sewell, C.A. Seymour. 'Notes on some old Siamese guns'. Journal of the Siam Society, XV, 1 (1922), 1–43.

Shahrum b. Yub. 'Kelantan black art: three examples'. Federation Museums Journal, n.s. XI (1966), 38–46.

―――― 'Four Kelantan Malay games'. Ibid., XII (1967), 35–52, plates.

Sharom Ahmat. 'Report on Malay documentary sources in the former Unfederated Malay States.' Journal of the Historical Society, University of Singapore, I (1966/67), 8–13.

Shaw, William & Mohd. Kassim *Haji* Ali. Coins of north Malaya. Kuala Lumpur, Muzium Negara, 1971. [Esp. pp. 19–31].

Sheppard, M.C.ff. 'Makyong—the oldest form of Malay drama'. Straits Times Annual (1960), illust.

Sheppard, Mubin. 'The magic kite and other Ma'Yong stories. Kuala Lumpur, Federal Publications, 1960.

——— 'Four historic Malay timber buildings'. Federation Museums Journal, n.s. VII (1962), 87–92, plates. [Includes Istana Tengku Bendahara, Kota Bharu, pp. 88–9, pl. V–VII.]

——— 'Malay palaces of the past: part one'. Malaya in History, VIII, 1 (1962), 20–5.

——— 'Malay shadow play figures in the museum of archaeology and ethnology, University of Cambridge'. Federation Museums Journal, n.s. VIII (1963), 14–17, plates.

——— 'Leaf shadow puppets'. *Ibid.*, IX (1964), 37–8, plates.

——— 'Processional birds of Kelantan'. Malaya in History, X, 1 (1965), 26–30, plates.

——— 'Pa' Dogol and Wa' Long: the evolution of the comedians in the Malay shadow play in Kelantan'. JMBRAS, XXXVIII, 1 (1965), 1–5.

——— 'The giant bird'. Straits Times Annual (1965), 46–8, illust.

——— 'A recording of the Ma'Yong, the dance drama of Kelantan'. Federation Museums Journal, n.s. XII (1967), 55–103, plates.

——— 'The Khmer shadow play and its links with ancient India. A possible source of the Malay shadow play at Kelantan and Trengganu'. JMBRAS, XLI, 1 (1968), 199–204.

——— 'Feast for sea djinns'. Straits Times Annual (1968), 38–41, illust.

——— 'Traditional Malay house forms in Trengganu and Kelantan'. JMBRAS, XLII, 2 (1969), 1–9.

——— 'Ma'Yong, the Malay dance drama'. Tenggara, V (1969), 105–13.

―――― 'The oldest mosque in Malaysia is moved to a safer site'. Malaysia in History, XIII, 2 (1970), 11–14, plates.

―――― 'The magic of the Ma'Yong'. Straits Times Annual (1970), 72–5, illust.

―――― 'Shadow play up-to-date'. *Ibid.* (1971), 91–3, illust.

―――― 'Two Ma'Yong stories'. TDR/The Drama Review, XV, 3 (T50) (Spring 1971), 115–21. [Entitled 'Dewa Muda' and 'Raja Muda Lembek', these originally appeared in Sheppard's The Magic Kite, *q.v.*, 1–8 and 37–9.]

'Kijang Puteh' (pseud. for Sheppard, Mubin). 'Puteri Sadong of Kelantan'. Straits Times Annual (1961), 78–80, illust.

―――― 'Malay kites'. *Ibid.* (1962), 8–11, illust.

―――― 'Kertok—the coconut drum of Kelantan'. *Ibid.* (1964), 78–89, illust.

―――― 'Talib, the boy dalang'. *Ibid.* (1967), 62–3 illust.

―――― 'Spirits of the bangau'. *Ibid.* (1969), 70–2, illust.

―――― 'The boats of Penarek'. *Ibid.* (1971), 52–4, illust.

―――― 'Harvest drums'. *Ibid.* (1972), 73–6, illust.

Sieveking, G. de G. 'Gua Cha and the Malayan stone age'. Malayan Historical Journal, I, 2 (1954), 111–25.

―――― 'Excavations at Gua Cha, Kelantan. 1954'. Federation Museums Journal, n.s. I/II (1954/55), 75–138.

Sieveking, G. de G. & Tweedie, M.W.F. 'Excavation of an important stone age site in the Malayan jungle, at Goa Cha, Kelantan'. Illustrated London News, CCXXVI (Mar. 5, 1955), 405–7.

Sim, Katherine. 'Up the Nenggiri'. Straits Times Annual (1960), 56–9, illust.

Skeat, W.W. Malay magic, being an introduction to the folklore and popular religion of the Malay peninsula. London, Macmillan, 1900.

―――― 'Report on Cambridge exploring expedition to the Malay provinces of lower Siam'. Report of the British Association for the Advancement of Science, LXIX (1900), 393–8.

―――― Fables and folk-tales from an eastern forest. Cambridge, University Press, 1901.

────── 'Report on 2nd Cambridge expedition to the Malay provinces of lower Siam'. Report of the British Association for the Advancement of Science, LXXI (1901), 411–24.

────── 'Notes on the ethnography of the Malay Peninsula'. Man, I (1901), Art. 142 (4 pp.)

────── 'Silk and cotton dyeing by Malays'. JSBRAS, 38 (1902), 123–7.

Skeat, W.W. & Blagden, C.O. Pagan races of the Malay Peninsula. London, Macmillan, 1906.

Skeat, W.W. & Laidlaw, F.F. 'The Cambridge university expedition to parts of the Malay Peninsula, 1899–1900. Personal accounts by the late W.W. Skeat and F.F. Laidlaw'. JMBRAS, XXVI, 4 (1953), 1–174.

Skinner, Cyril. The civil war in Kelantan in 1839. Singapore, Monographs of the Malaysian Branch, Royal Asiatic Society, No. 2, 1965.

────── 'Abdullah's voyage to the East Coast, seen through contemporary eyes'. JMBRAS, XXXIX, 2 (1966), 23–33.

────── 'The dating of the civil war in Kelantan referred to in the Kesah Pelayaran Abdullah'. Bijdragen tot de Taal-, Land- en Volkenkunde, 121 (1965), 433–7.

Slimming, John. Temiar jungle. A Malayan journey. London, John Murray, 1958.

Smith, T.E. 'Marriage, widowhood and divorce in the Federation of Malaya'. International Population Conference, V, 2 (1963), 302–9.

Smyth, H. Warington. Five years in Siam, from 1891 to 1896. London, John Murray, 2 vols., 1898. [Esp. vol. II].

────── 'Boats and boat-building in the Malay Peninsula'. Journal of the Society of Arts, L (1902), 570–86.

Stacey, Tom. The hostile sun. A Malayan journey. London, Gerald Duckworth, 1953.

Steffen, A. (with notes by N. Annandale). 'Clay tablets from caves in Siamese Malaya'. Man, II (1902), Art. 125 (4 pp.)

Stevens, Hrolf Vaughan. 'Materialen zur kenntnis der wilden staemme auf der Halbinsel Malaka' (ed. by A. Grünwedel). Veroeffentlichungen aus dem Koeniglichen Museum fuer Voelkenkunde (Berlin), II (1892), 81–163, III (1894), 95–100.

Stewart, K. 'Dream theory in Malaya.' Complex (New York), II (1951).

——— 'Culture and personality in two primitive groups'. *Ibid.*, IV (1953).

——— 'Mental hygiene and world peace'. Mental Hygiene, XXVIII (1945), 387-403.

——— 'The dream comes of age'. *Ibid.*, XLVI (1967), 230-7. [Note: The foregoing articles by Stewart contain material on the Temiar of Kelantan.]

Sturrock, A.J. 'Some notes on the dialect of Kelantan'. JSBRAS, 62 (1912), 1-7.

Suara siswa. Articles on Patani. Suara Siswa (Kuala Lumpur), II, 2 (1970), 3-63. [Complete issue contains a number of articles, reprinted, on the irredentist movement in Patani.]

Suhrke, Astri. 'The Thai Muslims: some aspects of minority integration'. Pacific Affairs, XLIII, 4 (Winter 1970-71), 531-47.

Sullivan, Frank. 'The batik art of Khalil Ibrahim'. Straits Times Annual (1970), 54-9, illust.

——— 'Painter of the epics'. *Ibid.*, (1972), 80-3, illust.

Sweeney, Amin. 'The Rama repertoire in the Kelantan shadow play: a preliminary report'. Tenggara, V (1969), 129-38.

——— 'The shadow-play of Kelantan. Report on a period of field research'. JMBRAS, XLIII, 2 (1970), 53-80, plates.

Swettenham, F.S. 'Some account of the independent native states of the Malay Peninsula'. JSBRAS, 6 (1880), 161-202.

Teeuw, A. & Wyatt, D.K. Hikayat Patani. The story of Patani. The Hague, Martinus Nijhoff, 2 vols., 1970.

Thamsook Numnonda. 'The Anglo-Siamese secret convention of 1897'. Journal of the Siam Society, LIII, 1 (1965), 45-61.

——— 'Negotiations regarding the cession of Siamese Malay states, 1907-9'. *Ibid.*, LV (1967), 227-35.

Thiphākǫrawong, *Čhaophrayā*. Phrarātchaphongsāwadān krung rattanakōsin chabap hǫsamut hāēng chāt; ratchakān thī 1 [dǫi Čhaophrayā Thiphākǫrawong ... lae] ratchakān thī 2 [dǫi Prince Damrong Rajanubhab] [Royal Chronicles of the Bangkok Era, National

Library ed.; First Reign (by Čhaophrayā Thiphākǭrawong) and Second Reign (by Prince Damrong Rajanubhab)]. Bangkok, Samnakphim Khlang Witthayā, 2505 (1962). [These standard chronicles, covering the years 1782-1824, include some references to Kelantan (pp. 125, 537-538) and many to Patani.]

—— Phrarātchaphongsāwadān krung rattanakōsin chabap hǭsamut hāēng chāt; ratchakān thī 3 ... ratchakān thī 4 [Royal Chronicles of the Bangkok Era, National Library ed.; Third Reign [and] Fourth Reign.] Bangkok, Samnakphim Khlang Witthayā, 2506 (1963). [Kelantan figures prominently in the Third Reign (1824-51), but is less in evidence in the Fourth (1851-68).]

Thomas, M. Ladd. 'Political socialization of the Thai-Islam'. In R.K. Sakai (ed.), Studies on Asia (Lincoln, Neb., University of Nebraska Press) 7 (1966), 89-106.

—— 'Some observations on interaction of local authority and development programs in the four Muslim provinces of Thailand'. In F.R. von der Mehden & David A. Wilson (eds.), Local Authority and Administration in Thailand (Los Angeles, Academic Advisory Council for Thailand, University of California at Los Angeles, 1970), 145-69.

Thompson, Geoffrey. Front-line diplomat. London, Hutchinson, 1959. [Thompson was British Minister to Bangkok from March 1946 to April 1950.]

Thompson, Virginia & Adloff, Richard. 'The Malays of south Thailand'. In their Minority Problems in Southeast Asia (Stanford, Calif., University Press, 1955), 158-65.

Tjoa Soei Hock. Institutional background to modern economic and social development in Malaya (with special reference to the East Coast). Kuala Lumpur, Liu & Liu Agency, 1963.

Trevor, J.C. & Brothwell, D.R. 'The human remains of mesolithic and neolithic data from Gua Cha, Kelantan'. Federation Museums Journal, n.s. VII (1962), 6-16, plates.

Tylor, E.B. 'Malay divining rods'. Man, II (1902), Art. 40 (2 pp.)

Tweedie, M.W.F. 'Report on excavations in Kelantan'. JMBRAS, XVIII, 2 (1940), 1-22.

—— Obituary of Anker Rentse. Ibid., XXIV, 1 (1951), 192-3.

────── 'An early Chinese account of Kelantan.' *Ibid.*, XXVI, 1 (1953), 216–19.

────── 'Obituary: W.W. Skeat, 1866–1953'. *Ibid.*, 225–8.

Udom Sombat, *Luang*. Čhotmāi lūang udom sombat [The letters of Luang Udom Sombat]. Bangkok, Funeral rites of Phra Rattanathatmunī, 2505 (1962).

Utusan Melayu. 'Perbadanan kemajuan iktisad negeri Kelantan'. In Kemajuan Melayu: Laporan Khas Utusan Melayu (Kuala Lumpur, Utusan Melayu Press, 1971), 53–7.

Vaughan, J.D. 'Puppet shows'. In N.B. Dennys, A Descriptive Dictionary of British Malaya (London, London & China Telegraph Office, 1894), 324.

Vella, Walter. Siam under Rama III, 1824–1851. Locust Valley, N.Y., J.J. Augustin, 1957. [Esp. chap. 5]

Wang Gungwu. 'An early Chinese visitor to Kelantan'. Malaya in History, VI, 1 (1960), 31–5.

Wansbrough-Jones, Ll. 'The Kelantan section of the East Coast railway, Federated Malay States railways'. Royal Engineers Journal, XLIV (1930), 647–56.

Waterstradt, J. 'Kelantan and my trip to Gunong Tahan'. JSBRAS, 37 (1902), 1–27.

Wavell, Stewart. The lost world of the east. An adventurous quest in the Malayan hinterland. London, Souvenir Press, 1958.

────── The Naga king's daughter. London, Allen & Unwin, 1964.

────── Trances. London, Allen & Unwin, 1966.

Wells, Carveth. Six years in the Malay jungle. London, Heinemann; New York, Doubleday, 1925. [Wells, a surveyor, was in Kelantan during the period of the To' Janggut rebellion.]

────── North of Singapore. New York, Robert M. McBride, 1940 [Chaps. 8 and 9 describe a return visit to Kelantan in 1939,]

Wenk, Klaus. The restoration of Thailand under Rama I, 1782–1809. Tucson, Arizona, University of Arizona Press for Association of Asian Studies, 1968. [Esp. pp. 100–3]

Whitney, Gaspar. Jungle trails and jungle people; travel, adventure and observation in the far east. New York, Scribner, 1905.

Whittingham-Jones, Barbara. 'Patani appeals to UNO', Eastern World, II, 4 (1948), 4–5.

Wichiankhiri, Phrayā. 'Phongsāwadān müang pattani' [Chronicle of Patani] In the Prachum phongsāwadān [Collected Chronicles] (Bangkok, Samnakphim Kāonā, 1964), II, 1–29. [First publ. 1914].

Wilkinson, R.J. The aboriginal tribes. Papers on Malay Subjects, Ser. 1, Supplement, Kuala Lumpur, Government Printer, 1910.

Williams-Hunt, P.D.R. An introduction to the Malayan aborigines-Kuala Lumpur, Government Printer, 1952.

Wilson, John Anthony Burgess. See Burgess, Anthony.

Wilson, T.B. The economics of padi production in north Malaya. Part I: Land tenure, rents, land use, and fragmentation. Kuala Lumpur, Ministry of Agriculture, 1958.

Winstedt, R.O. 'A Malay pantheist charm'. JSBRAS, 86 (1922), 261–7. [Probably from Kelantan].

——— Review of the 2nd (1922) edition of J.D. Gimlette's Malay Poisons and Charm Cures. JMBRAS, I (1923), 264–5. [Cf. also his review of the 3rd ed., 1929, in ibid., VII (1929), 376.]

——— 'Notes on Malay magic'. Ibid., III, 3 (1925), 6–21.

——— 'The great flood, 1926'. Ibid., V, 2 (1927), 295–309.

——— 'Obituary. John Desmond Gimlette'. Ibid., XII, 2 (1934), 184.

——— 'A Panji tale from Kelantan'. Ibid., XXII, 1 (1949), 53–60.

Wright, A. & Reid, T.H. The Malay Peninsula. A record of British progress in the Middle East [sic]. London, T. Fisher Unwin, 1912. [Esp. chaps. 10 and 11.]

Wyatt, David K. 'A Thai version of Newbold's Hikayat Patani'. JMBRAS, XL, 2 (1967), 16–37.

——— 'Thai sources for the study of Malaysia's history'. Peninjau Sejarah, II, 1 (1967), 19–24.

Wyatt, D.K. & Wilson, C.M. 'Thai historical materials in Bangkok'. Journal of Asian Studies, XXV, 1 (1965), 105–18.

Yahaya Ismail. 'Ulasan buku. Pertentangan (novel) karya S. Othman, Kelantan ... 1967'. Dewan Bahasa, XL (1967), 281–6.

Yahya Abdullah. Peperangan To' Janggut, atau balasan derhaka. Kota Bharu, Muslim Printing Press, 1955.

Yano, Toru. 'A socio-anthropological study in Songkhla province: a preliminary report'. Tonan Ajia Kenkyu (Kyoto), III, 1 (1965), 140-3.

——— 'Land tenure in south Thailand'. Ibid., IV, 5 (1966), 2-31. [In Japanese]

Yorke, Susan. 'Kelantan silver and silks'. Hemisphere (Sydney), XIII (May 1969), 9-13, illust.

Youngman, E.P. Mining laws of the Unfederated Malay States. Washington, United States Bureau of Mines, Information Circular No. 6633, 1932.

Yusop Zaki Yaakub. Pembongkaran rahsia Subud. Kota Bharu, Pustaka Dian, 1961.

Zakiah Hanum. 'Thai materials in the [Malaysian] national archives- Peninjau Sejarah, II, 2 (1967), 52-3.

Zakaria b. Haji Awang Soh. 'Sediments of Kelantan delta: grain-size distribution in different environmental conditions'. Nusantara, 2 (July 1972), 169-187.

INDEX

ABAS PA' NIK, 83.
Abbas b. Haji Muhammad, Haji, 168.
Abbas Taha, Haji, 161.
Abdul Aziz, Tengku, 295.
Abdul Aziz b. Omar, 188.
Abdul Ghani Azmi, Dr., 174.
Abdul Kadir, Engku (Engku Dir), 172.
Abdul Kadir Adabi, 177, 180.
Abdul Latiff, Inche, 71.
Abdul Majid, Tengku, 158.
Abdul Rab Attamini, 182.
Abdul Rahman, To' Semian Wan, 154, 156.
Abdul Rahman b. Daud al-Makki, Haji, 175.
Abdul Rahman b. Haji Wan Musa, Nik, 156.
Abdul Rahman b. Sultan Muhammad III, Tengku, 134, 135.
Abdul Razak, 75.
Abdul Razak, Tun, 303-4.
Abdul Samad, Haji (Tuan Tabal), 154-5, 156, 169.
Abdullah, Haji Nik, 92.
Abdullah, Imam Haji, 40.
Abdullah, Khatib Haji Wan, 138.
Abdullah b. Abdul Kadir, Munshi, 107, 171.
Abdullah b. Haji Wan Abdul Samad, Wan, 133, 146, 154, 155, 165.
Abdullah b. Haji Wan Musa, Haji Nik, 156, 161-4, 165, 169.
Abdullah b. Muhammad (Nakula), 185.
Abdullah b. Raja Zainal, Nik, 154, 155, 159.
Abdullah b. Sultan Ahmad, Tengku Chik, 32, 58, 158.
Abdullah b. Tengku Mahmud, Tengku, 158.
Abdullah 'Aqhas (Abdullah Al-Qari), 185.
Abdullah Muhammad, 184.
Abdullah Tahir b. Haji Ahmad, Tuan Guru Haji, 95, 96, 168.
Abdullah Zawawi, Haji, 97.
Abu Abdullah Sa'id Hasan b. Nur Hasan (To' Khorasani), 156, 162.
Abu al-Samah al-Zahiri, 162.
Abu Bakar, Khatib, 83.
Abu Hassan al-Azahari, Shaykh, 140.
Abu'l-Hasan ash-Shadhīlī, 155.
Achehnese, 174, 302.
Adam, Penghulu of Kelubi, 63, 70, 77, 80, 84.
Adams, Mr., 82.
Adat (custom), 101, 106, 176, 231; *adat temenggong*, 228.
Ad-Durus al-Kenaliyyat al-ibtida'iyyah, 95, 96.
Afghans, 141, 162.
Ahmad, father of To' Kenali, 88.
Ahmad, headman of Kampong Kenali, 88.
Ahmad, Haji, Penghulu, 84.
Ahmad, Sultan (1886-90) (Tuan Long Ahmad: 'Sultan Tengah'), 23, 24, 32, 107, 108, 156, 277.
Ahmad, Tengku Long, 8, 11, 12-14.
Ahmad, Tuan Guru Wan (Ahmad Patani), 91, 155, 172.
Ahmad b. Haji Abdul Manan, Haji, 121, 133.
Ahmad b. Haji Abdul Rahman, Haji, 121.
Ahmad b. Haji Ismail, Haji (To' Kemuning), 163.

Ahmad b. Haji Muhammad Yusof, Haji, 97.
Ahmad b. Haji Nik Hassan, Nik, 186.
Ahmad b. Isa Banjari, 179.
Ahmad b. Ismail, 94, 96, 175, 180.
Ahmad Asmara, 185.
Ahmad Kamil, Dato' Nik, 282–3, 284, 295.
Ahmad Mahir b. Haji Ismail, Haji, Mufti, 160, 167, 168, 173.
Ahmadiyyah *tarekat*, 140.
Ahmadiyyah-Shadhiliyyah *tarekat*, 158.
A'isyah, Nik, 156.
Al-Ahliyah Press, Kota Bharu, 185, 186.
Al-Asasiyah Press, Kota Bharu, 175, 180.
al-Azhar University, Cairo, 91, 96, 126, 172, 184, 187.
Alcohol, 122, 129–30, 225, 264.
al-Ghazzali, Imam, (1058–1111), 87, 99.
Al-Hedayah journal, 87, 94, 96, 175–7, 180.
Al-Hikmah journal, 96, 175, 180, 187.
Al-Hikmah Press, Kota Bharu, 175, 180.
Ali, accused in a theft case, 27–8.
Ali, *luang* Seri Paduka, 9.
Ali b. Kassim, Shaykh, 178.
Ali Kutan, Haji Wan, 172.
Ali Maliki, Shaykh, 156, 162.
Al-Imam journal, 171.
Ali Pulau Pinang, Haji, 95.
Ali Salahuddin, Tuan Guru Haji, 95–6.
al-Jam'iyyat al-'Asriyyah, 94.
al-jāddat al-qawiyyat al-Muhammadiyya, 163, 165.
Al-Kamaliah Press, Kota Bharu, 177, 178, 182, 183, 186.
Al-Kitab periodical, 174–5.
Allah: and magic, 195, 196–7, 200–2, 204, 213; and prayer, 293.
Alliance Party: publicity for, 187; founded, 273; in 1955 elections, 273, 284–6; and independence, 284–6, 291; in 1959 elections, 286; peasants disillusioned with, 288, 291–2, 307; and federal grants, 293, 296, 297, 303–5, 306.
Al-Ma'arif Press, Kota Bharu, 181.
al-Shafi'i, Imam, 96.
al-Umm, 96.
Aluwi b. Tahir al-Haddad, Sayyid, 168.
Amaluddin Darus, 183, 186.
Ambergris used in magic, 198.
Ambon Island, 182.
Anah, Ganah, Janah and Manah (spirits), 205, 211, 212.
Anderson, Sir John, 55, 57–8.
Anglo-Kelantan Treaty (1910), 58, 64, 68, 102, 119.
Anglo-Siamese Boundary Agreement (1899), 35, 38.
Anglo-Siamese Boundary Protocol (1908), 55.
Anglo-Siamese Convention (1897), 35, 38, 55.
Anglo-Siamese Treaty (1902), 33, 40–1, 47, 49–50, 52, 58, 64, 110.
Anglo-Siamese Treaty (1909), vii, 55–7, 58, 64, 68, 111, 119.
Angsa, Luang, 42.
Annam, 34, 45.
Anomeng Gerop Puteh (Hanuman, a spirit), 217.
Anti-colonialism, 279, 282.
Anwar Halim, 184.
Apostasy, 130.
Appeals: to Sultan, 106; to Mufti, 113, 121, 123, 124; to Majlis Ugama, 138, 139.
Arabic language: teaching of, 89, 144, 175, 265; students of, 90; To' Kenali's improved methods of teaching, 92, 94–5; translations from, 96, 142, 148, 154, 175, 179, 180, 181; verse in, 97; books written in, 103; *khatib* required to know, 105; scholars in, 145; Islam and literacy in, 263.
Arabic schools, 246, 247–9, 251, 254, 255, 262, 266, 268.
Arabs, 91, 180; and Islam, 165.
Aristocracy: traditional rural leaders, 66–7; inferior status for those outside, 67; and taxation, 72; guardians of Malay custom and Islam, 133, 244; promote nationalism, 273; support royal family's intrigues, 277; gain influence through Majlis Ugama, 278–9; peasants owe no allegiance to, 280; enjoy hegemony under colonial regime, 283; on State Council, 286; one of four classes in Malaya, 290.
Arjuna (spirit), 217.
Arts and crafts, v–vi, viii, 243.
Asa'ad b. Haji Daud, Haji, 96, 165.
Asa'ad Shukri b. Haji Muda, *see* Muhammad Asa'ad.
Ashari Muhammad, 188.
Asri, Dato', *see* Muhammad Asri, Dato'.
Asmupati (Angkatan Sasterawan Muda Partai Timur), 184.
Assaults, 63, 72.
Assistant British Advisers, 44, 64, 120.
Assistant District Officers, 175, 177.
Assistant *Kathis*, 113, 121, 124.
Assistant Muftis, 92, 138.
Audit, 148; Audit Office, 148.
Autonomy, vi, 278.
Awang Chik, 25.
Awang, To' Wali, 196–7.
Awang-Meh Sari, 193–5.
Ayub b. Haji Husain Kemboja, Haji, 165.
Ayudhya Kingdom (Siam), 2, 3.
Ayyuha'l-walad, 99.

BACHOK, 74, 78, 190, 192, 206, 221; To' Guru of, 90, 206, 208–9.
Bagheh (trance rite), 213, 214–16, 222.
Bahar, Long (Raja Thawọ: Long Yu-

nus), Governor of Kelantan (*circa* 1740), 5.
Baharuddin Latif, 183.
Baja, Wan, 17.
Bakti periodical, 185.
Balai besar (Raja's audience hall), 57, 81, 106, 125, 130; *balai menteri*, 3.
Balai Pustaka (Press), Djakarta, 178.
Bananas used in magic ritual, 193-4, 207.
Bandung, Java, 178, 182.
Banggu, 80.
Banggul, Tuan (Long Zainal), 5, 6, 7, 8, 11-14.
Bangkok, 8, 13, 14, 18, 51; Long Yusof visits, 7, 9, 11, 12, 16; *bunga mas* sent to, 17, 34; Dato' Maha Mentri visits, 25; news of Sultan Mansur's illness sent to, 29; Burney's negotiations in, 33; French influence in, 35; Duff visits, 37, 49; negotiations for 1902 Treaty in, 40; Graham and Thomson reach Kelantan from, 41; discussion on Duff's concession takes place in, 50; negotiations for 1909 Treaty in, 53, 55; Raja Senik refuses to visit, 56; Graham returns to, 57; historical records in, 109 (used also as an equivalent for Siamese Government).
Ban Phrai Wan (Kampong Belawan), Siam, 55.
Ban Tak Bai (Kampong Tabal), Siam, 55.
Bān Thāle, *phrayā* (Tuan Long Ismail), Raja Muda of Kelantan, 5, 6.
Batek dyeing, 243.
Batu Melintang, 55.
Batu Mengkebang (town), 43, 121, 124.
Batu Mengkebang (Ulu Kelantan) district, 95, 112.
Batu Sebutir, Pasir Puteh, 76.
Batu Tiga, Pasir Mas, 187.
Bayt ul-mal (treasury for religious revenue), 131, 136, 139.
Bengkelam, 80.
Bentong, Pahang, 182.
Beras fitrah (rice used for alms), 136, 146.
Beras kunyit (rice mixed with turmeric), 203-4, 207.
Berita Pertanian Kelantan, journal of Agriculture Department, 183.
Berkat (blessed), 263, 267.
Bersilat (art of self-defence), 73, 244.
Beserah, Pahang, 198.
Besut, Trengganu, 75, 82, 168, 192, 198.
Betel vines, tax on, 70, 73.
Bid'ah (innovations), 159, 161.
Bilal (*surau* official), 69, 105, 116.
Bintang Emas Press, Kota Bharu, 186.
Bishop, J.E., British Adviser (1910-13), 121-2.
Blood, *hantu* and, 216.
Boats, magic and, 198, 203-4.
Bomoh (spirit medium): important in village life, 105; and healing, 192, 212, 216, 238-9, 240, 264; and fishing, 199, 200-6; and *keramat*, 201, 207-8; and personal protection, 209-17; *penggawa* and, 215-17; and conjuring, 217-22; and exorcism, 264.
Bongsu, Tuan, 26, 32.
Books, reviews of, 175-6, 179.
Braddell, Thomas, 53.
Bribes paid to Siamese, 24, 28.
British: control west Malayan states, vii, 110; their views on *bunga mas*, 34; 'forward movement' by, 39-40, 68; in Kelantan Civil Service, 45, 119; in Siam, 51, 53, 55; planters in Kelantan, 75-6; send soldiers to Kelantan, 78, 79-80, 81, 82; and First World War, 79; and Islam, 102-3, 130-1; and reforms in Kelantan, 107; Graham in Kelantan copies their administration in F.M.S., 112; their regime in Kelantan, 114, 119, 172, 180, 261; and Majlis Ugama, 133; British law, 143, 172; in India, 166; introduce printing into F.M.S., 171; Japanese urge Malays to fight against, 181; colonial rule of, 273, 275, 276-7, 278, 281, 283, 286, 309; occasion for their intervention in Malaya, 277; their policy in Kelantan in 1920's and 1930's, 280; land policy of, 290.
British Advisers: Kelantan has to accept, vii, 119; powers of, vii, 58, 64-5; members of State Council, 44, 65; introduced, 57; confirmed by Anglo-Kelantan Treaty, 58; records of, 62; seconded from Malayan Civil Service, 119; administrative reforms of, 120-1; look for efficiency, 123; consulted by Mufti about appointment of his staff, 124, 138; indirect rule by, 277-8; and peasants, 288.
British Residents, vii, 28, 40.
Brownlow, Colonel, 78.
Brunei, 64, 169.
Buddhism, 253; Buddhist states, 53.
Bugis people, 256.
Bukit Abal, Pasir Puteh, 79.
Bukit Jawa, Pasir Puteh, 76, 79, 80.
Bukit Merbau, 196; Wali of, 208-9.
Bukit Mertajam, Province Wellesley, 95-6.
Bulan Melayu journal, 179.
Bull-fighting, 66, 118.
Bunga Mas, 5, 6, 9, 17, 32, 34.
Bunut Payong, Kota Bharu, 95, 96, 185.
Bureaucratization: of Islam, 103, 115, 131, 135, 149, 261, 279; of *imam*, of general administration, 118; of Mufti's office, 123-4, (*see also* Institutionalization).
Bureaucrats, 244, 245.
Burhanuddin Al-Helmi, Dr., 160, 182 279.
Burma, 41, 45.

Burney, Captain Henry, 33; his treaty (1826), 33.
Busu b. Tuan Long Ismail, Tuan, 6.
Busu b. *phrayā* Temenggong, Tuan, Raja Muda of Kelantan, 6, 7, 8–11, 14.

Cadmus, H.M.S., 79.
Cairo, 89, 91, 96, 126, 174, 187, 280.
Calcutta, 166.
Calypso, H.M.S., 81.
Cambodia, 35, 91, 92, 155, 165.
Candles used in magic, 203–4, 205.
Cattle-theft, 63, 72.
Central Court, 43, 112.
'Centrality', 253–6, 257.
Ceylon, 166.
Chaiphonphak, *luang*, 7.
Chaiyā province, Siam, 12.
Chaiyā Thāinām, *phrayā*, 12–14.
Chakri dynasty of Siam, 3, 16.
Chāngwāng (title), 7.
Chāngwāng, *phrayā*, 7, 9–11, 13, 14, 15.
Charity, 136.
Charoon, Chao, 41–2.
Che', Tengku (Engku Na Nik), 15.
Che' Ha', Dato', Dato' Maha Mentri, 24, 108 (see Sa'ad).
Cherang Tuli, Pasir Puteh, 63, 76–7.
Che' Wan, Sgt., 73–5, 76.
Chief Minister of Kelantan, 30, 89, 92, 94, 125, 134, 278, 282–3, 286, 287.
Chief Police Officer, 36, 76, 83, 119.
Ch'ih-t'u, 2.
Chik, Tengku, Tengku Chik Penambang, 23, 26–8.
Chi-lan-tan (Kelantan), 2.
Children: upbringing of, 226–7; and spirits, 227, 239.
China, 2, 34, 38.
Chinese in Kelantan, v, 16, 27, 37, 44, 75, 129, 280, 289–90; travellers, 23; trial of, 122; love gambling and opium-smoking, 129–30; marry Malay girls, 130; supply goods to conjurers, 218–19; economic dominance of, 245, 256–7; Malays and, 246, 280; schools for, 246, 247, 251; Chinese students' sense of values, 251, 254, 256; and religion, 253; endogamy among, 256; race-formation among, 256; in Alliance Party, 273.
Chinese records, 2.
Christians, 158, 169.
Chuang Bunnag, Regent of Siam (1868–73), 16, 17.
Chulalongkorn (Rama V), King of Siam (1868–1910), 4, 16, 31, 36, 39, 52, 56.
Chung Hwa School, Kota Bharu, 248–50, 251.
Civil Procedure Code, 112.
Civil servants, 133–4, 144, 244, 245, 250, 278, 282, 291.
Clifford, Hugh, 28, 30, 33, 36, 107.

Cochin China, 35.
Cockfighting, 66, 73, 107, 108, 197.
Coconuts: plantations of, 63, 75, 76; tax on, 73, 77, 88; planters of, 75–6; used in magic ritual, 193–4.
Coffee shops, 261, 271.
Colonial Office, Britain, 52, 53, 58, 62.
Commerce, 280, 281 (*see also* Trade).
Commercialization, 290.
Communalism, 256–7, 281, 289; communal tension, 245.
Concessions, 36–9, 41, 48, 50, 111, 118, 120.
Conjuring, 190, 217–22.
Corruption in courts, 113, 120.
Cotton threads used in magic, 202, 203, 207, 218, 219, 221.
Conterfeiting, 46–7.
Courtesy (*budi bahasa*), 226, 231, 234, 245, 253.
Courts: Raja's relatives usurp functions of, 32; Small Courts, 43, 71, 72; Courts of Small Causes, 43, 67, 112; criminal, 106; Central Court, 112; corruption in, 113, 120; jurisdiction of, 139, 142 (*see also* High Court: Shari'a Court).
Courts Regulation, 112.
Crime: in Kelantan, 63, 71–2; reporting of, 178.
Criminal Procedure Code, 112.
Crop assessment, 112.
Currency: tin, 39, 45–7; Siamese, 39, 47–8; crisis over, 45–7.
Customs, Supervisor of, 119.

Daerah (district), 44, 45.
Dagang, Tuan, 14.
Damrong, Prince, 29, 37, 49–50.
Danes, 38.
Dareh, Tengku, 11.
Darul-'Ulum, Deoband, India, 156, 162, 165.
Dasuki Ahmad, 187.
Dato' Maha Mentri, *see* Sa'ad, Dato'.
Dato' Sri Paduka, *see* Nik Yusof.
Daud, Haji Wan (appointed to Majlis Ugama, 1917), 146.
Daud b. Wan Suleiman, Imam Haji Wan, Mufti (?1893–1907), 108, 121, 155.
Daud b. Abdullah al-Patani, Shaykh, 91, 154.
Daud b. Che' Husain, Haji (Haji Daud Kechik), 154.
Davies, R.D., 110, 113.
Delhi, 165, 166.
Deli, Sumatra, 147.
Demarcation of *mukim* boundaries, 138.
Deoband, India, 156, 162, 165, 166.
Derahman, Penghulu, 84.
Deraman b. Diah, 83.
Deru journal, 188.
Devawongse Varoprakar, Prince, 55.

Dictionaries, 174, 183.
District Officers: established, 45, 63, 112; supplant local chiefs, 63, 65, 67, 69–70; grant licences, 213; appoint *penghulus*, 231.
Districts, 44–5, 68, 112.
Dit Bunnag (*čhaophrayā* Phra Khlang), 8, 16.
Divorce, 156; *imam* and, 104; cases heard in Shari'a Court, 106, 139; Regulations concerning, 114; fees for registration of, 128; of prostitutes, 141; common in Kelantan, 228–9; wives and, 229, 235.
Djakarta, Java, 178.
Dogs, cleanliness of, 160–1, 279.
Doves used in conjuring, 218–22.
Dreams, 162; magic and, 193.
Dress and piety, 166, 263–4.
Duff Development Company, 33, 36, 39, 45, 48–50, 52, 111, 132; Duff Syndicate, 32–3, 37, 38, 39.
Duff, Robert William, 32–3, 36–40, 48–9, 52, 111, 277.
Durian, tax on, 77, 88.
Dutan, Nebeng, 84.
Dutch historical records, 2.

ECONOMIC DOMINANCE, of Chinese, 245, 256–7.
Economics, communal interaction in, 256.
Education: reforms in, 43; secular, 43, 103, 112, 137; religious, 43, 96, 103, 104, 145, 157, 158, 231, 265, 266, 268; Majlis Ugama and, 142–3, 147, 148–9, 278; 'English', 144, 167, 284; in *pondok*, 155; 'Malay', 175; belief in magic reduced by, 190, 223; and marriage, 227; and status, 231; and tradition, 241; in Pasir Mas, 245–57; purposes of, 246; primary, 268; vernacular, 268, 279; colonial, 282 (*see also* Schools).
Eggs used in magic, 203, 204, 211, 216.
Egypt, 91, 159, 163.
Egyptians, 161.
Elong river, 55.
Elections: (1955), 273, 277, 283, 284, 285–6, 288; (1959), 273–4, 286, 287, 292, 294, 296; (1964), 294; (1969), 295, 297.
Elephant, and magic, 207.
Elites: rural, 72, 277, 286; administrative, 273, 284; in politics, 276; urban, 277, 280; religious, 279, 280; traditional, 281, 283–5, 287, 293, 295, 309; in PMK, 282; new, 283; local, 286; non-traditional, 286.
Embung, Tengku, 156–7.
Embung, Wan, 156.
Emergency (1948–60), 282.
Emigration from Kelantan, 289.
Emotional support: between parents and children, 226; between close relations, 229.
Employment for Kelantanese, 278.
Enactments, 114, 139, 140, 179.
Endogamy, 256.
Engku (title), 23.
England, 289; study in, 145–6, 158, 283.
English-educated aristocrats, 273, 282.
English historical records, 2.
English language: as medium of education, 144, 167, 177, 188, 246, 248–9, 250, 251–2, 278; translations from, 148, 173, 181.
Ethnicity, 243, 250, 251–4, 256–7.
Europeans: and commerce, 2, 257, 280; in Kelantan, 75; as officials in Kelantan, 119; and alcohol, 129.
Exorcism, 213, 264.
Extraterritorial rights, 51–2, 55, 57.

FAISAL, AMIR OF IRAQ, 174.
Family, importance of, 226–7, 230.
Faridah, Nik, 183.
Farrer, R.J., British Adviser, 62, 73, 129, 134, 142, 143, 144.
Fasting month (Ramadhan), 104, 108, 117, 122, 127, 136, 140, 232, 263, 265, 294.
Fatimah, Hajjah (mother of To' Kenali), 88, 91.
Fatimah bte Haji Wan Musa, Nik, 156.
Fatimah Haji Karim, Nik, 183.
Fatwa (legal rulings on religion), 102, 124, 140, 141, 146, 157, 172.
Federal Legislative Assembly, 183, 274.
Federated Malay States (F.M.S.): not the only source of Malaysia's institutions, 1; some officials in Kelantan recruited from, 42; and Kelantan's financial crisis, 47–8; gives Siam a loan to build a railway, 51, 55, 57; railway system in, 57; Kelantan not part of, 58–9; Islam in, 103; British administration in, 112; Adviser to Kelantan an official of, 119; administration of justice in, 120; fees from marriage and divorce spent on religious purposes in, 128; makes loans to Kelantan, 132 (*see also* Straits Settlements).
Federated Malay States Government, 51, 53; High Commissioner, 1, 40, 55, 57, 62, 63–4, 118, 119, 125, 129, 143, 144; Governor, 35, 64; Resident-General, 57.
Federated Malay States Service, 41, 119.
Federation of Malaya, vii, 1, 273.
Festivals, expenditure on, 126–7, 136.
Feudalism, 261, 279, 289.
Fikh (jurisprudence), 145, 154, 160, 165, 167.
Filsafat Berumahtangga, 168.
Finances: of Kelantan, 45–8, 69–73, 109, 111, 119, 132; of Majlis Ugama and,

126, 133, 135–7, 145, 146, 147–9.
Fines, 114, 115, 117–18, 122, 124, 126–7, 128.
First World War, 79, 84, 162, 166, 175.
Fishermen, 243; and agricultural magic, 192, 193; master-fishermen, 195, 196–7, 200, 203, 219.
Fishfighting, 66.
Fishing: licences for, 112; magic and, 195–206, 209, 215.
Fitrah (tax for alms), 105, 106, 136–7, 143, 145, 146, 147, 148, 294 (*see also Zakat*).
Foreign Office, Britain, 37, 38, 52.
Foreign relations in Kelantan, 34, 41, 58.
Forests, magic against animal damage in, 192.
France, 35, 51, 289.
Franco–Siamese Treaty (1907), 51, 53.
French, 35, 38, 53.
French historical records, 2.
Friday prayers, 270; Imam's duties at, 104, 117, 264–5; Regulations for, 108, 114; punishment for non-attendance at, 109, 115, 126–7, 128, 139; exemptions from attending, 115, 127, 128; Majlis Ugama and attendance at, 140; social pressure ensures attendance at, 232 (*see also Pemereksa Juma'at*).
Funerals, 104.

GA'AFAR, LONG, chief of Jeram, 66.
Gaal, Pasir Puteh, 78.
Gabongan Melayu Patani Raya (GEMPAR), 182.
Galas district, 44.
Gambling: common in Pasir Puteh district, 63; To' Janggut addicted to, 66, 74; Munshi Abdullah on, 107; prohibited for Malays, 108, 129–30; *surau* officials and, 118; Chinese love of, 129–30; a cause of crime, 142; welfare funds obtained through, 294.
Ganah (spirit), 205, 211, 212.
Germans, 38, 51, 55, 79.
Germany, 40, 51.
Gold, vi, 44.
Golok river, 55.
Government departments, 42–5.
Graham, William Armstrong, 67; Siamese Adviser (1903–9) to Kelantan, vii, 33, 41; opposes Duff, 33, 48–50, 111; his administration, 42–8, 65, 111–15, 118–20; opposes transfer of Kelantan to Britain, 56; leaves Kelantan, 57; his appointment starts British forward movement in Kelantan, 68; and Islam, 111, 112–13, 115, 119, 123; supports Raja Muhammad, 277.
Great Britain: Trengganu, Kedah and Kelantan transferred to, 1, 3, 111; and Kelantan, 22, 32–5, 38, 40, 50, 110; and Siam, 22–3, 33–5, 38, 40–1, 50–7, 58, 108; 'forward policy' of, 22, 39–40, 68; and Trengganu, 35, 40; wants to keep Siam independent, 35; and currency, 47; Duff Development Company and, 49, 50; fears foreign rivals in Malaya, 51; in First World War, 79, 84.
Green, Mr., 75.
Gua Musang area, Galas district, 44.
Gunboats: Siamese, 41, 57; British, 80.
Gunong, Pasir Puteh district, 75–6, 79, 80.
Gunong Semanggol, Perak, 182.
Gunong Telaga, Legeh, 84.
Guru, 265, 266, 267–8, 269–70; *guru jajahan* (travelling teacher), 116, 123–4, 138, 148; *guru pondok*, 262, 269, 271 (*see also To' Guru*).

Hadith, 87, 89, 98, 108, 155, 162, 165, 172.
Haj (Mecca pilgrimage), 107, 262; women and, 263–4.
Haji, 262, 263, 264, 271.
Hakim (judge), 27, 104, 106, 113, 121, 125, 133, 138.
Halus (refined), 234, 254.
Ham, G.L., 81.
Hamilton, A.W., 83.
Hamzah b. Tengku Zainal Abidin, Tengku, 283, 286, 295.
Hamzah Masri, Shaykh, 156.
Hantu (evil spirit), 191, 196, 198, 203, 222; and *Keramat*, 202, 207–8; cause illness, 207, 210, 211, 213–14, 238; on the sea-edge, 211, 212; fostering of, 215; compared with *penggawa*, 216, 217; children threatened with, 227; and possession of men, 237.
Hanu, Wan, 15.
Hanuman (spirit), 217.
Haram (forbidden), 264, 270.
Hari Raya festival, 232, 233, 237.
Harta pesaka (inheritance), 131.
Hasan b. Nik Abdul Majid, 38.
Hasan b. Pa' Nik Jid, Nik, Orang Kaya Seri Akar Raja, 171.
Hashim Ahmad, 184.
Hasil Nyior and Hasil Padi Regulations (1905), 69, 70.
Hassan b. Haji Wan Mohd., Haji Wan, 121.
Hassan, Wan, 29.
Hassan b. Haji Omar, 173, 175.
Hassan b. Haji Wan Mohammad, Wan, 138.
Hassan b. Haji Ya'acub, 96, 174, 184.
Hassan b. Haji Yunos, Haji, 96.
Hassan b. Idris, Haji, 172.
Hassan b. Tengku Muhammad, Tengku Muda, 134–5, 158.
Hassan Adli, 183.
Hassan Bandung, 178.
Headman, 44, 292 (*see also Penggawa: Penghulu: To' Kweng*).

Healing, 264, 267; magic and, 190, 192, 204, 206, 207, 208, 209, 212, 213, 216–17, 222.
Hejaz, 89, 90.
High Court, 43, 71, 112, 120, 134, 154, 158, 179.
Hikayat, 171.
Hikayat Isma Dewa Pekerma Raja, 171.
Hikayat Patani, 2.
Hikayat Seri Kelantan, 94, 172.
Hindus, 253.
History: historical sources, 2, 4, 94, 109; articles on, 173, 174, 179, 182, 184, 185, 186, 187.
Hizbul Muslimin movement, 182.
House of Lords, Duff Development Company and, 33, 50.
Hsieh Ching-kao, 23.
Hujjat Allāh al-Bālighah, 164, 165.
Husain Pulau Pinang, Haji, 165.
Husband and wife, 228–9, 235, 240.
Husein, To', 83.
Husin, Wan, 28.
Hussin, Sayyid, 37, 38, 40.

IBN KALDUN, 162, 165, 169.
Ibrahim, Haji, 89.
Ibrahim, Inche, 67, 70–1.
Ibrahim, Tengku, Raja Kelantan, 158, 163; (later) Sultan Ibrahim (1944–60), 93, 160.
Ibrahim, Wan, 185.
Ibrahim b. Haji Yusoff, Haji, Mufti (1927–41), 160.
Ibrahim Chandu, 25.
Ibrahim Teleng, 80, 84.
Idris, Tuan Long (Tengku Petra Semerak), 23, 24, 32, 37.
Idris b. Haji Hassan, Haji, Mufti (1921–7), 89, 92.
Ilham journal, 188.
Ilmu (knowledge), 191, 205, 208.
Imaduddin Abil Fida' Ismail b. Kathīr, 94.
Imam: as village teachers, 43, 263; originally in charge of village administration, 44, 104–5; tax exemption for, 69; powers of, 104; duties of, 104, 115–16, 117, 139; and To' Kweng, 105, 110, 111–12, 118; under Mufti's control, 106, 109, 115; collect taxes, 106; help with land survey, 110, 123; in charge of land registration, 112; bureaucratization of, 113; *imam tua*, 116, 117; *imam muda*, 116; importance of, 118; penalties for, 122; payments of commission to, 123, 135, 136; and Friday attendance, 127; Sultan and Mufti disagree over powers of, 131; Majlis Ugama and, 139, 146; training of, 143; difficulties of, 146; responsible for repair of buildings, 148; and magic, 206; village leaders, 231, 236, 292; larger villages have resident *imam*, 232; links between villagers and Majlis Ugama, 244; in *surau*, 263, 264–5, 271; in mosques, 263, 264–5, 270; strike by, 294; and PMIP, 295.
Imprisonment, Royal Family usurps powers to impose, 32.
Independence, political parties and, 273, 276, 284, 285–6, 287–8, 291.
Independence of Malayan Party, 283.
India, viii, 156, 162, 164–5, 166.
India Office, Britain, 52.
Indians in Kelantan, v, 29, 129, 134, 251, 253, 254, 273.
Indirect rule by British, 278, 283.
Indo-China, 35.
Indonesia, 91, 92, 178, 182, 186, 266, 268, 285.
Indonesian language, 178.
Industrialization, 290.
Inheritance: jurisdiction to hear cases of, 114, 120, 121, 139; Sultan and Mufti disagree over rules of, 122, 123, 131, 139, 156–7; stresses caused by, 235, 236.
Institutionalization: of Islam, vi, 116, 119, 126, 149; of Imams' remuneration, 123; of *fitrah*, 143 (*see also* Bureaucratization).
Integration of races, 257.
Intelligentsia, 170, 182, 279, 280, 282, 284, 285.
Interest, charging of, 145, 167.
Ishak b. Abdul Kadir, Haji Wan, 156.
Ishak b. Abdul Rahman, Haji Wan, Mufti (1907–8), 121.
Ishak Lutfi Omar, 178, 180, 292.
Islam: renovation of, 87, 99, 108, 110, 154, 268; knowledge of, 88, 94, 96; instruction in, 90; education under, 93; governance of, 103, 106–8, 112, 118, 122, 126, 129, 130–1, 137, 140, 278; organization of rural, 104–6, 116; Siam and, 110; British and, 126, 130–1; state role of, 126, 129, 131–2; modernism in, 132, 154, 155, 159–61, 162, 164–9, 178, 264, 268, 279–80; books and articles on, 145, 171, 183, 188; established in Kelantan, 153; its development in Kelantan, 154–5; accretions to, 161, 279–80; and magic, 191, 195–6, 199, 201, 202–3, 205–6, 222; differing interpretations of, 245; endogamy in, 256; party politics and, 259–60, 268–71, 272, 274, 276, 293, 300–10; has no priests, 262; and remedy for peasants' grievances, 272, 275–6, 306–8; and nationalism, 273; traditional, 279 (*see also* Bureaucratization: Institutionalization: Religion).
Islamic Law (*see* Muslim law).
Ismail, headman of Kampong Kenali, 88.
Ismail b. Jamaluddin, Hakim Haji Wan 89, 91, 92, 94, 121, 125.

Ismail, Tengku, 133, 172, 283; (later) Sultan Ismail (1920-44), 94, 133, 159, 163, 172, 175.
Ismail, Tengku, Tengku Sri Indera Mahkota, 58.
Ismail, To' Wali, 208.
Ismail, Tuan Long (Bān Thāle), Raja Muda, 5, 6.
Ismail, Wan, 185.
Ismail Patani, Haji, 91.
Ismail Pekerma, Tengku, 177.
Ismail Shauki, 185.
Ismail Yusoff, 173.
Istanbul, 174, 175.

JA'AFAR, SAYYID, 27.
Ja'afar, Tengku Muda Tuan, 79.
Ja'afar, Tuan Long (Tuan Abdul Ghafar: Tengku Petra), 23-4, 25, 28, 30, 31, 32.
Ja'afar b. Haji Muhammad, Inche, 172.
Ja'afar b. Haji Nik Abdul Kadir, Nik, Dato' Bentara Dalam, 134.
Jackson, Chief Inspector, 75.
Jackson, Colonel, 58.
Jah, Nik, 156.
Jail, 29, 75; reform of, 43; religious teachers and, 141.
Jalan Chepa, Kota Bharu, 167.
Jalan Sultan, Kota Bharu, 171.
Jalan Tengku Putera Semerak, Kota Bharu, 94.
Jalor (Yala) state, Thailand, 53.
Jama'ah Penerbit (Publications Committee), Kelantan, 185.
Jambangan Melayu, 144-5.
Jami'a Merbau, Kota Bharu, 165, 173, 175, 182, 186.
Jami'a Milliyya-i Islamiyya, Delhi, 165, 166.
Janah (spirit), 211, 212.
Japanese: occupy Malaya, 156, 173, 181, 182, 273, 282, 290; intrigue against Britain, 181, 279.
Japanese historical records, 2.
Jawi Peranakan newspaper, Singapore, 171.
Jelapang, To', 90.
Jensen, Mr., 75.
Jeram, 63, 66, 67, 74; Engku Besar of, 63, 65-8, 70, 75, 77, 84, 125.
Jering (Yaring) state, Siam, 53.
Jews, 158, 169.
Jinn (spirits), 203, 204, 205, 213, 237; Jinn Tanah (Earth Spirit), 205; Jinn Merah, 205, 211; Jinn Puteh, 205; Jinn Kuning, 205, 211, 212; Jinn Hitam, 211, 212; Jinn Islam, 218.
Jogjakarta, Java, 186.
Johore, 96, 130, 168, 171, 172, 178.
Johore Bahru, Johore, 179.
Journalism, 182, 279, 282; religious, 96.
Journal Persatuan Sejarah Kelantan, 186.
Journals, 170-88.

Judges, 120, 134, 158; European, in Siam, 55.
Judicial reforms, 43.
Judiciary, 109; salaries of, 123.
Jurisprudence, 103-4, 155 (*see also Fikh*).
Juru selam, 198, 204.
Juru Sukat Sempadan Mukim (demarcators of *mukim* boundaries), 124, 125, 127.
Justice, administration of, 39, 44, 45, 71, 120.

KADIR LEBAI, 76-7, 78.
Kalāhom Ministry, Siam, 8, 17, 18.
Kalthum bte Wan Abdul Rahman, Wan, 154.
Kalthum bte Wan Musa, Nik, 156.
Kamaluddin Muhammad (Keris Mas), 182-3.
Kampongs, 230, 250, 265; not isolated, 204; ideology of, 244-5, 251, 254, 256.
Kampong Atas Banggul, Kota Bharu, 156, 158, 161.
Kampong Ayer Lubok Bunga, Tanah Merah district, 55.
Kampong Banggul, Kota Bharu, 89, 154, 164.
Kampong Batang Merbau, Tanah Merah district, 55.
Kampong Belawan (Ban Phrai Wan), Siam, 55.
Kampong Che' Hel, Siam, 55.
Kampong China, Kota Bharu, 44.
Kampong Jedok, Tanah Merah district, 55.
Kampong Jeli, Tanah Merah district, 55.
Kampong Kangkung, Pasir Mas district, 165.
Kampong Kemuning, Pasir Puteh district, 83.
Kampong Kenali, Kubang Kerian, 88, 92, 97.
Kampong Laut, Kota Bharu district, 106.
Kampong Masjid, Kota Bharu, 182.
Kampong Merbol, Pasir Puteh district, 83.
Kampong Paya, 95.
Kampong Penambang, 25, 27-8.
Kampong Pupoh, Pasir Puteh district, 83.
Kampong Pura-pura, 226, 227, 230, 231, 232, 233, 236-7.
Kampong Repek, Pasir Mas, 27.
Kampong Sering, Pasir Puteh district, 81, 82, 83.
Kampong Sireh, Kota Bharu, 95.
Kampong Sungei Golok, Siam, 55.
Kampong Tabal (Ban Tak Bai), Siam, 55.
Kampong Tabal Tempoyak, Siam, 154.
Kampong Tanjong, Siam, 55.
Kampong Telosan, Pasir Puteh district, 83.

Kampong To' Akib, Pasir Puteh district, 73.
Kampong To' Semian Tua, Kota Bharu, 154.
Kapitan China, 16, 44.
Karimah Zainab, 183.
Kathis: Mufti has one as his assistant, 106; scarcity of qualified men for post, 113; try cases involving religion and inheritance, 120; under Mufti's control, 124; salaries and travelling allowances for, 124, 126; *Kathi Besar* (Chief *Kathi*), 138, 160, 173; training of, 143.
Kathis' courts, 121, 122, 124, 126, 127, 128, 141.
Kaum muda (modernists), 132, 134, 159, 178, 179.
Kayu Kelat river, 55.
Kebun Mengseta, Kota Bharu, 27, 36.
Kechil, Tengku, 14.
Kedah, 183; Siam and, vii, 3, 22, 33; civil war in, 8; Siam willing to transfer to Britain her rights in, 51–2, 53; cession of, 55, 56; steps taken against immorality in, 130.
Kelana Jayaputera, 182.
Kelantan: mainly Malay, v, 280–1; population of, v, 289; its people mostly agricultural, v, vi, 63–73, 243, 260, 279, 280, 281; isolated, v, viii, 2, 275; whether backward, v, 275, 303, 305; arts and crafts in, v–vi, viii, 243; and Patani, vi, 2–3; and Trengganu, vi, 4–5; Siam and, vi–vii, viii, 1–18, 24–6, 28, 30–4, 36, 38–9, 41, 49, 58, 64, 107, 171; dynastic disputes in, vii, 7–14, 23–9, 30–2, 36; Civil War (1839) in, vii, 3, 4, 104, 171; British and, vii–viii, 2–3, 33–5, 40, 50, 58, 110; an Unfederated Malay State, vii, 59, 281; transferred (1909) from Siam to Britain, 1, 55, 56–8, 62, 64, 111, 119; period of transition (1900–10) in, 22–59; rivalry of Britain and Siam over, 22–3, 32–6, 108, 110; in Burney's Treaty, 33–4; 'new regime' in, 41–8, 57, 68; finances of, 45–8, 69–73, 111, 119, 132; strongly Muslim, 153–5, 243, 275; intra-Malay tensions in, 289–91, 293, 296.
Kelantan Court, 112.
Kelantan Land Office, 68, 109, 123, 124, 133, 135, 171, 172, 175.
Kelantan river, v, vi, 81.
Kelantan State Assembly, 181, 182, 183.
Kelantan State Civil Service, 42, 45, 57, 58, 67, 175, 284.
Kelantan State Council, 44, 65, 101, 103, 112, 126–7, 139, 141, 142, 148, 286–7.
Kelantan State Treasury, 43–4, 45, 46–7, 69, 75, 127, 136, 137.
Kelubi, Pasir Puteh district, 63.
Kemasin river, 192.

Kembang Meriam, Tengku, 156–7.
Kemubu Irrigation Project, 296.
Kemuning, Pasir Puteh district, 80.
Kenchana periodical, 179.
Keping (coin), 45–6.
Keramat (having supernatural power), 160, 191, 199, 200–1, 202, 217, 218, 222; concept of, 206–17.
Kesatuan Guru2 Melayu Kelantan, 185.
Kesatuan Melayu Muda (KMM) (Young Malay Union), 173, 182, 279, 282, 285.
Ketereh, 201, 208.
Ketua kampong, 231, 236.
Khadijah bte Wan Musa, Nik, 156.
Khaidir Khatib, 182, 183, 186.
Khalid b. Tengku Chik Abdullah, Tengku, 158.
Khalwat (improper association with opposite sex), 108, 139.
Khatib (*surau* official), 69, 105, 116, 123, 133, 146, 172.
Khazīn, Imam, 94.
Khuzaimah Kesmani, 188.
Kinship, 210, 228–30, 233; stress in, 235–6, 240–1; in politics, 284.
Kitab Chahaya Pernama, 145.
Kitab Khoja Maimun, 171.
Kite-flying, vi, 233.
Klang, Selangor, 156.
Kōchā Ishak, *luang*, 16.
Kongres Pemuda Kelantan (Kelantan Youth Economic Congress), 188.
Korea, 34.
Kota, Tuan, *phrayā* Čhāngwāng, 6, 7, 8, 9–10.
Kota Bharu district, 45, 112.
Kota Bharu (town), 70, 88, 110, 125, 160, 221; railway near, viii; Siamese Commissioner in, 25, 26, 32, 35–6, 41; jetty and ceremonial ground of, 27; Norman visits, 28; Siamese officials in, 30, 31, 39; Siamese soldiers in, 31–2, 36; Duff visits, 37, 39; Swettenham visits, 41; police-station built in, 42; jail at, 43; courts at, 43, 109, 112; district chiefs live in, 44; Chinese suburb of, 44; cession of Kelantan to Britain announced in, 57–8; and Pasir Puteh rising, 75, 77, 78–9, 81–2; To' Kenali in, 89, 91, 93; mosque in, 89, 92, 93, 95, 106, 107, 117, 126, 127, 133, 136, 142, 143, 144, 145, 146–9; religion in, 94–5, 106, 107, 112, 154–5; schools in, 95–6, 133, 142–4, 147, 156, 165, 172, 175, 177, 183, 186, 187, 248–50, 251, 254; exercise of central authority outside, 106; Shari'a Court in, 106, 121, 128; immorality in, 107, 130, 141; reforms in, 109; Land Office in, 171; periodicals published in, 74–5, 179–88; printing-presses in, 177–87; demonstrations against Malayan Union in, 282; politics in, 284; elec-

tions in, 286.
Kota Jeram, Pasir Puteh district, 70.
Kuala Kangsar, 144, 147; Malay College in, 177.
Kuala Kelantan district, 45.
Kuala Krai, 82.
Kuala Lebir district, 45.
Kuala Lebir (town), 38.
Kuala Lumpur, Selangor, viii, 147, 182, 282, 289, 291, 295.
Kuala Semerak, Pasir Puteh district, 80.
Kuala Trengganu, Trengganu, 175.
Kuasa (authority), 79, 104, 105, 117, 139.
Kubang Golok, 207.
Kubang Kerian, Kota Bharu district, 88.
Kubang Labu, Raja of, 161.
Kucha, Phra, Siamese Commissioner, 42.
Kuliah Sharī'a, Mecca, 97.
Kundor, Tuan, 25.
Kundor b. Tuan Long Ahmad, Tuan Long, 23 (*see also* Muhammad III, Sultan).
Kuran: study of, 65, 88, 263, 268; reciting of, 97, 104, 264, 266; quotations from, 98; Kuranic schools, 104, 112; and other religions, 166; stresses need for the family, 168; translation of, 174-5, 178; and magic, 196, 204, 205; saints in, 209; instruction in, 232, 265; egalitarianism in, 301.
Kutan, 89.

LABOUR: under corvee (*kerah*) system, 8, 32, 78, 80; by jail prisoners, 43; hard, 115.
Lah (Leh), Haji Nik, 121.
Lamiswayer, Lieutenant, 80.
Land: British introduce new land system, 63, 70, 72-3, 77; alienation of, 67, 112; duty of *imam* in regard to, 104-5, 110, 112, 118, 123; disputes over division of, 104-5; registration of, 105, 107, 112, 261; tenure of, 107, 261, 289-90; survey of, 110, 123, 171; assessment of, 112, 123; registers for, 117; fees in transactions over, 123; reserved for Malays, 280-1, 289; scarce, 289, 291; market-value of, 290-1; peasants' anxiety over, 291, 292, 297; grants made by PMIP, 298 (*see also* Concessions).
Land Officers, 45, 63, 112, 120.
Land revenue: District Officer in charge of, 45, 63, 67, 69-70, 112; collection of, 67, 111, 112; new system of, 70, 72, 77 (*see also* Revenue).
Lands, Superintendent of, 119.
Lands Commission, 110, 171.
Langgar, Kota Bharu district, 106.
Langham-Carter, W., British Adviser (1913-15), 63, 72, 73, 75, 78, 79, 80, 82-3, 84, 122, 127-9, 138.
Langkat, Sumatra, 147.

Langkawi Islands, 54, 55.
Laos, 35.
Latifah bte Haji Daud, Nik, 183.
Latiff, Che', 71-5.
Latrines in villages, 142.
Laws: enactment of, 65, 114-18, 122; certification and revision of, 103, 283.
Layar river, 55.
Lebai (religious man), 196, 205, 263, 271.
Lebar, Nik Wan, 156.
Legal costs, 114, 115.
Legeh state, Siam, 53, 55.
Leh (Salleh), Inche, 71.
Licences: for fishing-boats, 112; for *main puteri*, 213.
Ligor province, Siam, 33.
Literacy, vi, 170; of women, 179.
Loans: by Siam to Kelantan, 46, 47; by F.M.S. to Siam, 51, 55, 57; among relations, 229.
London, 39, 52, 283 (used also as an equivalent for British Government).
Low, Sir Hugh, 53.
Lupa (trance), 206, 214 (*see also* Trances).

McLEAN COMMISSION on Higher Education (1938), 180.
Madina, Hejaz, 89.
Madoh, Tengku, 15.
Madrasah (schools), 95, 232, 265, 266.
Madrasah al-Ahmadiah, Pasir Mas, 182.
Madrasah al-'Arfiah, Mecca, 97.
Madrasah al-Falāh, Pulau Pisang, 95-6.
Madrasah Diniah Bakariah Terusan, Pasir Tumboh, 187.
Madrasah Ma'ahad Ihya al-Sharif, Gunong Semanggol, 182.
Madrasah Manābi' al-'Ulūm wa Maṭāli'an-Nujum, Bukit Mertajam, 95-6.
Madrasah Muhammadi, Kota Bharu, 143-4, 172, 173, 178.
Madrasah Zainal Abidin, Kuala Trengganu, 175.
Magic, 190-223; and spiritual authority, 107; peasants' pragmatic attitude towards, 190, 192, 195, 197, 199, 201, 209, 222; and agriculture, 190, 192-5; and fishing, 190, 195-206, 209, 215; for personal protection, 190, 192, 209-17; and healing, 190, 192, 204, 206, 207, 208, 209, 212, 213, 216-17, 222; Islam and, 191, 195-6, 199, 201-2, 203, 205-6, 222; defined, 191; ritual and formulae in, 191, 192, 193-5, 196, 197, 200, 202-4, 205, 206, 209, 213, 214, 216; faith and scepticism about, 191, 201-2, 206, 209, 212, 215, 216, 218, 220, 221-3; lucky and unlucky days, 192, 198; *sejuk*, 193, 194; blessings, 196, 197, 199, 201, 208; taboo, 198; and health, 201; good and bad, 218; possession of magic powers, 255.
Magistrates, 45, 63, 69, 175.
Mahkamah Adat, 134.

INDEX

Mahkamah Balai, 106.
Mahkamah Jumaat, 113, 115, 121.
Mahkamah Kelantan (High Court), 154.
Mahkamah Shari'a, 113, 115 (*see* Shari'a Court).
Mahmud b. Dato' Lundang, Nik, 77.
Mahmud b. Haji Wan Daud, Haji Wan, 173.
Mahmud b. Haji Wan Ismail, Dato' Haji Nik, Dato' Bentara Setia and, later, Chief Minister: helps to put down Pasir Puteh rising, 76–8, 79, 80, 125; Chief Minister, 89, 94, 134, 163, 171, 173; a friend of To' Kenali, 91, 92, 93, 94, 126; in Mecca, 91; becomes Dato' Bentara Setia, 92; helps to found Majlis Ugama, 93, 126, 132–3, 147; becomes Muhammad IV's closest adviser, 125; a friend of Muhammad Said, 126, 173; and payment of costs of festivals, 128; a member of Majlis Ugama, 134–5; supports appointment of Wan Muhammad to Council of State, 138; articles written by, 145, 172; lists Majlis Ugama's aims, 147–8; opposes Wan Musa, 158; as Chief Minister, helps British, 278; during Japanese occupation resigns as Chief Minister, 282.
Mahmud b. Haji Wan Musa, Nik, 156.
Mahmud b. Khatib Haji Muhammad Said, 175.
Mahmud b. Tuan Long Ahmad, Tuan Long, 23, 24, 25, 32.
Mahmud Zohdi, Tengku, 159.
Mahyuddin ibn al-'Arabi, Imam, 155.
Main puteri (*petri*), (psycho-drama), v, viii, 107, 109, 206, 212, 213–14, 238–41.
Maintenance, 139, 141.
Majallah al-Kamaliah periodical, 178–9.
Majallah al-Riwayat periodical, 180–1.
Majallah Dian periodical, 184–5, 186.
Majallah Kelantan periodical, 185–6.
Majlis Ugama dan Isti'adat Melayu (Council of Religion and Malay Custom), 101–49; To' Kenali and, 87, 92, 93, 100; founded (1915), 93, 124, 126, 131, 132, 171, 172, 278; members of, 95, 96, 133–4, 165, 172, 174, 175; helps modernization, 126, 132, 142, 149; finances of, 126, 133, 135–7, 145, 146, 147–9; organization of, 133; its achievements, 134–5, 139–45, 146–9; becomes chief administrator of Islam, 137; administrative and judicial powers of, 138–40; manages a printing press, 144, 145, 183; publications of, 144–5, 171, 172; staff of, 145, 182; its schools, 145, 172, 173, 175, 177, 182, 186, 268, 283, 292; criticized, 146, 278–9, 280; Haji Wan Musa and, 157; issues teaching certificates, 167, 244; and Haji Nik Salleh, 167–8; *Al-Hikmah*'s dispute with, 180; *imams* connect *kampongs* with, 244; revision of laws governing, 283; and politics, 293, 294–5.
Mak Saman, 84.
Mak Sengaroh (spirit), 211.
Mak Yong (traditional folk play), v, viii, 108, 140.
Malacca Sultanate, 1, 2, 160.
Malayan Union (1946), 273, 282.
Malay College, Kuala Kangsar, 144, 177.
Malay Congress (1946), 182.
Malay historical records, 2.
Malay language: translations into, 148, 154, 174; publications in, 170, 171, 172, 177, 184; as medium of education, 175, 188, 278; the only language of many Kelantanese, 243.
Malay Nationalist Party, 285.
Malay peninsula: west coast states, vii, 1, 171, 288; British 'forward policy' in, 22; British rule in, 51–2, 110; east coast states, 275; north-west states, 275, 291.
Malay Reservations Act (1930), 280–1, 289.
Malaysian Railways, 27.
Malays: synonymous with Muslims, 243, 253; have political dominance, 245, 246, 256–7; and Chinese, 246; Malay students' sense of values, 248–54; endogamy among, 256; formation of ethnicity among, 256; grievances of, 272, 287–9; and land, 289.
Malay schools, 246, 247.
Malay states: Siam and, 2, 8, 22–3, 29, 33–4, 35, 39, 51–2, 56; rivalry between Siam and British over, 22–3, 53–6; British paramountcy in, 51–2, 57–8.
Malay States Guides, 80, 82.
Malu (embarassed), 234–5, 237, 239.
Mamat, Che' (a conjuror), 218–22.
Mamat, Che' (a rebel), 84.
Mamat (Che' Mat) (a servant), 199, 210, 218, 219, 220, 222.
Mamat, To', of Kota Bharu and Sungei Besar, 205.
Mamat Mindok, To', 206, 211, 214, 215, 216, 217, 219, 222.
Manah (spirit), 211.
Manir Tendung, Pasir Mas, 172.
Mansur, Tuan Long, 23–4; Raja Kelantan (1891–7), 24, 25–9, 107; Sultan (1897–1901), 23, 29, 30, 31, 64, 171.
Mansur Shah, Sultan of Trengganu (1740–93), 4.
Markes and Owen, Messrs., 76.
Market forces and peasant security, 289.
Markets, 232–3.
Marriage(s): *imam's* right to perform, 104, 117, 265; Shari'a Court's juris-, diction over, 106, 114, 139; fees for, 117, 123, 128; plural, 122, 235, 240;

usual time for, 227; age for, 228; stress in, 235; religion and, 253; ceremonies in, 268.
Masjid al-Azhar, Cairo, 89.
Masjid al-Ḥarām, Mecca, 89, 90–1.
Masjid an-Nabawīy, Madina, 89.
Masjid Muhammadi, Kota Bharu, 156, 157, 165.
Mason, James Scott, British Adviser (1909–10), 57, 119–21, 130.
Mat, Nik, 77.
Mat b. Haji Wan Daud, Nik, 172.
Mat Besar, Nik, 28, 30.
Mat Hassan, Haji (To' Janggut), 63, 65–6, 70–1, 73–5, 77–8, 82, 83–4, 125.
Mat Kechil, Shaykh Nik, 175.
Matahari weekly paper, 181.
Matba'ah Majlis Ugama (Religious Council Press), 144, 145, 172.
Maxwell, W.G., 62, 83, 134, 144.
Mecca, 140, 208; pilgrimage to, 65, 107, 163, 218, 232, 262; To' Kenali in, 88, 89–91, 92, 95; publications in, 89, 159; education in, 90–1, 125, 154, 155, 161–2, 165, 180–1; visitors to, 95, 156; Malays' birthplace, 96, 175; Malays live in, 97; judges from, 113; Nik Mahmud in, 125; Wan Musa in, 155–6; Nik Abdullah in, 161–2; pervaded by Arabic custom, 165; fanaticism in, 166; Prophet's journey to Jerusalem from, 168; ambergris imported from, 198; and magic, 203, 205; peasants travel to, 244, 262; children taken to, 262.
Medicine: Western, 213, 238; and magic, 216–17, 223.
Mek Ngah, To', 88.
Menara river, 55.
Menora (folk play derived from Thailand), v, 108, 140.
Merbau, Kota Bharu, 165.
Mercantile Bank, Kota Bharu, 81, 171.
Meshuarat Ulama (Council of Religious Scholars), 95, 141, 173.
Mexican dollars in Malaya, 47.
Middle class, 289.
Middle East, viii, 87, 126, 172, 184.
Midwives, 136.
Minah, Che', 217.
Minangkabau, Sumatra, 74, 182; Malays from, 65, 256.
Mindok, 238–9.
Mingguan Kota Bharu newspaper, 187.
Mirik, Kong, 29, 31.
Modernization: and *imam*, 112; Majlis Ugama promotes, 126, 132, 142, 149; continuity important for traditional societies faced with, 149; in villages, 231, 241; in hinterland of Kelantan, 243; brings pressures, 245; and education, 246; schools accept value structures of, 252, 257; emphasizes ethnic differences, 256; and integration, 257; and Islam, 268; and politics, 268; class-based conflict due to, 289; Alliance Party and, 305, 306.
Mohammed Amin b. Wan Musa, Nik Wan, 134, 138.
'Mohammedan religion and Malay custom': Advisers not to interfere with, 41, 58, 68, 111, 119, 120, 128.
Mohammed Hassan b. Mohd. Salleh, Dato' Mentri, 76.
Mohammed Yusof b. Sultan Ahmad, Tengku, 158.
Moneylenders, 296–7.
Mongkut (Rama IV), King of Siam (1851–68), 15–16.
Monopolies, 38, 118.
Montgomery, Mr., 76.
Morality, 263–4; offences against, 43, 113.
Morkill, Mr., 81.
Morrison, Mr., 76.
Mortgages, 289–91, 296.
Mosques: Kuran studied in, 43; *pondok* centred on, 89, 266; supervision of, 102, 138, 139; maintenance of, 136, 142; Majlis Ugama to build, 137, 146, 147–9; *imam* in charge of, 263, 264, 265; built by UMNO, 269, 305; PMIP and building of, 270; federal grants for building, 293–4, 295.
Mosques and Surau Enactment (1916), 139.
Muang Ban Tapan, Siam, 35.
Muar, 96.
Mufti of Johore, 96, 168.
Mufti of Kelantan: holders of the post, 89, 92, 97, 108, 121, 157, 173; has state-wide authority, 106; controls *imam* and *surau*, 109, 114–15, 123; Graham increases powers of, 111; legal jurisdiction of, 113, 122–3; responsible for maintenance of *surau*, 116; advices on creation of new *surau*, 117; his disagreements with Sultan, 119, 122–3, 131, 139, 157–8; hears appeals, 121, 123, 124; officials under control of, 124, 138; and non-attendance at prayers, 127; Majlis Ugama and, 134, 137, 157, 279; his powers reduced, 137–8, 139; rivalry for post of, 163–4.
Mufti of Pahang, 168.
Mufti of Trengganu, 168.
Muhammad, Long (Long Pandak), Raja of Kubang Labu, 161.
Muhammad, Sayyid (To' Hakim Engku Sayyid), 27–8.
Muhammad, The Prophet, 178, 206; his sayings (*hadith*), 98, 155; his birthday (*Maulud Nabi*), 127, 237, 265; his teachings, 156, 157; whether literate, 158–9; and dreams, 162; and *waliyy al hay'ah*, 163; strengthens the Caliphate, 163; his journey to Jerusalem,

168; *Mi'rāj* of, 168-9; and magic, 203, 213; descent from, 263; tribulations endured by, 295; progress in the time of, 305.
Muhammad, Tuan Long, Sultan Muhammad I (1794-1837), 5-7.
Muhammad II, Sultan (1837-86), 6-8, 9-11, 12-14, 15, 16-17, 23-4, 26, 27, 30, 32, 66, 88, 104, 107, 108, 118, 156-7, 277 (*see also* Senik, Tengku).
Muhammad III (Tuan Long Kundor), Sultan (1890-1), 23-4, 26, 28, 30, 107, 134, 157.
Muhammad IV (Tuan Long Senik), Sultan (1910-20), 172; becomes Sultan, vii, 63-4, 107, 119, 277, 283; whether fully sovereign, vii, 64-5; and Pasir Puteh rebellion, 63-4, 65, 68, 76, 78-80, 82, 84, 125; depends on British, 64-5, 125, 131, 277, 278, 279; visits Pasir Puteh (1916), 85; and Islam, 94, 120, 122, 128, 130, 137, 140, 146; and Majlis Ugama, 101-2, 103, 132-4, 147-8, 149; benefits from centralization of government, 103, 118; disagrees with Mufti, 119, 122-3, 131, 139, 157-8; and Shari'a Court, 120, 122; and Langham-Carter, 129; and Kota Bharu mosque, 146, 147; death of, 148, 158; his wife, 156; printing under, 171-2 (*see* Senik, Tuan Long).
Muhammad b. Haji Abdul Samad, Imam Hakim Haji Wan, Mufti (1916-21), 92, 133, 135, 138-9, 146, 155.
Muhammad b. Haji Ibrahim Kota, Haji, 164.
Muhammad b. Haji Muhammad Yusof, Haji, 97.
Muhammad b. Haji Nik Muhammad Salleh, Haji, 186.
Muhammad b. Haji Sulong, 175.
Muhammad b. Haji Wan Musa, Nik, 168.
Muhammad b. Khatib Haji Muhammad Said, Haji, Dato' Bentara Jaya, 93, 126, 132, 134-5, 145, 147, 172, 173, 174-5, 283.
Muhammad b. Salleh, Haji, Dato' Kaya Bakti, 172.
Muhammad Abduh, Shaykh, 159.
Muhammad Abdullah, Shaykh, 183.
Muhammad Adnan b. Mohd. Arifin, Haji, 173, 175.
Muhammad al-Ghazali Kartosuwirjo, 187.
Muhammad Ali, Haji Wan (Wan Ali Kutan), 89.
Muhammad Ali, Maulvi, 174-5.
Muhammad Ali ar-Rashidi, Shaykh, 97.
Muhammad al-Jauhari, 173.
Muhammad al-Sidqi, Haji Nik, 164.
Muhammad Amin, Wan, 40.
Muhammadan Religious Fund, 124, 126-7, 128.
Muhammad Asa'ad b. Haji Muda (Asa'ad (or Sa'ad) Shukri), 177-8, 179, 183.
Muhammad Asri b. Haji Muda, Dato', 181, 182-3, 304-5.
Muhammad Daud b. Haji Muhammad Salleh, 177.
Muhammad Daud b. Salim (Che' Wok Johor), 110, 133, 172, 173.
Muhammad Ghazali, Dato' Bentara Luar, 133, 172, 175.
Muhammad Idris al-Marbawi, Shaykh, 96.
Muhammad Mahyuddin b. Wan Musa, Nik, 156.
Muhammad Nur ul-Din b. Wan Musa, Nik, 156.
Muhammad Radhi b. Puteh, 188.
Muhammad Said, To' Khatib Haji, 133, 135, 172.
Muhammad Salleh b. Haji Muhammad Yusof, Haji, 93, 97.
Muhammad Salleh b. Haji Wan Musa, Haji Nik (Haji Nik 'Leh), 156, 164-9.
Muhammad Yusof, Haji (To' Kenali: Awang), 87-100, 185; his influence and work, 87, 93-100, 155; his early youth, 88-9; in Mecca, 88-91; friend of Nik Mahmud, 91, 92, 93, 94, 126; a religious teacher in Kelantan, 92, 95-7; his death, 92-3; helps to found Majlis Ugama, 92, 126, 132; edits *Pengasoh*, 93, 100, 141, 172; a member of Majlis Ugama, 133, 134, 138; pupils of, 156, 162, 165, 175.
Muhammad Zain b. Salleh, 187.
Mukhtar b. Haji Ahmad, Haji, 168.
Mukim, 44, 105, 115, 146, 265; *mukim surau*, 44, 117, 123, 127.
Mulut Merah, Sultan, 23, *see also* Muhammad II, Sultan.
Munas, 66.
Muqaddimah, 162, 165, 169.
Muratha, Siamese gunboat, 31, 41.
Musa b. Haji Abdul Samad, Haji Wan, Mufti (1908-16): controls Shari'a court, 121; Muhammad IV disagrees with, 122-3, 131, 139, 157-8; Majlis Ugama and, 134, 140, 159, 164, 279; resigns as Mufti, 138, 157; his brother is also a Mufti, 138, 146; a religious modernist, 154, 155, 159-61, 162-3, 165; a leading teacher, 155, 156, 169; in Mecca, 156; his marriages and family, 156; appointed Mufti, 157; respected by Sultan Ismail, 158.
Muslim law: Majlis Ugama to administer, 102, 140; status of women under, 228; divorce under, 228; inheritance under, 236; contrasted with secular law, 302 (*see also* Shari'a law).
Muslim Press, Kota Bharu, 183, 185, 187.
Muslim states in southern Siam, 53.
Mustaffa Fadhil b. Haji Nik Mahmud,

Haji Nik, 163.
Mustafa Kamal, 161, 174.
Muzaffar, Raja, Sultan of Perak (acceded, 1511), 52.
Mysticism, 140 (see also Sufism).

NABILAH RUSHDI, 186.
Nafsu and *akal*, 160, 302–3, 304, 306.
Nakhǭn (Nakorn) Sī Thammarāt province, Thailand, 8, 9–10, 13–14, 15, 17–18, 41; Governor of, 6, 9–10, 12, 13, 15.
Nang Klao (Rama III), King of Siam (1824–51), 3, 6, 9, 16.
Nanik, Engku, 156–7.
Narāthiwāt province, Thailand, 14, 15.
Nationalism: whether Pasir Puteh rising was inspired by, 84; Burhanuddin and, 160; *Petra* journal and, 178; in Indonesia, 182; beginnings of, 273; Islamic, 273, 274, 292–3; populist, 273, 274, 279, 292–3; elitist-administrative, 273; anti-colonial, 282; PMIP and, 285.
National loyalty, 250, 252, 254.
Nawang, *luang*, 42.
Negri Sembilan, 184, 230.
Nenek Batara Guru, 213.
Neng Rumek, 171.
Nering, Pasir Puteh district, 63.
Nets: rites performed over, 196, 197–8, 199, 200, 202, 203; blessing of, 197, 199; cursing of, 198.
Newspapers, 170, 171, 177–8, 187.
Niat (intention), 155, 159.
Nidorahan, Tengku, 15.
Nik, Tuan, of Gagap, 6.
Nilam journal, 188.
Nilam Puri Centre of Higher Islamic Studies, Kota Bharu, 188.
Nǭi, Governor of Nakhǭn Sī Thammarāt (1811–39), 6.
Nǭi Iat, Deputy Governor of Nakhǭn Sī Thammarāt, 13.
Nǭngchik state, Thailand, 11–15, 53.
Non-Malays and religion, 253.
Noor Sabia, 185.
Norman, Henry, 28–9.
Notices (*Notis*), legal: on Shari'a Court, 114–15, 139; on *zakat* and *fitrah*, 115, 136; on Friday prayers, 117, 127, 128, 140; forbidding Malays the use of alcohol and opium, 129; on protection of Kelantan girls, 130; repeating Surau Regulation, 137; restricting theatres, etc., 140; on gambling, 142.
Nuh b. Ali Bafdzal, Haji, 178–80.

OIL PALM, 177.
Omar b. Haji Abdul Samad, Wan, 155.
Omar b. Ismail, Haji, 144–5.
Omar b. Tambi Kechik, Tambi, 134.
Omar Hamdan, Shaykh, 156, 162.
Ong Chao Seri, Phra, 42.
Onn b. Ja'afar, Dato', 282–3, 284.

Opium, 129–30.
Osman Abdullah, 183.
Othman b. Sayyid Omar, Sayyid (S. Othman Kelantan), 184, 185, 188.
Othman b. Ali, Megat, 173, 174.
Othman Jalaluddin al-Kelantani, Tuan Guru Shaykh, 95–6.

PADANG, SUMATRA, 89.
Padang Bank, Kota Bharu, 83.
Padang Bongor, Kota Bharu, 156.
Padang Garong Malay School, Kota Bharu, 182.
Padi: tax on, 88, 109, 115; *padi zakat*, 117; growing *padi* as main occupation in Kelantan, 250; price of, 291 (see also Rice).
Padi river, 55.
Paget, Mr., British Minister in Bangkok, 51, 54, 55, 56.
Pahang, vi, 37, 168, 170, 182, 198; British Resident in, vii; Siam and, 23; Duff a police-officer in, 33, 36; British rule in, 110; oil palm in, 178.
Pai, 84.
Pak Dogol (shadow play figure), 207.
Palembang, Sumatra, 155.
Pangkor Engagement (1874), 102.
Pan-Malayan Islamic Party (PMIP: Partai Islam), 160, 181, 182, 183; controls State Legislature in Kelantan, vi, 254, 272–7; its journals, 183, 186–7; rival of UMNO, 259–60, 268–71, 274, 283, 285, 296, 303–5, 308; in Pasir Mas, 259; wins 1959 elections, 268, 286; peasants and, 272, 275, 277, 297; and religion, 273, 276, 302, 310; formed from UMNO, 273, 283; objectives of, 274–5; reasons for support for, 276–7, 289, 292, 297–300, 305, 309; in 1955 elections, 285; consolidates, 286; village leaders and, 292; and federal grants, 293–4, 304–5; *imams* in, 295; and Islamic appeal, 305–7.
Pan-Malayanism, 279, 285.
Pantai Timur periodical, 185.
Paramountcy of Britain in Malaya, 51–2, 57–8.
Parsi merchants, 180.
Partai Rakyat Malaya, 273, 285.
Party Negara, 273, 283, 284–5, 287, 297.
Pasir Mas district, 89, 165, 172, 187, 245.
Pasir Mas (town), 122, 180, 201; schools in, 144, 182; first branch of PMIP in Kelantan founded at, 183; educational system in, 245–57; organization of Islam in, 259–71; PMIP in, 259.
Pasir Mas Hulu, 187.
Pasir Pa' Anor, Pasir Puteh district, 74.
Pasir Pekan, 83.
Pasir Puteh district, 177; formed, 45, 65, 66, 67, 69–70, 112; rebellion (1915) in, 62–85, 124–5, 128, 130, 132, 134,

INDEX

277–8; treasury of, 127.
Pasir Puteh (town), 62, 65, 93; courts at, 43, 121, 124, 128; in 1915 rebellion, 73, 74–5, 76–7, 78, 80–1, 83; Muhammad IV visits (1916), 85; school in, 144.
Pasir Tumboh, 187.
Patani, 66, 110, 156, 170; and Kelantan, vi, 2–3; Siam and, vii, 2–3, 22, 29, 33–4, 35, 107, 113; Tengku Besar settles in, 11; divided (1832) into seven provinces by Siam, 14, 39, 54; Tengku Besar becomes ruler of, 15–16; visited by King Mongkut, 16; Swettenham's intrigues in, 39, 40; Siam refuses to cede, 53–4; Pasir Puteh rebels flee to, 84; religious teachers and scholars from, 91, 107, 154, 172, 173, 175; religious students from, 92; Islam in, 154, 155, 159, 260; history of, 182; trade in, 260, 266; *pondok* in, 266.
Paternalism, 273, 281.
Pathalung, Siam, 51.
Peasants: economic divisions among, 244; and PMIP, 272, 275, 277, 297; grievances of, 272, 287–9, 291, 292, 297; reject UMNO and Alliance Party, 274, 277, 287–8, 303, 307, 308–9; prefer traditionalism to modernism, 279–80; and politics, 281, 286, 297, 298; security for, 289; and Islamic ideals, 306–7.
Pedoman Masharakat Islam journal, 187.
Pelopor periodical, 187.
Pemereksa Jumaat (Friday inspectors), 109, 123–4, 126, 138.
Penambang, Kota Bharu district, 44, 81.
Penang, 134, 165.
Pendukong journal, 188.
Pengasoh journal, 87, 92–3, 96, 100, 141, 145–6, 148, 171–5, 176, 179.
Penggawa (familiar spirit), 213, 215–16, 217, 218–22.
Penggawa (headman), 72, 244.
Penghulu (headman), 231, 232.
Penyedar journal, 182–3, 282.
Perak, vii, 23, 36, 133, 144, 173, 182, 285.
Pergau river, 55.
Perhentian islands, 198.
Peringat, Pasir Puteh district, 78.
Periodicals, 170–88, 279.
Perkumpulan Wanita Kelantan (Kelantan Women's Association), 183.
Perlis, 22, 54, 56, 228.
Persatuan Guru2 Ugama Sa-Malaya (All-Malayan Association of Religious Teachers), 188.
Persatuan Islam, 178.
Persatuan Penulis Kelantan (Writers' Association of Kelantan), 188.
Persekutuan New Club, Pasir Puteh, 177.

Persekutuan Persetiaan Melayu Kelantan (PPMK) (League of Malay Loyalists), 180, 182, 282, 292.
Perupok, 200, 204, 209.
Pesantren (religious schools), 266.
Petchaburi, Siam, 51.
Petra newspaper, 177–8.
Petra Kelab, Kota Bharu, 177–8.
Pha Kong, 29, 31.
Phiphitphakdī, *luang*, 12, 13.
Phiphitphakdī, *phra*, (Tengku Besar), 15, 16.
Phitthayam Ranayut, Siamese warship, 18.
Phisa, Phra, 57.
Phongsāwadān mūang kalantan (PMK) (Chronicle of Kelantan), 3–18.
Phrayā (Siamese title), 34.
Phuket province, Siam, 51.
Piety (*beribadat*), 166, 263, 267.
Pigs, 192, 198.
Pilgrimage (*haj*), 260, 262, 263 (*see also* Mecca).
Pitis (tin money), 45–7.
Poems in periodicals, 170, 182, 184, 188.
Police: force formed, 29; Chief Police Officer, 36, 76, 83, 119; reorganized, 42; in Pasir Puteh rising, 73–6, 81–2, 83; the force increased, 109; To' Kweng's police powers, 112; Superintendent of, 119; religious teachers in 141; and peasants, 244.
Police Regulation, 112.
Politics: articles on, 171, 174, 182, 183; stresses caused by, 235; and tradition, 241; political dominance by Malays, 245, 246, 253, 256; communalism and, 256–7; Islam and, 259–60, 268–71, 272, 274, 276, 293, 300–10; during colonial period, 277; pre-eminence in, 287.
Pondok, 180, 185; characteristic of Kelantan and Patani, vi, 266; To' Guru teach in, 43, 105, 107; built round mosques, 89, 266; one founded by To' Kenali, 91; To' Kenali improves instruction in, 94; formal education based on, 155; standard of values in, 246, 247, 254, 255; description of, 265–8; in Pasir Mas, 266–7; and politics, 269–70, 271; peasants like the traditional ideas of, 280.
Pondok Ahmadiyyah, Bunut Payong, 95, 96, 168, 185.
Pondok Kenali, Kota Bharu district, 91, 92, 95.
Pondok Kubang Pasu, Kota Bharu, 89, 92.
Pondok Lubok Tapah, Pasir Mas, 248–9.
Population: assessment of, 112; of Kelantan, 289, 290; increase in, 291.
Populism, 274, 279, 282, 285, 292.
Pork, 264.
Portuguese historical records, 2.

Praphāt Udǭn Sayām, Siamese steamboat, 16–17.
Prathētsongkhrām, *luang*, 10.
Prestige in Islam, 263.
Printing presses, 144, 148, 171–2, 175.
Printing Presses and Seditious Publications Enactment (1931), 179.
Prong, *luang*, 31.
Property, women's ownership of, 228.
Prospecting and mining, 37, 38, 120.
Prostitution, 108, 130, 141.
Protected Malay States, vii, 120.
Protection, British, 34, 58, 111, 283; protectorate, 58, 64, 278.
Province Wellesley, 95.
Pryde, W., 78.
Public administration, reforms in, 42–5, 50, 58, 68, 107, 109, 111, 120, 278.
Publications, 142, 145, 170–88.
Public buildings, 132.
Public health, 142.
Public Works Office, 43, 109; public works, 45; Director of Works and Surveys, 119.
Pulai area, Galas district, 44.
Pulau Pisang, Kota Bharu, 95–6.
Puloh (coin), 45, 46.
Purnama journal, 185.
Pustaka Aman Press, Kota Bharu, 96, 174, 184–5.
Pustaka Dian press, Kota Bharu, 96, 178, 184, 186, 187.
Pustaka Permai, 183.
Puteh, Tengku, 15.

QAMUS AL-MARBAWI, 96.

RADICALISM: in Majlis Ugama, 134; Wan Musa and, 164; in intelligentsia, 178, 279, 280, 282, 284; in Hizbul Muslimin, 182; one form of nationalism, 273, 279, 292–3; in KMM, 282; in PMIP, 285, 292–3.
Radio and television, 244, 254.
Raffles, Sir (Thomas) Stamford, 53.
Rahman Talib Report on Education (1960), 246.
Railways, viii, 49, 50–1, 55, 57.
Rajaburi province, Thailand, 53.
Rama I, King of Siam (1782–1809), 5–6.
Rama III (Nang Klao), King of Siam (1824–51), 3, 9, 16.
Rama V, King of Siam, see Chulalongkorn.
Raman province, Siam, 53, 54, 55, 56.
Rangae, *phraya*, 14.
Rashid Ridha, 159.
Razak Report on Education (1956), 246.
Razaleigh b. Tengku Hamzah, Tengku, 295.
Razim, M.S., 186.
Reconstruction, post-war, 290.
Reforms: in administration, 42–5, 50, 58, 68, 107, 109, 111, 120, 278; in religion, 159, 161, 164.
Regulations, 112, 114, 116, 126.
Religion: enthusiasm in Kelantan for, v–vi, 252–3, 254; education in, 43, 92, 96, 103, 104, 142, 143, 157, 158, 231, 265, 266, 268; reform of, 87, 159; books and articles on, 96, 107, 167–8, 179, 187; and custom, 101; Sultan the head of, 102, 118–19, 126, 131, 132–3, 279, 282, 294; Mufti's authority over, 111, 157; its growth in Kelantan, 153; villages as rural centres of, 232; PMIP and, 273, 276, 302, 310; meaning of changes in, 310 (*see also* Islam).
Religious schools, 259, 261, 262, 265 (*see also* Pondok).
Religious teachers: in villages, 43, 44, 232; *imams* as, 44; payment to, 136; for police force and jail, 141; certificates for, 167, 244; and magic, 199, 206; and politics, 269–70; as rural leaders, 292 (*see Guru*).
Residency Surgeon, 119, 142.
Revenue: collection of, 35, 39, 44, 68–9; miscellaneous, 71; Inspectors of, 112; Superintendent of, 119 (*see also* Land Revenue: Taxation).
Revenue Officers (Collectors), 45, 63, 116.
Rice: staple crop of Kelantan, v, 243, 250, 281, 290; tax on, 136, 137; 'dry' and 'wet' methods of growing, 192, 194, 260; used in magic, 196, 197, 201, 203–4, 208, 212, 213; rice paste, 197, 204; mixed with turmeric, 203–4, 207; Kelantan not self-sufficient in, 289; imported from Thailand, 290 (*see also Padi*).
Richards, Henry, 43.
Ritual: observance of, 113; *imam* and, 118, 263; payment for ritual service, 136; religious, 159; in magic, 191, 192, 193–5, 196, 197, 200, 202, 203–4, 205, 206, 209, 213–14, 216; in conjuring, 219; sacred water, 264; ritual feasts, 265; ritual life, 270–1; ritual reversals, 307–8.
Roads, viii, 43, 71, 109, 132.
Rokiah bte Haji Mahmud, 97.
Roles: fulfilment of, 227–8, 230; dissatisfaction with, 235, 240–1.
Royal family, members of: cemetery of, 4; choose Rulers, 5, 6; intrigues among, 7–14, 23–9, 30–2, 36, 42, 45, 107, 110, 131, 278; and state treasury, 43; as territorial chiefs, 44; become state officials, 45; and minting of coins, 46; object to Siam's loss of suzerainty, 56; dislike Graham's control, 118; and plural marriage, 122; and Islam, 133; mostly excluded from Majlis Ugama, 134; Wan Musa's advice to, 158, 161; respect Wan Musa, 159; respect Nik Abdullah, 163.

Rubber, 26; estates of, 122, 134, 145; smallholdings of, 243, 290–1.
Ruhusna, 185.
Ruling class in Kelantan: regards State as a source of personal revenue, 67; and Islamic bureaucracies, 103; resents Graham's control, 118; loses concessions, 120; and Pasir Puteh rising, 125; increased penalties for, 129; intrigues against Sultan, 131; opposes Wan Musa, 157, 158, 161.
Rumaja Pantai Timur magazine, 185.
Rural areas: administration of, 42, 44–5, 109–10, 111–12, 116, 118; leaders in, 66, 280, 292, 293.
Russians, 38.
Ryukyan historical records, 2.

SA'AD B. NGAH (CHE' HA'), DATO' MAHA MENTRI, 24–6, 27–8, 30, 108, 109.
Sa'ad Shukri, *see* Muhammad Asa'ad b. Haji Muda.
Sabasu, Tengku, 15.
Sabri, A., 186.
Safiah bte Haji Karim, Nik, 184.
Sahak Inche, of Nering, 63, 70.
Sai, Phra Ong Chao, 42.
Sāi (Narāthiwāt) province, Siam, 14, 53.
Sāiburī (Sāi: Teluban), Patani: *māēkǭng Lamai* of, 14; Raja of, 35.
Sa'id, Haji, of Cherang Tuli, 63, 70, 84.
Sa'id, Haji Wan, Hakim, 121.
Sa'īd Husain Ahmad Madani, Maulana, 165.
Salaries: judges, 114, 123; Mufti and his staff, 123–4; *imams* do not receive, 123; To' Kwengs, 123; Kathis, 124; local religious officials, 126; Majlis Ugama members and, 134; Majlis Ugama officials, 130, 145; officials of central mosques, 136; religious teachers, 148; salariat, 244, 245; civil officials, 261.
Salleh, Che' (To' Leh), 88.
Salleh, Penghulu, 27.
Salleh b. Tuan Long Ahmad, Tuan Long, 23, 24.
Sallehuddin Abdullah, 186.
Salmān al-Farisi, 163.
Salor, 180, 187.
Samretphāsā, *khun*, 12.
Sanēhāmontrī, *phrayā*, 13–15, 18.
Sang Gana (spirit), 205.
Santajiwa journal, 186.
Sastra Tarakit, Phra, 39, 42.
Saudi Arabia, 97.
Schools, 132; secular, 43; Koranic, 112; vernacular, 133, 144; Majlis Ugama to build, 137, 142–3, 147; Majlis Ugama and, 144, 145, 148, 172, 182; magazines produced by, 188; value-tests in, 243–57; primary, 246, 255, 266; secondary, 246, 248–52, 254–5, 257, 266; 'English', 283 (*see also* Education).
Schoolteachers: status of, 250; and politics, 269.
Science, education in, 251.
Seberang Prai, Province Wellesley, 95.
Second World War, 59, 166, 170, 175, 177, 180, 268, 272 (*see also* Japanese).
Sejarah Melayu, 2.
Sekolah Kebangsaan, Pasir Mas, 246.
Sekolah Menengah Zainab, Kota Bharu, 183.
Selangor, 133, 156, 159.
Semangat (soul), 191, 207, 209, 222; *semangat padi* (rice soul), 192–5.
Semar (spirit), 205.
Semerak, Pasir Puteh district, 74–6, 78, 80, 198.
Senik, Tengku ('Red Mouth'), 4, 5, 6 (*see also* Muhammad II, Sultan).
Senik, Tuan Long, Raja Kelantan (1900–11); becomes Raja Kelantan, vii, 30–1, 64, 107, 119; forced to accept Anglo-Siamese Treaties of 1902 and 1909, vii, 40, 64; passed over in 1891, 23–4; a weakling, 24, 42; recognized by Siam as heir to the throne, 25; warns Siam about Sultan Mansur's illness, 29–30; opposed by his relations, 31–2, 36; and Duff's concession, 37–8, 48–9, 111; Siam wants to take Kelantan over from him, 39; refuses to support opposition to transfer of suzerainty to Britain, 56–7; signs Anglo-Kelantan Agreement and becomes Sultan, 58, 64 (for details of his later life, *see also* Muhammad IV, Sultan).
Senik (Nik), Tuan, of Gagap, Tengku Seri Indera Perata Mahamenteri, 6, 7–8, 9–11, 14.
Sensibility in Malays, 228, 233, 234–5.
Seri Perak newspaper, 171.
Setul (Satun) state, Siam, 22, 53–4.
Sexual knowledge among students, 255.
Shadow play (*wayang kulit*), v, viii, ix, 107, 140, 207, 217, 244, 302.
Sha'er Musoh Kelantan, 171.
Shafi'i School of Law, 167.
Shafiq Deoband, Maulana, 166.
Shamsul Haqq Fashawar, Maulana, 166.
Shamsulnaeem, 185.
Shari'a (Shari'a law: *hukum shara'*), 187; Majlis Ugama's legal position under, 102, 138; codification of, 103, 114; and early religious institutions in Kelantan, 104; only a part of religious law, 104; strict enforcement of, 104, 108, 131; fixed penalties under, 114; *zakat* and *fitrah* under, 114, 136, 146; institutionalization of *surau* by, 116; and new *surau*, 117; Sultan's control of populace through, 118; peasants' right to choose their *surau* under, 127; sometimes slackly enforced, 130; and religious revenue, 131; inheritance

under, 139, 157; trial of offences against, 139; *Meshuarat Ulama* to answer questions on, 141; usury forbidden by, 145; study of, 155; Wan Musa's sons and, 161, 162.
Shari'a Court, 71; jurisdiction of, 43, 106, 114, 139; and inheritance, 43, 114, 120, 121, 139; under Mufti, 106; appeals from, 106, 121, 123, 124, 138; strengthened, 109, 111, 115, 119; separated from other courts, 111, 114; Graham dislikes, 112–13; help from civil authorities for, 113; imams to give offenders' names to, 115, 117; imams can be reported to, 116; can levy fines, 118, 124, 126–7, 128; friction possible between Sultan and, 119; criticized by Mason, 120; its powers reduced, 120, 121; British attitude to, 120–1; its membership unstable, 121; Hakims of, 121, 133, 138; post of Hakim abolished (1911), 121; Kathis' courts to be branches of, 121; the name abandoned (1919), 121, 138; growth of its powers halted, 122, 131; Sultan wants to abolish, 122–3; salaries in, 124; and expulsion of prostitutes, 141.
Shari'a Court Notices (1907), 114–16, 126.
Shari'a Court Regulations (1907–9), 113–18, 124, 126.
Sharikat al-Ittihad al-Islamiah, 180.
Sī Phiphat, *phrayā* (That Bunnag), 8.
Sī Suriyawong, *čhaophrayā*, 16.
Siak, Sumatra, 155.
Siam: and Kelantan, vi–vii, viii, 1–18, 22, 24–6, 28, 30–4, 36, 38–9, 41, 49, 58, 64, 107, 171; and Patani, vii, 2–3, 22, 29, 33–4, 35, 107, 113; transfers (1909) Kelantan to Britain, 1, 55, 56–8, 62, 64, 111, 119; and Malay States, 2, 3, 8, 22–3, 29, 33–4, 35, 39, 51–2, 53–6; and Trengganu, 3, 5, 33–4, 51, 53–6, 58; and Britain, 22–3, 33–5, 38, 40–1, 50–7, 58, 108; and Kelantan currency, 39, 47–8; loans to Kelantan from, 46–7; and Duff Development Co., 49; Kelantan rebels flee to, 84; and Islam, 110; *bomoh* from, 217 (*see also* Thailand).
Siamese Adviser, vii, 41, 50, 52, 57, 67, 68, 110–11, 113, 118, 119.
Siamese in Kelantan: in Civil Service, 45; officials, 120.
Siamese Commissioners, 25, 32, 35–6, 37, 39, 41, 42, 52, 109, 110.
Siamese–Kelantan Treaty (1902), 100.
Siamese Railway Department, 51, 55.
Siaran PAS Kelantan journal, 186–7.
Sikhs, 29, 83.
Silversmithing, v, 243.
Simpang Kubang, Pasir Puteh district, 76.

Sinaran I'tiqad, 168.
Singapore: police recruited from, 29; Kelantan's trade with, 46; Pasir Puteh rising reported to, 63; officials appointed in Kelantan from, 67, 71; troops sent from against rebels, 78–9, 125; troops return to, 81; *kathi* of, 160; publications in, 171; Sultan Mansur visits, 171; Japanese capture, 181; used as equivalent for Government of F.M.S., 47, 50.
Singaporeans, 71, 133, 172, 178.
Singgora, Siam, 29, 41, 110 (*see also* Songklā).
Siti Aspah bte Haji Wan Omar, 183.
Siup technique in magic, 192, 209, 212.
Skeat, W.W., 109, 110.
Skull caps (*kupiah*), 264, 267.
Sleight of hand, 220, 221.
Socialism, 285.
Social mobility, 246, 250–1, 256, 290.
Social welfare lottery, 294.
Songkhlā (Singgora), Siam, 5, 8, 9, 12, 13, 14, 16, 29; Governor of, 11, 12, 13.
Sǫnsēnī, *luang*, 8–9.
Sorcery (*seher*), 218, 220.
Sovereignty of Sultan of Kelantan, 64–5.
South China Sea, v, 2.
Spirit mediums, 209 (*see also* Bomoh); Chinese, 253.
Spirits: of the sea, 195, 196, 197, 199, 201, 203–4, 205, 215; and illness, 210, 211–15, 238–9, 240; of water's edge and tide-rip, 211, 212; fear of, 217; and relief of stress, 241.
State Assemblies, 274, 287, 292; members of, 298–300.
Status, 232, 234, 235; differences in, 231, 244; religious, 263–4.
Straits Dollars, x, 45–6, 47–8.
Straits Settlements, 42, 48, 107, 171.
Straits Settlements, Government of, 47–8, 52; Governor of, 40, 55, 57, 63.
Straits Settlements Service, 119.
Strobel, Herr, 51, 54.
Stubbs, R.E., 58.
Su, Haji, 76, 78.
Suara Islam periodical, 183.
Suara journal, 179–80.
Subsistence economy, 243, 288, 290, 291.
Succession to Small Estates Act (1910), 120.
Sufism, 89, 98, 99, 140, 155, 160.
Sugar used in magic, 218, 219, 221, 222.
Sugar cane used in magic, 193–4.
Sukhum, Phya, 29–30, 31, 39.
Sulaiman b. Tuan Long Ahmad, Tuan Long, 24, 25, 32.
Suloh Pelajar journal, 184.
Sulong b. Tuan Kota, Tengku, 14, 15.
Sulong b. Tuan Senik, Tengku (later Sultan Ahmad), 14, 16, 23.
Sultan: head of Islam in Kelantan, 102,

118–19, 126, 131, 132–3, 270, 282, 294; and charity, 106, 136; judicial powers of, 106; religious powers of, 116–17, 123, 124, 139; possibility of tension with Shari'a Court, 119, 131; and Mufti, 119, 123, 124, 131; federal government and, 294.
Sultanate, British support for, 125, 131, 277–8, 280, 289.
Sultan Ibrahim School, Pasir Mas, 246, 248–50, 251.
Sultan Idris Teachers' Training College, 185.
Sultan Ismail College, Kota Bharu, 248–9, 251.
Sumatra, 89, 91, 92, 147, 155, 182.
Summons, 108, 115, 117.
Sungei Besar, 205.
Sungei Budur, Kota Bharu, 89.
Sungei Pinang, 8, 29.
Sunthǫnnurak, *phra*, 13.
Supernatural powers, 65, 190, 206, 208.
Surarik, Phra, 32.
Surau (village prayer houses); religious teaching in, 43, 112, 154; *mukim* based on, 44; Majlis Ugama to supervise, 102, 137–8, 139; ritual centre of rural Islam, 104, 137, 232; *surau besar* (larger *surau*), 104–5, 106, 116, 117, 127, 137; *surau kechil* (smaller *surau*), 104, 116, 127, 137; can be the object of a religious trust, 105, 262; upkeep of, 105, 115, 135, 136, 148, 269; attendance at Friday prayers in, 108; inspection of, 109, 139–40; laws governing, 114, 116–17, 139; supervised by Mufti, 114–15, 123; Sultan and, 118, 123; friction between Sultan and Mufti over, 131; finances of, 136–7; Wan Musa's *surau* replaced, 167; *imams* attached to, 263, 264–5, 272; may be centre of *pondok*, 266; and politics, 271; grants for building of, 293.
Surau officials: tax exemption for, 69; controlled by Mufti, 106, 109; duties of, 114, 115, 116–17; penalties against, 118; payments to, 123–4, 136; come under Majlis Ugama, 137, 139 (*see also* Imam).
Surau Regulation (1908), 116, 137, 139.
Surawong Waiyawat, *čhaophrayā* (Wǒn Bunnag), 17.
Suzerainty: Siamese, 3, 29, 34, 35, 38–9, 64; British, 39–40, 58; transferred to Britain, 56–7, 64, 111.
Swettenham, Sir Frank, 39–41, 52, 53.

TABOO, 198, 207–8, 217.
Tafsīr al-Khazīn, 94.
Tafsīr Ibn Kathīr, 94.
Taib, Tuan Guru Haji (Tuan Padang), 89.
Taiping, Perak, 171.
Tajul Ariffin, 184.

Tali Harus (tide-rip), 211, 212.
Taman Wanita journal, 183–4.
Tamils, 122, 178.
Tan, Tuan Long, 5, 23.
Tan Busu Setia, 182.
Tanah Merah district, 55.
Tanah Merah (town), 81.
Tanjong Mas, Siam, 84.
Tanjong Pauh, Pasir Puteh district, 80.
Taoism, 253.
Tasrīfal-'Arf, 95–6.
Taxation: poll-tax, 9–10, 73, 105, 111; collection of, 44, 68–9, 70, 71, 72, 231 Duff Development Co.'s rights of, 48; Duff Development Co.'s liability to, 49; chiefs' rights of, 67, 69, 118; exemption from, 69, 72, 73; of produce, 70, 72–3, 77, 88, 105, 109, 111, 261; of padi and rice, 70, 88, 109, 115, 136, 137; boycott of, 70, 125; the cause of Pasir Puteh rebellion, 77, 82, 84; religious, 106, 117, 265; remission of lumber tax, 116; regularized, 118, 261; peasants and, 298 (*see also* Fitrah: Revenue: Zakat).
Taylor, Sir William, 57.
Teaching certificates, 166, 244.
Teh, Tengku, Sultan of Lingga, 11.
Telephone service, 109.
Tengah, Tengku, 6, 7, 8.
Tengku (title), 23.
Tengku Besar, *see* Yusof, Tuan Long.
Tengku (or Tuan) Besar b. *phrayā* Bān Thāle, 6–9, 11–16; Tengku Sulong confused with, 16–18.
Tengku Chik Penambang, *see* Chik, Tengku.
Tengku Petra, 23 (*see also* Ja'afar, Tuan Long).
Tengku Seri Indera Perata Mahamenteri, *see* Senik (Nik), Tuan, of Gagap.
Tengku Seri Petera Maharaja, 8.
Tengku Sri Indera Mahkota, 58.
Terok monthly magazine, 177.
Territorial chiefs, 63, 65, 66–70, 84, 105, 261.
Terutau islands, 54.
Tests for school-children's sense of values, 247–57.
Thai historical records, 2–4, 109.
Thailand, 169; ethnically Malay, v, viii; and Kelantan, viii, 3; irredentist movement in Malay provinces of, 182; students from, 266; *pondok* in, 266; rice from, 290 (*see also* Siam).
That Bunnag (Sī Phiphat), *phrayā*, 8.
Thawǫ, Raja (Long Bahar), Governor of Kelantan (*circa* 1740), 5.
Theft, 63, 72, 80, 142, 215, 227.
The Kelantan Printing Press, Kota Bharu, 172.
The Torch journal, 177.
Thomson, H.W., 41.
Tical (Siamese coin), 39, 47.

Tigers, 198.
Timur journal, 184.
Tin, vi, vii; coins made from, 45–7.
Tipakosa, Phraya, 42.
Title to land: British give peasants deeds of, 72, 289; security of, 291.
Tiup 'blowing' in magic, 210, 222.
To' *Guru*, 43, 105, 107 (*see also Guru*).
To' Janggut, 63–4, 65, 187 (*see also* Mat Hassan, Haji).
To' Janggut Rebellion (1915), 62–85, 124–5, 277–8.
To' Kenali, *see* Muhammad Yusof, Haji.
To' Khorasani, *see* Abu Abdullah Sa'id Hasan.
To' *Kweng* (circle headmen): introduced during reforms of rural administration, 44–5, 105, 107; manage tax assessment and collection, 68–70, 88; assist in dealing with Pasir Puteh rebellion, 74, 78, 80; and *imams*, 105, 110, 111–12, 118, 139; help in resurvey, 110; under District Office, 112; Superintendent of, 134; to investigate *surau* affairs, 139–40.
To' *Nebeng* (village headmen), 44, 45, 69.
Top spinning, 215, 233, 244.
To' Wali, 197, 208.
Trade: trade routes of South China Sea, 2; Chinese, 2; European, 2; Burney Treaty and, 33–4; British with Siam, 35; Duff and, 37–8; currency and, 46–7; in Kelantan, 46; British in Malaya, 53; revenue from taxation of, 67; in Patani, 260, 266.
Traders, petty, 232, 243, 250, 267, 284, 296, 297.
Traditionalism: ruling class, 68–70, 103, 118, 281, 283; in magic, 192–3, 194, 202, 214, 222–3; parents arrange marriages, 227; village is centre of many activities, 231; rural society, 231–2, 237, 244, 281, 292, 293; methods of relieving stress, 240–1; erosion of, 241, 243–4, 261; and kampong ideology, 245; and Islamic social organization, 259; and piety, 263; PMIP and, 275, 285; in Islam, 279–80, 310; preferred to modernism by peasants, 280; and land tenure, 289; village economy, 291, 297; politics in colonial period, 309.
Trances, 206, 213–14, 216, 221, 238–9, 244.
Trang, Thailand, 51.
Translation: from Arabic, 94, 142, 148, 154, 175, 179, 180, 181; Majlis Ugama and, 144, 148; from English, 148, 173, 181; of Kuran, 174–5, 178.
Travelling expenses of *surau* officials, 124, 126.
Travelling religious teacher (*guru jajahan*), 89, 116, 123–4, 138, 148.
Treaty of Bangkok (Burney's Treaty) (1826), 33, 34.
Trengganu: and Kelantan, vi, 4–5, 11; Siam and, 3, 22, 52; Banggul and Long Ahmad in, 12, 14; in Burney's Treaty, 33–4; British and, 33–5, 40; counterfeit coins minted in, 46; Siam willing to cede it to Britain, 51, 53–4; cession of, 55, 56; under British protection, 58; adjoins Kelantan, 62–3, 75, 112; lawless, 63; Pasir Puteh rebels and, 76, 84; Wan Musa in, 158; religious teacher from, 168; PMIP in, 183, 273–4; divorce rate in, 228.
Trengganu State Assembly, 183.
Tua, Tengku Sri Maharaja, of Jeram, 66.
Tuan (title), 23.
Tuan Besar, 6 (*see also* Tengku Besar).
Tuan Tabal, *see* Abdul Samad, Haji Wan.
Tumpat, 14, 75, 76, 78, 79.
Tuntut (revelation), 191.
Turks, national struggle of, 175.

Ubat (medicine), 191, 198, 218, 221, 222.
Ubayd-Ullāh as-Sindhī, Maulana, 156, 162, 165, 166.
Ulama (religious scholars), 178; Kelantan noted for, vi, 153; To' Kenali, 99; in Majlis Ugama, 133–4; in *Meshuarat Ulama*, 141, 173; from Patani, 154; develop Islam in Kelantan, 154; Wan Musa and his sons, 155, 158, 161, 164, 165, 169; Wan Musa opposed by many of, 157, 159, 160; in Deoband, 162, 166; grant teaching certificates, 244; in PMIP, 285, 302.
Ulu Kelantan district, 36, 43, 45, 112, 124, 128.
Umar, Tengku (later, Sultan of Trengganu), 11.
Umar b. Haji Taib, 177, 178.
Umi Salmah, 183.
Unfederated Malay States, vii, 59, 281.
United Malays National Organization: founded (1946), 18, 72, 273, 282–3; journal of, 187; rival of PMIP, 245, 259–60, 268–71, 274, 283, 285, 293–4, 296, 303–5, 308; standards of value in, 254; defections from, 273, 283, 284; and independence, 273, 284–5; in 1955 elections, 273, 284, 286; in 1959 elections, 273–4, 287–8, 292; its organization in Kelantan, 284, 295; intelligentsia in, 285; federal officials appointed by, 291; and Majlis Ugama, 295; in 1969 elections, 297; rejected by peasants, 298–9, 303–5, 307–9 (*see also* Alliance Party).
United States, 40.
University, 180, 251, 255.
University of Malaya, 184.
Usemain Pari (spirit), 211.

VALUE SYSTEMS, 243–57.
Victory Bonds, 145.

Villages: social status in, 226–33; harmony in, 227, 228, 232, 233, 235, 237; religion in, 232; social values in, 233–5; social stress in, (a) overt, 235–7, (b) covert, 237–41; social life in, 237, 244, 281, 292 (*see also* Rural areas).
Visits to friends, 232, 233, 237, 241.

WAKAF BERANGAN, Pasir Puteh district, 77.
Wak Long (shadow play figure), 207.
Wali (saints), 98, 208, 209, 262, 263; *waliyy al-hay'ah* (saintly), 162–3.
Waliyullāh al-Dihlawī, Imam Shah, 159, 162, 163, 164, 165, 167, 169; Waliyullāhi Movement, 162.
Wan (title), 23.
Wang, Che, 15.
Water: used in magic, 201, 214; sacred, 264.
Wealth: and status, 231; desire for, 252, 254; peasants and, 261, 290; Islam and, 262.
Weld, Sir Frederick, 53.
Women: journals for, 176, 179, 183–4; literacy among, 179; as teachers, 179, 183; status of, 228; and mental illness, 240; and *wali*, 263; and religion, 263; and the *haj*, 263–4.
Wōn Bunnag, 17.
Wood, W.A.R., 110.

YA'ACOB, HAJI (Haji Ya'acob Lorong Gajah Mati), 96.
Ya'acob, Wan, 29.
Yahya, Tuan (Tuan ya), 25.
Yahya Petra, Sultan (acceded 1960), 295.
Yamani, Sayyid, 156.
Yaring (Jering) state, Thailand, 15.
Yim, Inche, 67.
Yoke Eng School, Pasir Mas, 246.
Young, Sir Arthur, 64.
Yunus, Long, Sultan (1756–94), 23, 161, 186.

Yusof, Tuan Long, Tengku Besar, 23, 24, 25, 32.
Yusof b. Nik Abdul Majid, Nik (Nik Soh), Dato' Sri Paduka, 24, 26–9, 30, 38, 108.
Yusof Mustafa, 185.
Yusof Zaki Ya'acub, Ustaz Haji, 96, 178, 184, 186.

ZAHRAH IBRAHIM HAJI OMAR, 183.
Zainab, Nik Wan (later, Sultanah Zainab), 156.
Zainab bte Nik Yahya, Nik, 156.
Zainab Karim, Nik, 185.
Zainab Yusof Idris, 183.
Zainal Abidin b. Tuan Long Kundor, Tuan Long, Raja Muda, 25, 29–30, 31, 172, 283; his Diary (DRM), 28, 29, 31, 32, 39.
Zakat: only *surau besar* can collect, 104, 117; *surau* officials paid from, 105, 123; pays for upkeep of mosques, 106, 142; Regulations on, 114–15, 117, 148; *surau* officials must not conceal names of those liable to pay, 118; pays for building of new mosques, 126, 142; Majlis Ugama to take part of, 133, 136, 146; distributed between *surau*, charity and Majlis Ugama, 136; systematic collection of, 136, 143; revenue received from, 137; Wan Musa disagrees with Majlis Ugama over use of, 138, 157; Majlis Ugama intends to pay for education and the building and maintenance of mosques out of, 142; criticism of the way it is distributed, 146; Majlis Ugama not to interfere with expenditure on *surau* upkeep, 148; Nik Salleh differs from Majlis Ugama over, 167–8; articles on, 182.
Zakir Husayn, Dr., 165–6.
Zin bte Suleiman, Hajjah, 179.
Zinc coins, 47.